THE

MARCUS GARVEY

AND

UNIVERSAL NEGRO
IMPROVEMENT ASSOCIATION

PAPERS

SUPPORTED BY
The National Endowment for the Humanities
The National Historical Publications and Records Commission

SPONSORED BY
The University of California, Los Angeles

EDITORIAL ADVISORY BOARD

Marcus Garvey

THE
MARCUS GARVEY

AND

UNIVERSAL NEGRO
IMPROVEMENT ASSOCIATION

PAPERS

Volume I
1826–August 1919

Robert A. Hill
Editor

Carol A. Rudisell
Assistant Editor

University of California Press
Berkeley   Los Angeles   London

University of California Press
Berkeley and Los Angeles, California

University of California Press, Ltd.
London, England

The preparation of this volume was made possible in part by a grant
from the Program for Editions of the National Endowment for the
Humanities, an independent federal agency. In addition, support
was also received from the National Historical Publications and
Records Commission, Washington, D.C., and the University of
California, Los Angeles.

Documents in this volume from the Public Record Office are ©
British Crown copyright 1914 and are published by permission of
the Controller of Her Brittanic Majesty's Stationery Office.

Designed by Linda Robertson and set in Galliard type.

Library of Congress Cataloging in Publication Data
Main entry under title:

The Marcus Garvey and Universal Negro Improvement Association
   papers.

   1. Garvey, Marcus, 1887–1940. 2. Universal Negro Improvement
Association—History—Sources. 3. Black power—United States—
History—Sources. 4. Afro-Americans—Race identity—History—
Sources. 5. Afro-Americans—Civil rights—History—Sources.
6. Afro-Americans—Correspondence. I. Hill, Robert A.,
1943–   . II. Garvey, Marcus, 1887–1940. II. Universal Negro
Improvement Association.

E185.97.G3M36   1983   305.8'96073   82-13379
ISBN 0-520-04456-8

Printed in the United States of America

I   2   3   4   5   6   7   8   9

To
Frank Augustus Hill
1910–1980
Walk good

CONTENTS

THE DOCUMENTS

CONTENTS

CONTENTS

CONTENTS

CONTENTS

CONTENTS

CONTENTS

ILLUSTRATIONS

J. Robert Love
Courtesy of the National Library of Jamaica

S. A. G. Cox
Courtesy of the National Library of Jamaica

Birkbeck College
A Short History of Birkbeck College (London, 1924)

Edward Wilmot Blyden
Courtesy of the British Library

Dusé Mohamed Ali
ATOR, September 1913

Booker T. Washington
Booker T. Washington National Monument

Amy Ashwood
National Archives, Records of Immigration and Naturalization Service

H. A. L. Simpson
ATOR, April 1913

E. Ethelred Brown
Courtesy of Dorice Leslie

Emmett J. Scott
WWCA, vol. 1

R. R. Moton
Tuskegee Institute Archives

John E. Bruce
ATOR, September 1913

W. A. Domingo
American Recorder, February 1929

Nicholas Murray Butler
Courtesy of Columbiana Collection, Columbia University

Hubert H. Harrison
WWCA, vol. 1

William Monroe Trotter
Association for the Study of Afro-American Life and History

Ida Wells-Barnett
Courtesy of Joseph Regenstein Library, University of Chicago

Eliézer Cadet
Courtesy of Eliézer Cadet

Allen Weston Whaley
School of Theology, Boston University

William H. Ferris
WWCA, vol. I

Benjamin E. Burrell
Courtesy of Mrs. Benjamin E. Burrell

Edward D. Smith-Green
Lusk Papers, New York State Library, Albany

Edgar M. Grey
Amsterdam News, 31 August 1927

Fred D. Powell
Lusk Papers

Jeremiah M. Certain
Lusk Papers

George Tobias
Lusk Papers

Joshua Cockburn
Lusk Papers

Henrietta Vinton Davis
National Archives, Records of the Federal Bureau of Investigation

Walter H. Loving and Roscoe Conkling Simmons
Courtesy of Edith Loving

R. D. Jonas with the Abyssinian delegation
National Archives, Records of the Military Intelligence Division

A. Philip Randolph
WWCA, vol. I

Chandler Owen
New York Public Library

Cyril V. Briggs
Federal Bureau of Investigation

Edwin P. Kilroe
Courtesy of Robert Kilroe

J. Edgar Hoover
Federal Bureau of Investigation

J. W. H. Eason
Negro World, 1 November 1919

Chief Alfred C. Sam
Courtesy of Akua Bua

ACKNOWLEDGMENTS

Historical documentary editing depends to an extraordinary degree upon the willing collaboration of many individuals and institutions to assemble and coordinate numerous misplaced, scattered, or fragmented historical sources. This volume gives significant testimony to their contributions which have been essential to the Marcus Garvey project. While the store of personal and professional debts the project has accumulated has become extensive, such debts are a true pleasure to acknowledge.

The greatest debt of appreciation is owed to those sponsors who can take credit not only for initiating but for sustaining the project: the National Historical Publications and Records Commission (NHPRC), the National Endowment for the Humanities (NEH), and the University of California, Los Angeles (UCLA). An especially fond word of appreciation goes to Fred Shelley, who helped launch the project under the auspices of NHPRC. His continuous encouragement and advice to historical editors throughout his long years of service with the commission have earned him the deserved admiration of the entire profession. Since Shelley's retirement, his successor as NHPRC's Director of Publications, Roger Bruns, as well as Assistant Director George Vogt, have maintained this NHPRC tradition of consistent and efficient helpfulness. Similarly, George Farr, Deputy Director of NEH's Division of Research Programs, and the capable staff of the Research Materials Section, have rendered splendid assistance. The support received from UCLA's Center for Afro-American Studies is also gratefully acknowledged, as is the assistance of the Institute of the Black World, the independent black research center in Atlanta, where the editor began his collection of Garvey and UNIA material in the United States and Europe in 1971 and 1972.

The distinguished members of the project's editorial advisory board have provided invaluable support. Their assistance was critical during the project's difficult beginning, and they have cheerfully continued to share their advice and expertise. The volume has benefited greatly from their critical comments.

Many individuals have helped to secure valuable historical manuscripts. Others have obtained rare materials required for the detailed preparation and annotation of the texts. Although it has not been possible to identify every

one of these persons by name, in each instance the editor is deeply apprecia-
tive. Thanks go to the following individuals for their special assistance: Rev.
H. Armstrong, formerly of Jamaica, Superintendent, Methodist Church in
the Caribbean and the Americas, now of County Antrim, Northern Ireland;
Arthur Basco, Davis Town, St. Ann's Bay, Jamaica; Sibthorpe Beckett,
Kingston, Jamaica; Dr. Randall K. Burkett, College of the Holy Cross,
Worcester, Massachusetts; Mrs. Benjamin E. Burrell and her daughters,
Vivian Burrell and Eileen R. Mayer, of San Diego, California, and her son,
Louis Burrell of Jamaica, New York; Claudius Burrowes, Bronx, New York;
Rudolph E. Burrowes, St. Ann's Bay, Jamaica; Eliézer Cadet, Port-de-Paix,
Haiti; Neville N. Clarke, Honorary Jamaican Consul, San José, Costa Rica;
Paul Coates, Baltimore, Maryland; Prof. Gregson Davis, Stanford Univer-
sity; Mabel Domingo, Eulalie Domingo, and Max Dorsinville, New York;
Fritz Dorsinville, Port-au-Prince, Haiti; Theodore Draper, Hoover Institu-
tion on War, Revolution, and Peace, Stanford, California; W. F. Elkins,
London; Charles Golbourn, Wilford Stanford Goulbourne, and John Rob-
inson Graves, Port Limón, Costa Rica; Dr. Marcel Herard, Petite Rivière de
l'Artibonite, Haiti; William Hiss, Bates College, Lewiston, Maine; Dr.
Calvin B. Holder, City University of New York, Staten Island; H. P. Jacobs,
Kingston, Jamaica; Paul Jenkins, Basel, Switzerland; Rev. Sydney Judah,
S.J., Kingston, Jamaica; Kwesi Kambon, New York; Thomas F. Kilroe,
Honesdale, Pennsylvania; Mary-Jo Kline, Editor, Papers of Aaron Burr,
New-York Historical Society, New York; Bro. Ephrem Le Mat, Principal,
Institute Saint-Louis de Gonzague, Port-au-Prince, Haiti; Edna McCormack
Lee (daughter of Thaddeus A. McCormack), St. Elizabeth, Jamaica; Dorice
Leslie (daughter of Rev. E. Ethelred Brown), Queens, New York; Blanche
Loutet, Vancouver, British Columbia; Dr. Joan M. Jensen, New Mexico
State University, Las Cruces; Dr. Donal McCartney, University College,
Dublin; Malcolm George McCormack, Kingston, Jamaica; Richard New-
man, New York; Gregory Organ, formerly of Stanford, California; Rev.
Francis J. Osborne, S.J., St. Ann, Jamaica; the Rerrie family, St. Ann's Bay,
Jamaica; James A. Phillips and Dr. Rupert Rogers, San Pedro de Macoris,
Dominican Republic; James P. Rodechko, Wilkes Barre, Pennsylvania; Isaac
Rose, St. Ann's Bay, Jamaica; Richard Small, Kingston, Jamaica; Rosalie
Schwartz, San Diego, California; Taiyi Goldie Seifert and Enid Smith-
Green, New York; Edward D. Smith-Green, Jr., Washington, D.C.; A. J. P.
Taylor, London; Robert Taylor, Bluefields, Nicaragua; William Taylor (d.),
Los Angeles; Werner Ustorf, Hamburg, West Germany; Eleanor Veira,
Kingston, Jamaica; Ben Waknin, New York; Bishop William J. Walls (d.),
Yonkers, New York; and Lionel M. Yard, Brooklyn, New York.

The annotation of Chief Alfred C. Sam posed special problems, and the
project extends its most sincere appreciation to James Anquandah, Senior
Lecturer in Archaeology at the University of Ghana, Legon, for conducting
the necessary fieldwork in Ghana. We would also like to thank the following
interviewees: Fred Agyemang, Accra, Ghana; Joseph Kwamena Baffoe and

Justice Acquah Felbah (formerly Nana Kurantsi III, chief of Saltpond), Saltpond, Ghana; Kwesi Anana, Akua Twumasiwaa Buaa (daughter of Chief Alfred Sam), Efua Kuma (first wife of Chief Alfred Sam), and Timothy Kwame Owusu, Akyem Swedru, Ghana; Akua Duraa, queenmother of Apasu, and Kojo Anokye, Apasu, Ghana; and Opanyin Ofosuhene, Amanfopon, Ghana.

The invaluable contributions made by various archives, libraries, and governmental agencies to the location and collection of the Papers have resulted in a large debt of gratitude, which is owed to the following institutions: Aberdeen University Library, Aberdeen, Scotland; American Baptist Historical Society, Rochester, New York; Association of the Bar of the City of New York; Bates College, Lewiston, Maine; Beaverbrook Library, London; Biblioteca Nacional, San José, Costa Rica; Bibliothèque de l'Institution Saint-Louis de Gonzague, Port-au-Prince, Haiti; Birkbeck College, University of London; Bodleian Library, Oxford, England; Boston College, Chestnut Hill, Massachusetts; British Museum, London; British Newspaper Library, Colindale, England; University Research Library, University of California, Los Angeles; Canal Zone Library and Museum, Canal Zone; Chicago Historical Society Library; Chicago Public Library; Historical Society of the Episcopal Church, Austin, Texas; Butler Library, Columbia University; Curtis Memorial Library, Brunswick, Maine; State of Delaware, Corporation Department, Dover; University of Durham Library, Durham, England; Emory University Library, Atlanta; Federal Archives and Records Center, Archives Branches: Bayonne, New Jersey, East Point, Georgia, Philadelphia, and Suitland, Maryland; Federal Bureau of Investigation of the United States Department of Justice, Washington, D.C.; Fisk University Library, Nashville; Fordham University Library, Bronx, New York; Foreign and Commonwealth Office Library, London; General Theological Seminary Library, New York; Georgetown University Library, Washington, D.C.; Golders Green Crematorium, London; Guildhall Library, London; Harvard University Library; Historical Commission of the Southern Baptist Convention, Nashville; Honorable Society of the Middle Temple Library, London; House of Commons Library, London; House of Lords Record Office, London; Illinois State Historical Society, Springfield; Irish Genealogical Society, Dublin; Island Record Office, Kingston, Jamaica; Jamaica Archives, Spanish Town, Jamaica; Japanese Ministry of Foreign Affairs, Diplomatic Record Office, Tokyo; Kansas State University of Agriculture and Applied Science, Manhattan; League of Nations Archives, Geneva; Library of Congress, Washington, D.C.; Lloyd's Registry of Shipping, London; University of Maine at Orono Library; Maryland State Bar Association; Massachusetts Bar Association; Massachusetts Office of the Secretary of State; University of Massachusetts Library, Amherst; British Ministry of Defence Library, War Office, London; Moorland-Spingarn Research Center, Howard University, Washington, D.C.; Morgan State University Library, Baltimore, Maryland; National Archives and Records Service, Washington, D.C.; National Library of Jamaica (formerly the West India Reference Library), Kingston; National Personnel Records Center, St. Louis; Nebraska State Historical Society, Lincoln; University of New Hampshire Library, Durham; Roman Catholic Archdiocese of New York Archives, Yonkers; New York County City Registers Office; New York County Court; New York County Lawyers Association; New York Public Library; New York State Assembly, Albany; New York State Department of Health, Bureau of Vital Records, Albany; Office of the New York Secretary of State, Albany; New York State Library, New York State Archives, Albany; New York University Library; University of North Carolina Library, Chapel Hill; Northwestern University Library, Evanston, Illinois; Northwestern University School of Law Library, Chicago; Oklahoma Department of Libraries, Oklahoma City; Panama Canal Company, Washington, D.C.; Panama Canal Zone Government, Balboa Heights, Canal Zone; Pejepscot Historical Society, Brunswick, Maine; Public Archives of Canada, Ottawa; Public Record Office, London; Rhodes House Library, London; Royal Commission on Historical Manuscripts, London; Schomburg Center for Research in Black Culture, New York; Senate of the Inns of Court and the Bar, Gray's Inn, London; Sheffield City Libraries, Sheffield, England; Royal Society of Genealogists, London; University of South Carolina Library, Columbia; State Bar of Texas, Austin; Tuskegee Institute Archives, Tuskegee Institute, Alabama; United States Army Military History Institute, Carlisle, Pennsylvania; United States Army Intelligence and Security Command, Fort Meade, Maryland; United States Department of the Army, Washington, D.C.; United States Department of Commerce, Bureau of the Census, Personal Census Service Branch, Pittsburg, Kansas; United States Department of Justice, Office of Privacy and Information Appeals, and Records Management Division, Washington, D.C.; United States Department of Justice, Immigration and Naturalization Service, Washington, D.C.; United States Military Academy Library, West Point, New York; United States Postal Service, Office of the Postmaster General, Washington, D.C.; United States Veterans Administration, Los Angeles; Virginia Historical Society, Richmond; Department of Human Resources, Vital Records Section, Government of the District of Columbia, Washington, D.C.; Washington and Lee University, Lexington, Virginia; Booker T. Washington Papers Project, University of Maryland, College Park; Wayne County Historical Society, Honesdale, Pennsylvania; West India Committee Library, London; University of the West Indies Library, Mona, Jamaica; Western Reserve Historical Society, Black History Archives Project, Cleveland; Woodrow Wilson Papers, Princeton University; and Sterling Memorial Library, Yale University.

The archival research staff of the National Historical Publications and Records Commission in the National Archives in Washington, D.C., has been of extraordinary assistance to the project. The editor wishes to express the project's considerable gratitude for the sustained help that it received from this archival research team.

Appreciation also goes to the librarians of the *Christian Science Monitor*, Boston, the *Daily Telegraph*, London, and the *Philadelphia Inquirer*.

The complexities of the United States copyright law (Public Law 94-553, passed by Congress on 19 October 1976) affect the use of certain documents. The project was fortunate in being able to turn for advice to Alan F. Charles, Assistant Chancellor–Legal Coordinator, University of California, Los Angeles, and to his Assistant Counsel, Susan Amateau.

For permission to reprint selected documents, the project acknowledges: the Afro-American Company of Baltimore City, Baltimore; the *Chicago Daily Defender*; Agnes Conway, Brooklyn; the *Crisis*, New York; Mrs. Frederick Douglass III, Bethesda, Maryland; Her Majesty's Stationery Office, London; Marcus Garvey, Jr., Framington, Massachusetts; Mabel I. Domingo, New Rochelle, New York: University of Massachusetts Press and University of Massachusetts Library, Amherst; Rare Book and Manuscript Library, Columbia University; the Gleaner Company Limited, Kingston, Jamaica; House of Lords Record Office, Clerk of the Records, London; Jamaica Archives, Spanish Town, Jamaica; Onnie Millar, Brooklyn, New York; Rhodes House Library, Oxford, England; and Tuskegee Archives, Tuskegee Institute, Alabama.

Each new historical edition is privileged to begin by standing on the shoulders of previous editions for inspiration and guidance. The project also benefited greatly from the sagacious advice of Arthur S. Link, Editor of the Woodrow Wilson Papers, who is justly acknowledged as the doyen of the historical editing profession.

Photographs used both for research and for illustration in the present volume were generously provided by numerous sources: School of Theology, Boston University; Brown Brothers, Sterling, Pennsylvania; Akuu Twumasiwaa Buaa, Akyem Swedru, Ghana; City of New York, Department of Records and Information Services; Low Memorial Library, Columbiana Collection, Columbia University; Culver Pictures, Incorporated, New York; Margo Davis, Stanford, California; University of Massachusetts Library, W. E. B. Du Bois Papers, Amherst; United States Federal Bureau of Investigation; Agatha Fraser, New York; Free Library of Philadelphia; Freelance Photo Guild, New York; Dr. Gilbert Geis, South Laguna, California; University Library, Office of Public Relations and Special Collections Division, George Washington University, Washington, D.C.; Georgetown University Library, Special Collections, Washington, D.C.; Harvard University Library University Archives; Illinois State Historical Library, Springfield; Robert H. Kilroe, Honesdale, Pennsylvania; Knights of Columbus, New Haven, Connecticut; Library of Congress, Prints and Photographs Division, Washington, D.C.; Museum Library of the Mariners Museum, Newport News, Virginia; Moorland-Spingarn Research Center, Howard University, Washington, D.C.; National Library of Jamaica; National Portrait Gallery, Smithsonian Institution, Washington, D.C.; Photo Trends, New York; Joseph Conrad Library of the Seamen's Church Institute of New York, New York;

Mrs. Taiyi Goldie Seifert, New York; Women's History Archive, the Sophia Smith Collection, Smith College, Northampton, Massachusetts; the Steamship Historical Society Library, University of Baltimore; Underwood and Underwood News Photos, Incorporated, Chicago; United Press International, New York; Special Collections, University of Chicago; University of Notre Dame Archives, Notre Dame, Indiana; James T. White and Company, Clifton, New Jersey; Wide World Photos, Incorporated, New York; Fritz Dorsinville, Port-au-Prince, Haiti; and Joyce Loutet, Vancouver, British Columbia.

A special debt of gratitude is owed to several persons for their helpful criticism of the Introduction: Randall K. Burkett, George E. Carter, Howard Dodson, St. Clair Drake, Nathan I. Huggins, Michael Lofchie, Richard Sklar, Richard Weiss, and Eugene Victor Wolfenstein. Their numerous insights have resulted in significant improvements, even though I must alone remain responsible for the final statement.

The present volume has benefited greatly by the technical assistance and wise counsel of James E. Kubeck and Shirley Warren, Sponsoring Editor and Senior Editor of the University of California Press, Los Angeles. The design of the volume by Linda Robertson and the copy editing of the manuscript by Sylvia Tidwell and Gretchen Van Meter have greatly helped the final stages of the manuscript. Their gracious accommodation of numerous editorial demands in the area of design and in the rendering of a complicated manuscript has added to the rewards of a working partnership with the University of California Press.

The editor's debt of appreciation to the project's coworkers is very great. For their valuable contribution and dedication, the editor wishes to thank Diane Lisa Hill, Administrative Assistant; Ruth Schofield, Secretary; Althea Silvera, Staff Research Associate; Michael Furmanovsky and Gregory Pirio, Graduate Research Assistants; Deborah Forczek, NHPRC Fellow in Advanced Historical Editing for 1979–80 and now the project's Publications Coordinator; and Carol A. Rudisell, Assistant Editor. The process of revision in the draft manuscript was significantly aided by the careful reading of Emory Tolbert, who joined the project in July 1981 as Senior Editor and whose critical comments have improved the quality of the final work in all its aspects.

The documents presented here represent the most complete historical record of the achievement of Marcus Garvey and the Universal Negro Improvement Association that we have been able to reconstruct. We again thank all those whose help and support have made the work and final fruition of this volume possible and, we hope, worthwhile.

GENERAL INTRODUCTION

Marcus Garvey and the Universal Negro Improvement Association (UNIA) form an important link in the historical struggle of black Americans for freedom, justice, and equality. This struggle has encompassed a wide range of popular movements that, in turn, have established a distinctive tradition of black thought and action within American history. The shifting course of this struggle has brought both hope and despair to black Americans, especially when they have undertaken independent efforts to achieve self-emancipation. This independence was particularly evident in the struggle spearheaded by Marcus Garvey and the UNIA in America, when unprecedented numbers of black Americans sought to define a dignified existence outside the dominant power of white American society.

The result has been a unique moral and political discourse through which black Americans have articulated a profound racial consciousness.[1] Indeed, in the African diaspora and in Africa itself, the discourse of social and political protest has borrowed significantly from the idiom of freedom forged by the black American.[2] Similarly, with each wave of black movement in America, a strategic identification with Africa has reaffirmed the cultural bonds and has broadened the historical meaning of black freedom.[3]

1. The study of race consciousness forms a chapter in American sociology; see E. Franklin Frazier, *The Negro in the United States* (New York: Macmillan, 1949), pp. 492–563; Oliver C. Cox, *Race Relations: Elements and Social Dynamics* (Detroit: Wayne State University Press, 1976); Robert E. Park, "Negro Race Consciousness as Reflected in Race Literature," *American Review* 1 (September–October 1923):505–16; W. O. Brown, "The Nature of Race Consciousness," *Social Forces* 10 (October 1931):90–97; T. G. Standing, "Race Consciousness as Reflected in the Negro Press," *Southwestern Social Science Quarterly* 19 (December 1936):375–77; Elizabeth A. Ferguson, "Race Consciousness among American Negroes," *Journal of Negro Education* 7 (January 1938):32–40; and James P. Pitts, "The Study of Race Consciousness: Comments on New Directions," *American Journal of Sociology* 80 (November 1974):665–87.

2. An impressive corpus of scholarly literature now exists on the subject of Afro-American linkages with Africa. Some of the most significant accounts are to be found in the various works of George Shepperson, St. Clair Drake, Robert G. Weisbord, Imanuel Geiss, Ian Duffield, J. Ayodele Langley, and Hollis Lynch.

3. The metaphor of black movement as a historically regenerative current is to be found in Vincent Harding, *There Is a River: The Black Struggle for Freedom in America* (New York: Harcourt Brace Jovanovich, 1981); see also Lerone Bennett, Jr., *Wade in the Water: Great Moments in Black History* (Chicago: Johnson Publishing Co., 1980). The same metaphor also informs Langston Hughes's memorable elegy "The Negro Speaks of Rivers" (1926).

Marcus Garvey and the UNIA present a sizable enigma, however, in the history of those manifold black movements. Over sixty years have passed since Garvey and the UNIA came to America and shortly thereafter confronted a startled world, but the questions that they posed have remained only imperfectly understood.[4] Garvey himself in his latter days was struck by the force of the enigma. This is particularly reflected in his efforts to find an explanation for the UNIA's meteoric rise and its decline:

> The Universal Negro Improvement Association was the greatest and strongest movement ever started among Negroes. In a comparatively short time this organization enrolled more members throughout the world than almost all other Negro Organizations put together. Thousands of Branches were established, and by indications it would have seemed almost impossible for such a movement to wane, but the unexpected happened. The movement did wane, and the wild enthusiasm of its millions of members cooled down, and in some instances to indifference. One would wonder at the cause of this.[5]

It becomes essential, therefore, to attempt to elucidate the development of Garvey and the UNIA. Nevertheless, it is not the purpose of the present introduction to detail the myriad functions of the UNIA throughout the over nine hundred divisions and chapters that operated in the United States, Canada, the British Isles, Africa, the Caribbean, and Central and South America. Nor does it attempt to review every controversy in which Garvey and the UNIA became embroiled. All that it is possible to attempt within the limits of an introduction is an overview that will clarify the underlying stance of Garvey and the UNIA in relation to their historical context.

Foundations of Garveyism

At the simplest level, Marcus Garvey and the UNIA symbolize the historic encounter between two highly developed socioeconomic and political traditions: the social consciousness and drive for self-governance of the Caribbean peasantry and the racial consciousness and search for justice of the Afro-American community. The dominant social consciousness of the Caribbean was the special creation and possession of a fiercely proud and independent peasantry. As the black majority, their real achievement throughout the postemancipation period was the development of a dynamic and expanding

4. See Lenwood G. Davis and Janet L. Sims, comps., *Marcus Garvey: An Annotated Bibliography* (Westport, Conn.: Greenwood Press, 1980), for a list of references to existing scholarship.

5. Marcus Garvey, "A Message to Members of the Universal Negro Improvement Association and Allied Organizations," *Black Man* 1 (February 1934):3 (reprint ed., Robert A. Hill, comp. and ed. [Millwood, N.Y.: Kraus-Thomson Organization, 1975]; hereafter cited as *BM*). Garvey's *Blackman*, published in Kingston, Jamaica, from March 1929 to February 1931, should not be confused with this later periodical.

peasant economy that, in some places, even challenged the dominance of the plantation system. By 1860, the former slaves in Jamaica were thus able to forge themselves, in the words of Thomas Witter Jackson, into "an independent people . . . notwithstanding their humble position."[6]

Garvey came to America endowed with this Caribbean ideology. His early views had been shaped by the nexus within the peasant economy of Jamaica, in which independent peasant cultivators and artisans played an important role. Garvey's father was an artisan of some repute, a bricklayer in the rural town of St. Ann's Bay, Jamaica. His mother's family were small farmers. The rural integration of artisan and peasant groups frequently occurred at the level of the extended family, which provided much of the labor force in agriculture. At a political rally in Kingston in September 1929, Garvey described his own early connection with the economy of peasant production through his relationship with his maternal uncle, Joseph Richards:

> He worked and planted out 25 acres of land in canes, ground provisions and every imaginable agricultural produce you can think of in Jamaica. He had one farm that brought him an income of about £100 per year. He had up to his mule sending his bananas to market on Mondays, and he was expanding and he was intelligent and he was able to educate me because my father would not do it. I helped to keep his books and so at the week end I got a commission of 13/- for selling bananas, some of which I got honestly and some I stole [laughter].[7]

As a printer trained by his godfather in St. Ann's Bay, Garvey belonged to the artisan elite, but he always honored his peasant roots in postemancipation Jamaican society. His choice of 1 August, the anniversary of slave emancipation in the British West Indian colonies, as the annual date for the holding of the UNIA conventions, is significant.[8]

Racial caste oppression in the United States bequeathed to the Afro-American community a different legacy. Garvey always acknowledged this difference, declaring the "difficulty about the West Indies [to be] that the Negroes there haven't the racial consciousness possessed by the Negroes of

6. PRO, CO 137/349, Thomas Witter Jackson to Hugh Austin, 22 February 1860, enclosed in no. 49, Charles Darling to Duke of Newcastle, 28 March 1860 (quoted in Monica Schuler, *"Alas, Alas, Kongo": A Social History of Indentured African Immigration into Jamaica, 1840–1865* [Baltimore: Johns Hopkins University Press, 1980], p. 44). See Trevor G. Marshall, *A Bibliography of the Commonwealth Caribbean Peasantry, 1838–1974*, Occasional Bibliography Series no. 3 (Cave Hill, Barbados: Institute of Social and Economic Research, Eastern Caribbean, University of the West Indies, 1975), for an extensive listing of sources.

7. "Second Part of Hon. Marcus Garvey's Political Talk at Cross Roads," *Blackman*, Thursday, 12 September 1929, p. 1. Garvey's uncle (better known as "Ba Joe") was also the steward of the Lauriston Presbyterian Church; for statements about him, see Amy Jacques Garvey in *Garvey and Garveyism*, 2d ed. (New York: Collier-Macmillan, 1970), p. 3, and "The Early Years of Marcus Garvey," pp. 30–31, in John Henrik Clarke, *Marcus Garvey and the Vision of Africa* (New York: Random House, 1974).

8. See B. W. Higman, "Slavery Remembered: The Celebration of Emancipation in Jamaica," *Journal of Caribbean History* 12 (1979):55–74.

the United States nor those of Africa."[9] The paradoxical source of a strongly motivated and highly developed racial consciousness did not escape his notice:

> The American Negroes are the best organized and the most conscious of all the Negroes in the world. They have become so because of their peculiar position. They live in very close contact with organized racial prejudice, and this very prejudice forces them to a rare consciousness that they would not have had otherwise.[10]

Garvey's failure to make headway with the UNIA in Jamaica, which was what impelled him to visit the United States in 1916, could be attributed to the absence of a clear-cut racial consciousness in Jamaica. One of his early Jamaican benefactors, R. W. Bryant, confirmed the reality of Garvey's early failure: "Marcus Garvey had . . . an uphill fight in Jamaica. He did not meet with the success he was hoping for."[11] Garvey's assessment was that in 1916, Jamaicans "were not sufficiently racially conscious to appreciate a racial movement because they lived under a common system of sociological hypocrisy that deprived them of that very racial consciousness." Conversely, he felt that the American Negro would respond to his calls to racial action because in the United States, "the Negro was forced to a consciousness of his racial responsibility."[12]

In America, the climate of opinion amply confirmed Garvey's estimate. A *Washington Bee* editorial of July 1918, entitled "A Moses Needed," stands as an important prolegomenon foreshadowing the role of prophet that Garvey would ultimately attain: "The colored race is greatly in need of a Moses—one that is not hand-picked or controlled by the blandishments of official environment—a man of the people and designated by the people."[13] The

9. Marcus Garvey, "Centenary of Negro Emancipation," *BM* 1 (May–June 1934):11. For Garvey's opinion on the role of the West Indian in his scheme of racial emancipation, see "The W.I. as Guide," *BM* 2 (September–October 1936):14.

10. Marcus Garvey, "A Dialogue: What's the Difference?" chap. 2, *BM* 1 (August–September 1935):14. For additional comments by Garvey on the superiority of the racial consciousness possessed by black Americans, see "The West Indian Negro," *BM* 1 (May–June 1934):17; "The American Negro," *BM* 1 (June 1935):3–6; "The Confusion in America," *BM* 1 (December 1935):6–7; "The U.S. as Teacher," *BM* 2 (September–October 1936):14; "The American Negro," *BM* 3 (November 1938):20; and "Garvey Speaking in Toronto," *BM* 4 (February 1939):8.

11. *Gleaner*, Saturday, 13 December 1919. Likewise, Garvey made it known in March 1921 that "when he was trying in Jamaica, his own race 'turned him down' and all the assistance and encouragement he received were from men of the white race" (*Gleaner*, Saturday, 26 March 1921, p. 10); see also Robert A. Hill, "Marcus Garvey: The First England Years and After, 1912–1916," pp. 62–66, in Clarke, *Marcus Garvey and the Vision of Africa.*

12. Marcus Garvey, "What Is the U.N.I.A.?" *BM* 1 (December 1933):5.

13. "A Moses Needed," *Washington Bee*, 25 November 1918, p. 4. The same notion of prophetic deliverance would later be applied to Garvey, namely, "Because he [Garvey] had a definite program and propaganda, the Negroes hailed him as a New Moses" (William Ferris, "Garvey and the Black Star Line," *Favorite Magazine* 4 [July 1920]:397); Claude McKay, "Garvey as a Negro Moses," *The Liberator* 5 (April 1922):8–9; K. L. Fenner, "Marcus Garvey, the Negro Moses," *Negro World* (hereafter *NW*), Saturday, 4 November 1922, p. 9; E. U. L.

time was thus ripe for the convergence of the contrasting traditions of racial and social consciousness that the program and ethos of the UNIA would comprise. The appearance of Garvey and the UNIA on the American scene would help to precipitate a new era of militant black leadership and would, indeed, answer the contemporary call for a "black Moses."[14] To the powerful racial consciousness of Afro-American nationality, Garvey and the UNIA would join a Caribbean consciousness of popular sovereignty and an intense preoccupation with the structure of the state. Writing to the *Negro World* (12 February 1921) from Chicago, J. Arthur Davis made the following assessment of Garvey: "This leader from the West Indies, the freedom of whose people antedates that of the American Negro and who are better schooled in the science of government and the arts and devices of Caucasian domination, henceforth will be our foremost American." When observers at a later stage commented that the UNIA constituted, in fact, a black government in exile, they were testifying to the successful imbrication of the two traditions that constituted the framework of Garveyism.

Garvey as the Self-made Man

When Garvey arrived in America, not only did he enter "a country of self-made men," to quote Calvin Colton (*Junius Tracts*, 1844), but he came to Harlem, the emerging capital of black success in America, which had super-seded such traditional centers of black achievement as Philadelphia, Atlanta, Durham, North Carolina, and Washington, D.C. Garvey's meteoric rise to fame and international prominence was simultaneous with Harlem's attain-ment of recognition as the political and cultural capital of the "new Negro."[15] Going forth from this heightened atmosphere of racial optimism and enterprise, Garvey preached a doctrine of racial success and political achievement. Moving beyond his earlier failure in Jamaica, Garvey geared

Allick, "Marcus Garvey Our Moses" (poem), *NW*, Saturday, 10 September 1921, p. 7; see also Truman Hughes Talley, "Marcus Garvey: The Negro Moses?" *World's Work* 41 (December 1920):153–66. The biblical allusion had long been used to describe the redemptive mode of black nationalist leaders in America, e.g., Thadeus Edgar Horton, "A Black Moses," in James T. Haley, comp., *Afro-American Encyclopaedia* (Nashville: Haley & Florida, 1895), a biographi-cal account of Bishop Henry McNeal Turner, the major exponent of Afro-American national-ism and African emigration in the United States before Garvey (see Edwin S. Redkey, "The Flowering of Black Nationalism: Henry McNeal Turner and Marcus Garvey," in Nathan Huggins, Daniel M. Fox, and Martin Kilson, eds., *Key Issues in the Afro-American Experience* 2 [New York: Harcourt Brace Jovanovich, 1971]:107–15, and *Black Exodus: Black Nationalist and Back-to-Africa Movements, 1890–1910* [New Haven, Conn.: Yale University Press, 1969]).

14. This phrase also provided the title for E. David Cronon, *Black Moses: The Story of Marcus Garvey and the Universal Negro Improvement Association* (Madison: University of Wisconsin Press, 1955).

15. David Levering Lewis, *When Harlem Was in Vogue* (New York: Alfred A. Knopf, 1981); see also Jervis Anderson, *This Was Harlem: A Cultural Portrait, 1900–1950* (New York: Farrar, Straus, Giroux, 1982).

himself for success, admitting in 1919, "the world has laughed at me, but I am going to strike a blow."[16] An ever-present anxiety over failure and a compensatory insistence on measurable success would remain constants underlying Garvey's radically shifting policies and political methods. Garvey's single-minded preoccupation with achieving success at all costs would give him decisiveness and would contribute to his significant ability as a propagandist by allowing him to seize every opportunity, no matter how superficial, to advance his cause. However, while this decisiveness was his great strength as a leader, it also proved to be the cause of his many costly misadventures.

Garvey drew parables from his own life for the moral and intellectual instruction of his followers: "I am trying to make everyone a Marcus Garvey personified," he stated in 1937, and, in truth, he always presented himself as the prototypical self-made man.[17] Holding his life up as a mirror before his public, Garvey carried this message to listeners in the West Indies in 1937. In Montserrat he announced, "I came from a surrounding not better than many of you, but my mind lifted me out of my surroundings."[18] In St. Kitts he told his audience, "If you know the world you know that the greatest men had humble beginnings."[19] Looking back on his crowded life in 1934, Garvey tried to draw out its defining quality:

> I was born in the country town of St. Ann's Bay. . . . And in my tender years I went to . . . [my father's] books and I gathered inspiration, and what inspiration I gathered, changed my outlook from the ambition of wanting to be a wharf-man or a cow-boy, and made me look forward to being a personality in the world. Nobody helped me toward that objective except my own mind and God's good will, and during 44 years of struggle I brought myself from the possibility of a cow-boy to a man who is known in many continents."[20]

Garvey's essential proposition for his black readers and audiences was always the same: success as the basis of equality and recognition. Speaking before a Liberty Hall audience on 11 July 1920, Garvey again referred to his own youthful experience:

16. DNA, RG 165, 10218–364/1, "Negro Agitation."

17. "Marcus Garvey Addressing the People of Detroit," *BM* 2 (December 1937):10.

18. "The Rule of Intelligence. Marcus Garvey Glorifies the Mind of Man," *BM* 3 (July 1938):14.

19. "Marcus Garvey Speaks in St. Kitts, B.W.I.," *BM* 2 (December 1937):16.

20. "Councillor M. Garvey Will Appeal to Heart of England," *Daily Gleaner*, 21 July 1934, p. 17. See also Garvey's interview in the *Toronto Daily Star* (26 August 1936): "Denying that he has been chosen by God as savior of his race, he [Garvey] attributes his success in life to 'grit, determination and refusal to bow to anyone but God.'" The year before this Garvey had stated, "The biographies and auto-biographies of individuals have shown that some of the humblest boys in the world become the world's greatest men" (Marcus Garvey, "A Dialogue: What's the Difference?" chap. 1, *BM* 1 [June 1935]:10–11).

I can recall having read and studied in the same class room with white boys, but up to now none of them has made a better success in life than I have on their own initiative. Hence, I come to the conclusion that I am as good as any white man.[21]

Garveyism as the Religion of Success

As the evangel of the gospel of black success, Garvey's program of racial self-determination conceptualized and instituted an important political variation on the white norm of success. "I have been trying to lift men out of themselves," he declared, calling upon his racial compatriots with his famous injunction: "Look Up, You Mighty Race."[22]

The success ideal was central to Garvey's racial perspective, and the ideology of the American cult of success exerted a profound influence on the evolution of his program for racial independence. Furthermore, Garvey's guiding philosophy was entirely in accord with the long-standing Afro-American struggle to succeed despite white opposition. This identity of aim might explain in part the immediacy with which black Americans gravitated toward the program of the UNIA. In 1944, Gunnar Myrdal, in his classic *An American Dilemma* (New York: McGraw-Hill Book Co., 1964), made special note of the fact that the "vicarious satisfaction [taken] in the present-day achievements of individual Negroes" was important, since according to him, its effect was to "help build up a 'tradition of success,' the lack of which has helped to keep Negroes down in the past" (p. 755). This "tradition of success" went back much further, however, as attested by the fact that the home reading libraries of many black Americans from the turn of the century onward included a significant number of success manuals produced by black authors (e.g., James T. Haley, comp., *Sparkling Gems of Race Knowledge Worth Reading* [Nashville: J. T. Haley & Co., 1897]; I. Garland Penn et al., *Afro American Home Manual and Practical Self-educator, Showing What to Do and How to Do It; Being a Complete Guide to Success in Life* [Philadelphia: National Publishing Co., 1902]; G. P. Hamilton, *Beacon Lights of the Race* [Memphis: E. H. Clarke & Bro., 1911]; and Joseph R. Gay, *Progress and Achievements of the Twentieth Century Negro. . . . A Handbook for Self-Improvement Which Leads to Greater Success* [n.p.: 1913]).

---

21. *NW*, Saturday, 17 July 1920; see also "A Dialogue," chap. 1, *BM* 1 (June 1935):10. The classic study of the American ideal of the self-made man is Irvin G. Wyllie, *The Self-Made Man in America: The Myth of Rags to Riches* (New Brunswick, N.J.: Rutgers University Press, 1954); see also John G. Cawelti, *Apostles of the Self-Made Man* (Chicago: University of Chicago Press, 1965), p. 39. There are also references to Garvey as a self-made man in Imanuel Geiss, *The Pan-African Movement* (New York: Africana Publishing, 1974), p. 281, and Tony Martin, "Some Aspects of the Political Ideas of Marcus Garvey," in Clarke, ed., *Marcus Garvey and the Vision of Africa*, p. 430.

22. "The Rule of Intelligence: Marcus Garvey Glorifies the Mind of Man," *BM* 3 (July 1938):15; Marcus Garvey, "Look Up, You Mighty Race," *BM* 2 (September–October 1936):3–4.

Finally, what Merle Curti has termed "the cult of getting ahead through one's own efforts" was the doctrine retailed by Garvey in frequent exhortations, such as his *Negro World* editorial headline of 1 October 1921:

Negro Must Climb in the Achievement of Higher Things—Race Must Conquer the Alps of Oppression—There Should be a Will Not to Surrender—Negro Should Feel Himself a Sovereign Human Being— Man Should Harness the Elements and Nature and Use Them to His Will.

In an editorial in the *Negro World* of 11 October 1919, William Ferris underscored the radical significance of Garvey's translation of the doctrine of business success into a new belief in emancipation for black Americans:

What we want is another Emancipator who will tell the Negro youth, "You can succeed in big business just as you have succeeded along other lines of intellectual and mechanical endeavor, if you study business as you study the other subjects and trades and learn the detail necessary to success. You can even sail the high seas and run a steamship line . . ."

In his promotional pamphlets and speeches, Garvey not only quoted at length from Elbert Hubbard,[23] American author of the popular and influential success manuals *A Message to Garcia* (1899) and *Health and Wealth* (1908), but he recommended a degree of discipleship: "Get a copy of [Hubbard's] *Scrap Book*. Ask any publisher in your town to get it for you. It contains invaluable inspiration."[24] In 1922, a Negro Factories Corporation advertisement for shares declared that "Enthusiasm Is One of the Big Keys to

23. David A. Balch, *Elbert Hubbard, Genius of Roycroft: A Biography* (New York: Stokes, 1940); and Freeman Champney, *Art and Glory: The Story of Elbert Hubbard* (New York: Crown Publishers, 1968). For a collection of Hubbard's writings, see *The Philosophy of Elbert Hubbard* (New York: W. H. Wise & Co., 1930). The imagery contained in Hubbard's famous *Message to Garcia* was later adapted by Garvey: "The Negro has slept too long. He has waited for the letter or for the message from someone too long. Sometimes a letter never comes nor the bearer brings the message. The greatest message a man can expect is a message from his own deep-seated soul, is a message delivered by his own mind, and his mind should always say to him—man, go and work; man, go and find your place in the sun" ("Find Your Work!" *BM* 1 [March–April 1934]:4). For a discussion of "The Self-Made Man and the Cult of Success," see Merle Curti, *The Growth of American Thought* (New York: Harper & Bros., 1951), pp. 644–50. Quotations from *Success Magazine* appear in C. Howard Blackman, "The Philosophy of the Color Question," *NW*, Saturday, 27 August 1921. The most illuminating analysis to date of the evolution of the gospel of success in America, and one filled with numerous subtle insights, is Richard Weiss, *The American Myth of Success: From Horatio Alger to Norman Vincent Peale* (New York: Basic Books, Inc., 1969); see also works on the same subject by Kenneth S. Lynn, Rex Burns, Richard M. Huber, and Lawrence Chenoweth.

24. Marcus Garvey, "Intelligence, Education, Universal Knowledge, and How to Get It," lesson 1, "School of African Philosophy," September 1937, p. 18. Garvey was referring to *Elbert Hubbard's Scrap Book, Containing the Inspired and Inspiring Selections, Gathered during a Life Time of Discriminating Reading for His Own Use* (New York: W. H. Wise & Co., 1923).

Success," averring that "from the time Marcus Garvey was twenty, he held an enthusiastic vision of great accomplishment for himself and his race."[25] In a 1925 editorial entitled "The Person Who Succeeds," veteran black journalist and later editor of the *Negro World* T. Thomas Fortune wrote, "in his front page article in The Negro World last week, President-General Marcus Garvey talks about success. . . . Is this not a splendid picture to frame in the mind and shape the conduct by? We think so."[26] Garvey's inspirational maxims appeared regularly on the cover of each issue of *Black Man*, his last journal, edited in Jamaica and later in England, reinforcing the mind-power credo of the success cult: "Be a Man by Doing the Deeds of Men" (*BM*, 1 December 1933); "Blackman! What Is in Thy Bosom? Pluck It Out—Is It Genius? Is It Talent for Something? Let's Have It!" (*BM*, 1 February 1934). His poems were couched in the same idiom: "Go and Win" (*BM*, 1 December 1933); "Find Yourself" (*BM*, 1 February 1934); "Be King of Circumstances" (*BM*, 1 October 1935). In like fashion, a front-page article in Garvey's *Blackman* newspaper in Jamaica declared in the headline:

> Let Us Give off Success and It Will Come
> *As Man Thinks So Is He*[27]

Popular response to Garvey's success myth enabled his racial ideal to become transformed into a militant eschatology of racial redemption. A surviving fragment from an unidentified black Philadelphia magazine proclaims:

> Ride on, Marcus Garvey. You haven't begun to spend till you have spent billions of dollars and millions of lives. Ride on, Marcus Garvey. Thinking men and women are with you. Let the Black Horse ride and hold the balances high that the world may see justice for all mankind. If billions must be spent to hold the balances high, spend God's billions and call for millions more.

In this perspective, white society was thus seen as vanquished by the triumphant and avenging black prophet of a millennium of racial success. Such beliefs, held by numerous black adherents and sympathizers, created a constant counterpoint to Garvey's shaping ideas and ultimately invested Garvey himself with a transcendent mythic meaning. In consequence, an important feature of Garvey's broader legacy has been its continuing influence at a

---

25. *NW*, Saturday, 1 April 1922, p. 10.
26. *NW*, Saturday, 6 June 1925, p. 4.
27. The original biblical epigram was, "For as he thinketh in his heart, so is he" (Prov. 23:7); it was also the title of James Allen's influential book *As a Man Thinketh* (Chicago: Sheldon Press, 1908), which by 1960 had gone through eight editions. The phrase might also have been adapted by Garvey from Marcus Aurelius Antoninus's *Meditations*, which work seems to have also provided him with the model for *Selections from the Poetic Meditations of Marcus Garvey* (1927). The themes of the triviality, brutishness, and transience of the physical world were the same in both works.

fundamental level of folk consciousness. This folk legacy augments the legacy of influence used by cultural and political activists at various stages throughout the Pan-African movement.[28]

Radical millennial sects, such as the Black Muslims in America and the Rastafarians in Jamaica, have provided the principal expression in the folk idiom of the retention of Garveyism.[29] In essence, Garvey's inspirational message of success had an effect tantamount to religious conversion upon many of his followers. A UNIA devotee in Panama informed the *Negro World* in December 1921: "We people down this way regard your movement as a religion."[30] Even so, Garvey outspokenly declared himself to be not religious in the traditional sense and repeatedly defined his concerns as secular. In closing the second UNIA convention (1921), he asserted that "we are living in a material world, even though it is partly spiritual, and since we have been very spiritual in the past, we are going to take a part of the material now, and will give others the opportunity to practice the spiritual side of life."[31]

Garvey's position was, indeed, problematic for many black religionists who were otherwise sympathetic. Robert Athlyi Rogers, founder of "The Afro-Athlican Constructive Gaathly" and author of *The Holy Piby* (Woodbridge, N.J.: Athlican Strong Arm Co., 1924), articulated his doctrine of Ethiopian divinity in part by assigning to Garvey the leading role among the three prophets of "the redemption of Ethiopia and her suffering posterities." Rogers was forced to acknowledge Garvey's clear lack of piety. He could not conceal his dilemma, but he divested himself of the burden of its

28. For a description of the ideological legacy of Garveyism, see E. David Cronon, *Black Moses*, chap. 8, "Echoes and Reverberations"; and Theodore G. Vincent, *Black Power and the Garvey Movement* (Berkeley: Ramparts Press, n.d.), chap. 9, "Twilight Achievements."

29. The relationship between Garveyism and the origins and development of the "Nation of Islam" in America has best been described in E. U. Essien-Udom, *Black Nationalism: A Search for an Identity in America* (Chicago: University of Chicago Press, 1962). For Garvey's influence on the Rastafarian movement in Jamaica, see M. G. Smith et al., *The Ras Tafari Movement in Kingston, Jamaica* (Mona, Jamaica: Institute of Social and Economic Research, University College of the West Indies, 1960); Ken W. J. Post, "The Bible as Ideology: Ethiopianism in Jamaica, 1930–1938," in C. H. Allen and R. W. Johnson, *African Perspectives* (Cambridge: Cambridge University Press, 1970), pp. 185–207. The relevance of Garveyism to the rise of black power in the 1960s is positively assessed in Walter Rodney, *The Groundings with My Brothers* (London: Bogle-L'Ouverture Publications, 1969), chap. 2, "Black Power: A Basic Understanding."

30. Quoted in William H. Ferris, "The Question of Survival" (editorial), *NW*, Saturday, 25 February 1922, p. 4; see also Campbell MacRaw Lewistall, "Religion and Garveyism: A Successful Philosophy in Practice," *NW*, Saturday, 23 April 1921, p. 6; Felix Britton, "The U.N.I.A. as a Religion," *NW*, Saturday, 18 March 1922, p. 5; Rev. James M. Webb, "The Garvey Movement Is Biblical," *NW*, Saturday, 17 December 1921, p. 10; and "A Spiritual Movement" (editorial), *Negro Churchman* 1 (July 1923):1–2. For a discussion of the religious dimension, see Randall K. Burkett, *Garveyism as a Religious Movement: The Institutionalization of a Black Civil Religion* (Metuchen, N.J.: Scarecrow Press and American Theological Library Association, 1978), and *Black Redemption: Churchmen Speak for the Garvey Movement* (Philadelphia: Temple University Press, 1978).

31. *NW*, Saturday, 10 September 1921, p. 6; Garvey, "The U.N.I.A. Considered in Light of New Religion," *NW*, Saturday, 16 October 1919.

resolution by placing the issue (and Garvey) outside the realm of mortal controversy:

> In the year of 1921 Garvey spake, saying: I have no time to teach religion.
>
> Because of this saying Athlyi took up his pen and was about to declare him not an apostle of the twentieth century.
>
> And it came to pass that the word of the Lord came to Athlyi saying, blame not this man, for I the Lord God, hath sent him to prepare the minds of Ethiopia's generations, verily he shall straighten up upon the map [of life].
>
> [*The Holy Piby*, p. 23]

Throughout his life Garvey remained impatient with what he saw as the piety of traditional black religion and with anything else that he felt might interfere with the pursuit of worldly personal success. In a 1937 article, significantly entitled "The Cold Truth," Garvey urged blacks "to argue their way out to success" by recognizing that "with all its religion and its philosophy, the most potent factor of the world's civilization is its austere materialism, through which races and individuals see themselves enthroned, guaranteed and protected by the strength of their own practical achievements, in politics, in industry, in commerce, in education, and in the general field of economics."[32]

In view of Garvey's explicit stance, it would be wrong to assume that his fundamentalist followers simply failed to grasp the secular basis of his doctrine of racial success. Actually, their traditional religious fervor was converted into a new spiritual inspiration through Garvey's advocacy of the metaphysic of success. When Garvey declared that "there are people who would not think of their success but for the inspiration they receive from the U.N.I.A.," he recognized that his followers had eminently practical reasons for supporting the UNIA.[33] The fact that their reasons were frequently cloaked in the mystique of traditional religious inspiration should not obscure the pragmatism of their actions.[34] The UNIA rank and file essentially experienced Garvey's teachings on two distinct levels, the one mundane, the other mystical. In this context, what Garvey taught can be reconciled with what his followers actually chose to believe. This merger of realism and faith pervaded all aspects of the Garvey movement and was given frequent, vivid

---

32. *BM* 2 (August 1937):6.
33. Marcus Garvey, "The Work That Has Been Done," *BM* 3 (July 1938):8.
34. The combination of the mundane and the mystical can be seen in the following recollection by an original charter member of the Toronto UNIA: "[Garvey] even went as far as to say Black people should have a religion of their own, a God of their own, a Black God, because when you worship someone else who doesn't look like you, then you are in trouble. And I agree with that, I really do. To me, a humble Black fellow in the street, Garvey gave me a real bit of hope. He said get brains, get learning, go to school, learn" (Donna Hill, ed., *A Black Man's Toronto, 1914–1980: The Reminiscences of Harry Gairey* [Toronto: The Multicultural History Society of Ontario, 1981], p. 12).

testimony. At the 1926 UNIA convention, for example, the secretary-general presented the following resolution:

> Everything points to the star of hope, born 38 years ago, and which came upon our horizon in 1918. In him we behold our one destiny, outlined and emerged into a program, comprehensive, all-inclusive, and sane. It goes without saying, that Marcus Garvey, this star of hope, has given to the black peoples of the world new life, desire, and ambition.[35]

This resolution followed the collapse of the Black Star Line Steamship Company and Garvey's imprisonment for mail fraud in 1925. The Black Star Line represented perhaps the most ambitious of Garvey's efforts to channel his success gospel and the fervor of his followers into racially oriented commercial ventures, even though the Black Star Line proved to be a financial disaster, with the total operational deficit on its three vessels estimated at $476,169.58.[36] Garvey's constant faith in what he termed "the possibility of achieving success and glory," particularly through the stock promotions of his shipping and investment schemes, was, in fact, symptomatic of more than racial nationalism or the disturbed conditions of postwar racial strife.[37]

Garvey was not the first black figure with an imaginative shipping scheme as part of a program of African return. The idea dates back to Paul Cuffee in the early nineteenth century.[38] In 1918 and 1919, the first man to announce plans for launching such a program was not Garvey but an itinerant East African known as Prince U. Kaba Rega, who had smuggled his way from Canada to the United States in 1916.

The "prince" claimed to have been born in Unyoro, Uganda, on 18 July 1876. A United States Bureau of Investigation informant described him in August 1920 as "nothing more nor less than a negro agitator attempting to stir up trouble among the negroes of this country and the south in particular, exhorting them to radical actions on account of the lynchings, and also exhorting them that they have no flag."[39] But Prince Kaba Rega devoted

35. G. Emonie Carter, "Report of Secretary General of the Universal Negro Improvement Association," *NW*, Saturday, 27 March 1926.

36. DNA, RG 267, appellate case no. 30924, *Marcus Garvey* v. *U.S.A.*, government exhibit 134, pp. 2648–49; government exhibit 142, pp. 2657–58; government exhibit 137, pp. 2650–51; government exhibit 138, p. 2652. The financial data of the Black Star Line were reconstructed by government accountants from stock ledgers, cash books, journals, vouchers, and minute books, obtained under subpoena of 5 January 1922 (government exhibit 119, pp. 2636–37). The team of government accountants built up "practically a new ledger" (p. 996), a task that required the full-time services of four accountants working for approximately two months (p. 1062).

37. Marcus Garvey, "The Negro and Character," *BM* 1 (May–June 1934):6.

38. For an account of various contemporary attempts to develop a black merchant marine, see Ian Duffield, "Pan-Africanism, Rational and Irrational," *Journal of African History* 18 (1977):602–7.

39. DNA, RG 65, file OG 388465.

most of his time and effort to preaching the religion of African missions in America on behalf of the body he founded, known variously as the African Interland Missionary Society or the Ethiopian Interland Interdenominational Missionary Society. Its American headquarters was in New Orleans, and its African headquarters was listed as "Unyoro, British East Africa," no doubt a reference to Bunyoro in Uganda. Prince Kaba Rega communicated his desire to organize an African return in a letter dated 23 April 1918 to the principal of Tuskegee Institute, R. R. Moton. The prince mentioned having spent the last three years "appeal[ing] to the people of my race." He wrote Moton of his plans:

> I have plans by which means I will be able to raise a great deal of money from my race for shipping facilities providing that the Government of the United States will grant me the privilege of demonstrating the possibilities and opportunities of the resources of Liberia to my people. I believe within a short time, I can raise money enough from my people for the purchasing of a steam ship for the usage of this Government and to the credit of my race.[40]

This letter is dated a full year before Garvey's formal announcement in April 1919 of his plan for establishing the Black Star Line. Because he did not, however, articulate possible stock investment plans and because he had no access to a propaganda organ along the lines of Garvey's *Negro World*, it is understandable that Kaba Rega's plan would fail.

The frenzy of economic speculation that swept the United States after World War I provided the psychological context that goes far toward explaining why Garvey couched the proposal of the Black Star Line in the manner that he did. In the words of W. P. G. Harding, this was "a time of fatuous optimism and of reckless extravagance, a period of expansion, speculation, extravagance, the like of which has never before been seen in this country or perhaps in the world" (*The Formative Period of the Federal Reserve System* [Boston: Houghton Mifflin, 1925], pp. 163, 297–98). The speculative mania that fueled this postwar economic revival reached such fantastic proportions between April 1919, the month when Garvey launched the Black

40. Tuskegee Institute Archives, box 27, file 192, Robert Russa Moton Papers, general correspondence, Rev. Prince U. Kaba Rega to the president of Tuskegee Institute, 23 April 1918. The name probably derived from Mwami Kabarega (Kabalega) of Bunyoro, Uganda, ca. 1850–1923, the last independent ruler of the Nyoro kingdom, from 1869 until 1899. A resistance leader against British conquest of Uganda, Kabarega was deported by the British to the Seychelles Islands in 1899; although he was allowed to return to Uganda as a private citizen in 1923. (For information, see *Dictionary of African Historical Biography* [Chicago: Aldine Publishing Co., 1978], pp. 95–96). A report by the Bureau of Investigation's New York section, General Intelligence Report No. 10, 13 January 1921, stated: "Rev. V. Kaba Rega, said to be an African prince, is delivering a series of addresses at various negro churches in the city" (DNA, RG 65, bureau section file 202600–9–10, p. 7). The phenomenon of itinerant African "princes" in the United States during the early decades of the twentieth century is one that merits careful study.

Star Line stock promotion, and the early summer of 1920 as to threaten the credit structure of the United States, causing Treasury Secretary Carter Glass to state in his annual report for fiscal 1919: "All sense of values seems to have departed from among us" (quoted in Joseph S. Davis, *The World Between the Wars, 1919–1939: An Economist's View* [Baltimore: Johns Hopkins University Press, 1975], p. 85).

Black Americans were by no means immune to the speculative fever of the postwar economic boom. The outbreak of a parallel mania of speculation in the black community was disclosed by Charles E. Hall of the Department of Labor, writing in November 1919 in response to an inquiry from National Association for the Advancement of Colored People (NAACP) assistant secretary Walter F. White. While Hall's standpoint was negative, his statement nonetheless conveys something of the speculative quality that characterized an important aspect of the racial activism of blacks in the immediate postwar period:

> They [blacks] are being "welfared" to death. Every little grafter and graftee, every pseudo sociologist and every hypocritical preacher, every angel and every gambler, every orator and every shyster, every good natured simpleton and every sycophant, every bully and every weak-brained pretentious fool and every highwayman and liar are working overtime with an alleged welfare scheme to help (?) the "man and brother."[41]

At the time of the first UNIA convention in August 1920, the idea of the speculative stock mania was picked up by the *New York Age* and applied to the proceedings. The newspaper commented in its editorial of 14 August that "the persistent appeal for subscriptions gives the whole meeting the appearance of a gigantic stock jobbing scheme, put forth under the guise of racial improvement."

In 1921, Hodge Kirnon ventured to analyze the source of popular motivation that accounted for the fantastic pace at which the UNIA's various stock promotion schemes were propelled. Kirnon observed that "the enterprising investors supported [the Black Star Line] largely on the basis of the extraordinary remunerations which were promised in a very limited time."[42] Within little more than two and a half years (July 1919 to February 1922), the Black Star Line was to sell approximately 153,026 shares of stock. At $5 per share, the total invested was nearly $765,130, a sum subscribed by approxi-

41. DLC, records of the NAACP, special correspondence, series C, container 76, Charles E. Hall to Walter F. White, assistant secretary, NAACP, Washington, D.C., 14 November 1919.
42. Hodge Kirnon, " 'As to Marcus Garvey,' " *NW*, Saturday, 16 July 1921, p. 3.
43. DNA, RG 65, file OG 258421, "P-138," New York, 6 August 1920; Marcus Garvey, "Our Lesson—Remember It," *BM* 1 (August–September 1935):12.

mately 35,000 individual stockholders, according to the estimate of the government auditors.

Despite the failure of the Black Star Line steamship line as well as the other commercial undertakings, Garvey's translation of the enthusiasm of traditional black religion into the new metaphysic of success remains a seminal accomplishment. "So far as I can see the movement has ceased to be simply a nationalist movement," reported a Bureau of Investigation confidential informant in August 1920; accordingly, the agent claimed, "among the followers it is like a religion," with Garvey "looked upon as a black Moses." In retrospect, it is not surprising to find that Garvey characterized his career as "20 years of inspirational agitation."[43]

Hodge Kirnon's discerning eye caught this fundamental quality of Garvey's appeal: "It is to be observed that Garvey is gradually succeeding in idealizing even the business end of the U.N.I.A.," he declared, adding: "Garvey is spiritualizing a commercial affair."[44] In the context of the times, Garvey's teaching shared an important affinity with New Thought, the influential and popular religion of mind power as the key to success. This was the essential meaning underlying the *Negro World's* front-page caption, "The UNIA Considered in Light of New Religion," which accompanied Garvey's weekly editorial greeting on 16 October 1920. New Thought represented, in the words of Richard Weiss, "a new gospel of success which came to supplant the earlier rags-to-riches myth [and] gave belief in the individual's power for self-direction a new lease on life by providing it with a rationale viable in the context of an industrialized society."[45] Its appeal was manifest throughout the years of Garvey's "inspirational agitation." In promoting the sale of the volumes of his *Philosophy and Opinions*, Garvey described it as "the Text-Book of Negro Inspiration," assuring purchasers: "When you read this Book you will be ready for the Battle of Life."[46] The transcendent height to which Garvey's thought aspired derived from his belief that "we have kept in communion with the Source of all knowledge, with the Source of all Wis-

44. "Hodge Kirnon Analyzes the Garvey Movement," *NW*, Saturday, 28 January 1922, p. 7); see also William Bridges, "Garveyism—A Cult," *Challenge* (June 1921), quoted in the *NW*, Saturday, 2 July 1921, p. 2.

45. Weiss, *The American Myth of Success*, pp. 130–31; see also Charles S. Braden, *Spirits in Rebellion: The Rise and Development of New Thought* (Dallas: Southern Methodist University Press, 1963); A. Whitney Griswold, "New Thought: A Cult of Success," *American Journal of Sociology* 40 (November 1934):309–18; and Carl T. Jackson, "The New Thought Movement and the Nineteenth Century Discovery of Oriental Philosophy," *The Journal of Popular Culture* 9 (1975):525–48. According to Richard M. Huber, "As a point of view, a way of looking at reality, New Thought has exerted its most extensive influence through public lectures and writings, which have not necessarily been labeled as such" (*The American Idea of Success* [New York: McGraw-Hill, 1971], p. 217). William Bridges, editor of *Challenge* magazine, observed that "the spirit of radicalism and new thought was dominant in the very atmosphere" of a Harlem Liberty Loan rally in 1918 (*Challenge* 2, no. 5 [n.d.]:140). The application of the system of "thought dynamics" to the goals of the UNIA can also be seen in Euston R. Matthews, "The Redemption of Africa," *NW*, Saturday, 30 July 1921.

46. Advertisements appearing in *BM*.

dom."[47] In the closing stages of his career, Garvey explicitly alluded to the importance of New Thought for blacks.[48]

Garvey's radicalizing influence on organized black religion was confirmed in the select band of talented black clergy who entered the ranks of the UNIA and contributed significantly to spreading its success gospel. William H. Ferris, who was not only an ordained minister but one of the UNIA's top elected officials and the editor of its official organ, was probably first to recognize the crucial importance of this particular achievement. Ferris told a Liberty Hall audience that "this UNIA has preached a new gospel to [the Negro race] and has in it the potency of a new religion" (*NW*, Saturday, 26 June 1920). Ample evidence pointed to a fusion between the radical wing of the black church and Garvey's doctrine of success. It is instructive to note that Rev. J. D. Brooks, secretary-general of the UNIA in 1920, in describing the feeling that his membership in the UNIA had produced in him, should have told the same Liberty Hall audience that Ferris addressed that "I feel now that I am a full-fledged minister of the African gospel." This synthesis was perhaps best exemplified in the person of Rev. J. W. H. Eason, who so "caught the vision" that he won election as the "Leader of American Negroes" at the UNIA's convention in August 1920.

Civilization as the Mirror of Success

In 1938, with only two years remaining to his life, Garvey reflected on the moral of existence before his last audience in the West Indies: "At my age I have learnt no better lesson than that which I am going to impart to you to make a man what he ought to be—a success in life." In summary, he advised that "there are two classes of men in the world—those who succeed and those who do not succeed."[49] For Garvey, however, success was measured solely according to the criteria of white Europe's achievements, despite

47. "Garvey Closes Convention with Classic Speech," pp. 17–18. Garvey's allusion to the operation of mental harmony was highly reminiscent of Ralph Waldo Trine's *In Tune with the Infinite; or, Fullness of Peace, Power, and Plenty* (1897), a work that made Trine, according to Weiss, "the most popular mindpower inspirationalist of his day" (*The American Myth of Success*, pp. 12, 231). Garvey also cautioned his followers that "the world in which we are environed has no patience with any group or set of people who are not sufficiently tuned to the harmony of their own self-protection and accomplishment" ("We Must Support a Good Cause," *BM* 2 [January 1937]:6). In 1922 Garvey received support from Robert T. Browne, the black American author of a metaphysical treatise, *The Mystery of Space: A Study of the Hyperspace Movement in the Light of the Evolution of New Psychic Faculties and an Inquiry into the Genesis and Essential Nature of Space* (New York: E. P. Dutton & Co., 1919), (*NW*, Saturday, 24 June 1922, p. 10).
48. "A Call to Action," *BM* 2 (August 1937):3; "A Dialogue: What's the Difference?" chap. 3 *BM* 1 (September–October 1935):13–14; "The Unsteady World," *BM* 3 (July 1938):3; and "The Rise of African Sentiment," *BM* 3 (July 1938):5.
49. Marcus Garvey, "A Straight Talk to the People," *BM* 3 (March 1938):8.

Garvey's being the most outspoken black opponent of continued European domination of Africa in the postwar period. Paradoxically, he held up to blacks the system of European civilization as a mirror of racial success. In this context Garvey expressed strenuous opposition to black folk culture, which he viewed as inimical to racial progress and as evidence of the retardation that for generations had made for racial weakness. "Spiritual and Jazz Music are credited to the Negro," Garvey conceded, but "it was simply because we did not know better music."[50] Garvey's overriding concern with cultural replication rested on the assumption that "the future of our world holds very little for groups not organized on the basis of our present civilization."[51] In refracting black aspirations through the cultural and historical mirror of the dominant civilization, Garvey came to believe that all history was a process of duplication in which the positions of Africa and Europe had at one time been reversed:

> The World today is indebted to us for benefits of civilization. They stole our arts and sciences from Africa. Then why should we be ashamed of ourselves? Their MODERN IMPROVEMENTS are but DUPLICATES of a grander civilization that we reflected thousands of years ago, without the advantage of what is buried and still hidden, to be resurrected and reintroduced by the intelligence of our generation and our posterity.[52]

From this hypothesis, Garvey could perhaps rationalize his rejection of black folk culture as incidental to his vaunting of a much different and prototypical black civilization inherited by white Europe. In mirroring European civilization, blacks could reclaim their own.

50. *BM* 3 (November 1938):14; see also "[William] Isles Points Out Danger in Perpetuation of Slave Songs," *NW*, Saturday, 1 July 1922, p. 2.
51. "We Must Support a Good Cause," *BM* 2 (January 1937):6. The parallel was the process of "Darwinian mimicry" adopted by Theodore Herzl, founder of Jewish Zionism (see Theodore Herzl, *The Complete Diaries of Theodore Herzl*, Raphael Patai, ed., and Harry Zohn, trans. (New York: Herzl Press, 1960), 1:10 [quoted in Jacques Kornberg, "Theodore Herzl: A Reevaluation," *Journal of Modern History* 52 (June 1980):229]). Gershom Schocken ("Revisiting Zionism," *New York Review of Books*, 28 May 1981) points out that "Kurt Blumenfeld, the important ideologue of German Zionism, said with good reason: 'Zionism is the gift of Europe to the Jewish people' " (p. 42). Imanuel Geiss takes the view that Garvey was "striving to institute a basically modern social and political order" (*The Pan-African Movement*, pp. 279–82). Garvey's "modernizing" predisposition was criticized in 1925, however, by the Gold Coast exponent of African traditional polity, William Esuman-Gwira Sekyi (1892–1956), also known as Kobina Sekyi, in his seminal work of nationalist philosophy, *The Parting of the Ways* (Cape Coast: n.p., 1925). For a discussion of Sekyi and his ideas, see J. Ayodele Langley, "Modernization and Its Malcontents: Kobina Sekyi of Ghana and the Re-Statement of African Political Theory, 1892–1956," *Research Review* 6 (University of Ghana, Institute of African Studies, 1970):1–61; see also *Pan-Africanism and Nationalism in West Africa, 1900–1945* (Oxford: Clarendon Press, 1973), pp. 97–103.
52. *NW*, Saturday, 6 June 1925, p. 1.

When asked where the Negro could "build [his] nation, kingdom or empire [and lay] the foundation of his industrial and commercial marts," Garvey's answer contained no trace of doubt:

> There are more than two hundred million Negroes in Africa with a continent that is large and resourceful. Let him build there, let him build his own nations, let him build his own civilization, let him show the world a duplicate in Africa of what exist[s] in Europe.[53]

For Garvey, then, history conformed to a cycle of success and failure: "Just as the Negro ruled once and lost his power, so some of the races that are ruling now will in the cycle of things lose their power." He foresaw "great hope for the Negro to be restored to his true political position, because sooner or later some of these dominant nations and races will fall."[54] Garvey at other times could not help but inveigh against his racial compatriots' failure:

> Our civilization to-day is the positive result of the creative thought of those who are actually mastering our politics, our sciences, our industry. The Negro laments his position in the midst of these changes, whether they be upward or downward, but has failed within modern times to apply himself to the willingness of doing—of creating for himself, thereby establishing his own place in civilization.[55]

In 1925 Garvey assured his followers: "It is because we have studied history that we of the Universal Negro Improvement Association have started toward empire."[56]

Garvey deliberately orchestrated a set of cultural and political parallels to inculcate a "success mentality" among blacks. As early as 1914, he urged blacks to "look around and take a leaf out of the book of EXAMPLES set before you by our [white] friends and benefactors—our brothers of Salvation." In America, he stated "that even as there is a White Star Line owned by white men, there is going to be a Black Star Line owned by black men."[57] In 1920 Garvey also declared in presenting the prospectus of the UNIA's $2 million "Liberian Construction Loan": "The Gold Cross of African Redemption will be to Negroes what the Victoria Cross of England has been to Englishmen, and the Iron Cross of Germany has been to the Germans." He adopted the aristocratic titles, honorary degrees, and the assorted panoply of devices symbolizing the grandeur of Europe's achievements. Garvey defended these controversial actions by exhorting his followers:

53. Marcus Garvey, "A Dialogue: What's the Difference?" chap. 2, *BM* 1 (July 1935):15.
54. Marcus Garvey, "A Dialogue: What's the Difference?" chap. 1, *BM* 1 (June 1935):12. Elsewhere Garvey stated: "Civilization is a cycle. It changes." ("The Work That Has Been Done," *BM* 3 [July 1938]:9).
55. Marcus Garvey, "The Willingness to Do," *BM* 1 (December 1935):3.
56. "Building Empires," *NW*, Saturday, 3 October 1925, p. 1.
57. *NW*, Saturday, 21 June 1919.

You can have your own king, your own emperor, your own pope, your own dukes, your own everything—therefore, don't bow down to other races for recognition. . . . A white king has no more right to drive in a golden coach than your king and sovereign. Their pope has no more right of putting on sacred robes than your pope. . . .[58]

Equality was the goal behind such strict correspondences: not to overtake the white race but to elevate the black man to "a normal existence" as "a standard creature."[59] He also desired "the Negro . . . coming into his own as a standardized race."[60] This was "the philosophy taught in a nutshell by the UNIA." Garvey added: "Until you can produce what the white man has produced you will not be his equal."[61] A 1934 article in Garvey's *Black Man* reaffirmed the view that "when the Negro can produce scientists, statesmen, philosophers, leaders, creators, similar to those of the white race, and when he can lay down a proper system of civilization, which is of the standard of the white man, [will] the prejudice from which he now suffers . . . disappear as the mist before dawn of day."[62] He readily admitted: "In fact, I am criticising the black man. I am a queer critic, but I am a logical one."[63] He regularly inveighed against the perceived failures of his race:

Unfortunately, among the sentimental, emotional and sometimes superstitious, people of ultra mental slackness are members of the Negro race who dream and see visions, not in the sober practical way but as actuated and influenced by pure emotion. Such a practice has led the race to no appreciative goal, but to the contrary has left us dumped in the gutter of practical life.[64]

In Garvey's view, any support to the aesthetic revival of black folk culture had to be rejected, and he viewed such exercises as further perpetu-

58. "Aims and Objects of the UNIA," lesson 3, "School of African Philosophy." The curriculum of the School of African Philosophy encompassed "over forty-two subjects touching vitally every phase of human life" ("The School of African Philosophy," *BM* 2 [December 1937]:4).

59. Marcus Garvey, "The Negro and Himself," *BM* 1 (December 1933):12; see also "Addressing the People of Detroit," *BM* 2 (December 1937):11.

60. "A United Wish," *BM* 4 (June 1939):1.

61. "Addressing the People of Detroit," p. 12.

62. "If I Were a Negro (by a White Man)," *BM* 1 (January 1934):7.

63. "Addressing the People of Detroit," p. 11.

64. Marcus Garvey, "The Cold Truth," *BM* 2 (August 1937):6–7. Kornberg comments: "Herzl fits a type, described by Rupert Emerson [*From Empire to Nation: The Rise to Self-Assertion of Asian and African Peoples*, Cambridge, Mass.: Harvard University Press, 1960], dominating the first phase of nationalist leadership among a colonized people. Westernized, torn loose from their roots, these leaders are at the same time spurned by the dominant Europeans. . . . Once bitten by Europe, these men absorb its perspectives, and suffer from . . . uncritical self-humiliation and [the] acceptance of alien superiority. Measured against Europe, native history seems a despised catalog of superstition, ignorance, and political impotence. Their people must be remade into masters by adapting the West's instruments of power—modern government, science and technology" (pp. 234–35).

ating the cultural and political humiliation of Africa. Garvey thus pronounced his anathema upon the entire body of literature produced during the Harlem Renaissance of the middle and late 1920s. "Our race, within recent years," he declared, "has developed a new group of writers who have been prostituting their intelligence, under the direction of the white man, to bring out and show up the worst traits of our people." He named the key literary figures, spurning them all: "Claude McKay, the Jamaican Negro, is not singular in the authorship of such books. W. E. B. Du Bois, of America; Walter White, Weldon Johnson, Eric Waldron [*sic*], of British Guiana, and others, have written similar books, while we have had recently a large number of sappy poems from the rising poets."[65]

Culture served, in Garvey's view, as a propaganda vehicle for the concept of dominance. To be justifiable, black literature should inculcate in the black man the same "dominant idea of control" monopolized by the white man: "He [the white man] feels he must govern, that no one must be above him. Such a feeling inspires him to its accomplishment and so he is a ruler everywhere you find him."[66] Garvey's own literary efforts exemplified this intent. *Coronation of an African King*, a three-act play written and produced in 1930 by Garvey in Kingston, dramatized those ceremonial symbols of regnant power adopted officially by the UNIA at its second convention in 1921. The *Negro World* headlined in the following terms: "ANCIENT ETHIOPIAN CEREMONIAL COURT RECEPTION REVIVED AMID SCENES OF UNUSUAL POMP, MAGNIFICENCE AND SPLENDOR BY U.N.I.A."[67] Like his great hero Napoleon, Garvey "took to believing in Semblances," to quote Thomas Carlyle. Indeed, his first wife went so far as to remark on the manifestation of Garvey's "Napoleonic complex." The same association also appears in the fictionalized portrait that Garvey received in Dusé Mohamed Ali's auto-

65. " 'Home to Harlem,' Claude McKay's Damaging Book, Should Earn Wholesale Condemnation of Negroes," *NW*, Saturday, 29 September 1928, p. 1. For McKay's defense of the cultural import of his novel against an earlier attack by William Ferris (*Pittsburgh Courier*, 31 March 1928), see Claude McKay to James Ivy, 20 May 1928, in Wayne F. Cooper, ed., *The Passion of Claude McKay: Selected Poetry and Prose, 1912–1948* (New York: Schocken Books, 1973), p. 145. The Harlem Renaissance is analyzed in Lewis, *When Harlem Was in Vogue*; Nathan I. Huggins, *The Harlem Renaissance* (New York: Oxford University Press, 1971); Bernard Bell, "Folk Art and the Harlem Renaissance," *Phylon* 36 (June 1975):155–63; and Chidi Ikonne, *From Du Bois to Van Vechten: The Early New Negro Literature, 1903–1926* (Westport, Conn.: Greenwood Press, 1981). Hodge Kirnon noted that "Garveyism has accounted for a period in the intellectual life of the race that might well be called the 'Negro Renaissance.' " (*NW*, Saturday, 28 January 1922, p. 7). The *NW* acted as an outlet for some of the early writing of the Harlem Renaissance, e.g., Zora Neale Hurston, "Bits of Our Harlem" and "Passion" (Saturday, 15 April 1922, p. 6); Hodge Kirnon, "Claude McKay's 'Harlem Shadows,' " (Saturday, 3 June 1922, p. 6). Eric Walrond's highly praised book of short stories, *Tropic Death* (New York: Boni & Liveright, 1926), was also serialized in the *NW*.

66. "A Dialogue," chap. 2, p. 14.

67. See William H. Ferris's lengthy editorial, "The Psychology of Robes and Pageants" (*NW*, Saturday, 15 October 1921, p. 4), written in response to a critique by the *New York Freeman* (5 October 1921); and J. A. Rogers's comment: "Though he was opposing British imperialism, he [Garvey] imitated its forms. Apparently he had never been able to throw off the impression British folderol and glitter had made on him in his childhood" (John Henrik Clarke, ed., *World's Great Men of Color*, rev. ed. [New York: Collier-Macmillan, 1972], p. 419).

biographical story, "Ere Roosevelt Came," wherein he appears in the thinly disguised character Napoleon Bonaparte Hatbry.[68]

Climbing the Ladder of Success

At the age of eighteen Garvey said that he had felt "a yearning for service of some kind, because of [his] training in the first government—government in the family."[69] This search for service involved Garvey in the simultaneous pursuit of material success. In his view, success was a requisite to leadership, just as leadership was a requisite to effective service. Thus, the paradigm of the self-made man was integral to Garvey's governing conception of racial leadership and service.

Garvey's adherence to the ideals of service and success, on the one hand, and to the practical boosterism of the self-made man, on the other, created a peculiar tension in his later relationships with both W. E. B. Du Bois and Booker T. Washington. The antagonism between Du Bois and Garvey was more cultural than political. It stemmed from the struggle between the nineteenth-century New England patrician ideal, translated by Du Bois into his concept of "the Talented Tenth," and the competing ideal of the self-made man that provided Garvey with his rationale. "Many American Negroes," Du Bois asserted, viewed Garvey's meteoric rise as the "enthroning of a demagogue, who with monkey shines was deluding the people and taking their hard-earned dollars."[70] Garvey, for his part, accused Du Bois of setting himself up as "the highest social dignitary." Garvey saw in himself the idealized self-made man who triumphed over continual disadvantage in a heroic struggle for success and survival. On this basis he drew a harsh distinction between Du Bois and himself:

> Marcus Garvey was born in 1887; Du Bois was born in 1868; that shows that Du Bois is old enough to be Marcus Garvey's father. But what has happened? Within the fifty-five years of Du Bois' life we find him still

68. Thomas Carlyle, *On Heroes, Hero-Worship, and the Heroic in History*, lecture 6, p. 241, in *The Works of Thomas Carlyle*, Centenary Edition, vol. 5 (London: Chapman and Hall Limited, 1897); Amy Ashwood Garvey, unpublished MS, "Marcus Garvey: Portrait of a Liberator"; Dusé Mohamed Ali, "Ere Roosevelt Came: A Record of the Adventures of the Man in the Cloak", serialized in *Comet* (Lagos), chap. 2 (3 March 1934); chap. 5 (24 March 1934); chap. 10 (28 April 1934); chap. 13 (26 May 1934); chap. 14 (9 June 1934); chap. 20 (21 July 1934); chap. 25 (8 September 1934); and chap. 30 (13 October 1934). (The editor wishes to thank Dr. Ian Duffield of Edinburgh University for bringing this important source to his attention.) According to J. A. Rogers, Garvey "worshipped Napoleon" (*World's Great Men of Color* 2:415). For an interesting psychohistorical perspective on the subject, see E. Tangye Lean, *The Napoleonists: A Study in Political Disaffection, 1760–1960* (London: Oxford University Press, 1970).

69. *Daily Gleaner*, Tuesday, 22 January 1935.

70. W. E. B. Du Bois, "Back to Africa," *Century Magazine* 105 (February 1923):539; "The Talented Tenth," in Booker T. Washington et al., *The Negro Problem* (New York: James Pott, 1903), pp. 31–75.

living on the patronage of good white people, and with the thirty-six years of Marcus Garvey's (who was born poor and whose father, according to Du Bois, died in a poor house) he is able to at least pass over the charity of white people and develop an independent program originally financed by himself to the extent of thousands of dollars, now taken up by the Negro people themselves. Now which of the two is poorer in character and manhood?

Then, in a bold assertion of his self-worth against "Du Bois [who] personally had made a success of nothing," Garvey declared:

Suppose for the proof of the better education and ability Garvey and Du Bois were to dismantle and put aside all they possess and were placed in the same environment to start life over afresh for the test of the better man? What would you say about this, doctor? Marcus Garvey is willing now because he is conceited enough to believe that in the space of two years he would make you look like a tramp in the competitive rivalry for a higher place in the social, economic world.[71]

This ethic of "competitive rivalry" that aroused such hubris in Garvey was strongly abhorrent to Du Bois on philosophical and cultural grounds. Beyond the special Afro-American quality of Du Bois's experience, his social outlook had been profoundly shaped by the New England morality of patrician service and sacrifice. Du Bois could not have viewed with equanimity the brash and headstrong claims to "competitive rivalry" of his self-made Jamaican antagonist.[72]

Conversely, Garvey shared with Booker T. Washington a deep commitment to the success ethic and its application to the goal of racial improvement. Washington rooted his racial uplift program in the gospel of the self-made man, and he "wished to be seen by the world, as the American success hero in black."[73] Indeed, Garvey perceived similarities between his

71. Marcus Garvey, "W. E. Burghardt Du Bois as a Hater of Dark People," *NW*, Saturday, 13 February 1923; reprinted in Amy Jacques Garvey, comp., *Philosophy and Opinions of Marcus Garvey; or, Africa for the Africans* (New York: Universal Publishing House, 1926; reprint eds., London: Frank Cass, 1967, and New York: Atheneum, 1969), 2:313, 315, 319. For Garvey's "Swapping Stories of Success" against Du Bois, A. Philip Randolph, Chandler Owen, and Cyril V. Briggs, see "Marcus Garvey Asks Malicious Negroes Who Criticize Him to Prove Their Ability," *NW*, Saturday, 8 July 1922, p. 1.

72. For a discerning analysis of Du Bois's "championing of the elitism of the 'talented tenth' " on the basis of the New England tradition of "Puritan moral elitism" (p. 7), see Arnold Rampersad, *The Art and Imagination of W. E. B. Du Bois* (Cambridge: Harvard University Press, 1976). Rampersad underscores the importance of Du Bois's "moral fervor" and views it correctly as the basis of Du Bois's "hunger for an aristocratic tradition" (p. 10); see also E. Digby Baltzell, *Puritan Boston and Quaker Philadelphia: Two Protestant Ethics and the Spirit of Class Authority and Leadership* (New York: The Free Press, 1979).

73. Louis R. Harlan, ed., *The Booker T. Washington Papers*, vol. 1: *The Autobiographical Writings* (Urbana: University of Illinois Press, 1972), p. xv. Harlan also notes that "when

own confrontations with Du Bois and the earlier Washington–Du Bois controversy. "When Booker T. Washington, by his own effort and energy, attempted to climb the ladder of success among his people," Garvey claimed, "we had the sage of Atlanta, Berlin, and Harvard, who attacked him most viciously from every quarter."[74]

Du Bois, in his famous critique of Washington in *The Souls of Black Folk* (1903), attributed Washington's possession of the "mark of the successful man" to what he said was "his singleness of vision and thorough oneness with his age." This was an expansion upon Du Bois's earlier *Dial* magazine critique (16 July 1901) of Washington's autobiography, *Up from Slavery*, in which Du Bois asserted that Washington had "by singular insight . . . intuitively grasped the spirit of the age that was dominating the North," mastering "the speech and thought of triumphant commercialism and the ideals of material prosperity." This capacity explained "Mr. Washington's success, North and South, with his gospel of Work and Money."

Such attributes were, of course, entirely synonymous with the reigning gospel of success, but in Du Bois's view, they "raised opposition to him [Washington] from widely divergent sources." This was, indeed, the crucial factor that gave the split between Washington and Du Bois the character of "two warring ideals," to borrow the phrase made famous by Du Bois in another context. The two men represented opposing American ideals of civilization, within and through which each sought to legitimize his separate vision of the "strivings" of Afro-Americans.[75]

Booker T. Washington was in fact responsible for producing his own impressive body of conduct-of-life literature, on which the character-ethic stage of the success cult rested to a significant degree. These are, in addition to his major autobiographical writings, *The Story of My Life* (1900) and *Up from Slavery* (1901), *Black Belt Diamonds* (1898), *Sowing and Reaping* (1900), *Character Building* (1902), and *Putting the Most into Life* (1906). This nineteenth-century philosophy of the character ethic also deeply pervaded Garvey's outlook, which he translated into essays with such titles as "The Character of Races" (*Philosophy and Opinions* 2:134), "The Negro and Character" (*BM* 1 [May–June 1934]:5–6), and "Character! Character! Character! A Vital Necessity" (*BM* 2 [September–October 1935]:6–7).

---

raising funds in the North he [Washington] drew the admiration and the contributions of such men as Andrew Carnegie, for like the steel millionaire Washington had sprung from obscurity and by hard work and good management had achieved success" (*The Booker T. Washington Papers* 2:xxviii–xxix).

74. *NW*, Saturday, 20 September 1922, p. 1.

75. W. E. B. Du Bois, *The Souls of Black Folk* (Rpt., New York: Fawcett Publications, 1961), p. 43; "The Evolution of Negro Leadership," *The Dial* 31 (16 July 1901):54; "Strivings of the Negro People," *Atlanta Monthly* 80 (August 1897):194. Amy Ashwood Garvey recalled that "[Booker T.] Washington had been a man after his [Garvey's] own heart; a self-made man who had triumphed over many an obstacle, but who, in his hour of success, never failed to remember the less fortunate or less gifted members of his race and did his utmost to assist them" (unpublished MS, "Portrait of a Liberator: Biographical Sketch of Marcus Garvey," p. 82).

But significant differences in viewpoint between Washington and Garvey reflected the impact of societal change. In holding up "the self-made black capitalist as a hero of his race," C. Vann Woodward notes that "Washington went back to a bygone day for his economic philosophy," which he describes as consisting "of the mousetrap-maker-and-beaten-path maxims of thrift, virtue, enterprise, and free competition." Woodward also notes that "it was the faith by which the white middle-class preceptors of his youth had explained success, combined with a belief that, as he expressed it, 'there is little race prejudice in the American dollar.' "[76] In short, Washington's philosophy of uplift reflected the nineteenth-century character ethic, with worldly success rewarding such homely virtues as diligence, industry, and frugality. Its emphasis, as noted by Richard Weiss, "was on the balanced, ordered, harmonious nature of the social organism."[77] In effect, Woodward suggests, Washington's philosophy "dealt with the present in terms of the past," and, in economic terms, was "more congenial to the pre-machine age than to the twentieth century," when massive industrial expansion in America progressively reduced the options for success to the petty entrepreneurial trades.[78]

Conversely, Garvey was the archetypal black spokesman of the success cult's most optimistic phase, at the end of World War I, when the vision of success became subsumed by the rush to financial speculation. Nontraditional opportunities became available to the small entrepreneur with the dramatic rise of finance capital to a position of dominance in the American political economy. The process was already well under way by the war's beginning, and postwar America emerged as the new banking capital of the world, bringing with it large-scale financing and control of industrial development.[79] Garvey's philosophy of success would come to incorporate the chief mental attributes imparted by the period of industrialization and by the new era of American economic growth. These were the aggressive virtues of self-mastery, mind power, determination, energy, ambition, force of will—all the virtues of personal dominance, which, according to Garvey, assured "that [one would] win the battle over others."

76. C. Vann Woodward, *Origins of the New South, 1877–1913* (Baton Rouge: Louisiana State University Press, 1951), p. 365.

77. Weiss, *The American Myth of Success*, p. 117.

78. Woodward, *Origins of the New South*, pp. 365–66.

79. Douglas F. Dowd, *The Twisted Dream: Capitalist Development in the United States Since 1776*, 2d ed. (Cambridge, Mass.: Winthrop Publishers, Inc., 1977), pp. 94–98; see also Derek H. Aldcroft, *From Versailles to Wall Street, 1919–1929* (Berkeley: University of California Press, 1977). According to Aldcroft, "by the later 1920s speculation had moved into the realms of fantasy—a gambler's paradise seemingly without end—which bore little relation to the current or prospective business conditions or to the level of profits." It is Aldcroft's opinion that "probably the share market mania can only be satisfactorily explained in psychological terms" (pp. 195–96).

Confraternity and Self-culture

When he left Jamaica for America, however, Garvey's point of view had reflected Booker T. Washington's nineteenth-century ethic. With the launching of the UNIA in 1914, Garvey had renounced participation in local Jamaican politics, declaring that "the society [UNIA] is non-political" and reportedly asking his followers "to eschew politics as a means of social improvement."[80] Establishing a collegiate and social fund within the UNIA, he had proposed an industrial farm and institute in Jamaica, to be based "on the same plan as the Tuskegee Normal and Industrial Institute of which Doctor Booker T. Washington is head."

At the outset of the UNIA, in 1914, Garvey's decision to eschew politics was perfectly suited to the organization's social program, which espoused the principles of confraternity, liberal humanitarianism, and self-culture. As Garvey himself proudly admitted during its first year of operation, the UNIA was like "any other humanitarian society in the British Empire."[81] Its essential purpose was "to achieve the highest standard of civilised culture," and its stated aim was "to establish a Universal Confraternity among the race," from which came the word *universal* in the title of the UNIA.[82]

Garvey actually established two separate entities in 1914 under the combined title of the Universal Negro Improvement and Conservation Association and African Communities League. The distinction was not merely semantic, since it reflected a basic dichotomy of purpose which made the UNIA, as originally conceived by Garvey, only the fraternal-benevolent arm of the wider movement. This was conveyed in the first five of the original list of ten "General Objects":

> To establish a Universal Confraternity among the race.
> To promote the spirit of race pride and love.
> To reclaim the fallen of the race.
> To administer to and assist the needy.
> To assist in civilizing the backward tribes of Africa.

Objects six through ten, conversely, described the "imperial" character of the African Communities League (ACL), a concept that Garvey used as a metaphor for his ideal of racial dominion. Garvey's view of empire stemmed from the same conception that had become enshrined in the ethos of late Victorian England and the age of high imperialism that it ushered in. It paralleled, moreover, the Edwardian view of the British Empire, which Lord Curzon defined as "a great historical and political and sociological fact which is one of the guiding factors in the history of mankind." Historian Michael Howard declared that in pre-1914 Britain, "Empire, Race and War . . . were seen as

---

80. *Gleaner*, Thursday, 23 September 1915.
81. *Gleaner*, Thursday, 28 January 1915.
82. *Daily Chronicle*, Friday, 26 March 1915.

lix

facts of life to be accepted if not indeed welcomed; certainly ones that presented challenges to be met and problems to be solved if disaster was not to ensue." Garvey, in disclosing that the full title of the ACL was the "African Communities (Imperial) League," provided an important clue to certain characteristics that it shared with the program of the Imperial Federation League (IFL) in Great Britain. Between 1884 and 1887, this body was largely responsible for moving the ideology of imperialism beyond that of a general sentiment and translating it into a specific program that looked toward "the permanent unity of the Empire" on the basis of closer union between Great Britain and her white self-governing colonies.[83]

A similar vision of imperial union animated Garvey's declaration, in 1914, that the objectives of his organization were also "to strengthen the imperialism of independent African States," and "to establish Commissionaries or Agencies in the principal countries of the world for the protection of all Negroes, irrespective of nationality." Equally important, Garvey's initial concept of racial unity rested on a perspective of imperial federation that was similar to that enunciated by the IFL. In his October 1913 article published in the *African Times and Orient Review*, entitled "The British West Indies in the Mirror of Civilization—History Making by Colonial Negroes," Garvey not only voiced his support for a future federation of the British West Indian islands, which he said was "sure to come about because the people of these islands are all one," but even more important, he prophesied that this "turning point in the history of the West Indies" would make "the people who inhabit that portion of the Western Hemisphere . . . the instruments of uniting a scattered race who, before the close of many centuries, will found an Empire on which the sun shall shine as ceaselessly as it shines on the Empire of the North to-day" (p. 160). In reality, therefore, Garvey's racial vision accurately expressed the prevailing ideology of race and empire that to a significant degree shaped the political consciousness of the Edwardian era and the language that expressed it.

The distinguishing feature of the UNIA and ACL was thus their respective embodiment of the fraternal and imperial principles. Not until the middle of 1918 did the two entities became fused politically, at which time the

83. George Nathaniel Curzon, Marquis Curzon of Kedleston, *Subjects of the Day* (London: George Allen and Unwin, 1915), p. 5; Michael Howard, "Empire, Race, and War in pre-1914 Britain," in Hugh Lloyd-Jones et al., *History and Imagination: Essays in Honour of H. R. Trevor-Roper* (London: Duckworth, 1981), pp. 340, 342; M. D. Burgess, "Lord Rosebery and the Imperial Federation League, 1884–1893," *New Zealand Journal of History* 13 (October 1979), p. 165; see also M. D. Burgess, "The Imperial Federation Movement in Great Britain, 1869–1893," (Ph.D. diss., Leicester University, 1976); J. E. Tyler, *The Struggle for Imperial Unity, 1868–1895* (London: Longmans, 1938); and H. C. G. Matthew, *The Liberal Imperialists: The Ideas and Politics of a Post-Gladstonian Elite* (Oxford: Oxford University Press, 1973). Garvey's subsequent proposal for "Colonial Representation in the Imperial Parliament," contained in the first plank of his election campaign manifesto in Jamaica in 1929, was also very similar to the proposal of the Imperial Federation League to have colonial delegates sit in the House of Lords ("A Thought from Jamaica," *BM* 4 [February 1939]:15; Burgess, "Lord Rosebery and the Imperial Federation League," pp. 167, 169, 175, n. 42).

UNIA-ACL's *Constitution and Book of Laws* declared in its statement of aims (article 1, sec. 3), that among its objectives was "to assist in the development of Independent Negro Nations and Communities." Even so, the UNIA maintained a distinct role as the membership organization of the movement, while the ACL was its avowedly propagandistic and commercial wing.

The essential fraternal character of the UNIA did not go unnoticed. In 1922, in his perceptive analysis of Garvey and the UNIA, Hodge Kirnon stated that "there is no indication that Garvey meant it [the UNIA] to be anything more than a fraternal order." Harry Albro Williamson, the leading bibliophile of black Masonry, later wrote an important article on Prince Hall Masonry for the *Negro World* (3 June 1922). Amy Jacques Garvey later recalled that Garvey became a Mason "through the influence of John E. Bruce and Dr. [F. W.] Ellegor [but] he did not attend Masonic meetings, he was always too busy, so the connection dropped." Moreover, she disclosed that UNIA chapters operated quite freely within the ranks of black fraternities.[84]

During the final four years of his life, Garvey turned even more emphatically toward the Masonic ideal based on secret knowledge. With the defeat of Ethiopia in the Italo-Ethiopian War of 1935–1936 and the rapid escalation of militarism throughout Europe and Asia, Garvey revised dramatically his previous estimates of what political movements alone could be expected to accomplish. Thus, he viewed as problematic the absence of "masonry in his [the Negro's] political ideals," noting that "there is nothing secret in what he is aiming at for his own hope of preservation."[85] Garvey was alluding to the evolution of the fraternal idea from its earlier craft stage into a potent

84. "Hodge Kirnon Analyzes the Garvey Movement," *NW*, Saturday, 28 January 1922, p. 7; Western States Black Research Center, Los Angeles, Amy Jacques Garvey to Theodore G. Vincent, 15 July 1970, and 6 June 1972; see also Vincent, *Black Power and the Garvey Movement*, p. 158. The role of fraternal and benevolent organizations among blacks still awaits major research; however, see W. E. B. Du Bois, ed., *Economic Co-operation among Negro Americans* (Atlanta University Publications, no. 12, 1907); Monroe N. Work, "Secret Societies as Factors in the Social and Economical Life of the Negro," in James E. McCulloch, ed., *Democracy in Earnest . . .* (Washington, D.C.: Southern Sociological Congress, 1918), pp. 342–50; Charles Harris Wesley, "Jonathan Davis and the Rise of Black Fraternal Organizations," *Crisis* 84 (1977):112–18; Gunnar Myrdal, "Voluntary Associations," chap. 43, sec. 5, *An American Dilemma*; James B. Browning, "The Beginnings of Insurance Enterprise among Negroes," *Journal of Negro History* 22 (1937):417–32; Edward Nelson Palmer, "Negro Secret Societies," *Social Forces* 23 (December 1944):207–12; Alvin J. Schmidt, *Fraternal Organizations* (Westport, Conn.: Greenwood Press, 1981). For accounts of the craft of Masonry among blacks, see Charles Harris Wesley, *Prince Hall: Life and Legacy* (Washington, D.C.: United Supreme Council, Southern Jurisdiction, Prince Hall, Affiliation, 1977); and William A. Muraskin, *Middle Class Blacks in a White Society: Prince Hall Freemasonry in America* (Berkeley: University of California Press, 1975).

85. Marcus Garvey, "A Warning to the Negro," *BM* 2 (May–June 1936):9. Students who were enrolled in Garvey's School of African Philosophy were required to sign an oath swearing themselves to secrecy (unpublished MS, notebook of Elinor White, School of African Philosophy, 23 September 1937). Garvey also issued instructions about the use of his poem *The Tragedy of White Injustice*: "Never allow it to get into the hands of a white man if possible" (lesson 1, "School of African Philosophy," pp. 11–12).

political vehicle, one based on the organization of secret revolutionary brotherhoods.[86]

From the start, the UNIA shared numerous features with fraternal benevolent orders. The UNIA's governing *Constitution and Book of Laws* held the same status and function as Freemasonry's *Book of Constitutions* and *Book of the Law*. The UNIA's titular "potentate" was clearly analogous to the "imperial potentate" of the Ancient Egyptian Arabic Order of the Nobles of the Mystic Shrine, or black Shriners. The High Executive Council of the UNIA and ACL reflected the Imperial Council of the black Shriners and the Supreme Council of Freemasonry in general. The elaborate and resplendent public displays by the UNIA, particularly during its annual conventions, drew upon the example of the black Shriners and other fraternal groups. On 6 August 1921, the *Negro World* reported that at the opening of the Second International Convention of the UNIA, the potentate, Gabriel Johnson, "wore a military-shaped helmet, with large flowing white feather, closely resembling the uniform hat worn by Masons on special parade occasions" (p. 3). Other features shared with fraternal orders included solemn oaths and binding pledges, special degrees of chivalry (such as the Cross of African Redemption, Knight of the Sublime Order of the Nile, and Knight of the Order of Ethiopia), and an auxiliary Ladies' Division with its own "lady president" (article 5, sec. 5). An editorial in the *Negro World* (30 April 1921) entitled "A Word Regarding Titles," pointed out that "the Order of Free and Accepted Masons, the Grand United Order of Odd Fellows and other religious and fraternal bodies have a hierarchy of titles. And we do not see wherein the U.N.I.A. is introducing an innovation."

The UNIA and ACL performed an important benevolent function through provision of death benefits to members, a service all black fraternal orders had been obligated to offer because insurance companies did not extend coverage to blacks. "The distinctive thing about Negro [voluntary] associations," wrote Gunnar Myrdal in *An American Dilemma*, "has been the death benefit and sickness insurance features of some Negro lodges and benevolent societies" (p. 955). In like fashion, the UNIA and ACL financed its benefit program through assessment of dues and fees: a monthly subscription of twenty-five cents; the annual Parent Body tax of one dollar; and the death tax of ten cents (article 8, secs. 1 and 3).

The principles of organized benevolence were formally enunciated in the third and fourth objects listed in article 1, section 3, of the constitution of the UNIA, namely, "to reclaim the fallen of the race," and "to administer to and assist the needy." The UNIA's separate charter of incorporation was filed in June 1918, "to promote and practice the principles of Benevolence, and for the protection and social intercourse of its members." Similarly, the preamble to the constitution stated that "the Universal Negro Improvement

---

86. E. J. Hobsbawm, *Primitive Rebels* (New York: W. W. Norton & Co., 1965), shows that ritual organizations in Europe "all tended to belong to a single family" of Masonic groups that were descended from the eighteenth century (p. 162).

Association and African Communities' League is a social, friendly, humanitarian, charitable, educational, institutional, constructive and expansive society, and is founded by persons, desiring to the utmost, to work for the general uplift of the Negro peoples of the world." Article 5, sections 47 and 48, provided for loans to members and for an employment bureau for members in each local division.

This extensive commitment to fraternal and benevolent endeavor directly reflected the fact that Garvey's own position as a printer had made him a member of the Jamaican artisanry elite.[87] Mutual improvement associations had served for many years as vehicles for the social aspirations of this group within urban Kingston. Prominent among these were the Jamaica United Brotherhood, Jamaica Labourers' Cooperative League, Royal Prince Albert Mutual Society, Jamaica Workmen's Mutual Aid and Benevolent Society, the Franklin Town Benevolent Society, and numerous branches of Masonic lodges.

In addition to the goals of mutual improvement and organized benevolence, the UNIA also sought to develop among blacks the ideal of cultural self-improvement. The stated aim of the UNIA's Collegiate Industrial and Social Fund in October 1914 was "to establish educational and industrial (day and evening) training colleges for the purpose of the further education and culture of our boys and girls." This was echoed in the *Constitution and Book of Laws*, which declared that the UNIA undertook "to establish Universities, Colleges, Academies and Schools for the racial education and culture of the people." A contemporary close acquaintance of Garvey, one who "during the years came into daily contact with him," later would write that "even in the days when Garvey was just another youngster about town . . . he went about forming debating groups and societies for promoting culture and racial pride."[88] This might help to account for the UNIA's extensive program of lectures and debates, which provided a community forum for the principle of self-culture and improvement. Weekly UNIA lectures included such subjects as "Self-industry," "Self-appreciation," "Duty of Citizenship," "Despair and Its Cure," "Music," "Spiritual and Moral Law of Man," "Hygiene and Its Relation to Public Health," "Character," "Cooperation," "Sanitation," "Education and What It Means," "The Signs of the Times," "What Shall We Do with the Child," and "Thrift." Similar discussion programs had popular precedence in the existing agencies of self-culture in Kingston, such as the Wesley Guild and the East Queen Street Baptist Temperance and Literary Society.

The UNIA charter of incorporation promised to serve the development of its members' "mental and physical culture." When Garvey settled down to

---

87. For the parallel ethnic linkage between fraternal organizations and social and political struggles of labor, see Mary Anne Clawson, "Brotherhood, Class, and Patriarchy: Fraternalism in Europe and America" (Ph.D. diss., State University of New York at Stony Brook, 1980).

88. Randolph Williams, "This *Is* Marcus Garvey," *Jamaica Standard*, Thursday, 26 January 1939, p. 6.

organizing the UNIA in New York, he immediately promoted what he termed "social uplift work." He proposed the erection of a $200,000 building in Harlem to be, in his words, "the source from which we will train and educate our people to those essentials that will make them a more cultured and better race."[89]

In effect, through the organization of the UNIA, Garvey devised a combination fraternal body and popular lyceum. The fusion of the two distinct but overlapping traditions of fraternalism and self-culture was made explicit in the UNIA's constitution in the section governing the issuance of charters and the setting up of local bodies:

> Sec. 4. A charter may be issued to seven or more citizens of any community whose intelligence is such as to bring them within respectful recognition of the educated and cultured of such a community, provided there is no chartered division in such a community.

A constant throughout Garvey's career was his self-proclaimed role of public lecturer. As Garvey himself put it:

> I am a public lecturer, but I am President-General of the Universal Negro Improvement Association. As a public lecturer I endeavour to help to educate the public, particularly of the race, as I meet that public . . . if the public is thoughtful it will be benefited by the things I say. I do not speak carelessly or recklessly but with a definite object of helping the people, especially those of my race, to know, to understand to realise themselves.[90]

The influence on Garvey of the combined lyceum-chautauqua[91] era requires further research, but it is apparent that Garvey achieved through the organization of the UNIA a dynamic linkage between the traditional forms of racial confraternity and the educational programs of self-culture. This organization was also responsible for "generat[ing] the national industrial education movement, emphasizing self-help and economic and moral uplift"; out of it eventually emerged the whole system of "Negro industrial and

89. NNC, NMB, circular appeal letter, New York, ca. April–June 1918.
90. "A Straight Talk to the People," p. 8. For the history of the nineteenth century lyceum, see Carl Bode, *The American Lyceum: Town Meeting of the Mind* (New York: Oxford University Press, 1956); and Donald M. Scott, "The Popular Lecture and the Creation of a Public in Mid-Nineteenth-Century America," *Journal of American History* 66 (March 1980):791–809. According to Robert Weaver, "the [lyceum] movement as a whole provided a foundation for the lecture-lyceum, the chautauqua, and for adult education" ("Josiah Holbrook: Feeding the Passion for Self-Help," *Communication Quarterly* 24 [Fall 1976]:10).
91. The Chautauqua movement took its name from the Chautauqua Literary and Scientific Circle, founded in 1878 at Chautauqua, New York; see Joseph Gould, *The Chautauqua Movement: An Episode in the Continuing American Revolution* (New York: State University of New York, 1961); Theodore Morrison, *Chautauqua: A Center for Education, Religion, and the Arts in America* (Chicago: University of Chicago Press, 1974).

agricultural education" between 1880 and 1900.[92] "Negro industrial training" was, in reality, an applied branch of the system of vocational education pioneered by the self-culture movement during the second half of the nine-teenth century for the education of artisans and adult workers. According to John Cawelti, moreover, the self-culture movement provided "another important ideological source of the philosophy of success."[93] Through the Jamaica period (1914–1916), Garvey advanced the goals of benevolence and self-culture, not only as the basis of his social program but as the alternative to local political involvement.

Garvey adopted methods characteristic of the established agencies of self-culture and moral and intellectual improvement, including lectures, de-bates, adult classes, popular entertainments, religious exercises, and the publication of correspondence courses. A typical report of a 1914 UNIA meeting, for example, stated that "Mr. H. B. Green spoke on the value of a 'stock of good information combined with character.' "[94] Typical, also, were programs including musical and elocutionary performances. The UNIA became noted for the excellence of its large choirs and orchestras and its recitation programs. At Edelweiss Park, the UNIA headquarters in Jamaica, Garvey added an amphitheater for large musical programs and promenade concerts, which were in addition to the usual UNIA agenda of political meetings, inspirational lectures, recitations, elocution contests, and histori-cal pageants. As a result, the UNIA in Jamaica exerted a powerful formative influence on the evolution of popular theater.[95]

92. James D. Anderson, "The Hampton Model of Normal School Industrial Education, 1868–1900," in Vincent P. Franklin and James D. Anderson, eds., *New Perspectives on Black Educational History* (Boston: G. K. Hall, 1978), p. 61; see also Clyde Hall, *Black Vocational and Industrial Arts Education: Development and History* (Chicago: American Technical Society, 1973).

93. Cawelti, *Apostles of the Self-Made Man*, pp. 174–75. The author locates "the classic expressions of the ideal of self-culture" (p. 84) in the thought and writings of William Ellery Channing (1780–1842) and Ralph Waldo Emerson (1803–1882); see also Andrew Delbanco, *William Ellery Channing: An Essay on the Liberal Spirit in America* (Cambridge, Mass.: Harvard University Press, 1981); and David Robinson, *Apostle of Culture: Emerson as Preacher and Lecturer* (Philadelphia: University of Pennsylvania Press, 1982). William E. Channing's "lengthy discourse on emancipation" was claimed by a *Negro World* contributor to be "in accord with the spirit of the U.N.I.A." (Willis C. Perry, "A Fulfilled Prophecy—the Character of the African," *NW*, Saturday, 30 July 1921). For expositions of the self-culture ideal in relation to the character ethic stage of the success cult, see O. S. Fowler, *Self-Culture and Perfection of Character* (1851); Edwin P. Whipple, *Success and Its Conditions* (1888); Newell Dwight Hillis, *A Man's Value to Society: Studies in Self-Culture and Character* (1899); and *The Contagion of Character: Studies in Culture and Success* (New York: Fleming H. Revell Co., 1911).

94. *Gleaner*, Thursday, 8 October 1914; see also the article by Jamaican Rev. G. E. Stewart, D.D., high chancellor of the UNIA, "The Relation of Christian Principles to Mental Culture," *NW*, Saturday, 17 December 1921, p. 5.

95. Errol Hill, unpublished MS, "Garvey's Contribution to West Indian Drama," May 1971. In 1932 the entertainments at Edelweiss Park were promoted by "the Edelweiss Amusement Company, Ltd.," of which Marcus Garvey was chairman and Daisy L. Whyte, secretary; see also William Lawrence Stout, *Theatre in a Tent: The Development of a Provincial Entertainment* (Bowling Green, Ohio: Bowling Green University Popular Press, 1972), for the parallel with popular chautauqua entertainments.

As with the era's renowned speakers of the lyceum-chautauqua lecture circuit, Garvey's popular image was that of "an orator of exceptional force." In January 1919 a handbill for an address in Washington, D.C., described Garvey as "the Greatest Orator of the Negro Race" whose "reputation as an orator is world-wide, having addressed thousands in England, Scotland, France, Germany and America." In December 1920, Garvey was again termed "the Greatest Negro Orator of the Twentieth Century." The Black Star Line was described in November 1920 as "the result of a Herculean effort on the part of Marcus Garvey, world-famed Negro orator."[96] "Again and again the Negro is brought back," the editor of Garvey's *Negro World*, William H. Ferris maintained, "to the Fable of Hercules and the Wagoner and to Emerson's doctrine of Self-reliance."[97] In fact, Ferris argued, Garvey "preached with telling force and earnestness Emerson's gospel of self-reliance."[98] Furthermore, Ferris averred that "there is something in Emerson's advice to 'Hitch your wagon to a star,' " which was undoubtedly the same inspiration as the advice that Garvey used in his exhortation to "lift up yourselves men, take yourselves out of the mire and hitch your hopes to the stars; yes, rise as high as the very stars themselves."[99]

Transition to Radicalism

Garvey originally came to America to learn more about Tuskegee and to enlist support for his own Jamaican version. Instead, he became converted in America to the primacy and efficacy of political goals. "[The] new spirit of the new Negro does not seek industrial opportunity," Garvey said in 1921. He "seeks a political voice, and the world is amazed, the world is astounded that the Negro should desire a political voice, because after the voice comes a political place, and nobody thought the Negro would have asked for a place in the political sun of the world."

In abandoning his earlier static view of political abstinence, Garvey was not renouncing "the teachings of the great sage of Tuskegee"; he was assessing the needs of the time. Speaking at Liberty Hall in New York in October 1921, Garvey prefaced his analysis of the evolution of the UNIA into a political organization:

96. *NW*, Saturday, 1 November 1920, p. 5.
97. "Socialism and the Negro," *NW*, Saturday, 25 October 1919, p. 2.
98. Ferris, "Garvey and the Black Star Line," *Favorite Magazine*, p. 397.
99. *NW*, Saturday, 19 June 1920, p. 3; *The Philosophy and Opinions of Marcus Garvey* 1:78. While speaking at Liberty Hall during the same month, June 1920, Ferris returned to the subject of Emerson: "The wisest words uttered by Ralph Waldo Emerson were these: 'If you wish men, black or white is insignificant'" (*NW*, Saturday, 26 June 1920). According to Weiss, "Just as the Puritanism of Boston gave birth to the old success myth, so the transcendentalism of Concord gave birth to the new. . . . The new movement acknowledged Emerson as its 'great prophet'" (*The American Myth of Success*, pp. 134–35).

Unfortunately the world is about to have a rude awakening, in that we have started to evolve a new ideal. The new ideal includes the program of Booker T. Washington, but it does not stop there. The new ideal does not mean to exclude anything that Dr. Booker T. Washington did or said, but we have taken all that and have even gone further. And it seems that the world has been slow in appreciating the fact that there is a new ideal.

Garvey believed that "if Washington had lived he would have had to change his program." In the place of Washington's outdated accommodationism, Garvey claimed to offer "a correct interpretation of the new spirit of the new Negro," which presented "a new problem—a problem that must be solved not by the industrial leader but by the political leader." All this resulted from Garvey's discovery in the United States that "politics is the science that rules the world . . . although industry has a great deal to play in it."[100] An immense distance separated Garvey's "non-political" program in Jamaica from his radically transformed vision of political independence. This vision made him the foremost beneficiary of the nationalist mood that emerged full-scale among blacks after 1918.

When we trace the development of the original interrelationship within the UNIA of programs of racial confraternity and self-improvement through cultural and educational uplift, the question must arise: Why did Garvey's political outlook shift from these original priorities? Indeed, this shift coincided with the onset of what Garvey aptly termed "the great rush toward the Organization by the masses." At this turning point, the UNIA became converted from a fraternal and educational organization and mushroomed into a mass political movement with "the momentum that was necessary to bring it forcibly before the world as a great racial factor."[101]

The catalyst was the outbreak in this period of intense racial conflicts signaled by the pogromlike East St. Louis riot of July 1917. During this time, the black populations of many northern industrial cities had almost doubled with the great wave of black migration from the south. The veritable explosion of postwar race riots, climaxing in May through September 1919, was also sparked by the awakened racial consciousness of black soldiers returning from France. Black racial militancy regarding the riots led the Department of Justice to acknowledge in its 1919 report on "Radicalism and Sedition Among the Negroes as Reflected in Their Publications" that a "dangerous spirit of defiance and vengeance [was] at work among the Negro leaders and, to an ever increasing extent, among their followers."[102] At about the same

100. "Negroes Determined to Do for Themselves in Africa What White People Have Done in Europe and Elsewhere," *NW*, Saturday, 22 October 1921, p. 2.

101. Marcus Garvey, "What Is the U.N.I.A.?" *BM* 1 (December 1933):5–6.

102. U.S. Congress, Senate, *Investigative Activities of the Department of Justice*, exhibit 10 of A. Mitchell Palmer, s. doc. 153, 66th Cong., 1st sess., 1919, 12:187.

time, Major J. E. Cutler of the Military Intelligence Division of the War Department reported a "growing influence of radical publications and of a new type of radical race leader," which he said "constitute[d] a critical juncture in the history of the colored race in this country." After studying the conditions that gave rise to the "race consciousness among the colored people today which is of recent origin," Cutler concluded: "Beyond a doubt, there is a new negro to be reckoned with in our political and social life."[103]

Richard Maxwell Brown, in his study of American violence, notes that "during the period of the first World War and after . . . there were 13 major race riots (and at least 15 minor ones in 1919 alone)." Brown describes the emergence of a new level of armed black resistance: "Although whites were still generally dominant, the riot activity was more equal, featuring 'mass, uncoordinated battle' in which 'large, relatively evenly-matched sections of each community attacked members of the other communities.'"[104] Major riots took place in Houston, Texas (1917), Knoxville, Tennessee (1919), Washington, D.C. (1919), and Chicago (1919). Race riots also occurred in Charleston, South Carolina, Longview, Texas, Omaha, and Elaine, Arkansas.

A new era had begun in the evolution of racial consciousness among blacks. The impact of mass resistance by blacks, who faced unprecedented levels of white racial violence both during and after the war, emboldened Garvey to enlarge the range of his political discourse and action. Impelled by the explosive racial crisis, Garvey quickly sought a new political legitimacy for the UNIA, seeking relevance within the contending currents of black resistance. Garvey's associate, William H. Ferris, would later note that "the East St. Louis, Chicago, Washington, D.C., Tulsa, Oklahoma, and Elaine, Arkansas, riots fed Garvey's agitation fires and he loomed upon the horizon as a dauntless and fearless race champion."[105]

The Mirror of Nationalism

The metamorphosis of the UNIA did not go unnoticed at the time. In January 1922, Hodge Kirnon noted that "an association of Negro peoples with the redemption of Africa as its ideal and 'Africa for the Africans' as a slogan seemed entirely foreign to Garvey's mind at the time (of the founding of the UNIA in New York in the spring or early summer of 1918)." But, Kirnon observed, "they have become the cardinal and distinctive features of

103. DNA, RG 165, 10218-361, 15 August 1919.
104. Richard Maxwell Brown, *Strain of Violence: Historical Studies of American Violence and Vigilantism* (New York: Oxford University Press, 1975), p. 211. Arthur I. Waskow puts the number of such incidents at eleven (*From Race Riot to Sit-in, 1919 and the 1960s* [Garden City, N.Y.: Doubleday & Co., 1967], pp. 12, 304–7), while William Cohen speaks of "no fewer than thirteen lesser conflicts between the races" ("Riots, Racism, and Hysteria: The Response of Federal Investigative Officials to the Race Riots of 1919," *Massachusetts Review* 13 [Summer 1972]:375).
105. *Philadelphia Tribune*, Thursday, 27 June 1940.

the movement; also the shaping and inspiring forces to both its numerical and spiritual growth." Kirnon suggested that these changes in Garvey's original views "were simply the outcome of a broader perspective which Garvey had gained in the course of time; aided in all probability by his native keenness and shrewdness which permitted him to see their effectiveness at the time."[106]

At the critical moment, spurred by the crises of war and racial riot, Garvey moved beyond the premises of benevolence and self-improvement to articulate a *political* program of "African Redemption." The immense up-heavals that also engulfed the world during and after the Great War wrought a major change in Garvey's entire outlook. In November 1920 Garvey wrote, "never before in the history of the world has the spirit of unrest swept over as it has during the past two years." He termed it "the age of unrest, the age of dissatisfaction," perceiving its impact as broader and more complex than that of the French Revolution and the Napoleonic wars:

> The Napoleonic wars which disturbed nearly all of Europe did not usher in the universal sway of unrest as did the recent World War. When an American President began to talk about making the world safe for democracy and about the self-determination of peoples and nations, he gave voice and expression to the pent-up thoughts and feelings of men, and oppressed classes, races and nations felt that at last the much talked-of millennium had come. The failure of the Peace Conference at Versailles and the fact that Ireland, India, Egypt, Africa, the Negroes of the Western Hemisphere and the toiling masses everywhere continued to groan under the yoke of oppression, soon disillusioned them. Then came the recoil and the reaction, and we have as a result the present unrest.[107]

Garvey continued to emphasize the central importance of the postwar nationalist conjuncture. Speaking before the second UNIA convention, in August 1921, he declared: "All other races are on strike now.... Four hundred million Negroes are striking (applause) and we are striking now with a vengeance, never to be abused, never to be tossed about, never to be kicked about again, because we have found a way to liberty."[108] William H. Ferris editorialized in February 1922 that "the same desire for justice and liberty which De Valera has voiced for Ireland, Mahatma Ghandi [*sic*] for India and Egyptian leaders for Egypt, Marcus Garvey has voiced for Africa."[109]

106. "Hodge Kirnon Analyzes the Garvey Movement," *NW*, Saturday, 28 January 1922, p. 7.
107. Marcus Garvey, "In Every Land Demanding a New Order of Things," *NW*, Saturday, 6 November 1920, p. 1.
108. "First Week's Evening Sessions of Great Convention Attended by Large Numbers Who Display Much Enthusiasm," *NW*, Saturday, 13 August 1921, pp. 2–3.
109. "The Question of Survival," *NW*, Saturday, 25 February 1922, p. 4; see also "Gandhi, Garvey, and De Valera—Martyrs in Jail for Ideals," *NW*, Saturday, 25 August 1923, p. 10. The

The Influence of Ireland

Far more than any other nationalist struggle, the Irish revolutionary struggle assisted in focusing Garvey's political perspective. Dramatically symbolized in the "blood sacrifice" of the Easter Week Rising of 1916, the Irish cause provided the major ideological mainspring for Garvey's radical political transformation. Even the slogan made famous by Garvey, "Africa for the Africans at home and abroad," echoed the oft-repeated Irish slogan "the Irish race at home and abroad."[110]

Garvey was not alone in his response to the Irish revolt, just as he had not been alone in his proposal for a black merchant marine nor in his advocacy of African emancipation. In one sense the split among black radicals of the period along nationalist or socialist-communist lines was expressed in the primacy assigned either to the Irish or to the Bolshevik revolutions. Hubert H. Harrison, the chief intellectual spokesman of the "new Negro" nationalism, broke with the Socialist party in 1914, and in 1917 he suggested that "the colored people rise against the government just as the Irish against England unless they get their rights."[111] Strong support for the Irish cause also came from Cyril V. Briggs during his radical-nationalist phase, prior to his joining the Workers' party in 1921. In the August 1919 issue of his journal, the *Crusader*, Briggs commented on "Approaching Irish Success." In February 1921 he heralded the Irish struggle with an editorial, "Heroic Ireland—the Irish Fight for Liberty the Greatest Epic of Modern Times and a Sight to Inspire to Emulation All Oppressed Groups."[112] The *Crusader*'s exchange of subscription advertisements with the Irish revolutionary journal *Sinn Feiner* evoked favorable comments from Irish readers.[113] Moreover, Briggs's creation of the secret African Blood Brotherhood for African Liberation and Redemption (ABB) in the summer and fall of 1919

---

historical conjuncture of nationalism was taken as a basic political axiom by Garvey: "On every hand there is a swelling tide of nationalism, and a materialism of races and peoples. . . . Can the Negro not see then that it is necessary for him to form a part of this universal wave of racial human consciousness?" (Marcus Garvey, "The Call to a Purposeful Life," *BM* 1 [May–June 1934]:20); "The Negro must stretch out and reach beyond his narrow orbit. His politics must become more centred and more determined and those politics must be based upon an objective nationalism" ("A Call to Action," *BM* 2 [August 1937]:3).

110. Quoted in Conor Cruise O'Brien, *States of Ireland* (London: Hutchinson, 1972), p. 48. According to Eric Walrond, it was "hearing the great cry of 'Jerusalem for the Jews—Ireland for the Irish—India for the Indian'" that the UNIA came to believe "that it is about time for the negroes to raise the cry of 'Africa for the Africans,' at home and abroad" ("Imperator Africanus—Marcus Garvey: Menace or Promise?" *Independent* 114 [January 1925]:9). Walrond was an associate editor of the *Negro World*.

111. *Afro-American*, 30 June 1917. According to Hodge Kirnon, "An interest in Africa and matters of culture relating to Africa and the Africans . . . were being shaped and brought to a near maturity by [Hubert H.] Harrison before Mr. Garvey came upon the scene" (" 'As to Marcus Garvey,' " *NW*, Saturday, 16 July 1921, p. 3).

112. *Crusader* 1 (August 1919):8; ibid. 4, no. 2 (February 1921):5; see also "The Irish Boycott on British Goods," ibid. 4, no. 3 (March 1921):9–10.

113. "From an Irish Patriot," *Crusader* 4, no. 3 (March 1921):27–28.

drew upon the example of the Irish Republican Brotherhood, the body responsible for planning and executing the Irish Easter Week Rising of 1916. The motto of the ABB was, "Those only need apply who are willing to go the limit."[114]

If the most compelling contemporary model for postwar black nationalist revolutionaries was the Irish revolution, just as the inspiration for ideological conversion among blacks to socialism and communism was the model of the Russian revolution, it was also true that Garvey's familiarity with the ideas and rhetoric of Irish nationalism dated from before the war. As early as 1910, Garvey was assistant secretary of the National Club of Jamaica, a group whose activities marked the first attempt by Jamaicans to create a nationalist political platform.[115] The club's founder, S. A. G. Cox, absorbed the influence of the Sinn Fein movement while he was enrolled as a student, beginning in 1905, at the Middle Temple in England. Representing a radical break with the established tradition of the Irish home rule movement, Sinn Fein offered a program of Irish national restoration through the winning of political independence for Ireland and the revival of Gaelic culture. The Jamaican historian Richard Hart has pointed out that "for [the National Club's] newspaper Cox chose the name *Our Own*, a rough translation of the Irish nationalists' *Sinn Fein*."[116] In a manner similar to Garvey's later Black Star Line, the constitution of the national council of Sinn Fein in 1906 proposed in its economic program to advance the objective of a national government in Ireland by "the re-establishment of an Irish mercantile Marine to facilitate direct trading between Ireland and the countries of Continental Europe, America, Africa, and the Far East."[117] From its first convention in November 1905, Sinn Fein also proposed the establishment of an Irish consular service abroad. This was essentially the same idea enunciated by Garvey in 1914 based on his plan "to establish Commissionaries or Agencies in the principal countries of the world for the protection of all Negroes, irrespective of nationality."

114. *Crusader* 2 (October 1919):27. The IRB was founded by James Stephen in 1858 in Dublin; see Leon Ó Broin, *Revolutionary Underground: The Story of the Irish Republican Brotherhood, 1858–1924* (Dublin: Gill and Macmillan, 1976); and Sean Cronin, *Irish Nationalism: A History of Its Roots and Ideology* (New York: Continuum Publishing Co., 1981).

115. For the founding of the National Club and its political platform and rules of membership, see "A New Political Movement: Mr. Cox Initiates Political Clubs," *Jamaica Times*, Saturday, 6 March 1909; "Formation of Political Club," *Gleaner*, Friday, 5 March 1909; "National Club: Principles for which Mr. Cox Stands," ibid., Wednesday, 14 April 1909; "Aims of the National Club," ibid., Thursday, 17 June 1909, and Wednesday, 23 June 1909. S. A. G. Cox was described in 1920 as a "nationalistic political agitator who had incurred the wrath and antagonism of the British officials in Jamaica by advocating Jamaica for the Jamaicans" (Anselmo R. Jackson, "An Analysis of the Black Star Line," *Emancipator*, Saturday, 27 March 1920).

116. Richard Hart, "Jamaica and Self-Determination, 1660–1970," *Race* 13 (January 1972): 282; and "The Life and Resurrection of Marcus Garvey," *Race* 9 (October 1967):219. The National Club's journal, *Our Own*, was published from July 1910 until July 1911. Literally, *sinn fein* means "ouselves alone" or "we ourselves."

117. *The Sinn Fein Policy* (Dublin: James Duffy, 1906), p. 36; see F. S. L. Lyons, "The Rise of Sinn Fein," in *Ireland since the Famine* (London: Weidenfeld & Nicolson, 1971), pp. 243–55; and

Garvey's subsequent stay in England during 1912 to 1914 coincided with the period of uninterrupted crisis in both England and Ireland over Irish home rule, which climaxed in the Irish independence struggle, the Easter Rising of 1916.[118] After World War I, Garvey repeatedly acknowledged his identification with the heroic epic of the Irish struggle. Speaking at the formal dedication of Liberty Hall, the UNIA's general meeting place, in July 1919, Garvey announced that "the time [had] come for the Negro race to offer up its martyrs upon the altar of liberty even as the Irish [had] given a long list from Robert Emmet to Roger Casement."[119] The name chosen for the UNIA meeting place reflected an appreciation for Liberty Hall, Dublin, the symbolic seat of the Irish revolution and the site where the Irish Citizen Army had launched the Easter Rising on 23 April 1916.[120]

Garvey consistently accorded the Irish independence struggle primacy among all other national movements of the era, including those in India, Egypt, China, the eastern European states, and the movement to secure a Jewish homeland in Palestine. His strong identification with Ireland's tradition of patriotic martyrdom inspired him to proclaim in a Chicago speech in 1919, "Robert Emmet gave his life for Irish independence . . . and the new negro is ready to give his life for the freedom of the negro race."[121] Ulti-

Robert Kee, "Arthur Griffith and Sinn Fein," in *The Green Flag: A History of Irish Nationalism* (London: Weidenfeld & Nicolson, 1972), pp. 438–60. The political and ideological contributions made to the Irish nationalist struggle by the Gaelic cultural revival were principally the result of the Gaelic League (founded in 1893) and D. P. Moran's *Leader* (founded in 1900) and his book *The Philosophy of Irish Ireland* (Dublin: Duffy & Co., 1905); see Donal McCartney, "Gaelic Ideological Origins of 1916," in O. Dudley Edwards and Fergus Pyle, eds., *1916: The Easter Rising* (London: MacGibbon & Kee, 1968), pp. 41–49; Lyons, "The Battle of Two Civilisations," in *Ireland since the Famine*, pp. 219–42; and Kee, "Growth of National Consciousness," in *The Green Flag*, pp. 426–37. A suggestive parallel between the Harlem Renaissance and the Anglo-Irish literary revival can be found in Huggins, *Harlem Renaissance*, pp. 203, 231.

118. Patricia Jalland, *The Liberals and Ireland* (Brighton: Harvester Press, 1980). For the Ulster crisis of 1912–1914, see Lyons, "The Road to Revolution" and "The Rising," in *Ireland since the Famine*, pp. 328–79; see also Thomas M. Coffey, *Agony at Easter: The 1916 Irish Uprising* (New York: Macmillan & Co., 1969).

119. "Liberty Hall Dedicated at Great Mass Meeting," *NW*, Saturday, 2 August 1919, p. 1. Garvey would later state: "We have established this Liberty Hall as the centre from which we send out the sparks of liberty to the far corners of the world" (*NW*, Saturday, 20 August 1921, p. 2). Henrietta Vinton Davis, first UNIA assistant president-general, declared that "the Liberty Hall in New York city, the first Liberty Hall established for the Universal Negro Improvement Association, is like a great central sun that sends its rays afar, reaching unto all the uttermost parts of the world" (*NW*, Saturday, 25 August 1923, p. 8). William H. Ferris also described Liberty Hall as "the originating source of the movement" (*NW*, Saturday, 2 December 1922, p. 2). In 1917, the Department of Justice reportedly raided a dwelling in Chicago also named "Liberty Hall." The raid involved a neutrality violation and it is possible that the building, located on South Dearborn Street, near Whiteside and Wentworth, was used in support of Irish activities. (DNA, RG 65, file OG 154434, American Protective League report, Chicago, 5 September 1918).

120. See Cathal O'Shannon, ed., *Fifty Years of Liberty Hall* (Dublin: Irish Transport and General Workers Union, 1959), During the hostilities of the Easter Rising, Liberty Hall was shelled and destroyed by a British gunboat, but it was subsequently rebuilt.

121. DNA, RG 65, BS 198940, "Marcus Garvey (Negro)." For a summary account of the "blood-sacrifice" ideal inspiring the political messianism of the leaders of the Irish Easter

mately, Garvey was to be compared by William Ferris to Saint Patrick, the Irish patron saint: "the same courage which St. Patrick showed in defying the pagan gods of Ireland Marcus Garvey shows in defying Anglo-Saxon caste prejudice."[122]

The UNIA's call for an "International Convention of the Negro Peoples of the World," issued on 1 March 1919, followed by one week the Third Irish Race Convention attended by six thousand Irish-Americans on 22 to 23 February 1919 in Philadelphia. The Philadelphia convention, which climaxed a series of Irish-American mass meetings begun in December 1918, calling for official American recognition of Ireland as an independent republic, was sponsored by the Friends of Irish Freedom, which had itself grown out of the first meeting, in 1916, of the Irish Race Convention. One of the principal informers on "Negro subversion" for the Military Intelligence Division (MID) alleged that Garvey and the Friends of Irish Freedom were linked. MID disclosed in its confidential "Weekly Situation Survey" of 23 June 1920 that its informer, R. D. Jonas, had publicly declared that "the Friends of Irish Freedom had aided in establishing the Black Star (negro) Steamship Line which would ultimately carry arms to Africa." Beyond the timing of the UNIA's convention call, however, Garvey's statement inaugurating a "$2,000,000 Convention Fund" has a further significance. "We think the time has come for the Negro to find a universal leader," Garvey declared, adding, "if Germany is to follow the Kaiser, if England is to follow George V . . . and Ireland is to follow De Valera, then the time has come for four hundred million Negroes to follow a Negro elected by themselves."[123]

Rising, in particular the mystical character of the leadership of Padraic H. Pearse, see F. X. Martin, "The 1916 Rising—a *Coup d'Etat* or a 'Bloody Rising,' " *Studia Hibernica* 8 (1968): 106–37; "The Evolution of a Myth—the Easter Rising, Dublin 1916," in Eugene Kamenka, ed., *Nationalism: The Nature and Evolution of an Idea* (London: Edward Arnold, 1973), pp. 74–78; and William Irwin Thompson, *The Imagination of an Insurrection, Dublin, Easter 1916* (New York: Harper & Row, 1967), chap. 4.

122. "Garvey Likened to St. Patrick—Virtues and Qualities as Leader Extolled in Contrast with Saint," *NW*, Saturday, 2 April 1921, p. 4. The first week's session of the UNIA's Second International Convention was addressed by "a representative of the Society of Irish Freedom [*sic*]" (William H. Ferris, "The U.N.I.A. Convention," *NW*, Saturday, 3 September 1921, p. 4). James A. McCurrien represented the National Committee of the Friends of Irish Freedom, and the report of his address stated that "by the frequent applause from the audience, it was quite evident that the aims and objects of the two great peoples are identical and that their efforts are mutual" (H. Vinton Plummer, director of Bureau of Publicity, "U.N.I.A. Convention Notes," *Washington Bee*, 27 August 1921, p. 2). The political example of the Friends of Irish Freedom might also have exerted an important influence on the formation of the "Friends of Freedom for India" (N. G. Rathore, "Indian Nationalist Agitation in the United States: A Study of Lala Lajpat Rai and the India Home Rule League of America, 1914–1920," [Ph.D. diss., Columbia University, 1965], pp. 116–17); see also Horst Kruger, "India's Freedom Struggle and Beginnings of Solidarity between National Liberation Movements before World War I in Various Countries" (section entitled "Contacts between the Indian and Irish National Liberation Movement") in P. M. Joshi and M. A. Nayeem, eds., *Studies in the Foreign Relations of India, from the Earliest Times to 1947* (Hyderabad, India: State Archives, Government of Andhra Pradesh, 1975), pp. 304–8.

123. Copy found in DNA, RG 59, Department of State, Office of the Counselor, file 504-69,

Garvey's reference to the president of both Sinn Fein and the Irish republic, Eamon de Valera, was especially meaningful. De Valera's arrival in America on 11 June 1919 received spectacular coverage by the American press.[124] Although de Valera's American visit was ultimately not an unqualified political success, he scored a major propaganda triumph for the Irish cause during the eighteen months he spent in the United States through an "incalculable but far-reaching" impact on American public opinion. "Above all, in anything he said and did," state his biographers, "he showed that the Irish were in deadly earnest and engaged in a life and death struggle from which there would be no turning back."[125]

When the long-awaited UNIA convention opened on Sunday night, 1 August 1920, amid great pomp in Madison Square Garden, Garvey began his speech by announcing dramatically:

> I have in my hand . . . a telegram to be sent to the Hon. Edmund De Valera, [*sic*] President of the Irish Republic: "25,000 Negro delegates assembled in Madison Square Garden in mass convention, representing 400,000,000 Negroes of the world, send you greetings as President of the Irish Republic. Please accept sympathy of Negroes of the world for your cause. We believe Ireland should be free even as Africa shall be free for the Negroes of the world. (loud applause) Keep up the fight for a free Ireland. Marcus Garvey, President-General of the Universal Negro Improvement Association." (applause)[126]

On 30 August, the convention elected Garvey to the post of "provisional president of Africa," while a banner in the convention's closing parade on 31 August 1920 was emblazoned: "A President for Ireland; Why Not One for

---

p. 17; "$2,000,000 Convention Fund for Great Race Movement," *NW*, Saturday, 19 April 1920, p. 9; Alan H. Ward, *Ireland and Anglo-American Relations, 1899–1921* (Toronto: University of Toronto Press, 1969), pp. 171–72. For the successive meetings of the Irish Race Convention in 1916, 1918, and 1919, see Charles C. Tansill, *America and the Fight for Irish Freedom, 1866–1922* (New York: Devin-Adair, 1957), pp. 188–90, 270–74, and 296–302. The Irish Victory Fund launched by the Third Irish Race Convention raised the sum of $1,500,000 when the fund ended on 31 August 1919.

124. Eamon de Valera's visit to the United States and its political results are examined critically in Donal McCartney, "De Valera's Mission to the United States, 1919–1920," in Art Cosgrove and Donal McCartney, eds., *Studies in Irish History* (Dublin: University College, Belfield, Department of Modern History, 1979), pp. 304–23; see also Patrick McCartan, *With de Valera in America* (New York: Brentano, 1932).

125. The Earl of Longford and T. P. O'Neill, *Eamon de Valera* (Dublin: Gill and Macmillan, 1970), p. 114

126. *Negro World Convention Bulletin*, no. 2, Tuesday, 3 August 1920, p. 1; *New York Times*, Tuesday, 3 August 1920, p. 7; see also "Sympathy for Ireland at Negro Convention," *Gaelic American*, 14 August 1920, p. 5; Thomas E. Hackey, "The Irish Question: The British Foreign Office and the American Political Conventions of 1920," *Eire-Ireland* 3 (1968): 92–106.

Africa?"[127] The same symbolic identification was also present in the UNIA leaflet of December 1920 announcing the meeting that de Valera was to have addressed. While the address by de Valera did not take place as planned, the leaflet pointed to his significance for the UNIA:

> *Come and See the Irish President*
> Among the Speakers will be
> His Excellency Hon. MARCUS GARVEY
> Provisional President of Africa
> His Excellency Hon. EAMON De VALERA
> Provisional President of Ireland

Although the convention's original call spoke of the founding of an "African Empire," Garvey told Charles Mowbray White on 18 August 1920 that he was "leaving for [Africa] . . . to set up a Republic."[128] In another interview conducted in August 1920 by Charles Mowbray White, W. E. B. Du Bois revealed his belief that Garvey and his followers were "allied with the Bolsheviks and the Sinn Feiners in their world revolution. . . ."[129] The example of de Valera's clandestine travel between America and Ireland also became an object of emulation for Garvey. In his speech at Liberty Hall on the evening of 6 January 1921, he alluded to his impending departure for the Caribbean and Central America: "Two weeks from this I shall suddenly disappear from you for six or seven weeks," he told his audience. "You won't hear from me during that time, but don't be alarmed because we Negroes will have to adopt the system of underground workings like De Valera and other white leaders."[130] Two weeks later, Garvey told a UNIA meeting in Philadelphia: "They said that they are going to keep me out of Africa. They said they were going to keep De Valera out of Ireland, but he is there."[131]

---

127. "Leaders of Race Elected by International Convention of Negroes Assembled at New York, U.S.A., August 1 to 31," *NW*, Saturday, 11 September 1920, p. 1; "UNIA Convention Closes in Triumph," ibid., pp. 8ff. In January 1922, Garvey made note of the fact that while Eamon de Valera "gained millions of Irish adherents in this country [and] they printed his name as Provisional President of Ireland," they nonetheless "inclosed it in inverted commas, to try to show those who were his enemies that his claim to that title was ridiculous" (*NW*, Saturday, 14 January 1922, p. 2). Garvey's identification with de Valera was pointed out by the black American sociologist Charles S. Johnson: "Just prior to the first international convention [of the UNIA], De Valera was elected Provisional President of Ireland. Garvey then became Provisional President of Africa" ("After Garvey—What?" *Opportunity* 1 [August 1923]:233).

128. NN, NCF, "The Negro," box 152. According to White, Garvey assigned the following symbolic meaning to the UNIA's tricolor: "The Red showed their sympathy with the 'Reds' of the world, and the Green their sympathy for the Irish in their fight for freedom, and the Black—The Negro."

129. Ibid.

130. DNA, RG 65, BS 202600-667-16X, "Negro Activities."

131. DNA, RG 65, BS 198940, "Marcus Garvey." Garvey prefaced his statement with the injunction: "Do not question my being away as I am about to bring you success."

Shortly after the close of the first UNIA convention, Liberty Hall was the scene of a meeting attended by about fourteen Irish sympathizers. Speeches were delivered by Dudley Field Malone and other leaders of the boycott of English ships, which had been called by Irish longshoremen in order to try to force the British government's release of Terence MacSwiney, the lord mayor of Cork. MacSwiney's hunger strike, according to Robert Kee, "uniquely concentrated attention from all over the world on the spirit and determination of Irish militants" (*The Green Flag*, p. 696). Indeed, at the closing session of the first UNIA convention, Garvey announced that he had dispatched a telegram "to Father Dominick, confessor of the Lord Mayor of Cork, and it read 'Convey to McSwiney [*sic*] sympathy of 400,000,000 Negroes'" (*NW*, Saturday, 11 September 1920).

Following the convention, the Bureau of Investigation reported that Garvey sent Rev. J. W. Selkridge "down to the docks to urge all the Negro longshoremen not to load British ships, which act pleased the Irish strikers, who learned that Garvey had sent him down to aid them" (DNA, RG 65, file OG 329359). A measure of Garvey's immense reverence for MacSwiney, who finally died on the seventy-third day of his hunger fast, can be gained from his declaration: "Hundreds and thousands of Irishmen have died as martyrs to the cause of Irish freedom. . . . They compelled the attention of the world and I believe the death of McSweeney [*sic*] did more for the freedom of Ireland today than probably anything they did for 500 years prior to his death" (*NW*, 17 December 1921).

At the start of the Second International Convention of Negroes, in August 1921, Garvey dispatched cables to Eamon de Valera in Dublin and to King George V in London. In his cable to de Valera, Garvey assured him: "We, the Representatives of 400,000,000 Negroes of the World assembled in the 2nd Annual International Convention, send GREETING, and pray that you and your fellow COUNTRYMEN will receive from the hands of the British your merited freedom."[132] Garvey informed the British monarch that "on principle, nothing would please the 400,000,000 Negro peoples of the World more, except the freedom of Africa, than the granting of freedom to the four and a half million people of Ireland, and also the emancipation of the poor people of India, and Egypt."[133]

Shortly afterward, Garvey's support of the Irish republican cause reached its apogee. On 6 December 1921 the Anglo-Irish Treaty was signed, leading to the end of hostilities and to the eventual establishment of the Irish Free State. The treaty itself was a compromise agreement, however. It represented a good deal less than the independent republic that the Irish nationalists who had fought since the Easter Rising had demanded. Eamon

132. DNA, RG 165, 10218-261/68. On 31 August 1921, at the close of the convention, Garvey announced in Liberty Hall: "The news has come to us, and I have a cable in my pocket that comes from Ireland that the Irish are determined to have liberty and nothing less than liberty. (Applause)" (*NW*, Saturday, 10 September 1921, p. 2).
133. DNA, RG 165, 10218-261/67.

de Valera and many other Irish nationalists denounced the treaty as a betrayal of Ireland's national sovereignty. The consequent fateful split among the Republican leadership would bring on the Irish civil war and ultimately dismember Sinn Fein.

While the future of Ireland hung precariously in the balance, Garvey did not delay in declaring his stand on the treaty. On 11 December 1921, before the critical debate in the Irish parliament, Garvey summoned a special mass meeting at Liberty Hall. He spoke on "Ireland and Africa," stating that "we have a cause similar to the cause of Ireland." Garvey made plain his support for the negotiated settlement with England: "I am glad that Ireland has won some modicum of self-government. I am not thoroughly pleased with the sort of freedom that is given to them, but nevertheless I believe that they have received enough upon which they can improve. . . ."[134] Garvey then read a cable, to be sent to the leading Irish treaty negotiator Arthur Griffith, signed "Marcus Garvey, Provisional President of Africa." The cable informed Griffith: "Six thousand of us assembled in Liberty Hall, New York, representing the four hundred million Negroes of the world, send you congratulations on your masterly achievement of partial independence for Ireland. The stage is set for a greater day for Ireland. Long live the new Irish Free State."[135] Immediately after the treaty was ratified by the Irish Republican parliament, Garvey issued the following announcement:

> The Irish have succeeded, first among the trio of Egypt, India and Ireland, in winning a place of mastery among the nations of the world. Some time last night the Irish Parliament, with a majority of seven, voted for the ratification of the agreement . . . thus elevating Ireland and the Irish people from the position of serfs, peons, to that of masters.[136]

The evolution of Garvey's ideology of political nationalism closely mirrored the rise and fall of the two historic phases of the Irish nationalist movement, namely, the constitutional nationalism of home rule and the

134. "Hon. Marcus Garvey, as spokesman for 400,000,000 Negroes, Telegraphs Arthur Griffith and Lloyd George on the Settlement of the Irish Question and Creation of a Self-Governing Irish Free State," *NW*, Saturday, 17 December 1921, p. 1. For accounts of the treaty negotiations and the tragic aftermath of the Irish Civil War, see Joseph M. Curran, *The Birth of the Irish Free State, 1921–1923* (University: University of Alabama Press, 1980).

135. Ibid.

136. "Hon. Marcus Garvey Comments on Establishment of Irish Free State and Efforts of Hindus and Egyptians to Gain Their Independence—Points out Meaning to Negro Peoples of World," *NW*, Saturday, 14 January 1922, p. 2. On the occasion of the British government's publication of the Peel Report, in July 1937, which recommended the ending of the Palestine mandate and the creation of a separate Jewish and Arab state by the partitioning of Palestine, Garvey wrote: "This recognition of the Jew may help the Negro to force his argument for his free State. . . . When he gets serious and lines up behind the U.N.I.A. as the Jews lined up behind Zionism the Negroes may surprisingly benefit from the recommendation of some Royal Commission that may recommend in Africa, as well as elsewhere—Free States for the race" ("The Jews," *BM* 2 [August 1937]:2).

revolutionary nationalism of Sinn Fein.[137] The harsh and violent transition between the two paved the way for Garvey's own transitional development. From being dependent on his alliance with the "liberal-minded" wing of the colonial and imperial establishments, Garvey found that his admiration of the revolutionary nationalism of Sinn Fein, under conditions of violent racial upheaval in America, refocused his articulation of the race question: "Africa must be for the Africans, and them exclusively."[138] This ideological transition, moreover, was enhanced and deepened by Garvey's identification with the awe-inspiring blood sacrifice of Irish patriotic martyrdom, which symbolized in very dramatic ways both the recovery of Irish political independence and racial redemption. Thus, if Garvey's rapid entry into the swirling currents of postwar nationalist agitation did contribute to the turbulent quality of the epoch, he was guided to a remarkable degree by the example of the Irish struggle waged both in Ireland and from America.

The figure most symbolic of the Irish movement was Eamon de Valera. As Garvey admitted in July 1932, "we have watched his career for several years both in Ireland and the U.S.A., where he carried on a relentless propaganda in the interest of Irish Republicanism." He stated further, "we understand him (de Valera) and the spirit of the people he represents."[139] In the long shadow cast by the totemic figure of Eamon de Valera, Garvey's perception of politics experienced a radical new life, while the black republicanism of the UNIA's political program of African self-determination was emblematic of revolutionary Irish republicanism between 1919 and 1921.

Retreat from Radicalism

Garvey's speeches after July 1921, when compared to his prior revolutionary rhetoric, reveal the start of a new political phase. Typical of his earlier revolutionary posture was his famous exhortation, delivered in Madison Square Garden on 30 October 1919, which not only electrified the black world but also alerted European governments to the danger inherent in the movement's spread, particularly in Africa. Garvey boldly proclaimed: "It will be a

137. For the failure of the Irish nationalist party, see F.S.L. Lyons, "The Passing of the Irish Parliamentary Party (1916–1918)," in T. Desmond Williams, ed., *The Irish Struggle, 1916–1926* (London: Routledge and Kegan Paul, 1966), pp. 95–106; and R. Dudley Edwards, "The Decline and Fall of the Irish Nationalists at Westminster," in Kevin B. Nowlan, ed., *The Making of 1916: Studies in the History of the Rising* (Dublin: Stationery Office, 1969), pp. 127–56.

138. *NW*, Saturday, 5 April 1919.

139. "The Character of de Valera," *New Jamaican*, Monday, 18 July 1932, p. 2; see also "De Valera and Ireland," *Blackman*, July 1930 (reprinted in Amy Jacques Garvey and E. U. Essien-Udom, eds., *More Philosophy and Opinions of Marcus Garvey* [London: Frank Cass, 1977], 3:126–27); "The Irish Situation," *New Jamaican*, Friday, 5 August 1932, p. 2; "De Valera, the Strong," ibid., Wednesday, 17 August 1932, p. 2; "The Great de Valera," ibid., Monday, 12 September 1932, p. 2. Garvey disclosed in one of his statements: "We have already confessed, and this is not of today, but of years, our sympathy with Ireland in securing national independence" (17 August 1932).

terrible day when the blacks draw the sword to fight for their liberty. I call upon you 400,000,000 blacks to give the blood you have shed for the white man to make Africa a republic for the Negro."[140] Garvey's speeches employed the same general rhetoric until his departure from the United States on his tour of the West Indies and Central America in February 1921. On the eve of his departure from America, while addressing a mass meeting in Philadelphia in January 1921, Garvey reportedly urged: "Get together from now on and be ready to get into Africa. . . . [B]uild battleships and raise armies, after we get a good foothold in Africa, which must positively be in the next twelve months."[141]

For over four months Garvey languished in the Caribbean while his repeated applications for a reentry visa to the United States were denied. Suddenly, on 25 June 1921, Charles L. Latham, the American consul in Jamaica, notified Garvey that the State Department had approved his visa application. In the view of J. Edgar Hoover, the principal architect and coordinator of Garvey's exclusion, the abrupt change in the State Department's policy was a disappointment, and the unusual circumstances warranted a special Bureau of Investigation inquiry. Suspicions fell upon Harry Alexander McBride, an official in the Visa Control Section of the State Department. Prior to taking his position on 27 December 1920, McBride had served as the acting general receiver of customs and financial adviser in Liberia. Although in the end the bureau's investigation remained inconclusive, indications were that McBride granted approval for Garvey to receive a visa on the basis of a bribe from the UNIA's assistant counsel-general, William C. Matthews. Matthews was said to have acted through Henry Lincoln Johnson, the recorder of deeds in Washington, D.C., and probably the leading black politician in the Republican party. Johnson had also earlier consulted Secretary of State Charles Evans Hughes on the matter of Garvey's request for readmission.[142]

140. "Negroes Sharpen Swords for War of Races, Says Garvey," *New York World*, Friday, 31 October 1919; see also "Dangerous Talk—Negro War Threats—Black Men 'Sharpening Swords' for Race War," *African World*, Saturday, 8 November 1919.

141. DNA, RG 65, BS 198940, "Marcus Garvey—President, Universal Negro Improvement Association.

142. DNA, RG 65, BS 198940-249, and 198940-262; see also RG 59, 811.108G191/29. The details of the bureau's investigation are discussed in Robert A. Hill, "Marcus Garvey and the Federal Prosecution Efforts, 1918–1927" (Paper presented at the Eighteenth Annual National Archives Conference, Washington, D.C., 21–22 September 1978). For a recounting of the prevalence of political bribery and corruption during the Harding administration, see Charles L. Mee, Jr., *The Ohio Gang: The World of Warren G. Harding* (New York: Evans, 1981); see also Francis Russell, *The Shadow of Blooming Grove: Warren G. Harding in His Times* (New York: McGraw-Hill, 1968). Henry Lincoln Johnson (1870–1925) had a reputation for selling federal appointments in his position as a member of the Republican National Committee and as recorder of deeds in Washington, D.C.; in 1912–13, when he was collector of internal revenue in Atlanta, he was charged with soliciting political subscriptions and violating civil service law; later, in 1921, he was charged with forgery (see DNA, RG 65, files 160962, 215059, 223955-1, 35-51-1, and 3617); however, see Du Bois's highly favorable obituary of Johnson in *Crisis* 31 [November 1925]:11. Henry Lincoln Johnson was also responsible for securing the admission in 1921 of the UNIA potentate, Gabriel Johnson, mayor of Monrovia, Liberia. According to

Whatever the cause of the abrupt change in the government's policy of exclusion, the impact on Garvey's political course was immediate. Garvey had prepared the ground to some extent by his policy of noninterference in local affairs during his Caribbean travels. Wherever he visited, Garvey was careful to point out his respect for the established order. Thus, he told an audience on his first stop in Cuba: "I do not come here to interfere with the labor question or the political question where governments are concerned." On his return, the first signal of a volte-face came during Garvey's speech at the mass meeting in Liberty Hall welcoming him back to Harlem after nearly five month's absence. A special agent of the Bureau of Investigation who attended the meeting reported that "this change in Garvey's attitude is not yet fully understood." But it did not take too long for others in the leadership of the UNIA to understand. Within a few days the same agent noted that the acceptance of Garvey's new political line was spreading: "For some unknown reason all the officials of the Black Star Line and Garvey's other organizations seem to have undergone a change of mind. They are very patriotic in their speeches and have eliminated all the antiwhite talks and in its place [are] preaching loyalty to the U.S.A." After speaking personally with Garvey two days later, the same agent provided additional evidence that Garvey had embarked on a major change in political direction: "Garvey is now more patriotic and is preaching nothing but loyalty to the flag. His recent experience must have taught him to take another sane course."[143] Less than two months later, on 1 September 1921, Garvey filed his declaration of intention to become a citizen of the United States of America.[144]

Surrender to Racial Purity

Until Garvey's departure from America in early 1921, the militancy of his commitment to the struggle for black rights was unsurpassed in both eloquence and fervor. Thus, after the Washington riot in July 1919, Garvey reportedly announced that "the Universal Negro Improvement Association will be the most powerful factor in freeing the black man in the United States."[145] With his political change of course in July 1921, however, Garvey abandoned his earlier espousal of resistance. Garvey's retreat from radicalism

William C. Matthews, UNIA assistant counselor-general, "Colonel [Henry Lincoln] Johnson gladly and willingly assisted me in bringing to a successful termination this splendid piece of work, and it was made possible by the high regard in which he is held by the Secretary of Labor, Hon. James J. Davis" ("Col. Henry Lincoln Johnson Commended by Wm. C. Matthews," *NW*, Saturday, 30 July 1921).

143. "Hon. Marcus Garvey Delivers Stirring Address at Blair's Park, Cuba," *NW*, Saturday, 18 June 1921; DNA, RG 65, files BS 198940-217 and 198940-218.

144. U.S. Department of Labor, Naturalization Service, declaration no. 101706.

145. DNA, RG 165, 10218-364/1, "Negro Agitation."

acquired a special logic, so that the dogma of racial purity now became the basis of the UNIA's search for legitimacy. The main target of the policy was Du Bois, whom Garvey accused, together with Emmett Scott, of "using their influence with the government after I had left the country to prevent my return."[146] In reality, however, Garvey was seeking to neutralize the political influence that he presumed his opponents possessed by trying to distinguish himself on the basis of racial purity.

Garvey first articulated this new strategy in August 1921 at the second convention of the UNIA. He then cabled a lengthy resolution to the League of Nations, the ostensible purpose of which was to inform the league of the UNIA's "repudiation" of Du Bois's forthcoming Second Pan-African Congress, scheduled for later that month in London, Brussels, and Paris. The cable stated "that the said W. E. B. Du Bois and his associates who call the Congress are making an issue of social equality with the white race for their own selfish purposes, and not for the advancement of the Negro Race, and that the idea of their holding a Congress in European Cities is more for the purpose of aggravating the question of social equality to their own personal satisfaction, than to benefit the Negro Race."[147] This statement's strong echo of Booker T. Washington's famous indictment of "social equality," delivered at the Atlanta Exposition in 1895 was not accidental.[148] The UNIA's resolution went on to make explicit the fears that "social equality" evoked among whites:

> We further repudiate the [Pan-African] Congress because we sincerely feel that the white race like the Black and Yellow Races should maintain the purity of self, and that the Congress is nothing more than an effort to encourage Race suicide, by the admixture of two opposite Races . . . and [the Negro] therefore denounces any attempt on the part of dissatisfied individuals who by accident are members of the said Negro Race, in their attempts to foster a campaign of miscegenation to the destruction of the Race's purity.

146. *NW*, Saturday, 13 August 1921, p. 5; DNA, RG 65, file BS 198940-218.

147. League of Nations Archives, Geneva, file 1/14410/13940; see also file 1/15499/13940 for a second telegram, sent on 7 August 1921. A transcript of the first resolution can also be found in DNA, RG 165, file 10218-261/65; see also *NW*, Saturday, 6 August 1921, p. 5. Within the UNIA camp, the first person to espouse the doctrine of racial purity was Hubert H. Harrison. In his lecture "Racial Imperatives," delivered on 23 April 1921, Harrison was reported to have "discussed the relation of hybrid populations to their opposite racial progenitors as often being a menace to either of the stronger ancestral races and as being often raceless at a time when race pride should be pronounced." Harrison also "strongly emphasized" that there was "the tendency in America for mulattoes to pose as leaders of their brothers of a darker hue, and, at the same time, ostracising them on the grounds of color, more baseless than the color line between them and the whites" (Thomas M. Henry, "Mr. H. H. Harrison Lectures in New York," *NW*, Saturday, 7 May 1921).

148. See "The Standard Printed Version of the Atlanta Exposition Address," in *The Booker T. Washington Papers* 3:583–87; see also Rayford W. Logan, *The Betrayal of the Negro from Rutherford B. Hayes to Woodrow Wilson*, new enl. ed. (New York: Collier Books, 1965), chap. 14, pp. 276–312.

In a statement published shortly afterward by the *New York World*, on 9 September 1921, Garvey upbraided "the Dr. Du Bois group" and called attention to the fact that "the Universal Negro Improvement Association believes that both races have separate and distinct destinies, that each and every race should develop on its own social lines, and that any attempt to bring about the amalgamation of any two opposite races is a crime against nature."[149] The following month Garvey praised President Harding's Birmingham, Alabama, speech, which had emphasized that "race amalgamation there can never be." Harding justified his position on the ground that the maintenance of "natural segregations" between the races was the result of "widely unequal capacities and capabilities."[150] In springing to the support of Harding amid the controversy that his remarks created, Garvey called upon blacks everywhere to "follow President Harding's great lead," and he urged them to "stand uncompromisingly against the idea of social equality." Garvey further asserted that Harding's speech made him "one of the greatest statesmen of the present day."[151]

The other side of Garvey's attack against "social equality" took the form of an assertion that "America is [a] White Man's Country."[152] "Why should I waste time in a place where I am outnumbered and where if I make a physical fight I will lose out and ultimately die," Garvey asked.[153] Garvey also managed to shift the blame for white America's racial exclusivity from white prejudice to black failings. In another broadside against Du Bois, Garvey argued that "[Negroes] have done nothing praiseworthy on their own initiative in the last five hundred years to recommend them to the serious consideration of progressive races. . . . [T]hey have made no political, educational, industrial, independent contribution to civilization for which they can be respected by other races, thus making themselves unfit subjects for free companionship and association with races which achieved greatness on their own initiative."[154]

Garvey was, in fact, attempting to present himself before the white American establishment as the potential architect of a new racial "compro-

149. See also "James Weldon Johnson and Marcus Garvey in a Tilt—the Immortal Question of Social Equality," *NW*, Saturday, 1 October 1921, p. 5; also Marcus Garvey, "Race Assimilation," *The Philosophy and Opinions of Marcus Garvey* 1:26; "Purity of Race," ibid., 1:37; "Race Purity a Desideratum," ibid. 2:62. In January 1924, in a statement entitled "What We Believe" (*NW*, Saturday, 5 January 1924, p. 1 and passim), Garvey called for "the purity of the Negro race and the purity of the white race" as well as "the social and political physical separation of all people to the extent that they promote their own ideals and civilization, with the privilege of trading and doing business with each other."

150. "President Harding Pleads Negro's Cause; Whites Silent as He Touches Big Question," *NW*, Saturday, 5 November 1921, p. 5.

151. "President Harding Has Rendered a Signal Service Not Only to America, but to the Whole World, Says Marcus Garvey, Declaring him a Sage and Man of Great Vision, Destined to Rank with Washington and Lincoln," *NW*, Saturday, 5 November 1921, pp. 2–3; see William H. Ferris, "President Harding vs. His Critics," *NW*, Saturday, 19 November 1921, p. 4.

152. *NW*, Saturday, 1 July 1922, p. 1.

153. *NW*, Saturday, 5 November 1921, p. 2.

154. Marcus Garvey, "Negro Self-Assertion," *New York Tribune*, Sunday, 18 September 1921, sect. 4, p. 11.

mise." This was, indeed, a far cry from the sentiment that Garvey voiced when, at the close of the August 1920 convention, he was reported in the *Negro World* of 11 September as having "hurled defiance at the 'crackers' of the South." During this period of political retreat, Garvey embarked on his various flirtations with Senator T. S. McCallum of Mississippi and with the infamous Ku Klux Klan, setting the precedent for his subsequent alliances with John Powell, leader of the Anglo-Saxon Clubs of America, with Earnest Sevier Cox, leader of the White America Society, and still later in the 1930s with Sen. Theodore G. Bilbo, the scourge of Mississippi blacks. When Garvey spoke at Carnegie Hall on "The Future of the Black and White Races," on 23 February 1923, the audience was assured that "the Universal Negro Improvement Association believes in the purity of all races and respects the rights of all peoples." It was no mere accident, moreover, that the second volume of Garvey's *Philosophy and Opinions* should have begun with the statement written in October 1923 entitled, "An Appeal to the Soul of White America" (pp. 1–6).

Garvey's espousal of the doctrine of racial purity, beginning in the summer of 1921, however, did not originate with his alleged West Indian misreading of the supposedly different system of racial segmentation in America. "Not only did Garvey advocate race purity," E. D. Cronon comments in *Black Moses*, "but as a Jamaican black he attempted to transfer the West Indian three-way color caste system to the United States by attacking mulatto leaders" (p. 191). This view echoed Du Bois's earlier statement in his essay "Back to Africa," in which he claimed that Garvey brought to America "the new West Indian conception of the color line" (p. 541). "Imagine, then, the surprise and disgust of these Americans when Garvey launched his Jamaican color scheme," Du Bois recounted (p. 542). The same view, with only minor modification, was taken by the black sociologist Charles S. Johnson in his essay in *Opportunity*, August 1923, wherein he adjudged that Garvey "hated intensely things white and more intensely things near white" (p. 232). Yet in proposing the creation of a "United States of Africa" in June 1922, Garvey made it plain that his whole outlook was based upon "the White Man's civilization [as] a splendid example to Negroes."[155]

In their attempts to comprehend the rationale behind Garvey's stance on racial purity, observers have missed the significance of Garvey's political change of course in the summer of 1921. Garvey's promulgation of the doctrine at this precise juncture served a more fundamental political purpose. If, indeed, Garvey was guilty of using the Jamaican or West Indian color-class system as his model (which American commentators have described incorrectly as a "color caste" and have said he counterposed to the traditional American system of proscription based on racial caste), such usage merely facilitated the real import of his revised political message. Prior to his reentry crisis in 1921, Garvey had not found it necessary to resort to the argument of

155. *NW*, Saturday, 10 June 1922, p. 1.

racial purity or to attack "social equality." Garvey's decision to seek a resolution of his conflict with the American state brought about the change. His belief at the time that his political opponents conspired to use the state against him prompted him to challenge their influence by provoking the issue of "social equality" while promoting his commitment to the ideal of racial purity. This shift was made all the easier by the fact that it came after Garvey's protracted absence from America. His loss of critical contact with the pulse of the movement's rank and file probably led him to overestimate the importance of his political critics and, correspondingly, the readiness of the American state to enter into meaningful dialogue with him. Garvey's new strategy, moreover, increased the competition within black American leadership, a competition based in part on ideological differences but prompted, as well, by the desire for official sanctions and rewards.

Garvey undoubtedly felt justified in making a concerted pitch for official backing because the threat of continued official harassment would have further aggravated the twin crises of the Black Star Line's bankruptcy and the dismal collapse of the UNIA's initial attempt at Liberian colonization in the summer of 1921. For these reasons, therefore, much more was at stake than the question of opposing typologies of racial classification. Indeed, the disintegration of the UNIA as a radical political force began the moment Garvey resorted to the ideology of racial purity.

The Nadir

As the popular thrust of the Garvey movement was blunted, the UNIA paled in contrast to the phase when, in Garvey's own words, "the organization flared forth in all its mighty ways, and for years after held the theatre of the world spell-bound, forcing men as well as races and nations everywhere to think, and some to immediately act."[156]

In his first published message from Jamaica following his deportation from the United States in December 1927, Garvey called for patience from his followers. "It will take me some little time," he advised them, "to write the new creed of the Association and to perfect the sign by which we shall conquer."[157] But this was never to happen. Everything that Garvey tried would fail to reignite the old enthusiasm among the black masses.

156. "The Next Move!" *BM* 1 (November 1934):1.
157. "Marcus Garvey Sends Special Message to Members and Friends," *NW*, Saturday, 10 December 1927, p. 1. Garvey had intended his epistle on "African Fundamentalism: A Racial Hierarchy and Empire for Negroes" (*NW*,, 6 June 1925, and repeated over the next three consecutive *NW* issues [13, 20, and 27 June 1925]) to have served this purpose. The use of the term *fundamentalism* in the title, however, showed the influence of the contemporary controversy raging between Christian fundamentalism and the scientific theory of evolution. According to Merle Curti, the Scopes trial proceedings, which became the focus of national and world attention during 1925, signalled that the "battle between fundamentalism and modernism had reached its highest point" (*The Growth of American Thought*, "The Conflict Between Fundamentalism and Science," pp. 704–7). See also R. M. Cornelius, "Their Stage Drew All the

As Garvey tried to "re-establish the confidence that the masses have in the U.N.I.A.," he contrasted his efforts to the UNIA's earlier phase of mass mobilization. "Unlike the first period of the Organization's existence," Garvey explained, "there is no flare of trumpets, there is no wave of banners, there is no beating of drums, because the time is too serious and our experiences are too rich in knowledge to make us still resort to this method of getting people together."[158] In his last journal, the *Black Man*, he instituted a much less militant line in the editorial policy than had been the case with the *Negro World*: "The policy of the [*Black Man*] Magazine is based upon conditions as they actually are, and the thoughtful method of solution as far as our race is concerned. The *Negro World*, the official organ of the Universal Negro Improvement Association in early days was a propaganda organ. *The Black Man* will be a constructive mouthpiece."[159]

Garvey made a last attempt from Jamaica to revive the demoralized UNIA with the Seventh International Convention of the Negro Peoples of the World, in August 1934. He seized upon the opportunity of his opening address to give some justification for the change in his leadership and in his outlook:

My American co-workers and whole-hearted supporters wondered why for nearly three years I remained quiet, why I did not send to them fiery messages, why I did not attempt to continue stirring them up in enthusiasm. I could not have done that to their good and benefit, because of the peculiarity of the new order. I knew they would have been hungry, I knew that they did not follow my advice in the thirteen years prior, that of economically entrenching themselves, so that they could be their own producers and masters. I realized that in the new order they were still seeking the goodwill of the man who still controlled them. This is my explanation, my friends.[160]

The explanation reflected Garvey's decision, however, to jettison once and for all his belief in a strategy of resistance as the key to popular mobilization. He determined instead to settle on a return to the UNIA's original abstinence from political struggle. Although claiming that he viewed it as only a temporary setback, Garvey clearly admonished the delegates at the seventh convention: "Others are learning that they cannot gain much to-day by being too aggressive; we have to be very compromising, and if we have to

World: A New Look at the Scopes Evolution Trial," *Tennessee Historical Quarterly* 40 (Summer 1981).

158. Marcus Garvey, "An Advice and Statement," *BM* 1 (May–June 1934):12; "A Drifting Race," *BM* 1 (March–April 1934):11.

159. "Our New Start," *BM* 1 (June 1935):1.

160. "Marcus Garvey Opens International Convention with Great Speech—Sound Advice to the Race—New Spirit of U.N.I.A.," *BM* 1 (November 1934):6–11.

be more compromising than other peoples, it is because of our peculiar position—a position that we have invited [upon] ourselves." In the year following the convention, Garvey again reminded his adherents that "today, the scenes have somewhat changed, and the great fight toward racial salvation has to be undertaken from different angles."[161]

At the UNIA's eighth convention, in August 1938 in Toronto (which was to be his last), Garvey was forced to defend his leadership, not against external opposition but against criticism from within his own organization. He asserted that the administration of the UNIA "has not changed in its ultimate object, it has not differed, it has said nothing that would cause anybody with a reasonable mind to think that the UNIA is not the same Association that was started when you all knew it in the United States of America." Nonetheless, Garvey did concede that the UNIA "may have to change methods of operation, but it has not in any way changed its object."[162]

Africa as the Site of Success

However complete the denouement of Garvey and the UNIA, Garvey's underlying purpose remained fixed. Fundamentally, Garvey conceived his racial mission as the achievement of black success. "Negroes, get busy quickly looking after yourselves and your business," Garvey exhorted, "and your business is to get as much out of the earth in common with other people as you can."[163] The novel feature of Garvey's success creed was its combination with the doctrine of nationalism.

Because they were denied the vivifying message of success, in his view the most terrible denial of all, Garvey sought to implant in blacks an energizing vision that he translated into the philosophy of racial pride. "There is a destiny of human success, of human accomplishment, being the result of human labour and human energy," Garvey declared; "let us look forward then to these things as our natural right."[164] Garvey's black creed of pride in success promoted an autonomous Africa as the political precondition for translating his "inspiring vision" of racial progress. "Why should I lose hope, why should I give up and take a back place in this age of progress?" he asked.[165] Instead, he linked politics and success as parts of a single vision of racial regeneration: "If I had the power of a Divine Magician," declared Garvey, "I would reach into the mind of every Negro and stir him to

161. "Garvey's First Message from London—Our Cause Is Just," *BM* 1 (June 1935):18.
162. "Garvey Speaking in Toronto—Suggestions for the Good and Welfare of the Race," *BM* 4 (February 1939):8.
163. "Opening of Conference at Toronto," *BM* 2 (December 1937):7–9.
164. *BM* 2 (July–August 1936):11–12.
165. Marcus Garvey, "The Future as I See It," in *The Philosophy and Opinions of Marcus Garvey* 1:78.

individual and collective action: yes, I would set him to restore the Empire of the glorious Ethiopians."[166]

Africa thus existed ontologically for Garvey on two separate levels. The first level was vividly illustrated in the iconography of the Black Star Line, which declared: "Africa, the Land of Opportunity." Speaking at the Second International Convention of Negroes in August 1921, Garvey assured his listeners that "by our success of the last four years we will be able to estimate the grander success of a free and redeemed Africa" (*Philosophy and Opinions* 1:93). Through this dream of success, Garvey perceived Africa as the land of the black self-made man: "We want to build up Cities, Nations, Governments, Industries of our own in Africa," he appealed during the same year, "so that we will be able to have a chance to rise from the lowest to the highest positions in the African commonwealth." The second level was cultural and was summed up in Garvey's belief that the "world is looking for culture in the highest civilisation and that culture may be recognised as being national in its many branches."[167] Garvey had originally assented to the older, providential view that it was necessary, as the UNIA General Objects expressed it, "to assist in civilizing the backward tribes of Africa." As events transpired, however, the belief in the redemption of a benighted Africa became transformed into a belief in the political primacy of Africa, now seen as the locus and agency of a regenerated national culture and of racial success. Said Garvey: "We may make progress in America, the West Indies and other foreign countries, but there will never be any real lasting progress until the Negro makes of Africa a strong and powerful Republic to lend protection to the success we make in foreign lands. Let us therefore unite our forces and make one desperate rush for the goal of success." Garvey thus found a reciprocal basis for what he termed "the work of redemption and accomplishments," by which he meant, simply, the gospel of success for Africans "at home and abroad."[168]

The Success of Propaganda

If Garvey and the UNIA sounded the possibilities of success, the cultural and political dimensions of their program were dependent on forging an expansive vision of Pan-African solidarity. Garvey spelled out the theme of Pan-African fusion succinctly: "Africa will be the natural centre of Negro salvation, but Africa can only and will only play her part when properly inducted into the necessary knowledge which is to be her salvation. That knowledge must come from America, the land of present opportunities."[169]

166. Marcus Garvey, "Wake Up, Black Men!" *BM* 1 (February 1934):15–16.
167. "An Appeal from Marcus Garvey—Every Negro Man and Woman Should Read This Appeal and Do Something to Improve the Race" (found in DNA, RG 165, file 10218-261/62); "The Force of Organized Life," *BM* 4 (June 1939):4.
168. *NW*, Saturday, 1 November 1919, p. 1; "Dialogue," *BM* 1 (August–September 1935):15.
169. Marcus Garvey, "The Confusion in America," *BM* 1 (December 1935): 7.

The force that sustained this Pan-African amalgam was what Garvey himself described as the UNIA's "twenty-five years of propaganda activity."[170] In this view, the UNIA was a veritable black international, and, indeed, Garvey's organizing skills were well suited to this purpose: "I am reputed to be a good organizer and a good speaker and a good writer, and that has brought me into prominence."[171] Garvey's training as a printer and journalist and its contribution to his extraordinary skill as a propagandist have yet to be sufficiently appreciated. Claude McKay, otherwise a harsh critic of Garvey, was probably the first to emphasize this aspect of Garvey's achievement when he affirmed that "[organized propaganda] was Marcus Garvey's greatest contribution to the Negro movement," adding that he saw Garvey's "pioneer work in that field [as] a feat that the men of broader understanding and sounder ideas who will follow him must continue."[172] Hodge Kirnon offered the same assessment in 1921: "Garvey is primarily an organizer and a propagandist. . . . In these fields he is supreme."[173] In fact, William Ferris would recall at the time of Garvey's death in 1940 how he had "sprung sensation after sensation upon a startled world, almost rivalling the tale of Aladdin's lamp and of the Arabian Nights."[174] C. L. R. James would also stress Garvey's significance as a propagandist: "When you bear in mind the slenderness of his resources, the vast material forces and the pervading social conceptions which automatically sought to destroy him, his achievement remains one of the propagandistic miracles of this century. . . . In little more than half of ten years he made [the cause of Africa and of people of African descent] a part of the political consciousness of the world."[175]

The ultimate justification Garvey offered for his various commercial ventures was their propagandistic function. Its acceptance was well stated by William L. Sherrill when he explained to a Liberty Hall audience in August

---

170. "The New Way to Education," *BM* 4 (February 1939):7.
171. *Daily Gleaner*, Saturday, 21 July 1934, p. 17.
172. Claude McKay, "Soviet Russia and the Negro," *Crisis* 27 (December 1923):61–62.
173. Hodge Kirnon, " 'As to Marcus Garvey,' " p. 3.
174. *Philadelphia Tribune*, Thursday, 20 June 1940. Garvey commented in 1934 that "the man who is to lead must be from the shock battalion, he must be able to, by his force and personality arrest the attention of men by his shocking or daring deeds or expressions" (*BM* 1 [March–April 1934]:3). The prevalence of propaganda as an especially salient feature of contemporary politics was commented upon by Garvey in "Propaganda," *The Philosophy and Opinions of Marcus Garvey* 1:15, and "Propaganda," lesson 16, "School of African Philosophy." For studies of the impact of propaganda during and immediately after the First World War, see Alice Goldfarb Marquis, "Words as Weapons: Propaganda in Britain and Germany During the First World War," *Journal of Contemporary History* 13 (1978):467–98; Philip M. Taylor, "The Foreign Office and British Propaganda During the First World War," *Historical Journal* 23 (1980):875–98; Taylor, *The Projection of Britain: British Overseas Publicity and Propaganda, 1919–1939* (Cambridge: Cambridge University Press, 1981); and Catte Haste, *Keep the Home Fires Burning: Propaganda in the First World War* (London: Allen Lane, 1977); see also Elliott M. Rudwick, "Du Bois versus Garvey: Race Propagandists at War," *Journal of Negro Education* 28 (Fall 1959):421–29.
175. C. L. R. James, *The Black Jacobins: Toussaint L'Ouverture and the San Domingo Revolution*, 2d ed. (New York: Vintage Books, 1963), appendix, pp. 396–97.

1923, "The Black Star Line was only a means to an end; the grocery stores and laundries were only means to that end. We started these things in an effort to show Negroes that commercially they could do big things in commercial lines."[176] At the same time, however, Sherrill's statement is an example of the UNIA's consistent overvaluation of propaganda, which led Garvey always to link a scarcity of resources with the need to propagandize. Garvey himself made this overvaluation clear when, for instance, he declared in August 1920 that "in the conduct of a movement of the vast size and all-embracing scope as the UNIA, money is required, is indispensable; otherwise it would be impossible to spread the propaganda necessary to continue its life and gain new adherents and followers."[177] The success of the UNIA did not ultimately extend beyond the organized propaganda stage. Sherrill admitted as much in 1923, when he reported that after five years of mass mobilization, "the program of the U.N.I.A. is in its propaganda stage."

Paradox and Prophecy

The history of Marcus Garvey and the UNIA therefore consists essentially of the several complex stages through which a "vision of success" came, in Garvey's words, to be "undertaken by an organized race group."[178] The legacy of this phenomenon, which inspired unprecedented feelings of black unity at the time, is still felt in different parts of the black world.

Yet the relationship between Garvey and the UNIA was paradoxical. On the one hand, as Hodge Kirnon noted, the UNIA was "the outgrowth of the ideas, convictions and persistent and energetic activities of Garvey." On the other hand, the UNIA possessed an objective historical reality with a powerful dynamic all its own, and over which Garvey could exercise very little control. This phenomenon, the independent and intractable reality of the UNIA, was therefore separate from the personality of Garvey. "Once [Garvey] dominated the U.N.I.A. movement," Kirnon declared; "now, while he is the soul of it, he is very much the servant of it."[179]

A further irony was the paradox that animated the vision behind Garvey's program of African renascence. When he spoke about "the average Negro [who] doesn't know much about the thought of the serious white man," Garvey was alluding to the side of the vision that drew upon the intellectual traditions of Euro-American culture.[180] At the same time, however, Garvey also sought after an original source in the black racial experience as the basis for the vindication of his ideas: "What is in my mind," he told the

---

176. NW, Saturday, 25 August 1923, p. 10.
177. NW, Saturday, 21 August 1920.
178. BM 1 (December 1935):5.
179. NW, Saturday, 28 January 1922, p. 7, and Saturday, 16 July 1921, p. 3.
180. Marcus Garvey, "Building a State," BM 3 (March 1938):3–4.

final UNIA convention in 1938, "is purely Negro." On this basis, Garvey's definition of a Negro leader was "a man who has nothing else in his head than what concerns the Negro and leading the Negro towards it."[181] In truth, this paradox made Garvey, in the words of Amy Ashwood Garvey, his first wife and UNIA cofounder, "a strange mixture of a man—[a mixture of] racial doubts and racial aspirations."[182]

Despite this paradox, Garvey possessed a genuine, prophetic vision of the emancipation of Africa. In 1935, as he surveyed the world's approaching return to the battlefield, Garvey proclaimed, "There is no doubt that the Negro's chance will come when the smoke from the fire and ashes of twentieth-century civilization has blown off."[183] This impending clash would "come with a mighty rush—a sweeping rush that will take men off their feet everywhere."[184] When the final outbreak of war was only a matter of months away, Garvey, amid dire penury and personal and political isolation, boldly announced, "Africa is a country of the future. Her inhabitants, her everything tend toward an Africa of the natives, where they will rise to govern as other men are governing."[185] Garvey would not live to see Africa independent, but within two decades, history would begin to prove the accuracy of Garvey's vision and give credence to his claim that it was "the Universal Negro Improvement Association that breathed the spirit of nationalism in 1918 [which] was really the precursor or forerunner to an age when nationalism would be necessary for the protection and existence of the Negro."[186]

LOS ANGELES   ROBERT A. HILL

181. "Garvey Before the Convention—Can the Negro Find His Place," *BM* 4 (Febuary 1939):12.

182. Amy Ashwood Garvey's statement is contained in a printed brochure advertising the "Black Man of Destiny," described by her as a forthcoming "intimate biography of Marcus Garvey" (Rev. George A. Weston Papers, Stanford, California).

183. "The World a Battlefield," *BM* 1 (July 1935):2.

184. "The World Crisis Is Coming," *BM* 2 (December 1937):3.

185. "Africa's Sovereignty," *BM* 4 (February 1939):2.

186. "The Negro Does Not Prepare—That Is Why He Loses Every Time," *BM* 2 (May–June 1936):10; see also Garvey's other statements: "Now we have started to speak, and I am only the forerunner of an awakened Africa that shall never go back to sleep" (*Minutes of Proceedings of the Speech by the Hon. Marcus Garvey at the Century Theatre, Archer Street, Westbourne Grove, London, W. 11, on Sunday, September Second, 1928* [London: Universal Negro Improvement Association, 1928]:22); and "Be assured that I planted well the seed of Negro or black nationalism which cannot be destroyed even by the foul play that has been meted out to me" (Marcus Garvey, "First Message to the Negroes of the World from Atlanta Prison," 10 February 1925, in *The Philosophy and Opinions of Marcus Garvey* 2:237–38).

THE PAPERS

The Marcus Garvey and UNIA Papers project formally began in June 1976 at Northwestern University in Evanston, Illinois, under the sponsorship of the National Historical Publications and Records Commission. The edition was transferred the following year to the Center for Afro-American Studies, University of California, Los Angeles. In July 1979 a two-year grant from the National Endowment for the Humanities, Research Materials Division, was awarded to the edition for work on the first three volumes of the Papers.

The Collection

The Marcus Garvey and Universal Negro Improvement Association Papers are based on a comprehensive survey of all the presently available historical manuscripts and records pertaining to the life and work of Marcus Mosiah Garvey as well as to the popular worldwide organization that he founded and led from its inception in 1914 until his death in 1940. As the record of the only organized international mass movement of persons of African descent and as the history of a mass social phenomenon, these Papers go beyond a preoccupation with the fortunes of a single, even if major, historical figure. Their focus is as much on the participation of members and supporters as on Garvey's activities as the political leader of the movement.

During its collection phase, the project undertook a far-reaching search for the widely scattered manuscript sources. Unlike most other large-scale editions, the Garvey and UNIA Papers project was not blessed with an original, parent collection of personal or organizational records. The documents in the present collection, therefore, have been retrieved from 93 official archives that contain 119 relevant record groupings; 35 manuscript collections; and 25 private manuscript holdings, personal as well as institutional. Source locations have included the United States, Canada, Central America, the Caribbean, western Europe, Africa, and Asia. This process of recovery has made for an important methodological advantage, however, since the problem of locating the surviving documents has revealed much about how the movement spread. As the underlying process of the movement's proliferation became clearer, the process of collection was enhanced in turn.

For this edition, the project has collected approximately twenty-five thousand archival documents and original manuscripts, which represent the most comprehensive historical profile of the Garvey phenomenon ever assembled. The documents thus recovered, and upon which the edition bases its selection, fall into seven principal categories: personal correspondence of Garvey, official correspondence of the UNIA and governmental officials, organizational records of the UNIA, investigative intelligence records, legal and court records, published newspaper documents, and iconographic materials.

Mere numbers of documents and repositories, however, do not tell the complete story. Even more important than the extensive compass of the documentary sources has been their lode of rich detail, which describes the myriad organizational problems that confronted Garvey and the UNIA at each step. Moreover, close diplomatic relations between the United States and western European countries with colonial possessions in Africa created a considerable traffic of political intelligence relating to Garvey and the UNIA, which fills a critical aspect of the movement's international character.

Recovery of these important official records compensates in part for the destruction or loss of most of the UNIA's organizational records, which, along with the loss of Garvey's personal papers, represents a great liability to historical research. The major loss has been the records of the UNIA's supervising parent body, which underwent a major disturbance when the United States District Attorney's office seized the records in 1922 as evidence to be used in the mail fraud trial of Garvey and his associates. Later, in September of the same year, a fire in the basement of the three-story brick building that housed the main offices of the UNIA and the *Negro World* destroyed a part of their joint archives. The parent body's remaining records were further dispersed after February 1925 because of the outbreak of violent factional strife within the UNIA's leadership immediately following Garvey's imprisonment for mail fraud. Soon afterward, successive foreclosures caused the UNIA parent body to move to rented quarters, a fact that further disrupted the records. Whether the remaining parent body's records or only a portion of them were transferred to Jamaica after Garvey was deported is still not known. Finally, when he moved his headquarters from Jamaica to London, in March 1935, Garvey was forced to leave behind in Jamaica the great majority of his records, which were subsequently lost when the UNIA's headquarters in Jamaica fell under the auction hammer as a result of mortgage foreclosure. Finally, the wartime devastation of London in 1941 and 1942 destroyed the records accumulated and stored at Garvey's final headquarters.

A similar loss has afflicted the documentary sources of other black radical movements throughout the greater part of Afro-American history.

For our immediate purposes, however, when we examine the period after 1918, we see that the record of destruction presents the same limiting picture. In a list of "colored newspapers" by the National Negro Press Association in November 1923, it was reported that there were "upward of 300 Negro [weekly] newspapers published in the United States," a number more than double the 141 newspapers published in the period of 1916 to 1919.[1] Of the 18 cited as "the better publications" by the National Negro Press Association in 1923, copies of only 6 newspapers are available today, representing approximately 2 percent of the overall total. For the entire period of 1916 to 1923, the number of surviving black newspapers increased to 12 out of a total of more than 300.[2] The only factors to alleviate this bleak situation are the newspaper clipping collections developed by Hampton Institute's George P. Peabody Library and the Tuskegee Institute News Clippings File, 1899–1966, begun by the famous Tuskegee Institute archivist and sociologist Monroe N. Work.[3]

Garvey's Literary Legacy

To date there has been only a single attempt to edit Garvey's extant speeches and writings. This was *The Philosophy and Opinions of Marcus Garvey*, compiled by Garvey's second wife, Amy Jacques Garvey, from material that had appeared mostly in the *Negro World*. Published in two volumes, the entire work was intentionally propagandistic and apologetic. When the first volume was published in early 1923, Garvey was engaged in a campaign to attract support for his legal defense against a federal mail fraud indictment, and this placed a politically self-serving character on the production of the text. This fact also explains why none of Garvey's speeches and writings from the UNIA's radical phase, between 1918 and February 1921, were chosen for the volume. Yet this radical period holds the key to an understanding of the explosive rise of the movement. Garvey's earlier controversial statements, however, were obviously considered a political liability, in light of his attempt to cultivate a "liberal" image in order to create a degree of acceptability to the American establishment as well as to highlight the element of political persecution in the government's indictment. Thus, the first volume of Garvey's *Philosophy and Opinions* serves mainly to delineate the strategic

1. DLC, Papers of Calvin Coolidge, National Negro Press Association to C. Bascum Slemp, 10 November 1923; DNA, RG 65, file 384671, *Proceedings of the National Negro Press Association and Executive Committee Sessions for the Years of 1916, 1917, 1918, 1919.*

2. The twelve papers are the *Baltimore Afro-American, St. Paul Appeal, Chicago Broad Ax, Chicago Defender, Cleveland Gazette, Houston Informer and Texas Freeman, Norfolk Journal and Guide, New York Age, Philadelphia Tribune, Pittsburgh Courier, Cincinnati Union*, and *Washington Bee.*

3. The Tuskegee collection has now been microfilmed. An important reference tool for black history developed by the Frederick Douglass Papers is John W. Blassingame and Mae G. Henderson, eds., *Anti-Slavery Newspapers and Periodicals: An Annotated Index of Letters, 1817–1871* (Boston: G. K. Hall, 1980), vols. 1 and 2.

turn in the political line of the UNIA; unfortunately, it has institutionalized a distorted picture of the militant stage of the UNIA and its mass following.

The second volume merely continued this revisionist strategy. When it appeared in the fall of 1925, Garvey had begun serving sentence in the Atlanta federal penitentiary, and his overriding objective at this time was to secure an executive pardon and commutation of his five-year prison sentence. His wife-editor later described how Garvey intended to attract political support through the publication of the second volume:

> I thought I had done almost the impossible, when I was able to rush a first copy of Vol. II to him, but he callously said, 'Now I want you to send free copies to Senators, Congressmen and prominent men who might become interested in my case, as I want to make another application for a pardon.' . . . After two weeks he telephoned me to come and bring all acknowledgements of books sent; then he informed me that as soon as I was stronger, I should make a list of the favorable ones, and go to the capital to lobby on his behalf.[4]

It should be clear from such testimony that both volumes of Garvey's *Philosophy and Opinions* have to be used with care in the scholarly evaluation of his literary legacy. There is also a further reason for caution. In attempting to establish the text of a speech by Garvey contained in the first volume of *Philosophy and Opinions*, Randall K. Burkett discovered that "the religious language has there been altered by Mrs. Garvey so that the familiar passage from Psalms 68:31 is substituted in place of some of Garvey's more rhapsodical passages concerning Jesus." Burkett also disclosed that "numerous other changes from the *Negro World* versions have been made in this and many of the speeches published in *Philosophy and Opinions*."[5]

Principles of Editorial Selection, Transcription, and Annotation

The Marcus Garvey and Universal Negro Improvement Association Papers will be published as a letterpress edition of selected documents reflecting: first, the personal and political career of Garvey; second, the history and spread of the UNIA; and third, the external response to both Garvey and the UNIA from official and unofficial quarters. It is thus our objective to offer, as far as is possible, a comprehensive reconstruction of the origin, development, and spread of the UNIA under Garvey's leadership, between its founding in 1914 and his death in 1940. While a few areas remain for which documenta-

4. Amy Jacques Garvey, *Garvey and Garveyism*, pp. 167–68.
5. Randall K. Burkett, *Black Redemption: Churchmen Speak for the Garvey Movement*, p. 185, n. 11.

tion is not yet available, we hope that as the edition progresses, new discoveries of documents will continue to be made. These will be announced and published whenever possible.

Among the documents that are now recovered, highest priority in selection is given to Garvey's correspondence and written manuscripts. In cases where Garvey wrote identical letters to several individuals, the one selected has been the letter considered to have had the greatest impact. Garvey's published writings have been selectively used to avoid unnecessary repetition of subject matter. Recipients' copies of letters are used whenever possible, but file copies, retained draft copies, and transcripts are used in the event that an original text cannot be located.

The next priority of selection is given to second- and third-party material. Second-party documents comprise letters and documents addressed to Garvey and/or the UNIA, while third-party documents consist of contemporary letters, documents, and published material containing information about Garvey and/or the UNIA. Third-party documents, particularly intelligence dossiers and secret or confidential official correspondence, frequently contain, in addition to data on Garvey and the UNIA, extensive information about other closely related individuals and groups. In such cases, the relevant material has been extracted from the document, and the extrapolation has been indicated by ellipses.

The transcription of the text is governed by rules that are set out in detail in the statement of Editorial Principles and Practices (see p. xcvii). The text thus etablished also employs specific textual devices, so that a critical text as well as one that is authentically descriptive of the original document is produced. The edition has not encountered the usual dilemma of most historical editing, namely, a choice between "exact reproduction" and "modernization" of text, since the documents conform to modern usage throughout.

Regarding annotation, information pertaining to biographical, textual, historical, and bibliographical matters is provided in two ways: first, in a fully descriptive source note showing the provenance of the document as well as its textual character by means of editorial abbreviations and symbols, and second, in a series of numbered explanatory footnotes. All reasonable effort has been made to identify personal names, but many of the persons who were active participants in the UNIA have proved impossible to identify. Annotation of individuals is made upon their first appearance, although additional information may be presented at subsequent stages where necessary. Extended biographical essays on a number of key figures annotated in the text are presented in appendix I. The essays, based on original primary research, were necessitated by the scarcity of reliable biographical data in the secondary literature. The reader can either consult them in conjunction with the relevant texts in the volume or they can be read separately. Since many documents frequently are valuably annotated by information contained in documents that appear elsewhere in the volume, cross-referencing will be possible through the Index.

Plan of Publication

Publication of the edition is based on three broad divisions. The *Main Series* consists of documents that record both the political career of Garvey and the history of the UNIA in the United States of America. It will include the records of Garvey's leadership which directly relate to the evolution of the UNIA in America, in spite of his absence from the country following deportation to Jamaica in 1927. The *African Series* contains the documents recording the spread of the UNIA and Garvey's ideology throughout sub-Saharan Africa. The *Caribbean Series* records the impact of the UNIA throughout the Caribbean as well as among the circum-Caribbean population areas of Central and South America.

Decisions on ordering the documents have been far from easy. Criteria have been the principal relevance of a document and its origin. For example, the UNIA's spread throughout Europe's colonial empire in Africa and the Caribbean moved centrifugally from the UNIA's American base. At the same time, the UNIA's spread confronted a wide array of political counter-responses from European imperial governments. Most of the documents recording these responses have been placed within the African and Caribbean series. The Main Series, however, was chosen for documents that relate chiefly to evaluation of the United States government's request for information or investigative findings. Similarly, correspondence between European diplomats in America and various officials of the United States government has been retained as part of the Main Series. In essence, the three series encompass the whole range of reciprocal actions that trace the network established between the UNIA's parent body in America and UNIA divisions and chapters throughout the United States, the Caribbean, and Africa, and, correspondingly, between interests that felt threatened by the Garvey movement. A reading of all three series is ultimately essential to an accurate understanding of the UNIA's complexity as an international movement.

EDITORIAL PRINCIPLES AND PRACTICES

I. Arrangement of Documents

Documents are presented in chronological order according to the date of authorship of the original text. Enclosures and attachments to documents, however, do not appear in strict chronological sequence, but are printed with their original covering documents. Enclosures have been set in italic type in the table of contents for identification.

The publication date of news reports and periodical articles is given on the place and date line within square brackets. In the case of news reports and periodical articles containing the date of original composition, that date chronologically supersedes the date of eventual publication and is printed within double square brackets on the place and date line of the document.

In the case of reported speeches, the date of publication supersedes chronologically the date of original delivery and is printed within single square brackets on the place and date line of the document.

When investigative reports give both the date of composition and the period covered by the report, they are arranged according to the date of the period covered by the report.

Documents that lack dates and thus require editorial assignment of dates are placed in normal chronological sequence. When no day within a month appears on a document, it is placed after the documents specifically dated on the latest date within that month. Documents that carry only the date of a year are placed according to the same principle. Documents that cover substantial periods, such as diaries, journals and accounts, will appear according to the date of their earliest entries.

When two or more documents possess the same date, they are arranged with regard to affinity to the subject of the document that immediately precedes them or that which immediately follows them.

II. Form of Presentation

Each document is presented in the following manner:

A. A caption introduces the document and is printed in a type size larger than the text. Letters between individuals are captioned with the names of the individuals and their titles; captions, however, include a person's office only upon that person's first appearance. The original titles of published materials are retained with the documents; however, the headlines of some news reports are abbreviated or omitted, in which case this is indicated in the descriptive source note to the document.

B. The text of a document follows the caption. The copy text of letters or reports is taken from recipients' copies whenever possible, but in the absence of a recipient's copy, a file copy of the letter or report is used. If the file copy is not available, however, and a retained draft copy of the letter is found, the retained draft copy is used as the basic text.

C. Following the body of the text, an unnumbered descriptive source note describes editorially the physical character of the document by means of appropriate abbreviations. Moreover, a repository symbol gives the provenance of the original manuscript or, if it is rare, printed work. Printed sources are identified in the following manner:

   1. A contemporary pamphlet is identified by its full title, place and date of publication, and the location of the copy used.

   2. A contemporary essay, letter, or other kind of statement that appeared originally in a contemporary publication is preceded by the words "Printed in . . .," followed by the title, date, and, in the case of essays, inclusive page numbers of the source of publication.

   3. A contemporary printed source reprinted at a later date, the original publication of which has not been found, is identified with the words "Reprinted from . . .," followed by the identification of the work from which the text has been reproduced. The same applies to any originally unpublished manuscript printed at a later date.

D. Numbered textual annotations that explicate the document follow the descriptive source note. The following principles of textual annotation have been applied:

   1. Individuals are identified upon their first appearance, with additional information about them sometimes furnished upon their later appearance in a document where such data provide maximum clarification. Pseudonyms are identified, wherever possible, by a textual annotation.

   2. Reasons for the assignment of dates to documents or the correction of dates of documents are explained in those instances where important historical information is involved.

3. Obscure allusions in the text are annotated whenever such references can be clarified.

4. Printed works and manuscript materials consulted during the preparation of textual annotations appear in parentheses at the end of each annotation. Frequently used reference works are cited in an abbreviated form, and the complete table may be found in the list of Abbreviations of Published Works.

III. Transcription of Text

Manuscripts and printed material have been transcribed from the original text and printed as documents according to the following principles and procedures:

A. Manuscript Material

1. The place and date of composition are placed at the head of the document, regardless of their location in the original, but exceptions are made in the cases of certificates of vital registration and documents in which original letterhead stationery is reproduced. If the place or date of a letter (or both) does not appear in the original text, the information is supplied and printed in italics at the head within square brackets. Likewise, if either the place or date is incomplete, the necessary additional information is supplied in italics within square brackets. Superscript letters are brought down to the line of type, and terminal punctuation is deleted.

   In the case of Bureau of Investigation reports that were submitted on printed forms, the place and date are abstracted and placed at the head of each document, while the name of the reporting agent is placed at the end of the document on the signature line. In the case of United States Postal Censorship reports, which were also prepared on printed forms, the narrative section of the report is printed in roman type. The other sections of the censorship reports, containing recorded analytic and filing information, have been treated as printed forms.

   The formal salutation of letters is placed on the line below the place and date line, with the body of the text following the salutation.

   The complimentary close of letters is set continuously with the text in run-in style, regardless of how it was written in the original.

   The signature, which is set in capitals and small capitals, is placed at the right-hand margin on the line beneath the text or complimentary close, with titles, where they appear, set in uppercase and lowercase. Terminal punctuation is deleted.

When a file copy of a document bearing no signature is used to establish the text but the signatory is known, the signature is printed in roman type within square brackets.

The inside address, if significant and not repetitive, is printed immediately below the text.

Endorsements, docketings, and other markings appearing on official correspondence, when intelligible, are reproduced in small type following the address, with appropriate identification. In the case of other types of documents, such as private correspondence, endorsements and dockets are reprinted only when they are significant.

Minutes, enclosures, and attachments are printed in roman type following their covering documents and placed after the annotation material of their covering documents. Whenever minutes, enclosures, or attachments are not printed, this fact is always recorded and explained. Whenever a transmission letter originally accompanying an enclosure or attachment is not printed, the omission is noted and the transmission document identified and recorded in the descriptive source note.

2. Printed letterheads and other official stationery are not reproduced, unless they contain significant information, in which case they are reprinted above the date line. In cases where they are not reprinted, they are sometimes abstracted, and the information is placed in the descriptive source note. Printed addresses are reproduced only upon the first appearance.

3. In general, the spelling of all words, including proper names, is preserved as written in the manuscript and printed sources. Thus, personal and place names that are spelled erratically in the original texts are regularized or corrected only in the index. However, serious distortion in the spelling of a word, to such an extent as to obscure its true meaning, is repaired by printing the correct word in italics within square brackets after the incorrect spelling. Mere "slips of the pen" or typographical errors are corrected within the word and printed in roman type within square brackets; however, some typographical errors that contribute to the overall character of the document are retained.

4. Capitalization is retained as in the original. Words underlined once in a manuscript are printed in italics. Words that are underlined twice or spelled out in large letters or full capitals are printed in small capitals.

5. Punctuation, grammar, and syntax are retained as found in the original texts. In the case of punctuation, corrections that are essential to

the accurate reading of the text are provided within square brackets. If, however, a punctuation mark appears in a document as a result of typographical error, it is corrected in square brackets or, in some instances, silently deleted.

6. All contractions and abbreviations in the text are retained. Abbreviations of titles or organizations are identified in a list of abbreviations that appears at the front of the volume. Persons represented by initials only will have their full names spelled out in square brackets after each initial on their first appearance.

7. Superscript letters in the text are lowered and aligned on the line of print.

8. Omissions, mutilations, and illegible words or letters have been rendered through the use of the following textual devices:

   a) Blank spaces in a manuscript are shown as [   ]. If the blank space is of significance or of substantial length, this fact is elaborated upon in a textual annotation.

   b) When a word or words in the original text must be omitted from the printed document because of mutilation, illegibility, or omission, the omission is shown by the use of ellipses followed by a word or phrase placed in square brackets in italics, such as: . . . [*torn*], . . . [*illegible*], . . . [*remainder missing*].

   c) Missing or illegible letters of words are represented by suspension points within square brackets, the number of points corresponding to the estimated number of letters omitted. The same holds true for missing or illegible digits of numbers.

   d) All attempts have been made to supply conjecturally missing items in the printed document, according to the following rules:

   (1) if there is no question as to the word, the missing letter is supplied silently;

   (2) if the missing letter(s) can only be conjectured, the omission is supplied within square brackets and printed in roman type. Uncertainty of the conjecture, however, is indicated by a question mark within the square brackets in the document.

9. Additions and corrections made by the author in the original text have been rendered as follows:

   a) Additions between the lines are brought onto the line of type and incorporated into the body of the text within diagonal lines / /.

   b) Marginal additions or corrections by the author are also incorporated into the printed document and identified by the words [*in the margin*] italicized in square brackets. Marginal notes made by someone other than the author are treated as an endorsement and are printed following the text of the document.

   c) Words or groups of words deleted in the original, as in a draft, are restored in the printed document. The canceled word or phrase is indicated by ~~canceled type~~ at the place where the deletion occurs in the original text. If a lengthy deletion is illegible, this is indicated by the words [*deletion illegible*].

B. Printed Material

Contemporary printed material has been treated in the same manner as were original texts and has been transcribed according to the same editorial principles as was manuscript material.

1. In the case of originally published letters, the place and date of composition are uniformly printed on the place and date line of the document, regardless of where they appear in the original, and placed within double square brackets. Those elements that have been editorially supplied are italicized.

2. Newspaper headlines and subheads are printed in small capitals. Headlines are punctuated as they are in the original; however, they are reproduced in the printed document in as few lines as possible. Unless the headline would otherwise become distorted, ornamental lines appearing within the headlines are not retained.

3. Words originally printed in full capitals for emphasis or for other reasons are usually printed in small capitals. Boldfaced type that appears within the text is retained.

4. The signature accompanying a published letter is printed in capitals and small capitals.

5. Obvious typographical errors and errors of punctuation, such as the omission of a single parenthesis or quotation mark, are corrected and printed within square brackets in roman type.

6. In the case of a printed form with spaces to be filled in, the printed words are designated in small capitals, while the handwritten or typewritten insertions are designated in italics with spaces left before and after the small capitals to suggest the blank spaces in the original form.

TEXTUAL DEVICES

[ ]	Blank spaces in the text.
[. . .], [. . . .]	Suspension points indicate approximate number of letters or digits missing in words or numerals (not to exceed four) and not conjecturable.
[[ ]]	Double square brackets are used to give the composition date of a published letter or news report if the publication date differs.
/ /	Incorporation into the text of addition or correction made above or below the line by author.
[roman]	Conjectural reading for missing, mutilated, or illegible matter, with a question mark inside the square bracket when the conjectural reading is doubtful. Also used in editorial correction of typographical errors in original manuscript or printed document. Also used to indicate the publication date of a news report or periodical article.
[*italic*]	Assigned date of any undated document; editorial comment inserted in the text, such as [*endorsement*], [*illegible*], [*remainder missing*], [*sentence unfinished*], [*torn*], [*enclosure*], [*attachment*], [*in the margin*].
~~canceled~~	Textual matter deleted in the original but restored in the text.

SYMBOLS AND ABBREVIATIONS

Repositories and Collections

The original locations of documents that appear in the text are described by use of symbols. The guide used for American repositories was the *Symbols of American Libraries*, 11th ed., (Washington, D.C.: Library of Congress, 1976). Foreign repositories and collections have been assigned symbols that conform to the institution's own usage. In some cases, however, it has been necessary to create acronyms containing the initials of the main words of the repository title. Acronyms have also been created on this basis for private manuscript collections. In a few instances, location symbols have also been provided for identification of record groups in the National Archives, Washington, D.C., and the Public Record Office, London, which have been used in the annotation of documents printed in the volume.

Repositories

AFRC	Federal Archives and Records Center, East Point, Georgia
	RG 163 Records of the Selective Service System (World War I)
ATT	Hollis Burke Frissell Library, Tuskegee Institute, Tuskegee, Alabama
BM	British Museum Archives, London
DHU	Moorland-Spingarn Research Center, Howard University, Washington, D.C.
DLC	Library of Congress, Washington, D.C.
DNA	National Archives, Washington, D.C.
	RG 28 Records of the Post Office Department, records relating to the Espionage Act, World War I, 1917–1921
	RG 36 Records of the Bureau of Customs, returned crew lists
	RG 38 Records of the Office of the Chief of Naval

	Operations, Office of Naval Intelligence confidential, "suspect," and general files, 1913–1924
RG 59	General records of the Department of State, records of the post-1906 period, decimal file; records of the Office of the Counselor
RG 60	General records of the Department of Justice
RG 65	Records of the Federal Bureau of Investigation
RG 74	Records of the Bureau of Ordnance
RG 165	Records of the War Department General and Special staffs, records of the Office of the Chief of Staff

HLRO	House of Lords Record Office, London
IRO	Island Record Office, Spanish Town, Jamaica
JA	Jamaica Archives, Spanish Town, Jamaica
MU	University of Massachusetts Library, Amherst
NA1DS	Office of the Secretary of State, State of New York, Albany
NN-Sc	The Schomburg Center for Research in Black Culture, New York Public Library, New York
NNC	Butler Library, Columbia University, New York
PRO	Public Record Office, London
	Cab. Cabinet Office
	CO Colonial Office
	T. Treasury
RHL	Rhodes House Library, Oxford, England
TNF	Fisk University Library, Nashville

Symbols for Manuscript Collections

ABL	Andrew Bonar Law Papers, *HLRO*
AJG	Amy Jacques Garvey Papers, *TNF*
ASAPS	Anti-Slavery and Aborigines Protection Society Manuscripts, *RHL*
BTW	Booker T. Washington Papers, *DLC*
JEB	John E. Bruce Papers, *NN-Sc*
NCF	National Civic Federation Papers, *NN*
NMB	Nicholas Murray Butler Papers, *NNC*
RRM	Robert Russa Moton Papers, *ATT*
TR	Theodore Roosevelt Papers, *DLC*
W	The *World* Collection, *NNC*
WEBDB	W. E. B. Du Bois Papers, *MU*

Symbols for Private Collections

AEB	Alfred E. Burrowes Papers, St. Ann's Bay, St. Ann, Jamaica
EDSG	Edward D. Smith-Green Papers, New York
RF	Rerrie Family Papers, Winders Hill, St. Ann, Jamaica
TAM	Thaddeus A. McCormack Papers, Barton, St. Elizabeth, Jamaica
WAD	Wilfred A. Domingo Papers, New York

Descriptive Symbols

The following symbols are used to describe the character of the original documents:

ADS	Autograph document signed
ALS	Autograph letter signed
AMS	Autograph manuscript
AMSS	Autograph manuscript signed
AN	Autograph note
ANI	Autograph note initialed
D	Document
DS	Document signed
L	Letter
LS	Letter signed
MS	Manuscript
N	Note
TD	Typed document
TDS	Typed document signed
TL	Typed letter
TLI	Typed letter initialed
TLR	Typed letter representation
TLS	Typed letter signed
TMS	Typed manuscript
TN	Typed note
TNI	Typed note initialed
TNS	Typed note signed

Abbreviations of Published Works

ATOR	*African Times and Orient Review*
BFQ	*Bartlett's Familiar Quotations*
BM	*Black Man*
CBD	*Chambers's Biographical Dictionary*
CQ	*Caribbean Quarterly*
DAB	*Dictionary of American Biography*
DG	*Daily Gleaner*
DNB	*Dictionary of National Biography*
EA	*Encyclopedia Americana*
EB	*Encyclopaedia Britannica*
EWH	*Encyclopedia of World History*
HJ	*Handbook of Jamaica*
NCAB	*National Cyclopedia of American Biography*
NW	*Negro World*
NYT	*New York Times*
PP	*Parliamentary Papers*
WBD	*Webster's Biographical Dictionary*
WWCA	*Who's Who of Colored America*
WWCR	*Who's Who of the Colored Race*
WWJ	*Who's Who in Jamaica*
WWW	*Who Was Who*
WWWA	*Who Was Who in America*

Other Symbols and Abbreviations

Included are abbreviations that are used generally throughout annotations of the text. Standard abbreviations, such as titles or scholastic degrees, are omitted. Abbreviations that are specific to a single annotation appear in parentheses after the initial citation and are used thereafter in the rest of the annotation.

ABB	African Blood Brotherhood
ACL	African Communities' League
AFL	American Federation of Labor

AME	African Methodist Episcopal Church
AMEZ	African Methodist Episcopal Zion Church
ASAPS	Anti-Slavery and Aborigines' Protection Society
BSL	Black Star Line
BWI	British West Indies
CB	Companion of the Order of the Bath
CMG	Companion of the Order of Saint Michael and Saint George
CSO	Colonial Secretary's Office
DSM	Distinguished Service Medal
IWW	Industrial Workers of the World
KB	Knight of the Order of the Bath
KBE	Knight of the British Empire
KCMG	Knight Commander of the Order of Saint Michael and Saint George
MP	Minute Paper
NAACP	National Association for the Advancement of Colored People
OBE	Order of the British Empire
RG	Record Group
UNIA	Universal Negro Improvement Association

Monetary Symbols

d.	English pence
s.,/-	English shilling
£	English pound

GARVEY CHRONOLOGY

August 1887–August 1919

1887

17 August   Birth of Malcus Mosiah Garvey, Jr., at St. Ann's Bay, parish of St. Ann, Jamaica.

1889

15 December   Marriage of Garvey's parents, Malchus Mosiah Garvey, Sr., and Sarah Jane Richards.

1890

28 October   Garvey is baptized into Wesleyan Methodist church.

ca. 1895

Attends Church of England school in St. Ann's Bay.

1897

22 June   *Queen Victoria's Diamond Jubilee*

1901

22 January   *Death of Queen Victoria; accession of Edward VII to throne.*

ca. 1901

Garvey begins printer's apprenticeship with Alfred E. Burrowes, master printer, St. Ann's Bay.

ca. 1903

Leaves school after completing the sixth standard; employed as compositor in printery of Alfred E. Burrowes and Company.

ca. 1904

Leaves St. Ann's Bay to work in branch printery established by Alfred E. Burrowes at Port Maria, in the adjoining parish of St. Mary.

ca. 1906

Leaves Port Maria and moves to capital city of Kingston; employed in printing department of P. A. Benjamin Manufacturing Company.

1907

14 January	*Kingston is destroyed by disastrous earthquake and fire.*
November	Garvey is elected vice-president of the compositors' branch of Kingston Typographical Union, organized as affiliate (no. 98) of International Typographical Union of the American Federation of Labor.

1908

18 March	Death of Sarah Jane Garvey, age fifty-six, in Kingston.
December	Kingston printers begin strike.

1909

January	Printers' strike collapses and union disintegrates.
?	Publication by Garvey of a weekly newspaper, *Garvey's Watchman*; discontinued after third issue.
3 March	*S. A. G. "Sandy" Cox forms the National Club of Jamaica.*
17 November	*Cox wins St. Thomas seat in the Legislative Council by large majority.*

1910

20 April	Garvey is elected an assistant secretary of the National Club.
6 May	*Death of Edward VII, accession of George V.*
18 May	*The Legislative Council suspends Cox for making "ill-founded charges against certain public officers."*
May	Garvey publishes *The Struggling Mass*, a pamphlet in defense of Cox's role as elected member of the Legislative Council.
July	*S. A. G. Cox starts publishing Our Own, magazine of the National Club.*
24 August	Garvey competes in island elocution contest representing the parish of St. Ann.
?	Garvey leaves Jamaica for Central America.

1911

19 January	*Cox is reelected to the Legislative Council at the general election.*
8 February	*Election petition is filed against Cox by Henry Cork.*
7 June	*Cox is unseated from the Legislative Council.*
?	Garvey resides for several months in Port Limon, Costa Rica, and edits *La Nacion/The Nation*, a daily newspaper; afterward, travels to Panama, where he edits a triweekly newspaper in Colon.
?	Garvey returns to Jamaica from Central America.

1912

ca. February	Garvey is employed by Government Printing Office in Kingston as extra hand.
12 February	Outbreak of Streetcar Riot in Kingston; Garvey comes to assistance of the governor, Sir Sydney Olivier.
?	Garvey is connected with *Catholic Opinion*, official organ of the Roman Catholic diocese in Jamaica.
ca. April–May	Garvey leaves Jamaica for England.
ca. July	Indiana Garvey, his sister, accompanies Judah family to England to join Garvey.
?	Garvey attends Birkbeck College in London.

1913

8 July	Garvey applies to British Colonial Office for financial assistance to return to Jamaica.
October	Article by Garvey, "The British West Indies in the Mirror of Civilization: History Making by Colonial Negroes," is published in *African Times and Orient Review*.
post 10 December–January 1914	Garvey visits Paris, Madrid, Boulogne, Monte Carlo, and other cities in Europe.

1914

ca. 14 January	Garvey visits Edinburgh and Glasgow in Scotland.
ca. mid-January	Garvey returns to London from Scotland; attends classes at Birkbeck College.
29 May	Garvey visits the Colonial Office in London requesting financial assistance to return to Jamaica.
17 June	Garvey leaves England for Jamaica aboard S. S. *Trent*.
June	Article by Garvey, "The Evolution of Latter-Day

	Slaves: Jamaica, A Country of Black and White," is published in the *Tourist*.
8 July	Garvey arrives in Jamaica.
20 July	First meeting of the UNIA and ACL and the election of officers.
ca. July–August	Garvey publishes pamphlet, *A Talk with Afro-West Indians: The Negro Race and Its Problems*.
4 August	*Great Britain declares war on Germany.*
8 September	Garvey writes to appeal to Booker T. Washington, principal of Tuskegee Institute, Alabama, for support.
3 October	Washington invites Garvey to visit Tuskegee Institute.
12 November	Garvey and UNIA delegation inspect Hope Farm School.
21 November	*Dr. J. Robert Love, pioneer nationalist of Jamaica and Garvey's proclaimed mentor, dies in Kingston.*
1 December	Special UNIA memorial meeting for Dr. J. Robert Love.

1915

12 April	Garvey writes to Booker T. Washington informing him of impending trip to America and requesting his assistance.
ca. 14 April–1 May	*W. E. B. Du Bois visits Jamaica on brief vacation.*
27 April	Washington responds to Garvey welcoming his proposed visit to America.
17 May	Opening of the UNIA Reading Room in Kingston.
June	Garvey's father, Malchus Mosiah Garvey, Sr., is committed to St. Ann Poor House.
24 August	Garvey announces plan to establish industrial farm and institute in Jamaica.
8 September	Dr. Leo S. Pink, Jamaican dentist, writes letter to the *Daily Chronicle* requesting an accounting of UNIA funds; also states he will write Booker T. Washington to warn him against Garvey.
11 September	Garvey writes to Washington defending himself against Dr. Pink's published attacks.
27 September	Garvey writes further to Washington explaining reasons for recurrent published attacks against UNIA in Jamaica.
29 October	Garvey visits St. Ann's Bay to hold first UNIA meeting outside Kingston.

14 November	*Death of Booker T. Washington.*
22 November	Garvey delivers address on "Life and Work of the Late Booker T. Washington" at special UNIA memorial meeting.
?	St. Ann parish inspector of the poor serves court summons against Garvey for disobeying court order to provide maintenance costs for his father.

1916

29 February	Robert Russa Moton, newly appointed principal of Tuskegee Institute, on visit to Jamaica receives lengthy memorandum from Garvey regarding conditions in Jamaica.
6 March	Garvey leaves Jamaica for America aboard S.S. *Tallac.*
24 March	Garvey arrives in New York City.
25 April	Garvey visits the *Crisis* office.
9 May	Garvey holds first public lecture in America at St. Mark's Church Hall in New York City.
ca. May–June	Garvey embarks on yearlong speaking tour throughout the United States.
16 June	Distress warrant is issued in Jamaica against Garvey by the St. Ann parish inspector of the poor.

1917

January	Article by Garvey, "West Indies in the Mirror of Truth," is published in Chicago in the *Champion Magazine.*
6 April	*America declares war against Germany.*
May	Garvey returns to New York City after speaking tour through thirty-eight states.
May	Thirteen members join to form the New York branch of UNIA organized by Garvey.
5 June	Garvey registers for selective service.
12 June	Inaugural meeting of Liberty League of Negro-Americans in New York City is addressed by Garvey.
2 July	*Outbreak of racial rioting in East St. Louis.*
8 July	Garvey delivers address on "The Conspiracy of the East St. Louis Riots."
October	First split in New York branch of the UNIA.
6 November	*The Bolshevik Revolution triumphs in Russia with the seizure of power by the Bolsheviks in Petrograd.*

1918

8 January	*President Woodrow Wilson in address to Congress unveils his peace program, consisting of celebrated Fourteen Points.*
ca. 9–13 January	New York branch of UNIA again splits into opposing factions.
February	Garvey reorganizes New York branch of the UNIA.
3 March	Garvey is hospitalized with pneumonia.
24 March	UNIA holds debate on "Self-Government of Africa."
5 May	UNIA holds meeting "to foster the spirit of race co-operation between the White and Black peoples of the world."
3 June	Bureau of Investigation receives report that Garvey speaks nightly at outdoor meetings on Lenox Avenue in Harlem.
17 June	UNIA is incorporated in New York State.
31 July	ACL files for incorporation in New York State.
July	Publication of *Constitution and Book of Laws Made for the Government of the Universal Negro Improvement Association and African Communities' League.*
17 August	The *Negro World*, official UNIA organ, begins publication.
7 November	Postal censorship authorities intercept parcel mailed by Garvey containing "twelve copies of an appeal to the racial instinct of the negroes (calculated to incite hatred for the white race)."
8 November	*Armistice is signed.*
10–11 November	UNIA formulates and sends "Peace Aims" to Allied governments.
1 December	UNIA elects delegation to attend peace conference in Paris.
9 December	Emmett J. Scott, special assistant to the secretary of war, interviews Garvey in Washington, D.C., at request of Military Intelligence Division.
December	Mutiny by members of the Eighth Battalion, British West Indies Regiment, at Taranto, Italy, reportedly organized by the Caribbean League; mutiny quelled by Col. Maxwell Smith, who reports the dissemination of the *Negro World* among battalion members.

1919

19–21 February	*Pan-African Congress, organized by W. E. B Du Bois, meets in Paris.*
21 February	Garvey appeals to the U.S. Congress to reject ratification of the League of Nations.
February	UNIA opens restaurant in Harlem.
February	*Negro World* banned in British Honduras (Belize) by the acting governor; governor of Trinidad orders seizure of *Negro World* on grounds that it is seditious.
1 March	Eliézer Cadet, UNIA high commissioner to the peace conference, arrives in Paris.
9 March	Cadet delivers the UNIA's "Peace Aims" to the president and secretary of the peace conference, with request that they be published.
9 March	UNIA meeting in New York hears "Report of the 'Negro High Commissioner' at the Peace Conference."
26 March	Garvey denounces W. E. B. Du Bois at public meeting in Harlem after receiving cable from France from Eliézer Cadet.
27 April	Garvey announces his plan for launching black steamship venture.
May	British Guiana censor seizes copies of *Negro World*.
6 June	*Trinidad attorney general recommends that the British colonial secretary approve passage of legislation by West Indian colonies to suppress publications deemed seditious.*
16 June	Garvey is questioned by New York Assistant District Attorney Edwin P. Kilroe about financial aspects of the Black Star Line.
18 June	Copies of the *Negro World* seized by the colonial authorities in Trinidad.
20 June	Executive Council in British Guiana instructs postmaster general to prohibit importation of the *Negro World* and other black American newspapers.
27 June	BSL files for incorporation under the laws of the state of Delaware.
12 July	Bureau of Investigation requests New York division to forward all information on Garvey; also instructs Chicago division to observe closely activities of Garvey and other "negro radicals."

20–21 July	*Race riot in Washington, D.C.*
22 July	Uprising in Belize, British Honduras, attributed in part to popular dissatisfaction with the suppression of the *Negro World*; martial law proclaimed.
27 July	UNIA Liberty Hall is established in the old Metropolitan Baptist Church in Harlem at 120 West 138th Street; a mass meeting is held the same evening to dedicate the building.
27–31 July	*Race riot in Chicago.*
28 July	Garvey is again questioned about BSL by New York Assistant District Attorney Kilroe.
July	W. A. Domingo resigns as editor of the *Negro World*.
July	*British colonial secretary instructs governor of British Guiana to use his powers to suppress publications "inciting to racial hatred."*
2 August	Garvey dismisses Edgar M. Grey and Richard E. Warner as BSL directors and officers.
2 August	The *Negro World* publishes editorial entitled "Two Negro Crooks Use Office of Deputy District Attorney Kilroe to Save Themselves from Jail."
4 August	Kilroe swears out warrant for Garvey's arrest on charge of publishing a criminal libel.
5 August	New York district attorney Edward Swann questions Garvey regarding relationships with the IWW, socialists, and anarchists.
5 August	Garvey is arraigned before City Magistrate George W. Simpson.
6 August	Acting governor of Jamaica orders postmaster to open and detain all copies of the *Negro World*.
13 August	Attorney general requests the commissioner-general of immigration to inquire into the case of Garvey, "relative to the institution of deportation proceedings against subject."
15 August	Bureau of Investigation instructs New York division to immediately forward summary of its file on Garvey and to prepare "at the earliest moment a case for deportation."
16 August	Attorney general is informed by commissioner-general of immigration that the Bureau of Immigration has never instituted a warrant of deportation against Garvey.

19 August	Legislation to ban the *Negro World* in the Windward Islands advocated by the governor, G. B. Haddon-Smith.
19 August	Governor of Grenada recommends to the British colonial secretary granting special executive power to West Indian governors to exclude newspapers considered seditious, such as the *Negro World*.
20 August	Copies of the *Negro World* confiscated by the authorities in Port Limón, Costa Rica.
25 August	Garvey speaks in Carnegie Hall.

THE PAPERS

VOLUME I
1826–August 1919

Chapter in Autobiography

"The Negro's Greatest Enemy," published in *Current History* (September 1923), was Marcus Garvey's most extensive autobiographical statement, and the first to be written for the American public. It was written during his incarceration in the Tombs Prison in New York City, while he awaited the outcome of his appeal for bail after conviction on a charge of mail fraud. Garvey attempted to meet two objectives with his statement: to present a brief account of his background and to answer the attacks of his critics. The essay thus represents Garvey as he wanted the public to view him during a critical phase of his career. Although his autobiographical writings were few, studies of Garvey are numerous: Len Nembhard, *The Trials and Triumphs of Marcus Garvey* (Kingston: Gleaner, 1940); E. David Cronon, *Black Moses: The Story of Marcus Garvey and the Universal Negro Improvement Association* (Madison: University of Wisconsin Press, 1955); Amy Jacques Garvey, *Garvey and Garveyism* (London: Frank Cass, 1963; rpt, New York: Collier-Macmillan, 1970); Adolph Edwards, *Marcus Garvey* (London: New Beacon, 1967); Theodore Vincent, *Black Power and the Garvey Movement* (Berkeley: Ramparts, 1971); Daniel S. Davis, *Marcus Garvey* (New York: Franklin Watts, 1972); Elton C. Fax, *Garvey: The Story of a Pioneer Black Nationalist* (New York: Dodd, Mead and Co., 1972); Tony Martin, *Race First: The Ideological Struggles of Marcus Garvey and the Universal Negro Improvement Association* (Westport, Conn.: Greenwood, 1976); and Emory J. Tolbert, *The Universal Negro Improvement Association and Black Los Angeles* (Los Angeles: Center for Afro-American Studies, UCLA, 1980).

THE NEGRO'S GREATEST ENEMY

By MARCUS GARVEY

This article, which is largely a chapter of autobiography, was written by the author—the founder of the Universal Negro Improvement Association

Starting a movement in opposition to negroes who do not want to be negroes—A country for the black man—Attempts to capture the Universal Negro Improvement Association

I WAS born in the Island of Jamaica, British West Indies, on Aug. 17, 1887. My parents were black negroes. My father was a man of brilliant intellect and dashing courage. He was unafraid of consequences. He took human chances in the course of life, as most bold men do, and he failed at the close of his career. He once had a fortune; he died poor. My mother was a sober and conscientious Christian, too soft and good for the time in which she lived. She was the direct opposite of my father. He was severe, firm, determined, bold and strong, refusing to yield even to superior forces if he believed he was right. My mother, on the other hand, was always willing to return a smile for a blow, and ever ready to bestow charity upon her enemy. Of this strange combination I was born thirty-six years ago, and ushered into a world of sin, the flesh an[d] the devil.

I grew up with other black and white boys. I was never whipped by any, but made them all respect the strength of my arms. I got my education from many sources—through private tutors, two public schools, two grammar or high schools and two colleges. My teachers were men and women of varied experiences and abilities; four of them were eminent preachers. They studied me and I studied them. With some I became friendly in after years, others and I drifted apart, because as a boy they wanted to whip me, and I simply refused to be whipped. I was not made to be whipped. It annoys me to be defeated; hence to me, to be once defeated is to find cause for an everlasting struggle to reach the top.

I became a printer's apprentice at an early age, while still attending school. My apprentice master was a highly educated and alert man. In the affairs of business and the world he had no peer. He taught me many things before I reached twelve, and at fourteen I had enough intelligence and experience to manage men. I was strong and manly, and I made them respect me. I developed a strong and forceful character, and have maintained it still.

To me, at home in my early days, there was no difference between white and black. One of my father's properties, the place where I lived most of the time, was adjoining that of a white man. He had three girls and two boys; the Wesleyan minister, another white man whose church my parents attended, also had property adjoining ours. He had three girls and one boy. All of us were playmates. We romped and were happy children playmates together. The little white girl whom I liked most knew no better than I did myself. We were two innocent fools who never dreamed of a race feeling and problem. As a child, I went to school with white boys and girls, like all other negroes. We were not called negroes then. I never hea[r]d the term negro used once until I was about fourteen.

At fourteen my little white playmate and I parted. Her parents thought the time had come to separate us and draw the color line. They sent her and another sister to Edinburgh, Scotland, and told her that she was never to write or try to get in touch with me, for I was a "nigger." It was then that I found for the first time that there was some difference in humanity, and that there were different races, each having its own separate and distinct social life. I did not care about the separation after I was told about it, because I never thought all during our childhood association that the girl and the rest of the children of her race were better than I was; in fact, they used to look up to me. So I simply had no regrets. I only thought them "fresh."[1]

After my first lesson in race distinction, I never thought of playing with white girls any more, even if they might be next door neighbors. At home my sister's company was good enough for me, and at school I made friends with the colored girls next to me. White boys and I used to frolic together. We played cricket and baseball, ran races and rode bicycles together, took each other to the river and to the sea beach to learn to swim, and made boyish efforts while out in deep water to drown each other, making a sprint for shore crying out "shark, shark, shark." In all our experiences, however, only one black boy was drowned. He went under on a Friday afternoon after school hours, and his parents found him afloat half eaten by sharks on the following Sunday afternoon. Since then we boys never went back to sea.[2]

"YOU ARE BLACK"

At maturity the black and white boys separated, and took different courses in life. I grew up then to see the difference between the races more and more. My schoolmates as young men did not know or remember me any more. Then I realized that I had to make a fight for a place in the world, that it was not so easy to pass on to office and position. Personally, however, I had not much difficulty in finding and holding a place for myself, for I was aggressive. At eighteen I had an excellent position as manager of a large printing establishment having under my control several men old enough to be my grandfathers. But I got mixed up with public life. I started to take an interest in the politics of my country, and then I saw the injustice done to my race because it was black, and I became dissatisfied on that account. I went traveling to South and Central America and parts of the West Indies to find out if it was so elsewhere, and I found the same situation. I set sail for Europe to find out if it was different there, and again I found the same[3] stumbling-block—"You are black." I read of the conditions in America. I read "Up From Slavery," by Booker T. Washington, and then my doom—if I may so call it—of being a race leader dawned upon me in London after I had traveled through almost half of Europe.

I asked, "Where is the black man's Government?" "Where is his King and his kingdom?" "Where is his President, his country, and his ambassador, his army, his navy, his men of big affairs?" I could not find them, and then I declared, "I will help to make them."

Becoming naturally restless for the opportunity of doing something [for] the advancement of my race, I was determined that the black man would not continue to be kicked about by all the other races and nations of the world, as I saw it in the West Indies, South and Central America and Europe, and as I read of it in America. My young and ambitious mind led me into flights of great imagination. I saw before me then, even as I do now, a new world of black men, not peons, serfs, dogs and slaves, but a nation of sturdy men making their impress upon civilization and causing a new light to dawn upon the human race. I could not remain in London any more. My brain was afire. There was a world of thought to conquer. I had to start ere it became too late and the work be not done. Immediately I boarded a ship at Southampton for Jamaica, where I arrived on July 15, 1914. The Universal Negro Improvement Association and African Communities (Imperial) League was founded and organized five days after my arrival, with the program of uniting all the negro peoples of the world into one great body to establish a country and Government absolutely their own.

Where did the name of the organization come from? It was while speaking to a West Indian negro who was a passenger with me from Southampton, who was returning home to the West Indies from Basutoland with his Basuto wife, that I further learned of the horrors of native life in Africa. He related to me in conversation such horrible and pitiable tales that my heart bled within me. Retiring from the conversation[4] to my cabin, all day and the following night I pondered over the subject matter of that conversation, and at midnight, lying flat on my back, the vision and thought came to me that I should name the organization the Universal Negro Improvement Association and African Communities (Imperial) League. Such a name I thought would embrace the purpose of all black humanity. Thus to the world a name was born, a movement created, and a man became known.

I really never knew there was so much color prejudice in Jamaica, my own native home, until I started the work of the Universal Negro Improvement Association. We started immediately before the war. I had just returned from a successful trip to Europe, which was an exceptional achievement for a black man. The daily papers wrote me up with big headlines and told of my movement. But nobody wanted to be a negro. "Garvey is crazy; he has lost his head," "Is that the use he is going to make of his experience and intelligence?"—such were the criticisms passed upon me. Men and women as black as I, and even more so, had believed themselves white under the West Indian order of society. I was simply an impossible man to use openly the term "negro;" yet every one beneath his breath was calling the black man a negro.[5]

I had to decide whether to please my friends and be one of the "black-whites" of Jamaica, and be reasonably prosperous, or come out openly and defend and help improve and protect the integrity of the black millions and suffer. I decided to do the latter, hence my offence against "colored-black-white" society in the colonies and America. I was openly hated and persecuted by some of these colored men of the island who did not want to be classified as negroes, but as white. They hated me worse than poison. They opposed me at every step, but I had a large number of white friends, who encouraged and helped me. Notable among them were the then Governor of the Colony, the Colonial Secretary and several other prominent men. But they were afraid of offending the "colored gentry" that were passing for white. Hence my fight had to be made alone. I spent hundreds of pounds (sterling) helping the organization to gain a footing. I also gave up all my time to the promulgation of its ideals. I became a marked man, but I was determined that the work should be done.

The war helped a great deal in arousing the consciousness of the colored people to the reasonableness of our program, especially after the British at home had rejected a large number of West Indian colored men who wanted to be officers in the British army. When they were told that negroes could not be officers in the British army they started their own propaganda, which supplemented the program of the Universal Negro Improvement Association. With this and other contributing agencies a few of the stiff-necked colored people began to see the reasonableness of my program, but they were firm in refusing to be known as negroes. Furthermore, I was a black man and therefore had absolutely no right to lead; in the opinion of the "colored" element, leadership should have been in the hands of a yellow or a very light man. On such flimsy prejudices our race has been retarded. There is more bitterness among us negroes because of the caste of color than there is between any other peoples, not excluding the people of India.

I succeeded to a great extent in establishing the association in Jamaica with the assistance of a Catholic Bishop, the Governor, Sir John Pringle, the Rev. William Graham, a Scottish clergyman, and several other white friends. I got in touch with Booker Washington and told him what I wanted to do. He invited me to America and promised to speak with me in the Southern and other States to help my work. Although he died in the Fall of 1915, I made my arrangements and arrived in the United States on March 23, 1916.

Here I found a new and different problem. I immediately visited some of the then so-called negro leaders, only to discover, after a close study of them, that they had no program, but were mere opportunists who were living off their so-called leadership while the poor people were groping in the dark. I traveled through thirty-eight States and everywhere found the same condition. I visited Tuskegee and paid my respects to the dead hero, Booker Washington, and then returned to New York, where I organized the New York division of the Universal Negro Improvement Association. After instructing the people in the aims and objects of the association, I intended returning to Jamaica to perfect the Jamaica organization, but when we had enrolled about 800 or 1,000 members in the Harlem district and had elected the officers, a few negro politicians began trying[6] to turn the movement into a political club.

POLITICAL FACTION FIGHT

Seeing that these politicians were about to destroy my ideals, I had to fight to get them out of the organization. There[7] it was that I made by first political enemies in Harlem. They fought me until they smashed the first organization and reduced its membership to about fifty. I started again and in two months built up a new organization of about 1,500 members. Again the politicians came and divided us into two factions. They took away all the books of the organization, its treasury and all its belongings. At that time I was only an organizer, for it was not then my intention to remain in America, but to return to Jamaica. The organization had its proper officers elected, and I was not an officer of the New York division, but President of the Jamaica branch.

On the second split in Harlem thirteen of the members conferred with me and requested me to become President for a time of the New York organization so as to save them from the politicians. I consented and was elected President. There then sprung up two factions, one led by the politicians with the books and the money, and the other led by me. My faction had no money. I placed at their disposal what money I had, opened an office for them, rented a meeting place, employed two women secretaries, went on the streets of Harlem at night to speak for the movement. In three weeks more than 2,000 new members joined. By this time I had the association incorporated so as to prevent the other faction using the name, but in two weeks the politicians had stolen all the people's money and had smashed up their faction.

The organization under my Presidency grew by leaps and bounds. I started The Negro World. Being a journalist, I edited this paper free of cost for the association, and worked for them without pay until November, 1920. I traveled all over the country for the association at my own expense, and established branches until in 1919 we had about thirty branches in different cities. By my writings and speeches we were able to build up a large organization of over 2,000,000 by June, 1919, at which time we launched the program of the Black Star Line.

To have built up a new organization, which was not purely political, among negroes in America was a wonderful feat, for the negro politician does not allow any other kind of organization within his race to thrive. We succeeded, however, in making the Universal Negro Improvement Association so formidable in 1919 that we encountered more trouble from our political brethren. They sought the influence of the District Attorney's office of the County of New York to put us out of business. Edwin P. Kilroe, at that time an Assistant District Attorney, on the complaint of the negro politicians, started to investigate us and the association. Mr. Kilroe would constantly and continuously call me to his office for investigation on extraneous matters without coming to the point. The result was that after the eight or ninth time I wrote an article in our newspaper, The Negro World, against him. This was interpreted as criminal libel, for which I was indicted and arrested, but subsequently dismissed on retracting what I had written.

During my many tilts with Mr. Kilroe, the question of the Black Star Line was discussed. He did not want us to have a line of ships. I told him that even as there was a White Star Line, we would have, irrespective of his wishes, a Black Star Line. On June 27, 1919, we incorporated the Black Star Line of Delaware, and in September we obtained a ship.

The following month (October) a man by the name of Tyler came to my office at 56 West 135th Street, New York City, and told me that Mr. Kilroe had sent him to "get me," and at once fired four shots at me from a .38-calibre revolver. He wounded me in the right leg and the right side of my scalp. I was taken to the Harlem Hospital, and he was arrested. The next day it was reported that he committed suicide in jail just before he was to be taken before a City Magistrate.

RECORD-BREAKING CONVENTION

The first year of our activities for the Black Star Line added prestige to the Universal Negro Improvement Association. Several hundred thousand dollars worth of shares were sold. Our first ship, the steamship Yarmouth, had made two[8] voyages to the West Indies and Central America. The white press had flashed the news all over the world. I, a young negro, as President of the corporation, had become famous. My name was discussed on five continents. The Universal Negro Improvement Association gained millions of followers all over the world. By August, 1920, over 4,000,000 persons had joined the movement. A convention of all the negro peoples of the world was called to meet in New York that month. Delegates came from all parts of the known world. Over 25,000 persons packed the Madison Square Garden on Aug. 1 to hear me speak to the first International Convention of Negroes. It was a record-breaking meeting, the first and the biggest of its kind. The name of Garvey had become known as a leader of his race.

Such fame among negroes was too much for other race leaders and politicians to tolerate. My downfall was planned by my enemies. They laid all kinds of traps for me. They scattered their spies among the employes of the Black Star Line and the Universal Negro Improvement Association. Our office records were stolen. Employes started to be openly dishonest; we could get no convictions against them; even if on complaint they were held by a Magistrate, they were dismissed by the Grand Jury. The ships' officers started to pile up thousands of dollars of debts against the company without the knowledge of the officers of the corporation. Our ships were damaged at sea, and there was a general riot of wreck and ruin. Officials of the Universal Negro Improvement Association also began to steal and be openly dishonest. I had to dismiss them. They joined my enemies, and thus I had an endless fight on my hands to save the ideals of the association and carry out our program for the race. My negro enemies, finding that they alone could not destroy me, resorted to misrepresenting me to the leaders of the white race, several of whom, without proper investigation, also opposed me.

With robberies from within and from without, the Black Star Line was forced to suspend active business in December, 1921. While I was on a business trip to the West Indies in the Spring of 1921, the Black Star Line received the blow from which it was unable to recover. A sum of $25,000 was paid by one of the officers of the corporation to a man to purchase a ship, but the ship was never obtained and the money was never returned. The company was defrauded of a further sum of $11,000. Through such actions on the part of dishonest men in the shipping business, the Black Star Line received its first setback. This resulted in my being indicted for using the United States mails to defraud investors in the company. I was subsequently convicted and sentenced to five years in a Federal penitentiary. My trial is a matter of history. I know I was not given a square deal, because my indictment was the result of a "frame-up" among my political and business enemies. I had to conduct my own case in court because of the peculiar position in which I found myself. I had millions of friends and a large number of enemies. I wanted a colored attorney to handle my case, but there was none I could trust. I feel that I have been denied justice because of prejudice. Yet I have an abundance of faith in the courts of America, and I hope yet to obtain justice on my appeal.

ASSOCIATION'S 6,000,000 MEMBERSHIP

The temporary ruin of the Black Star Line in no way affected the larger work of the Universal Negro Improvement Association, which now has 900 branches with an approximate membership of 6,000,000. This organization has succeeded in organizing the negroes all over the world and we now look forward to a renaissance that will create a new people and bring about the restoration of Ethiopia's ancient glory.

Being black, I have committed an unpardonable offense against the very light colored negroes in America and the West Indies by making myself famous as a negro leader of millions. In their view, no black man must rise above them, but I still forge ahead determined to give to the world the truth about the new negro who is determined to make and hold for himself a place in the affairs of men. The Universal Negro Improvement Association has been misrepresented by my enemies. They have tried to make it appear that we are hostile to other races. This is absolutely false. We love all humanity. We are working for the peace of the world which we believe can only come about when all races are given their due.

We feel that there is absolutely no reason why there should be any differences between the black and white races, if each stop to adjust and steady itself. We believe in the purity of both races. We do not believe the black man should be encouraged in the idea that his highest purpose in life is to marry a white woman, but we do believe that the white man should be taught to respect the black woman in the same way as he wants the black man to respect the white woman. It is a vicious and dangerous doctrine of social equality to urge, as certain colored leaders do, that black and white should get together, for that would destroy the racial purity of both.

We believe that the black people should have a country of their own where they should be given the fullest opportunity to develop politically, socially and industrially. The black people should not be encouraged to remain in white people's countries and expect to be Presidents, Governors, Mayors, Senators, Congressmen, Judges and social and industrial leaders. We believe that with the rising ambition of the negro, if a country is not provided for him in another 50 or 100 years, there will be a terrible clash that will end disastrously to him and disgrace our civilization. We desire to prevent such a clash by pointing the negro to a home of his own. We feel that all well disposed and broad minded white men will aid in this direction. It is because of this belief no doubt that my negro enemies, so as to prejudice me further in the opinion of the public, wickedly state that I am a member of the Ku Klux Klan, even though I am a black man.

I have been deprived of the opportunity of properly explaining my work to the white people of America through the prejudice worked up against me by jealous and wicked members of my own race. My success as a[n] organizer was much more than rival negro leaders could tolerate. They, regardless of consequences, either to me or to the race, had to destroy me by fair means or foul. The thousands of anonymous and other hostile letters written to the editors and publishers of the white press by negro rivals to prejudice me in the eyes of public opinion are sufficient evidence of the wicked and vicious opposition I have had to meet from among my own people, especially among the very lightly[9] colored. But they went further than the press in their attempts to discredit me. They organized clubs all over the United States and the West Indies, and wrote both open and anonymous letters to city, State and Federal officials of this and other Governments to induce them to use their influence to hamper and destroy me. No wonder, therefore, that several Judges, District Attorneys and other high officials have been against me[10] without knowing me. No wonder, therefore, that the great white population of this country and of the world has a wrong impression of the aims and objects of the Universal Negro Improvement Association and of the work of Marcus Garvey.

THE STRUGGLE OF THE FUTURE

Having had the wrong education as a start in his racial career, the negro has become his own greatest enemy. Most of the trouble I have had in advancing the cause of the race has come from negroes. Booker Washington aptly described the race in one of his lectures by stating that we were like crabs in a barrel, that none would allow the other to climb over, but on any such attempt all would continue[11] to pull back into the barrel the one crab that would make the effort to climb out. Yet, those of us with vision cannot desert the race, leaving it to suffer and die.

Looking forward a century or two, we can see an economic and political death struggle for the survival of the different race groups. Many of our present-day national centres will have become overcrowded with vast surplus populations. The fight for bread and position will be keen and severe. The weaker and unprepared group is bound to go under. That is why, visionaries as we are in the Universal Negro Improvement Association, we are fighting for the founding of a negro nation in Africa, so that there will be no clash between black and white and that each race will have a separate existence and civilization all its own without courting suspicion and hatred or eyeing each other with jealousy and rivalry within the borders of the same country.

White men who have struggled for and built up their countries and their own civilizations are not disposed to hand them over to the negro or any other race without let or hindrance. It would be unreasonable to expect this. Hence any vain assumption on the part of the negro to imagine that he will one day become President of the Nation, Governor of the State, or Mayor of the city in the countries of white men, is like waiting on the devil and his angels to take up their residence in the Realm on High and direct there the affairs of Paradise.

Printed in *Current History*, 18:6 (September 1923), pp. 951–57.

1. This sentence was omitted from the version printed in *The Philosophy and Opinions of Marcus Garvey*, edited by Amy Jacques Garvey (Vol. 1, 1923, Vol. 2, 1925; reprinted in one volume, New York: Atheneum, 1969; hereafter cited as *P & O*), pp. 124–34.

2. In *P & O*, this sentence reads: "since then we boys never went sea bathing," p. 125.

3. The word "same" was omitted from *P & O*, p. 126.

4. The phrases "in conversation" and "from the conversation" were omitted from *P & O*, p. 126.

5. In *P & O*, the phrase reads: "calling the black man a nigger," p. 127.

6. This reads "tried" in *P & O*, p. 128.

7. This reads "Then" in *P & O*, p. 128.

8. In *P & O*, it is "three" voyages, not "two," see p. 130.

9. In *P & O*, the phrase reads "very light colored," p. 133.

10. In *P & O*, "opposing" is used rather than "against," p. 133.

11. "Combine" appears in *P & O* rather than "continue," p. 133.

Extract from the St. Ann Register of Slave Baptisms

[St. Ann, 1826]

Name	Belonging To
Charlotte Garvey[1]	(Roaring River Estate)[2]
William Garvey[3]	''
Richard Garvey	''
Henry Garvey	''
Robt Garvey[4]	''
James Garvey[5]	''
Amelia Grant Garvey[6]	''
Jane A. Garvey	''

IRO, 1B/11/8/2, Parish of St. Ann, "A Register of Baptisms of Slaves, 1826." AMS. Unfortunately, the baptismal register made no mention of any age or birth information of the slaves, nor was there any indication given of the possible kinship relations among the eight Garvey slaves.

1. The name Garvey was introduced into Jamaica from Ireland. Christopher Garvey, a captain in the British army, settled in Jamaica around the middle of the eighteenth century. He was the fourth and youngest son of John O'Garvey, lord of the manors of Murrisk, Lehinch, Tully, Kiggall, Annfield and other lands in County Mayo. Michael Garvey, Jr., was the legal executor of his father's estate in St. Ann, Orange Hall. In 1784, Dr. Anthony Garvey, the proprietor of 139 acres in the Ocho Rios area of St. Ann, held the post of surgeon of the St. Ann's militia. In Gaelic, the name "Garvey" means warlike; also rough (*garbh*), (Edward MacLysaght, *The Surnames of Ireland* [New York: Barnes and Noble, 1969], p. 97). For additional information on the early Irish presence in the West Indies, see Rev. Aubrey Gwynn,

"Early Irish Migration to the West Indies (1612–1643)," Part 1, *Studies* (September 1929): 377–93; and Part 2, (December 1929): 648–63; and "Documents Relating to the Irish in the West Indies," *Analecta Hibernica* (October 1932): 139–286.

2. The return for Roaring River in 1826 listed a total of 188 slaves and 119 stock ("Return of Proprietors, Properties, etc., Given to the Vestries," *The Jamaica Almanac for the Year 1826*, [Kingston, Jamaica]). When slavery was abolished in 1834, however, the receiver of Roaring River claimed compensation from the British Crown for a total of 221 slaves, for which he was awarded £4,086 (*PP, Accounts of Slave Compensation Claims*, 1837–38 [215] 48, Claim No. 331, List E). The British Parliament under the terms of the Slavery Abolition Act awarded the West Indian slave owners an outright sum of £20 million, out of which Jamaican slave owners received £6,149,939 for their 311,070 slaves. This figure was 20,049 slaves fewer than the 331,119 registered in the triennial registration of slaves in 1826. (*PP, Slave Registration*, 1833 [539] 26).

3. William Garvey (ca. 1805–1891), a mason, was Marcus Garvey's grandfather (IRO, Death Certificate, Parish of St. Ann, No. 1061 GA). He eventually owned a home on Winders Hill, a slope behind the town of St. Ann's Bay. His land bordered on the large Cloisters property of the Wesleyan Methodist church and extended onto the Winders Hill estate of Anthony Rerrie, a prominent St. Ann's Bay businessman. After William Garvey's death, his son, Mosiah Garvey, moved his family to Winders Hill, where Marcus Garvey lived until early manhood. The land was finally sold in June 1916.

4. In May 1837, during the probationary period of apprenticeship that followed the abolition of slavery, Robert Garvey succeeded in purchasing his freedom as a nonpraedial apprentice for 30 pounds (*PP, Papers Relative to the Abolition of Slavery in the British Colonies, Part 5, Jamaica* [1], 1838 [154] 49, *"Return of Valuations Concluded by the Special Magistrates from the 1st of November 1836 to the 31st of July 1837 Inclusive,"* Centre District, St. Ann's).

5. James Garvey was listed in a will entered July 1911 as "late of Steer Town in the parish of St. Ann[,] Labourer" (IRO, Liber No. 10, 1908–1911, Folio 426).

6. The Slave Register of 1832 referred to a "William McBean, birth—negroe 2 [years] and 4 [months]—Creole—of Amelia Garvey" (PRO, T.71/50). The Scottish absentee planters who owned Roaring River before it went into receivership were William and Alexander McBean. In the other Roaring River slave registration records, "Amelia" was also listed as the mother of "Sammy—Negro—2 yrs/1821" (PRO, T.71/45, 1823), of "John—Negro/C[reole] b. 24 Nov. 1823" (PRO, T.71/46, 1826), and of "Dennis—Negro—2 months/C[reole]" (PRO, T.71/47, 1829).

Extract from the St. Ann Register of Baptisms

[St. Ann, 1838]

No.	Date	Name	Abode
2	Jan. 7, 1838 (6 mos.)	Mosiah Garvey[1] (Apprentice)[2]	Roaring River

IRO, 1B/11/8/2, St. Ann, Parish Register, Baptisms Index 1826–1848, Vol. 5. AMS.

1. Mosiah Garvey (1837–1920) was the son of William Garvey and later the father of Marcus Garvey. The only source for the name that has been found is *The Book of Mormon*, first published in 1830, in which the "Book of Mosiah" was one of its fifteen books.

2. Under the provisions of the Slavery Abolition Act, after 1 August 1834 slave children under six years of age, and children subsequently born to slave mothers, were legally free, unless they became destitute, when they might be apprenticed by a special magistrate to the mother's former slave owner. For a recent discussion of the system of apprenticeship, see Izhaz Gross, "Parliament and the Abolition of Negro Apprenticeship, 1835–1838," *English Historical Review* 96 (July 1981): 560–76; William A. Green, *British Slave Emancipation: The Sugar Colonies and the Great Experiment, 1830–1865* (Oxford: Clarendon Press, 1976).

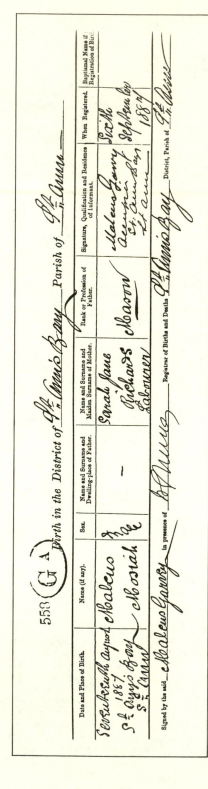

Garvey's Birth Certificate (Source: IRO).

Record of Birth of Malcus Mosiah Garvey

Birth in the District of St. Ann's Bay Parish of St. Ann

Date and Place of Birth.	Name (if any).	Sex.	Name and Surname and Dwelling-place of Father.[1]	Name and Surname and Maiden Surname of Mother.
Seventeenth August 1887 St. Ann's Bay St. Ann	Malcus[2] Mosiah	Male	—	Sarah Jane Richards Labourer

Rank or Profession of Father.[3]	Signature, Qualification and Residence of Informant.	When Registered.	Baptismal Name if added after Registration of Birth and Date.
Mason	Malcus[4] Garvy Occupier St. Anns Bay St. Ann	Sixth September 1887	

SIGNED BY THE SAID *Malcus Garvey* IN PRESENCE OF [*W G ?*] *Nunes Registrar of Births and Deaths* *St. Ann's Bay* DISTRICT, PARISH OF ST. ANN

15

IRO, Registration of Births, St. Ann, No. 558 GA. DS, Printed form with manuscript insertions.

1. The blank space in the certificate reflects the fact that the child's parents were unmarried. In such cases the birth certificate would normally omit the rank or profession of the father. However, for some reason this practice was not followed in the case of Garvey's father.

2. "Malcus" was the original Christian name given to Garvey at birth which he later changed to Marcus. Garvey's boyhood friend and schoolmate Isaac "Corpie" Rose (1884–) has recounted the name change in various interviews: "As a boy in school we called him Mosiah, he changed his name to Marcus when he went away. His father's name was Mosiah Garvey, he gave him his name." (Interview by Richard Small, St. Ann's Bay, 20 July 1971); and, "He (Garvey) put Marcus to his name . . . we called him Mosiah Garvey but he changed his name to Marcus." (Editor's interview with Isaac Rose, St. Ann's Bay, 14 December 1977). A relative of Garvey on his father's side has also affirmed that "they used to call him Moziah Garvey" (Interview with Miss Edith Williams, St. Ann's Bay, 20 December 1977). In 1905 Garvey moved from St. Ann's Bay to the nearby town of Port Maria where many of his relatives lived. Port Maria is the principal town of St. Mary Parish, which is adjacent to St. Ann's Parish. On 25 January 1910, a twenty-six-year old bachelor named Marcus Garvey died in St. Mary Parish. It is possible that in his honor Garvey adopted the Christian name Marcus in 1910. (IRO, Death Certificate, Parish of St. Mary, No. 356 FE).

3. Garvey, Sr., was the father of three separate sets of children. The first group consisted of four children: Norman, Bridget, Semana Venetia, and Isabella. Their mother, Caroline Trail, resided at the town of Moneague in St. Ann. The second group consisted of Bathsheba and Desmond, whose mother was Charlotte Lawrence of Higgin Town. The third and last group were the children of Sarah Jane Garvey: Trueman, Indiana, Rosanna, and Malcus Mosiah. Amy Jacques Garvey, however, states that there were a total of eleven children from the last union. (*Garvey and Garveyism*, [New York: Collier-Macmillan Books, 1970], p. 2; Record of Baptism of Trueman Shepherd Garvey, JA, 5/6/11, Methodist Church Archives, Records of Baptism in St. Ann's Bay Circuit, Western Division, Vol. 1; Record of Birth of Rosanna Garvey, IRO, Registration of Births, St. Ann, No. 1664 GA).

4. The name *Malcus* came from the name of the high priest Caiphas' servant whose ear the apostle Peter severed with a sword (Matt. 26:51). *The Century Dictionary* (1890) cites as one of the meanings of the word, "a short cutting sword." Since the elder Garvey was a stonemason by profession, the name was clearly appropriate.

Record of Marriage of Malchus and Sarah Jane Garvey

MARRIAGE REGISTER

No.	When Married.	Name and Surname.	Condition.	Calling.	Age.	Parish and Residence at the time of Marriage.	Father's Name and Surname.
68	1889 December fifteenth	Malchus[1] Moziah Garvey	Bachelor	Brick-layer	fifty two	St. Anns Bay	William Garvey
		Sarah Jane Richards	Spinster		forty two	Davis Town	George Richards (dec'd)

brace joining St. Anns Bay and Davis Town: St. Ann

MARRIED AT *St. Anns Bay*, BY (OR BEFORE) ME *JOHN DUFF*, A MARRIAGE OFFICER OF THE PARISH OF ST. ANN.

THIS MARRIAGE WAS CELEBRATED BETWEEN US { *Malcus Moziah Garry* / *Sarah (x) Richards* } *her*

IN THE PRESENCE OF US { *William Lawrence* / *Mary ann Morris* }

THIS *Fifteenth* DAY OF December 18 89

THE CROSS (OR CROSSES) OF *Sarah Jane Richards* WAS (OR WERE) ADDED IN MY PRESENCE *John Duff*

IRO, Marriage (Duplicate) Register, Parish of St. Ann, No. 851. DS, Printed form with manuscript insertions.

1. The change in the spelling is in the original.

17

Record of Baptism of Malchus Moziah Garvey

RECORD OF BAPTISM

No.	Child's Name.	Parents' Name.	Residence.	Father's Occupation.	When Born.	When Baptized.	Minister.
71	Malchus Moziah[1]	Malchus Garvey; wife, Sarah Jane Garvey	St. Ann's Bay	Mason	May 1887[2]	28 Oct. 1890[3]	W. R. Griffin

JA, 5/6/11, Methodist Church Archives, Records of Baptism in St. Ann's Bay Circuit, Western Division, Vol. I. AMS.

1. The change in the spelling of both names is in the original.
2. The difference in the date of birth is also in the original.
3. The long lapse of time between birth and baptism was characteristic of the era.

Record of Death of Sarah Garvey

Death in the District of *Kingston* Parish of *Kingston*

Date and Place of Death	Name and Surname	Sex	Condition	Age last Birthday.	Rank, Profession or Occupation.
Eighteenth march, 1908 *Public Hospital, Kingston.*	*Sarah Garvey*	*Female*	*married.* [1]	*56* [2] *years.*	*Domestic Servant.* [3]

Certified cause of Death and duration of illness.	Signature, Qualification and Residence of Informant.	When Registered.
apoplexy cerebral. Certified by Florizel de L. Myers, M.B., ChB.	*Certificate received from G. H. K. Ross, Chief Resident Officer, Public Hospital, Kingston.*	*Thirtieth march, 1908.*

SIGNED BY THE SAID *Entered from the Chief Resident Officer's Certificate as above by me* IN PRESENCE OF *C. N. M. Croskery* REGISTRAR OF BIRTHS AND DEATHS *Kingston* DISTRICT, PARISH OF *Kingston*

19

IRO, Death Certificate, Parish of Kingston, No. 9943 AA. DS, Printed form with manuscript insertions.

1. Garvey offered this account of his parent's separation. "I, as a poor man, did all that was possible for me to do to assist a father who had money to provide for himself and made no good use of it. My father gave me at the age of fifteen [1902] the care of my mother and an elder sister [Indiana Garvey] when he himself was in a position to care for his family. . . ." (*Gleaner*, 9 April 1921). According to Amy Jacques Garvey, "Ma Garvey was in desperate straits, as all her crops were lost. Mose confided only to her his plans to go to Kingston to his maternal uncle, and get a job as a printer, so that later on he could send for her." (*Garvey and Garveyism*, p. 4).

2. There was a discrepancy between Sarah Garvey's age given at the time of death and that given on her marriage certificate. In the latter her age was listed as forty-two in 1889, which, if correct, would have made her sixty-one in 1908 at the time of her death.

3. This was Sarah Garvey's customary occupation in St. Ann's Bay. Interviews with people who knew her have revealed that she was employed as a cook with the family of the Wesleyan minister, Rev. Arthur F. Lightbourn, stationed in St. Ann's Bay between 1900 and 1907. Before that, she was employed as the housekeeper and cook for Sylvester Cotter, the agent of the Boston Fruit Co. (later the United Fruit Co.) in St. Ann's Bay.

Election of Officers of the National Club of Jamaica

[*Gleaner*, 22 April 1910]

TUMULTOUS MEETING OF THE NATIONAL CLUB

A split in the camp marks the advent of the second year of the National C[l]ub of Jamaica,[1] and the Club is now without a President, although one was re-elected only on Wednesday night [*20 April*].

The Club had its regu[l]ar monthly meeting on Wednesday night last in the temporary building on the grounds of the Collegiate Hall.

The termination of the meeting was dramatic. Its outstanding features are the high tribute paid to the Hon. S. A. G. Cox[2] for his work in the Legislative Council, striking denunciation of the Press and all members (except Mr. Cox) of the Legislative Council, the presence of the Hon. H. Cork[3] (who came in for some strong criticisms), and, lastly, a clash between the President and the Senior Vice-President, Mr. Cox.

The attendance was large and Mr. H. A. L. Simpson[4] (President) occupied the chair. On the platform were Mr. Alexander Dixon,[5] Hon. H. Cork and Mr. W. T. Connolly.[6] . . .

Mr. Garvey in moving a vote of confidence in the Hon. S. A. G. Cox with regard to his service in the Legislative Council, spoke in glowing terms of their Vice-president.

The [se]conder followed in the same strain and the resolution was carried amidst cheers.

Mr. Cox returned thanks for the resolution and announced that the Club was in the 13th month of its existence and that night they were to elect officers to serve for the ensuing term. He proposed Mr. Simpson as President for another year, and in doing so he might say that Mr. Simpson had carried the position of the Club to a high standard.

Mr. Simpson was unanimously re-elected President.

Hon. Cox, Messrs. Dixon and Connolly were proposed by Mr. Simpson as Vice-presidents and these gentlemen were unanimously elected.

Exchanges of compliments followed.

Messrs. G. [B.] Parker, Henry and Garvey were elected secretaries.

A committee was appointed to deal with a letter of Dr. Meikle[7] suggesting the affiliation of the National Club with the Labour Union of America.[8] . . .

Printed in the *Gleaner*, Friday, 22 April 1910. Original headlines have been abbreviated and subheads omitted.

1. Founded on 3 March 1909, the National Club was Jamaica's first nationalist political organization. It was created to expose and redress the abuses of crown colony government in Jamaica, focusing on "coolie" immigration, the judicial system, education, and the autocratic methods of the governor, Sir Sydney Olivier. It proposed to develop a "more liberal policy" for Jamaica by contesting the seats of members in the Legislative Council who in the general election of 1911 did not pledge to support the policy of the National Club. By this means it hoped to control a political majority in the council. The National Club's manifesto declared that only native-born Jamaicans could be members and that each member must pledge himself to Jamaican self-government. The official organ was *Our Own*, a bimonthly that appeared from July 1910 to July 1911. The title of the journal was influenced by the Irish Sinn Fein movement (in Gaelic *Sinn Fein* means "our own").

2. Solomon Alexander Gilbert Cox (1871–1922), more popularly known as "Sandy" Cox or "The People's Sandy," was the founder and moving spirit of the National Club. He entered the Jamaica government service at an early age and worked as a legal clerk in the Judicial Department for twenty years before studying law at the Middle Temple in London. He was called to the bar in July 1908, and returned to Jamaica to become deputy clerk of the Court for the Parish of St. James. Cox left the post in January 1909 amid charges by the governor that he was absent from duty without leave. Cox instituted proceedings against the governor for libel, but lost.

On 3 March 1909, the National Club launched a concerted political campaign against the governor, and in December Cox submitted a statement to the secretary of state for the colonies seeking the removal of Governor Olivier from Jamaica. Prior to this action, Cox had won election to the Legislative Council as the member for the parish of St. Thomas, only to find himself suspended from the council six months later, in May 1910, for publishing the proceedings of a select committee appointed to examine charges that Cox had made against certain prison officials. But at the January 1911 general election, Cox was again returned as the member for St. Thomas. A court petition challenged the legality of his election on technicalities regarding the residency requirement and income, and Cox was unseated by a court decision in June 1911. Denied its principal voice in the legislature, the National Club soon floundered for lack of support. In October 1911, Cox went to Panama and Costa Rica to raise funds to revive his antigovernment newspaper in Jamaica, *The Daily News* ("The People's Paper"), which had discontinued publication in June 1911. But instead of returning to Jamaica, he migrated to the United States in November 1911, where he practiced as an attorney in Boston. Despite his residence abroad, Cox continued to write frequent letters to the Jamaican press on political subjects, though it appears that he disavowed politics completely after he became a Christian Scientist in 1913. When he died, the *Gleaner* noted that "Cox swayed remarkable influence over large sections of the masses of the country." (*HJ*, 1923; *Gleaner*, 13 December 1922).

3. Henry Cork served as a member of the Legislative Council for the parish of St. Catherine. He later became a candidate for the St. Thomas Legislative Council seat in the general election of January 1911, and it was his election petition that unseated Cox from membership in the Legislative Council. Cork was a planter and valuator from the parish of Portland as well as a justice of the peace for St. Thomas, Portland, and St. Catherine. (*WWJ*, 1921–24).

4. Hubert Ashton Laselve Simpson (1872–1938) was renowned as one of Jamaica's most

brilliant solicitors and political figures. He was educated at the Kingston Collegiate School and admitted to practice as a solicitor in 1898. He was elected a councillor of the city of Kingston and later was appointed vice-chairman of the city council. At the general election in January 1911, Simpson was elected to the Legislative Council as the member for Kingston and the following year he was elected the city's mayor. Reelected on three successive occasions, Simpson finally resigned in September 1916. For his services during the war, in 1918 he was awarded the OBE. Elected mayor of Kingston and St. Andrew in 1925, he was defeated in the general election of that year. At the general election in 1930, he again contested the seat for Kingston as a member of Marcus Garvey's newly formed People's Progressive party, but he was defeated. However in 1935, Simpson was elected to the Legislative Council, and between 1935 and 1937 he was again the mayor of Kingston. (*DG*, 21 December 1938; *HJ*, 1939).

5. Alexander Dixon (1852–1917), with S. A. G. Cox and H. A. L. Simpson, was a cofounder of the National Club. He was also the first black Jamaican to be elected to the Legislative Council in 1899, an event that caused a considerable political stir. Born in Kingston and educated at Mico College, Dixon was a teacher at Coke Chapel, but he soon moved to the parish of St. Elizabeth, where he established a business at Santa Cruz. Upon his return to Kingston, Dixon influenced local politics as a member of the Legislative Council and the city council. It was claimed that Dixon's wide popularity helped S. A. G. Cox to secure his sweeping electoral victories. For several years Dixon was also one of the trustees of Wolmer's School Trust. The *Gleaner's* obituary of 15 October 1917 noted that Dixon "was looked up to by people of his race with great esteem and respect, and was a doughty champion of their rights." (*WWJ*, 1919–20; *HJ*, 1918).

6. William Thomas Connolley (1859–1930) served as head clerk in the army pay office for over forty years and as a member of the City Council of Kingston for twelve years. (*WWJ*, 1919–20; *HJ*, 1931).

7. Dr. Louis Sancroft Meikle, M.D., D.D.S., (1874–1937) was born in Jamaica in the parish of Manchester; he graduated in dentistry from Howard University, Washington, D.C., and lectured in its dental college. Later, he studied medicine and after graduating went to Panama, where he worked for the U.S. Public Health Service during the construction of the canal. Meikle wrote *The Confederation of the British West Indies versus Annexation to the United States of America: A Political Discourse on the West Indies* (London: S. Low, Marston and Co., 1912), in which he advocated the establishment of a British Caribbean federation. Meikle claimed that there could be no real "United Empire" until the West Indies joined the white dominions as fully self-governing territories. (*DG*, 2 March 1937).

8. The National Club proposed to amalgamate with the Labor Federation of Trinidad in order to form a National League of the West Indies, but nothing came of the idea. At the outset of the National Club, Cox had also proposed to affiliate it with the Labour party in England to promote trade unions in Jamaica. For the early history of trade unionism in Jamaica, see George Eaton, "Trade Union Development in Jamaica," *Caribbean Quarterly* 8:1 (n.d.):43–53.

Report of a Pamphlet by Marcus Garvey

[*Jamaica Times Supplement*, 28 May 1910]

'THE STRUGGLING MASS'

Mr. Marcus Garvey has issued a pamphlet[1] in which he upholds the policy of Mr. Cox and deals severely with the Press which he declares is now the enemy of the people.

Printed in the *Jamaica Times Supplement*, Saturday, 28 May 1910.

1. This pamphlet has not been found. Garvey may not have been its sole author. W. A. Domingo, who was a fellow member of the National Club, later recalled the appearance of "a

pamphlet which, in a sense, we both wrote in Kingston and he [Garvey] published" (TNF, AJG, W. A. Domingo to Amy Jacques Garvey, 15 January 1961).

Island Elocution Contest

[*Gleaner*, 20 August 1910]

THE PARISH DEFEN[D]ERS.

Next Wednesday evening, 24th inst., what is known as an Island Elocution Contest will take place in the Collegiate Hall, Kingston. Then Recitations of leading Authors will be given by representatives from the various parishes of the Island. The best will be awarded prizes of £5, £3, and £2, respectively, and will be regarded as the Champion Elocutionists for the time being.

The Judges will be Rev. W. Graham,[1] of Kingston, Barrister Hector Josephs,[2] B.A., L.L.B., and Mr. William Morrison[3] Solicitor.

Following are the names of those who will represent the different parishes, the passages they will recite, the parties who "named" them, and facts about the reciters, so far as are known.

MR. R. W. THOMPSON, Kingston, "The Battle of Naseby" (T. H. Mac-Dermot[4] Esq., Editor JAMAICA TIMES): An able reciter, has acquitted himself well at the Kingston Athenaeum, a worthy defender of the premier parish.

MR. J. D. BURROW, St. Andrew, "The Dream of Clarence" from Richard III. (R. C. Guy Esq.,). With such a capital selection Mr. Burrow ought to make an able showing.

MR. S. BARNES, St. Thomas, "My Mother's Picture," (W. R. Durie Esq.). A selection calling forth much elocutionary powers, which Mr. Barnes is likely to display.

MR[.] PERCIVAL BURKE, Portland. "Mary Queen of Scots' Farewell to France" (Mr. J. L. King, B.A., L.L.B., and W. H. Plant Esq.) A capital selection in capable hands.

MR. H. LAWRENCE, Manchester, Scott's "Lady of the Lake". (Mr. A. L. Walcott). As a schoolmaster Mr. Lawrence ought to acquit himself nobly.

MR. G. W. T. KNIGHT, Clarendon, "The Burial March of Dundee" (Mr. T. S. Phillips). Master Knight fresh from Wolmers will nobly defend this parish.

MR. M. MOZIAH GARVEY. St. Ann, "Chatham on American War".[5] (Dr. Ernest Murray,[6] M.B. B.S.). The "Garden Parish" will be fittingly represented by this energetic elocutionist.

MR. S. MCCORMACK, St. Catherine, "Paradise Lost," (A. L. Walcott, Esq,). A "West Branch Boy" who ought to "show his colours."

MR. E. J. IRONS, St. Mary, "Coeur de Leon at the Bier of his Father." (R. H. Haughton, Esq)

MR. J. BEECHER, Trelawny, Extracts from "Pope's Homer" (N. A. Parker, Esq., *Telegraph and Guardian*.)

MR. A. H. BONITTO, Hanover, "John Maynard" (Rev. Father Mulligan, S. J.)

MR. S. SMYTHE, Westmoreland, "The Bridge-Keeper's Story" (E. Morand, Esq.) Mr. S. has been an Elocution Prize Winner in England.

MR. G. J. BINNS, St. Elizabeth, "The Women of Mumble's Head" (W. R. Durie, Esq.)

MR. E. M. WATSON, St. James, "The Dream of Eugene Aram" (W. R. Durie, Esq.,) Mr. Watson has been winner at similar contests at St. George's College.

MR. N. J. PURDON, Port Royal, "The Bride of Collin's Grave," (W. R. Durie, Esq.,) Mr. Purdon has won a medal offered by Custos McGrath.

In connection with the Contest there will also be a Concert to which the Jamaica Choir may contribute, as well as other well-known artists.

Admission will be 2s and 1s and the Contest promises to be highly interesting.

Printed in the *Jamaica Times*, Saturday, 20 August 1910. Original headlines have been abbreviated. The contest was organized by Mr. T. S. Phillips of the *Jamaica Times* on behalf of local charity (R. N. Murray, ed., *J. J. Mills, His Own Account of His Life and Times* [London and Kingston: William Collins and Sangsters (Jamaica) Ltd., 1969], p. 108).

1. Rev. William Graham (1859–1922) was a white Presbyterian who was the pastor of Scotch Kirk in Kingston, Jamaica, where he also published a monthly church magazine, *Scotch Kirk Pulpit*. For some time, Rev. Graham also served as the editor of the *Gleaner*. On 22 March 1921, in an address of welcome delivered in the Collegiate Hall on Garvey's return to Jamaica, Graham disclosed that: "When Mr. Garvey was much younger than he was to-day, he used to come to him for advice; and on those occasions he gave Mr. Garvey the very best possible advice in sympathy with the Negro Race in Jamaica. . . . Mr. Garvey knew as well as he did (because he was going back to a conversation he had with him), what the Negro race owed to his race. . . ." ("Big Reception Given Mr. Marcus Garvey," *Gleaner*, 24 March 1921, p. 11; see also *Gleaner*, 11 July 1922).

2. Hector Archibald Josephs (1871–?) in 1912 became the first black Jamaican to be appointed assistant attorney general, which was for some time the highest ranking position held by a Jamaican in the colonial civil service. Educated at the Collegiate School, Kingston, and at York Castle, St. Ann, Josephs was the Jamaica Scholar in 1891. In the same year he entered Trinity College, Cambridge, and was a prize-winning student. In 1896 he was called to the bar at Lincoln's Inn. He subsequently held a variety of civic positions in Jamaica, including president of the Kingston Citizen's Association, 1910–11, and member of the Jamaica Schools Commission, 1907–09. (*WWJ*, 1921–24).

3. William Morrison (1875–1951), lawyer and sportsman, was admitted to practice as a solicitor of the Supreme Court of the Judicature of Jamaica in 1899. He served as a nominated member of the Legislative Council of Jamaica from 1922 until 1941. (*WWJ*, 1916).

4. Thomas Henry MacDermot (?–1933) was an elementary school teacher for many years before he turned his attention to journalism. Working first with the *Christian Chronicle*, MacDermot later became assistant editor of the *Jamaica Post*, a special writer for the *Gleaner*, and eventually editor of the *Jamaica Times*. Under the pseudonym of "Tom Redcam," he wrote a variety of verse and fiction. He is traditionally considered the poet laureate of Jamaica. (*HJ*, 1935).

5. John James Mills (1888–1966), a well-known Jamaican educator who was also born in St. Ann, was in the audience when Garvey delivered his addresses at the elocution contest. He recalled in his autobiography:

Garvey chose a poem of vigour and action for his first "number." The audience learnt later that he had been placed first in that effort. His second rendition was the well-known extract from Lord Chatham's speech in the House of Lords, thundering against the evils of the War of Independence. Garvey's rendition, though convincing, provoked smiles and tittering because of his sometimes squeaking voice. At last, a member of the audience sitting near the front interrupted loudly with a humorous remark. This caused loud laughter which noticeably affected Garvey's performance, for he was eventually placed third. An echo of this was heard weeks later in the law courts.

The man who so rudely interrupted was tried and found guilty of maliciously contriving to deprive Garvey of his chances of winning total championship of the contest . . . (*J. J. Mills*, p. 109).

For the contest winners, see "The Elocution Contest," *Jamaica Times*, Saturday, 27 August 1910. The report shows that Garvey did not place among the winners.

6. Dr. Ernest E. Murray (1869–1953) attended the Wesleyan Church's York Castle High School of Boys in St. Ann and was named Jamaica Scholar in 1888. He was awarded a medical scholarship to study at University College in London and received his M.B. and B.S. degrees in 1894. After his return to Jamaica, he became president of the Wesleyan Conference and later the principal of his old high school. (*WWJ*, 1916).

Record Item

[*Colonial Office, London*] 8 July 1913

Garvey, M. Assistance, applies for—in circumstances stated.[1] Ansd. [and ret.?] 12 Aug. [*1913*].

PRO, CO 351/21, No. 27424, Jamaica Register of Correspondence, Ind. 18937. AN. The original correspondence was destroyed.

1. Garvey arrived in England in the spring or early summer of 1912. The "circumstances" to which the register referred were probably due to Garvey's straitened financial condition at the time.

Marcus Garvey to Sir Frederic George Kenyon, Director, British Museum[1]

176, Borough High Street, S.E. [*London*]
October 6th. 1913

Dear Sir,

I hereby beg to make application to be admitted as a permanent reader in the Reading Room of the Museum for the purpose of research and reference.

Enclosed please find testimonial from the Editor of "The African Times & Orient Review".[2]

I am a journalist and student. Yours faithfully,

MARCUS GARVEY

[*Endorsement*] BLS. 34 7/10/13

BM, TLS. Recipient's copy. Handwritten endorsement.

1. Sir Frederic George Kenyon (1863–1952) became director of the British Museum in 1909 and published a variety of works on its manuscript collection. (*WWW*).

2. The *African Times and Orient Review*, (*ATOR*) which for a period in 1913 employed Marcus Garvey in its editorial office on Fleet Street as a messenger and handyman, was edited and published in London by Dusé Mohamed Ali. In Garvey's obituary in *The Comet*, Dusé Mohamed Ali remembered that Garvey was employed "for the greater part of a year" (*The Comet*, 8: 6 [17 August 1940], p. 1).

ATOR appeared as a monthly from July 1912 to December 1913, but as a weekly after that, from 24 March to 18 August 1914. Publication was suspended because of the war for over two years, but it was resumed on a monthly basis from January 1917 until October 1918. After another suspension of publication, it reappeared under the slightly changed title of *Africa and Orient Review*, from January to December 1920. In June 1928 a final single issue was published in New York under the title *Africa*. Originally, *ATOR* intended to fill the need "for a Pan-Oriental Pan-African journal at the seat of the British Empire which would lay the aims, desires, and intentions of the Black, Brown and Yellow races—within and without the Empire—at the throne of Caesar" ("Foreword," *ATOR* 1 [July 1912]: iii). Nonetheless, the editorial policy also took care to express its essential loyalty and a professed belief in racial harmony. The official British attitude toward *ATOR* was summarized by the recollections of two British colonial officials in November 1917: "In the old days, the magazine was considered to be of doubtful loyalty, owing to Duse Mohamed's pan-Ethiopian programme"; followed by "Duse Mohammed, the editor of the *African Times and Orient Review*, is a rather doubtful character whose paper, before the war, was *suspect*, being inclined to the Ethiopian movement and believed to be in touch with undesirable elements in India and Egypt" (PRO, CO 554/35/55259, "African Times and Orient Review, and Duse Mohamed Ali"). The "pan-Ethiopian" character of *ATOR* was reflected in the quality of the magazine's agents: Rev. Attoh Ahuma, West Africa; John E. Bruce, United States; H. C. Solomon, Panama Canal Zone; and F. Z. S. Peregrino, Cape Town, South Africa. *ATOR* was represented in Jamaica, its only West Indian base, by the *Jamaica Times*.

Enclosure

158, FLEET STREET, LONDON, E.C.
6th. October, 1913

Dear Sir,

I beg to recommend Mr. Marcus Garvey as being a fit and proper person to use the Reading Room of the British Museum. Yours truly,

DUSE MOHAMED[1]

[*Address*] The Director, British
Museum, W.C.

BM. TLS, Recipient's copy. Printed on the stationery of the *African Times and Orient Review*.

1. Writing under the pen name "Delta," Dusé Mohamed Ali offered readers of the *ATOR* Christmas annual in 1912 an extensive commentary on "British Museum Types in the Reading Room" (pp. 39–41). For further information on his career, see the Biographical Supplement, Appendix I.

Marcus Garvey to Sir Frederic George Kenyon

176 Borough High Street, S.E. [*London*]
Oct., 8, 1913

Dear Sir:

Re my letter of the 6th inst making application for admission to your reading room I further beg to inform you that the special purposes for which I would like to use the said room are "Reading the works of the late Dr. Edward Blyden LL.D[1] and other works that are not obtainable in any of the other libraries of London, as also to scan certain copies of old journals that are /not/ obtainable elsewhere.

Knowing your willingness to assist those in need of that knowledge that is under your keeping I now feel assured that you will consider my purpose befitting the condition under which your department is seen.[2] Yours faithfully

MARCUS GARVEY

[*Endorsements*] Let me see previous papers
1 month call R/R Adm 1 month 11. 10.
13   Call 10/10/13   F. G. Kenyon

BM. ALS, Recipient's copy. Handwritten endorsements.

1. Edward Wilmot Blyden (1832–1912), born in St. Thomas, Danish West Indies (now known as the Virgin Islands), migrated to Liberia from the United States in 1851. In addition to being a prolific writer and pioneer of Pan-Africanism, Blyden also rose to become Liberian secretary of state, 1864–66, minister plenipotentiary of the Republic of Liberia to the Court of St. James, 1877–78, president of Liberia College, 1880–84, and the Liberian minister of the interior and secretary of education, 1880–82. (See Hollis R. Lynch, *Edward Wilmot Blyden, Pan-Negro Patriot, 1832–1912* [New York: Oxford University Press, 1967]; *WBD*).
2. Garvey was granted a reading ticket (no. 11199) for one month, dated 11 October 1913.

Article by Marcus Garvey in the *African Times and Orient Review*

[London, October 1913]

THE BRITISH WEST INDIES IN THE MIRROR OF CIVILIZATION.
HISTORY MAKING BY COLONIAL NEGROES.

BY MARCUS GARVEY, JUNR.

In these days when democracy is spreading itself over the British Empire, and the peoples under the rule of the Union Jack are freeing themselves from hereditary lordship, and an unjust bureaucracy, it should not be amiss to recount the condition of affairs in the British West Indies, and particularly in the historic island of Jamaica, one of the oldest colonial possessions of the Crown.

It is right that the peoples of the vast Empire to which these colonies belong should be correctly informed on things affecting the welfare of these islands, being a comparatively neglected, if not unknown, region of the Atlantic Archipeligo.

The history of the British possession of these islands is very interesting, as it reveals the many conflicts between the various powers that have been struggling for occupancy and supremacy in the Carrib[b]ean waters for three hundred years.

These islands were discovered by Christopher Columbus,[1] in the latter part of the fourteenth century, and the major portion of them were handed over to the Spanish throne. England and France laid claim to certain of these colonies, and the former, with her justifiable (?) means of warfare, succeeded in driving the Spaniards from their tropical "Gold Mines" with much regret on the part of the ejected, who had extinguished the Aborigines, an action quite in keeping with the European custom of depopulating new lands of their aboriginal tribes. The British West Indian Colonies to-day, comprise Jamaica, Trinidad and Tobago, Barbadoes, British Guiana, Grenada, St. Vincent, St. Lucia, Dominica, Antigua and Montserrat, St. Kitts, and Nevis, the Virgin Islands and one or two others, scattered over the groups known as the Greater and Lesser Antilles, with a population of over three million souls.[2]

When the Spaniards took possession of these islands they introduced cotton and sugar growing. To supply the labour that was necessary to make these industries solid and profitable, they started the slave traffic with Africa, from which place they recruited thousands of Negro slaves whom they took from their congenial homes by force. The sugar industry developed wonderfully with Negro labour, and the great output of sugar, as exported to Europe, brought incomputable wealth to the landed proprietors, which they used in gambling and feasting; and for exploration and further development of the veritable "gold mines" of the Western Hemispheres.

Piratical and buccaneering parties used to frequent the waters of the Carib[b]ean, where they held up on the high sea merchant vessels laden with their rich cargoes bound for Europe and the West Indies. Filibustering was carried on in a daring fashion on land, where a buccaneering invader would hold up one of these islands and force the wealthy landlords to capitulate on conditions suitable to filibustering requirements.

During the sixteenth century England drove the Spaniards from the wealthiest of these islands and established herself in possession. To the Plantations, as they were called, a large proportion of her criminal class was deported, as also a few gentlemen. The new occupiers took over the paying sugar industry, and, with their superior knowledge of agriculture, gave a new impetus to it. These new owners found it necessary to replenish their labourers with new arrivals to foster the industry, hence an agreement was entered into with John Hawkins, of infamous memory, who clandestinely obtained a charter from his sovereign to convey Negroes from Africa to the West Indies, thereby giving new life to the merciless traffic in human souls.

Jamaica was the most flourishing of the British West Indian Islands, and the ancient capital, Port Royal, which has been submerged by earthquake,[3] was said to be the richest spot on the face of the globe. The chief products of this colony were sugar and rum, but its assets were largely added to by its being the headquarters of European pirates and buccaneers who took their treasures thither, where they gambled and feasted in great luxury. It is amusing to note that many of the pirates who traversed the West Indies had been deprived of their ears as the result of unsuccessful piratical encounters. Some of the early Governors of these islands, such as Sir Henry Morgan, were known as subtle rogues, and were themselves at some time or another, pirates and buccaneers.

Among the many piratical and buccaneering heroes or rogues, whichever you wish to call them, may be mentioned Teach, otherwise known as Blackbeard, Morgan, Hawkins, Rogers, Drake, Raleigh, Preston, Shirley, Jackson and Somers. Such terror did these villains strike in the heart of the people of these islands, that up to the present day their names are held as auguries of fear among the people. It is common to hear a black or coloured mother, in trying to frighten her child, count "One, two, three, four," and then shout, "Preston, ah, com!" at which intimation the child runs away in terror.

Owing to the limit of space I shall confine myself to a few facts relating to the island of Jamaica, but I may say that the condition in the various islands are the same, and what is true of one is true of the whole.

Jamaica became a colony of England in 1665, under Oliver Cromwell,[4] and has since remained under her control. The country has passed through many forms of local government; at one time it was self-governing; then it became a Crown Colony. For the last twenty years, it has enjoyed a semi-representative government,[5] with little power of control, the balance of power resting in the hands of the red-tapists, who pull the strings of colonial conservatism from Downing Street, with a reckless disregard of the interests and wishes of the people.

When the English took possession of this island they exploited it agriculturally for all it was worth, which was a great lot. As I have already mentioned they imported Negro slaves from Africa who tilled the soil under the severest torture, and who are the real producers of the wealth that the country has contributed to the coffers of Europe, and the pockets of English adventurers who, in the early days, were men of foul and inhuman characters.

The slaves were inhumanly treated, being beaten, tortured and scourged for the slightest offence. One of the primitive methods of chastisement was to "dance the treadmill," an instrument that clipped off the toes when not danced to proper motion. In self-defence, and revenge of such treatment, the slaves revolted on several occasions, but with little or no success, as being without arms, they were powerless in the face of the organised military forces of the ruling class. In 1851 [*1831*] the Negro slaves in one of the North Western parishes of the island revolted, but were subdued with the loss to the planting proprietors of over three-quarters of a million sterling.[6] They again revolted in 1865 in the East, under the leadership of the Hon. George William Gordon,[7] a member of the Legislative Council, and Paul Bogle.[8] They sounded the call of unmolested liberty, but owing to the suppression of telegraphic communication, they were handicapped and suppressed, otherwise Jamaica would be as free to-day as Hayti, which threw off the French yoke under the leadership of the famous Negro General, Toussaint L'Ouverture.[9] The Gordon party[10] killed fifteen of the native despots and a savage plutocrat by the name of Baron von Ketelhodt[11] who had great control over the Governor, Edward John Eyre.[12] The victorious party hanged Gordon, Paul Bogle and several hundred negroes, for which crime Governor Eyre was recalled to England and indicted for murder, but escaped by the "skin of his teeth."[13]

In 1834[14] a law was passed by the Imperial Parliament declaring all slaves within the British Empire free for ever, with the promise that such slaves should undergo an apprenticeship for a few years. On the 1st August, 1838, the Negro slaves of the West Indies became free. Twenty millions sterling was paid to the planters by the Imperial Government for the emancipation of the people whom they had taken from their sunny homes in Africa. The slaves got nothing; they were liberated without money, proper clothing, food or shelter. But with the characteristic fortitude of the African, they shouldered their burdens and set themselves to work, receiving scanty remuneration for their services. By their industry and thrift they have been able to provide themselves with small holdings which they are improving, greatly to their credit.

Since the abolition of slavery, the Negroes have improved themselves wonderfully, and when the Government twenty or thirty years ago, threw open the doors of the Civil Service to competitive examination, the Negro youths swept the board, and captured every available office, leaving their white competitors far behind. This system went on for a few years, but as the white youths were found to be intellectually inferior to the black, the whites persuaded the Government to abolish the competitive system,[15] and fill vacancies by nomination, and by this means kept out the black youths. The service has long since been recruited from an inferior class of sychophantic weaklings whose brains are exhausted by dissipation and vice before they reach the age of thirty-five.

The population of Jamaica, according to the last census,[16] was 831,383, and is divided as follows: —White, 15,605; Black, 630,181; Coloured, 163,201; East Indian, 17,380; Chinese, 2,111 and 2,905 whose colour is not stated. Thus it can be seen that more than two-thirds of the population of Jamaica (as also of the other West Indian Islands), are descendants of the old African Slaves.

The question naturally arises, How comes this hybrid or coloured element? This hybrid population is accountable for by the immoral advantage taken of the Negro women by the whites, who have always been in power and who practice polygamy with black women as an unwritten right. The old slave-owners raped their female slaves, married or unmarried, and compelled them into polygamy much against their will, thus producing the "coloured" element. The latter day whites, much to their regret, have not the opportunity of compelling black girls to become their mistresses, but they use other means of bewitching these unprotected women whom they keep as concubines; thus perpetuating the evil of which their fathers were guilty. The educated black gentleman, naturally, becomes disgusted with this state of affairs; and in seeking a wife he generally marries a white woman. These are the contributing causes to the negroid or hybrid population of the West Indies. Unlike the whites in the United States the negroes do not lynch white men when they rape and take advantage of black girls; they leave them to the hand of retributive justice.

There have been several movements to federate the British West Indian Islands, but owing to parochial feelings nothing definite has been achieved. Ere long this change is sure to come about because the people of these islands are all one. They live under the same conditions, are of the same race and mind, and have the same feelings and sentiments regarding the things of the world.

As one who knows the people well, I make no apology for prophesying that there will soon be a turning point in the history of the West Indies; and that the people who inhabit that portion of the Western Hemisphere will be the instruments of uniting a scattered race who, before the close of many centuries, will found an Empire on which the sun shall shine as ceaselessly as it shines on the Empire of the North to-day. This may be regarded as a dream, but I would point my critical friends to history and its lessons. Would Caesar have believed that the country he was invading in 55 B.C. would be the seat of the greatest Empire of the World? Had it been suggested to him would he not have laughed at it as a huge joke? Yet it has come true. England is the seat of the greatest Empire of the World, and its king is above the rest of monarchs in power and dominion. Laugh then you may, at what I have been bold enough to prophecy, but as surely as there is an evolution in the natural growth of man and nations, so surely will there be a change in the history of these subjected regions.

Printed in the *African Times and Orient Review* 2 (Mid-October 1913): 158–60. Garvey's article was described in a later issue of *ATOR* as "a powerful and telling summing up of the History of the West Indies" (William H. Ferris, "A Colored American's Estimate of the A.T.O.R.," [14 April 1914], p. 77).

1. Columbus made his four voyages from 1492 until 1502, and not in the latter part of the fourteenth century as Garvey stated.

2. According to the 1913 *World Almanac* and *Whittaker's Almanacs*, the population of the British West Indies was 1,890,000.

3. On 7 June 1692 the town of Port Royal, built on a long spit of sand opposite the present capital city of Kingston, was totally destroyed by an earthquake. The entire town was enveloped by the sea, and an estimated two-thirds of the population of Port Royal drowned. (Clinton Black, *Port Royal* [Kingston, Ja.: Bolivar Press, 1970]).

4. While he was lord protector, Cromwell sent a expeditionary force to the Spanish West Indies in 1655, which resulted in Britain's first colonial holdings in the Caribbean. Jamaica was seized in May 1655, not 1665 as Garvey claimed. (S.A.G. Taylor, *The Western Design: An Account of Cromwell's Expedition to the Caribbean* [Kingston: Institute of Jamaica & Jamaica Historical Society, 1966]).

5. In 1883 a petition was sent from the inhabitants of Jamaica for a change in the Constitution of the colony, which after 1865 had been administered as a crown colony. By an order in council of 19 May 1884, a "moderate step in advance" was granted: nine members of the previously entirely appointive Legislative Council were to be elected by the people. Then in 1895 the elected members were increased to fourteen (one for each parish), the nominated members being increased to ten (and four kept in abeyance). In 1899 the governor added the four nominated members held in reserve in order to pass the Tariff Bill. They were later withdrawn but reinstated in 1900. (Graham Knox, "British Colonial Policy and the Problems of Establishing a Free Society in Jamaica, 1838–1865," *Caribbean Studies* 2 [1963]: 3–13).

6. On 27–28 December 1831 slaves burned the buildings of Kensington estate in the parish of St. James, signaling the beginning of the revolt led by Sam Sharpe, who had been a member of Rev. Thomas Burchell's congregation in Montego Bay. Sharpe thought that Jamaican slave owners might prevent the widely anticipated emancipation of slaves. He came to believe that emancipation had already been granted by the English Crown but was being denied to the slaves. Working through black Baptist leaders, Sharpe planned a work strike for the day following the Christmas holidays, to continue until slave owners gave the promise of pay for work. However, the subsequent burning of Kensington and other neighboring estates destroyed his nonviolent plan. In the harsh repression that followed, Sam Sharpe and his associates were hanged for inciting rebellion. The final death toll included a dozen whites, while over four hundred blacks were killed during the military suppression of the revolt, and another hundred were executed following courts-martial. Approximately sixty properties in western Jamaica were destroyed by fires set by the slaves. In all, 626 slaves were tried for participating in the revolt. (See Mary Reckard, "The Jamaica Slave Rebellion of 1831," in Richard Frucht, ed., *Black Society in the New World* [New York: Random House, 1971], pp. 50–66; Richard Hart, *Slaves Who Abolished Slavery*, vol. 2, *Blacks in Rebellion* [Mona, Ja.: Institute of Social and Economic Research, University of the West Indies, 1982]).

7. Although important for his role as the chief spokesman of the political opposition to Gov. Edward John Eyre in the House of Assembly, George William Gordon (ca. 1820–1865) was not a leader in the rebellion. Gordon was a planter, successful businessman, and a former justice of the peace for St. Thomas. (Ansell Hart, *The Life of George William Gordon* [Kingston, Jamaica: Institute of Jamaica, 1973]; "George William Gordon and 1865" [By the Observer], *Gleaner*, 19 February 1913).

8. Paul Bogle, a native Baptist preacher and a small property owner in the village of Stony Gut in St. Thomas, was the chief leader of the rebellion. On 23 October 1865 he was captured, tried and convicted by court-martial, and hanged. (Francis J. Osborne, S.J. "Morant Bay, 1865," *Jamaica Historical Society Bulletin* 4 [December 1966]: 151–58; "The Part that was played by the celebrated Paul Bogle in the Rebellion which occurred in the Parish of St. Thomas Nearly Fifty years ago" [By the Observer], *Gleaner*, 7 April 1913).

9. Pierre Dominique Toussaint L'Ouverture (1746–1803) was born near Cape François, Haiti, of African slave parents. In 1791 he joined the slave insurgents in a successful rebellion that resulted in their freedom in 1793. French Republicans made him commander in chief of Haiti at their convention in 1794. Garvey's speeches frequently mentioned L'Ouverture. (*WBD*; Francis J. Osborne, S. J. "The Haitian Revolution and Jamaica," *Jamaica Historical Society Bulletin* 5 [December 1967]: 227–41).

10. The reference to the "Gordon" party was in error. On 11 October 1865, Paul Bogle and about four hundred supporters marched on the court house in Morant Bay. The building was set afire and some eighteen people, including the custos, were killed as they fled from the flames. (*Report of the Jamaica Royal Commission, 1866* [London, 1866]).

11. Baron Maximilan Augustus von Ketelhodt was custos of St. Thomas-in-the-East, 1862–65. A German who had married a Jamaican widow at Aix-la-Chapelle, he came to Jamaica to manage her estates. He became a naturalized English subject and a prominent public figure in

Jamaica. (H. P. Jacobs, *Sixty Years of Change, 1806–1866: Progress and Reaction in Kingston and the Countryside* [Kingston, Ja.: Institute of Jamaica, 1923], pp. 76–78, 93–95; "The Parish of St. Thomas on the Eve of the Morant Bay Rebellion," *Jamaica Historical Society Bulletin* 4 [September 1966]: 135–43).

12. Edward John Eyre (1815–1901), explorer and colonial governor, was born in England, but he immigrated to Australia in 1832 where he became a successful sheep farmer. He was appointed magistrate and protector of aborigines affairs, and was later made lieutenant governor of New Zealand. He held this office until 1853, when he was appointed governor of St. Vincent (1854–60) and the Leeward Islands (1860–61). During the absence of Sir Charles Darling, governor of Jamaica, Eyre was appointed commander in chief (1861–64). When Darling resigned in 1864, Eyre was confirmed as governor of Jamaica. In October 1865, the Morant Bay Rebellion occurred, and Eyre declared martial law. His actions and those of the British troops were quite controversial; consequently, Eyre was recalled in 1866 and a royal commission of inquiry was established. On 9 April 1866 the commission reported that although Eyre had acted with commendable promptness in stopping the riots, his unnecessary rigor resulted in many improperly conducted courts-martial. Eyre retired in England, though the controversy regarding his actions in Jamaica raged for many years. (*DNB*).

13. It is not known how many rioters were killed or wounded on 11 October by the parish militia, but in the subsequent violent military suppression of the rebellion, at least 85 people were killed by the troops, either by shooting or hanging without trial. 354 were executed by sentence of court-martial, and about 600 men and women were flogged brutally. It was estimated that the troops destroyed nearly one thousand cottages, houses, and other buildings. In June 1868 criminal proceedings were begun in England against Eyre under the Colonial Governors Act, but the grand jury threw out the bill of mandamus brought by the Jamaica Committee. (B. A. Knox, "The British Government and the Governor Eyre Controversy, 1865–1875," *The Historical Journal* 19 [1976]: 877–900).

14. Though the Slavery Abolition Act became law on 28 August 1833, its provisions allowed the slave owners one year's grace period by specifying that the law would not go into effect until 1 August 1834.

15. Open competitive examination for civil service posts in Jamaica was introduced in October 1885. Prior to this, the governor filled vacancies in the public service department on the recommendation of the department's head. Some of the public as well as certain civil servants opposed the new system, and in response, changes were made allowing specific exemptions from the examinations. However, in 1905 these amendments were disallowed and open competition returned. Competitive examinations were discontinued once again in 1911, and the system of appointments by the governor was reinstated. (*HJ*, 1887; *HJ*, 1912).

16. These figures were taken from the 1911 census.

Marcus Garvey to T. A. McCormack[1]

14 Durley Rd. Stamford Hill London, W.

10/12/13

[*First four pages of letter missing*] I hope you have received some money from Mr. Scott   Adrian[2] is taking advantage of my absence for when he says that there was no decided bargain he has simply reversed the truth. Any how we wont fall out for that if he doesnt pay, ask him to keep the books safely till my return.

I will write you from Paris but you must answer my letters for the present and address them in care of Miss Indiana Garvey[3] at above address as I shall be globe-trotting for a while.

There is an old man by the name of Phillips who works at the office of Mr. Orett, a solicitor, who was American Vice-Consul. His office is in Duke Street in an Earthquake wrecked bldg adjoining Cargill & Cargill opposite the Mayor & Council he owes me five shillings please receive it and take same. I will send you some cash in the New Year. Yours sincerely /Happy Christmas & Prosperous New Year/

MARCUS GARVEY

Re SON'S MEMORIAL

Dear Mr. Phillips

I am hereby asking you to be good enough to pay to Mr. T. A. McCormack the sum of 5/- for Memorial and oblige   Yours faithfully

MARCUS GARVEY

TAM. ALS, Recipient's copy.

1. Thaddeus Alexander McCormack (1878–1953) was born in Kingston, Jamaica, and educated at West Branch School. He was a tailor and worked as a cutter for a number of the city's large department stores. As an outstanding elocutionist, and the winner of several medals, it is possible that he initiated Garvey into the art of elocution. After Garvey arrived in Kingston, he boarded with the McCormack family; he was given a small room adjoining the main house at 13 Pink Lane, which was located near the central market in the area of the city then known as Smith Village. Garvey became a lifelong friend of T. A. McCormack and his family. Following Garvey's return to Jamaica from the United States in 1927, McCormack worked as the secretary for Garvey's *Blackman* and *New Jamaican* newspapers (Interview with Malcolm George McCormack [nephew of T. A. McCormack], 1979; letter to editor from Edna L. McCormack [daughter of T. A. McCormack], 26 April 1979).

2. A possible reference to Adrian Daily, one of the founding members and associate secretary of the UNIA in 1914. Daily was a baker by profession.

3. Indiana Garvey (ca. 1882–1956) was Garvey's elder sister and later the wife of Alfred Uriah Peart. She joined Garvey in England in the summer of 1912. George Fortunatus Judah, Kingston city engineer and leader of the Roman Catholic laity, granted Garvey's request to have her accompany his family to England that year. Indiana Garvey returned to Jamaica sometime after Garvey, though the exact date is not known. She was to join Garvey again in the United States, working as his housekeeper in New York until the early spring of 1920 when she and her husband returned to Jamaica. (Interview with Ruth Peart Prescott [daughter of Indiana Garvey], 1976; IRO, Death Certificate, S-48,956/78).

Marcus Garvey to T. A. McCormack

Hotel Cecil, 128 Trongate,
Glasgow, Scotland, January, 14, 1914

My Dear Friend,

Just a few lines to inform you that I am still in the land-of-the-living. As you will see from heading I am in "Bonny Scotland" among the Highland folk. I expect leaving here at the week end for London. I have just run over to Edinburgh to take a glance of the ancient domains of "Mary Queen of Scots" *for the scene was changed*[1] I have visited Manchester, Liverpool, Leeds, Shiefield and New-castle-on Tyne before coming here and after my European tour. I have seen wonders, I have learnt wonders and I hope to teach wonders   It is bitingly cold in these parts, but since I am a tourist I have provided all the necessaries for such a season. At some places I have visited I have been the only black man seen for a good time and as you know me well, I have had access to places that only the aristocracy would think of going. Some of the people I meet as tourists are wondering how a black man can travel about so much, some take me for an African millionaire   I have met some of the same people at Monte Carlo, Paris, Boulogne, London, Madrid and elsewhere. If I wanted white heiresses I could have startled Jamaica on my return; but . . .[*remainder of letter missing*]

TAM. AL, Recipient's copy.

1. This is a reference to the poem, "Mary, Queen of Scots," written by Henry Glassford Bell (1805–1894), which details the demise of Mary Stuart. It was a favorite dramatic piece, often recited at elocution contests (Frank McHale, ed., *Pieces That Have Won Prizes* [New York: Noble and Noble, 1917], pp. 232–36).

Marcus Garvey to Alfred E. Burrowes

14 Durley Rd. Stamford Hill,
London, N. March 2, 1914

Dear Mr. Cap:[1]

I trust that by now you have received samples from firms . . . [*several words mutilated and illegible*] same. I have been travelling about the Continent a great deal[2] and returned to College[3] a couple of weeks ago.

I am asking that you be good enough to send me a testimonial to the effect that I /am a practical printer and/ have been managing office as such.[4] I have been unfortunate enough to lose my testimonial and references during my stay in Paris. I loss them in my hand case along with other valuables. You could word the letter of explaination or testimonial to the effect that I have been managing your office in Port Maria,[5] Jamaica, and that I relinquished such post for journalism.

When I left Port Maria I went . . . [*word illegible*] [to manage] Benjamin's office and I subsequently started a paper of my own,[6] and latterly I have been running and editing my own papers in Port Limon[7] [*Costa Rica*] and Colon[8] [*Panama*] respectively. I have asked Benjamin's to send me a testimonial also.

You can please oblige me by having the testimonial typewritten.

I am now breaking the news to you as the only person in Jamaica, that I am engaged to a Spanish-Irish heiress[9] whom I had the pleasure of meeting during my tour on the Continent. It is somewhat destructive of my principle, hence the ~~matter~~ news is not yet co[nveyed] to the Jamaica press. I hardly think I can change my mind in marrying her, although it will be some . . .

[*word mutilated*] time . . . [*two words mutilated*] and arrangements.
I trust you and family are well. I am yours faithfully

MARCUS GARVEY

AEB. ALS, Recipient's copy.

1. Alfred Ernest "Cap" Burrowes (1857–1928) was a master printer of St. Ann's Bay with whom Marcus Garvey served his apprenticeship, and who may also have been his godfather. Garvey always remained on close terms with Burrowes after leaving St. Ann's Bay.

2. The precise date on which Garvey left England for the continent is still not known, nor is the date of his return to England.

3. A reference to Birkbeck College. In 1920 Birkbeck College was recognized as a school of the University of London for evening and part-time students. Birkbeck catered to working class students without formal qualifications; however, the college's records for 1910–16 show no trace of Garvey's enrollment. The registrar of students during 1912–14, who was said to have had an exceptional memory for detail, stated later that he had a very definite recollection of Garvey and believed that he attended some courses in law (D. Dakin, Registrar, Birkbeck College, to E. D. Cronon, 23 November 1953). Garvey later alluded to Birkbeck as "the College where we spent a little time (twenty years ago)." ("Birkbeck College," *New Jamaican*, Saturday, 19 November 1932).

4. Garvey was referring to his employment in the printing department of P. A. Benjamin Manufacturing Co., a Kingston firm of manufacturing chemists. In addition to printing labels and advertising leaflets, the P. A. Benjamin press also published the *Commercial Messenger* as "the business helper to the general public" (*Daily News*, Tuesday, 24 January 1911). Garvey worked with P. A. Benjamin Manufacturing Co. from the time of his arrival in Kingston from Port Maria, which may have been in 1905, until the ill-fated printers' strike at the end of November 1908. The strike was called by the Kingston Typographical Union (KTU) (Affiliate No. 98 of the International Typographical Union of the American Federation of Labor). Garvey was the vice-president of the compositors' branch. With the collapse of the strike after four weeks, in January 1909, the KTU disintegrated and the executive members of the union's three branches (bookbinders, pressmen, and compositors) were denied reemployment with the print shops closed by the strike (Richard Hart, "The Life and Resurrection of Marcus Garvey," *Race* 9:2 [1967]:219).

5. On a visit to Port Maria in 1921, Garvey "recalled the fact that during his boyhood days he laboured in Port Maria" (*Gleaner*, Saturday, 9 April 1921). Alfred Burrowes was apparently operating in partnership with his brother in Port Maria at that time.

6. A reference to *Garvey's Watchman*, about which, however, Garvey's own evidence was contradictory. Unfortunately no copies of this paper, which appeared following the collapse of the printers' strike in 1909, have ever been found; only three issues of the paper were published. In a speech in January 1935, Garvey told his Kingston audience that "when he was eighteen years old he owned and edited a little paper called *Garvey's Watchman*" (*Gleaner*, Tuesday, 22 January 1935). If this statement is correct, the publication date would have been 1905. On the other hand, in testimony given during his mail fraud trial in June 1923, Garvey stated: "I edited a paper in Jamaica, I believe, in 1912, and in the same year I sailed for Europe—England" (*Garvey* v. *United States*, No. 8317 [Ct. App., 2d Cir. Feb. 2, 1925], p. 2327). The newspaper's name showed the influence of the famous *Watchman* newspapers published in Jamaica in the nineteenth century. The first paper, known as *The Watchman and Jamaica Free Press* (also called *The Watchman* or *The Jamaica Watchman*), was published by the leader of the Jamaica free colored community, Edward Jordon (1800–1869), from 1830 to 1836. The second newspaper, known as *The Watchman* and *Kingston Free Press*, was published in 1853 and acquired in 1858–59 by George William Gordon. There was a third paper, *The Watchman and People's Free Press*, for which only a single extant issue (21 January 1864) has been found. (For additional information on the *Watchman*, see W. Adolphe Roberts, "Edward Jordon," in *Six Great Jamaicans: Biographical Sketches* [Kingston: The Pioneer Press, 1951], pp. 3–24; Roberts, "Civil Liberties from Jordon to Love," *Jamaica Historical Society Bulletin* 2 [September 1958]:114–16; Mavis Christine Campbell, *The Dynamics of Change in a Slave Society: A Sociopolitical History of the Free Coloreds of Jamaica, 1800–1865* [Teaneck, N.J.: Fairleigh Dickinson University Press, 1976], chap. 4; Gad J. Heuman, "Robert Osborn: Brown Power Leader in Nineteenth Century Jamaica," *Jamaica Journal* 11 [1977]:76–81; Heuman, *Between Black and White: Race, Politics, and*

the Free Coloreds in Jamaica, 1792–1865 [Westport, Conn.: Greenwood Press, 1981]; and Heuman, letter to editor, 3 November 1981).

7. Garvey lived in Port Limón with the family of his maternal uncle, Henry Richards, and he did engage in some kind of newspaper work while living there. There were two bilingual daily newspapers published in Port Limón at the time; the *Times/El Tiempo*, published between 12 November 1910 and 28 June 1913, and the *Nation*, but no copies of this latter paper have been found. Garvey claimed that he was "the owner and managing editor of a daily paper in Costa Rica by the name of 'La Nacion'" (*NW*, Saturday, 19 June 1920, p. 4). *La Tribuna* (Saturday, 15 April 1921) shortly after also reported: "He [Garvey] spent nine years [*sic*] in Limón and edited a newspaper in English, the Nature [Nation?], in partnership with Mr. Aguilera."

8. According to the account given by Amy Jacques Garvey of Garvey's travels in Central America, his uncle helped him to go to Bocas-del-Toro in Panama, where "(he) worked for some months, then went to Colon and started another paper called *La Prensa*" (*Garvey and Garveyism*, p. 7). Garvey himself claimed that he was the "editor of a tri-weekly paper in Colon [Panama]" (*NW*, Saturday, 19 June 1920, p. 4). No copies of this newspaper have been located. J. Charles Zampty, one of the organizers of the Colon Federal Labor Union, states that he remembers meeting Garvey in Colon during October–November 1912, and that "he was publishing little pamphlets" (Interview with J. Charles Zampty, Detroit, Michigan, 1976). Since Garvey was already in England by that date, it is possible that in reality the year was 1911.

9. Garvey's first wife, Amy Ashwood Garvey, recalled in her unpublished memoir that "he [Garvey] had been engaged to an Englishwoman and contemplated marriage." Upon his return to Jamaica, Garvey was reported to have written to her: "Marriage between us is now impossible. You will be far happier with a member of your race; so will I be with one of mine. I have seen a girl, blood of my blood, and of my own race. Forgive me, but if I marry you now that you know the truth, I shall revert to my own kind every time the opportunity presents itself . . ." (Amy Ashwood Garvey, "Portrait of a Liberator: Biographical Sketch of Marcus Garvey," unpublished MS, n.d., pp. 19–20). This was probably a paraphrase and not a quote from the original letter.

Alfred E. Burrowes on Marcus Garvey

St. Ann's Bay, Ja., B.[W.I. *ca.
April–May 1914*]

I have much pleasure in [te]stifying that Mr. /Marcus/ Garvey has been with me for quite [a] number of years first as an apprentice learning [the] art of printing and subsequently as Manager of [a] Branch /Printing/ Establishment which I opened up in the town of Pt. Maria, Jamaica. I have found him always intelligent, honest and reliable workman. He . . .[*illegible*] for journalism and . . .[*illegible*] [printing newspapers.] and acted as . . .[*words illegible*] also been editing (and /supervising/ the typographical part of the work) papers both in Colon and Republic /Pt. Limon/.

I am confident that with /his very studious disposition and/ the ~~experience~~ knowledge he has gained by travelling that ~~he will~~ there is a bright future in store for him in ~~either of the~~ the field of journalism and I wish him every success.

ALF. E. BURROWS
Printer, Book-binder & Stationer

AEB. AMSS, Draft copy.

Repatriation of Marcus Garvey

[*Colonial Office, London*] 28 May 1914

From Anti-Slavery & Aborigines Prot. Soc.[1] Re Repatriation of M. Garvey. If it is possible to provide fund for—Soc. will be willing to assist by a contribution. He [*Garvey*] is bearer of this letter. Ans. 30 May [*1914*].[2]

PRO, CO 351/21 Misc. 19719/14, Jamaica Register of Correspondence. AN. The original correspondence was destroyed under statute.

1. The Anti-Slavery and Aborigines' Protection Society (ASAPS) was the product of the merger in June 1909 of the two similar but separate humanitarian societies. The British and Foreign Anti-Slavery Society, founded in 1839, was dominated by the Buxton family and had a distinguished history reaching back to the abolitionist campaign of William Wilberforce. Its largely aristocratic membership was led from 1899 by Sir Thomas Fowell Buxton (1837–1915), president, and Travers Buxton, honorary secretary. The Aborigines' Protection Society was founded in 1837 as a product of the early Victorian reform movement. From 1889, Henry Richard Fox Bourne (1837–1909), the descendant of a famous Whig family, headed the society. Bourne grew up in Jamaica, but after a lengthy career in England as a journalist he devoted himself to the representation and protection of native peoples in the colonial territories of the world. Shortly after Bourne's death in January 1909, the membership of the two societies agreed to amalgamate. Both organizations, however, retained their own executives. (H. R. Fox Bourne, *The Claims of Uncivilised Races* [London: Aborigines' Protection Society, 1900]; A. F. Madden, "Changing Attitudes and Widening Responsibilities, 1895–1914," in *The Cambridge History of the British Empire*, vol. 3, *The Empire-Commonwealth, 1870–1919* [Cambridge: Cambridge University Press, 1967], pp. 351–53).
2. This letter of reply has not been found.

Anti-Slavery and Aborigines' Protection Society to Marcus Garvey

[*London*] 29th May, 1914

Dear Sir,

As promised to you yesterday, I enclose a letter[1] for the Colonial Office, which I suggest your taking there at an early opportunity. I also return the papers which you handed to me. Yours faithfully.

[TRAVERS BUXTON][2]

[*Address*] Marcus Garvey, Esq., Argosy
Hotel, 71, Borough High Street, S.E.

RHL, ASAPS, Brit. Emp. s. 19, D/1/14 (256). TL, Carbon copy.

1. A copy of the original, which Garvey delivered in person to the Colonial Office, has not been found in the ASAPS Papers.
2. Travers Buxton (1864–1945) was a lifelong crusader against slavery and colonial misrule. In 1898 he became full-time secretary of the Anti-Slavery Society and initiated a campaign to expose King Leopold II's maladministration and the concomitant atrocities in the Congo Free State. Buxton's agitation received international attention, and in 1908, following Leopold's death, the Leopoldian system was ended. In 1909 Buxton became secretary of the ASAPS as

well as editor of its journal, the *Anti-Slavery Reporter and Aborigines' Friend*. Over the next three decades, Buxton worked for the ASAPS as well as other reform causes. (*WWW*; Wm. Roger Louis and Jean Stengers, eds., *E.D. Morel's History of the Congo Reform Movement* [Oxford: Clarendon Press, 1968]).

Anti-Slavery and Aborigines' Protection Society to the British Colonial Office

[*London*] 8th June, 1914

Mr. Marcus Garvey has applied to the Anti-Slavery and Aborigines Protection Society stating that, having been robbed of a large sum of money, he finds himself destitute in London and unable to return to his home in Jamaica. He desires help to enable him to raise his passage money and pay off a few debts incurred here. From examination of Mr. Garvey's papers I believe his story to be a genuine one, but the Society has no funds for purposes of relief. Understanding, however, that he is willing in part to work his passage back, if sufficient funds can be raised to meet the amount needed, the Committee will subscribe one guinea to help him. If desired, I shall be glad to receive contributions for Mr. Garvey at this office.

RHL, ASAPS, Brit. Emp. s. 19, D/1/14 (291). TN, Carbon copy.

Case of Marcus Garvey

[*Colonial Office, London*] 9 June, 1914

Anti-Slavery & Aborg. Prot. Soc. Case of M. Garvey. He is endeavouring to raise a fund to meet passage money. If CO will contribute the Socy will give an equal amt. Ans. 12 June [*1914*].[1]

PRO, CO 351/21, No. 21181, Jamaica Register of Correspondence. AN. Original correspondence was destroyed under statute.

   1. The letter has not been located.

Record Item

[*Colonial Office, London*] 19 June 1914

Anti-Slavery Soc. Case of Mr. Garvey—He did not think it necessary to fill up form. He [*Garvey*] left for Jam on 17 June, necessary funds having been raised by private charity.

PRO, CO 351/21, No. 22368, Jamaica Register of Correspondence. AN. Original correspondence was destroyed under statute.

Case of Indiana Garvey

[*Colonial Office, London*] 24 June, 1914

Patronage. Garvey, Miss I[ndiana]. Passage to Colony [*Jamaica*], states her circumstances and asks for assist to obtain. Ans copy corres. [COS ?]—26 June [*1914*].[1]

PRO, CO 351/21, No. 22915, Jamaica Register of Correspondence. AN. Original correspondence was destroyed under statute.

1. The Colonial Office's answer has not been found.

Article by Marcus Garvey in the *Tourist*

[London, June 1914]

THE EVOLUTION OF LATTER-DAY SLAVES
JAMAICA, A COUNTRY OF BLACK AND WHITE

Among the little groups of islands scattered in the Caribbean Sea, to the southeast of North America, is the historic and much-talked-of island of Jamaica, known as the "Pearl of the Antilles," one of the oldest colonial possessions of England. It was discovered by the redoubtable and adventurous Christopher Columbus in 1494; and, in common with other West Indian discoveries, was handed over to Ferdinand and Isabella of Spain, who were the patrons of the discoverer's wanderings.

The island remained under Spanish rule for a little more than a century and a half, during which time the aboriginal tribes were completely extinguished.

In 1656, during the Commonwealth of Oliver Cromwell, the island was annexed, and became a colony of England. Since that time it has remained loyal to the Crown.

Sugar, rum and allspice were the chief products of the little island, and at the time when Admiral Rodney[1] defeated the Spaniards and hoisted the English ensign thereon, a brisk and profitable trade had already been established with Europe, and daring adventurers were waxing rich with the bountiful returns of the island exports.

English, Scotch and Irish adventurers were not slow to grasp the great possibilities of exploiting the country, and immediately England took possession a great flow of emigration from the British Isles commenced. Independent gentlemen went out and established themselves as planters, and a goodly number of troublesome English citizens were also shipped away to the country by the Government.

When the new "land lords" arrived they found that the country was very productive, and could yield enormous wealth out of sugar and rum. They therefore set themselves to the practical management of the estates and plantations that were inaugurated by the late Spaniards[.]

The labour force of the country was not equal to the demands of the new planters, so that, to increase the insufficient number of slaves who were already in service, and who were imported by the Spaniards, the English masters turned their attention to Africa, whence they knew they could recruit fresh supplies of negro slaves.

At this time Sir John Hawkins appeared. He negotiated with the reigning sovereign and obtained a Charter which empowered him to take negro slaves from Africa to supply the demand in the West Indies; hence a new start was given to the already established custom of using African negro slaves for developing productive wastes. Thousands of slaves were landed in Jamaica through the agency of Sir John Hawkins, and they were quickly portioned out to different masters, and scattered all over the country. Husbands, wives and chidren were, in the majority of cases, separated from each other, never to meet again, owing to the fact that the estates on which they served were owned by different masters, and were non-communicative and far apart.

There was no doctrine of brotherhood in those days; the slave was but the chattel of his master, and as such he had to work and exist. The slave had no rights to be observed, and he was, therefore, treated as a beast of burden. The task-master's whip was used as the lash of correction, and it echoed minutely day by day—in chastisement and tyranny.

The majority of the imported slaves succumbed to the different abuses to which they were subjected. Only a comparative few were able to withstand for any length of time the harsh treatment meted out to them.

The dancing on the tread-mill, an instrument that clips off the toes when not danced to proper motion, was one of the many observances that kept the negro slave in strict subservience. Very few of them would have courage enough to face the terrors of this death-dealing machine.

For fully a hundred years the slaves were kept as mere labouring animals, and nothing was done to raise them to the higher plane of manhood. But at last the missionaries entered the field in the personal characters of men like Knibb[2] and Knox and with the true spirit of godliness they taught and preached to the enslaved masses, who were anxiously yearning for some hope of salvation.

The doctrines of the missionaries took deep root in the hearts of the suffering people, and they began to realise that they were human like their masters, and claimed affinity with the common God.

The planters did not favour the teachings of the missionaries, and they often opposed their interference with the slaves; but the Christian teachers were determined to liberate the unfortunate creatures both in body and soul.

Broad-minded men in England began to interest themselves in the conditions of the slaves, and they formed themselves into a league to protect and help them.

In 1831 the negro slaves in the western parishes of the island revolted, and did great damage to the properties of their masters. The uprising was crushed by the militia, and a large number of the slaves were executed and maimed. The revolt and its consequences tended to inspire the friends of the slaves to more determined action, and their cause was represented to the British nation in Parliament, thus opening their eyes to the iniquities being carried on under their protection and government.

A great cry was raised against slavery and its horrors, in which a partial section of the Press, headed by THE TOURIST, took the matter up[.] The outcry reached the ears and hearts of all noble-minded Englishmen. Buxton,[3] Clarkson,[4] Wilberforce,[5] Birchell, Knox, and dozens of other zealots, fought the negro's battle, and on August 1st. 1838, the slaves of Jamaica were declared free.

It is just seventy-six years since the Jamaican negro emerged from his shackles, and within this period of time he has accomplished wonders.

The negro who could not decipher his own name in the dark days has become the grandfather of a race of men who are now proclaiming to the world that there is "something" of *capacity* and *action* about them.

In Jamaica the descendants of the old slaves are to be found in all departments of social, intellectual, administrative, commercial and industrial activity. They have become heads of Government departments, Privy Councillors, Attorneys-General, King's Counsel, Companions of Knighthood and controllers of finance.

The population of the country at the present time is 831,383, and is divided as follows:—White, 15,605; black, 630,181; coloured, 163,201; East Indian, 17,380; Chinese, 2,111, and 2,905 whose colour is not stated.

The presence of the East Indian coolies in the island is accounted for by the fact that they were imported from India by the present-day planters—with subsidised assistance from the local Government to take the place of cheap labourers, no longer plentiful in Jamaica.[6]

The negro, having evolved into a state of enlightenment, claims all the concessions and privileges under the constitution of his country, and practically refuses to do manual work except when properly paid.

The standard of wages offered to labourers on the estates and plantations varies from 9d. to 1s. 6d. per day, and for these amounts no Jamaican labourer would move an inch. Hence the importation of indentured coolies who earn the above-mentioned pay.

For the past twenty years the bulk of native labourers have been emigrating to Central America,[7] where they have found employment in laying-out farms and constructing railroads, and subsequently digging and assisting in carrying through the work of the Panama Canal.[8]

The white inhabitants live quite peacefully with their black and coloured fellow citizens; and all men within the State have equal rights.

The laws are framed by the local Legislative Council, of which white, coloured and black men are members, elected by popular suffrage.[9] There is no friction of colour, and the day is yet to come for anyone to hear anything disparaging said about the difference of race among the people. The churches, which are the living voices of the classes as well as the masses, are governed by men of all colour, and they preach the one doctrine of brother-hood and love to their mixed congregations.

Unlike the American negro, the Jamaican lives in an atmosphere of equality and comradeship, hence the outrages that are characteristic of Amer-ica are quite unheard of in the island. White Americans, both Northerners and Southerners, have come to realise that all negroes are not pugnacious and vicious, for when they go over to Jamaica to spend their winter holidays they befriend and associate with the black natives just the same as they do with people of their own race.

Verily, there has been a marked change in the slave of a century ago, and all those who visit the famous tropical pleasure and health resort can testify to the benign influence of English justice, liberality and philanthropy.

Such pleasing results as those presented by the Jamaican negro of to-day cannot fail to satisfy English hearts that it was good that slavery should have been abolished, and peace and equality set up in its place.

The Jamaica of the present time is partly forgetful of the past, and although the 1st of August of each year is observed as "Emancipation Day," very few of the younger generation seem to connect the date with the horrors of the past.

"It's a holiday, and we must get merry," is the only thought that is given to that historic day when their forefathers' shackles fell off and liberty was proclaimed.

Printed in the *Tourist* 19 (June 1914): 61–63. Reprinted in Jamaica in the *Gleaner*, Monday, 13 July 1914, five days after Garvey's arrival from England.

1. George Brydes Rodney (1719–1792) was the naval commander in the Caribbean (1759–1782) who extended the British holdings by capturing the islands of St. Lucia, Grenada, and St. Vincent, as well as the Dutch settlements in the West Indies. (*WBD*).

2. Rev. William Knibb (?–1845), a Baptist missionary, arrived in Jamaica in 1824, where he worked to improve conditions among slaves. However, hostility over the slave rebellion in 1832 led slaveholders to accuse Knibb of inciting the rebellion, and they subsequently destroyed his chapel and mission. He returned to England to lecture for the immediate abolition of slavery.

3. Sir Thomas Fowell Buxton (1786–1845) was a member of Parliament from 1818 to 1837, where he advocated the abolition of slavery in British dominions. (*WBD*).

4. Thomas Clarkson (1760–1846), English abolitionist, led the crusade against the African slave trade. (*WBD*).

5. William Wilberforce (1759–1833) led the agitation in the House of Commons against the slave trade, which was abolished in 1807. In 1823 he was a founder of the Anti-Slavery Society, which urged the abolition of slavery itself. (*WBD*).

6. It is estimated that during the period 1845–1917, a total of 38,681 East Indians arrived in Jamaica, and of this number, 11,959 chose to return to India. (See K. O. Lawrence, *Immigration*

into the West Indies in the Nineteenth Century [Mona, Ja.: Caribbean Universities Press, 1977]; George Roberts, *The Population of Jamaica* [reprint ed., Millwood, N.Y.: KTO, 1979]).

7. In 1911–12, as many as 10,829 Jamaicans migrated to Central America, mainly to Costa Rica and Panama, and approximately 60,000 Jamicans resided or were employed in Central America at that time. As an example of the high rate of Central American emigration in 1911, it was reported that "of the 1,421 persons [who] left Jamaica during the month of January for proclaimed places under the Emigrants Protection Law . . . 621 went to Colon (Panama), 415 to Costa Rica, 70 to Guatemala, 182 to Cuba, and the balance to Hayti, etc." (*Daily News*, Friday, 3 March 1911). In 1927, the Costa Rican census recorded that 19,136 Jamaicans were living in that country. (Roy S. Bryce-Laporte, "West Indian Labor in Central America: Limon, Costa Rica, 1870–1948," Paper presented at the symposium on the Political Economy of the Black World, Center for Afro-American Studies, UCLA, 1978; Michael D. Olier, "The Negro in Costa Rica," Ph.D. diss., University of Oregon, 1967).

8. The Panama Canal was built largely with West Indian labor. American contractors campaigned to attract West Indian labor in 1904 and by 1907 had brought twenty thousand laborers mainly from Jamaica, Trinidad, Barbados, and Martinique. These laborers were subject to discrimination by many Panamanians, white Americans, and the local police. Wages were paid on an unequal basis for similar or identical work. In 1904 there was a general strike of colored workers on the Panama Railroad and this gave the impetus to an attempt to unionize West Indian labor. However, national and language barriers hindered unionization efforts, while employer and police opposition also impeded union growth. With the canal's completion in 1914, many West Indians elected to remain in Panama in their own separate communities. (See L. L. Lewis, "The West Indian in Panama; Black Labor in 1850–1914," Ph.D diss., Tulane University, 1975; Olive Senior, "The Colon People," *Jamaica Journal* 11 [March 1978]: 62–71, Part Two, [September 1978]:87–103).

9. Garvey's assertion concerning the nature of the colonial electoral system in Jamaica was not reflected in the number of registered voters or in the number of votes cast at Legislative Council elections between 1896 and 1920. The following table of election returns shows a different picture:

Year	Registered Voters	Population	% Population Registered	Votes Cast
1896	38,376	694,865	5.5	11,544
1901	16,256	755,730	2.1	2,310
1906	8,607	820,437	1.0	1,628
1911	27,257	831,383	3.2	6,643
1920	42,267	853,123	4.9	3,858

(Sources: *Blue Book of the Government of Jamaica [1896–1920]*; HJ *[1896–1920]*).

The restricted nature of colonial suffrage, which remained more or less constant until 1944 when universal adult suffrage was introduced following the labor disturbances of 1938, was due entirely to the property qualification requirements of electors. (See Robert A. Hill, "Marcus Garvey and the Racial Economy of the Crown Colony State: A Study in Colonial Political Protest," M.Sc. thesis, University of the West Indies, Mona, Ja., 1974, Appendix I).

Arrival of Marcus Garvey in Jamaica

[*Gleaner*, 11 July 1914]

MR. MARCUS GARVEY.

Mr. Marcus Garvey, who left Jamaica last year[1] for the purpose of taking the B.A. degree at the University of London, returned to the island on Thursday [*8 July*], on the S.S. Trent.[2] While in England, Mr. Garvey studied at Berbeck [*Birkbeck*] College and matriculated; and is now in the intermediate stage.

During his stay abroad, Mr. Garvey visited Paris, Madrid, Glasgow and Edinburgh, and met Sir Sydney Olivier,[3] Lord Balfour of Burleigh,[4] and Mr. J. Pointer, M.P.[5]

Printed in the *Gleaner*, Saturday, 11 July 1914.

1. Garvey actually left Jamaica in 1912.

2. Garvey returned to Jamaica as one of only three third-class passengers on the S.S. *Trent*. On the passenger manifest, Garvey listed his occupation as journalist. The S.S. *Trent* left port from Southampton, England, on 17 June 1914; she stopped in Barbados, Trinidad, and Panama before arriving in Jamaica on 7 July 1914.

3. Sir Sydney Haldane Olivier (1859–1943) served as colonial secretary of Jamaica from 1900 to 1904 and in 1907 was appointed captain-general and governor in chief. His most urgent task was to repair the damage to the city of Kingston caused by the earthquake and fire which occurred on 14 January 1907. During the Kingston Streetcar Riot of February 1912, Olivier stopped his car while on a tour of the city in order to rescue policemen who were trapped inside a bar. While standing outside, Olivier was struck on the head with a brick. Some years later, Garvey declared that "he was an eye-witness, and was one of the two men—Mr. Elliot the photographer being the other—who shielded the Governor of the day from attack" (*Gleaner*, Wednesday, 23 January 1935). Sir Sydney Olivier's tenure as governor of Jamaica ended in January 1913 when he was offered the post as secretary of the Board of Agriculture in England. A noted Fabian socialist and authority on colonial questions, Olivier was the author of many works, including *The Myth of Governor Eyre* (London: L. & V. Woolf, 1927); and *Jamaica, the Blessed Island* (London: Faber & Faber, 1936). (*WWW*).

4. Alexander Hugh Bruce (1849–1921), sixth baron Balfour of Burleigh, had visited the West Indies in 1909 as a member of the Royal Commission on Closer Trade Relations between Canada and the West Indies. As a leading figure in the Church of Scotland, he also visited the various Presbyterian stations in the West Indies. (*WWW*).

5. Joseph Pointer (1875–1914) was the Labour party member of Parliament for Sheffield from 1909 to 1911. From October to December 1912, he visited Trinidad and Jamaica as a representative of the Labour committee inquiring into the indentured immigrant labor system and exploring the possibility of representative government for the West Indian colonies. (*WWW*; *Daily Citizen*, 8 November 1912, p. 3).

Postscript by W. G. Hinchcliffe to the *Gleaner*

[[72 Tower Street, Kingston;
July 13, 1914]]

FOR CIVIC HONOURS.[1]

. . . P.S.—Mr. Editor, why did you give space to the latter part of Mr. Marcus Garvey's letter which appeared on the tenth page of your issue of to-day's?[2] Under the caption: "What freedom has done for the Natives of this Island." As a black man like Mr. Garvey, and a struggling Jamaica[n] like himself too, I am of the opinion that he could not in his sane moments have written to the English papers some of what he has written.

W. G. H.[3]

Printed in the *Gleaner*, Tuesday, 14 July 1914.

1. The title of Hinchcliffe's letter was "For Civic Honours" and dealt with the announced candidacy of Rev. T. A. Glasspole in the general election for the Legislative Council.

2. A reference to Garvey's article in the *Tourist* reprinted as "The Progress Made by the People of Jamaica—What Freedom had Done for the Natives of this Island," *Gleaner*, Monday, 13 July 1914.

3. W. G. Hinchcliffe, a carpenter and house-builder, was one of the founders and officials of the early Carpenters', Bricklayers', and Painters' Union (otherwise known as the Artisans' Union) in 1899. He later headed the Jamaica Trades and Labour Union, which was affiliated with the American Federation of Labor. (*Gleaner*, 11 January 1899).

Marcus Garvey to the *Gleaner*

[[34 Charles St., July 15, 1914]]

Sir:—

My attention was called to postcript of Mr. Hinchcliffe's in a letter which he wrote to your paper yesterday, in which he asked you why you gave space to a certain portion of an article which I contributed to an English paper last month whilst in England. I suppose you satisfied yourself in publishing the article in question but as for Mr. Hinchcliffe's inference that I could not have been sane when I wrote the article I can assure him that I have never been off my head for even once. According to his inference he would suggest that he knows me to be insane at times. On the whole I am not surprised at anything certain people in Jamaica say or do: one can be so easily vilified and outraged here.

I have written many articles for the English Press, and I did so because I was paid for them. I did not write for the "Joke of the thing," neither did I sell my conscience. In my writings I was always careful to stand by the people.

The majority of people abroad really think that we have some savages here, as they are not well acquainted with little places like Jamaica, and so much of the dark picture has gone abroad that I did not realize that I was doing wrongly to write favourably of the Jamaican Negro. I suppose I would have pleased Mr. Hinchcliffe highly if I had gone about telling the English world about the darkest side of Jamaica Negro life. I do not think it conducive to the interest of a people to characterize them always from the lowest standard, when there are other standards of comparison that would do good in adding to the status of a people generally thought little of.

Being a Negro myself, and knowing the ignominious place he occupies in the outer world, I could not but have written in the strain which seems to displease Mr. Hinchcliffe. But I am not cognisant that I have said anything unworthy or un[t]rue, so I am not inclined to waste time in profitless controversy. Mr. Hinchcliffe has a lot of time to spend in writing, being an author, poet, etc., I have very little time to spend away from the great problem that confronts me in the word "Afric."[1]

Some day my brother-friend might know that he is not the only one striving to do something to help the fallen African race to which we are both connected . . . and I feel sure that he can well realize that all people engaged with particular ideals do not always "travel" the same way.

I hardly think that I have displeased anyone else other than Mr. Hinchcliffe so I am not going to weep severely this time; I only beg of my brother to pardon me for disturbing his noble spirits, and to think or write no more of

MARCUS GARVEY

Printed in the *Gleaner*, Friday, 17 July 1914. Original headline has been omitted.

1. A possible retort to the assertion made by Hinchcliffe in his letter, "I feel that the Afric's blood is coursing through my veins ready to help . . ."

Charles S. Shirley to the *Gleaner*

[[Lawrence Tavern, July 15, 1914]]

The Editor, Sir,

Kindly permit space in your columns to reply to some things stated by Mr. Marcus Garvey in your issue of July 13th, regarding the condition of the black man in Jamaica. In the latter part of the gentleman's letter, he leaves the impression with folks who don't know anything about conditions in Jamaica, that the black man's bread is buttered, at least on one side. It is impossible to figure out what is anyone's idea of prosperity who thinks that the black man of Jamaica is prospering fairly well. Not only is his bread not buttered on any side, but he hasn't any bread to be buttered.

No fair-minded man who knows the actual condition of the black man in Jamaica—and the brown or colored people too as far as that's concerned—can conscientiously say that the black man's lot in Jamaica is anything desirable. There is actually no comparison between the condition of the black man in Jamaica, and his brother in America. In America he is better off in every respect than he is in Jamaica. Any one who says he isn't either doesn't know or doesn't care to state the facts. The average American Negro is more intelligent, better housed, better clothed, better fed, has greater opportunities for education than his poor unfortunate brother in Jamaica. The writer spent 15 years in the States, four in the South, and 11 in the North, and unqualifiedly makes this statement, that the average American Negro family eats his food at table with silver knives, forks and spoons, a clean table cloth and eats meat at least once a day, has pictures on the wall and a piano in the parlour. His children are not forbidden free education at the age of fourteen, just the age when they are beginning to know what education means. Education is free—from kindergarten to the bachelor's degree. The daily and weekly newspaper in an American Negro family is a necessity; in Jamaica it is so rare that it is a luxury.

The poor, unfortunate Jamaica negro submits to his fate more with the stolidity of the brute than with the resignation of the philosopher. He tries to console himself with the thought that he is a British subject! He never stops to think that that doesn't put any food in his stomach, clothes on his back, money in his pocket, or ambition in his make-up. He really couldn't exactly tell what good being a British subject does for him. He is told that it does some good, and he allows faith to do the rest. He is not like his American brother who has Booker T. Washington[1] and other men of their race who have attained affluence, and influence, and who can plead their cause at the bar of public opinion. Mr. Garvey has heard a whole lot, but he certainly doesn't know very much about the condition of the American negro. The Jamaica negro of to-day presents anything but "pleasing results." During my fifteen years' stay in the States I never saw such poverty-stricken, woe-begone people as I have seen in Jamaica during the four months I have been here, and this compels me to speak out. I am, etc.,

CHAS. S. SHIRLEY[2]

Printed in the *Gleaner*, Saturday, 18 July 1914. Original headline has been omitted.

1. Booker Taliaferro Washington (1856–1915) became unquestionably the most powerful black man of his era in America following his famous Atlanta address in 1895. In 1872, he enrolled at Hampton Normal and Agricultural Institute, where he became the leading scholar in his class, graduating with honors. He taught at various schools, including Hampton, before becoming principal of Tuskegee Institute in Alabama in 1881. Concentrating on the need for industrial education, Tuskegee Institute became the foremost black college in the country under Washington. To maintain his power and influence, Washington also built a political machine to administer federal and state patronage to his followers and to silence some of his opponents. Washington's espousal of the philosophy of improvement attracted white philanthropists and industrialists from the North, and allowed him to attain an unprecedented level of influence with the blacks as well as white elite groups. Eventually, however, this attitude led to the alienation of a growing section of the northern intelligentsia, both black and white, culminating in the formation of the NAACP in 1909. Washington reached the pinnacle of his power in the first few years of the century; by the time of his death in 1915, however, his influence was in decline. (*WBD*; Louis R. Harlan and Raymond W. Smock, eds. *The Booker T. Washington Papers* [Urbana: University of Illinois Press, 1972—]; and Harlan, *Booker T. Washington: The Making of a Black Leader, 1856–1901* [New York: Oxford University Press, 1973]).

2. Rev. Charles Samuel Shirley (1878–ca. 1968), Jamaican-born, attended the Southern Christian Institute, Edwards, Miss., from 1898 to 1902, and Eureka College, Eureka, Ill., from 1902 to 1905. He studied briefly at the University of Chicago before returning to Jamaica in 1914 to enter the ministry. During the next thirty-seven years he served as a minister for several churches. In 1920, Shirley was one of the founders of the Lawrence Tavern People's Co-operative Loan Bank Ltd., serving as secretary-manager until 1966. During his years in the ministry, Shirley was a member of the Jamaica Christian Council and the Kingston Ministers Fraternal; he retired from the ministry in December 1951. (Obituary, n.d., Institute of Jamaica newspaper clipping file).

Marcus Garvey to the *Gleaner*

[[34 Charles Street, Kingston.
July 18, 1914]]

Sir,—

I am very sorry to see that one or two of your readers who read the article you reproduced from "The Tourist" of London, which I contributed to that paper, have gone so far from its meaning and intention.

The two gentlemen who have written criticising the latter part of the article have not said anything in print to show that they have read the article from any other standpoint than narrow prejudice. They are not satisfied with the general condition of the Jamaica Negro, and I can tell them that there is no man any where in this country, or elsewhere, who feels more keenly the depressed state of the coloured people of this country than I do. I love the negro; I have fought many battles for him. I have suffered for him, and it is my life's purpose to continue to suffer for him, in the hope that in the end some good will be achieved in the interest of the struggling race.

Those who know me long enough, know that I am one of those negroes who are not ashamed of the blood Afric, but who think that there is as much nobility and courage about the negro as any other race. I have had the opportunity of studying the "true history" of the negro, and I can tell all those who are ignorant of it that the negro has an ancestry of which he should be proud.

Mr. Shirley is misunderstanding me when he thinks that I am comparing the Jamaican and the American negro on the same platform of industrial or commercial progress. I have already written that the American negro is far in advance of the West Indian negro, commercially and industrially, meaning thereby the Jamaican negro also.[1] I don't know for certain, as I have only spent a short time in America,[2] if the average American negro 'is more advanced educationally, than the Jamaica negro. I know that there is something like 13,000,000 American negroes and 600,000 Jamaican negroes, and I know that America offers good opportunity to its citizens, but I do not know if the average American negro citizen take full advantage of same.

The English press is publishing, of late, tales in big headlines about the negro that tend to show him up as a pugnacious person. If he marries a white woman (a thing he has no right to do) and there is a little family quarrel and the press gets hold of it, it is published broadcast with glittering headlines, which has a moral of its own. If he strikes a white woman he is held up as the example of racial brutality, and so on we go.

Well, the Colonial negro in England is a gentleman either at the Inns of Court or at a University College, and he has a lot to lose and suffer by being classified, as is the wont of the foreign races with the "stage dancing coon" (not meant offensively) who prides himself in going about with two and three white women, and generally ending up his gambles in a fight or brawl.

The misconduct of one negro in England reflects against the others through free publicity, hence I was compelled to write about the difference of characteristics between the two people. God knows how much I hated doing it, but if low class Americans will go over to England and misbehave themselves, it is but fair that Colonial negroes should seek to protect themselves against the strange characteristics of individuals of a particular nationality. I am, etc.,

MARCUS GARVEY

Printed in the *Gleaner*, Monday, 20 July 1914. Original headline has been omitted.

1. A reference to the sentiment Garvey expressed in a pamphlet, which is printed below, that he was either about to publish or had recently published titled *A Talk with Afro-West Indians*. The relevant passage, which occurred on the first page of the pamphlet, declared that "he [the negro] has no status socially, nationally, or commercially (with a modicum of exception in the United States of America)." The date of Garvey's letter, 18 July, and the fact that he had arrived in Jamaica on 8 July, strongly suggest that the draft of the pamphlet had been written either while Garvey was still in England or during his return voyage to Jamaica.

2. Garvey may have stopped briefly at an American port on his way to England in 1912. There is no evidence, however, of such a visit to America during this period of Garvey's life.

[*Gleaner*, 26 August 1914]

WEST INDIAN FEDERATION

Mr. Marcus Garvey, Jnr., writes that he read with great pleasure Dr. Meikle's letter in last Saturday's Gleaner.[1] He is in accord with Dr. Meikle's scheme and he favours general federation, for he thinks it the only way by which the West Indian colonies can get proper representation within the Empire. Mr. Garvey regards Dr. Meikle[2] as a true West Indian patriot, who has given a great deal of time and serious thought to this movement, and he thinks Dr. Meikle must have been moved to take up the idea of federation from observing the disadvantages under which the various West India Islands labour.

During his stay in England, Mr. Garvey was surprised to see the number of colonial representatives there and particularly in London. By means of their representatives the Dominions[3] have succeeded in cornering a large amount of capital and trade. Outside of Crown Agents[4] the little West India Islands have no proper representation in the British Isles, and there is no agency for advertising their natural resources and importance. One could go the whole round of London and he would see nothing to inform him that there are countries in the West Indies by the name of Jamaica, Trinidad, Barbados, etc. Our correspondent realises that little countries like ours cannot afford to advertise and keep up large representative staffs in England independently, but if they were to federate, they could easily establish and support a large commissionary department in the mother country to serve them in the same way as the commissioners serve the bigger colonies.

There are many reasons why we should federate, Mr. Garvey thinks, and those mentioned by Dr. Meikle are only part objects in the great boon of federal realization. Mr. Garvey cannot see his way to agree with Mr. Gideon Murray, who thinks that Jamaica and British Honduras should be left out of such a federation; for if the people of the West Indies are to reach out to a higher destiny they must all move together. Mr. Garvey ap[p]eals to "all critics of sense and reason to lend their support to Dr. Meikle and help to bring about the realization of a united West Indies." With regard to the location of the seat of Government in case of the adoption of such a scheme, Mr. Garvey is of opinion that Trinidad has equal rights with Jamaica in claiming the presence of the chief administrator.

Printed in the *Gleaner*, Wednesday, 16 August 1914.

1. *Gleaner*, 22 August 1914, p. 10. For additional reports on federation, see "A West Indian Commonwealth: The Possibility of Federation," *The Times*, 24 May 1910.

2. Dr. Michael MacFarlane Meikle (?–1931), was born in Manchester and educated at the Collegiate School in Kingston. He was the medical officer for the parish of Manchester from January 1905 until August 1914. He was the brother of Louis S. Meikle. (*HJ*, 1932).

3. Canada, New Zealand, Australia, and South Africa.

4. The crown agents handled commercial and financial business for the colonies but were appointed in Britain by the colonial office and were obliged to obey the secretary of state for the colonies. The crown agents succeeded the older West Indian colonial agents, whose power was progressively reduced and entirely abolished in 1852. (Graham Knox, "Political Change in Jamaica, [1866–1906] and the Local Reaction to the Politics of the Crown Colony Government," in F. M. Andic and T. G. Matthews, eds., *The Caribbean in Transition* [Rio Piedras, Puerto Rico: Institute of Caribbean Studies, University of Puerto Rico, 1965], pp. 141–62; Ronald V. Sires, "The Experience of Jamaica with Modified Crown Colony Government," *Social and Economic Studies* 4 [June 1955]:150–67; and John Manning Ward, "The Crown Colony System . . . The Jamaica Problem: Retrogression of Colonial Self-Government," in *Colonial Self-Government: The British Experience* [Toronto: University of Toronto Press, 1976], pp. 114–23).

ONE GOD! ONE AIM! ONE DESTINY!

JAMAICA DIVISION.

The Universal Negro Improvement and Conservation Association
—AND—
AFRICAN COMMUNITIES LEAGUE.

Cable Address: "AFRICANUS," Jamaica.

MARCUS GARVEY,   T. A. McCORMACK, Secretary General
President and Travelling Commissioner.   ADRIAN DALEY, Associate Secretary.

121 ORANGE STREET & 34 CHARLES STREET,
Kingston, Jamaica, W. I.

........August..27th..............191...4.

Travers Buxton, Esqre.M.A.
    Anti-Slavery and Aborigenies Protection Society
           Denison House
              Vauxhall Bridge Rd.
               London S.W.

Dear Mr. Buxton,

      I now take the opportunity and pleasure of informing you that I have arrived home. I would have written to you before this, but I have been unwell for a little time, and I have been having a rather busy time going about the country, lecturing and meeting onligations, in connection with my position as President and Travelling Commissioner of the above named Society.

      I hereby beg that you convey my best regards to Mr. Harris and the lady Typist, and your Clerk, who were very knid to me during my time there.

      I shall ever remember your kindness and trust to repay same in the immediate future.

      As promised I shall be sending on to you later, after the immediate depression of the War, the monies for distribution to the different gentlemen, which you have promised to do for me.

      I leave Jamaica on a lecturing tour throughout North, South and Central America, as also Canada and the West Indies, in the fall of the present year. I may be away from Jamaica for about six months. We publish a fortnightly journal named "THE NEGRO WORLD", the first appearance will be next week.

      Please and us your journal in exchange for same. With best wishes.

              Yours faithfully,

              Marcus Garvey

Marcus Garvey to Travers Buxton (Source: RHL, ASAPS)

Marcus Garvey to Travers Buxton, Secretary, Anti-Slavery and Aborigines' Protection Society

ONE GOD!   ONE AIM!   ONE DESTINY![1]

JAMAICA DIVISION.

THE UNIVERSAL NEGRO IMPROVEMENT AND CONSERVATION ASSOCIATION

AND

AFRICAN COMMUNITIES LEAGUE.

Cable Address: "AFRICANUS," Jamaica,

MARCUS GARVEY,

President and
Travelling Commissioner.

T. A. MCCORMACK,
Secretary General

ADRIAN DALEY,
Associate Secretary

121 ORANGE STREET & 34 CHARLES STREET,[2]
Kingston, Jamaica, W.I.

August 27th 1914

Dear Mr. Buxton,

I now take the opportunity and pleasure of informing you that I have arrived home. I would have written to you before this, but I have been unwell for a little time, and I have been having a rather busy time going about the country, lecturing and meeting o[b]ligations, in connection with my position as President and Travelling Commissioner of the above named Society.[3]

I hereby beg that you convey my best regards to Mr. Harris[4] and the lady Typist, and your Clerk, who were very k[in]d to me during my time there.

I shall ever remember your kindness and trust to repay same in the immediate future.

As promised I shall be sending on to you later, after the immediate depression of the War, the monies for distribution to the different gentlemen, which you have promised to do for me.

I leave Jamaica on a lecturing t[o]ur thoughout North, Sou[t]h and Central America, as also Canada and the West Indies, in the fall of the present year. I may be away from Jamaica for about six months. We publish a fortnightly journal named "THE NEGRO WORLD", the first appearance will be next week.[5]

Please s[e]nd us your journal[6] in exchange for same. With best wishes. Yours faithfully,

MARCUS GARVEY

[*Address*] Travers Buxton, Esqre. M.A.
Anti-Slavery and Aborigines Protection
Society, Denison Hallouse, Vauxhall
Bridge Rd. London S.W.
[*Endorsement*] rec. Sept 21/14

RHL, ASAPS, Brit. Emp. s. 19D 2/6. TLS, Recipient's copy. Endorsement is handwritten.

1. The UNIA's motto was similar to the phrase, "One God, one law, one element," in Alfred Lord Tennyson's *In Memoriam*. Garvey's appreciation of the English poet is reflected in the fact that a UNIA-sponsored elocution contest offered a volume of Tennyson's poetry as the prize. (*Daily Chronicle*, 27 February 1915). Garvey later gave the following interpretation of the UNIA motto: "Like the great Church of Rome, Negroes the world over MUST PRACTICE ONE FAITH, that of Confidence in themselves, with One God! One Aim! One Destiny!" (*NW*, Saturday, 6 June 1925, p. 1).

2. In an unpublished biography of Amy Ashwood Garvey by Lionel M. Yard, entitled *The First Amy Tells All*, the following disclosure is made:

> After the establishment of the paper organization, Garvey invited Amy to attend a committee meeting. As Amy described the situation, 'He (Garvey) invited me to attend a Committee meeting at his office in Orange Street, Kingston. The address turned out to be a room in a hotel where Garvey lived. I asked him if he lived there although it was quite obvious for there were signs in the little room of his residence, for I saw a cot in a corner of the room. He replied that the address was very central and he sometimes rested there. I informed him that I would not be able to return there to attend any meeting and that my mother was very dubious about the whole affair.['] (p. 21).

According to the author, Garvey found an alternative meeting place on Charles Street. In Amy Ashwood Garvey's unpublished biographical sketch of Garvey, *Portrait of a Liberator*, she cites different circumstances:

> Since my father had made me the family treasurer in his absence, I decided to rent a house at 36 Charles Street, Kingston. Although my mother had consented to the move, half of the house was immediately put at the disposal of [the] UNIA for use as offices and as a meeting place. It was in this new headquarters that Marcus, I, and a few enthusiasts began to elaborate the aims and principles of our Association in a thorough and systematic manner. We were laying the first foundations of what was to grow into a world-wide, mass Negro movement. (p. 67).

There is a discrepancy between the Charles Street address given in this account and the address of "34 Charles Street" listed in the document. At subsequent dates, still other Charles Street addresses appeared on official UNIA stationery: "32 Charles Street," "30 Charles Street," and "30 & 34 Charles Street."

3. The dedicatory service for the new society was originally scheduled for 16 August in the Ward Theatre, but it was postponed and no record has been found of it having been rescheduled (*Daily Chronicle*, 14 August 1914). In a lecture given by Garvey on "the history and growth of the Universal Negro Improvement Association and African Communities' League" which took place near the close of the "Second International Convention of the Negro Peoples of the World," on 29 August 1921, it was reported:

> He [Garvey] said he first conceived the idea of founding the organization in 1914 after traveling through England, Scotland, Ireland, France, Italy, Spain, Austria-Hungary, and Germany. Extensive travels in those countries revealed to him the disabilities under which Negroes lived, politically and otherwise. It occurred to him that, if the Negro must become a recognized factor in world government, the race must solidify itself through the medium of one great organization based on international principles. With this idea in mind he sailed from England in June 1914, arriving in Jamaica on the 15th of July. His plans having been mapped out on board ship, he called the first meeting of the

U.N.I.A. and A.C.L. on the 20th of July, and elected officers. (*NW*, Saturday, 10 September 1921, pp. 5–6).

4. Rev. John H. Harris (1894–1940) served as the ASAPS organizing secretary and later as the ASAPS secretary. He was knighted in 1933 and was the author of several works on African conditions. (*WWW*).

5. This journal was never published in Jamaica, instead it was to become the UNIA's official organ, published weekly in the United States between 1918 and 1933.

6. *The Anti-Slavery Reporter and Aborigines' Friend.*

Pamphlet by Marcus Garvey

[*Kingston, Jamaica, ca. July–August 1914*][1]

A TALK WITH AFRO-WEST INDIANS.
The Negro Race and its Problems.

by Marcus Garvey, Jnr.,
President of The Universal Negro
Improvement and
Conservation Association and African
Communities League.

Dear Friend and Brother:

I am moved to address you through the great spirit of love and the kindred affection that I have for the race Afric; and I am asking you to be good, loyal and racial enough as to take this address in the spirit of goodwill, and lend yourself to the world-wide movement of doing something to promote the intellectual, social, commercial, industrial, and national interest of the down-trodden race of which you are a member.

For the last ten years I have given my time to the study of the condition of the Negro, here, there, and everywhere, and I have come to realize that he is still the object of degradation and pity the world over, in the sense that he has no status socially, nationally, or commercially (with a modicum of exception in the United States of America) hence the entire world is prone to look down on him as an inferior and degraded being, although the people as a whole have done no worse than others to deserve the ignominious snub. The retrograde state of the Negro is characterized as accidental and circumstantial; and the onus of his condition is attributable to the callous indifference and insincerity of those Negroes who have failed to do their duty by the race in promoting a civilized imperialism that would meet with the approval of established ideals.

Representative and educated negroes have made the mistake of drawing and keeping themselves away from the race, thinking that it is degrading and ignominious to identify themselves with the masses of the people who are still ignorant and backward; but who are crying out for true and conscien-

tious leadership, so that they might advance into a higher state of enlightenment whence they could claim the appreciation and honest comradeship of
the more advanced races who are to-day ignoring us simply because we are so
lethargic and serfish.

The prejudices of the educated and positioned Negro towards his own
people has-[*in the margin*: have] done much to create a marked indifference
to the race among those of other races who would have been glad and willing
to help the Negro to a brighter destiny. Yet these very Negro "gentlemen"
who have been shunning their own people do not receive better treatment
from the hands of the other races when they happen to meet away from their
own sphere of influence[.] They are snubbed and laughed at just the same as
the most menial of the race, and only because they are Negroes, belonging to
the careless and characterless race that has been sleeping for so many centuries. In the majority of cases the "aristocratic" Negroes who have refused
to ident[i]fy themselves with the race are thought less of, and they are
secretly "talked" and "gamed" at, by individuals of the progressive races who
are true to themselves, and who do not believe that environments or position
removes one from the tie of blood relationship in race.

In America, Europe, Africa, and Australia the Negro is identified by his
colour and his hair, so it is useless for any pompous man of colour to think
because his skin is a little paler than that of his brother that he is not also a
Negro. Once the African blood courses through the veins you are belong to
"the company of Negroes," and there is no getting away from it.

God places us in the world as men, so whether we are of an identical
species or not, as far as accidental details are concerned, does not matter,
what matters is, that we are all human, and according to the philosophy of
human relationship, all of us have one destiny, hence there should be no
estrangement between the people who form the groups of mortals scattered
in the different parts of the world.

It is true, that by accident and unfavourable circumstances, the Negro
last [*in the margin*: lost] hold of the glorious civilization that he once
dispensed, and in process of time reverted into savagery, and subsequently
became a slave, and even to those whom he once enslaved, yet it does not
follow that the Negro must always remain backward. There is no chance for
the Negro to-day in securing a comfortable place with the PROGRESSIVES of
mankind, as far as racial exclusiveness protects the achievements of the
particular race; but there is a great chance for the Negro to do something for
himself on the same standard of established customs among the ADVANCED;
and the ADVANCED are eagerly waiting to stretch out the hand of compliment
to the Negro as soon as he shall have done the THING to merit recognition.

The Negro is ignored to-day simply because he has kept himself backward; but if he were to try to raise himself to a higher state in the civilized
cosmos, all the other races would be glad to meet him on the plane of
equality and comradeship. It is indeed unfair to demand equality when one
of himself has done nothing to establish the right to equality.

But how can the Negro ever hope to rise when the very men who should have been our props and leaders draw themselves away and try to create an impossible and foolish atmosphere of their own, which is untenable and never recognised.

The appeal I now make is: "For God's sake, you men and women who have been keeping yourselves away from the people of your own African race, cease the ignorance; unite your hands and hearts with the people Afric, and let us reach out to the highest idealism that there is in living, thereby demonstrating to others, not of our race, that we are ambitious, virtuous, noble, and proud of the classification of race.

"Sons and daughters of Africa, I say to you arise, take on the toga of race pride, and throw off the brand of ignominy which has kept you back for so many centuries. Dash asunder the petty prejudices within your own fold; set at defiance the scornful designation of "nigger" uttered even by yourselves, and be a Negro in the light of the Pharaohs of Egypt, Simons of Cyrene,[2] Hannibals of Carthage,[3] L'O[u]ve[r]tures and Dessalines[4] of Hayti, Blydens, Barclays[5] and Johnsons[6] of Liberia, Lewises[7] of Sierra Leone, and Douglas's[8] and Du Bois's[9] of America, who have made, and are making history for the race, though depreciated and in many cases unwritten.

To study the history of the Negro is to go back into a primative civilization that teems with the brightest and best in art and the sciences.

You who do not know anything of your ancestry will do well to read the works of Blyden, one of our historians and chroniclers, who have done so much to retrive the lost prestige of the race, and to undo the selfishness of alien historians and their history which has said so little and painted us so unfairly. Dr. Blyden is such an interesting character to study that I take pleasure in reproducing the following passages from his "Christianity, Islam and the Negro Race":[10]

There was, for a long time, in the christian world considerable difference of opinion as to the portion of the earth and the precise region to which the term Ethiopia must be understood as applying. It is pretty well established now, however, that by Ethiopia is meant the continent of Africa, and by Ethiopians, the great race who inhabit that continent. The etymology of the word points to the most prominent physical characteristics of this people.

To any one who has travelled in Africa, especially in the portion north of the equator, extending from the West Coast to Abyssinia, Nubia and Egypt, and embracing what is known as the Nigritian and Soudanic countries there cannot be the slightest doubt as to the country and people to whom the terms Ethiopia and Ethiopian, as used in the Bible and the classical writers were applied. One of the latest and most accurate authorities says: "The country which the Greeks and the Romans described as Ethiopia and the Hebrews as Cush, lay to the South of Egypt, and embraced, in the most extended sense, the modern Nubia, Senaar, Kordofan, etc., and in its more definate sense, the kingdom of Meroe, [f]rom the junction of the Blue and White branches of the Nile to the border of Egypt.["]

Herodotus the father of history, speaks of two divisions of Ethiopians who did not differ at all from each other in appearance except in their language and hair; "for the Eastern Ethiopians", he says, "are straight haired, but those of Libya [(]or Africa) have hair more curly than that of any other people." "As far as we know," says Mr. Gladstone,[11] "Homer recognized the African Coast by placing the Lotophagi upon it, and the Ethiopians inland, from the east, all the way to the extreme w[e]st." There has been an unbroken line of communication between the West Coast of Africa, through the Soudan, and through the so called Great Desert and Asia, from the time when portions of the descendants of Ham, in remote ages, began their migrations westward, and first saw the Atlantic Ocean.

Africa is no vast island, separated by an immense ocean from other portions of the globe, and cut off throu͜gh the ages from the men who have made and influenced the destiny of mankind. She has been closely connected, both as source and nourisher, with some of the most potent influences which have affected for good the history of the world. The people of Asia and the people of Africa have been in constant intercourse. No violent social or political disruption has ever broken through this communication. No chasm caused by war has suspended intercourse. On the contrary, the greatest religious reforms the world has ever seen—Jewish[,] Christian, Mohammedan—originating in Asia, have obtained consolidation in Africa. And as in the days of Abraham and Moses, of Herodotus and Homer, so to-day, there is a constantly accessible highway from Asia to the heart of the Soudan. Africans are continually going to and fro between the Atlantic Ocean and the Red Sea. I have met in Liberia and along its eastern frontier, Mohammedan Negroes, born in Mecca, the Holy city of Arabia, who thought they were telling of nothing extraordinary when they were detailing the incidents of their journeyings and of those of their friends from the banks of the Niger,—from the neighbourhood of Sierra Leone and Liberia—across the continent of Egypt, Arabia and Jerusalem. I saw in Ca[iro] and Jerusalem, some years ago, West Africans who had come on business, or on religious pilgrimage, from their distant homes in Senegambia.

Africans were not unknown, therefore, to the writers of the Bible. Their peculiarities of complexion and hair were as well known to the Ancient Greeks and Hebrews, as they are to the American people to-day. And when they spoke of the Ethiopians, they meant the ancestors of the black-skinned and woolly-haired people who, for two hundred and fifty years[,] have been known as labourers on the plantations of the South (America). It is to these people, and to their country, that the Psalmist refers, when he says, "Ethiopia shall soon stretch out her hands unto God." The word in the original which has been translated "soon" is now understood to refer not so much to the time as to the "manner" of the action. Ethiopia shall "suddenly" stretch out her hands unto God, is the most recent rendering. But even if we take the phraseology as it has been generally understood, it will not by any one acquainted with the facts, be held to have been altogether unfulfilled.

There is not a tribe on the continent of Africa, in spite of the fetishes and greegees which many of them are supposed to worship—there is not one who does not recognize the Supreme Being, though imperfectly understanding His character—and who does perfectly understand his character? They believe that the heaven and the earth, the sun, moon, and stars, which they behold, were created by an Almighty personal Agent, who is also their own Maker and Sovereign, and they render to him such worship as their untutored intellec[t]s can conceive.[12] ... And if the belief in a common creator and Father of mankind is illustrated in the bearing we maintain towards our neighbour, if our faith is seen in our works, if we prove that we love God, whom we have not seen, by loving our neighbour whom we have seen, by respecting his rights, even though he may not belong to our clan, tribe, or race, then I must say, and it will not be generally disputed that more proofs are furnished among the natives of interior Africa of their belief in the common Fatherhood of a personal God by their hospitable and considerate treatment of foreigners and strangers than are to be seen in many civilized christian community. Mungo Park[13] "a hundred years ago" put on record in poetry and in prose—and he wished it never to be forgotten—that he was the object of the most kindly and sympathetic treatment in the wilds of Africa, among a people he had never seen before and whom he never could requite. The long sojourn of Livingstone[14] in that land in contentment and happiness, without money to pay his way, is another proof of the excellent qualities of the people, and of their practical belief in a universal Father. And, in all history, where is there anything more touching than the ever memorable conveyance, by "faithful ha[n]ds" of the remains of the missionary-traveller from the land of strangers over thousands of miles, to the country of the deceased, to be [d]eposited with deserved honour in the "Great Temple of Silence."

And this peculiarity of Africans is not a thing known only in modern times. The Ancients recognised these qualities, and loved to descant upon them. They seemed to regard the fear and love of God as the peculiar gift of the darker races. In the version of the Chaldean Genesis, as given by George Smith,[15] the following passage occurs[:] ["]The word of the Lord will never fail in the mouth of the dark races whom he has made." Homer and Herodotus have written immortal eulogies of the race. Homer speaks of them as the "blameless Ethiopians" and tells us that it was the Ethiopians alone among mortals whom the Gods selected as a people fit to be lifted to the social level of the Olympian divinities. Every year, the poet says, the whole Celestial Circle left the summits of Olympus and betook themselves for their holidays to Ethiopia, where, in the enjoyment of Ethiopian hospitality, they sojourned twelve days.

> The sire of gods and all the ethereal train
> On the warm limits of the farthest main
> Now mix with mortals, nor disdain to grace

The feasts of Ethiopia's bla[m]eless race;
Twelve days the Powers ind[u]lge the genial rite,
Returning with the twelfth revolving night.

["]Luscian represents a sceptic, or freet[h]inker of his day, as saying, in his irreverence towards the gods, that on certain o[c]casions they do not hear t[h]e prayers of mortals in Europe because they are away across the ocean, perhaps among the Ethiopi[a]ns, with whom they dine frequently on their own invitation.

It shows the estimate in which the Ancients held the Africans, that they selected them as the only fit associates for their gods. And in modern times, in all the countries of their exile, they have [n]ot ceased to commend themselves to those who have held rule over them. The testimonies are numerous and striking to the fidelity of the Africans. The newspapers of the land are constantly bearing testimony to his unswerving faithfulness, not-withstanding the indignities heaped upon him.[16] But there is another quality in the Ethiopian or African, closely con[n]ected with the preceding, which proves that he has stretched out his hands unto God. If service rendered to humanity is service rendered to God, then the Negro [an]d his country have [b]een, during the ages, in spite of untoward influences, tending upward to the Divine.

Take the country,—It has been called the cradle of civilization, and so it is. The germs of all the sciences and of the two great religions now professed by the most enlightened races were fostered in Africa. Science, in its latest wonders, has nothing to show equal to some of the wonderful things even now to be seen in Africa. In Africa stands that marvellous architectural pile—the great Pyramid—which has been the admiration and despair of the world for a hundred generations. Scientific men of the present day, mathe-maticians, astronomers and divines, regard it as a sort of key to the uni-verse—a symbol of the profoundest truths of science, of religion, and of all the past and future history of man. Though apparently closely secluded from all the rest of the world, Africa still lies at the gateway of all the loftiest and noblest traditions of the human race—of India, of Greece, of Rome. She intermingles with all the Divine administrations, and is connected, in one way or another with some of the most famous names and events in the annals of time[.]

The great progenitor of the Hebrew race and the founder of their religion, sought refuge in Africa from the ravages of famine. We read in Gen. XII, 10, "And there was a famine in the land; and Abram went down into Egypt to sojourn there, for the famine was grevious in the land." Jacob and his sons were subsequently saved from extinction in the same way[.] In Africa, the Hebrew people from three score and ten souls multiplied into millions. In Africa Moses, the greatest lawgiver the world has ever seen, was Greece and Rome, to gaze upon its wonders and gather inspiration from its arts and sciences. Later on a greater than Moses and than all the prophets and

born and educated. To this land also resorted the ancient philosophers of philosophers, when in infancy, was preserved from death in Africa. "Arise," was the message conveyed by the Angel to Joseph, "Arise, and take the young child and his mot[h]er and flee into Egypt, and be thou there until I bring thee word; for Herod will seek the young child to destroy him.["] When in his final hours, the Saviour of mankind struggled up the heights of Calvary, under the weight of the cross, accused by Asia and condemned by Europe, Africa furnished the man to relieve him of his burden[.] "And as they led him away they laid hold upon one Simon a Cyrenian, coming out of the country, and on him they laid the cross that he might bear it after Jesus.[17] And all through those times, and times anterior to those, whether in sacred or profane matters Africa is never out of view as a helper. . . ."

The glories of the past should tend to inspire us with courage to create a worthy future. The Negro to-day is handicapped by circumstances; but no one is keeping him back. He is keeping back himself, and because of this, the other races refuse to notice or raise him. Let the Negro start out seriously to help himself and ere the fall of many more decades you will see him a "new man," once more fit for the association of the "gods" and the true companionship of those whose respect he lost.

I am pleading, yea, I am begging, all men and women within the reach of the [b]lood Afric to wake up to the responsibility of race pride and do something to help in promoting a higher state of appreciation within the race. Locally, we are suffering from a marked shade prejudice, among ourselves, which is foolish and distructable. The established truism reigns the world over,—that all people with the African blood in their veins are Negroes. The coloured man who refuses to acknowledge himself a Negro has only to step into the outer world of Europe, Australia, or America, and even South Africa, to find his level and "place" whence he will find it even more advantageous, from a moral point of view, to be a "black nigger." It is so disgusting to hear some foolish people talk sometimes about their s[u]perior[i]ty in shade of colour. The Caucasian is privileged to talk about his colour for there is a standard in his breeding, and all of us have to respect him for his prowess and his might and his mastery, over established ideals. The Negro can attain a like position by self-industry and co-operation, and there is no one more willing to help him to attain that position than the genuine MAN of Europe, the lord of our civilization[,] to-day.

The MAN of Europe is longing to see the Negro do something for himself, hence I am imploring one and all to join hands with those millions across the seas, and particularly those in the Fatherland Africa, America, Brazil, and the West Indies, and speed up the brighter destiny of race in the civilized idealism[18] of the day.

Let us from henceforth recognize one and all of the race as brothers and sisters of one fold. Let us move together for the one common good, so that those who have been our friends and protectors in the past might see the good that there is in us.

N.B.—Mr. Marcus Garvey, Jnr., President and Travelling Commissioner of the Universal Negro Improvement and Conservation Association and African Communities League, will be pleased to communicate or speak with any one d[e]siring to help in the world-wide moveme[n]t for the advancement of the Negro. Mr. Garvey will be leaving Jamaica shortly on a lecturing tour through the West Indies, North, South and Central America, in connection with the movement; but all communications received during his absence will be dealt with by the officers in charge of the local division, 121, Orange Street and 34, Charles Street, Kingston, Jamaica.

SOME OF OUR OBJECTS

To Establish a Universal Confraternity among the Race,

To Promote the Spirit of Race Pride and Love.

To Reclaim th[e] Fallen of the Race.

To Administer to, and help the Needy.

To Assist in Civilizing the Backward tribes of Africa.

To Strengthen the Imperialism of Bas[u]toland, Liberia, etc.

To Establish [C]ommissionaries in the Principal Countries of the World, for the Protection of all Negroes, Irrespective of Nationality.

To Promote a Conscientious Christian Worship among the Native Tribes of Africa.

To Establish Universities, Colleges and Secondary Schools for the Further Education and Culture of our Boys and Girls.

Etc.,   Etc.,   Etc.

Donations, bequests or any voluntary help thankf[u]lly received and acknowledge[d] so as to help in carrying out the objects of the League. All Negroes are invited to membership which is [n]on-restrictive, free, a[n]d open to adults and children of the race. Communications should be addressed to the General Secretary The Universal Negro Improvement and Conservation Association and African Communities League, 121, Orange Street and 34, Charles Street, Kingston, Jamaica, W.I.

Our Motto:
One God, One Aim, One Destiny.
LOOK OUT
——FOR——
The Appearance of
THE NEGRO WORLD,
The Official Organ of The African
Communities League,
Edited by MARCUS GARVEY.

DLC, BTW. Printed and published by the African Communities League, n.d. Manuscript corrections in Garvey's hand.

1. It has not been possible to establish the exact date in 1914 of the pamphlet's publication.

2. Simon of Cyrene helped Jesus bear the cross (Luke 23:26); Cyrene was an ancient city situated in modern-day Libya. (*WBD*).

3. Hannibal (247–183 B.C.) was the Carthaginian general who engineered a brilliant attack against the Romans by crossing the Alps into Italy. (*WBD*).

4. Jacques Dessalines (ca. 1760–1806) was a former slave who served as Toussaint L'Ouverture's first lieutenant in the slave uprising of St. Domingo. Dessalines carried through the Haitian War of Independence, and was proclaimed the emperor of Haiti on 8 October 1804, but he was later shot and killed during an insurrection led by Henri Christophe. (*WBD*).

5. Arthur Barclay (1854–1938), a Barbadian immigrant to Liberia, was president of Liberia, serving from 1904 to 1912. (Mark R. Lipschutz and R. Kent Rasmussen, *Dictionary of African Historical Biography* [Chicago: Aldine Publishing, 1978]).

6. This may have been a reference to Elijah Johnson, an early Liberian pioneer, or to his son, Hilary R. W. Johnson, the first native-born president of Liberia (1884–1892). (See Tom W. Shick, *Behold the Promised Land: A History of Afro-American Settler Society in Nineteenth-Century Liberia* [Baltimore: Johns Hopkins University Press, 1977]).

7. Sir Samuel Lewis (1843–1903), a barrister and member of the Sierra Leone Legislative Council for more than twenty-nine years, was also a leading figure of the Krio community at the height of its influence. Lewis was instrumental in the establishment of the Freetown Municipal Council and in 1895 became Freetown's first mayor. In 1896 he was knighted—the first African to be so honored. A friend of Edward Wilmot Blyden, Lewis wrote the preface in 1886 for Blyden's *Christianity, Islam, and the Negro Race*. (*Dictionary of African Biography*, vol. 2, [Algonac, Mich.: Reference Publications, 1977]).

8. Frederick Douglass (ca. 1817–1895) was born a slave in Tuckahoe, Md. He escaped from slavery in 1838 and settled in New Bedford, Mass. He became active in antislavery circles and in 1845 published his autobiography, *Narrative on the Life of Frederick Douglass*. A lecturer and editor of the *North Star*, after the Civil War Douglass served in various government positions, including minister to Haiti (1889–91). (*WBD*; John Blassingame, ed., *The Frederick Douglass Papers*, vol. 1 [New Haven: Yale University Press, 1979]).

9. William Edward Burghardt Du Bois (1868–1963) was the leading figure in the black protest movement in the United States before the First World War. Born in Great Barrington, Mass., Du Bois was educated at Fisk College, Nashville, Harvard University, and the University of Berlin. At the time that Garvey's pamphlet was published, Du Bois had already made a significant contribution to the historiography of blacks in *The Suppression of the African Slave Trade*, written in 1897, and had pioneered in the study of the sociology of blacks in *The Philadelphia Negro* and the Atlanta University studies. Du Bois's early interest in the international status of blacks was reflected in his attendance at the First Pan-African Conference in London in 1900. In 1911, he spoke before the International Races Conference in London, outlining the conditions black Americans faced, and in 1919 he revived the Pan-African movement by organizing a meeting in Paris during the peace conference at the end of World War I. He also served as the principal architect of the Pan-African Congresses of 1921, 1923, and 1925, as well as chairman of the 1945 congress. (Herbert Aptheker, ed., *The Correspondence of W. E. B. Du Bois* [Amherst: University of Massachusetts Press, 1978]; Philip Foner, ed., *W.E.B. Du Bois Speaks*, vol. 1, 1890–1919; vol. 2, 1920–1963 [New York: Pathfinder Press, 1970]; and Arnold Rampersad, *The Art and Imagination of W. E. B. Du Bois* [Cambridge: Harvard University Press, 1976]).

10. Edward Wilmot Blyden, *Christianity, Islam, and the Negro Race* (London: W. B. Whittingham, 1887; 2nd ed., 1888), pp. 130–49. The passage which Garvey quoted was from the chapter, "Ethiopia stretching out her hands unto God: or, Africa's Service to the World (Discourse delivered before the American Colonization Society, May 1880)." Blyden's book, a collection of speeches, articles, and reviews, did much to establish his scholarly reputation. The essays dealt with the influence of Christianity and Islam on Africans, the achievements of the black race, and the role of blacks in Africa's past and future. Blyden articulated the thesis that Islam, with its lack of color distinctions, had beneficial effects for blacks, whereas he attacked the treatment of blacks within Christianity, especially Protestantism. Another major theme of Blyden's book concerned his belief that blacks could never be free except in Africa, and he urged Western blacks to emigrate.

11. William Ewart Gladstone (1809–1898) served as the Liberal prime minister of England (1868–74, 1880–85, 1886, 1892–94). (*WBD*).

12. The remainder of the paragraph in the Blyden original was omitted (see p. 132).

13. Mungo Park (1771–1806), the Scottish explorer of Africa, was the author of *Travels in the Interior of Africa* (London, 1799). (*WBD*).

14. David Livingstone (1813–1873), Scottish missionary and explorer, organized many African expeditions, discovering Lake Ngami (1849), the Zambesi River (1851), and Victoria Falls (1855). After he became lost on a trip to find the source of the Nile River, he was rescued by Henry M. Stanley in 1871. (*WBD*).

15. George Smith (1840–1876) was an English antiquarian who deciphered the Chaldean account of the flood from the cuneiform tablets discovered during Sir Austin H. Layard's excavations of ancient Nineveh. (*WBD*).

16. Paragraph ending in Blyden original.

17. Paragraph ending in Blyden original.

18. The phrase "civilized idealism" expressed Garvey's concept wherein each race existed on the basis of its own separate civilization. Garvey spelled this out while addressing the eighth UNIA convention in Toronto, Canada, in August 1938:

> . . . each group must find a sphere from which to operate[,] a sphere that is specifically different from the other group, so that th[e] group may be able to maintain itself in the future as it has maintained itself in the past. Each group must find its place in the world of humanity and must arrange to so effectively maintain itself, irrespective of what the other groups of humanity may say and may do.
>
> Unfortunately, the Negro within recent years of the history of man . . . has completely lost his idealism in this respect. The idealism of maintaining and securing himself always as a separate the distinct unity of general humanity. (Marcus Garvey, "The Purpose of Man's Creation: The Negro's Fullest Part," *BM* 3 [November 1938], p. 15).

Pamphlet by Marcus Garvey

[*Kingston, Jamaica, ca. July–August 1914*]

THE DESTINY OF THE NEGRO.

By MARCUS GARVEY, JNR.

President of The Universal Negro Improvement and
Conservation Association and African Communities
Imperial League.

The destiny of the Negro is a thought-compelling problem that is occupying the minds of the world. Great men and women of all nations have given their views on the Negro question, and there is an abundance of pessimism and optimism in the recorded opinions of these wise thinkers.

Some people think that the Negro will never be better than he is, because he is too serfish, self-content, childish and spiteful to himself[.] Others think that by educating him to the dignity of race pride, and pointing out to him that, by education and industry, he can raise himself to the level of the superior races, the problem of his insignificance shall be solved, and the era of a better man ushered in.

Whatsoever might be said about the Negro, there is one truth that we, as a people, have to admit, and that is "We do not love one another." And until we grow to appreciate the fact that "blood is thicker than water," we shall ever be the outcast and refuse of human society—a people worthy of no good, but a degraded lot fit only as "hewers of wood and drawers of water."

Now, I am speaking to you as fellow Negroes, and as one who loves you in all s[i]ncerity and who is prepared to go to the front to fight your educational, industrial and social battles. I want you from henceforth to meet your brother and your sister with the smile of friendship, and stretch out the hand of fellowship to every member of the race, thereby sinking that foolish pride, hatred and grudge which you have held against each other for so long a period. Please look around and take a leaf out of the book of EXAMPLES set before you by our friends and benefactors—our brothers of Salvation. Some of you are stupid enough to think that you are unfairly dealt with by the other people of this community. Now, let me tell you right here, that you are entirely wrong. You have consistently been unfair to yourselves, because you hate and despise yourselves.

No one in the wide world is handicapping the Negro, the sleeping Negro has handicapped and is still handicapping himself and not until he realizes the danger of this self-inflicted burden shall he find the way to the post that marks the path to success[.] I have asserted that you are your own handicappers in the race of life—you supply and strengthen the source of "drawback[.]" If you think this assertion misleading, I am asking you to enquire of yourselves individually[:] "Have I ever begrudged, d[e]spised, slander, treat unkindly or spoken ill of my brother, simply because he is of my own race?" And I know well the answer shall be in the affirmative.

Dear brother and sister let us throw off that slavishness of the past, join hands and hearts together and march forward to the new era of progress[.] "God helps those who help themselves[,]" hence if we want the help for success we must first help ourselves. You know well our position as a people, it is quite unfavourable. Others who are not of our fold have helped us in the past, and they are still helping us: do, let us try too, even now, and help ourselves,

  ....Be thine
To bring man nearer man,
And with all worthy works combine
In one far reaching plan.

N[.]B[.]—The Universal Negro Improvement and Conservation Association and African Communities Imperial League has a world scope, and it aims at unifying the people of the African race all over the world. It recognizes the brotherhood of man, and it is our desire to clasp hand with all men of every nation, race and tribe, in the perfected state of a developed manhood. Our motto is—One God! one aim! one destiny! Some of our objects are: To establish a universal confraternity among the race; to promote the spirit of race pride and love; to reclaim the fallen of the Race; to administer to, and help the needy; to assist in civilizing the backward tribes of Africa; to establish Commissionaries in the principal countries of the world for the protection and representation of all Negroes, irrespective of nationality; to strengthen the imperialism of Liberia, Basutoland, etc; to establish a conscientious Christian worship among the tribes of Africa, the fatherland; to establish and support universities[,] colleges, and secondary schools for the further education and culture of our boys and girls, etc. etc.

We want every man[,] woman and child who claims the designation of "Negro" to join the universal confraternity. There is no fee. Send in your name and address and we shall send you a card of membership. If you are far away you can send a penny stamp for postage[.]

We distribute thousands of educational literature every week, so those who can afford to give a donation to help in the propagation and other work, in enabling us to reach the millions yet outside the fold, can please enclose and send same to us, which donation shall be acknowledged in the columns of "The Negro World" the fortnightly official organ of the League. All within the blood Afric, men[,] wom[e]n and children are requested to address or call on Mr. Marcus Garvey, Jnr. President and Traveling Commissioner[,] The Universal Negro Improvement and Conservation Association and African Communities Imperial League or to the General or Associate Secretaries, 121 Orange Street, and 34 Charles Street, Kingston, Jamaica, B.W.I.

A copy of the pamphlet "The Negro Race and its problems" by Marcus Garvey, Jnr. will be posted on application, price 2d; but if you can't afford the 2d, send or call and you will be supplied with a copy free of cost. To read it, is to get a deep insight into the history of the Negro. Good wishes for success—Au revoir.

Read and Subscribe to "The Negro World" 2d, per copy, 4/- per year. If you are too poor to purchase a copy or subscribe for the year, write or call on us and let us arrange to send you a free copy. We do not want your money, we want you to help yourself, and be one of the loyal brotherhood in the circle of world-wide Ethiopia.

DLC, BTW. Printed and published by The African Communities Imperial League, n.d. At the beginning of the pamphlet was printed the following: "Educational Series—Impression 250,000. Suppl[e]ment to 'The Negro World.' "

Marcus Garvey to Booker T. Washington

Kingston, Jamaica, W.I.
September 8 1914

Dear Sir & Brother

I have been informed by our Commissioner in London that you are expected to be in Europe during the month of April and /or/ May of next year, and that you shall be engaged addressing Meetings in London and other cities of the British Isles on the subject of "The progress of the Negro.["]¹ Please be good enough to inform me if this is correct.

I have been keeping in touch with your good work in America, and although there is a difference of opinion on the lines on which the Negro should develop himself, yet the fair minded critic cannot fail in admiring your noble efforts. The two schools of America² have gone as far as to give us, who are ~~article~~ /outside/ the ~~dread~~ /real/ possibility/ies/ of the industrial and intellectual scope for Negro energy. We are organized out here on broad ~~lives~~ /lines/ and we find it condu[c]ive to our interest to pave our way both industrially and intellectually.

The prejudice in these countries is far different from that of America. Here we have to face the prejudice of the hypocritical whitemen [(]who nevertheless are our friends) as also to /fight/ down the prejudice of our race in /shade/ colour.

Our organization is marching steadily on and we hope to extend [*in the margin*: our] ~~sphere~~ /scope/ all over the world within the next few years. I have just returned from a tour in Europe where I spent two years studying the Negro's place there. I am also hoping to be in England about March next year after paying a visit to the U.S.A. I intend lecturing in a few of the European cities on the condition of the West Indian Negro.

I enclose you a Circular Appeal which I feel sure will interest you, and I am asking that you be good enough as to help us with a small ~~danation~~ /donation/ to carry out our work.

We publish for the first time next week our paper "THE NEGRO WORLD" a copy of which we shall send you regularly. If you publish any journals in connection with Tuskegee³ please be good enough to send us same in Exchange.

Wishing you well and praying for the salvation of World Wide Ethiopia. Yours in the bonds of Fellowship

MARCUS GARVEY
President and Travelling
Commissioner

DLC, BTW. TLS, Recipient's copy. Corrections in Garvey's hand.

1. In July 1914, the Anti-Slavery and Aborigines' Protection Society of London announced Washington's scheduled visit to Europe, which was to begin the following March. During the months of March–May, Washington was to speak in several cities in England, as well as Brussels, Berlin, and Paris. (*African Mail*, 17 July 1914, p. 423).

2. A reference to the rival Afro-American schools of thought regarding education and social philosophy, as typified on the one hand by Booker T. Washington's program of industrial education and self-improvement and on the other hand by W. E. B. Du Bois's advocacy of liberal humanistic education for the training of the "Talented Tenth."

3. The official publications of Tuskegee Institute were the *Tuskegee Student*, which appeared every alternate Saturday under the editorship of Albon L. Holsey, and the *Negro Year Book* (1912–1952), an annual encyclopedia, under the editorship of Monroe N. Work (1866–1945), director of Tuskegee's Department of Records and Research. One of the principal features of the *Tuskegee Student* was the reprinting of Booker T. Washington's Sunday-evening talks.

Enclosure

Kingston, Jamaica, W.I.
Sept 8 1914

DEAR SIR & BROTHER:

Having organised ourselves into a Society for the purpose of helping the struggling masses of this community to a higher state of industry and self-appreciation, we take the opportunity of acquainting you of our aims, and we hereby beg to solicit your assistance in helping us to carry out our most laudable work.

As you are aware the people of this [c]ommunity have had seventy-six years of unfettered liberty, during which period of time they have made all possible progress; but at our best we are still backward, and fall short of that appreciative standard which is expected of us by the more progressive races.

Throughout the country we have abundance of evidence of the backwardness of our people, hence we have determined to do our best to raise them by education and industry, to a higher status among the civilized peoples of the world. With the assistance of our friends and supporters from abroad, we intend, at no distant date to erect several colleges, (educational and industrial) at different centres in the island for the purpose of supplying free secondary and industrial education to our boys and girls.[1] We are having travelling lecturers to visit the various centres of the Island, lecturing to the people on "Self-Industry" and "Self-appreciation."

The following are a few of our objects for which we ask your support:—

To establish educational and industrial colleges for the further education of our boys and girls.

To reclaim the fallen and degraded (especially the criminal class) and help them to a state of good citizenship.

To administer to and assist the needy.

To promote a universal confrate[r]nity and strengthen the bonds of brotherhood and unity among the races.

We, therefore, beg to solicit a small donation in helping us to carry out this work, and knowing your deep interest in the country and its struggling people makes us feel sure of your kind help.

With best wishes for success, and trusting you will be one of those to lay the foundation of a brighter future, Yours faithfully

MARCUS GARVEY
President and Travelling
Commissioner

[*Address*] Dr. Booker T. Washington
Tuskegee

DLC, BTW. L, printed on official UNIA stationery, with the date and inside address handwritten by Garvey.

1. Garvey's plan to set up an industrial school in Jamaica was not novel. Some two years earlier, at the International Conference on the Negro held at Tuskegee Institute during 17–19 April 1912, the West Indian students and faculty of Tuskegee presented a series of resolutions to the visiting Jamaican delegates headed by the island's director of education. In the resolutions, they asked "that the delegates use their influence to secure for the West Indies a school like Tuskegee Institute, where the masses of the people will have an opportunity to learn trades. They also urged upon them to invite Dr. Booker T. Washington to visit Jamaica, and other West Indian islands, and give the coloured people there the benefit of his advice and counsel." (*African Times and Orient Review* [July 1912]).

Newspaper Reports

[*Gleaner*, 14 September 1914]

A New Society.

At their meeting in the Collegiate Hall to-morrow evening at 7.30 o'clock, the Universal Negro Improvement Association will pass a patriotic resolution expressive of their sympathy with the English people at home during this their time of trouble and anxiety. The resolution will be forwarded to Mr. E. Robbins of the English Press Association,[1] for distribution among the Press. Copies of the resolution will also be sent to members of Parliament who are patrons and supporters of the Society, as also to the Society's representatives in England.

The debate for the evening will be: "Has politics greater influence on the world than religion?" Mr. Marcus Garvey, supported by Mr. S. Trott, will speak for the affirmative; whilst Mr. Adrian Daily,[2] supported by Mr. T. A. McCormack,[3] will speak for the negative. Visitors will be allowed to take part in the debate. A debate takes place once weekly. The object of the Association is to improve the elocutionary and literary tastes of the youth of our community. One evening is set apart for lectures, and the other evenings of the week for classes and social and charitable work. The subjects to be taught at the evening classes include Latin and Roman History, English, French, Spanish, English History, Geography, Logic, Mathematics, Lectures in Chemistry, Botany and Agriculture; as also subjects for general accomplishments.

Several University graduates have consented to take the classes so as to assist those of the people who desire to assist themselves. A cordial invitation is extended to ladies and gentlemen interested.

Printed in the *Gleaner*, Monday, 14 September 1914.

1. Sir Edmund Robbins, KBE (1847–1922) served as a journalist for the *Launceston Weekly News* (1858–65), leaving to join the Central Press Agency. On the formation of the Press Association in 1870, he was appointed subeditor; by 1880 he was appointed manager and served in that position until 1917. (*WWW*).
2. UNIA associate secretary.
3. UNIA secretary general.

[*Gleaner*, 17 September 1914]

RESOLUTION ADOPTED BY NEGRO IMPROVEMENT ASSOCIATION AT TUESDAY'S MEETING EXPRESSIONS OF LOYALTY TO SOVEREIGN AND SYMPATHY FOR PEOPLE OF BRITAIN AND FRANCE

The Universal Negro Improvement Association held a general meeting at the Collegiate Hall on Tuesday night last, [*15 September*] when there was a large and representative gathering.

Mr. Marcus Garvey, Jnr., President and Travelling Commissioner of the association, delivered an interesting address, urging the co-operation of one and all for the general improvement and widening of human fellowship. In part, he said that the true lesson that must be taught is that which expresses the brotherhood of man and the general relationship we bear to one another in the plan of God.

After the address, a debate took place, the subject of which was: "Have politics a greater influence on the world than Religion?" Mr. Garvey spoke for the affirmative, and Mr Adrian Daily, Mr. T. A. McCormack and Mr. W. T. Knight, for the negative. The debate was warm and interesting, and when the vote was taken, the affirmative won with a two to one majority.

Two resolutions were passed by the meeting, copies of which are to be sent to His Excellency the Governor,[1] Mr. E. Robbins of the London Press Association, Lord Balfour of Burleigh, Sir Sydney Olivier, Members of Parliament, who are patrons and supporters of the Society, as also the Editor of *Le Matin, Le Journal, The African Times*, and the Society's representatives in London.

The resolutions follow:

Resolution (1)—"Be it resolved that we the members of the Universal Negro Improvement and Conservation Association and African Communities League, assembled in general meeting at Kingston, Jamaica, B.W.I., being mindful of the great protecting influence of the English nation and people, and their justice to all men, and especially to their negro subjects scattered all over the world, hereby beg to express our loyalty and devotion to His Majesty the King[2] and Empire, and our sympathy with those of the people who are grieved and in difficulty in this their time of trouble and anxiety. We further hope for the success of British arms on the battlefield of Europe, and at sea, in crushing the common foe of Europe and the enemy of peace and further civilization. We rejoice in British victories and the suppression of foreign foes. Thrice we hail: "God save the King! Long live the British Empire."

[Resolution (2) "Be it resolved that we the members of the Universal Negro Improvement and Conservation Association and African Communities League, assembled in general meeting at Kingston, Jamaica, B.W.I., hereby beg to express our sympathy with the President of France[3] and the French people in this their time of trial. We pray for the defeat of the common foe of Europe and the enemy of peace and further civilization. May continuous victory follow the French army against the foe, and France once more resume her peaceful and civilizing influence on the world."][4]

Printed in the *Gleaner*, Thursday, 17 September 1914.

1. Brigadier-General Sir William Henry Manning, KCMG, KBE, (1863–1932), succeeded Sir Sydney Olivier as governor of Jamaica in January 1913. (*HJ*, 1933–1934).
2. George V (1865–1936) was the king of England from 1910 to 1936. (*WBD*).
3. Raymond Poincaré (1860–1934) was elected president of France in 1913; he stepped down from the presidency in 1920 to return to the senate. (*WBD*).
4. The published *Gleaner* report omitted the second resolution but it was reported in the *Daily Chronicle*, Thursday, 17 September 1914. The square brackets in which the second resolution has been placed in the text indicate that it was excerpted from the latter source.

Booker T. Washington to Marcus Garvey

[*Tuskegee Institute, Alabama*]
September 17, 1914

My dear Sir:

I have your very kind favor of some days ago.

I have given up altogether my plans for the European trip which I had planned for next March. Matters are in such unsettled condition in that country that I fear I could not accomplish what I hope to do. I shall keep the matter in mind and hope to be able to make the trip at some other time.

I have read what you say with reference to the advance being made in educational facilities for the Negroes of that section. I hope that when you come to America you will come to Tuskegee and see for yourself what we are striving to do for the colored young men and women of the South.

I thank you for the printed matter which you sent. I shall give it a careful reading at the earliest convenience. I regret, however, that I am not able now to make a contribution toward your work.

We shall be very glad to receive copies of The Negro World, and shall be glad to send you in exchange The Tuskegee Student, published at this Institution. Yours very truly,

BOOKER T. WASHINGTON
PRINCIPAL

F

DLC, BTW. TL, Carbon copy.

Sir William Henry Manning,
Governor of Jamaica, to Marcus Garvey

Kings House Jamaica.
19th September, 1914

Sir,

I have the honour to acknowledge the receipt of your letter of the 16th Instant[1] enclosing a Resolution from your Association to be forwarded to His Majesty's Secretary of State for the Colonies,[2] concerning which you will receive a further communication.

I have to thank you for your expressions and offers of readiness to serve in any way, which I much appreciate. I have the honour to be, Sir, Your obedient servant,

W. H. MANNING
GOVERNOR

TNF, AJG. TLS, Recipient's copy.

1. This letter has not been found.
2. Viscount Lewis Harcourt (1863–1922) was secretary of state for the colonies from 1910–1916 after a long career as a free-trade Liberal (*WWW*).

Marcus Garvey to Travers Buxton

Kingston, Jamaica, W.I.
September 19th 1914

[Dear S]ir:—

I have the honour to forward you the enclosed resolu[tion][1] [w]hich was passed at a General Meeting of our Society, [assemb]led at Kingston, Jamaica, on the 15th September, 1914.

This resolution is a genuine expression of our feelings [towar]d His Majesty and people, and I hereby beg that you [accep]t same as a token of our esteem for you and yours. Believe me Sir To be Your Humble Servant

MARCUS GARVEY
PRESIDENT & TRAVELLING
COMMISSIONER

RHL, ASAPS, Brit. Emp. s. 19, D/6. TLS, Recipient's copy. Corrections in Garvey's hand.

1. The resolution was contained in the press clipping taken from the *Gleaner*, Thursday, 17 September 1914.

Travers Buxton to Marcus Garvey

[*London*] 23rd September, 1914

Dear Mr. Garvey,

I was glad to have your letter of the 27th ultimo last week. We shall be pleased to send you our quarterly journal in exchange for *The Negro World*, which you kindly speak of sending me. I am very glad to know that you reached home safely and that you are busy in connection with the Universal Negro Improvement Association. I hope your six months' lecturing tour will be a useful and satisfactory one.

Mr. Harris joins me in good wishes, Yours faithfully,

[TRAVERS BUXTON]

RHL, ASAPS, Brit. Emp. s. 19, D/1/14 (698). TL, Carbon copy.

Newspaper Reports

[*Gleaner*, 25 September 1914]

SOCIETY MEETS.

The Universal Negro Improvement Association held their general weekly meeting in the Collegiate Hall, on Tuesday evening last [*22 September*], at which a letter was read from His Excellency, the Governor, acknowledging the receipt of a resolution forwarded to him by the President of the Association for transmission to the Right Hon. Lewis Harcourt, the Secretary of State for the Colonies. His Excellency expressed his appreciation of the Society's willingness to help in any way in meeting the local situation, created by the war.

The Rev. Alfonso Dumar[1] was the guest of the evening, and he delivered an eloquent and interesting address which was greatly appreciated by the large and enthusiastic audience. Mr. George McCormack, Miss As[h]wood[2] and Mr. Marcus Garvey also contributed to the evening's programme, which was brought to a close by the singing of the National Anthem. Next Wednesday evening [*30 September*] at 7.30, the Association holds a debate, the subject of which is: "The Press or the Platform, which has the greater influence." An address will also be delivered by a prominent citizen.

Printed in the *Gleaner*, 25 September 1914.

1. Rev. Alfonso Dumar (1862–?) was the founder and incorporator of the African Methodist Episcopal Church in Jamaica. He was born in America and educated at Wilberforce University, Wilberforce, Ohio. Dumar later spoke at a UNIA meeting in New York in June 1924, saying:

Twelve years ago it was his good fortune to sail to Jamaica from the United States of America, and the second public meeting he addressed in the Island of Jamaica was a meeting at which the Hon. Marcus Garvey was presiding, a meeting of the Universal Negro Improvement Association. . . . He remembered visiting the office of Mr. Garvey on Charles Street in the city of Kingston and intimating to him that his scheme was a mammoth one, one that Jamaica was too small to put over, and that if he went to the United States he would find himself inside of ten years at the head of the greatest Negro movement ever inaugurated in the world. (*NW*, Saturday, 14 June 1924).

2. Amy Ashwood (1897–1969) was born at Port Antonio, parish of Portland, on 10 January 1897, the third child of Michael and Maudraine Ashwood. Her father was economically secure and owned a bakery in Port Antonio; subsequently he immigrated to Panama with his family, including his two sons, Michael and Claudius. He ran a food-catering service and restaurant in Panama City for several years, but he moved his business to Santa Marta, Colombia, shortly after completion of the construction of the Panama Canal in 1914. When she was about eleven years, Amy Ashwood returned to Jamaica with her mother and enrolled as a boarding student at the Westwood High School for Girls at Stewart Town, Trelawny. She remained in Jamaica after leaving Westwood High School, and in July 1914, at a debate sponsored by the East Queen Street Baptist Literary and Debating Society, where she was an active member, she met Marcus Garvey for the first time. As one of the founding members of the UNIA, she played a principal role in helping to organize UNIA fund-raising activities and the women's auxiliary of the UNIA. Sometime late in 1915, she became secretly engaged to Garvey, but her parents strongly disapproved and prevailed upon her to return to Panama early in 1916. Eventually she rejoined Garvey in New York on 3 September 1918; she played an important organizing role in the burgeoning American UNIA as Garvey's chief aide, and she was made a director of the Black Star Line on 20 September 1919. They were finally married on 25 December 1919 in an elaborate wedding ceremony held in the UNIA's Liberty Hall. Within a few months, on 6 March 1920, Garvey separated from her and sought an annulment of the marriage. He withdrew his suit as a result of the adverse publicity which his wife's disclosures in the case attracted. From the time of their separation in 1920, however, Amy Ashwood Garvey developed an expansive career as a social worker, publicist, lecturer, political activist, playwright, theatrical producer, educator, restauranteur, and world traveler. Garvey succeeded in obtaining a divorce in Missouri on 5 July 1922, and later that same month he married his secretary, Amy Jacques (1896–1973). But legal entanglements continued for several years as a result of suits that Amy Ashwood brought against him for financial support, bigamy, and divorce, though she never succeeded in obtaining the latter, so that at the time of Garvey's death in 1940 and subsequently, there arose some dispute over the question of which of Garvey's two wives was to be recognized as his legal widow. Amy Ashwood died in Kingston, on 3 May 1969, leaving several drafts of her unpublished memoir of Garvey and the UNIA, as well as other unpublished manuscripts on the history of Liberia and on the subject of African women in history. (Lionel M. Yard, *The First Amy Tells All*, unpublished MS; Amy Ashwood, *Garvey, Portrait of a Liberator*, unpublished MS).

[*Gleaner*, 3 October 1914]

A NEW SOCIETY.
UNIVERSAL IMPROVEMENT ASSOCIATION.

The Universal Negro Improvement Association held their general weekly meeting in the Collegiate Hall, on Thursday evening last [*1 October*]¹, at 7.30, when there was a large turn out of members and visitors. The guest of the evening was Councillor R. W. Bryant,² who delivered an eloquent and inspiring address on the "Duty of Citizenship." Mr. Bryant outlined the many duties incumbent on both men and women in living the lives of good citizens. He impressed his hearers with the important part sanitation played in the proper upkeep of city li[fe], the absence of which tends to spread disease and infectious maladies.

A letter was read from Dr. Booker T. Washington, Principal of the Tuskegee Normal and Industrial Institute, inviting the President of the Association to visit, his institution, during his forth coming visit to America, so as to gain some practical knowledge of the work being done in the South, in the industrial interests of the people of America. Dr. Washington also informed the President, that he has cancelled his lecturing tour of Europe for 1915, when he was to have spoken on the "Progress of the Negro."

Letters were also read from Dr. Wm. Ferris, M.A.,[3] author of a popular volume entitled "The African Abroad" and M. C. Regulus, the Haytian Consul promising to give some assistance in helping to establish industrial and educational colleges for the creation of a better class of workers and cultured citizens among the people. A letter was also read from the Hon. J. H. Levy,[4] sympathizing with the aims of the society in trying to assist in creating a better state among the masses.

A debate on "The Press or the Platform, which has the greater influence?" followed a finely rendered dialogue between Miss A. Ashwood and Mr. A. Daily, entitled "Sixteen." Mr. Marcus Garvey led for the Press supported by Mr. Daily and Miss Ashwood, whilst Mr. L. Small, led for the Platform, supported by Mr. L. Fraser, and members of the audience. When the issue was put to the vote Mr. Small's side won with a large majority. Next Tuesday [6 October] at 7.30 the association holds its next general weekly and musical and literary evening to which members and the public are cordially invited.

Printed in the *Gleaner*, Saturday, 3 October 1914.

1. The meeting had been postponed from Wednesday, 30 September, since the intercessory service for soldiers and sailors engaged in the European war was scheduled for that day.

2. Robert William Bryant, (1865–1948), was born in England; he arrived in Jamaica in July 1887 and was admitted to practice as a solicitor in 1898. He was appointed mayor of Kingston in January 1911, serving until October 1912; then, in October 1916, he won the first in a series of Kingston mayoral contests, as a result of which he served as mayor until the creation of the Kingston and St. Andrew Corp. in 1923. In 1919 he was awarded an MBE for his wartime services as mayor of Kingston. (*DG*, 4 June 1948).

3. William Henry Ferris (1873–1941) was later assistant president general of the UNIA as well as associate editor of the *Negro World*. After attending Yale Graduate School, 1895–97 (M.A. 1899), Harvard Divinity School 1897–99, and Harvard Graduate School, 1899–1900 (M.A. 1900), he worked briefly as a correspondent for both the *Boston Guardian* and the *Colored American* in 1902–03. He began lecturing on African history in 1905 and traveled extensively in the United States and Canada gathering material for his book, *The African Abroad; or, His Evolution in Western Civilization: Tracing His Development under Caucasian Milieus*, 2 vols. (New Haven, Conn.: Tuttle, Morehouse and Taylor, 1913). Ferris "first heard of Marcus Garvey in November, 1913," as the result of Garvey's article in *ATOR*. "I heard no more of Garvey until the summer of 1914, when he wrote to me that he had organized the Universal Negro Improvement Association and desired to arrange for me a West Indian lecture tour under the auspices of the association," he reported, "but the World War blocked his plans" (*Philadelphia Tribune*, 27 June 1940). Ferris recorded the details of his first meeting with Garvey thus: "I first met him in Chicago, Ill., in the late fall of 1916, when I was Associate Editor of the Champion Magazine, of which Fenton Johnson was editor, Mr. William M. Kelley, the business manager, and Mr. and Mrs. Jesse Binga, the patrons. Marcus Garvey impressed both Fenton Johnson and myself as being ambitious, wide-awake and energetic, and we published his article in the January number. He lectured in Chicago and various western,

eastern and southern cities" (ATT, Monroe N. Work Newspaper Clipping Files, William Ferris, "Duse Mohamed and Marcus Garvey," n.p., n.d.; Yale University Obituary Record of Graduates Deceased during the year ending July 1, 1942, pp. 69–70).

4. Joseph Henry Levy (1843–1927), Jamaican-born general merchant, was elected a member of the St. Ann Parochial Board in 1885 and in 1896 became its chairman. In 1892 he was elected member of the Legislative Council for St. Ann and St. Mary; in 1913 he was nominated by the governor for the same position. He was appointed justice of the peace and chairman of the District Recruiting Committee for the parish of St. Ann in 1918. (*WWJ*; *HJ*, 1928).

[*Gleaner*, 8 October 1914]

THE UNIVERSAL NEGRO IMPROVEMENT ASSOCIATION.

On Tuesday evening [*6 October*] at 7.30, the Universal Negro Improvement Association held their weekly general meeting in the Collegiate Hall, when there was a large and representative attendance. The chair was occupied by the President of the Association and the visitor of the evening was the Rev. Theo. Glasspole.[1] Many interesting and enjoyable items were contributed to the musical and literary part of the programme. Mr. A. Daily read a paper on "Despair and its Cure," and Miss A. Ashwood also read one on "Music" which was highly appreciated. Mr. H. B. Green spoke on the value of a "stock of good information combined with character." Mr. J. C. Beecher[2] recited passages from Byron's "Darkness" which were well rendered. Mrs. L. Livingstone recited some beautiful selections from the works of the poet Paul Laurence Dunbar.[3] Mr. and Mrs. George McCormack were cheered for their musical renditions.

The Rev. Theo. Glasspole gave an instructive address which was well received. The following resolution was moved by Mr. A. Daily and seconded by Mr. T. A. McCormack, and was passed unanimously. "That the Universal Negro Improvement Association take steps to organize a brass band in connection with the society for the purpose of supplying the existing need of a city band, and that the band thus organized be utilised for discoursing free music to the people of Kingston, and especially playing in the Victoria Gardens three times a week, and at such places as the citizens of Kingston might request for the benefit of one and all."

Next Tuesday evening [*13 October*] at 7.30 a debate takes place, the subject of which is: "Rural or city life, which helps more in the development of the State?" The visitor for Tuesday 20th, will be the Rev. Jno. Graham,[4] who will speak on the "Spiritual and Moral Law of Man."

Printed in the *Gleaner*, Thursday, 8 October 1914.

1. Rev. Theophilus A. Glasspole was pastor of the Watsonville and Guy's Hill Wesleyan churches in St. Catherine. (*WWJ*, 1916).

2. John Coleman Beecher later became a Kingston city councillor in 1937. (*HJ*, 1938).

3. Paul Laurence Dunbar (1872–1906) gained his reputation for articulating the language of black Americans in *Lyrics of Lowly Life* (New York: Dodd, Mead & Co., 1896). His *Complete Poems* (New York: Dodd, Mead & Co.) appeared posthumously in 1913. (*WBD*).

4. Archdeacon John Henry Heron Graham (1852–1936), an Anglican priest, was stationed

for over thirty years at Port Maria, St. Mary. At the 13 October UNIA meeting, however, it was Rev. William Graham, and not Rev. John Henry Heron Graham, who spoke. (*WWJ*, 1916; *DG*, 10 December 1935; *HJ*, 1936).

Sir William Henry Manning to Lewis Harcourt, British Colonial Secretary

Kings House Jamaica.
9th October 1914

JAMAICA. NO: 435
Sir,

At the request of the Universal Negro Improvement and Conservation Association and African Communities League, I have the honour to transmit to you herewith, a letter [*in the margin*: $\frac{16.\ 9.14.}{\text{In duplicate.}}$] which has been addressed to you by the President of the Association conveying an expression of the loyalty and devotion of the Members of His Majesty the King and to the British Empire. I have the honour to be, Sir, Your most obedient, humble Servant,

W. H. MANNING,
GOVERNOR

PRO, CO 137/705, Jamaica No. 435. TLS, Recipient's copy.

Enclosure

Kingston, Jamaica, W.I.
September 16th 1914

Dear Sir,

I have the honour to ~~foward~~ /forward/ you, through His Excellency the Governor, the following resolution, passed by our Association at a general meeting, held in the Collegiate Hall, Kingston, on Tuesday evening the 15th Sept, 1914., which I beg that you accept as the genuine feeling of our members. Our love for, and devotion to, His Majesty and the Empire, stands unrivalled and from the depths of our hearts we pray for the ~~comming~~ /crowning/ victory of the British Soldiers now at war.

I, therefore, beg that you convey the feelings of this resolution to His Gracious Majesty and people.

"That we the members of the Universal Negro Improvement and Conservation Association and African Communities League, assembled in general meeting at Kingston, Jamaica, being mindful of the great protecting and civilizing influence of the English nation and people, of whom we are subjects, and their justice to all men, and especially to their Negro Subjects scattered all over the world, hereby beg to express our loyalty and devotion to His Majesty the King, and Empire and our sympathy with those of the people who are in any way grieved and in difficulty in this time of Natio[n]al trouble. We sincerely pray for the success of British ~~Armies~~ /arms/ on the battle fields of Europe and Africa, and at Sea, in crushing the "Common Foe," the enemy of peace and further civilization. We rejoice in British Victories and the suppression of foreign foes. Thrice we ~~shall~~ hail: "God save the King!" "Long live the King and Empire["].

I am, Sir, Your Obedient Servant,

MARCUS GARVEY
PRESIDENT—
THE UNIVERSAL NEGRO IMPROVEMENT
AND CONSERVATION ASSOCIATION AND
AFRICAN COMMUNITIES LEAGUE

PRO, CO 137/705, Enclosure in Jamaica Despatch No. 435, 9 October 1914. TLS, Recipient's copy. Corrections in Garvey's hand.

Minute

[*London*] 28.10.14

Mr. Grindle[1]

I blush to think that I once suggested to Mr. Marcus Garvey that he shd go to the workhouse.

? ack. with expression of appreciation of H. M. of the loyal sentiments expressed by the Association.

RHW

[*Endorsement*] G.G. 29.10.14 . . . [*word illegible*]

PRO, CO 137/705, Jamaica No. 435. ANI. Endorsement is handwritten.

1. Sir Gilbert Edmund Augustine Grindle, KCMG (1869–1934), was Oxford-educated; he became a barrister in 1895 and entered the Colonial Office the following year. In 1898 he was appointed assistant private secretary to Joseph Chamberlain (1836–1914), later serving as assistant undersecretary of state (1916–25), and deputy permanent undersecretary of state (1925–31). (*WWW*).

Newspaper Report

[*Daily Chronicle*, 16 October 1914]

IMPROVEMENT ASSOCIATION
CITY LIFE AND THE DEVELOPMENT OF THE STATE
DEBATE IN KINGSTON

The Universal Negro Improvement Association held a meeting in the Collegiate Hall on Tuesday night last [*13 October*]. There was a very large turn out of members and visitors.

The main item on the Agenda was a debate, the subject of which was:—"Rural or City Life, which helps more in the development of the State?"

Mr. A. Leo. Rankin[1] was the leader for rural life, supported by Mr. Marcus Garvey; and Mr. A. Bain Alves[2] led for city life supported by Mr. T. A. McCormack.

Mr. Rankin asked the audience not to consider the issue from mere parochial loyalty or feelings, but to decide *pro* and *con* from the soundest reason and facts. He pointed out that the cities could not exist and the fast life of the Metropolitans kept up, independent of the resources and bounty of the country. Mr. Rankin was most impressive and convincing all through.

Mr. Alves followed, and in a clever and masterly manner, moved the audience with the picturesque descriptions of city life as against the crude and rustic simplicity of the rural throng. He quoted Adam Smith on Political Economy, and he also read extracts from the *Jamaica Handbook* to bear out his arguments that Kingston as a city, was far more valuable to the State, as a contributing source of revenue, than any of the parishes. He asserted that 75 per cent of the revenue was collected in Kingston. Broadly speaking, Mr. Alves drew attention to the great manufacturers, commercial houses, and general activity of the large cities where millions of the people are employed and who live in such a way as to compel the circulation of money.

In reply to Mr. Alves, Mr. Garvey said that the question was not whether the country or rural parts were brighter or gayer than the city, it was which of the two places, country or city, contributes more to the development of the State. He submitted that in every country in the world where there is a system of industry, the rural parts are regarded as the main sources of the nation's upkeep. Manufactories, commercial houses and the general activity of the city people, could not be kept up without the great supplies of the country. Manufacturing cities like Manchester [*England*] with their cotton mills did not grow cotton or rear sheep, neither did London, Liverpool or the cities of Yorkshire grow cane, beet, or produce ore. He went on to say that the theories of Adam Smith, in many instances, are absolutely obsolete and should, therefore, be ignored in the light of modern reason. He cited the agricultural workers of France as an illustration of the great importance attached to the rural industrialism of a country. He said that immediately after the Franco-Prussian war of 1870, when the Prussians imposed an indemnity of several hundred millions on the French nation, and there was no money in the treasury, the President and Government did not ask the cities to come to the rescue of the State, but they appealed to the agricultural and industrial workers of France to rally around them and clear off this heavy debt, and within a short space of time all these millions were paid, and, through the stalwart agriculturists of that country. "Let us suspend our banana cultivations and cocoa, coffee and sugar industries in this island for one year," Mr. Garvey said, "and the whole country will go into bankruptcy."

Mr. McCormack followed in support of Mr. Alves and he also quoted Adam Smith, pointing out the educational and political advantages gained through city life.

Several speakers from the audience gave their support to the respective sides and when the question was put to the vote city life won with a majority of two, twenty-nine voted for rural life and thirty-one for city.

A letter was read from Mr. Travers Buxton, M.A., Secretary of the Anti-Slavery and Aborigine[s] Protection Society, in London, in support of the Society and wishing the President success on his coming tour.

A resolution was unanimously passed empowering the Committee of Management to communicate with the Hon. H. H. Cousins, Director of Agriculture,[3] asking that he be good enough to receive a deputation from the society who are desirous of visiting the Industrial farm at Hope[4] so as to gain some knowledge of the demonstrative usefulness of the farming industry, a branch in which the Society is to start active work next year.

The meeting came to a close after the singing of the National Anthem.

Next Tuesday [20 October] at 7.30, the Society will hold a musical and literary evening. The Rev. William Graham will be the visitor and he will speak on the "Spiritual and moral law of man." All are cordially invited to attend these meetings. A concert will be held in the Collegiate Hall on Thursday, the 29th inst., in aid of the funds of the society.

Printed in the *Daily Chronicle*, Friday, 16 October 1914. Original headlines have been abbreviated.

1. A. Leo Rankin was involved in the Liberal Men's Association of Jamaica, a group led by Rev. E. Ethelred Brown; he served as the association's secretary in 1920. (*Daily Chronicle*, 8 August 1916).

2. A. Bain Alves, organizer of the Franklin Town Benevolent Society in Kingston in October 1914, was a former cigar maker and also a labor leader. During the 1890s he served as a private in the Kingston infantry militia. (PRO, CO 137/722; *Daily Chronicle*, 14 October 1914; George Eaton, "Trade Union Development in Jamaica," pp. 43–53).

3. Herbert H. Cousin, M.A., (1869–?) was educated at Merton College, Oxford. Appointed agricultural chemist in 1900 and director of agriculture in 1908, Cousin was a member of the Legislative Council from 1907 to 1923 and the editor of *Bulletin of Department of Agriculture*. (*WWJ*, 1916).

4. The object of the Agricultural Farm School, established by the Department of Agriculture in 1909, was to provide a three year training program in agricultural science for young

men. Encompassing 1700 acres of land, the school was situated on the old Hope estate (later known as the Hope Botanical Gardens). The school was formally opened on 25 January 1910.

Sir William Henry Manning to Marcus Garvey

Kings House Jamaica.
20th October, 1914

Sir,

I have the honour to acknowledge the receipt of your letter of the 16th Instant[1] enclosing Tickets for the Concert to which you ask me to give my patronage.

I am pleased to give you my patronage and I trust your Concert will be successful. I also enclose a Cheque for Two Pounds [*in the margin*: £2.0.0] towards the object of your Society. I have the honour to be, Sir, Your obedient servant,

W. H. MANNING
GOVERNOR

TNF, AJG. TLS, Recipient's copy.
  1. This letter has not been located.

Travers Buxton to Marcus Garvey

[*London*] 21st October, 1914

Dear Sir

I acknowledge with thanks the receipt of your letter of the 19th ultimo enclosing a cutting containing the resolution of the Negro Improvement Association. I am glad to know that this body has thus expressed its feelings in regard to the war, and I am obliged to you for letting me know of it. Believe me, Yours faithfully,

[TRAVERS BUXTON]

RHL, ASAPS, Brit. Emp. s. 19, D/1/14 (793). TL, Carbon copy.

Newspaper Report

[*Gleaner*, 23 October 1914]

THE UNIVERSAL IMPROVEMENT ASSOCIATION.
ADDRESS DELIVERED ON TUESDAY NIGHT LAST BY
REV. W. GRAHAM AT COLLEGIATE HALL.
WHAT IS CHRISTIAN LIBERTY AND WHAT WE OWE
TO IT.

The Universal Negro Improvement Association held their regular weekly musical and literary meeting in the Collegiate [H]all on Tuesday night last [*20 October*], and there was another large turn out of members and visitors. The guest of the evening was the Rev. William Graham, and among the officers on the platform, were: Mr. Marcus Garvey, President; Mr. T. A. McCormack, general secretary; Mr. Adrian Daly, assistant secretary; Miss Eva Aldred, president of the ladies' division; Miss Amy Ashwood, general secretary of the ladies' division; Mrs. G. Livingstone, vice-president of the ladies' division; and Mr. W. G. Hinchcliffe, in the chair.

A letter was read from His Excellency, Sir William H. Manning, expressing his pleasure in giving his patronage to the concert to be held in the Collegiate Hall, on Thursday night next week in aid of the Collegiate industrial and social fund of the society. His Excellency also sent a donation towards the

OBJECTS OF THE SOCIETY

which are: To establish educational and industrial (day and evening) training colleges for the purpose of the further education and culture of our boys and girls: To reclaim the fallen and degraded of the people (especially the criminal class) and help them to a state of good citizenship: To work among, administer to, and assist the needy: To rescue the fallen women of the island from the pit of infamy and vice: To promote a cordial relationship between all men and strengthen the bonds of brotherhood: To do all that is possible and reasonable to help the struggling masses to a higher state of moral appreciation.

The society is non-political and it has as its motto: "One God! One Aim! One Destiny!"

In introducing the visitor to the audience Mr. Garvey said that he was glad to welcome the Rev. Graham, not only as a visitor, but as a true-hearted friend and well-wisher of the society, and the backward masses. Mr. Graham had been most kind and willing in helping the people to help themselves. So long as he (Mr. Garvey) lived he would never forget the kind services the rev. gentleman rendered him in the interest of the cause for which he was working, namely: the development and improvement of his people on proper lines.

After several musical and literary items had been contributed to the programme by Mr. and Mrs. George McCormack, Mr. Cole, Mr. Victor Anderson and others, Mr. Graham rose to speak. He said:

REV. W. GRAHAM'S ADDRESS.

Mr. Chairman, ladies and gentlemen: First of all I want to say that it gives me pleasure to be with you to-night; and again I want to say what has already been said by Mr. Garvey, namely; that I wish to do everything in my power to advance the association. Its objects, I believe, are something like this; you meet together and associate yourselves in unity, in order to improve your own people. The object of this association is a grand object. A better object no association can have than the improvement of one's fellowmen, of one's own race, of one's own people. I have always, in my work in Kingston, had that object in view. Every time I open my mouth to preach a sermon (of course I am not preaching a sermon to-night) the object is to improve, to advance, to lift up someone of those who are there to listen. And I can say this, that although it is a great work, (and a greater work than that is not to be found in this world), yet it is a most difficult work for many reasons, the chief among them being this that people don't want to be lifted up. Speaking generally, people don't want to be improved and they take very little trouble of themselves to improve themselves; and one of the greatest difficulties is to get into the hearts of the people to make them better than they are. They need to be taught that there is

A HIGHER LIFE

to attain to. They need to realize there is a better life to get to, and they must know that these things can only be achieved by hard work, by great attention to and the use of proper means. That is a hard and a difficult thing; and I can promise Mr. Garvey, this, that if he is to succeed he has got to work, and he has not only to work, but to work hard. And I wish to say that if your people are to rise to a higher life and better things you have got to work and work hard.

I preached a sermon some time ago that among the things which never rust are a sword and a spade. A sword represents offence and defence, a spade represents hard work. There is nothing in this world worth having that has not been gained or achieved along the line of hard work.

I look back upon the advancement of peoples who have risen to high things, I find that the foundation underlying their efforts is this: that they learnt the dignity of hard work[.] We are not inclined to work. I myself will candidly admit that I will avoid as much work as I can. We want to have installed into us ambitions, to see an object to attain before we work. If you are starving you will work. If you are starving for the higher things you will work. There is no nation or people that has ever risen to any dignity in the world, or has become of any worth in the sight of God or man, that has not achieved it by means of hard work.

Another point which I would like to impress is that, to advance, you must be subject to the spiritual laws[.] All the universe in all its various aspects is under law[.] And I belong to that school of philosophy and theology which holds that since we have that law we must have had a law-giver. Law is not self-originated. Law came into being because there was a law-giver to establish it. And a Law-giver that can make laws to so regulate the universe must necessarily be able to change those laws according to his will. That is very plain and easy. The next point is this: being under law, the law of human life and progress is the law of obedience. Do you want to be a healthy man? Obey the laws of health, and even God Himself will not take away the health from you. Live in dirt and in the midst of accumulations of filth, and you have typhoid and the other diseases that kill the human body. You say that God did it. It was yourself that did it, because you disobeyed the great law of health which He Himself has established, namely; cleanliness— ["] be clean." If we obey that law we will be as God intended us to be—free of those diseases that hinder us from doing good work. It is the same with the mind. The mind works under law. God is not going to spiritualize one of you unless you come under His Law. God is not going to make you a preacher by bestowing His Holy Spirit upon you and then send you out to be a preacher. The Holy Spirit is not a thing that works to encourage man's laziness. If you want the Holy Spirit you have to work hard to get it. You must apply and use the means, think deeply of things, and as you go on His Spirit will come in the way of revelation.

We see therefore that if we want to progress as a people we must come under the laws of obedience. The first thing to know is that there is no liberty apart from obedience. The people who are freest are the people who live under and in obedience to the law of the land.

TRUE LIBERTY.

It is difficult to understand; but mark it well—liberty does not belong to you or me apart from obedience to the law. If we have no obedience to the law then liberty becomes license, and license soon ends in the uprooting and the driving away of everything that a man should have or that is worth anything. Then what is the best way by which we may obtain freedom. The freedom we have to-night to hold such a meeting as this we did not always have. One hundred and twenty years ago, it was not the same in Scotland. We have got liberty through the British Empire. I have thought that if a new race ever rises to anything dignified it has got to rise through the liberty enjoyed under British rule. (cheers). If ever we get into German hands we will be under the hand of militarism.

Now I think that we owe a deep debt of gratitude to any living soul who has ever preached to man—and I don't say it because I am a minister of the gospel, and if we ever owe a debt of gratitude to any preacher, to any man who sought to uplift humanity we owe it to the Lord Jesus Christ. And I will prove it to you in one word. This is what He said: "Ye shall know the truth and the truth shall make you free." There never was a preacher that proclaimed that before. That was the beginning of the freedom of you and me. It was the foundation of our "Imperial Life." Man has fought for liberty and died for it. There is another way to get liberty, by Act of Parliament, as in the case of Jamaica. But we don't want an Act of Parliament alone. We want something better. The thing that makes us freest is the truth. You will say—"Well now, what is truth?" I will tell you. It is the simplest thing in the world. What Jesus meant was the truth he proclaimed His liberty comes from the truth. The truth He proclaimed was very simple. It was the truth concerning man, the truth concerning God, the truth concerning immortality. If you don't get deep down into that you don't get very deep into the Christian religion. And the truth about God was that God was the Father of the human race, and He cannot be worshipped well except you worship Him in Spirit. That was never proclaimed before[.] Concerning man, He said the greatest thing about us was that we were the sons of God; that we had souls; we were children of the Almighty. What a feeling that must give a man, when he once knows that his life was but a preparation for the great habitation which God has prepared for him. It is that truth which will make you free.

All freedom lies in the spirit. Of all the means of obtaining freedom religion is the greatest. Religion is the greatest inspiration of everything in a man's soul. In that is the safety of the British nation. The fundamental principle amongst the great men who stand in the forefront of our ranks is that if ever you want to rise you must rise on the foundation of the Gospel of Christ.

I tell you, not as a prophet, but simply as man to man, that God is putting us to the test to see whether we are fit for Him to choose some of us. If you want to advance and uplift yourselves you must put yourselves under the spiritual law by bringing yourselves within the requirements of religion. And you can always reckon on me to do anything to assist towards the objects at which this association aims.

Next Tuesday [*27 October*] a debate will take place and on Thursday night of next week the society will give a high-class concert in aid of its funds. All are invited.

Printed in the *Gleaner*, Friday, 23 October 1914.

H. G. Price to Marcus Garvey

The Times. [London]
Oct. 27th., 1914

Dear Sir,

I am desired by Lord Northcliffe[1] to thank you for your letter,[2] and to inform you that he has had the resolution you sent printed in "The Times." I enclose a cutting. Yours faithfully,

H G PRICE
Private Secretary

TNF, AJG. TLS, Recipient's copy.

1. Alfred Charles William Harmsworth, viscount Northcliffe (1865–1922), journalist and owner of the *Evening News*, the *Daily Mail*, the *Observer*, and *The Times*, was the most important force in the creation of modern British journalism. He served as head of the British Ministry of Propaganda in 1918. During the course of the European war, Northcliffe transformed himself from a newspaper proprietor into a major public figure, placing himself at the head of many of the era's popular movements. (*WWW*; Philip M. Taylor, "The Foreign Office and British Propaganda During the First World War," *The Historical Journal* 23 [1980]:875–98; Taylor, *The Projection of Britain: British Overseas Publicity and Propaganda, 1919–1939* [Cambridge: Cambridge University Press, 1981]; J. M. McEwen, "Northcliffe and Lloyd George at War, 1914–1918," *The Historical Journal* 24 [1981]:651–72).
2. This letter has not been found.

Enclosure

[*The Times*, 27 October 1914]

NEGROES' LOYAL MESSAGE.

The Universal Negro Improvement and Conservation Association, a body which aims at raising the condition of the negro, at a meeting held at Kingston, Jamaica, passed the following resolution. Mr. Marcus Garvey, the president, in forwarding it says it is a genuine expression of the people's loyalty to the King and the British people. . . .[1]

Printed in *The Times* (London), Tuesday, 27 October 1914.

1. The first of the two resolutions originally passed by the UNIA was reprinted in *The Times*.

Newspaper Report

[*Daily Chronicle*, 31 October 1914]

RECENT FUNCTION IN KINGSTON
ENJOYABLE CONCERT GIVEN BY NEGRO
IMPROVEMENT ASSOCIATION.

The concert arranged by the Universal Negro Improvement Association under the patronage of His Excellency the Governor, the Hon. Major Hughes Bryan,[1] Sir John Pringle[2] and other distinguished gentlemen, came off in the Collegiate Hall on Thursday night [*29 October*]. There was a large turn out and the programme was most enjoyable.

The first item on the programme was a selection by the Alpha Cottage Band, which was well rendered; after which Mr. R. W. Bryant explained the objects of the association, which he said were most commendable.

Mr. and Mrs. McCormack opened the vocal part of the entertainment with a duet, for which they were loudly applauded. Mr. G. Livingston next followed with a humorous recitation. It was unique in its rendition. Mr. George McCormack followed with a solo, and his powerful baritone voice filled the building with its heavy, clear, musical tones.

Mr. J. C. Beecher recited "The Roman Sentinel" which was rendered in masterly style, and called forth great applause. Mrs. Markland's song "I CAN'T HELP LOVING YOU" was well received and Mr. Granville Campbell, as usual, took the audience by storm with his solo. This was followed by Miss C. E. Mitchell with a splended violin solo. Mr. Bobby Grieves had twenty minutes of pleasure and laughter-producing demonstrations in ventriloquism; and his Mr. Brown, Mrs. Brown and Tommy, were most amusing, Tommy making several attempts to kiss at Mrs. Brown.

Miss Ashwood's recitation "The lover and the moon" by Paul Lawrence Dunbar, was splendidly rendered; after which the curtain was drawn for ten minutes intermission, during which time the band discoursed sweet music.

After the intermission the principal item on the programme was a farce entitled "The Breach of Promise", in which Messrs. Adrian A. Daly, M. Daly, T. M. McCormack, H. Davidson, F. Smith, T. Cross, Miss Gwen Campbell,[3] Miss Amy Ashwood and others, took part. This farce was well staged, and reflected credit on the actors.

Several other musical items were down on the programme to be contributed by Mrs. McCormack, Mrs. A. Anderson, Miss Davis, Mr. A. Leo Rankine and Mr. C. Clive Irons, which were omitted for lack of time.

To repeat, the evening was most enjoyable. All those who attended gave expressions of satisfaction. Among those present were the Hon. H. Bryan, C.M.G., and Mrs. Bryan, Mr. T. Byndloss, Mr. R. W. Bryant, Monsieur Regulus, Mr. C. P. Lazarus[4] and other well-known persons.

Last Tuesday's Debate

On Tuesday night last [*27 October*] the Society held a debate at its weekly meeting in the hall, when there was a large turn out of members and visitors. The subject of the debate was, "The pen or the sword, which is mightier?" Mr. A. Leo Rankine, supported by Mr. Marcus Garvey, spoke for the pen, and Mr. A. Bain Alves, supported by Mr. Uriah Henry[5] and Mr. A. Samuel Burton, spoke for the sword. After an animated and interesting discussion, lasting for about two hours, the audience gave a verdict in favour of the pen with a majority of forty.

Next Tuesday evening [*3 November*] at 7.30, the Society will hold their regular musical and literary meeting, to which all are cordially invited.

At the last meeting a letter was read from the headmaster of the Hope Farm School intimating the pleasure to welcome a committee appointed from the association to visit the Farm School for the purpose of gaining practical knowledge, by demonstration, of the usefulness of the farming industry.

Printed in the *Daily Chronicle*, Saturday, 31 October 1914. Original headlines have been abbreviated.

1. Colonel Sir Herbert Bryan (1865–1950) served as Jamaican colonial secretary from September 1914 until his retirement in 1925. He began his career in the British army and served for several years in West Africa. In 1902, he entered the Colonial Office and between 1904 and 1914 was colonial secretary in the Gold Coast. (*WWW*).

2. Sir John Pringle (1848–1923) was the largest landowner in Jamaica; he was a member of the Privy and Legislative Councils, custos of the parish of St. Mary, chairman of the St. Mary Parochial Board, and a justice of the peace for St. Mary. He also served as vice-president of the board of management of the Jamaica Agricultural Society, chairman of the board of directors of the Jamaica Mutual Life Assurance Society, as well as a member of various fraternal and religious organizations. (*HJ*, 1924).

3. Gwendolyn Campbell worked as a private secretary for Garvey in 1914. In February 1920, she accepted a position as a stenographer for the American parent body of the UNIA and the Black Star Line. (*Garvey* v. *United States*, no. 8317 [Ct. App., 2d Cir., Feb. 2, 1925), pp. 1241, 1275).

4. Charles P. Lazarus (1836–1917) was a businessman and owner of the principal foundry in Jamaica. A member of the Mayor and Council of Kingston, he also served as a justice of the peace for Kingston in 1916. (*HJ*, 1918).

5. Uriah M. Henry was listed in 1916 as an unofficial member of the Progressive Negro Association. A frequent speaker at meetings of the Liberal Men's Association in Kingston, Henry later served as the secretary of the Unitarian Church of Kingston in 1920. (*Daily Chronicle*, 8 August 1916).

Lewis Harcourt to Sir William Henry Manning

Downing Street, [*London*]
2nd November, 1914

JAMAICA No. 337.

Sir,

I have the honour to acknowledge the receipt of your despatch No. 435 of the 9th October forwarding a letter from the Universal Negro Improvement and Conservation Association and African Communities League.

2. The letter has been laid before the King and I have it in command from His Majesty to express His appreciation of the loyal sentiments which it contains. I have the honour to be, Sir, Your most obedient, humble Servant,

L. HARCOURT

JA, CSO 1B/5/26/82. TLS, Recipient's copy.

Newspaper Reports

[*Daily Chronicle*, 5 November 1914]

LOCAL ASSOCIATION.

At a meeting held in the Collegiate Hall on Tuesday evening last [*3 November*] the Universal Negro Improvement Association decided to provide a dinner and Christmas treat for three hundred of the poor of Kingston on Christmas Day. The Association has also agreed to give a concert on Christmas morning, too, and distribute flowers among the inmates of the Union Poor House; as also to distribute flowers among the patients of the Kingston General Hospital, providing the head of the General Department will agree to such steps.

A committee of twelve from the association will visit the Hope Industrial Farm next week, so as to gain some practical knowledge of the scientific methods of the farming industry.

Next Tuesday evening [*10 November*], the Association will hold an elocution contest in the Hall; and on the same evening, Mr. M. Daily[1] will deliver a lecture on Hygiene.

The Hon. Hugh Bryan, C.M.G., Colonial Secretary, and Vernon E. Grosett, Esqr.,[2] of Port Antonio, have sent donations to the Society.

Printed in the *Daily Chronicle*, Thursday, 5 November 1914.

1. Samuel Manasseh Daily (1883–?) entered the Jamaican civil service in 1907 as an apprentice in the government laboratory. He eventually became chief laboratory assistant in the pathological and bacteriological laboratory of the medical department in 1936. (*WWJ*, 1916).

2. Vernon E. Grosett (1877–?) was born at Port Antonio, parish of Portland, and educated at York Castle School in Jamaica and Kent College in Canterbury, England. Grosett was admitted to practice as a solicitor of the Supreme Court of Jamaica in 1902. (*WWJ*, 1916).

[*Daily Chronicle*, 14 November 1914]

Visit to Hope Farm School by Members of the Negro Improvement Association of Kingston
Interesting Outing
Proposal is to Send a Few Students to Study Agriculture

On Thursday afternoon [*12 November*] a committee of thirteen ladies and gentlemen of the Universal Negro Improvement Association paid a visit to the Hope Farm School. Among those who formed the committee were: Mr. Marcus Garvey, President of the Association; Mr. T. A. L. McCormack, General Secretary; Mr. J. W. Milburn, Treasurer,[1] Mr. S. Jones, Mr. V. Anderston, Mr. E. Reid,[2] and Miss Eva Aldred, Miss Amy Ashwood, Miss Amy Aldred, Miss Gwen Campbell, Miss Evelyn Monroe, Mrs. E. Peart,[3] and Mrs. Maud Markland. The committee had arranged to leave Kingston at 1 o'clock in the afternoon, but owing to the state of the weather, they never started until 2 o'clock, arriving at Hope 20 minutes to 3.

The headmaster of the school had made all arrangements to give the committee every facility for gaining practical knowledge of the work done at Hope by himself and staff, and when the party arrived they were met by Mr. Thelwell,[4] an assistant master, and several of the students, who were engaged at work at their end.

The Hope Farm School is such an extensive and important institution that the work of carrying it on extends over hundreds of acres of land, hence the work has to be divided into sections over which the masters and students preside at regular hours daily. The committee were first taken to the second and third year boys' dormitory and shown through; they then passed through to the northside dormitory, which was also a mixture of second and third year boys. There was to be seen to the north of the second year boys' dormitory a large area of guinea corn, which is supposed to be ten acres. Mr. Thelwell explained that the guinea corn is grown for the purpose of providing fodder for the stock during drought. Through a process that he hopes will become general in drought stricken areas of this country, they are able to preserve the guinea corn in a green and nutritious state for a long period, during which time, were drought to visit them, they would have a sufficient supply of fodder to feed the stock.

After passing through the dining room, class-room, offices, into the manual training room, the committee was shown a large incubator for the hatching of chickens. Mr. Thelwell called upon Mr. Constable, a second year student, to explain the operation of the machine, and in a most instructive way he explained and demonstrated the use of the artificial hatcher. He says that the percentage of hatches were generally fifty per cent, and whether the eggs are good or not they are placed before a specially manufactured lantern and in the observation if a black speck appear it shows that the egg is not fertile.

From the incubator the committee were being conducted to the poultry department when the rains started falling, and inevitably brought the inspection to a close as far as the external working of the school is concerned.

For fully two hours several members of the committee enjoyed themselves in the large dining room by singing and playing at the piano to the amusement of students and themselves.

Another visit is to be paid to the Farm so as to carry out the intention of the association which will be arranged for a whole day.

Next year the association anticipates sending several students to the school.

Owing to the inclemency of the weather the lecture and elocution contest, which should have come off in the Collegiate Hall last Tuesday [*10 November*], has been postponed to the general meeting night on Tuesday next [*17 November*]. All are cordially invited to be present.

Printed in the *Daily Chronicle*, Saturday, 14 November 1914. Original headlines have been abbreviated.

1. J. W. Milbourne later served as the president of the Progressive Negro Association from July 1916 until 27 July 1917. (*Daily Chronicle*, 8 August 1916).

2. Edwin E. Reid and his brother Jonathan M. Reid, were engaged in restaurant and jewelry businesses in Kingston. They were founding members of the UNIA in Jamaica and they later helped to establish the UNIA Liberty Hall in Kingston. (Lionel Yard, interview with Reid, 1973).

3. The former Indiana Garvey.

4. Arthur Frederick Thelwell (1889–?) became secretary and treasurer of the Jamaica Agricultural Society in 1937. He was also supervisor of the All-Island Banana Growers Association and a member of the Legislative Council of Jamaica. (*HJ*, 1938).

[*Daily Chronicle*, 19 November 1914]

THE UNIVERSAL NEGRO IMPROVEMENT ASSOCIATION LETTERS READ FROM NOTABLE PERSONS IN THE MOTHER COUNTRY

On Tuesday night last [*17 November*] the Universal Negro Improvement Association held a meeting in the Collegiate Hall. There was a very large turn out of members and visitors.

Several important letters were read, among them being a communication from the Right Hon. H. H. Asquith, Prime Minister,[1] the right Hon. David Lloyd George, Chancellor of the Exchequer,[2] the Right Hon. A. Bonar Law, M.P., Leader in the House of Commons of the Conservative Party,[3] the Hon. Harry Lawson, M.P. of the London *Daily Telegraph*;[4] Lord Northcliffe[;] the Earl of Rosebery;[5] Sir Owen Phillipps, K.C.M.G., Chairman of the Royal Mail Company;[6] and Mr. Travers Buxton, M.A., of the Anti-Slavery and Aborigines Protection Society.[7]

The following letter from the Duke of Northumberland[8] was also read:

"Alnuick Castle,"
27th October, 1914

Dear Sir,

I am much obliged to you for your letter enclosing resolution passed by the Universal Negro Improvement Association. The loyalty it expresses to the mother country is very gratifying at a crisis like the present, and I am very sensible of the compliment paid me by the Association in forwarding it to me. I am, Sir, Yours faithfully

(Signed) NORTHUMBERLAND

"Marcus Garvey, Esq."

A clipping was received and read from Lord Northcliffe as published in the *Times*, of London, about the Society.

The main items of the evening's programme were a lecture by Mr. S. M. Daily, on Hygiene and its relation to public health, and an Elocution Contest. Mr. Daily's lecture was most instructive and was well received. . . .[9]

The Association is arranging to give a concert in the Ward Theatre for the purpose of supplementing their funds to give a treat and Christmas dinner to three hundred of the poor of Kingston, and to distribute flowers among the patients of the General Hospital and Union Poor House.

Printed in the *Daily Chronicle*, Thursday, 19 November 1914. Original headlines have been abbreviated.

1. Herbert Henry Asquith (1852–1928), first earl of Oxford, was prime minister of England from April 1908 to December 1916. Asquith's letter to Garvey has not been found. (*DNB*).

2. David Lloyd George (1863–1945) succeeded Asquith as chancellor of the exchequer in 1908. He was appointed minister of munitions in May 1915, and secretary of state for war in July 1916. He became prime minister in December 1916. His letter to Garvey has not been found. (*DNB*).

3. Andrew Bonar Law (1858–1923) was elected leader of the Conservative party in the House of Commons in 1911 after Arthur Balfour (1848–1930) resigned as party leader. In May 1915 he was appointed secretary of state for the colonies in the first wartime coalition ministry, and he was later appointed chancellor of the exchequer by Lloyd George as well as leader of the House of Commons. Bonar Law's letter to Garvey has not been found. (*DNB*).

4. Sir Harry Lawson Webster Levy Lawson (1862–1933) was the proprietor of the *Daily Telegraph*, 1903–28, and a leading figure in the British newspaper world. First a Liberal, and later a Conservative politician, Lawson served as a member of Parliament for various periods between 1885 and 1916. His letter to Garvey has not been found. (*DNB*).

5. Archibald Philip Primrose (1847–1929), fifth earl of Rosebery, was a leading British statesman, author, and exponent of the imperial idea of a commonwealth of nations. Ap-

pointed prime minister after Gladstone's resignation in May 1894, he resigned in June 1895; he also resigned his position as leader of the Liberal party in October 1896. (*DNB*).

6. Owen Cosby Philipps (1863–1937), baron Kylsant, was a shipowner, financier, and politician. He was chairman of the Royal Mail Steam Packet Co., and a Liberal member of Parliament from 1906 to 1910, switching to the Conservative party during his parliamentary term of 1916–22. In July 1931, Philipps was convicted on the charge of publishing and circulating a false shipping prospectus in 1928, for which he was sentenced to one year's imprisonment. His letter to Garvey has not been found. (*DNB*).

7. Travers Buxton's letter, dated 21 October 1914, is printed above.

8. Alan Ian Percy (1880–1930), eighth duke of Northumberland, served in the Boer War from 1901 to 1902, and with the Egyptian army from 1907 to 1910. He retired from the British army in 1912. On the outbreak of the European war, however, he rejoined his regiment, and served in France from 1914 to 1916. He was later appointed to the General Staff (Intelligence Department) at the War Office. The original of his letter to Garvey has not been found. (*DNB*).

9. The report of the lecture by Daily followed.

[*Daily Chronicle*, 28 November 1914]

IMPROVEMENT AND CONSERVATION ASSOCIATION

On Monday last [*23 November*] a committee of twelve ladies and gentlemen from the Universal Negro Improvement Association visited the Hope Farm School to continue an inspection of the Farm, and to gain knowledge of the methods used by the management in the outlay of Farms.

The committee was most courteously received, and every facility was afforded them to see everything worth seeing. They were taken from one department to another, and with the deepest interest, the officers of the Farm showed and explained all that was necessary. The Headmaster promised to render all possible assistance in helping the Association in their farming scheme as soon as they are ready and apply for such help as can be given.

On Tuesday night next week [*1 December*] the association will hold a memorial meeting on the life and work of the late Dr. J. Robert Love, JP.[1] Several prominent citizens will attend and take part. The address of the evening will be delivered by the Rev. T. Gordon Somers,[2] of Spanish Town.

On Wednesday, the 16th December, the Association will stage a Variety entertainment in the Ward Theatre under the patronage of His Worship the Mayor of Kingston, the Hon. H. A. L. Simpson, and other gentlemen, for the purpose of raising the funds to provide a dinner and treat for the poor of Kingston on Christmas Day.

The association opened an Employment Bureau and the members are endeavouring to get in touch with all shades of labour in the country so as to be able to help employers and workers in reaching one another. Communications from employers and the unemployed are invited. A special appeal is made to employers of domestic servants and planters applying to the society for reliable and honest workers.

The first term for the evening classes to be conducted in connection with the society commences on the 13th of January, and those interested are requested to communicate with the President, Mr. Marcus Garvey, or the General Secretary, Mr. T. A. McCormack, 121 Orange Street, Kingston.

Printed in the *Daily Chronicle*, Saturday, 28 November 1914.

1. Dr. J. Robert Love (1839–1914) was the first major political influence on Marcus Garvey. Garvey later acknowledged this influence: " . . . much of my early education in race consciousness is from Dr. Love" (*Gleaner*, 17 February 1930). Garvey also declared that it was "that great Jamaican Legislator and Patriot, Dr. Robert Love, to whom he owed his inspiration" (*Gleaner*, 3 August 1934). For additional information on Love's career, see the Biographical Supplement, Appendix I.

2. Rev. Thomas Gordon Somers (1866–1931), born at Camrose, St. James, served as the pastor of the First Baptist Church in Spanish Town and the Stewart Town Baptist Church in Trelawny. Somers was chairman of the Jamaica Baptist Union in 1908, and later its secretary in February 1918. In 1918 he was elected president of the Jamaica League, and he also served for a period as chairman of the St. Catherine Parochial Board. (*HJ*, 1932).

Sir Herbert Bryan to Marcus Garvey

Colonial Secretary's Office, Jamaica,
30th November 1914

Sir,

In continuation of the letter from this Office No: 13004/14926, dated the 9th October last,[1] I am directed by the Governor to inform you that the Secretary of State for the Colonies has intimated to His Excellency that the letter from the Universal Negro Improvement and Con[s]er[v]ation Association and African Communities League to him, dated the 16th September last, has been laid before the King and that the Secretary of State has it in command from His Majesty to express His appreciation of the loyal sentiments which it contains. I have the honour to be, Sir, Your obedient Servant,

H. BRYAN
Colonial Secretary

[*Address*] Marcus Garvey Esq, President of
the Universal Negro Improvement and
Conservation Association and African
Communities League, 121 Orange Street,
Kingston.
[*Docket*] No. 15628/S[*ecretary of*] S[*tate*] 337

TNF, AJG. TLS, Recipient's copy.

1. This letter has not been found, but the letter bore the same date as the letter from the governor to the secretary of state for the colonies, printed above, conveying the UNIA's patriotic resolutions.

UNIA Memorial Meeting

[*Daily Chronicle*, 4 December 1914]

On Tuesday night last [*1 December*] the Universal Negro Improvement Association held a memorial meeting on the life and work of the late Dr. J. Robert Love, M.D., J.P., Journalist and Politician. An appreciative audience assembled at the Collegiate Hall to listen to the noble fighter in the cause of his race and fellowmen.

Mr. R. W. Bryant, J.P., Vice Chairman of the Mayor and Council, occupied the chair.

Letters from the Colonial Secretary and the Right Hon. Arthur J. Balfour, M.P.,[1] to Mr. Marcus Garvey, jnr., President of the Society, were read. That from the Colonial Secretary's Office is as follows. . . .[2]

Writing from Whittingehame, Prestonkirk, Scotland, on October 31st, the Right Hon. A. J. Balfour states:

"Dear Sir,—I beg to acknowledge and thank you for the resolution which you have forwarded on behalf of the members of the Jamaica division of the Universal Negro Improvement Association. I need not say that I have read same with greatest gratification."[3]

After the reading of letters and the conveyance of a message of sympathy from Mr. T. H. McDermott, editor of the *Jamaica Times*, who was too ill to attend, the Chairman spoke of his acquaintance with the late Dr. Love.

Mr. George McCormack sang "Eternal Rest" which was beautifully rendered. Miss Amy Ashwood next recited "*In Memoriam*—Blessed are the Dead" from Longfellow, which was a masterpiece in rendition.

The Chairman called upon the Rev. T. Gordon Somers, J.P., for the address of the evening on the life and work of the late Dr. Love. The rev. gentleman was warmly received by the appreciative audience. After a few opening remarks he said:

Every country has had its great men, in intellect, in wealth, in achievement. In many instances the places that gave them birth receive the least direct benefit from their lives, while the lands of their adoption glory in their fame and are blessed by their services. Great men are the products of individual places and peoples, but in their service they are the property of the world. No particular race has the exclusive privilege to the production of such men, nor do they belong to any particular standard of civilization. Every race has had its shining star, every people its leaders, whose places are often difficult to fill when rendered vacant. Tonight we are met to do honour to the memory of one who occupied one of these vacant places—Dr. J. Robert Love. This name is known throughout the length and breadth of Jamaica. Twenty-five years ago there chanced to light upon the hospitable shores of Jamaica from the island of the "Black Republic" the subject of our address. He was a native of Nassau in the Bahamas and received his education both in that island and in the U.S.A. As we are told in an obituary notice of him, he followed first the profession of minister of the gospel, having been a priest in the Anglican Church;

subsequently he became a Doctor of medicine and for many years in Jamaica he graced the ranks of the journalists. We know little of Dr. Love's career previous to his coming to Jamaica but from the way he entered into the public life of this colony he has left behind the imprints of a strong character and a useful life. We may think of him from three points of view.

AS AN ARDENT POLITICIAN

A man of strong and pronounced views, of independent opinions and fearless in his expressions of them, he could hardly avoid the inducements which a political career offered. It was no surprise then when he early became a member of the Kingston City Council. His interest in the affairs of the city was deep and unselfish. His conscientious regard to duty was a marked feature in the service he rendered to the city. But his wide knowledge, his political aspirations, his thirst for social reform, his staunch advocacy of the needs of the people, his burning desire to use every available opportunity to voice the feelings of the masses, wanted a wider scope than the City Council Chamber, and so we find him in 1906 a member of the Legislative Council as representative of Aristocratic St. Andrew. He was then at the zenith of his fame. Jamaica expected much from him. Education, social reform, taxation, the labour question, were subjects he was expected to handle as opportunity afforded him with that masterly hand with which, in the columns of the *Jamaica Advocate* and on public platforms, he had again and again dealt with them. But, alas! we were to a large extent doomed to disappointment. That manly form that had aforetime traversed many a platform, thrilling audiences held spell bound by the rushing, gushing torrent of his unrivalled eloquence, was there, but the voice was seldom heard. Stricken at a time when Jamaica needed him by an affliction which compelled caution and restraint, he was bound to let his opportunities go by that he might in other ways less strenuous still serve his country. If he spoke but seldom he could always be counted upon to vote with his colleagues in the interest of the country. In this his conscience could be trusted. I think we do justice to his name in saying he was noted for his political integrity. He could not be bribed. It was impossible to intimidate him. He never swerved from his purpose even if he was beaten. He could not bend, he could only break.

(2) He was an uncompromising **Advocate of Equal Rights** for all. It was perhaps the experience he gained from his residence in U.S.A. that embittered his feelings so much against anything that savoured of class distinction. Petty prejudices that discriminate against a certain class, that, individual or racial self-consciousness which assumes an offensive attitude of superiority above others; the sacrifice of character and intellectual efficiency at the altar of favoritism; these and other evidences of unfair treatment were alike abhorrent to him and received either from his pen or from his lips the most scathing rebuke. When his soul became fixed from a sense of injustice to the weak and defenceless or where the iron heel of oppression crushed the life

of an unfortunate victim, Dr. Love arose in the fullness of his strength and his tongue became a tomahawk, his pen a scalping knife. He pleaded for the fullest opportunity to be given to everyone to be at his best; in this respect he did not ask favours—he claimed rights. He never [*ever?*] sought to strengthen the weakest point in the battle line but was never afraid to be in the thickest of the fight.

(3) He was **An Unflinching Champion** of the cause of his race. In connexion with no aspect of his work did his true nature stand out more conspicuously than in advocating the cause of his race. If he lacked the constructive ability, the genius, the organising powers of Booker T. Washington, he possessed his patriotism and enthusiasm for the race. His ideals were lofty, his outlook broad. He championed their cause without the slightest reference to the offence that his course of action might cause. It must be admitted that often he went to extremes and created enemies where he might have had friends. He taught that if the negro would rise and make his influence felt in this country, he must have education, money and landed property. In this he was misunderstood and severely criticised in some quarters. But who will conscientiously say he was not right. If he did not add to his triplet of great factors in the development of a people's life that greatest of all—godliness, it was because he did not think this fell within the scope of a social reformer's work. This was eventually the province of the religious leaders. Certainly he did not ignore it. He felt that personally and in behalf of his race he owed a deep debt of gratitude to those men through whom the people of his country obtained their freedom and whose life work as missionaries set before the emancipated, the finest examples of self-sacrifice and unselfishness. In order, therefore, to perpetuate this feeling he formed a socio-political institution known as the People's Convention which for about five years met annually in Spanish Town, on the 1st of August. Then public questions were discussed and from thence representations were made to the Government in the interest of the people. One of his desires was to bring to the front the more intelligent young women of the race and to some extent he succeeded admirably. The object of these convention gatherings was at first misconceived, and when the project was given out to the public, the press was unsparing in its criticism, individuals deprecated the idea, and prophesied the resurrection of racial animosities, and class antagonisms, but fortunately, they were disappointed. The management was wise, their leader was restrained and before the movement expired it deserved the encomium of the press and the public.

Dr. Love's sincerity was often questioned, but those who knew him best could come to no other conclusion than that he meant the best for his race and if his methods were defeated his motives were good and his heart beat true. He created enemies, but made many friends and it is a remarkable instance of the high esteem in which he was held, that many who failed to publicly identify themselves with him became **His Secret Disciples** and supporters.

Such was Dr. J. Robert Love, M.D., J.P., a man of scholarly attainments, the most brilliant orator of Jamaica in his day: fearless, dignified, independent, devoted to the best interests of the country in which he spent the fading years of his life. Truly as has already been said: "He made by force his merits known." Such a man was J. Robert Love that even when through ill-health he was obliged to be exceedingly careful he never absented himself, except unavoidably, from the City Council or the Parochial Board or the Legislative Council, and though that thrilling voice could not be heard there to gratify his admirers, yet everyone felt that he was conscientious, sincere, true to his convictions, unselfish in the motives that had led him into public life. He could be trusted always to vote conscientiously and in the interest of the unvoiced masses of the people.

A most touching notice has been given him, and one that appears true to the mark, in the Jamaica *Times* by one who took the trouble, no doubt, to study him properly more than other journalists have done.

Dr. Love was a man who for twenty-five years stood in the limelight of public opinion, sacrificed himself, and up to the very last that his strength permitted, stood up to his public duties, almost forgotten, except for the glimpses given him from time to time by the newspaper reporters. He has passed away to the grave, little thought of by the crowds that he helped, little remembered by those with whom he fought shoulder to shoulder, little honoured by those who sang his praises when he was a man to be counted with. But while his body moulders in the grave, his writings, the speeches he gave, the causes he advocated, the principles that ennobled his actions; the motives which lacked his efforts; the self-sacrificing efforts he ever bestowed, all seem to go marching on and will be a continuous record of one who, as the chairman has said, any country and any race can be justly proud of. We meet here to-night to honour that memory. He has left behind him lessons which it would do us well to copy: fearlessness in the expression of the opinions we have and feel to be right; high aims laid before us and the most strenuous efforts towards their attainment; the absence of partiality which makes us deal with some questions in a way that prejudices is put aside; a feeling broad enough to sweep all men within its folds; a general desire for the best good for the greatest number of the people at any time. Here was a man who strove to the best of his ability for the people of his race, and especially for the female element. I had the opportunity of listening to him and knowing his views with regards to them. He would speak of some plan in his mind which lack of means and other help prevented him realizing—all for the benefit of what he used to call the girls of this country.[4] If his efforts failed to achieve all the things he set himself out to realize, perhaps this was useful at the time. For those of us who are able to look at things in the proper perspective may be able to follow the leaders and do our best to follow their ideals and follow the pure motives which actuated them in their lifetime.

Dr. Love lives no more. His country lives on, his race lives on. He leaves behind footprints that are not easy to efface. Let it be ours to follow in those footsteps that when we too have passed away the influence left behind by each one in turn may be a source of blessing to those that survive.

Mr. J. A. Stuart and Mr. Marcus Garvey also spoke on the life of the Doctor, after which the meeting was brought to a close with the singing of the National Anthem. . . .

Printed in the *Daily Chronicle*, Friday, 4 December 1914. Original headlines have been omitted. The UNIA subsequently announced (ibid., Saturday, 9 January 1915) that it would publish in pamphlet form the panegyric delivered on the life and work of the late Dr. J. Robert Love; however, it has not been found.

1. Arthur James Balfour (1848–1930), first earl of Balfour and Conservative party leader, entered Parliament in 1874. He became leader of the House of Commons in October 1891, rising to the position of first lord of the admiralty in the wartime coalition government in May 1915. He was appointed as foreign secretary on Lloyd George's accession as prime minister in 1916. Balfour resigned as foreign secretary on 24 October 1919, but he retained his place in the British cabinet as lord president of the council. (*DNB*).

2. Printed above.

3. This letter has not been found.

4. Love hoped "that serious and earnest efforts are being made to lift the black girl up to the level of true, virtuous, self-respecting womanhood, conscious of the sacredness and dignity of her special mission in life" (*Jamaica Advocate*, passim). This aspiration was formally listed among the "Things Which the 'Jamaica Advocate' Would Like to See."

7th December, 1914.

Dear Sir,

        I have received your letter of the 5th Inst.
and I have much pleasure in enclosing a Cheque for
Two Pounds (£2. 0. 0.) towards the funds for providing
a Dinner and treat for the poor of Kingston on Christmas morning, and also to help to hold a Concert on
Christmas morning at the Union Poor House, and for
a distribution of flowers to the inmates of that
institution.

                        Believe me,

                        Yours truly,

Marcus Garvey, Esq.,
        President, The Universal
                Negro Improvement Association,
                        121 Orange St. & 32 Charles St.,
                                Kingston.

Sir William Henry Manning to Marcus Garvey (Source: EDSG)

Newspaper Reports

[*Daily Chronicle*, 11 December 1914]

COMING CONCERT

The concert arranged by the Universal Negro Improvement Association under the patronage of His Worship the Mayor of Kingston[1] to come off in the Ward Theatre on Wednesday of next week [*16 December*], promises to be a great success. This concert is arranged for the purpose of raising the necessary funds to provide a dinner and treat to the poor of Kingston on Christmas Day, and the management have also decided to hold a concert and distribute flowers at the Union Poor House as also the General Hospital on Christmas morning.

An appeal is made to all those who desire to help in any way in making the programme for Christmas a success. The arrangements call for a lot of helpers, and the opportunity is afforded friends and well wishers of the

Society to help either by attending the concert in the Theatre, assisting at the dinner, sending flowers or contributions to the Christmas morning concert programme. The arrangements are non-sectarian and the sole desire of the association is to reach the poor and unfortunate, irrespective of creed.

Those who desire to send flowers or help in any way, can communicate to Miss Eva Aldred, the lady President; Miss Amy Ashwood, General Secretary; or Mr. Marcus Garvey, President of the Male Division, or Mr. T A McCormack, General Secretary, 121 Orange Street.

Admission to the concert next Wednesday, is as follows:—Parquette 1/-, Gallery, sixpence, Dress Circle reserved for patrons,[2] tickets for which are *obtainable on application*.

The debate which should have been held by the society in the Collegiate Hall last Tuesday night [*8 December*] was postponed (owing to the threatened attitude of the rain) until January next year.

Printed in the *Daily Chronicle*, Friday, 11 December 1914.

1. H. A. L. Simpson.
2. Also listed as patrons of the concert were "His Lordship Bishop [John J.] Collins and other prominent members of the community" (*Gleaner*, Wednesday, 16 December 1914).

[*Gleaner*, 14 January 1915]

U.N.I.A. ADDRESSED BY MAYOR
THE JAMAICA DIALECT
MEMBERS NAME SOME FOREMOST REPRESENTATIVES OF COLOURED RACE

The last general meeting of the Universal Negro Improvement Association was held in the Collegiate Hall on Tuesday evening last [*12 January*]. The visitor of the evening was the Hon. H. A. L. Simpson who delivered an interesting address on the Abuse of Jamaica Dialect.

Several letters were read including one from Sir Sydney Olivier, asking that his best wishes be conveyed to the members of the society and wishing the society success in its objects.[1]

Mr. E. Morris Gordon of Boston, Mass.,[2] wrote to the President expressing his pleasure at the work being done by the society in helping to promote better conditions among the people of Jamaica. He also mentioned reading with interest articles written by the President on the Negro question in various English papers.

In opening the meeting the President said: "Your worship, ladies and gentlemen, I am pleased to welcome you here this evening to the first meeting of our association for the year, as also to thank you for the keen interest you have manifested in the past in our efforts to raise the people of our race of this community to a higher status among the classes. The Universal Negro Improvement Association has a programme to carry through that calls for the energy and grit obtainable of those who like working in the cause of improving the condition of an unfortunate and neglected people. We have been working as a society for some months in this community and to take a retrospective view of our efforts and endeavours, we can confidently say that we have achieved more than any other society started on similar lines within the short period of time. We say this not through conceit or bluff, but because it is true and the success of the past months has inspired us with new resolutions for this new year; hence we intend to be even more active in pushing forward the objects of our association and extend our scope of usefulness as far as possible under the circumstances of a trying and difficult time."

The President next introduced His Worship the Mayor to the meeting, who dealt at length with the dialect language of this country.

An important item of the evening's agenda was the election of the following gentlemen as representative men[3] of the race whose biography and autobiographies are to be used as requested by persons in America, for publication in the historical works of Dr. William Ferris, M.A. of Yale University, entitled "The African Abroad or His Evolution in Western Civilization." All Western Negro communities have submitted names of the worthy men of their countries, and the association was asked to make a selection.

After a lengthy nomination the following gentlemen were elected by fairly large majorities, except in two cases where the casting vote decided the election: Mr. Hector Josephs, K.C. representative of the law; Dr. J. Robert Love, M.D., J.P., (deceased) representative of literature and oratory; Rev. T. Gordon Somers, religion; Mr. Charles P. Lazarus, mechanics; Dr. J. J. Edwards, medicine;[4] Hon. David Corinaldi, politics;[5] Mr. Walter B. Parker (deceased) journalism;[6] Mr. B. de C. Reid, music.[7]

A resolution of condolence was passed on the demise of the Venerable Archdeacon Henderson Davis,[8] copies of which are to be forwarded to His Grace the Archbishop[9] and others concerned.

The next general meeting of the association will be Tuesday evening next [*19 January*] at 7.30 o'clock, when the postponed debate, "Is the intellect of woman as highly developed as of man's" will take place.

Printed in the *Gleaner*, Thursday, 14 January 1915.

1. The letter from Sir Sydney Olivier has not been located.

2. Egbert T. Morris Gordon, a Jamaican, lived in Boston and worked until 1919 as a bellman and a clerk. A branch of the Jamaica League was formed in Boston in 1920 with Gordon as president. He contributed articles to the *African Times and Orient Review*, and in an article in the *American Recorder* (16 February 1929) he listed his profession as publicist. (*Boston City Directory*, 1911, 1913, 1914–24; Gordon, "The Eureka Cooperative Bank," *ATOR* [July 1912]:375; "American Notes," *Africa and Orient Review* 1 [January 1920]:27).

3. The phrase "representative men" was the title of the collection of lectures given by Ralph Waldo Emerson (1803–1882), first published in 1849, each of which explained Emerson's choice of Plato, Swedenborg, Montaigne, Shakespeare, Napoleon, and Goethe as great men.

4. Dr. James Josiah Edwards, M.D., (1865–?) was born at Ulster Spring, Trelawny. He received his medical and master's degree in surgery from McGill University in Canada; he also held licentiates from the Royal College of Physicians and Surgeons (Edinburgh); and he was also a fellow of the Royal Institute of Public Health (London). (*WWJ*, 1916).

5. David Aurelius Corinaldi (1834–1920) served as a member of the Legislative Council for St. James for twenty-one years and as a justice of the peace and member of the St. James Parochial Board. An outstanding public debater and linguist, Corinaldi was consular agent in Jamaica for Colombia and the publisher and editor of the *New Century* newspaper. (The *Workman*, 13 March 1920, p. 2; *HJ*, 1921).

6. Walter Benjamin Parker (1877–1914) was the editor of the *Daily Chronicle*. Born in the parish of Manchester, Parker commenced his career as a journalist on *Gall's News Letter* and later became news editor of the *Gleaner*, before assuming his post as editor and manager of the *Daily Chronicle*. (See *Jamaica Historical Journal* 2 [June 1958]:94–97).

7. B. de C. Reid (b. 1872) was the composer of many sacred and secular musical works; the most famous was "Jamaica's Coronation Ode." He joined the Second West India Regiment band in 1886. He showed a marked musical ability and in a few years rose to the position of band sergeant. Subsequently he filled the position of acting band master for three years, but he could not receive a permanent appointment since a rule barred Jamaican natives from occupying the position. In 1906, however, he became band master of the Jamaica militia and also of the Montego Bay Citizens' Association band in 1908. (*Jamaica Times*, 5 August 1911).

8. Charles Henderson Davis (1846–1915) was ordained a deacon in 1870 and appointed curate the same year. He was appointed rector of Green Island (1871–81); Lucea, Hanover, (1881–95); and Savanna-la-Mar (1895–1915). On numerous occasions he acted as the senior archdeacon in the absence of the Anglican bishop of Jamaica. (*HJ*, 1916).

9. The Most Rev. Randall Thomas Davidson (1848–1930), archbishop of Canterbury, 1903–28. No copy of the UNIA's condolence resolution has been found. (*WWW*).

Article by Marcus Garvey in the *Jamaica Times*[1]

[16 January 1915]

THE UNIVERSAL NEGRO ASSOCIATION
WHAT IT AIMS AT.
REAL ARISTOCRACY OF RACE.
SPECIALLY WRITTEN FOR THE JAMAICA TIMES
BY MARCUS GARVEY, JR.

The Universal Negro Improvement and Con[s]er[v]ation Association and African Communities' League was found in Jamaica on the 1st of August, 1914, and since that time the Jamaica Division has been keeping itself before the sober world of reason and progress, and it is gratifying to say that the most cultured and liberal-minded of the people of this country have extended their good wishes for the success of the organization. There are, no doubt, a large number of people who do not properly understand the objects of the Association, and it is but right that the necessary information regarding its aims should be submitted to them, hence I take great pleasure in explaining and submitting the following:

In view of the fact that the Negro, in the classification of races, is regarded as a backward and inactive being, and that he is dubbed and believed to be capable of nothing worthy or elevating, thereby falling below the standard and appreciation of the more progressive races, it was thought fit to found an Association and League which should have for its object the raising of the standard of the Negro to the level of the more progressive of mankind, hence it was decided to found the Universal Negro Improvement and Conservation Association and African Communities' League. This society has been founded and is now in active operation, taking as its objects the promotion of a Universal Confraternity; the promotion of the spirit of pride and love; the reclamation of the fallen; the administering to, and assisting of the needy; the civilizing of the backward tribes of Africa; the administering of Commissionaries in the principal countries of the world for the protection and representation of all Negroes, irrespective of nationality; the promotion of a sound Christian worship among the non-Christian tribes of Africa; the establishing of Universities, Colleges and Secondary Schools for the further education and culture of the boys and girls; the establishing of Industrial and other Institutions for the general encouragement of industry, etc. These are the general objects of the society; but each community in which the Society operates has its own environments, hence local divisions are permitted to promote their objects according to such environment, providing the

LOCAL OBJECTS

in no way conflicted with the general ones.

The Jamaica division having adopted itself to local environments have decided on the following objects which are now being carried out to establish educational colleges, (day and evening) for the further education and culture of our boys and girls and to train them to a higher state of application among the more advanced classes; to reclaim the fallen and degraded of the people (especially the criminal class) and help them to a state of good citizenship; to work among, administer to, and help the needy; to rescue our fallen girls from the pit of prostitution and vice; to promote a cordial relationship between all men and strengthen the bonds of brotherhood; to help generally in the development of the country[.] No fair-minded and impartial observer can say that the condition of the Jamaica Negro is proportionately satisfactory. To take the people as a whole as all people are generally taken and judged, one can come to no other conclusion than that the Jamaica Negro is a social and moral nonentity. No people are judged

OF THE FEW

or the exceptions, but by the bulk, and when the fair-minded man comes to pass his opinion on our people, he can't but say that we are extremely backward. The backwardness of the masses of the race is accountable for through the callous indifference of one class of Negroes towards the other. The Negro who has just immerged from starving and who has been fortunate enough to find clean clothing and a comfortable home thinks himself an aristocrat, the imaginary descendant of an ancestral nobility other than that of Africa. He being ordinarily positioned, forgets that his brothers and sisters, who are from the same parentage, are barefooted and untidy and that his parents too are charges on the charity or poor rate of the country. Such is the blinding tomfoolery of the Negro towards the Negro, and until he realizes that there can be no aristocracy in race until such a race, as a whole, brings itself into respect, he shall be the "gaming-stock" of the cultured and progressive races, who do not admit nor believe that environments or circumstance remove one from the

TIE OF BLOOD

relationship in race.

If the dreaming aristocratic Negro of Jamaica would cease keeping up the [f]ar[ci]cal pride of exclusiveness in the race and his own family endeavour, every man, to raise his kin, there would really be no hardship in producing and presenting to the world within the next quarter of a century a class of Negroes comparable with the best of any other race, and then, but not until then, should the Negro think of aristocracy in race.

Jamaica can be a guide to the world on the reorganization of racial exclusiveness[.]

FORTUNATELY FOR US

the races do not ant[a]gonise one another here, the only difference between the Negro and his Caucasian brother is that the former is on the average crude and unrefined whilst the latter is wholly cultured and refined yet the latter is a true friend of the former, as far as friendship leads one into service to another. If our Negro populace were cultured and refined I feel perfectly sure that there would be no social exclusiveness, as far as the exclusiveness of one race protects itself against the social incursion of the other. But so long as the Negro elects to rem[a]in degraded and uncouth, so long must he expect to be debarred and excluded from the social companionship of his peers.

Any man who asserts that the average Jamaica Negro is equal to the White man in culture and refinement is an enemy of his race, he is void of fairplay and can, therefore, do the cause of the advancement of his race no good. In making these assertions I am fully aware that there are people of my race who will disagree with me, but methinks they are the very ones who feel themselves above their kindred.

Printed in the *Jamaica Times*, Saturday, 16 January 1915.

1. The *Jamaica Times*, in an article titled "Some Worthy Efforts" (17 October 1914), had previously reported the following: "Mr. Marcus Garvey, a young Jamaican, who has been to England for a course of study, has started here the Negro Universal Society which has excellent aims and has made a promising beginning."

Newspaper Report

[*Daily Chronicle*, 19 January 1915]

IMPROVEMENT ASSOCIATION

The Universal Negro Improvement Association at their meeting to-night in the Collegiate Hall, will pass a resolution praying that the bill of exclusion raised against negroes entering the United States,[1] be not made law, as in such a case inoffensive negroes from the West Indies and other places would be severely handicapped in their desire to acquire professions and study at their universities.

The subject for debate to-night is "Is the intellect of woman as highly developed as that of man's?" Mr. Marcus Garvey and Mr. A. A. Mends[2] will speak for the affirmative and Mr. L. Small and Mr. A. Daily for the negative. Members of the audience will be allowed to speak for five minutes. All are cordially invited to attend at 7.30.

Printed in the *Daily Chronicle*, Tuesday, 19 January 1915.

1. No report of the resolution has been found. On 7 January 1915, an immigration bill requiring a literacy test for aliens was sent to a joint House and Senate conference committee. It followed a vigorous debate over amendments added to the measure in the Senate excluding "members of the black or African race," while exempting Belgian agricultural immigrants from the literacy test and the contract immigration provisions of the law. Among those opposing the exclusion amendment was Booker T. Washington, who pointed to the important role played by West Indians (the principal black immigrants) in the construction of the Panama Canal. The exclusion amendment was finally defeated in the House by a vote of 252 to 75. (*NYT*, 1, 8 January 1915; David J. Hellwig, "The Afro-American and the Immigrant, 1880–1930: A Study of Black Social Thought" [Ph.D. diss., Syracuse University, 1973], pp. 212–15, 220–40; Hellwig, "Building a Black Nation: The Role of Immigrants in the Thought and Rhetoric of Booker T. Washington," *Mississippi Quarterly* 31 [Fall 1978]: 529–50).

2. Alfred Alexander Mends (1871–?) was active in a variety of reform movements in Jamaica. Prevented from legally practicing medicine, he earned his living as a homeopath and herbalist. He became the editor and manager of a number of short-lived newspapers as well as an activist in the Jamaica Federation of Labour. In 1923, following a brief period as general secretary of the Ethiopian Progressive and Cooperative Association Ltd., a UNIA-splinter group, he helped found the Jamaica Reform Club, an organization that played an important role in events leading to the Darling Street labor disturbance of 1924. A "radical democrat" rather than a socialist or trade unionist, Mends repeatedly called for "a restoration of the status quo ante, 1865." Mends also became the editor in 1935 of *Plain Talk*, the radical pro-Ethiopian organ that did much to channel popular feeling in the years immediately preceding the labor disturbances of 1938. Toward the end of his career, Mends cofounded a short-lived church at Bull Bay in eastern Kingston, "The Jamaica Reform Baptist Catholic and Apostolic Church." In the mid-1930s Mends became active in the British West Indian Labour party and in 1939 he submitted a memorandum to the visiting West India Royal Commission giving his explanation for the violent labor upheaval of the preceding year. (W. F. Elkins, *Street Preachers, Faith Healers, and Herb Doctors in Jamaica* [New York: Revisionist Press, 1977], chapter 7; Mends, "Can There Still be Hope for Reformation in Jamaica" [Kingston: The Temple of Fashion Printers, 1923]; "Things I Remember," [By the Cardinal], *Sunday Gleaner*, 14 January 1973).

Marcus Garvey to the *Gleaner*

[25 January 1915]

THE EDITOR, Sir,—

I hereby take the opportunity of returning thanks to you and to the other gentlemen of this community for the kind assistance you have rendered me in organizing and starting the Universal Negro Improvement Association in Jamaica.

For the six months of the society's existence we have been able to do a lot of good work on the lines of our objects as set forth from time to time, and we do hope that as soon as things shall have taken normal shape, we shall be in a position to carry through all the objects for which we labour.

The following gentlemen have given donations to help in bearing the expense of the general organization of the society: Sir W. H. Manning, £2; Mr. E. J. Wortley,[1] 5/; Rev. R. J. Ripley,[2] 2/6; Capt. J. Roser, 10/; Messrs. F. Chas. Fisher,[3] 5/; A. E. Motta,[4] 4/; S. Murad,[5] 5/; S. C. Lindo, 4/; J. H. Levy, 10/; G. P. Myers[6] 5/; A. Sept. Smith 5/; J. Wray & Nephew,[7] 10/; Geo. N. Penso,[8] 5/; Rev. Arthur Kirby,[9] 2/6; Messrs. Felix D. Rowe, 10/; E. R. Mordecai,[10] 5/; Pow Hing and Co., 10/; Vernon E. Grossett, £1 1s.; J. T. Hudson, 5/; Rev. Ernest Price,[11] 5/; Messrs. J. B. Lucie-Smith,[12] 6/; H. A. Cunha,[13] 5/; S. A. Nightingale, 5/; C. M. Ryan, 5/; K. Robinson, 5/; Prof. Monaghan,[14] 5/; Edwin Charley,[15] 10/; Mr. and Mrs. William Wilson,[16] £1 1s.; Palace Amusement Co., £1 1s.; Movies, Ltd., 5/; Messrs. A. deC. Myers,[17] 5/; W. Harris,[18] 5/; H. H. Cousins, 5/; Dr. Rerrie,[19] 5/; General Blackden,[20] 5/; Messrs. Gould,[21] 4/; Ralph Isaacs,[22] 4/; Ernest DeSouza,[23] 2/; Rev. S. O. Ormsby,[24] 5/; Messrs. H. I. C. Brown,[25] 5/; A. McDougal, 5/; T. R. Mac-Millan,[26] 5/.

Again thanking you and the above gentlemen as also the Rev. Mr. Graham for considerate help I am, etc.,

MARCUS GARVEY, PRESIDENT,
U.N.I.A.

Printed in the *Gleaner*, Monday, 25 January 1915. Original headline has been omitted.

1. Rev. Canon Edward Jocelyn Wortley, Anglican rector at Half-Way-Tree, was a canon of the Anglican cathedral in 1909, and an assistant commissary in 1910. (*WWJ*, 1919–20).

2. Rev. Reginald John Ripley became rector of St. Ann's Bay Anglican Church in 1891. He also served as rector of the Anglican parish church, Kingston, in 1909; rector and senior canon of the Anglican cathedral, Spanish Town, 1901–04; and a senior curate for the Kingston parish church, 1908–10. (*WWJ*, 1919–20).

3. Frederick Charles Fisher was a dry goods merchant and senior member of the Fisher Land and Lumber Co. (*WWJ*, 1916).

4. Alfred E. Motta, a solicitor, was admitted to practice 13 June 1904. (*WWJ*, 1916).

5. Salim Murad was a junior partner of the firm of Murad & Bro., wholesale dry goods merchants in Kingston. (*WWJ*, 1916).

6. George Paton Myers (?–1924), was a former engineer attached to the Naval Dock Yard at Port Royal; after retirement from the service of the Admiralty, he entered political life and became mayor of Kingston, and later member of the Legislative Council for Kingston. In 1916, he was unanimously elected chairman of the Kingston General Commissioners. (*HJ*, 1925).

7. Jamaica's leading rum manufacturer.

8. George Norman Penso was a carriage builder and at one time chairman of the St. Andrew Parochial Board, and chairman of the board of management of the Kingston and St. Andrew Union Poor House. (*WWJ* 1919–20).

9. Rev. Arthur Kirby served as pastor of the Coke Chapel (Wesleyan Methodist). (*WWJ*, 1921–24).

10. Ernest Rienzi Mordecai (1868–?) was a wholesale merchant who started his own business after the earthquake in 1907, having formerly been connected with the firm of A. Mordecai & Co. for thirty years. (*WWJ*, 1916).

11. Rev. Ernest Price, B.A., B.D. (1874–1965?) was invited to Jamaica from England in 1910 to become president of the Calabar Theological College. He also served as the senior representative in Jamaica of the Baptist Missionary Society of England. He reopened Calabar High School in 1912 and he became a member of the government's board of education in 1914. Rev. Price presided on various occasions at meetings of the Progressive Negro Association in 1916. He was also an ex officio member of the council of the Jamaica Baptist Union and the Jamaica Baptist Missionary Society. (*WWJ*, 1916).

12. John Barkly Lucie-Smith (1851–1915), postmaster of Jamaica, was the son of Sir John Lucie-Smith, the chief justice of Jamaica. (*HJ*, 1916).

13. Herbert A. Cunha was an associate of the Society of Accountants and Auditors, Great Britain. (*Jamaica Advocate*, 2 March 1895).

14. James Charles Monaghan (1857–1917), American consul at Kingston, entered the diplomatic service, serving as the American consul in various German cities from 1885–1900. He later taught at the University of Wisconsin (1900–03) and the University of Notre Dame (1906–08). In July 1915, during his tenure as consul at Kingston, he was reported to have delivered an address on Booker T. Washington at St. George's College in Kingston. (*Gleaner*, Saturday, 3 July 1915; *NCAB*, vol. 27; DNA, RG 84, file 842, "Industrial Education in Jamaica".)

15. Edwin Alexander Charley (1873–1940) was a wine and spirit merchant, a rum manufacturer, and the owner of Innswood Sugar Estate in St. Catherine. In 1937 his rum manufacturing business was acquired by Messrs. Fred L. Myers and Son. (*DG*, 19 June 1940).

16. William Wilson (1871–?), a Kingston businessman, was born in England and came to Jamaica in 1899. After the earthquake in 1907, he was instrumental in forming the Jamaica Policyholders Association, which fought the litigation over local insurance claims. He was also a member of many wartime and fraternal organizations, as well as justice of the peace for the parish of Kingston. (*WWJ*, 1916; Colonel Roger Willock, "Caribbean Catastrophe: The Earthquake and Fire at Kingston, Jamaica, B.W.I., 17–19 January 1907," *American Neptune* 29 [April 1968]:118–32).

17. Alfred de Cordova Myers (1879–?), a solicitor of the firm of Myers and de Cordova. (*WWJ*, 1916).

18. W. Harris (1860–?) was superintendent of the Jamaican public gardens and plantations. (*WWJ*, 1916).

19. Dr. Percy Rerrie was a medical officer for the Blue Mountain coffee estates, and a member of the Rerrie family of Winders Hill, St. Ann's Bay, Garvey's neighbors during boyhood.

20. Brigadier-General Leonard Shadwell Blackden, CBE (1863–1937), served as inspector of the West Indian local forces and general commanding officer of Jamaica, July 1914–August 1918. (*WWW*).

21. Henry Gould was the chief engineer of the Kingston General Commissioners and later the chief engineer of Kingston and St. Andrew Corp. (*WWJ*).

22. Ralph Henry Isaacs (1866–1922) was the managing commissioner of the Kingston General Commissioners beginning in 1913. He was also a justice of the peace for Kingston and St. Andrew. (*HJ*, 1923).

23. Ernest DeSouza was a commercial school principal.

24. Rev. Stephen Oliver Ormsby (?–1924) was the rector of St. Michael's Church, Kingston, beginning in 1903. (*HJ*, 1925).

25. Henry Isaac Close Brown (1874–1962) was educated at York Castle High School in Jamaica and Pembroke College, Oxford. He was acting solicitor general of Jamaica from 1905 to 1906; assistant to the attorney general from April 1906 to January 1912; and acting attorney general at various other times. He also served as judge of the Kingston Court for periods in 1912, 1914, and 1918. He was appointed a justice of the peace for Kingston in 1915 and appointed

puisne judge of the Supreme Court of Judicature of Jamaica in 1922. He was also the district grand master of English freemasonry in Jamaica. S. A. G. Cox, founder of the National Club, was married to Brown's sister. (*DG*, 26 March 1962; *Jamaica Standard*, 26 February 1938).

26. Thaddeus Rudolph MacMillan (1872–?) was a solicitor and member of the Mayor and Council of Kingston, a trustee of Wolmer's School Trust, member of the St. Andrew Parochial Board, and the board of management of the Kingston and St. Andrew Union Poor House. (*WWJ*, 1919–20).

Newspaper Reports

[*Gleaner*, 28 January 1915]

New Society
Meeting of Universal Negro Improvement
Assn. Paper on Character.
Address Delivered by the President on the
"Attitude of Race"

The general weekly meeting of the Universal Negro Improvement Association was held at Collegiate Hall on Tuesday evening last [*26 January*] when there was a large attendance of members and visitors. Amongst those present were: Messrs. Marcus Garvey, [(]President); Thomas Smikle (Vice-President)[1]; T. A. McCormack (General Secretary); Miss Amy Ashwood (Associate Secretary); Messrs. J. W. Milbourn (Treasurer); E. E. Reid, J. M. Reid, T. T. Brown, A. Peart, and Mrs. Peart, members of the Board of Management.

Read letter from Mrs. Gertrude A. Lane of Weatherills, Antigua, enquiring as to the objects of the Society,[2] and expressing the desire that the Association extends its scope of usefulness to other parts.[3]

After an entertaining recitation entitled "The Kaiser's God," by Mr. J. C. Beecher, Mr. Smikle read a paper on "Character," which was very instructive and interesting.

Mr. Bobbie Grieve followed with a sketch on ventriloquism and a song, both of which were well received.

The Secretary read a paper on "The Negro Fifty Years After the War of Retrospect," by Dr. Booker T. Washington. The paper was very engaging, and its contents were followed with the closest attention by those present.

The President delivered an address on the "Attitude of Race."

The paper was rather interesting. The speaker dealt with what he thought was an existing attitude of envy and dislike between the coloured man and his brother. In concluding he said: "For the present I am imploring the Negro to cease hating himself. Let him be more loyal to his own, and methinks that the next century will find him a man worthy of the true companionship of the ascendant race. To achieve the highest standard of civilised culture, it is not necessary for us to destroy or eliminate the good qualities that we have; what we must do is to add to them by loving ourselves."

The next general meeting of the Association will be held at the Hall next Tuesday evening [2 *February*], at 7.30 o'clock when a prominent citizen will deliver an address on "Thrift." The President and Vice-President will continue their discourses on "The Attitude of Race" and "Character," respectively.

Printed in the *Gleaner*, Thursday, 28 January 1915.

    1. Thomas Smikle, a teacher in Kingston, was one of the founding members of the UNIA.
    2. A parallel report published in the *Daily Chronicle* (Thursday, 28 January 1915) contained the following addition: "having seen mention of the society in the Christian Science Monitor of Boston." This referred to the published report, "Jamaican Negroes Express Loyalty in a Resolution," *Christian Science Monitor* (Thursday, 19 November 1914).
    3. The following addition to the sentence was contained in the report published in the *Daily Chronicle* (Thursday, 28 January 1915): "where similar conditions prevail, being also interested in the development of the people of these islands."

[*Gleaner*, 4 February 1915]

THE NEW SOCIETY.

The Universal Negro Improvement Association, held their weekly general meeting in the Collegiate Hall, on Tuesday evening last [2 *February*] when there was a large turn out of members and visitors. The chief speaker of the evening, was the Rev. R. A. L. Knight, M.A., B.Th., who delivered an interesting and instructive address on "Life in Canada."

The Chairman of the evening was the Vice-President, Mr. Thomas Smikle, and the programme was contributed to by Mr. V. Anderson, Mr. V. Hamilton, Mr. Marcus Garvey, Mr. S. McFarlane and Mr. H. B. Green. Speaking of his experience and observations of life in Canada, Mr. Knight said that there was no social distinction in that country; the people were truly democratic and they respected the rights of one and all. Agriculturally and industrially, the people had no prejudice against labour, for the dignity of labour was an understood and accepted principle throughout the Dominion. He exhorted his hearers to a keener appreciation of labour, and pointed out that it was by sticking to the soil here as elsewhere, and particularly in Canada, that the people and country could develop and go ahead. A debate will form one of the features of the general meeting next Tuesday night [9 *February*] to which the general public are invited.

Printed in the *Gleaner*, Thursday, 4 February 1915.

[*Gleaner*, 11 February 1915]

NEGRO IMPROVEMENT ASSOCIATION.
LECTURE ON "CO-OPERATION".

The last general weekly meeting of the Universal Negro Improvement Association was held in the Collegiate Hall on Tuesday night last [9 *Febru-*

ary]. There was a large turn out of members and friends. Among those present were Mr. Marcus Garvey, Jnr., President, in the chair, Mr. T. A. McCormack, general Secretary, Mr. Adrian A. Daily and Miss Amy Ashwood, associate secretaries, and Mr. and Mrs. Peart, Miss Amy Aldred, Miss Gwen Campbell, Mr. A. Murdock, Mr. T. T. Brown, Mr. E. E. Reid and Mr. J. M. Reid,[1] members of the Board of Management.

The debate for the evening was the question, "Is the intellect of woman as highly developed as that of man's?" Mr. A. A. Mends, supported by Miss G. Campbell and other members of the audience, spoke most forcibly for the affirmative, whilst Mr. L. Small and Mr. Adrian Daily and others of the audience argued for the negative. The negative won by a three to one majority.

ADDRESS BY THE REV. E. E. BROWN

The President next introduced the Rev. Ethelred Brown[2] to the meeting. This gentleman delivered an interesting address on the subject of "Cooperation". In the course of his remarks, Mr. Brown said, that one of the greatest needs of this island is the quality of co-operation. At the very outset there must be a oneness of aim and purpose. In the next place, successful co-operation requires mutual confidence among the persons co-operating. As a people, we are too much suspicious the one of the other. We refuse to believe in disinterested goodness, and suspect the motive of every man who sets out to work for the betterment of his fellows. Thirdly, there must be the absence of envy and jealousy. This is the potent cause of the failure of many attempts at co-operation in this country. And lastly, there must be loyalty to the ideals of the association, and obedience to its constituted authority[.] Individual pig-headedness has been the ruin of many promising institutions.

Mr. Brown then proceeded to point out the beneficial results of co-operation, and showed how it leads to economy of time and money by concentrating efforts; how it prevents disastrous competition; how it secures to the individual the powerful advocacy of the corporation, and how it secures to all the best contribution of each, and his lesson was expressed in the lines:

> "Bound by one great purpose
> In one living whole,
> Let us move together
> To the shining goal".

Printed in the *Gleaner*, Thursday, 11 February 1915.

1. One of the founding members of the UNIA in Jamaica, J. M. Reid served as a justice of the peace until 1955, when he was forced to retire because of failing vision. (Lionel Yard, interview with Reid, 1973).

2. Rev. Egbert Ethelred Brown (1875–1956) was a Unitarian minister who became a high official in the Jamaica League, a group organized in August 1914 to promote cooperative stores and local industries in Jamaica. He was also actively involved in organizing the Progressive

Negro Association and the Liberal Association, both of which were founded in 1916–17. During the labor disturbances that swept Jamaica in 1918–19, Rev. Brown emerged as a militant spokesman for the cause of the workers, publishing an original essay on labor conditions in Jamaica for the *Journal of Negro History* in 1919. Brown was one of the founders of the Jamaica Progressive League in 1936 in New York. (Mark Morrison-Reed, *Black Unitarians* [Boston: Universalist Unitarian Press, 1980]; interview with Mrs. Dorice Leslie [daughter of Rev. Brown], 1978; E.E. Brown Papers).

[*Daily Chronicle*, 27 February 1915]

Improvement Association
Musical & Literary Evening at the Collegiate Hall

One of the most successful of the weekly meetings of the Universal Negro Improvement Association came off at the Collegiate Hall on Tuesday night last [*23 February*]. The evening was a musical and literary one, an Elocution contest forming the chief feature of the evening's programme.

The large audience present bore testimony to the keenness in which the contest was held; and right heartily did they show their appreciation of the fine selections rendered by some of the contestants through their vociferous applauses. Mr. R. W. Bryant, Mr. A. L. Walcott,[1] and the Rev. Ethelred Brown acted as judges. The contributors to the musical part of the programme were:—Mr[.] Geo. McCorm[ac]k, whose splendid baritone solo charmed his auditors; Masters Alfred and Arthur Knight, who gave a beautiful pianoforte duet as an opening piece, and Master Michael Ashwood,[2] who rendered a comic song.

Eleven competitors c[a]me out to do battle for the various prizes, all of whom endeavoured to do full justice to their pieces; and when at the close of the contest Mr. R. W. Bryant ascended the platform to give out the judge's unanimous decision a breathless silence pervaded the hall. Before the result was given Mr. Bryant delivered a neat speech relative to young aspirants to the platform and the treatment they should receive. The beautiful gold filled watch presented by the Jamaica Tobacco Co., as first prize, was won by Mr. Marcus Garvey, who recited "Chatham on the American War".[3] Mr. Garvey's rendition was well received. The second prize was awarded Mr. T. L. McCormack which was of a dual nature, viz., a nickel watch and a gent's travelling case. This competitor recited "Byron's Darkness", and its delivery was very good.

Mr. Adrian Daily's interpretation of the "Battle of Trafalgar" was done in fine style; and right well did he deserve the loud applauses given him, as also the special remarks of congratulation by Mr. Bryant in handing the young gentleman the third prize, a beautiful electro-plated fruit dish. The consolation prize was won by Mr. A. Leo. Rankine. It was a volume of Tennyson's.

The lusty singing of the National Anthem brought a splendid evening to a close at about 10 o'clock.

Printed in the *Daily Chronicle*, Saturday, 27 February 1915. Original headlines have been abbreviated.

1. Master of West Branch school in Kingston and a member of the government board of education.

2. Younger brother of Amy Ashwood.

3. A reference to the one of four orations that William Pitt, earl of Chatham, gave concerning the American colonies. In November of 1777, Chatham addressed Parliament with his speech, "On the War in America," attacking the English conduct of the war and urging adoption of a spirit of compromise towards the Americans. His address became a favorite piece for recitation at elocution contests.

Address by Marcus Garvey

[*Daily Chronicle*, 26 March 1915]

PRESIDENT OF LOCAL SOCIETY ON ATTITUDE OF
RACE—ADDRESS BY PRESIDENT OF NEGRO
IMPROVEMENT SOCIETY ON RACIAL IDEALS
COMING VISIT OF MR. MARCUS GARVEY TO THE
UNITED STATES OF AMERICA
ON A LECTURE TOUR

The following address on the "Attitude of Race" was delivered by Mr. Marcus Garvey, Jnr., at a recent meeting of the Universal Negro Improvement Association of which he is President. Mr. Garvey is to leave for America shortly[1] where he is to lecture for three months among the coloured people of that country to raise funds to carry on the work of his association.

["]Ladies and gentlemen, I rise to continue my address before this Association on the "Attitude of Race",[2] and I am asking you to follow me through the discourse. To come to the solid points, I have, firstly, to draw your attention to the callous indifference our people manifest one towards the other in the development of racial ideals. The history of races has brought this to our knowledge—that all peoples belonging to particular races act differently in husbanding and propagating racial ideals quite different to the negro. The Jamaica negro has lived without a collective ideal: he lives a stranger to his own brother as if there was no natural affinity between the two. It is, indeed, strange, yet, ladies and gentlemen, it is fact and a lamentable one. Negroes as we are, domiciled in this country, away from our brothers who number millions, and who have their abode in different parts of the world, but especially in Africa and America, we cannot succeed in drawing ourselves away from them, yet we here possess traits which stamp us as being different from all other races and which is for me to-night, as a true friend and well-wisher, to point out to you and ask you to endeavour to train yourselves differently so that the observant onlooker and student of human nature might take a different view of us as a people.

["]We have had seventy-seven years of unfettered liberty to mould ourselves into appreciable beings. Through the clemency and brotherly kindness of the white man the opportunity of fostering an educational system, based on the highest civilized ideal, has been afforded us, and the seventy-seven years of application has not brought us up to an efficient state of culture, that culture which would stamp us as a different people to the crude and uncouth in race. These are not complimentary words to use to a people who apparently seem to be doing well to a point, but my friends, let us go beneath the surface of appearance, and I tell you boldly here to-night that the average Jamaica negro is anything but

FRIENDLY AND KINDLY DISPOSED

towards his own which is, indeed, a low trait or characteristic which should not even be found in the crude or untutored savage.

["]We find in Jamaica that people born in some districts who grow up under the same conditions, after taking on the serious responsibilities of life—such responsibilities that make one man responsible for his individual acts—get estranged towards one another, through the difference of success that comes to the particular individuals. One man makes the best of his time, and by his serious application to duty achieves success, he becomes an independent man, and through his independence and position he becomes somewhat raised from the others of his acquaintance who were not as sturdy and devoted as himself. Because of his elevated position above the others, a position, as I have pointed out, acquired through his own energy,—he is hated and spoken ill of by these former acquaintances, these schoolmates of his. The spirit of hatred and malice becomes rampant and in that spirit these acquaintances will plan and design all manner of tricks and unnatural methods to deprive the hated person of life itself, a thing which we all know and realize to be the prerogative of God. These are harsh things to say, yet they are true, and because they are true they need remedying. I, therefore, appeal to all the people of my race who are so disposed, to change your ways and live up to the brotherly loveliness of the other races, who by their actions and teachings point us to the value of the true spirit of racial unity and fellowship.

["]In Jamaica there is a stupid and frivolous idea existing in the minds of some of our people; and by this idea a goodly number of us think that when the negro is spoken of only the menial of the race is meant, and that one can speak of the negroes of this country without encircling the entire negro population of over 700,000.[3] When the student or man of letters speaks of the Negro, he does not mean to imply that the negro is only the man who walks the street barefooted and dirty or who ploughs the field in an unscientific way and who leaves his sphere of labour at noontide to return to an uncomfortable hovel where sanitation and cleanliness are strangers; but he also means the tailor-made or apparently respectable gentleman belonging to the same race, the gentleman who believes himself a high-born aristocrat, who claims kinship to the blood Africa.

["]What we better positioned negroes should realise is that we are in no way dissected from our unfortunate brothers and sisters who belong to the lowest strata of the one and same negro family. Respectable or not respectable, we all belong to the one and same negro race, and since we boast of a higher culture, a

LOFTY SPIRIT OF NOBLENESS

and would even believe ourselves aristocrats in race, it is for us to stretch our hands across and raise the fallen and degraded of our own people.

["]The history of the development of races teaches us that the first step to the up-growth of the people was not the establishment of a primary aristocracy, but the manifestation of a common interest in the advancement of the people, where one man tries to help and raise his brother and thereby establishes national independence and racial respect; and it is only after this independence and respect is established that the people think of aristocracy in race. How can a people speak of aristocracy when the aristocratic chap has his brother who belongs to the same kind loitering on the streets or idling in the gutter and being classified with the rogues and vagabonds of the country?

"What we want to do is to sink our selfishness and petty dislikes and join hands and hearts together and establish a sound system whereby all the members of our family can be held in regard, in the same respect as ourselves. We can achieve this only by encouraging and exhibiting the true spirit of love towards one another.

"Our Society, the Universal Negro Improvement Association, is founded for the purpose of helping to raise the people of our race to a higher state of appreciation among the more progressive races of the world. We have been criticised, not by the white man, for up to now he has been our truest friend, but by some of our own people and those who call themselves the aristocrats of the race. These people have been selfish enough as to say that they would not join a society of this kind, for they need no improvement. Well, ladies and gentlemen, it's not because you and I need individual improvement why we have founded this society; it is because we realise that our negro brothers and sisters who are not so fortunate as we are, need such improvement, and in improving them, in going into the lower life of the people and raising them to the higher and more congenial life, the life of respect, the life

OF CULTURE AND REFINEMENT

we shall be doing that which must commend us to the peoples of the other races who shall be willing to accept the negro on the pla[ne] of equality and comradeship when he (the Negro) shall have done the thing to merit respect. To achieve the ends on which this address is based, we propose to establish educational and industrial colleges for the further education and culture of our boys and girls; to reclaim the fallen and degraded, (especially the criminal class) and help them to a state of good citizenship, to administer to and assist the needy, to promote a wider taste for industry, etc., to promote a universal confraternity and strengthen the bonds of unity among the races, to rescue our fallen women from the pit of prostitution and vice, to help generally in the development of the country. We commend these objects to the people of Jamaica, and I feel sure that no broadminded man or woman, even though not of our race, will have aught to say against us.

"On the other hand, our white brothers have been the first to help and encourage us to improve ourselves, and if any good shall come out of this wide movement we have still to thank our white brothers for the start they have given us."

Printed in the *Daily Chronicle*, Friday, 26 March 1915.

1. A report published the previous day stated: "Mr. Garvey intends to leave Jamaica towards the end of April for the United States. . . ." (*Daily Chronicle*, Thursday, 25 March 1915).

2. The first half of Garvey's address was not published by any of the Jamaican newspapers.

3. The black population listed in the 1911 Jamaican census was 630,200 or 75.8 percent of the total.

Marcus Garvey to Booker T. Washington

Kingston, Jamaica, W.I.
April 12 1915

Dear Doctor Washington:

Some time last year I wrote to you informing you of my proposed visit to America to lecture in the interest of my Association and you were good enough to write to me inviting me to see your great institution.

I am expecting to leave for America between May and June and I shall be calling on you. I intend to do most of my public speaking in the South among the people of our race. I enclose you a manifesto of our Association which will give you an idea of the objects we have in view. I am now asking you to do your best to assist me during my stay in America; as I shall be coming there a stranger to those people.

I need not reacquaint you of the horrible conditions prevailing among our people in the West Indies as you are so well informed of happenings all over Negrodom.

Trusting to be favoured with an early reply With best wishes I remain Your Obedient Servant

UNIVERSAL NEGRO IMPROVEMENT
ASSOCIATN PER MARCUS GARVEY

P.S. I take the opportunity of enclosing your Patron's tickets for a concert to which we ask your patronage—as also envelope.

MG

DLC, BTW. ALS, Recipient's copy. List of officers included in Appendix III.

The Universal
Negro Improvement and Conservation Association and African Communities' League.

FOUNDED AUGUST 1, 1914.

In view of the universal disunity existing among the people of the Negro or African race, and the apparent danger which must follow the continuance of such a spirit, it has been deemed fit and opportune to found a Society with a universal programme, for the purpose of drawing the peoples of the race together, hence the organization above-named.

All people of Negro or African parentage are requested to join in with us for the propagation and achievement of the following objects.

GENERAL OBJECTS:

To establish a Universal Confraternity among the race.
To promote the spirit of race pride and love.
To reclaim the fallen of the race.
To administer to and assist the needy.
To assist in civilizing the backward tribes of Africa.
To strengthen the imperialism of independent African States.
To establish Commissionaries or Agencies in the principal countries of the world for the protection of all Negroes, irrespective of nationality.
To promote a conscientious Christian worship among the native tribes of Africa.
To establish Universities, Colleges and Secondary Schools for the further education and culture of the boys and girls of the race.
To conduct a world-wide commercial and industrial intercourse.

LOCAL (JAMAICA) OBJECTS:

To establish educational and industrial colleges for the further education and culture of our boys and girls.
To reclaim the fallen and degraded (especially the criminal class) and help them to a state of good citizenship.
To administer to, and assist the needy.
To promote a better taste for commerce and industry.
To promote a universal confraternity and strengthen the bonds of brotherhood and unity among the races.
To help generally in the development of the country.

MARCUS GARVEY, *President and Travelling Commissioner.*
THOS. SMIKLE, *Vice-President.*
EVA ALDRED, *President Ladies' Division.*
T. A. McCORMACK, *General Secretary.*

Office : 30 CHARLES STREET, KINGSTON, JAMAICA.

BOARD OF MANAGEMENT.

Marcus Garvey, Thomas Smikle, T. A. McCormack, Adrian A. Daily, E. E. Reid, T. T. Brown, J. R. Murdock, A. Peart, Arthur McKenzie, J. M. Reid, A. Knight, Robert Cross, Eva Aldred, Amy Ashwood, Gwen. Campbell, Connie Phillips, Mrs. A. Peart and Amy Aldred.

APPLICATION FOR MEMBERSHIP.

Secretary Universal Negro Improvement Association,
30 Charles Street, Kingston.

Dear Sir,
Please register me as an active member of our Society and send me from time to time all literature published by you. I enclose sixpence 6d. as my first monthly due.

Name...

Profession...

A..

(Source: TAM).

117

Booker T. Washington to Marcus Garvey

[*Tuskegee Institute, Alabama*]
April 27, 1915

My dear Mr. Garvey:

I have yours of April 12th advising of your proposed tour of this country and of your plan to visit Tuskegee Institute while in the South.

I am very glad indeed that you have decided to come here and it will give us all very great pleasure to make your stay as pleasant and as profitable as we can. Certainly I shall do what I can to help you while in this country.

I thank you for sending me the statement outlining the aim and purpose of the Negro Improvement Association. Yours very truly.

BOOKER T. WASHINGTON F

FES

DLC, BTW. TLR, Carbon copy. The signature is initialed "F," meaning that it was signed for Washington by Charles H. Fearing. Fearing was assistant secretary to the principal of Tuskegee Institute from 1908 until sometime after Washington's death in 1915. He was also associate editor of the *Tuskegee Student*.

Newspaper Reports

[*Daily Chronicle*, 28 April 1915]

VARIETY ENTERTAINMENT

To-night [*27 April*] what promises to be one of the best performances staged in Kingston for a long time is the Variety Entertainment and Band Concert to take place in the Collegiate Hall at 8 o'clock by the Universal Negro Improvement Association under the patronage of Sir John Pringle, K.C.M.G., Hon. Brig.-Genl. L. S. Blackden, Hon[.] D. S. Gideon,[1] Mr. J. H. Levy, Mr. William Morrison, Mr. A. E. Perkins and others of Kingston and St. Andrew who have intimated their intention of attending. The programme is very elaborate and those who attend can count on having an enjoyable time. The farce entitled "A Breach of Promise" will be staged.

Printed in the *Daily Chronicle*, Wednesday, 28 April 1915.

1. David Sampson Gideon CMG (1862–?), born in New York City, grew up in Jamaica and attended the Collegiate School in Kingston. He began his commercial career as a teenager and later rose to become chairman of the Jamaica Co-operative Fruit and Trading Co., resigning in 1894. In 1891 he was made a justice of the peace, and in 1896 he was elected member of the Legislative Council for Portland. He resigned his seat with the Legislative Council in 1900, and although reelected, he declined to sit as a protest against the government's manipulation of the constitution. In 1913, however, he reentered the council as a nominated member and became a permanent member of the Privy Council in 1917. In May 1923, he was appointed custos of the parish of Portland. (*HJ*, 1916; *WWJ*, 1916; F. L. Casserly, "Crown Colony Crisis: The

Hemming-Gideon Correspondence," *Jamaica Historical Review* 3 [March 1957]:39–78; and Frank Hill, "D. S. Gideon and Self-Government," *Jamaica Historical Society Bulletin* 2 [June 1957]:29–30).

[*Gleaner*, 29 April 1915]

LECTURE GIVEN ON THE WAR
GENERAL BLACKDEN AT THE NEGRO IMP. SOCIETY

The Negro Improvement Society had a successful time on Tuesday evening last [*27 April*], at the Collegiate Hall, when, after a fine musical programme, Brigadier General L. S. Blackden, Commander of the Forces, delivered a lecture on the war.

The building was crowded, a large number of visitors being in attendance, and the Rev. W. Graham occupied the chair.

After a masterly recital of "The Battle of Waterloo," by Mr. Glaister Knight, the Chairman, in a few appreciative remarks, welcomed General Blackden.

The lecturer was heartily received. He said he did not propose to give his audience a full history of the war, because that would take too much time. They had had war for nine months now—a war full of noble deeds and other things. He intended to give a lecture purely from the soldier's point of view, to show and explain the circumstances (not political) why the war was commenced, and the military and geographical reasons which forced the different armies to take up certain plans of campaign. . . .

The lecture lasted until after 10 o'clock, and General Blackden was accorded a hearty vote of thanks for having kindly accepted the invitation of the Society, and for the clear and masterly manner in which he had explained the whole situation.

The singing of the National Anthem brought the evening's entertainment to a close.

Printed in the *Gleaner*, Thursday, 29 April 1915. Original headline has been abbreviated.

Marcus Garvey to W. E. B. Du Bois (Source: MU, WEBDB)

Marcus Garvey to W. E. B. Du Bois

Kingston, Jamaica, W.I.
April 30, 1915

Mr. Marcus Garvey presents his compliments to Dr. E. B. Du Bois and begs to tender to him, on behalf of the Universal Negro Improvement Association, a hearty welcome to Jamaica, and trusts that he has enjoyed the brief stay in the sunny isle[1]

UNIVERSAL NEGRO IMPROVEMENT
ASSOCTN PER [*Marcus Garvey*]

MU, WEBDB, AN, Recipient's copy.

1. W. E. B. Du Bois spent over two weeks on vacation in Jamaica in April 1915, having just completed his pioneering work *The Negro* (New York: Henry Holt and Company, 1915). For reports of the event, see *Daily Chronicle*, 15 April 1915, 1 May 1915; and the editorial in the *Gleaner*, 1 May 1915.

J. C. Monaghan, American Consul, to Marcus Garvey

Kingston, Jamaica, May 14th, 1915

My dear Mr. Garvey:

I shall try to be at the meeting in the Collegiate Hall for any cause, such as your cause, appeals to me. Some time ago I lost my power to put things as I would like to put them, but if you deem anything that I say well enough said I will be glad to say something for you some night, selected by you, in June. I may be able to find a way to help you.

Your meeting calls for a "silver collection." I will find a little bit of silver, if not larger than a widow's mite, and I will see that it gets into the plate, even if I am not at the lecture itself.

I would be glad to select either one of the subjects selected by you, or one somewhat similar. I think, with God's help, that you can count on me saying something, certainly of doing something. Sincerely yours,

J. C. MONAGHAN
AMERICAN CONSUL

TNF, AJG. TLS, Recipient's copy.

Newspaper Report

[*Gleaner*, 19 May 1915]

IMPORTANCE OF EDUCATION

A fairly large attendance braved the weather last night [*18 May*] to listen to the lecture on Education, delivered by His Lordship Bishop Collins,[1] to the Negro Improvement Society at the Collegiate Hall.

His Lordship arrived at 8 o'clock accompanied by Rev. Fr. Patrick Mulry,[2] and in the absence of His Worship the Mayor, who should have taken the chair, Mr. Marcus Garvey introduced the Bishop.

THE LECTURE.

His Lordship, after thanking Mr. Garvey for his kind expression, said that the subject on which he had been asked to speak was a very broad one, and he did not think he would succeed in covering it during the course of the evening, but he would touch on a few of the essential points. The last time he spoke on the subject, someone said that education was not complete, unless it prepared a man or woman to earn a living. That was true in a sense. Education meant something that made a man ready to earn his living, no matter where he was placed. In every community, however, there should be men who were truly educated if that community was to be regulated and conducted along the right lines. There should be young men who gave themselves absolutely up to their studies, whose minds alone were developed, or whose minds chiefly were developed—men who received the training that would enable them to think for the whole of the community. When that did not exist then true education did not exist. Most people were born to work and earn a livelihood by their hands and their body, but there were others who were born to receive an education that would fit them to think for their fellows, and to know what was right and wrong. They could not expect the boy who went to college to spend his time with the hoe or fork. He might do a certain amount of physical labour for the exercise of his body, but the chief object of his life was the exercise of his mind so as to make himself a leader of men. All were not called for that, so that all were not called to that higher state of life, which was essential to every community. The great mass of mankind

DID NOT THINK.

He did not think God intended them to think. In all education, he claimed that the one thing was to make a teacher. If they failed to make the teacher, they failed to make the education; of course making the education was not all, there should be the necessary elements. They should however make the teacher, and that was particularly true in the Christian education. The great Master of life and death, our Lord and Saviour, was a teacher, and he said "I am the Light, the Truth, the Way." He was a teacher who by His life recommended the things He taught, a teacher whose conduct was beyond reproach. He was a great teacher. His own life was so attractive that it drew men to him. His life was an argument in favour of his doctrine. The life of every teacher should be a model for those he taught.

His Lordship then gave as illustration the Jesuit system of training teachers, showing how they devoted a lot of time to the study of the spiritual life, before they passed on to such subjects as mathematics, astronomy, philosophy, theology, history, ethics and everything within the range of human knowledge.

He said that if the Christian side was neglected, their education had been cut in halves, and the best side neglected, because they were only pilgrims here. An effort should be made to teach the people of Jamaica an intelligent love of the soil, because there was a lot in it. They should be taught to take an interest in the things around them and they would have far greater contentment, and life would be worth living. Sir Sydney Olivier once said, in very decisive tones, that the Agricultural Society did more good than the churches. He took exception to that statement at the time, and pointed out that the society had done nothing, except where the Priests and Ministers of religion started a branch society at Above Rocks, and now there were several around. It was the Priests and ministers who took up the work and spread it so that the churches had helped.

In conclusion His Lordship urged his hearers to take an intelligent interest in the things around them, and they would experience less of that pathos of the hardships of Jamaica life which was so impressive in some parts, where they thought life a real burden.

Mr. Garvey thanked his Lordship on behalf of the Association for his very able address and the singing of the National Anthem brought the meeting to a close.

Printed in the *Gleaner*, Wednesday, 19 May 1915. Original headlines have been abbreviated.

1. Bishop John J. Collins, S. J. (1856–1934) briefly held the position of president-rector of Fordham University before his consecration as vicar apostolic of Jamaica on 28 October 1907. He served in Jamaica until February 1920. (*HJ*, 1935).

2. Rev. Patrick F. X. Mulry, S. J. (1860–1922) was ordained in New York in 1892 and the following year he was sent to Jamaica, where he spent the next twenty years. For a time, Rev. Mulry held the positions of vice-chairman of the Kingston school board and member of the board of education. (*HJ*, 1923).

Robert Johnstone, Acting Colonial Secretary of Jamaica, to Marcus Garvey

Colonial Secretary's Office,
Jamaica, 31 May, 1915

Sir,

I am directed by the Governor to acknowledge the receipt of your letter dated the 27th Instant,[1] intimating that it is the desire of your Association to send through His Excellency a message of greeting and good wishes to His Majesty the King in connection with His Majesty's Birthday which message your Association desires should be sent by telegraph in order to reach His Majesty by the afternoon of the 2nd Proximo, at which time it is proposed that a resolution in terms of the message should be passed by your Association.

2.   I am to acquaint you in reply for the information of your Association that it will afford His Excellency pleasure to send the message as soon as the Resolution has been actually passed at the proposed meeting. A telegram will be prepared accordingly and will be issued as soon as you intimate to me on the afternoon of the 2nd June that the message has been adopted at the meeting.

3. I am to say however that the cost of the telegram will be Three pounds and Twelve shillings [*in the margin*: £3.12.0.] and that this amount should be remitted to this Office to be handed in with the telegram to the Direct West India Cable Office.

4. I am to say further that if your Association should so desire as an alternative His Excellency would be prepared to send the Message in a covering despatch through the Secretary of State for the Colonies[2] with the request that he would cause it to be laid before His Majesty.[3] I have the honour to be, Sir, Your obedient Servant,

ROBT. JOHNSTONE[4]
ACTING COLONIAL SECRETARY

[*Docket*] 7041   7961

TNF, AJG. TLS, Recipient's copy.

   1. Letter has not been found.
   2. Andrew Bonar Law.
   3. The resolution was sent to the king with a covering dispatch from the secretary of state for the colonies. (Sir William Henry Manning to Andrew Bonar Law, British Colonial Secretary, JA, CSO 1B/5/18/70, Jamaica No. 212).
   4. Robert Johnstone, CMG, (1861–1944) was made assistant colonial secretary in 1906 and acted as colonial secretary on numerous occasions. He also acted intermittently as governor of Jamaica during 1917–19. (*WWW*, 1941–50).

Newspaper Reports

[*Gleaner*, 4 June 1915]

ON CHILD LIFE.

The Universal Negro Improvement Association held their general meeting in the Collegiate Hall on Tuesday evening last [*1 June*] when there was a large turn out of members and visitors.

The Rev. Wilfrid Clarke, B.A., B.D. was the lecturer of the evening and spoke on "What shall we do with the child?" Mr. Thomas Smikle, vice-President of the association, occupied the chair.

After the reading of a letter from the Colonial Secretary relative to a cable message to be sent by the association through His Excellency the Governor to His Majesty the King, Mr. Marcus Garvey moved the following resolution:—"Be it resolved that the Universal Negro Improvement Association, in the name of the coloured people of Jamaica, sends greetings to His Majesty the King on this his 50th birthday and prays for a speedy and victorious termination of the war on the side of Britain and her Allies!" This resolution was seconded by Mr. J. R. Murdock,[1] and was carried with acclamation.

Rev. Clarke's Address.

On the Chairman introducing the Rev. W. Clarke to the audience, the rev. gentleman said:

Mr. Chairman, ladies and gentlemen. . . . I am very glad for the opportunity of speaking to the members and visitors of the Negro Improvement Association, because I feel it a duty to assist all good movements that have the uplifting of the people as their objects. The speaker continued to impress on his audience the helpful duty of assisting to make the life of the child a pleasant and useful one, after which he spoke about his coming departure to the front where he hopes to be placed in some Government office, telegraph office, hospital or somewhere where he shall be of some use. The revd. gentleman spoke of his strong attachment to Jamaica, because of its beauty and the people and expressed the hope to return some day to continue his work here, and trusted that he will have the opportunity of again visiting the association.

After the close of the address Mr. Adrian Daily moved a hearty vote of thanks to the speaker which was seconded by Mr. T. T. Brown[2] and heartily carried.

The singing of the National Anthem brought the meeting to a close.

On Tuesday night the 15th inst., the association will carry through the "Patriotic War Meeting" which should have come off yesterday afternoon in the Ward Theatre. The meeting will take place in the Collegiate Hall and will be in the interest of the "War Fund". The speakers for the occasion will be: Hon. H. A. L. Simpson, Mayor of Kingston, who will speak on "Jamaica's position in the War"; the Rev. W. Priestnal who will speak on "The War". Mr. R. W. Bryant, will speak on "The Effect of the War on the Empire", and the Rev. W. Graham will speak of "The influence of Christianity on the War."

Miss K. Craig, Miss F. Bennett, Mrs. Maud Markland and Miss C. G. Mitchell as also Mr. Geo. McCormack, Mr. T. A. McCormack, Mr. Cleve Irons will take part in the musical programme.

Printed in the *Gleaner*, Friday, 4 June 1915. Original headlines have been abbreviated.

1. Treasurer and member of the UNIA Board of Management.
2. Member of the UNIA Board of Management.

[*Gleaner*, 23 June 1915]

Talk on Thrift

The Hon. H. Cork, M.L.C. for the parish of St. Thomas, delivered a very entertaining and interesting lecture on "Thrift," at the weekly meeting of the Negro Improvement Society, which was held in the Collegiate Hall at 8 o'clock last night [*22 June*].

The President of the Society, Mr. Marcus Garvey presided, and the attendance was fairly large, Mr. Edwin Charley being among the visitors.

Mr. Garvey in introducing the lecturer said he had asked Mr. Cork to speak on the subject of "Thrift," because he knew that the hon. gentlem[a]n was a practical man and was responsible for his own development. . . .

The lecturer closed an interesting talk with a reference to one of Dickens most popular characters: Mr. Micawber's advice to his wife on thrift.[1]

Mr. T. Smikle, one of the officers of the society, emphasised the points laid down by the lecturer and thanked the hon. gentleman on behalf of the meeting for his interesting lecture.

The meeting then terminated.

Printed in the *Gleaner*, Wednesday, 23 June 1915. Original headlines have been abbreviated.

    1. Mr. Micawber was a character in *David Copperfield* (London, 1849–50); cf. chap. 12.

Andrew Bonar Law to
Sir William Henry Manning

[[Downing Street,
25th June 1915]]

. . . Sir—

I have the honour to acknowledge the receipt of your despatch No. 212 of the 2nd June and to inform you that the copy of the resolution which you enclosed has been duly laid before His Majesty the King who commands that his thanks should be conveyed to the Universal Negro Improvement Association for their loyal greetings on the occasion of his birthday. I have, etc.

(SGD.) A. BONAR LAW[1]

[*Address*] Governor, Brigadier-General
Sir W. H. Manning
K.C.M.G, C.B. Etc. etc.

Printed in the *Daily Chronicle*, Friday, 23 July 1915. Original headlines have been omitted. The initial portion of the newspaper report consisted of a transcription of Robert Johnstone's letter to Garvey.

    1. Robert Johnstone transmitted this Bonar Law letter to Garvey on 21 July 1915. (TNF, AJG).

GRAND CONCERT

—AT—

COLLEGIATE HALL,

Tuesday, 6th July, 1915, at 8 p.m.

—BY THE—

Universal Negro Improvement Association,

Assisted by other Ladies and Gentlemen.

Under the Distinguished patronage of His Excellency SIR WILLIAM H. MANNING, O.B., K.C.M.G., Governor of Jamaica, and The Hon. H. A. L. SIMPSON, M.L.C., Mayor of Kingston, in aid of

Feeding and Treating Four Hundred of the Poor of Kingston, 2nd August, 1915.

PROGRAMME.

PART I.

1.	March:	"Our Director"	Alpha Band
2.	Waltz:	"Sweet Voices"	M. J. H. Kesselo
3.	Piano Selection:	"Grand Opera"	Prof. A. Bosnifil
4.	Song:	"O Dry Those Tears"	Miss F. Bennett
5.	Song:	"Thora"	Mr. Geo. McCormack
6.	Violin Solo:	"As I Dream"	Miss Clem. E. Mitchell
7.	March:	"Oh Steer My Bark to Erin's Isle"	Alpha Band
8.	Recital;	"Battle of Trafalgar"	Mr. J. C. Irons
9.	Song:	"The Rosary"	Miss K. Craig
10.	Song:	"Selected"	Mrs. F. McCormack

10 MINUTES INTERMISSION.

PART II.

1.	Overture	"Star of the Sea"	Alpha Band
2.	Song:	"That Girl of Mine',	Mr. Geo. McCormack
3.	Violin Solo	"Parting no More"	Miss Clem. E. Mitchell
4.	Recital:	"The American War"	Mr. Marcus Garvey
5.	Song:	"When I Was Twenty One"	Miss E. Haughton
6.	Song:	"Selected"	Mr. Stanley Morand
7.	Recital:	"Downfall of Poland"	Mr. Adrian Daily
8.	Song:	"Dreaming"	Miss K. Craig
9.	Song:	"Selected"	Mr. V. Anderson
10.	Duet:	"Selected"	Mr. & Mrs. McCormack
11.	March:	"Col. Goetting's"	F. E. White

(Source: ATT, RRM).

127

Newspaper Report

[*Daily Chronicle*, 3 August 1915]

Improvement Association Proposal to Establish Industrial Farm in Jamaica

The Universal Negro Improvement Association is about taking up and putting through a scheme to establish in Jamaica a large industrial farm and institution on the same plan as the Tuskegee Normal and Industrial Institute of which Dr. Booker T. Washington is head. The object of the farm and institute will be to provide work for the unemployed and to provide the opportunity of training young coloured men and women for a better place in the moral, social, industrial and educational life of the country. Young men and women are to have the opportunity of learning a vocation and to gain a sound moral, literary and industrial training so that when they leave the institution they may by example and leadership help to change and improve the moral and industrial condition of the country.

Yesterday afternoon the Negro Improvement Association gave a treat to the poor at their hall in Charles Street. Two hundred persons participated in the treat.

Mr. Marcus Garvey, President of the Association, in addressing the large gathering, said it gave him pleasure to see such a large gathering of persons present this afternoon to partake of the things which have been got for them. He knew full well that there were some who would like to come and get something, but their past life has been such a good one that they do not come. But he could tell all those that in every country there are poor people, and furthermore, it is the duty of those who are in a better position than them to see that they are cared for. He would not weary them longer with a speech, but he would assure them that at all times when it was possible, his association would remember them. He then asked the ladies who were in charge to distribute the good things provided for those present. Among the officers of the Association present were Mr. T. McCormack, Mr. G. Murdock, Mr. I. Daly, Mrs. [*Maude*] Ashwood,[1] Miss [*Amy*] Ashwood and other ladies, who looked after the treat.

The President also conveyed the thanks of the Association to Sir John Pringle, K.C.M.G., Mr. H. I. C. Brown, K.C., Dr. G. C. Henderson, Mr. J. H. Cargill, and others, for contributions towards getting up the treat.

Printed in the *Daily Chronicle*, Tuesday, 3 August 1915. Original headlines have been abbreviated and subheads omitted.

1. The mother of Amy Ashwood.

First Annual UNIA Report

[*Gleaner*, 21 August 1915]

One year ago the Universal Negro Improvement Association was formed in Jamaica, during which period the organization has been making steady headway, and to-day it is known all over the world.

The scope of the organization is unbounded, as it aspires to embrace every phase of human life, and seeks to reach out to the remotest in its endeavor to serve the people. In a word, the scope of the society is in what the name implies.

After an extensive tour and study of the chief countries of Europe, the founder and President realized that the people of his race were far behind so far as progress and civilization—the ideal civilization of the day—were concerned. To him, the people of Africa were still in darkness, the coloured people of America were still far from the civilised ideal, and the peoples of the West Indies were outside the van of national pride and sentiments, and were in themselves little better than their brothers in Africa from the civilized and cultured standpoint. He realized that all the other races were so developed as to be properly represented and respected in Europe, but the darker man of Africa was without representation and was only regarded as a child of sympathy. There was, indeed a strong sympathy for him in Europe, a sympathy more warm and keenly felt than the sympathy for any other people. The rulers of Europe were anxious about the destiny of the negro, and the broadminded leaders of thought were eagerly awaiting the opportunity to do something to help the struggling son of Africa to raise himself to civilized manhood.

It was with the fullest confidence in the intention and desire of the liberty-loving and fairminded English people that the founder of the society planned and gave it a name with the approval of the liberal-minded of that country who are anxious to see the negro standing in the person of a recognizable brother and comrade. It takes a far way to go to realize all the objects of the society, but the founder, cognizant of this steadily forges his way on, and looks to the coming years to register the improvement of the people in general on the following lines:

A universal civilization; a universal confraternity; a universal spirit of pride and love; a universal brotherhood; the establishing of commissionaries or agencies in the principal countries of the world for the protection of the people irrespective of nationality; a universal university system; a better appreciation of Africa.

Locally, the society desires to establish educational and industrial colleges for the further education and culture of our boys and girls[,] to reclaim the fallen and degraded (especially the commercial class) and help them to a state of good citizenship, to administer to and assist the needy to establish industrial farms for the reclamation of discharged prisoners and finding work for the unemployed, to promote within the country a universal confraternity and strengthen the bonds of unity and brotherhood among the races; to rescue our young girls from the pit of prostitution and vice, to help generally in the development of the country.

Money is needed to make a success of the object of the society, and Europe would have supplied it, but to-day, unfortunately, Europe is at war, warring for the principles of the preservation of a higher civilization—and may God bless the Allies in this grand fight for liberty.

The society has friends and sympathisers all over the world, because its objects are good and commendable. The platforms of the Royal Albert Hall, the Guild Hall and Caxton Hall, as also the temporary stages of Hyde Park, Clapham Common and Trafalgar Square are as free and open to the principle of the society as they are to the Salvation Army, or any other humanitarian society in the British Empire, and the founder has laid the ground work of appealing to the liberal minded people of England, Scotland and Ireland whom he feels sure will help him in his efforts for the uplift of his race. For the present very little can be done until the Empire emerges from the war victorious.

Locally, the society has done a great deal of useful work for one year, and its thanks are due to the liberal minded of the gentry of this country who realize the necessity and possibility for improving the people to a better and higher appreciation among the cultured classes.

The founder begs to acknowledge the ungrudging support given him by His Excellency Sir William H. Manning, K.C.M.G., C.B., Hon. Robert Trefusis, Hon. H. Bryan, C.M.G., Hon. Brig. General L. S. Blackden, C.B., Hon. Sir John Pringle, K.C.M.G. Hon. Geo. McGrath,[1] Hon. D. S. Gideon, Hon. J. H. Levy, Hon. H. A. L. Simpson, Hon. H. T. Ronaldson, Hon. Henry Cork, Hon. H. H. Cousin, Hon. J. R. Williams, His Honour Sir Anthony Coll,[2] His Honour Mr. Justice C. Halman Beard,[3] Mr. H. I. C. Brown, B.A., LL.B., K.C., Mr. A. J. Corinaldi,[4] Mr. J. F. Milholland,[5] Mr. Alfred Pawsey,[6] Mr. H. Cunha, Mr. Vernon Grosett, Mr. K. M. Mallett-Pringle, Mr. J. Cohen,[7] Mr. Stainton Clarke,[8] Hon. B. S. Gosset,[9] Mr. Horace V. Myers,[10] Mr. Fred L. Myers,[11] Mr. A. deC. Myers, Mr. A. E. Motta, Mr. C. C. Anderson,[12] Mr. Archibald Munro,[13] Mr. Edwin Charley, Mr. J. A. Scott,[14] His Lordship Bishop Collins, S.J., D.D., LL.D., Mr. R. W. Bryant, Rev. S. O. Ormsby, Rev. Canon Wortley, Ven. Archdeacon Wm. Simms,[15] M.A., Ven. Archdeacon Sharp,[16] Mr. Wm. Cowper,[17] M.A., Mr. J. C. Ford,[18] Mr. Frank Cundall,[19] Rev. J. W. Williams, Rev. Ernest Price, B.A., B.D., Rev. J. T. Hudson B.A., B.D., Rev. Wilfred Clarke, B.A., B.D., Mr. Charles Fisher, Messrs. J. Wray and N[e]phew, Mr. Daniel Finzi,[20] Jamaica Tobacco Company, Mr. Alt. DaCosta, Mr. Thomas Leahong, Dr. Geo. C. Henderson, M.D. Dr. J. Huntley Peck,[22] Dr. Josleyn,[23] Dr. J. J. Edwards, M.D., Dr. Frank Saunders,[24] Dr. Lockett,[25] Dr. A. A. Ayton,[26] Dr. Oliver Crosswell,[27] Dr. E. E. Penso[28] and others.

The society will be glad to lend its assistance to any movement organization or individual that has the object of the development of the people and country at heart. The society is non-sectarian and non-political, the motto being "One God! One aim! One destiny!" The office of the society is 30 Charles Street, Kingston.

Printed in the *Gleaner*, Saturday, 21 August 1915. Original headlines have been omitted.

1. George McGrath was the custos of the parish of St. Catherine and ex officio member of the parochial board of the parish. He also served as justice of the peace for the parishes of St. Catherine, St. Ann and St. Mary. (*WWJ*, 1921–24).

2. Sir Anthony Coll (1861–1931) was appointed chief justice of Jamaica in 1911 and was knighted the following year; he retired from public life in 1922. (*HJ*, 1932).

3. Charles Halman Beard (1851–1927), born in St. Kitts, W.I., was a lawyer who acted as puisne judge, solicitor general, and attorney general of the Leeward Islands from 1886 until 1895. In 1898 he was made a resident magistrate in Jamaica; until 1921, he served in the positions of puisne judge of the Supreme Court and occasionally as chief justice. (*HJ*, 1928).

4. Adolphe Joseph Corinaldi (1859–?) was admitted to practice as a solicitor in 1880. In 1919 he was appointed crown solicitor of Jamaica and served until his retirement in 1924. (*WWJ*, 1919–20).

5. John Fitzalan Milholland (1865–1931) was admitted to practice as a solicitor in 1887, and he was appointed crown solicitor in 1912. In private practice he was senior member of the firm of Milholland, Ashenheim and Stone. (*HJ*, 1932).

6. Alfred Pawsey, planter and owner of Bog Estate, Clarendon, was also a dry goods merchant in Kingston. He was chairman of the Kingston Ice Making Co. Ltd., and director of several other companies. (*WWJ*, 1919–20).

7. J. G. Cohen served as the estate attorney for Sir John Pringle's property in St. Mary.

8. Stainton Clarke (1857–?) was a planter and penkeeper in the parish of Westmoreland; he served as justice of the peace for that parish as well as for St. Ann. He was a director of the Westmoreland Building Society. (*WWJ*, 1921–24).

9. Beresford Smyly Gosset (1852–1930) came to Jamaica in 1872 and became a penkeeper and a sugar and coffee planter. He served as a member of the Legislative Council for Hanover (1907–9), and as custos of St. Andrew (1907–20). (*HJ*, 1931).

10. Horace Victor Myers (1876–?) became a partner in his father's rum distilling firm of Fred. L. Myers & Son in 1897, and on his father's retirement became sole proprietor. He was active in the social, religious, and educational life of Kingston, but he was most noted for providing transportation in his ships for the Bahamas contingents in World War I. (*WWJ*, 1916).

11. Frederick Louis Myers (1853–1915) was a wholesale merchant and commission agent who built one of the most successful business operations in Kingston. He was also justice of the peace for that parish. (*HJ*, 1916).

12. Charles Campbell Anderson (1857–1921) was born in Nassau, Bahamas. He came to Jamaica in 1880 and served first as a clerk in the colonial secretary's office and later as assistant secretary to the Jamaica Mutual Life Association. In 1909 he was appointed tax collector for Kingston and, in 1912, he became the island treasurer and manager of the Government Savings Bank. (*HJ*, 1922).

13. Archibald Munro was a merchant and chairman of the People's Discount Co. He served as justice of the peace for Kingston, as deputy chairman of the Jamaica Cooperative Fire and General Insurance Co. Ltd., and as a director of the Kingston Ice Making Co. Ltd. (*WWJ*, 1919–20).

14. James Arthur Scott was director and chairman of Messrs. Nathan and Co. Ltd. (Jamaica) and of Nathan & Godfrey (London). (*WWJ*, 1919–20).

15. William Simms (1845–1932), archdeacon of the Anglican Church, was born in England; he came to Jamaica in 1875 as headmaster of Potsdam School. In 1882 he became headmaster of the Jamaica High School, later Jamaica College, a position he held until his resignation in 1915. He served as a member of the Jamaica Schools Commission, as a trustee of Mico College and Wolmer's School, and on the board of governors for the Institute of Jamaica. (*HJ*, 1933–34).

16. Ferrar Hughes Sharp, archdeacon of the Anglican Church, was ordained in Jamaica in 1863. He was rector for many of the mission stations of the Anglican Church between 1863 and 1897. He was a member of the Diocesan Council and Financial Board, as well as chairman of the Parochial Council for St. Ann; in 1906 he was made archdeacon. (*WWJ*, 1916).

17. William Cowper was the headmaster of Wolmer's Boys School in Kingston. (*WWJ*, 1916).

18. Joseph Charles Clitheroe Ford (1852–1921) was born at Wolverhampton, England; he came to Jamaica in the early 1870s as the business manager for Ford Brothers of Wolverhampton. For a time he was the editor of the *Gleaner* and in 1889–90 he served as secretary of the Institute of Jamaica. From 1891 to 1919, he was the government printer and coedited the *Handbook of Jamaica* with Frank Cundall. (*HJ*, 1922).

19. Frank Cundall (1858–1937), born in London, was later appointed secretary and librarian of the Institute of Jamaica in 1891 and served in that position until his death. Cundall established the West India Reference Library (1894), now the National Library of Jamaica, as an important collection of West Indian materials. He was a prolific writer, editor, and historian on a wide variety of Jamaican topics. (*HJ*, 1946; Glory Robertson, "The West India Reference Library of the Institute of Jamaica," *Jamaica Journal* 6 [March 1972]:15–20).

20. Eugene Daniel Finzi, wine and spirit merchant, was director of the firm of Daniel Finzi & Co. Ltd. He served as senior justice of the peace for Kingston. (*WWJ*, 1921–24).

21. Altamont E. Da Costa (1868–1936) was a merchant; he was appointed custos of the parish of Kingston beginning in 1928. He served as mayor of Kingston from January 1925 to November 1927 and as a member of the parish council from 1925 until 1936. (*HJ*, 1937–38).

22. Dr. John Huntley Peck (1857–1932) was born in India and entered the medical service of Jamaica in 1880 as the district medical officer for Linstead, St. Catherine. In 1899 he was transferred to Spanish Town, where he worked as surgeon of the St. Catherine district prison and medical superintendent of the lepers' home. He retired from government service in 1922 and established a private practice. (*HJ*, 1933–34).

23. Dr. Herbert Joselyn entered the public service on 1 April 1891 and served as district medical officer at Annotto Bay and justice of the peace for St. Mary. (*WWJ*, 1921–24).

24. Dr. Frank Saunders was president of the Jamaica branch of the British Medical Association and president of the Medical Council of Jamaica. (*WWJ*, 1919–20).

25. Dr. George Vernon Lockett (1866–1915) entered the government service of Jamaica on the staff of the Kingston public hospital, resigning as senior resident medical officer to work in private practice. Following the 1907 earthquake, he moved to Canada, but in 1915, he returned to practice in Jamaica. (*HJ*, 1916).

26. Dr. Albert Augustus Ayton (1878–1918) was born in Kingston and educated at Edinburgh University and also in London and Paris. He returned to Jamaica in 1906 and entered private medical practice. (*HJ*, 1919).

27. Dr. Louis Oliver Crosswell (1870–1923), a graduate of Aberdeen University (1894), entered public service as the medical officer of the Turks and Caicos Islands in April 1895. He served as the district medical officer of Black River, St. Elizabeth, Jamaica, from 1904 to 1908; in 1915 he was appointed medical officer of health for Kingston. (*WWJ*, 1919–20).

28. Dr. Everard E. Penso was a graduate of Howard University's school of dentistry. He was elected in 1939 as member of the Mayor and Council of Kingston and St. Andrew. (*WWJ*, 1919–20; 1940).

Address by Marcus Garvey

[*Daily Chronicle*, 26 August 1915]

. . . Mr. Chairman, ladies and gentlemen—On behalf of the Universal Negro Improvement Association I beg to lay before you the idea for establishing an Industrial Farm and Institute in the interest of our people and country and I am asking you as members, friends and sympathisers to follow me closely as I give expression to the executive feelings and desire of our society, which I feel sure will meet with your hearty approval and support.

The condition of our country and people is as much known to you as it is to me, but sometimes it becomes necessary for one to draw things in picture-like illustration to remind and impress those who ought to be interested. Hence I shall take the liberty to arrest your attention for a while in pointing out, even as you do know yourselves, the existing state of affairs.

Our people have had seventy-seven years of unfettered liberty in this country—a liberty given us by the liberty-loving and Christian British people—during which period of time we have tried our best to adopt ourselves to the environments of the country and to live up to the teachings of our Christian brothers. We have nothing to regret in adopting and living up to the teachings of our more fortunate and cultured friends, for in obeying their teachings and living up to their principles we have only done the right thing to bring us on par with the civilized habits and customs of the most cultured and civilized of mankind. Thank God there is no racial friction in Jamaica and I pray that the day may never dawn to see anything of racial friction or open racial prejudice in this country. Jamaica has a lesson to teach the world, and it is that people of different races can live together within one country as brothers and friends on the best of terms without prejudice upholding one government, ready to die for one flag, enjoying the same liberty of constitution (Christian and otherwise) and looking to one common destiny.

I say thank God for this state of affairs, and it shall be the principle of the Universal Negro Improvement Association to live up to and spread the

DOCTRINE OF BROTHERHOOD AND LOVE

among all mankind all over the world. We stand on the platform of humanity, and whether the man be black, white or blue, it shall be our mission to clasp his hand in fellowship. Any man who despises another because of his race only, is mean and in everyway a coward. God made us all to dwell on the face of the earth, so whether we are this, that or the other, we are all children of one common father. With Booker T. Washington, I repeat these words of wisdom, not for the people of America, but for the people of Jamaica:

"Different in race, in colour, in history, we can teach the world that, although thus differing, it is possible for us to dwell side by side in love, in peace, and in material prosperity. We can be one in sympathy, purpose, forebearance and mutual happiness. Let him who would embitter, would bring strife, between your race and mine be accursed in his basket and in his store, accursed in the fruit of his body and the fruit of his land. No man can plan the degradation of another race without being himself degraded. The highest test of the civilisation of any race is its willingness to extend a helping hand to the less fortunate."[1]

As President of the Universal Negro Improvement Association, I now declare that it is not my intention or the intention of the society to belabour any race question in this country as some may be inclined to believe and as some envious and wicked minds would care to suggest. The race question must never affect us, we must uphold the equity of the land, irrespective of race under our constitution. The British Constitution is free and liberal, and it dispenses justice to every man within the state. What concerns us here is the development of our people and country. As a society we realise that the negro people of Jamaica need a great deal of improvement. The bulk of our people are in darkness and are really unfit for good society. To the cultured mind the bulk of our people are contemptible—that is to say, they are entirely outside the pale of cultured appreciation. You know this to be true so we need not get uneasy through prejudice. Go into the country parts of Jamaica and you see there villainy and vice of the worse kind, immorality, obeah, and all kinds of dirty things are part of the avocation of a large percentage of our people and we, the few of cultured tastes, can in no way save the race from injury in a balanced comparison with other people, for the standard of races or of anything else is not arrived at by the few who are always the exceptions, but by the majority. Kingston, and its environs are so infested with the uncouth and vulgar of our people that we of the cultured class feel positively ashamed to move about, and through this state of affairs some of our most representative men even flatter themselves to believe that they are not of us and practically refuse to identify themselves with the people. Well, this society has set itself the task to go among the people and help them up to

A BETTER STATE OF APPRECIATION

among the cultured classes, and raise them to the standard of civil[iz]ed approval. To do this we must get the co-operation and sympathy of our white brothers. I know full well that the white people of this country sympathise with the struggling condition of their black fellow-citizens and that they would do anything that is reasonable and in their power to help the people to rise. Whatever we have achieved from slavery up that is commendable is due to their broadmindedness and help. The cultured within our fold have them to thank for all that they have achieved through their open institutions and philanthropic principles. They have done as much, and even more than should be expected of them, to advance our people. What we lack is self-help, and self-reliance, and even with our culture we lack this. We are always wanting somebody to do something for us. We depend too much on the large-heartedness of the individual and we expect too much of the state. As a people, we are always blaming someone else or the state for the lack of progress; but I swear it by God that it is the people who have kept back themselves. My opinion is that we are too envious, malicious and superficial, and because of this we keep back ourselves and eventually keep back the country. If we could succeed in producing a better class of people, less envious, less superficial, more industrious, real, cultured and appreciable, we could then boast of a country comparable with any other in any part of the world. We do not want you to envy the rich man and use his riches as an argument against him. Every rich man has his mission and a duty to perform;

and it is, therefore, good that we have rich men. Every country of consequence has rich men, and if we were to disgust our rich men, then the country would go to the dogs. Rich men are the props of all communities, and if it were not for the rich men of Jamaica the country would be no fit place to live in, for then villainy and vice and all kinds of evil would be more rampant. It is the rich men who provide work for us and help us to live for we have been unable to do anything for ourselves. Admire your rich men and [re]spect your superiors and do your best to

RISE ABOVE YOUR PRESENT CONDITION.

This is a better lesson than superficial bigotry and inactivity and the desire to force ourselves up to what we are not. Let us all join hands to lift the people, without prejudice to any class or colour. To achieve the ends of a better state among our people, our society desires to establish an Industrial Farm and Institute on these objects:

1. Providing work for the unemployed.
2. Training our men to a better knowledge and appreciation of agriculture and the soil.
3. Teaching our people to be industrious.
4. Providing better and more skilled agricultural workers;
5. Teaching the highest efficiency in the trades,
6. Fitting our young men and women for a better place in the moral and social life of the country.
7. Training our young women to be good and efficient domestics, etc.
8. Providing a good educational training for those who lacked the opportunity in earlier years.
9. And we desire to establish a department for reclaiming and providing ready work for discharged prisoners so as to keep the[m] from returning to crime, namely, praedial larceny, petty thefts, etc.

In a word, our society desires to establish a Tuskegee in Jamaica. These are objects that should commend themselves to every man who loves Jamaica and desires to see the people prosper. Who is against this let him show himself and we shall then say traitor. There is nothing to begrudge in the scheme, for if we are rendered able to achieve these things our country would become the better for our efforts. The better class would have to meet with a better class of peasantry, more intelligent, refined and cultured, the opposite of which they now meet and perforce mix with. The country would then be able to produce a better working class fit for association, controllable and tolerable. I am now appealing to Jamaica at large to help our society to establish this farm and institute. Now is the time for the true friends of the people to show themselves by helping the scheme. We haven't the money to start with so we are about to appeal to the generous people of Jamaica and our friends in America, and we shall be asking you to help us with your penny, shilling or pound to start this institution. Every penny given to this scheme shall be acknowledged in the newspapers, and a statement given to the people. We are passing through a difficult time, but we can still do something, and I feel sure that our white brothers are going to help us even as they have so willingly done in the past, for they wish us well and they have all along been our dear friends and protectors; and may God bless them in this

THEIR FIGHT FOR LIBERTY,

and we still sincerely pray that the day of victory for the Allies be not far off.

Dr. Booker T. Washington, America's "great man," has promised to help the society and he has written me this letter:[2] . . .

Now, friends, now countrymen, let us do something to help the people and country. Let us throw individual prejudice aside and help the scheme. I have done my best to bring into existence and keep alive this society that has been doing so much in this community. God alone knows what I have suffered and borne to keep the society, but those who desire to serve the people must be prepared for the criticism of the unjust and uncharitable. It is all well for men to sit by and talk and criticise; all this is cheap; what we want to-day is action backed up with a true manhood. I am not one of the "gassy crew". I am a man of action and every word I utter at anytime I mean to put into action and you can depend on it. I have given up myself to work in the interest of our people, and I mean to work, work, work, and I leave the rest to God. All of us can help in this effort; those who can't dedicate their lives to the cause, as I have done, can help with money and moral aid, and in some way or the other everybody can do something. I have been helped in my earlier efforts by several of the gentry of this country and I feel sure that they will give us a helping h[a]nd with this scheme. Dear friends, let us serve the people, let us serve Jamaica and God will bless us for our little efforts.

Printed in the *Daily Chronicle*, Thursday, 26 August 1915. Original headlines have been omitted. Address delivered at UNIA general meeting held Tuesday, 24 August 1915, in the Collegiate Hall.

1. It has not been possible to trace the exact reference of this quotation in the published writings and speeches of Booker T. Washington, who made several similar statements at various times.

2. Letter from Washington to Garvey, 27 April 1915, printed above.

M. de Cordova, Publisher of the *Gleaner*, to Marcus Garvey

148, 150 & 152 HARBOUR STREET.
KINGSTON JAMAICA Sept. 3rd. 1915

My Dear Mr. Garvey,

I have your letter of the 1st. inst., and shall be glad to see you anytime on Monday between the hours of 10 a.m. and 4 p.m. I am, Yours truly,

M. DE CORDOVA[1]
THE GLEANER CO. LTD.
PER [*blank*] MANAGER

EDSG. TLS, Recipient's copy. Written on the stationery of the Gleaner Co., Ltd.

1. Michael de Cordova (1870–?) was the Kingston-born editor and managing director of the *Gleaner*. (*WWJ*).

"Progress" to the *Daily Chronicle*

[[Kingston, 4th Sept. 1915]]

To the Editor; Sir,—

There is a disposition on the part of certain men who pose to be leaders of a section of the community in which they live to impose the condition of those people by wholesale condemnation. I think it very uncharitable on the part of the President of the Universal Negro Improvement Association to state as a fact that the bulk of our people are contemptible and are guilty of the worst kind of morality and all kind of dirty things. I can assure the President that I am not uneasy through prejudice, but only the impression such a statement will leave on the minds of people outside of Jamaica as at home we know to what extent such a statement is to be taken. I think I am right in saying that the association aim at the uplifting of the very people that the President criticises so severely. Not having a knowledge of the history of the association I expected to have found in the President's address a resume of the improvement, "if any," and work done for the benefit of the people who the association was intended for, during the year under review, thinking that to be an important factor and would act as an incentive to those who have been d[i]ffident in supporting so laudable a cause, also a proof to the general public whose aid the President solicits that the existence of such an association warrant their support. I am, etc.,

PROGRESS

Printed in the *Daily Chronicle*, Tuesday, 7 September 1915.

Leo S. Pink to the *Daily Chronicle*

[[Kingston Sept. 8, 1915]]

To the Editor: Sir,—

Please allow me space in your paper to express my opinion and at the same time supporting the article above the signature Progress *re* the Universal Negro Improvement Society. A short while ago, the President had the effrontery to make certain remarks in his address which, as Progress said, should have been a *resume* of past work so that the public could grasp and, if it could, to support the said society; but I think, from the remarks of Mr. Marcus Garvey, the President, he has driven the death-nail into the casket of the Universal Negro Society. Mr. Garvey's statements are too broad to be tolerated. If he will but think for a while he will see that the very people such damaging remarks are for, include his own flesh and blood; and his remarks reflect greatly on the gentleman. He refers to the cultured class of which he claims relation. I think he is living in a fool's paradise, as no cultured man would make such statements, and if such things exist, as Mr. Garvey said, the cultured-minded man having the interest and social uplifting of so many negroes at heart, should go about to right the wrong instead of mimicking the entire race for selfish, personal gain.

Booker T. Washington worked earnestly for his race and is entitled to the position he now occupies, and Mr. Garvey must not think for one moment he can be a Booker Washington, as great men are born, not made; and in these enlightened days the Government, I am sure, will be glad to welcome a man who has the ability to find a solution to our criminal problem. Such a man must firstly get into the confidence of our officials, must have influence, must be a man above the ordinary. All of the above enumerated qualities Mr. Garvey does not possess. Then how can he be successful in his venture? Mr. Garvey must account to the public for all moneys collected up to now, must know that his society is registered, also his officers must show that his intentions are square. Then when he has done all of these, the public can support his scheme whole-heartedly. Sir, if you will bear with me a while for the love I have for my people, for the love of the race which Mr. Garvey is mimicking, I must show the things as they exist. Mr. Garvey is not known in the community; outside of the dock which surrounds his abode the name of Marcus Garvey is foreign; he has collected moneys from men in high circles along with many of the poorer ones. What has he done with the money? People of my race, beware of your universal president; he wants to look for work, but you won't assist him; you are assisting him to abstain from honest labour by giving him your pennies. It is high time for this practice to stop. Sir, I am worked up to a pitch by the impertinence of this man, and I will write Mr. Booker Washington warning him against this gentleman.

Thanking you, sir, for space afforded. I am, etc.,

LEO S. PINK D.D.S.[1]

Printed in the *Daily Chronicle*, Friday, 10 September 1915. Original headlines have been omitted.

1. Dr. Leo S. H. Pink (1883–?) was a dental surgeon who was born in St. Ann's Bay, St. Ann. He traveled extensively for over fifteen years before settling permanently in Jamaica. He was among the guests invited to attend the banquet given to honor Du Bois on his visit to Jamaica in 1915. (*WWJ*, 1916; see also reports on the Du Bois banquet in the *Gleaner*, 1 May, 3 May, and 8 May 1915).

Appeal by Marcus Garvey

[*Gleaner*, 9 September 1915]

The Proposed Industrial Farm.

Mr. Marcus Garvey, President of the Universal Negro Improvement Association sends us the following:

The Universal Negro Improvement Association, desirous of doing its share in helping to raise the condition of the unfortunate of the people in assisting all agencies at work for that purpose, namely: the Government, the churches, philanthropic institutions and individuals, have decided to establish an industrial farm and Institute in the interest of the people, and they are now appealing to their members, friends and sympathizers to help them to realize and carry through the object. The Association realize that every good effort has its enemies as well as its friends, hence the appeal is confined only to those who are in sympathy with the aim of the association; namely, an earnest endeavour to lift the people of the struggling class to a better and more co[m]fortable state of living. The following are the objects for which the farm and Institute are to be established:

1, Providing work for the unemployed; 2, training our men to a better knowledge and appreciation of agriculture and the soil; 3, teaching our people to be industrious; 4, providing better and more skilled agricultural workers; 5, teaching the highest effi[ci]ency in the trade; 6, fitting our young men and women for a better place in the moral and social life of the country; 7, training our young women to be good and efficient domestics, etc; 8, providing a good educational training for those who lacked the opportunity in earlier years; 9, and the establishing of a department for reclaiming and providing ready work for discharged prisoners so as to keep them from returning to crime; viz praedial larceny, petty thefts, etc.

The idea of the farm is to teach, and illustrate to the people, the dignity, beauty, and civilizing power of intelligent labour; the object of the Institute is to supply literary and cultured training and to help in the production of a more efficient class of tradespeople and reliable servants.

Donation of any kind from those in sympathy with the Association can be sent to Mr. T. A. McCormack, General Secretary or Mr. J. R. Murdock Treasurer, 30 Charles Street, Kingston Jamaica, which shall be acknowledged by letter and through the press.

SUBSCRIPTION TO THE FUND.

Already received	. . . .	£15	0 0
Mr. A. J. Corinaldi	. . . .	1	0 0
Mr. Eugene Finzi	. . . .	1 1	0
		£17 1	0

Printed in the *Gleaner*, Thursday, 9 September 1915. Original headlines have been abbreviated.

"A Jamaican" to the *Daily Chronicle*

[[Kingston, 10th Sept., 1915]]

To the Editor; Sir,—
Dr. Pink has hit the President of the Universal Negro Improvement Association hard blows, but as an honourable and respected member of the race which Mr. Garvey has libelled, I think he, Dr. Pink, has done his duty. As hundreds of people, including myself, have never heard the proceedings of this society, I have enclosed a cutting from the President's address published in the newspapers sent to me by a friend and I will be glad if you will publish it so that the people of Jamaica can read it, and avoid Mr. Garvey. Mark you, our newspapers are read largely abroad. I wonder if the spirit of deadmanship has come over our people to allow Mr. Garvey's little business to live after his utterances. I am, etc.,

A JAMAICAN

Below is the cutting:—"The bulk of our people are in darkness and are really unfit for good society. To the cultured mind the bulk of our people are contemptible—that is to say, they are entirely outside the pale of cultured appreciation. You know this to be true, so we need not get uneasy through prejudice. Go into the country parts of Jamaica and you see there villainy and vice of the worst kind; immorality, obeah and all kinds of dirty things are parts of the avocation of a large percentage of our people."

Printed in the *Daily Chronicle*, Monday, 13 September 1915. Original headlines have been omitted.

Marcus Garvey to Booker T. Washington

Kingston, Jamaica, September 11th 1915

My dear Dr: Washington,

I take the opportunity of forwarding to you under separate cover, copies of our local papers, containing Reports relative to the Universal Negro Improvement Association which I trust will interest you.

I shall be writing you by next mail relative to my coming [*in the margin*: visit] to America.

As for Reports you will see that my Society has the support and recognition of the most influential men of this country.

I have up to the present been attacked in Jamaica by two correspondencets, one under the nom de plume of "Progress" and an unknown dentist by the name of "Mr: Leo: Pink." These attacks have been rather personal, but as my integrity stands above the malice and envy of these persons in Jamaica I am in no way affected.

I shall be able to furnish you and the American public with the best proofs of my integrity.

No one can understand more quickly than you the sacrifices and heart aches that accompany men who endeavour from the purest motives to do something in the interest of the people.

My task-to-/at/ this end is a hard one in that we have firstly to dislodge the prejudice existing among the people themselves before we can achieve the success that efforts of this kind demands.

With very best wishes for yourself and those at Tuskegee. Your most humble and obedient Servant

UNIVERSAL NEGRO IMPROVEMENT
ASSCTN
PER MARCUS GARVEY
President

DLC, BTW. TLS, Recipient's copy. Corrections in Garvey's hand.

Editorial Letters to the *Daily Chronicle*

[[Kingston September 13, 1915]]

TO THE EDITOR: Sir—

One of your correspondents, "Jamaican", submits in to-day's issue a quotation from the address recently delivered by Mr. Marcus Garvey, President of the Negro Improvement Society. The people of Jamaica now possess first-hand an unmistakable evidence of the opinions of the would-be "improver" of the negro race. Mr. Garvey in his Presidential address was reported as having given vent to the following utterance: "To the cultural mind, the bulk of our people are contemptible: that is to say, they are entirely outside the pale of cultured appreciation." Now, Mr. Editor, this saying of Mr. Garvey without doubt betrays an uncommon degree of colossal self-conceit and unmitigated snobbishness on the part of its author, who, from the lofty heights of his self-sufficient *culture*, gazes with supreme disdain d[o]wn upon the contemptible mass of his fellow-country men. I am far from denying that there is great room for improvement in the conditions of life and society among the peasantry of this island. They are indeed to be pitied and sympathized with: but CONTEMPTIBLE: NO SIR! By all means improve and educate the black race; but Mr. Garvey should be prevented from fouling our nest in the manner he has thought fit to do. His disgraceful utterance is nothing but a rank insult to the negro race, who, if this is the sort of "improvement" it is to expect had better fight shy of Mr. Garvey and his society. The word "*Contemptible*" supposes an attitude of mind which is not likely to be conducive to the betterment of the persons con[d]emned. Improvement is impossible without sympathy; but sympathy is incompatible with contempt. It is therefore evident that a man of Mr. Garvey's mental attitude is not likely to effect any improvement in the race which he affects to despise. I am almost tempted to suggest that he should try to improve himself before undertaking to improve others: that he should endeavour to remove the beam from his own eyes before trying to extract the mote from the eyes of his despised fellow-country men. If Mr. Garvey would learn the lesson of self-contempt he might be able to succeed in self-improvement: but this latter is inconsistent with the unfounded self-conceit with which he is inflated. I am, etc.

ANOTHER JAMAICAN

Printed in the *Daily Chronicle*, Tuesday, 14 September 1915. Original headlines have been omitted.

[[Kingston, Sept. 13th, 1915]]

TO THE EDITOR; Sir—

Sometime ago I noticed a Presidential address of the Negro Improvement Society, in your paper of Thursday, August 26th ult.

This address, as I read, was delivered by one Marcus Garvey, its President; setting forth *inter alia* what the society sought to do for the improvement of the negro. In that address, I, however, noticed that the very thing that this self-styled Negro leader-President should have espoused on behalf, and in the interest of the Negro, was defeated by his own calumnies against the Negro. I do not know this man, Marcus Garvey, at all, and I do not feel disposed to know him, anyhow; but I do say that, owing to the fact of his having maligned "three-fourths" of our race, I am impelled thereby to notice this man's effusions.

The particular reason for noticing them, is, because an reasonable person, and a man of straw as he is, taking upon himself to champion the cause of a people as "The Universal President of the Negro Improvement Association, in Jamaica," and having his effusions reported and printed in the newspapers, and such report subsequently coursing through British and other channels abroad, must necessarily reflect on the bulk of the Negro population here, and the British West Indies in general (if it were true).

I do not desire to quote from his address at all, as it speaks for itself. But I am only *en passant* assisting in warning the public against such a person as Marcus Garvey, having a smattering of intelligence, combined in a second sense with personal ambitions and aggrandisement to promote his own interests, will prostitute the claims of the best of a race to honesty, morality and otherwise, in order to achieve his own selfish ends. It is now, therefore, befitting time that this man Garvey should be made to understand that he cannot deceive and trade on public support and public confidence *re* his Negro Improvement Scheme any longer. The game is now up, so he must turn to something else by way of honourable labour whereby he might be kept from troubling. I have read letters from the pens of "Progress" and Dr. Leo Pink, D.D.S. and "Jamaican" and others, and these gentlemen have said enough by way of exposing Garvey's *laches*, hence I shall not say anymore but simply thank you for your indulgence and space.

Awaiting the publication of the Financial Statement of this society. I am, etc.,

DISGUSTED

Printed in the *Daily Chronicle*, Tuesday, 14 September 1915. Original headline has been omitted.

UNIA Cash Statement

[*Daily Chronicle*, September 14, 1915]

The "Daily Chronicle" has been asked by Messrs. T. R. Murdock (Treasurer), T. A. McCormack (Genl. Secretary) and Miss Amy Ashwood (General Secretary of the Ladies' Division) of the Universal Negro Improvement Association to publish the following cash statement for the year ended 1st August 1915:

Receipts

To Cash per subscription by friends and sympathisers	£20. 0.0.
To founders donation for organizing expenses	£40. 0.0.
To proceeds of concerts	£10.16.0.
To members subscriptions and grants	£10. 0.0.
	£80.16.0

Expenditure

By rental of Collegiate Hall and Ward Theatre for holding lectures, our weekly literary musical, general and public meetings and concerts	£20.17.0.
Rental for office and reading rooms	£15. 0.0.
Printing and stationery (organising literature)	£10.17.0.
Office furniture	£ 2. 0.0.
Organising clerical expenses and wages	£13. 0.0.
Magazines for reading room	£ 1.10.0.
Three prizes for elocution contest	£ 1. 0.0.
Charity, viz., poor dinners for 500 and gifts to poor persons	£15.14.0.
	£79.18.0.
Cash in Hand	18.0.
Total	£80.16.0.

J. R. MURDOCK, TREASURER
MARCUS GARVEY, PRESIDENT

Printed in the *Daily Chronicle*, Tuesday, 14 September 1915. Original headlines have been omitted.

Letters by Leo S. Pink

[[Kingston, Sept. 14, 1915]]

TO THE EDITOR: Sir—

I noticed in to-day's issue of your paper the financial statement of the "Universal Negro Improvement Association." I do not think this is satisfactory to the public, and through you I am asking Mr. Garvey for a detailed statement showing the names and amounts subscribed by each individual.

How much money paid for Collegiate Hall, Ward Theatre, etc., also how many dinners given to the poor? and where? the salaries of his staff, etc.

By immediate attention to the above he will be giving the public a chance to see how their monies were spent. I am, etc.

LEO S. PINK D.D.S.

Printed in the *Daily Chronicle*, Thursday, 16 September 1915. Original headlines have been omitted.

[[Kingston, Sept. 15th, 1915]]

Sir,—

I observed in the Gleaner of to-day's issue the following under Current Items:—"A general meeting of the Universal Negro Improvement Association will be held in the Collegiate Hall on Tuesday evening next [*21 September*] at 7.30 o'clock, when Mr. Marcus Garvey, the founder and President of the Association, will deliver an address in answer to public criticism. Mr. R. W. Bryant, Vice Chairman of the Mayor and Council, will preside. All friends and sympathisers of the Association are invited to attend."

Am I to understand that Mr. R. W. Bryant, the Vice Chairman of the City Council, after having read the calumnies, abuse and ridicule heaped upon the black and coloured population of this community by Marcus Garvey, the self-styled President of the Universal Negro Improvement Association in an address published in the Gleaner of the 26th ult., has come out to champion this man's cause and to further encourage him to hold up our people to ridicule by occupying the chair at the meeting advertised for Tuesday next, at the Collegiate Hall? I am, etc.,

LEO S. PINK, D.D.S.

Printed in the *Gleaner*, Thursday, 16 September 1915. Original headline has been omitted.

Newspaper Item

[*Jamaica Times*, 18 September 1915]

IN AND ABOUT "CULTURE."

When I read Mr. Garvey's address to his Society with the long name and big aims, I thought that if I knew anything about things in general and Jamaicans in particular, it would not be long before someone was looking for his head with a literary bludgeon. It has been even so. After a little shrapnel from anonymous sources, Dr. Pink has fired a portentous broadside at the

writer and we are all waiting curiously to see how much of Mr. Garvey is left
after the salvo. In fairness to both parties, I should mention that Dr. Pink is
identified with a Society[1] that is, in a way, the rival of the Universal Negro
Improvement Society, in the attempt to grapple the public affections to it
with links of steel, gold or gratitude or rather it may so be regarded, rightly
or wrongly. Perhaps this adds a little power to the critic's elbow in working
the range finder of his artillery. Anyway he goes for Mr. Garvey pretty
severely. One thing struck me, it is on the edge of the hurricane, so to speak,
and it is on the edge of things that triflers like myself are to be found. Mr.
Garvey after dealing faithfully with shortcoming members of his race here,
spoke of "us of the cultured class[.]" Dr. Pink hits him between wind and
water thus: He refers to the cultured class of which he claims relation. I think
he is living in a fool's paradise, as no cultured man would make such
statements." Now I am inclined to agree with the generalisation that may be
deduced from this, namely, that those who are cultured seldom speak of
themselves as so; but it also occurs to me very strongly that those who are
themselves cultured seldom indeed declare that such and such a person is not
in that happy state of being. They are not concerned with noting all the fever
of a "differing soul." Do I then suggest that critic and criticised both belong
to the outside of culture? All the little gods and goddesses of Hell as forbid. I
only suggest that we all sin and come short of that perfect land of culture that
shines before us. In fact the less we try to set the bounds of culture the better.
Cultured folk rarely speak of culture save in their uncultured moments.

Printed in the *Jamaica Times*, Saturday, 18 September 1915, from "Small Change for
News Notes."

1. The society referred to has not been identified.

Alexander Dixon to the *Daily Chronicle*

[20 September 1915]

TO THE EDITOR: Sir,—

In the *Gleaner* of August 26th under the caption of an address delivered
by the President of the Universal Negro Improvement Association at the
annual meeting, there was published the address of the President,
Mr. Marcus Garvey. In it is found the following statements: "The bulk of
our people are in darkness and are really unfit for good society. To the
cultured mind the bulk of our people are contemptible—that is to say, they
are entirely outside the pale of cultured appreciation. You know this to be
true, so we need not get uneasy through prejudice. Go into the country parts
of Jamaica and you see there villainy and vice of the worst kind; immorality,
obeah and all kinds of dirty things are parts of the avocation of a large
percentage of our people, and we, the few of cultured tastes, can in no way

save the race from infamy in a balanced comparison with other people, for the standard of races or of anything else is not arrived at by the few who are always the exceptions, but by the majority.

"Kingston and its environs are so infested with the uncouth and vulgar of our people that we of the cultured class feel

POSITIVELY ASHAMED

to move about, and through this state of affairs some of our most representative men even flatter themselves to believe that they are not of us, and practically refuse to identify themselves with the people."

Now, Mr. Editor, it is not reported that any resolution was passed at the meeting adopting the sentiments of the President, and one is left to believe that they were not endorsed.

It is not stated who were on the platform, or if there was a large gathering at the meeting. So the statement that the address was well received by the members, might mean, by very few persons, as it seems, from the financial statement published, only £10 was subscribed by the members for a whole year with grants included, whatever the grants may mean.

This address was delivered in the Collegiate Hall, and this hall is in connection with a denomination that exists for the purpose of enlightening the people. There are many other denominations existing for the same purpose; some have been operating for over a century; and I can testify from personal experience, as also from general observation, that the influence brought to bear upon the bulk of our population by these agencies has produced wonderfully good results, and 'tis a deliberate misstatement and a base calumny uttered Mr. Garvey when he said that the bulk of our people are "contemptible." If this were true, then the disgrace would be on the various agencies supported and sent out by the societies abroad. Mr. Garvey does not stop with besmirching those of his people whom he regards as immoral, villainous, vicious and contemptible, but tipping on his toes, he tries, *in vain*, to reach those of our people who tower head and shoulders above this self-inflated President, who up to now, according to his avowals, intends to get lands etc., for the people, and having received over £80 can only show a balance in hand of 18/- and not an inch of land.

This gentleman states that ["]some of our most representative men even flatter themselves to believe that they are not of us . . ." Now let me tell Mr. Garvey that I know of very many representative men of Jamaica who are not of *his* cultured class; and 'tis good for the island that they are not. But is there any truth in Mr. Garvey's statement that "some of our most representative men flatter themselves to believe that they are not of us?" I challenge him to prove it. Is he judging them from the fact that when they get professions or win to success in any of the walks of life, and prosperity, they live up to the standard warranted by the said success? Would he rather see them amid environments of poverty and lack of decency, so as to show to Mr. Garvey and his cultured class that they are identifying themselves with them?

As a proof that the assertion of Mr. Garvey is incorrect, we have letters from such real cultured representatives as "Progress," Dr. Leo. Pink, "Jamaican," "Another Jamaican," and "Disgusted," emphatically protesting against the unwarranted utterances of Mr. Garvey, who is very little known in Kingston, much less in the island of Jamaica.

But, Mr. Editor, perhaps Mr. Garvey is better known in Costa Rica, in connection with matters concerning which one who signs himself in another paper as "Interested," asked whether Mr. Marcus Garvey, who is now before the public of Kingston as President of the Negro Improvement Association, is *the* same individual who was in Costa Rica during 1911, while extensive arrangements were being made by British West Indians domiciled in that republic to mark the Coronation of His Most Gracious Majesty King George V., in London. This query of "Interested," demands a reply from Mr. Garvey or from any one who knows.

You see, Mr. Editor, how true is the adage, "Ebery dog hab him day." I, am etc.,

ALEX. DIXON

P.S.—My friends will, I am sure, be glad to know that I am much improved.

A. D.

Printed in the *Daily Chronicle*, Monday, 20 September 1915. Original headline has been omitted.

Address by W. G. Hinchcliffe

[*Daily Chronicle*, 22 September 1915]

Following is the full text of the address delivered by Mr. W. G. Hinchcliffe on the occasion of the recent anniversary of the Negro Improvement Association at the Collegiate Hall:

Mr. Chairman, Ladies and Gentlemen—The time has come when I can keep away no longer from becoming an active member of the Universal Negro Improvement Association.

Whether this association will die in its incipiency, or whether it will live to tell children yet unborn of the founder and those who are now associated with him, is not the thoughts that have inspired me so much, but I am inspired and propelled by the following words which sprang upon me: "Give help where help is needed when in Your Power so to do, and always give help in answer to a deserving cause.["] Those words that I have just uttered have been the fulcrum and lever that have landed me on this platform to-night.

The scheme, I must admit, is an august and ambitious one, but realising that ambition, aspiration and courage are some of the features that attend the actions of all true philanthropists, I sincerely hope that the founder will live to see his ideal hope realised. The good and true of every class have already come to back and help us in this unique endeavour:

"Let us then be up and doing
With a heart for any fate"—

Till we shall reach those heights that great men reached and kept, but which "were not attained by sudden fight."

It would be gross ignorance if we were to attempt to embark and launch out on such a great adventure without involving the guidance and help of the God of Israel, with faith in prayer. Prayer, says Beecher, is "the soul of a man moving in the presence of God," and for us to succeed we must unitedly let our souls move into the presence of God assisted by the psychological power of concentration. And we must believe that "faith is a power for God-inspired deeds when virtue points the way." We are aiming at good and great things—to save and reclaim the fallen, to rescue the perishing, and to do everything in our power in the interest and to the benefit of the race; while it will be incumbent on us, as we proceed, to let our demeanour give the most tangible and truest evidence that we are united in spirit, heart and mind centered on a pedestal of probity and honour.

We are already in the midst of harsh and distasteful criticisms and we must look forward to more of it in the future, while we must sincerely trust that our own people will begin to chant songs of love, unity and concord, instead of envy, disunion and discord. And may we pledge ourselves at this meeting tonight that we will endeavour and do all in our power to make it a lie in the future that: "The greatest enemy of the negro in Jamaica is the negro." We cannot live without being criticised, but we must have ourselves shelled like the rhinoceros that we may not be penetrated by the adverse criticism of our opponents. For it must be remembered that the Great Hawkesworth[1] died of criticisms. Tasso,[2] went mad by it and much is also said even of Sir Isaac Newton of the effects criticism had on him. So as there is danger in criticism it is best to walk farthest from it when it is in our power to do so.

There is before us a very long and wide field in Jamaica for progress, intellectually, industrially and otherwise; therefore, this organisation will not be moving in any direction that will impede, mar, or usurp any ideas, projects or workings of any other useful and beneficial society in our midst. If there be any such thought and desire that is lurking among the members of this association I would desire from this moment to disassociate myself. But I feel certain that this association will be helpful to others in the future. We will be interested in our praedial larceny brothers and sisters, the vagrants, in his diabolical and nocturnal career, and the sister who stands at the wayside and hedges who may be willing to be reclaimed. We want to find ourselves identifying the coal-carriers as our brothers and the ragged women who load

the ships with the bananas of our land as sisters, believing as I do in the
divinity and dignity of every honest toiling:

> Friends, to your reason I appeal.
> Why should the honest coal man shrink
>
> From mingling in the van
> Of Society and of wisdom, since,
> 'Tis mind that makes the man?

The late Paul Lawrence Dunbar, one of the greatest and most distinguished literary characters that ever lived in the United States of America,
was an ornament of special value to his race, tho' born of parents who were
held in slavery. And to-day, tho' he is now numbered among the Great
Majority, he yet speaketh; for, in writing his "Ode of Ethiopia,"[3] he has left
us some nice lessons in the following lines: —

> 'Be proud, my Race, in mind and soul,
> Thy name is writ on Glory's Scroll
> In characters of fire.
> High mid the clouds of Fame's bright sky
> Thy banner's blazoned folds now fly
> And truth shall lift them higher
>
> . . . .
>
> Go on and up! Our souls and eyes
> Shall follow thy continuous rise;
> Our ears shall list thy story
> From bards who from thy root shall spring
> And proudly tune their lyres to sing
> Of Ethiopia's Glory.[']

Personally, I am always pained when I see our less cultured brethren and
sisters in a group as prisoners brought in from the country parishes on the
trains; men handcuffed and with a long chain running amidst them to ensure
them being landed safely into the General Penitentiary. And I think that I
now see the ragged crowd of our civilised city following them as they go
along on the streets of this decent and respectable metropolis, some of whom
are half clad, some in rags bearing the marks of the colour of the soil from
whence they are, and others of the group are partly in a nude state that would
shock the modesty of the simplest lover of decency and morality. If we go to
the St. Catherine District Prison we will see upward of five hundred of our
brethren; fully ninety per cent. of them are of my complexion.

> They're steeped in vice and charged with crime
> They are outcasts—they have fallen.
> Still I'm a Brother all the time.

The time has come when we must use all our best and honest endeavours to assist in improving the general low condition of our people, who have been very much less favoured than we are, for we have really arrived at a point and stage whereby we can commence to show our desire and interest in our own people, and every lover of truth, honesty, morality, education, and general industry will in time see the necessity in aiding this cause which has been a long-felt want in this Beautiful Springing and envied land of ours. May God Speed the Endeavour.

Printed from the *Daily Chronicle*, Wednesday, 22 September 1915. Original headlines have been omitted. Address delivered at UNIA general meeting held Tuesday, 24 August 1915, in the Collegiate Hall.

1. John Hawkesworth (ca. 1715–1773) was an English author who founded the *Adventurer* magazine with Samuel Johnson. Hawkesworth also compiled a three-volume account of the South Sea explorations of Captain Cook, entitled *Voyages*, which he published in 1773. (*WBD*).
2. Torquato Tasso (1544–1595) was an Italian poet, astronomer, and mathematician, who suffered from various forms of mental illness and was committed to an insane asylum for many years (1579–86). (*WBD*).
3. Dunbar's "Ode to Ethiopia" was originally published in his *Lyrics of Lowly Life*. With the exception of some punctuation and indentations, the above excerpts appear as they do in the original publication.

Reply of Marcus Garvey to Critics

[Gleaner, 23 September 1915]

A general meeting of the Universal Negro Improvement Association was help in the Collegiate Hall on Tuesday night [*21 September*], when there was a very large turn out of members, friends and sympathisers of the society. The object of the meeting was to enable the founder and President, Mr. Marcus Garvey to reply to his critics and further explain the attitude of the association in the work for the uplifting of the people.

Among those present were Mr. R. W. Bryant who occupied the chair, Mr. W. G. Hinchcliffe, Mr. T. A. McCormack, general secretary, Mr. J. R. Murdock, treasurer[,] Miss Amy Ashwood, general secretary of the ladies division, Mr. Adrian Daily and other officers.

The chairman asked Mr. Garvey to address the audience.

Mr. Garvey was cheered vociferously, and in a forceful manner started to lay his case before the audience.

MR. GARVEY'S SPEECH.

Mr. Garvey said he was there to defend himself against the libel and imputations made against him by Dr. Leo Pink, his friends and followers. He had asked those present to come there so that he might explain his position, after which he felt confident that they would see "things really as they are."

He was a Jamaican of full African blood and so was unable to claim relationship with the Dukes and noble lords as some of his critics had done.

He was from humble parentage. Dr. Leo Pink was a fellow-townsman of his. He believed they were born at the same place. He believed they were at school together. He was in the juvenile department while Dr. Pink was in the advanced form. The doctor was a promising fellow. Later on they met and passed through the same office. They were apprenticed to the same master, Mr. A. E. Burrowes of St. Ann's Bay. He (the speaker) was always in a junior position to Dr. Pink when they worked together. Dr. Pink next left home. Mr. Garvey believed he went abroad where he studied along with a former apprentice of the old office who had become a dentist. Mr. Garvey never heard anything of Dr. Pink until a few days ago when he learnt that the gentleman who had been attacking him so ferociously was no other than the self-same Dr. Leo Pink.

Dr. Pink had written a lot of false things about him; but he challenged Dr. Pink to show a better record than his, a record of self-sacrifice, love, and devotion to the people and the cause he espoused. He had always been on the side that called for human and Divine help. His life had been one of service to the people.

He did not understand Dr. Pink when he wrote that he (the speaker) should get into the confidence of the officials. The chief officers of this country had such confidence in him and the cause he espoused that they had helped him in a small way. Some of the highest officials had visited the Association, among whom was the Colonial Secretary; and the Brigadier General had lectured to the Association. Nearly every high official had given them words of cheer. It was men of Dr. Pink's stamp who desired to keep back the hands of progress.

Mr. Garvey went on to say that had he no influence he could not have succeeded so far in his efforts. The accusation that he was not respected, deserved ridicule. The charge that he had collected money for his own purpose, was a wicked and cruel lie. He had given his own money to the Association. Mr. Garvey then explained his much criticised remarks in these words, the bulk of the people falls below cultured appreciation, if these were cultured, then all would be well.

Mr. Garvey then gave a history of his life, dealt at some length with Mr. Dixon, asked his hearers to eschew politics as a means of social improvement and repeated his intention of doing his utmost to continue in the work of the improvement of the condition of the masses of the island.

At the conclusion of Mr. Garvey's speech, the Chairman opened the meeting for free opinions, and after one speaker had addressed the audience in favour of the Society, the audience acclaimed, and accepted the explanation given by the President.

The meeting was brought to a close at 9.45 P.M. after the singing of the National Anthem.

Printed in the *Gleaner*, Thursday, 23 September 1915. Original headlines have been omitted.

Marcus Garvey to Booker T. Washington

Kingston, Jamaica, September 27th 1915

Dear Dr: Washington,

I send you under separate cover copies of local daily papers. I have been outrageously criticized in one of the local papers by an inspired Class of our coloured men numbering in all about four; although only two of the number had the courage to sign their names.

These persons have attacked me from Parochial, political and other personal reasons. They were (with one exception) unknown to the public and to the people until this attack.

I held a Public Meeting at the Collegiate Hall at which over four hundred of our Members, friends and sympathizers assembled and these persons were composed of the most intelligent and cultured of the black people. The Meeting was presided over by Mr. R. W. Bryant, an Englishman, Vice-Chairman of the Mayor and Council of this city and an Ex-Mayor. The Meeting was most enthusiastic and after I had spoken the Meeting was thrown open for free opinion. One Gentleman from the audience spoke in high favour of my attitude and the Society. The Meeting afterwards endorsed my attitude and supported me right through.

The Newspapers here are manned by a narrow minded lot of Journalists who sacrifice general interest at any time so as to ~~hear~~ /air/ personal views which are generally mingled with like or dislike of the individual criticized.

The News Editor of the paper that has attacked me through inspired correspondence has allowed this because I happen to pass his paper over when giving advertisements out ~~of~~ to the Press.[1] He is also among the coloured few who object to the name "~~n~~Negro" in connection with my Association. As I have explained to you already the difficulties in the development~~s~~ of the race rests with our own people as some do not like to call themselves "Negroes" which will eventually lead them into an awkward position later on if they be allowed to continue in their blind ignorance.

I am about to tour the country delivering addresses and I will write you later. With very best wishes   Your most humble and obedient Servant

MARCUS GARVEY
PRESIDENT

[*Endorsements*] Please handle.[*BTW*]
Have already written this man   ALH[2]

DLC, BTW. TLS, Recipient's copy. Corrections in Garvey's hand. Endorsements are handwritten.

1. Apparently a reference to the *Gleaner*, since no paid UNIA advertisements ever appeared in its pages. The only newspaper in which such advertisements were placed was the *Daily Chronicle*. At the time, the news editor of the *Gleaner* was Herbert George De Lisser (1878–1944). De Lisser, an editor, journalist, and novelist, started work at the *Gleaner* in 1895; two years later he joined the staff of the *Jamaica Times*. In 1903 he rejoined the *Gleaner* as its

assistant editor and within a year became editor in chief. De Lisser later wrote a series of historical novels on Jamaica; he also established *Planters Punch* (1920–44), a satirical magazine about Jamaican society, which also provided a vehicle for Caribbean historical and literary essays. (*DG*, 19 May 1944).

2. Albon Lewis Holsey was assistant secretary to the principal of Tuskegee Institute beginning in 1914. He was also associate editor of the *Tuskegee Student*. (Tuskegee Archives).

Marcus Garvey to the *Gleaner*

[29 September 1915]

Mr. Marcus Garvey, President of the Universal Negro Improvement Association, has sent a long letter to the Gleaner, in reply to the criticisms recently levelled at him by Dr. Pink. Mr. Garvey points out that only a summary of the speech he delivered at the last meeting of the Association, in answer to his "inspired critic," was published, and says he is quite satisfied that all present at that meeting upheld his attitude. The Association's cash statement, adds the writer, was published in detail as far as is compatible with decency and Dr. Pink, at no time ever subscribed to the funds of the Association. The doctor purchased one or two concert tickets, but this could not be held to be "contributing to the funds" of the Association, and with one exception all the concerts had been financial failures, he (Mr. Garvey) having to foot the bill. The writer declares that Dr. Pink is a member of a small party who objects to the use of the word "Negro," and also the advancement of the race as a whole; but he is of opinion that the Doctor's letter has helped the society, instead of doing it any harm. Mr. Garvey declares that he has hundreds of friends in England, Scotland, Ireland, and America, so that Dr. Pink's attacks can do him no harm. He has already acknowledged all the help given to the Association, but if subscribers in a body publicly request him to do so again, he will be quite willing to republish the details as often as may be desired.

Printed in the *Gleaner*, Wednesday, 29 September 1915. Original headlines have been omitted.

W. G. Hinchcliffe to the *Gleaner*

[1 October 1915]

Mr. W. G. Hinchcliffe in a letter to us, wishes that the controversy between Mr. Marcus M. Garvey, Jnr., and Dr. L. Pink might now end. Mr. Hinchcliffe who heard Mr. Garvey's speech at the Collegiate Hall in reply to his critics, thinks there can be no doubt that Mr. Garvey gave a very creditable and interesting account of himself, backed up by credentials, and that it would be a lamentable blow to the black people of Jamaica were it ever to be found out that probity, sincerity and honesty of purpose do not make up the platform on which Mr. Garvey is now standing. Mr. Hinchcliffe goes on to urge upon the members of the black race in Jamaica that they should rid themselves of envy and cease to justify the negro proverb, "dog nyam [*eat*] dog," and strive after true culture and endeavour to live in the spirit of those lines of John Wesley:[1] "We are friends of all and enemies of none."

Printed in the *Gleaner*, Friday, 1 October 1915. Original headline has been omitted.

1. John Wesley (1703–1791), English theologian and the founder of Methodism in 1739. (*WBD*).

Fund Raising Appeal by Marcus Garvey

[*Gleaner*, 1 October 1915]

Mr. Marcus Garvey sends us the following:

The Universal Negro Improvement Association is now calling on its members, friends and sympathisers to help them to establish an "Industrial Farm and Institute", in Jamaica. The need for industrial training for intelligent productive labour, for increased usefulness in agriculture and the trades, for self-respect and for the purification of home life is apparent, and the Association desires to help the people on the following lines through the agency of the Farm and Institute. . . .[1]

The appeal of the President is strictly confined to the members, friends and sympathisers of the Association and the objects. The benefits to be derived from the Association will be open to any member of the public, but as the Association realize[s] that it has enemies among individuals of the public it does not care to accept the help of "any-and-everybody" as in such a case more harm will be done the Society than good.

Parties in the country who are arranging meetings to be addressed by the President, in the interest of the "Farm and Institute["] ere his departure for America, are requested to mention their dates early so as to give him time to prepare for his visit to that place where he hopes to raise funds among members, friends and sympathisers of the Association. All help from British, American and local friends will be publicly acknowledged so as to show the state of the fund from time to time.

	£	s.	d.
Already acknowledged	15	0	0
Mr. A. J. Corinaldi	1	0	0
Mr. Eugene Finzi	1	1	0
Mr. Simpson	1	1	0
Messrs. F. L. Myers and Son	1	1	0
William Fox Film Corporation	1	0	0
Hon. F. E. Reed[2]	0	10	0
Rev. S. O. Ormsby	0	4	0
A.J.A.	0	2	0
Mr. E. B. Nethersole[3]	0	4	0
Mr. Michael Ashwood,[4] snr., Santa Marta [*Colombia*]	1	1	0
Mr. Aston Simpson[5]	0	10	0
	£22	14	0

Printed in the *Gleaner*, Friday, 1 October 1915. Original headlines have been omitted.

1. The aims and objectives that followed were identical to those printed in the *Gleaner* on 9 September 1915.

2. Francis Ernest Reed, OBE, (1852–1932), director of education, came to Jamaica in 1892 as inspector of schools, and in 1896 was appointed examiner in the education office. In 1911 he was made assistant director of education, and in 1916 he became its director, a position he held until his retirement in November 1919. From 1916 to 1919 and from 1925 to 1929 Reed was a nominated member of the Legislative Council. (*HJ*, 1933–34).

3. Ernest Bertram Nethersole (b. 1876) was born in Kingston and educated at Jamaica College. He joined the staff of the Jamaica Mutual Life Assurance Society in 1892. In 1913 he was appointed secretary of the society and held this position until his retirement in 1945. (Jamaica Mutual Life Assurance Society records).

4. The father of Amy Ashwood.

5. Aston Headley Laselve Simpson (b. 1882) was the younger brother of H. A. L. Simpson. He was admitted to practice as a solicitor in July 1907 and was the senior member of the legal firm of Messrs. Aston Simpson and Burrow. (*WWJ*, 1916).

Booker T. Washington to Marcus Garvey

[*Tuskegee Institute, Alabama*]
October 2nd 1915

My dear Sir:—

I am writing to acknowledge receipt of your letter of recent date relative to the organization of the Universal Negro Improvement Association and to say that I hope you may be wholly successful in putting the plans suggested in your letter into active operation.

This is the age of "getting together" and everywhere we look, we see evidences of that constructive accomplishment which are the result of friendly cooperation and mutual helpfulness. Such, I am sure, is the object of your Association and I am only too sorry that I cannot afford the time just now to give careful study to your plans as outlined.

Thanking you for your letter advising me of your plans and wishing you much success in your efforts, I am Yours very truly,

BOOKER T. WASHINGTON

ALH

DLC, BTW. TLR, Letterpress copy. Letter was signed for Washington by his secretary Emmett Jay Scott.

Newspaper Comment

[*Jamaica Times*, 9 October 1915]

DR. PINK AND MR. GARVEY.

I do not profess to like the tone in which Dr. Pink criticised Mr. Marcus Garvey, still less do I allow myself to imagine that the latter is not quite upright and straight, but it seems to me only fair to both parties to say that to leave things as they are is thoroughly unsatisfactory. If Dr. Pink has reason for challenging Mr. Garvey relative to funds he has collected from the public he is only fulfilling a public duty to do this, but why is he not more explicit or why does he not withdraw and apologise? On the other hand Mr. Garvey made a reply before his Club, but this has not been published except in very small part. Why not publish it all, just as his Presidential speech was published. The matter should be taken further, one way or the other.

Printed in the *Jamaica Times*, Saturday, 9 October 1915, from "Small Change for News Notes."

Alexander Dixon to the *Daily Chronicle*

[[Kingston, Oct. 18, 1915]]

Sir,—TO THE EDITOR:

Some time ago I sent you a letter disagreeing with the remarks made by Mr. Garvey, the President of the Universal Negro Association, as I believe the President was incorrect in saying that the bulk of our people were contemptible and so infested the city as to make him feel ashamed to move about.

The President never replied through the Press but, he did so at a meeting presided over by an ex-Mayor. At that meeting I am told he abused me, called me a liar and promised that when he was through with me there would not be a shred of Alex. Dixon remaining. I felt strange to know that a fellow councillor would sit down and allow a colleague to be abused without protest but, as I am feeling very much alive, I did not trouble myself with Mr. Garvey and his cultured class, feeling sure that such a society existing by abusing the race must come to naught. Your readers will be surprised to read the letter sent me by Mr. Garvey, dated Oct. 15th, asking if I am "opposed to the progress of the black people of this country or not," and wanting to find my attitude "towards his poor sisters and brothers."

Now, one good has been done to Mr. Garvey from the correspondence that has passed, for he comes to find that the people whom he described as working obeah and doing all kinds of dirty things are his "poor sisters and brothers". "Confession is good for the soul."

Mr. Garvey says that we worked together on the same platform. Does he mean the National Club of which Mr. Cox was founder? If so, how is it he came at the meeting of the National Club and asked the objects of the Club?[1]

I may tell Mr. Garvey I needn't trouble him or his association any more, he can ask any one in Jamaica that knows me whether I have protected "his poor brothers and sisters," and he will be told that not only have I done this but that I have never separated myself from them, by publishing to the world that I am better than they are, being of the cultured class.

I have sent this letter through the press as I do not require my autograph writing to be used by one who has up till now done nothing to elevate my race. From the time I read that Mr. Garvey had written in a paper in England, which was republished in Jamaica, that our people can get 1/6 per day and will not work[,][2] I, knowing this to be false, have kept aloof from him, and I am sure that even his poor brothers and sisters can expect little or nothing from such a brother.

It will be seen that Thomas Smikle, Esq's name has been struck out of the list of officers. He must have resigned, wise man. One by one the cultured class are going, and Mr. Garvey will find the old adage true, "You can[']t sidown pon cow, so cus cow kin."[3] I am, etc.,

ALEXANDER DIXON

MR. GARVEY'S LETTER.

30 Charles Street, Kingston, Jamaica,
Oct. 15, 1915

Dear Sir,—

As a negro who has the interest of my people at heart I now write to you asking that you be good enough to let me know by letter whether you are opposed to the progress of the black people of this country or not. I notice that you have attacked me most unjustly and uncharitably through the press, but I leave the answer to same, to the future.

Years ago, when I was associated with you on the same political platform I used to think that you had the interest of the "poor black, struggling people" of this country at heart, but, I now await your answer to find out your attitude towards my poor sisters and brothers. I also noticed that you have fallen under the influence of a few coloured "persons" who are opposed to the black people's progress. I accredited you for better judgment where the interest of the people is concerned.

I also beg to inform you that my association *is not a political organization*. Yours,

MARCUS GARVEY

[*Address*] Alexander Dixon, Esq., East Street.

Printed in the *Daily Chronicle*, Tuesday, 19 October 1915. Original headline has been omitted.

1. Alexander Dixon was one of the founders of the National Club and one of its vice-presidents. According to Dixon, the club failed to meet after S. A. G. Cox's departure from Jamaica in November 1911, due to the lack of a meeting place. The owners of the previous meeting place, Collegiate Hall, refused the club entrance after Cox gave what was considered an offensive speech. In early 1913, however, Dixon tried to revive the National Club by securing the support of the owner of a hall at the City Saw Mills in Kingston, and on 8 February 1913 the first meeting of the revived National Club was held there. The meeting was addressed by a visiting British Labour party M. P., Joseph Pointer, who promised to forward any resolutions that the club made to the British Parliament. In subsequent weeks, the club publicized the conditions of semistarvation allegedly prevailing in much of Jamaica because of oppressive taxation and drought, and it made a formal appeal to the governor to relieve this distress. Among those persons prominent in the revived National Club were the secretary, A. S. DeLeon, and Messrs. Lancelot Sherwood, Henriques, Quallo, Toledano, and Carson. (*Gleaner*, 8, 15 February 1913; 10 March 1913; 5 April 1913; 26 July 1913).

2. A reference to Garvey's article in the *Tourist* (June 1914), which was reprinted by the *Gleaner* on Monday, 13 July 1914.

3. "You can't depend upon the cow and curse the cow's skin" meant that one should not complain about the person from whom one gets one's living.

Marcus Garvey to the *Daily Chronicle*

[[30 Charles Street, Kingston, 20/10/15]]

TO THE EDITOR: *Sir*,—

Mr. Alexander Dixon, as is consistent with his policy, has been trying to misrepresent me to the public, and in replying to the letter published in your paper of the 18th I sent you a very long communication which I now think will take up about two columns of your paper. I am now asking you to publish this letter in the place of the other one,[1] and herein I beg to state, for the information of the people of Jamaica and the world at large, that I never made use of the remarks or words in the meaning as Mr. Dixon quoted them in his letter. He has changed, taken out and mixed up the words I used so as to suit his purpose. Mr. Dixon is too well-known as a misrepresenter of truth and he cannot be entrusted to interpret the simplest sentence on public questions. He says that he is finished troubling me, but I am not content with this, for Mr. Dixon will go back on his word too quickly to-morrow. I am prepared to finish with him once and for all times, and the best way to "finish up with him" is to meet him face to face on a public platform and there decide the issues by the judgment of the people. Letter writing can never set the issues involved, for if two or ten men write for one side or the other, the great majority's verdict is still unknown. Let us assemble together a few hundred of our thinking and serious-minded people and let them decide between both of us. I, therefore, ask Mr. Dixon through this medium to meet me on a public platform at some respectable building—not an open-air meeting—and then put his case to the people and let me do the same on my behalf, and that we both abide by the mandate of the people by majority vote. This, I think, will settle all the misunderstandings. I dispute Mr. Dixon's claim of being a leader because I think him incompetent and I guess he thinks the same of me, so the best way is to make the people settle the matter and the man who forfeits or loses to pay the expense of the meeting. I am, etc.,

MARCUS GARVEY

Printed in the *Daily Chronicle*, Thursday, 21 October 1915. Original headline has been omitted.

1. The longer version of the letter by Garvey has not been found.

UNIA Meeting in St. Ann's Bay

[*Jamaica Times*, 13 November 1915]

(*Specially Contributed.*)

On Friday night, 29th October, the Universal Negro Improvement Association held their first public meeting away from Kingston and the place appointed was St. Ann's Bay[,] the home of the President.

The meeting should have been on Thursday night, but a motor car accident occurred to the party four miles out of Spanish Town hence the President and his associates never reached the capital of the "Garden Parish" until eleven o'clock that night.[1] The meeting was therefore summoned for Friday night and right merrily did the people of the town turn out to listen to their fellow townsman in the person of the President of the Universal Negro Improvement Association. The meeting was held in the Baptist schoolroom and the Chairman was the Rev. J. T. Dillon.[2] Among those of the Association present on the platform were Mr. Marcus Garvey Jnr., Miss Amy Ash-wood, Mr. J. R. Murdock and Mr. M. Ashwood.

In introducing Mr. Garvey the Chairman said: It has fallen to my lot to preside at this meeting to-night, and I deem it not only a privilege but an honour and a good thing to do. I have had the opportunity of reading from the newspapers of the position Mr. Garvey was taking in the city of Kingston to inaugurate a society for the uplifting of the Negroes of this country. I want to say that anything that goes toward the

Betterment of the Masses

of this country we should welcome and give our support. We are all extending to Mr. Garvey a hearty welcome, I think Mr. Garvey feels glad to be among his own people in this town.

Mr. Ashwood was then called on to recite, after which the Chairman called on Mr. Garvey who rose amid the cheers and acclamation of the house.

Mr. Garvey said: Mr. Chairman, ladies and gentlemen, it comes to me to-night as a great privilege and pleasure to be able to address you the citizens of

My Native Town

in this Church Hall. But a short time ago, I mingled as a Sabbath-School scholar with many of the faces now present. I can never forget the pleasant years of childhood when I used to move among my boy friends both at day and Sunday Schools when each and every one of us used to do so much to make life happy and pleasant for the other. Youth is a period of life that lasts only for a short while, and those who used to mix and frolic on the play grounds during that human spring time generally pass out into life to become rivals and strangers afterwards. Friendship on the playgrounds or on the lawns either at [Et]on, Oxford, (as for some) or at our home elementary schools as is the common lot of most of us, does not always follow us into the world, hence sometimes you find two fellows passing from the same school or academy meet

Outside As Foemen

rather than colle[a]gues. I have come back to you to-night after a lapse of several years to talk to you on the important subject of the future of our race and country. Since I left you I have been travelling a great deal about the world; to America, North and Central, Europe and parts of the West Indies. It is needless to say that I have travelled a good bit about my own country and I am now speaking to you to-night as the President of the Universal Negro Improvt. Association, an organization that aims at raising the condition of our people. It is non political, but social and humanitarian. I guess you have been hearing a lot about me and this organization and especially of late since a fellow townsman of ours had thought it fit and proper to

ATTACK ME MOST OUTRAGEOUSLY

and wickedly. He tried to outrage me but the consensus of public opinion has been in my favour and since the attack the Association has sprang into greater favour and prominence and received truer support, in that I have been able at an instant to distinguish the friends from the enemies of the cause. I entertain no ill feeling against the man and it shall be my endeavour to do him a good turn always. But in writing the history of my Association I shall be having some interesting chapters to record. Mr. Garvey continued at length to explain the objects of the Association making reference to the work of the past. In closing Mr. Garvey said: "In a few words I will close with the policy of the Universal Negro Improvement Association of Jamaica: When a man is hungry[,] feed him; if a man wants a tidy suit of clothes and you have it to spare give it to him; if a man wants work and you can find it for him, help him, and see that he gets a living wage; if your brother is illiterate and

NEEDS HELP

do not prejudice him, exhibit a little patience and help him along; and more important than all help our women folk to be moral. If they ask you for help, help them for charity or love's sake, for God's sake don't take advantage of them, for in such a case they shall go from step to step until they enter the pit fall. If we want to rear a country of good and healthy men we must care [*for*] our women. They are the mothers of the nation and if they are weak and puny we cannot but produce a generation of weaklings."

At the conclusion of the President's speech the Chairman said: "I have listened carefully to the lecture of Mr. Garvey and that lecture has outlined a scheme that the Universal Negro Improvement Association has in view. He is not here simply to talk but for soliciting your help, as he has requested help of a practical nature. He is here to-night to form an auxiliary of the Association and I hope that the

CO-OPERATIVE SOCIETY

will materialize at some time. We as men in this country, as Mr. Garvey expressed, are not to believe that the "big man" is keeping us down and it is unfortunate to any man when he gets to that belief.["]

Miss Amy Ashwood arose amidst cheers to address the meeting. In part she said:

Mr. Chairman, ladies and gentlemen. I am here to-night as the General Lady Secretary of the Universal Negro Improvement Association, and I bring only a short message to you. It is the message of Co-operation, (hear! hear!) I say to you now co-operate and by so doing I feel sure that the future of our race and country will be assured.

I need not tire you with more of our objects for the President has already explained all. What we want to do is to come together and give each and every one some assistance to make the success of the Association assured.

To you ladies let me say that on you depend the making of our men. We want a country of good women, women whose influence in the home can be influence felt for good, that influence that will inspire our men to do good and noble things. It is a hard and difficult work that our President has undertaken, but God is our Shepherd and He will guide and help us through. Now it is for you, the people of St. Ann to give us a helping hand, and I am here to appeal to you to do your share in helping us to succeed. Finally I must say to you:

> Live for something,—Have a purpose
> And that purpose keep in view
> Drifting like an helmless vessel
> Thou cans't ne'er to self be true.[3]
> (Cheers.)

Printed in the *Jamaica Times*, Saturday, 13 November 1915. Original headlines have been omitted.

1. In 1921 Garvey recounted his version of the motor car incident: "Through some prejudice on the part of those who owned the motor car that I travelled in from Kingston, it was plotted to damage or destroy the car, so as to have me pay the cost of it, because these people were against my work! Whilst I was a few miles out of Spanish Town the chauffeur damaged the car. He returned to Spanish Town under the guise that he was going to seek help for repairing the damage. I gave him money, paid his fare on a train that was leaving the Spanish Town station back to Kingston, and he left me on the road waiting for him. I was scheduled to speak that night in St. Ann's Bay at 8, and it was then 6 o'clock. Since the man did not appear, I made enquiries and found out that he had deserted me. I was then forced to engage another car, from a Mr. Ellis in Spanish Town. The car took me to St. Ann's Bay and back." (*Gleaner*, Thursday, 21 April 1921).
2. Minister of the Jamaica Baptist Mission in St. Ann's Bay.
3. These lines were taken from a poem written by Ella Wheeler Wilcox (1850–1919), poet, novelist, and a leading exponent of New Thought. (*WBD*).

UNIA Farewell to the Jamaica War Contingent

[*Jamaica Times*, 13 November 1915]

FROM THE NEGRO IMPROVEMENT SOCIETY

This Society held a farewell meeting[1] in the Collegiate Hall, and bade good-bye, with hearty good wishes, to members of the Contingent who were present by invitation.[2] The President, Mr. Garvey, and Mr. A. Dayly, impressed on the men the good wishes of the meeting, and the duty of every true son of the Empire to rally to the cause of the Motherland.

Printed in the *Jamaica Times*, Saturday, 13 November 1915.

1. The date of the actual meeting has not been found.
2. The proposal to recruit a Jamaica war contingent was originally made by William Wilson in a letter to the *Gleaner* on 23 April 1915. The Legislative Council recommended that 500 men

(later increased to 550) should be sent to England to assist in the war. This number was later expanded to 2,550, with a commitment to provide reinforcing drafts of the same number for each year of the war. By the end of 1915, 789 men had been sent to England. The central recruiting committee set out in 1916 to recruit a total of 5,000 men to maintain the force of 2,550 in action. By the end of March this figure had reached nearly 4,000, and contributions of over £10,000 had been obtained to train and transport the men to England. (*HJ*, 1916; W. Adolphe Roberts, *The Gleaner Geography and History of Jamaica* [Kingston: United Printers, 1961] pp. 69–70).

UNIA Announcement

[*Jamaica Times*, 13 November 1915]

NEXT WEEK'S BIG EVENT

On Tuesday next week the 16th inst. the ladies of the Universal Negro Improvement Association along with their friends will sell flowers and bouquets to the members, friends and well-wishers of the Association in Kingston and St. Andrew for the purpose of raising a fund to be equally divided for providing a big dinner and treat to the poor [of] Kingston and St. Andrew at Christmas, and for the Society's "Industrial Farm and Institute Fund[.]" The proceedings will close on the day with a big concert in the Collegiate Hall at 7.30 p.m. when some of the best artistes of Kingston will take part, also Prof. C. A. Bryan, B.Sc., B. Mus. and his party. The proceedings are under the patronage of His Worship the Mayor of Kingston (Hon. H. A. L. Simpson, M.L.C.) R. W. Bryant, Esq., J.P., Alt. E. DaCosta, Esq., J.P., and others of the gentry of the City.

A rose can be bought for a 3d, 6d, 1/-, a pound or ten pounds to help the cause.

Any lady of the community who would like to help on the day by selling flowers, is asked to call on Miss Amy Ashwood, the Hon. Secretary, 30 Charles Street. All [t]ickets for the concert which should have [t]aken place on the 26th Oct. will hold [g]ood for the big concert on the 16th.

Printed in the *Jamaica Times*, Saturday, 13 November 1915. Original headlines have been abbreviated.

"ROSE DAY Here TO-DAY:

BUY A ROSE

For a 3d. 6d. 1s. 2s. £5 or £10

—AND HELP THE—

Universal Negro Improvement Association

OF JAMAICA.

TO ESTABLISH THEIR

Industrial Farm & Institute

To help the People of Jamaica.

A Bouquet can be bought from 2s 5s,. 10s, or any price the pur-
chaser cares to give to help the cause

THE OBJECTS OF THE FARM AND INSTITUTE ARE.

1—Providing work for the unemployed of Jamaica 2—Training our men to a better
knowledge and appreciation of Agriculture and the Soil   3 Teaching our people to be
industrious. 4—Providing better and more skilled Agricultural workers   5 — Teaching the highest efficiency in the Trades. 6—Fitting our young men and women for a
better place in the Moral and Social life of the Country. 7 Training our young women
to be good and efficient domestics, etc. 8—Providing a good educational training for
those who lacked the opportunity in earlier years. 9 And we desire to establish a
department for reclaiming and providing ready work for discharged prisoners so as to
keep them from returning to crime, namely Predial Larceny petty thefts, etc.

BUY A ROSE OR BOUQUET

And help the People to help Themselves.

See Dai   Papers and Jamaica Times for current reports and publications

GOD SAVE THE KING.

(Source: ATT, RRM).

165

UNIA Memorial Meeting for Booker T. Washington

[*Daily Chronicle*, 24 November 1915]

The Universal Negro Improvement Association held a memorial meeting on "The Life and Work" of the late Dr. Booker T. Washington[1] in the Collegiate Hall on Monday night last [*22 November*].

The Rev. D. A. Waugh[2] presided, and after the singing of hymns and the reading of psalms he called on the President of the Association to deliver the oration on the life and work of the great American Negro leader.

In an interesting speech lasting for more than an hour, Mr. Marcus Garvey gave a vivid description of the rise of Dr. Washington to the pin[n]acle of fame and world power. After giving an account of his life from slavery up, the speaker said: Under certain circumstances Washington should have been the acclaimed head of his race, but since the Negro has no national or set ideal of himself we in our humble way can only acclaim him as the greatest hero sprung from the stock of scattered Ethiopia.

Washington has raised the dignity and manhood of his race to midway, and it is now left to those with fine ideals who have felt his influence to lead the race on to the highest height in the adopted civilization of the age. He was the man for America. Without the presence of such a man the dominant race would have long ago obliterated the existence of the American Negro as a living force even as the Indians were outdone.

Every true negro mourns the loss of Dr. Booker T. Washington, scholar, orator, educa[to]r, race leader and philanthropist, and the man who does not feel over his demise is void of the feeling of humanity, for in him all that is good and representative of a struggling people is buried underground.

Printed in the *Daily Chronicle*, Wednesday, 24 November 1915. Original headlines have been omitted.

   1. Washington died on 14 November 1915, at Tuskegee, Alabama.
   2. A representative of the National Baptist Convention of America in Jamaica, Waugh also served as the vice-president of the Progressive Negro Association from 1916 until 1917. (*Daily Chronicle*, 8 August 1916).

Newspaper Report

[*Daily Chronicle*, 30 November 1915]

Owing to recent illness the lecture which should have been delivered by Mr. E. B. Hopkins[1] on the "Economic Value of Native Food" before the Universal Negro Improvement Association in the Collegiate Hall, to-night, has been postponed for a later date.[2]

By request the oration delivered on the life and work of the late Booker T. Washington by the President at the memorial meeting held in the Collegiate Hall on Monday of last week, will be published in the pamphlet form for circulation among members and friends of the Association.[3]

Persons desiring tickets for distribution for the poor dinner to be given by the association on Christmas Day can apply for same at the office of the society.

On Saturday of this week, 4th December, the lady members and friends of association at Spanish Town will sell flowers in their town to help the funds of the association.

Printed in the *Daily Chronicle*, Tuesday, 30 November 1915. Original headline has been omitted.

1. Elisha Baker Hopkins of Wellfleet, was one of the pioneers of the banana export trade in Jamaica and was an associate of the Jamaica Fruit and Shipping Co.

2. No report has been found that the postponed meeting was ever held.

3. No copy of the pamphlet of Garvey's address has been found, and it was probably never published.

UNIA Appeals

[*Daily Chronicle*, 30 November 1915]

A CALL TO THE MEMBERS, FRIENDS, AND SYMPATHIZERS, OF THE UNIVERSAL NEGRO IMPROVEMENT ASSOCIATION OF JAMAICA.

We desire to establish an Industrial Farm and Institute for the purpose of helping our people up to a better state of living on the following lines. . . .[1]

If you are a member, friend or sympathiser, we now ask that you help the association with a subscription to the fund; it can be a penny, shilling or a pound, it will be highly appreciated.

HELP US TO HELP THE PEOPLE.

Corr[e]spondence from Colon, Panama, Costa Rica, Bocas-del-Toro, Honduras, Guatemala, Nicaragua and other parts invited.

Address all communications to the General Secretary Unive[r]sal Negro Improvement Association, 30 Charles Street, Kingston, Jamaica.

Marcus Garvey, President and Travelling Commissioner; T. A. McCormack, General Secretary; J. R. Murdoch, Treasurer, Amy Ashwood[,] General Secretary, Ladies' Division.

Printed in the *Daily Chronicle*, Tuesday, 30 November 1915.

1. The aims and objectives that followed were identical to those printed in the *Gleaner* on 9 September 1915.

[*Daily Chronicle*, November 1915]

ACTIVE MEMBERS WANTED
FOR THE UNIVERSAL NEGRO IMPROVEMENT
ASSOCIATION OF JAMAICA

The object of the association is to unite and assist our government, the churches, the press and all societies and organizations to improve and help the bulk of the people who are regarded as ordinary members of the association. The intelligent must lead and assist the unfortunate of the people to rise, hence the appeal for intelligent active members whose lives and conduct should be of such as to act as a guide to the less fortunate[.] [T]eachers, artisans and tradesmen of all classes, doctors, ministers, clerks, lawyers, planters and every intelligent person should be an active member. Help us to raise the moral, educational, social, financial and industrial standard of our people. To raise the position of the masses is to strengthen and advance the position of the classes and society. Help our people in the bulk to become respectable members of society. In them lie the economic value of our country. If they live better, earn more and feel themselves true members of society, it means spending more with the capitalists class and those in business and the professions. If you are a friend or sympathizer send us a donation to help the work along. It can be a 1d, 1/- *a pound or ten pounds*.

All true friends of the people should help. Application for active membership (cut out and send in at once)

Secretary Universal Negro Improvement Association,
30 Charles Street, Kingston

Dear Sir or Madam,
Please register me as an active member of our Society and send me from time to time all literature published by you. I enclose a 6d as my first monthly subscription. Name ....
Address ....
Occupation ....
Marcus Garvey, President and Travelling Commissioner; T. A. McCormack, General Secretary; Amy Ashwood, General Secretary Ladies' Division; J. B. Murdock, Treasurer[.] Those willing to help the society by a donation can lodge same to the credit of the association at the Royal Bank of Canada or send direct to the office, 20 [30] Charles Street, Kingston.
Correspondence from all parts of the world solicited.

Printed in the *Daily Chronicle*, passim November 1915.

UNIA Meeting in Brown's Town, St. Ann

[[*14 December 1915*]]

Brown's Town, Tuesday.—The Universal Negro Improvement Association held its proposed meeting in the Tabernacle of Dr. James Johns[t]on[1] last night [*13 December*]. Mr. J. H. Levy occupied the chair for the evening, and the audience though somewhat disappointing in numbers; listened with rapt attention to the paper read by Mr. Marcus Garvey, President of the Association, setting forth his aims and ambitions for the improvement and uplifting of the race.

He was followed by Miss Amy Ashwood, Secretary of the ladies' department, dealing with this branch of the Association.

Mr. Levy in summing up, said he appreciated much the address of the speakers and he wished the association all success. He believed that success could be obtained if Mr. Garvey was faithful to the cause, and if he succeeded even in a part of his scheme he should be honoured and regarded. Mr. Levy made reference to the life of Dr. Booker T. Washington, who, engaged in a similar work, and in paying tribute to his worth and memory said it was the inconquerable spirit, backed by solid integrity that made success for him.

Dr. Johnston also wished the association success. He said he could add quite a lot about Washington. He was truly a great man, one who had so respected himself, and taught his race to respect themselves, and to be industrious, that he won the respect and admiration of his rankest opponent. Make a success, the Doctor declared, and you will have quite a number of friends, but make the success, the friends will follow. He thought the time just now inopportune for Mr. Garvey's scheme, there being so many matters of vital importance absorbing the attention of the people. He wouldn't, however, discourage him, but he hoped he would come again to the town, and when next he came he would give fuller details of his scheme, and say where he proposed to establish the Farm and Institute, how he proposed to run it, and from what resources he proposed to finance it, because, said the Doctor, the scheme will take an enormous sum of money to inaugurate.

Indications were not wanting that Dr. Johnston voiced the sentiment of the entire audience, who, though apparently in hearty sympathy with the aims of the association, expressed desire for something more concrete, and within practical grasp.

In moving a vote of thanks to Mr. Levy for being chairman, Dr. Johnston said that Mr. Levy, who, is here recognized as the universal chairman, was not a so-so man among them. He was Senior J.P. and Acting Custos. He should have been made Custos some twenty years ago, and so he thought it an honour when Mr. Levy came and presided. Mr. Levy and himself had carried on Brown's Town for the past forty years, and his only regret was that Mr. Levy did not visit the Tabernacle more often, for the two leading men of the community should meet more often. He had much pleasure in moving a vote of thanks to Mr. Levy, and to this, the audience signified their hearty assent, in the usual manner.

A collection was taken up for the cause and the lusty singing of the National Anthem terminated the proceedings.

Printed in the *Gleaner*, Saturday, 18 December 1915. Original headlines have been omitted.

1. Dr. James Johnston (1851–1921), Scottish-born physician and missionary, arrived in Jamaica in December 1874 and he began his missionary work in 1876 in the area of St. Ann's Dry Harbor Mountain. His mission was known as the Jamaican Evangelistic Mission, consisting of a tabernacle at Brown's Town and nine supplementary churches. He also practiced as a physician at Brown's Town, and for some years in the 1890s he represented the parish of St. Ann in the Legislative Council. In 1891, Johnston had the idea that black Jamaicans, because of their presumed adaptability to climate and their racial sympathy, could be employed successfully in the spread of Christianity in Africa. He led an expedition from Jamaica and over a period of twenty months the expedition crossed south-central Africa. Johnston's published memoir of the expedition appeared in *Reality versus Romance in South Central Africa: An Account of a Journey across the Continent* . . . (London: Hodder & Stoughton, 1893). (*HJ*, 1922).

W. G. Hinchcliffe to the *Gleaner*

[[44 John's Lane, Kingston,
Dec. 30, 1915]]

Sir,—

Some time since, I was moved by the Rev. W. Graham of this city to interest myself in the Universal Negro Improvement Association, of which Mr. Marcus Garvey is President. I must admit that after I had listened to the rev. gentleman's speech of interest towards the race, and the success that he would like to see attend the association, I decided that I would give the matter the consideration is deserved. During that time I received a letter from Mr. Garvey, asking me to become a member of an "advisory board" in connection with the association, and at the first meeting I attended I gave him my word of honour that I would serve him in the interest of the society to the best of my abilities. But having discovered since the 28th of October last, that I am still a novice relative to my conception concerning a class of mankind, and their methods, notwithstanding some very sad and memorable experiences of the past, I decided to leave the Universal Negro Improvement Association alone.

And it was not my intention to ask of you to give publicity to my withdrawal for reasons[1] I need not mention but as so many persons are still en[q]uiring of me concerning the association (the treasurer, Mr. Murdock, included), I think it wise to let the public know through this medium that I am no longer interested in the movement, as from the 28th October last. I am, etc.,

W. G. HINCHCLIFFE

Printed in the *Gleaner*, Friday, 31 December 1915. Original headline has been omitted.

1. The exact reasons for Hinchcliffe's withdrawal are still not known.

Newspaper Report

[[Montego Bay, Jan. 18 *1916*]]

Mr. Marcus Garvey, President of the Universal Negro Improvement Association, addressed a meeting here to-night in the First Baptist Church explaining the aims and objects of his Association. In the absence of the Rev. Webster who was kept away by business the Rev. J. W. Graham, M.A.,[1] presided. The Rev. gentleman introduced Mr. Garvey to the house. Mr. Graham said he had known Mr. Garvey for over six years, first meeting him as a rival in the newspaper world of Costa Rica. It was a pleasure for him to preside.

Mr. Garvey gave explanation of the intention of his association. The flag of England, he went on to say, afforded them liberty, and they should esteem it an honor to die for it. His association existed for assisting the many agencies at work in drawing the people closer together and bringing about a more common appreciation of each other. They did not want any division in Jamaica. They were all mortals the children of one Heavenly Father.

Mr. Garvey's speech was listened to with great interest, and he was heartily cheered.

Printed in the *Gleaner*, Friday, 21 January 1916. Original headline has been omitted.

1. Rev. Joseph William Graham (1868–?) was educated at the University of Durham, England; he first met Garvey while he was rector of St. Mark's Church in Port Limón, Costa Rica, where he was stationed from 1909 until 1911. (*WWJ*, 1916; *Crockford's Clerical Directory*, 1939). Graham was reported, however, to have run into a problem of ecclesiastical conflict during his missionary work in Port Limón. The report, entitled "Big Row Over Limón Church," appeared in January 1911 in the Jamaican *Daily News*.

BIG MEETING

AT
THE BAPTIST CHURCH, LUCEA.

Wednesday Night, 19th, at 7 O'clock

Mr. Marcus Garvey, President of the Universal Negro Improvment Association of Jamaica will deliver an address on the aim and object of the Society.

A cordial invitation is extended to every citizen to attend. No one should be absent.

THE ASSOCIATION AIMS AT THE UPLIFTING OF THE PEOPLE OF JAMAICA.

It is supported by the most representative and educated of the Island.

Dont Fail to Hear Mr. Garvey. He is an Able Orator.

A SILVER COLLECTION AND DONATIONS TAKEN TO HELP THE WORK OF THE SOCIETY

You may also buy a rose for a 3d, 6d, 1s, 2s, 5s or a £1 to be on sale to help.

ALL SHOULD ATTEND.

SANKEY HYMNS WILL BE SUNG.

God Save The King.

THE NORTHERN NEWS PRESS—MONTEGO BAY.

(Source: ATT, RRM).

Marcus Garvey to Emmett J. Scott,
Secretary of Tuskegee Institute

Kingston, Jamaica, Feby., 4 1916

My dear Mr. Scott,[1]

Apart from our local memorial meeting and organized mourning, it is the first I am writing to Tuskegee since the death of good Dr. Washington. A short time before his death I wrote to him telling him of my plans for touring this country before my visit to America. Through criticisms in my work and other causes I was kept back from visiting America months ago. Since I wrote Dr. Washington I have been lecturing up and down the country and I have taken the opportunity of bringing his life and work prominently before the sleeping Jamaica Negro public, so much so that his name and work are well known in the island.

Months before his death I wrote to him about my proposed visit to America and he promised that he would have done all possible to help me whilst there. I am to be over in April for lecturing in the interest of my Association and to get a little help on our Industrial Farm and Institute scheme at this end. I am hoping to call on you and I am now asking you personally to try and help me when there.

The work of Negro Improvement at this end is tough and it needs giant pluck and determination to succeed against the strong influence of Negro haters—a puzzle I can better explain by conversation.

I am hoping to be assisted by the "Jamaica Club"[2] in the North, so I am asking you to do your best for me in that portion of the South.

We held a very nice memorial meeting at our Collegiate Hall here for Dr. Washington. He is pretty well heard of in Jamaica of late since the formation of this Association.

If you were to turn his files for April of last year you will see where he promised to help me whilst there.

I am hoping to hear from you early   With best wishes Yours faithfully

MARCUS GARVEY

[*Endorsement*] answer fully

ATT, RRM. ALS, Recipient's copy. The official organizational title given in the letterhead did not include the phrase "and Conservation." Endorsement was handwritten.

1. Emmett Jay Scott (1873–1957), Booker T. Washington's private secretary from 1897 until Washington's death in 1915, was also secretary of Tuskegee Institute and its boad of trustees from 1912 to 1917. Following America's entry into World War I, he left Tuskegee to become special assistant to the secretary of war, advising in matters affecting black troops and civilians. Scott was born in Houston, Tex., and educated at Wiley College in Marshall, Tex., 1887–90. He began his career in 1891 as a newspaper man, working first for the white-owned *Houston Daily Post* and subsequently publishing his own weekly, *Freeman*, 1894–97. Scott moved to Tuskegee in 1897 and became in time, not only Washington's close personal friend, but also his principal political agent and advisor. In 1909 President William Howard Taft sent Scott as one of three

American commissioners to Liberia. He was also secretary of the International Congress on the Negro held at Tuskegee Institute in 1912. One of the founders of the National Negro Business League, the economic arm of the "Tuskegee machine," Scott was also the league's secretary from its founding in 1900 until 1922. A businessman himself, Scott invested in black real estate, insurance, and banking. When Washington died in 1915, Tuskegee's trustees passed over Scott and appointed Robert Russa Moton of Hampton Institute as the new principal. At the end of June 1919, after resigning as special assistant to the secretary of war, Scott was elected secretary-treasurer of Howard University, a position he held until 1934. From then until his forced retirement from the institution in 1939, Scott served as secretary. Throughout his career, Scott was also active in Republican party circles. (*WWCA*, vol. 2; *BTW Papers*, 4: 171–72).

2. The Jamaica Club of New York was formed as a social club in May 1891 by a group of twelve American citizens with an interest in the British colony. Its principal office was in the village of Jamaica, Queens, New York. There was also a Jamaica Club incorporated under Massachusetts law on 4 December 1886.

Letter of Recommendation

30 Charles Street, Kingston, Jamaica,
Feb[r]uary 18th. 1916

To Whom It May Concern.
- -

    This is to certify that the holder of this is Marcus Garvey Jnr. of Kingston Jamaica, the Founder and President of the Universal Negro Improvement Association of Jamaica who is travelling in America, the West Indies, South and Central America and Canada in the interest of the Association and that he is recommended by us for assistance in anyway possible to enable the Association to start and carry on our proposed "Industrial Farm & Institute" to help the Negro people of this country on the lines of the late Doctor Booker T. Washington/'s Institute/ of America. Signed on behalf of the Association.

GENERAL SECRETARY
T A. McCORMACK

ASSOCIATE SECRETARY
ADRIAN A DAILY

AMY ASHWO[OD]
GENERAL SECRETARY LADIES
DIVISION

REFERENCES.
- - - - - - - - - - - -
Sir John Pringle, K. C. M. G.
Clonmel P/O., Jamaica.

Hon. J. H. Levy,
Act. Cust[o]s of St. Ann,
Brown's Town, Jamaica.

Hon. J. R. Williams, M. A. J. P.
Ex. Director of Education,
Kew Park, Bethel Town, Jamaica.

Hon. F. E. Reid, B. A.
Act. Director of Education,
Kingston, Jamaica.

[*In the margin*:] Personally known to:
    [*signed*]   Rev D. A. Waugh
                    B.D
                    Kingston, Jamaica
                    B.W.I.
    [*signed*]   Alfonso Dumar, B D
                    A.M.E. Church
    [*Stamped*] UNIVERSAL NEGRO
                    IMPROVEMENT ASSOCN
                    Per [*blank*]

EDSG. TDS. Correction is written in Garvey's hand. The official UNIA letterhead included the following quotation: "One cannot hold another down in the ditch without staying down in the ditch with him; in helping the man who is down to rise, the man who is up, is freeing himself from a burden that would else drag him down. For this man who is down there is always something to hope for, always something to be gained. *Booker T. Washington.*"

Visit to Jamaica of R. R. Moton, Principal, Tuskegee Institute

[*Gleaner*, 26 February 1916]

Mr. Marcus M. Garvey, jnr., the President and Travelling Commissioner of the Universal Negro Improvement Association, writes on the coming visit of Major Moton,[1] the new head of the Tuskegee Institute, to Jamaica.

Mr. Garvey refers to a letter which appeared in our columns yesterday from the pen of Mr. Simeon De Leon which suggested that there is no organised negro society in this island to welcome Major Moton. Mr. Garvey states that he does not intend to enter into a controversy over this matter. In this connection Mr. Garvey dilates on his experience of local hypocrisy.

Mr. Garvey is glad Major Moton is coming here, "for as a 'great negro intellect' he will not take long to discover the blatant hypocrisy that exists among the people."

Mr. Garvey sends us a copy of correspondence which passed between himself and Mr. P. W. Murray[2] with regard to the reception of Major Moton. In a letter to Mr. Murray, Mr. Garvey informs that gentleman that he intends arranging a welcome meeting on the 29th inst. in honour of Major and Mrs. Moton and that a very prominent citizen will take the chair. Invitations will also be issued to prominent friends and well-wishers of Tuskegee.

Mr. Murray, in reply writes that the Major will not appreciate any meeting that Mr. Garvey may convene without his being first consulted in the matter, although he would certainly appreciate the desire of those who wished to offer him such a welcome. Later on meeting Mr. Garvey, Mr. Murray informed him that he hoped to hold a meeting at the Mico which everybody would have an opportunity of attending and at which representative men from the better classes will be present to meet Major Moton.

Printed in the *Gleaner*, Saturday, 26 February 1916. Original headline has been omitted.

1. Robert Russa Moton (1867–1940), formerly commandant of Hampton Institute, 1890–1915, was Booker T. Washington's successor as principal of Tuskegee Institute, a position he held until his resignation in 1935. After the armistice, President Wilson sent Moton to France to inspect black troops and report on their morale and the various charges that had been made against them. (*DAB*; Robert Russa Moton, *Finding a Way Out* [Garden City, N.Y.: Doubleday, Page, 1920]).

2. Percival Waterhouse Murray (b. 1880), superintendent of the government stock farm and graduate of Hampton Institute, was born in Kingston. Murray was appointed to the government service in November 1904 as superintendent of the sugar experiment station. He also served as the superintendent of school gardens in 1907 and became the headmaster of the farm school at Hope in January 1913. (*WWJ*, 1916).

Alexander Dixon to the *Gleaner*

[[York House, East Street,
Feb., 27, 1916]]

Sir,—

Letters were read to me in the newspaper, bearing on the subject of Major Moton's reception on his arrival in this colony, and I regret to see that Mr. Garvey has introduced friction. He wrote as follows: "As a great negro intellect he (Major Moton) will not take long to find out the blatant hypocrisy that exists amongst our people." Suppose this were true, is it proper for Mr. Garvey to begin to prepare another tirade of calumny and abuse to pour out before this strange gentleman by way of a reception? Be it remembered that in his presidential address last year, he discussed our people as being "contemptible," and if he has a reception for the Major he i[s] bound to tell him those things and repeat those vile abuses, and so it is well as it is now proposed, that a committee should be selected from "representative men" to meet Major Moton and give him a reception. Mr. Garvey seems to object to this. Does he feel that he will be left out if representative men will form the committee? As a humble citizen of Jamaica I most heartily endorse the proposed method to give this distinguished visitor a reception that will enable him to form a correct opinion of our people, and I know that the citizens will most cordially join in such an undertaking. I am, etc.,

ALEXANDER DIXON

Printed in the *Gleaner*, Wednesday, 1 March 1916. Original headline has been omitted.

Marcus Garvey to R. R. Moton

Kingston, Jamaica, Febry, 29 1916

My dear Major Moton/

As promised in my letter of yesterday's[1] I now send you the attached communication which I must ask you to read and study as the honest views of a true man who believes himself called to service in the interest of his unfortunate people.

I desired an interview with you, and I also desired that my Association be honoured justly by welcoming you and Mrs. Moton to our shores, and we were making arrangements to this end, but we were discouraged by the unkindly attitude of my personal enemies who have been using their unrighteous influence to defeat the purpose of having the Association do honour to an illustrious brother. I respect very much the desire of Mr. Murray to have you spend a pleasant time here, so I calmly withdrew my intention, feeling that you will all the same appreciate the desire of the Association.

My Association was founded in Jamaica eighteen months ago immediately after my return from a long tour and study of Europe. Personally I have spent nearly every cent I possessed to found the Society and keep it alive, and I can only say that the work has been most harassing and hard gene[rally.] My Association is well appreciated by the cultured white people of the country, and in a small way they have come to my assistance to help me along. From His Excellency the Governor down, among the whites, I have been helped by kindly encouragement, and I can say that some of the most influential of them have paid us the honour of coming amongst us. His Excellency the Governor, the Colonial Secretary, Hon. H. Bryan, C.M.G., Sir John Pringle, Hon. Brig-General L. S. Blackden, all members of the Privy Council, have been our patrons on several occasions and they are still friends of the Association. The Brig-General has lectured to us, as also His Lordship Bishop J. J. Collins, S.J., His Worship the Mayor of Kingston, Hon. H. A. L. Simpson, M.L.C., Mr. R. W. Bryant, J.P. Ex-Mayor of Kingston who has visited us more than a dozen times and many other prominent dignitaries of the country. The Hon. Colonial Secretary has himself attended a function along with his wife to which he was especially invited.

Whilst we have been encouraged and helped by the cultured whites to do something to help in lifting the masses[,] the so called representative[s] of our own people have sought to draw us down and ever since they have been waging a secret campaign to that end, hence even on your coming here you will find such men parading themselves as "wolves in sheep's clothing" who are desirous of destroying the existence of a Negro Society.

I am engaged in fighting a battle with foes of my own all around, but I am prepared to fight on with the strength given me by Almighty God.

I have many large schemes on my mind for the advancement of my people that I cannot expose at the present to the public as in such a case my hope of immediate success would be defeated, as my enemies are so many, and they are ever anxious to misrepresent me. I have firstly to fund a press of our own and to get some working start so as to demonstrate my true intention.

I have on my programme the establishing of an Industrial Farm and Institute here on the lines of the Tuskegee Institute where we could teach our people on the objects of race pride, race development, and other useful subjects.

I have been planning a tour of America where I am to lecture for five months and I am hoping to leave on Thursday this week if possible or later on in next month I intend visiting Tuskegee. Dr. Washington during his life time promised to assist me there under cover of 12th April 1915. I wanted was to have had an interview with you along with my secretaries, before I leave, if I go on Thursday, but up to now I have heard nothing definite from those to whom I have applied. If by accident I am unable to meet you here I hope to in America.

One of your experience, will readily realize what enemies in a cause mean.—They are the carrier of poison, so the "tongue" of the serpent sometimes stings without doing harm. I would really like to be able to interview you on Wednesday and I shall take the chance to call on you then so as to further explain the cause of my Association. Trusting you will enjoy your stay, With very best wishes   Yours faithfully,

MARCUS GARVEY

[*Address*]   Major R. Moton/ Tuskegee
Normal & Industrial Institute
   "On Visit to Jamaica"

ATT, RRM. ALS, Recipient's copy.
   1. This letter has not been found.

Attachment

30 Charles Street, Kingston,
Febry., 29th. 1916

Dear Sir,

You, being a prominent American Negro Leader, coming into a strange country, and I, being a resident here, and one who also claims the distinction of being a race leader, I think it but right that I should try to enlighten you on the conditions existing /amoung/ our people, hence I now take the opportunity of laying before you /my/ views on the local aspect of the Negro life.

Jamaica is unlike the United States where the race question is concerned. We have no open race prejudice here, and we do not openly antagonise one another. The extremes here are not between white and black, hence we have never had a case of lynching or anything so desperate. The black /people here/ forms the economic asset of the country, they number 6 to 1 of coloured and white combined and without them in labour or general industry the country would go bankrupt.

The black people have had seventy eight years of Emancipation, but all during that time they have never produced a leader of their own, hence they have never been led to think racially but in common with the destinies of the other people with whom they mix as fellow citizens. After Emancipation, the Negro was unable to cope intellectually with his master, and per-force he had to learn at the knees of his emancipator.

He has, therefore, grown with his master's ideals, and up to today you will find the Jamaica Negro unable to think apart from the customs and ideals of his old time slave masters. Unlike the American Negro, the Jamaican haves never thought of race ideals, much to his detriment, as instead of progressing generally, he has become a serf in the bulk, and a gentleman in the few.

Racial ideals do no people harm, therefore, the Jamaica Negro has done himself a harm in not thinking on racial ideals with the scattered Negroes of other classes /climes/. The coloured and white population have been thinking and planning on exclusive race ideals—race ideals which are unwritten and unspoken. The deplomacy of one race or class of people is the means by which others are outdone, hence the deplomacy of the other races prevent them leading the race question in Jamaica, a question that could have been understood and regarded without friction.

You will find the Jamaican Negro has been sleeping much to his loss, for others have gained on top of him and are still gaining.

Apparently you will think that the people here mix at the end of a great social question, but in truth it is not so. The mixture is purely circumstancial and not genuine. The people mix in business, but they do not mix in /true/ society. The whites claim superiority, as is done all over the world, and, unlike other parts, the coloured, who ancestrially are the illigitimate off-springs of black and white claim a positive superiority over the blacks. They train themselves to believe that in the slightest shade the coloured man is above the black man and so it runs right up to white. The black man naturally is kept down at the foot of the ladder and is trampled on by all the shades above. In a small minority he pushes himself up among the others, but when he "gets there" he too believes himself other than black and he starts out to think from a white and coloured mind much to the detriment of his own people whom he should have turned back to lead out of ~~the~~ surrounding darkness.

The black man lives directly under the white man's institutions and the influence over him is so great that he is only a play-thing in the moulder's hand. The blackman of Jamaica cannot think for himself, and because of this he remains in the bulk the dissatisfied "~~heart~~ /beast/ of burden." Look around and see to what proportion [t]he black man appears a gentleman in office. With a small exception the black man is not in office at all. The only sphere that he domunates in is that of the teaching profession and he domuinates there because the wage is not encouraging enough for others; and even in this department the Negro has the weapon to liberate himself and make himself a man, for there is no greater weapon than education; but the educated teacher, "baby-like" in his practice, does not think apart from the written code, hence he, himself, is a slave to what is set down for him to do and no more.

If you ~~should~~ /were/ to go into all the offices throughout Jamaica you will not find one per cent of black clerks employed. You will find nearly all white and coloured persons including men and women; for proof please go through our Post Office, Government Offices and stores in Kingston, and you see only white and coloured men and women in positions of importance and trust and you will find the black men and women, as store-men, messengers, attendants & common servants. In the country parts you will find the same order of things. On the Estates and Plantations you will find the blackman and woman as the labourer, the coloured /man/ as clerk and sometimes owner and the white man generally as master. /White and coloured women are absent from the fields of labor/ The professions are generally taken /up/ by the ~~by the~~ white and coloured men because they have the means to equip themselves.

Whenever a black man enters the professions, he per force, thinks from a white and coloured mind, and for the time /being/ he enjoys the apparent friendship of the classes until he is made a bankrupt or forced into difficulties which naturally causes him to be ostracised.

The entire system here is bad as affecting the Negro and the Negro of education will not do anything honestly and truly to help his brethren in the manss. Black Ministers and Teachers are moral cowards, they are too much afraid to speak to their people on the pride of race. Whenever the blackman gets money and education he thinks himself white and coloured, and he wants a white and coloured wife, and he will spend his all to get this; much to his eternal misery.

Black professionals who have gone abroad ~~of~~ /have/ nearly all married white women who on their arrival here leave them and return home. Others ~~many~~ /marry/ highly coloured women and others taking in the lessons of others refuse to marry in preference ~~if~~ to marrying the black girls. You will find a few educated blackmen naturally having black wives but these are the sober minded ones who have taken the bad lessons home. Our black girls are taught by observation to dispise blackmen as they are naturally poor /and of social discount/; hence you will find a black girl willing to give herself up to any immoral suggestion of white or coloured men, and positively refusing the good attentions of a /blackman at/ the outset.

Not until when she has been made a fool of by white and coloured before she turns back to the black man and wants him as a companion. Our morality is destroyed this way. Ninety per cent of the coloured people are off-springs of immorality, yet they rule next to the whites over the blacks.

This is shameful, but our men hav'nt the courage to stem the tide. Our ministers are funnying at the "teaching of the gospel" and they have been often criticised for their inactivity in correcting vice and immorality. I am sorry I have to say this; nevertheless it is true.

The blackman here is a slave of destiny, and it is only by bold and conscientious leadership that he can emancipate, and I do trust your visit will be one of the means of helping him. I am now talking with you as a man with a mission from the High God. Your education will enable you to understand me clearly. I do not mean ~~litter~~ literary education alone, for that we have here among a goodly number of Blacks as teachers and ministers. I mean the higher education of man's appreciation for his fellowman; of man's love for his race. Our people here are purely selfish and no man or people can lead if selfishness is the cardinal principle.

One Negro here hates to see the other Negro succeeds and for that he will pull him down every time he attempts to climb and defame him. The Negro here will not help one another, and they have no sympathy with one another. Ninety per cent of our people /are/ labourers and serfs, the other ten per cent are mixed up in the professions, trades and small proprietorships. /I mean the black people, not coloured or white. You look out for /here carefully/ We have no social order of our own   we have to flatter ourselves into white and coloured society to our own disgrace and discomforture, because we are never truly appreciated. Among us we have an excess of crimes and the prison houses, alm houses, and mad houses are over crowded with our people much to the absense of the other classes.

Our prisoners are generally chained and marched through the streets of the city while on their way to the Penitentiary. You should pay a visit to the Prisons, Alms house, and Asylum to test the correctness of my statements. We have a large prison in Kingston and another one at Spanish Town. You will find Alms Houses all over the Island, but the Union Poor House is near to Kingston in St Andrew.

Our women are prostituted, and if you were to walk the lower sections of Kingston after night fall you will see hundreds of Black prostitutes in the ~~dances~~ /lanes/, streets and all~~y~~ies.

Our people in the bulk do not live in good houses, they live in "huts" and "old shanties", and you will see this as you go through the country. If you care to see this in Kingston you can visit places like Smith's Village and Hannah's Town. Our people in the bulk can't afford to wear good clothes and boots. Generally /they/ wear rags and go bare-footed in the bulk during the week, and some change their garbs on Sundays when they go to church, but this is not general.

The people have no system of sanitation. They keep themselves /dirty/ and if you were to mix in a crowd on a hot day you would be stifled with the bad odour. You can only see the ragged and dirty masses on alarming occassions when you will see them running from all directions. If a band of music were to parade the city then you would /have/ a fair illustration of what I mean. Our people are not encouraged to be clean and decent because they are kept down on the lowest wage with great expences hanging over them.

Our labour~~ing we~~ get anything from nine pence (eighteen cent) 1/- (25 cents) 1/6 (36 cents) to fifty cents a day, on which they have to support a family.

This is the grinding system that keeps the blackman down ~~there~~, hence I personally, have very little in common with /the/ educated class of my /own/ people for they are the bitterest enimies of their own race. Our people have no respect for one another, and all the respect is shown to the white and coloured people.

The reception that will be given you will not be genuine from more than one reasons which I may explain later on to you.

Black men here are never truly honoured. Don't you believe like coloured Dr. Du Bois that the "race problem is at an end here"[1] except you want to admit the utter insignificance of the black man.

It was never started and has not yet begun. It is a paradox. I personally would like to solve the situation on the broadest humanitarian lines. I would like to solve it on the platform of Dr. Booker T. Washington, and I am working on those lines hence you will find that up to now my one true friend as far as you can rely on his friendship, is the whiteman.

I do not mean to bring any estrangement between black and white. I want to have Jamaica a country of "Black and White" all living in peace and harmony but with equal rights and opportunities.

I would not advise you to give yourself too much away to the desire and wishes of the people who are around you for they are mostly hypocrites. They mean to deceive you on the conditions here because we can never blend under the existing state of affairs—it would not be fair to the blackman.— To /blend/ we must all in equal proportion "show our hands." ~~XXX~~

Your intellect, I believe, is too deep to be led away by "sham sentiment." [*Inserted*:—XXX(1) See omission at bottom.]

[*Inserted*: (2)XXX] Impress this, and *let them answer* it *for publication*, and then you will have the whole farce in a *nut shell*. When you are travelling to the mountains parts, stop a while and observe properly the rural life of your people as against the life of others of the classes.

I have much more to say, but I must close for another time.

Again I wish you a pleasant stay. Yours in the Brotherhood,

MARCUS GARVEY

P/S. Another condition that I would like you to observe is how our people attend church. The churches are generally crowded with women with an opposite absence of men. The women are of different classes but the majority of them are people of questionable morality who parades themselves in the garbs of vice for which the men have to pay.

Omission X[*XX(1)*] Population of Jamaica   White 15,605, coloured 163,201; black *630,181*   East Indian 17,380, chinese 2,111   2,905 colour not stated omission XXX[(2)] If you desire to do Jamaica a turn, you might ask those around you on public platforms to explain to what proportion the different people here enjoy the wealth and resources of the country   XXX(2)

ATT, RRM. TLS, Recipient's copy. Insertions and corrections were handwritten by Garvey.

1. Garvey was probably referring here to a statement Du Bois originally made at a farewell dinner held in his honor in Jamaica on 30 April 1915. At the dinner, the press reported that Du Bois stated that Jamaica had "settled the race question" and that "there were few places in which that question was so well settled" (*Jamaica Times*, 8 May 1915, p. 2). Du Bois felt that the problem facing the peasantry of Jamaica was economic, rather than racial. The solution, Du Bois believed, was the creation of "a large number of small holdings" (*Daily Chronicle*, 1 May 1915).

Marcus Garvey to the *Gleaner*

[[Kingston, March 1st, 1916]]

Sir,—

Mr. Alexander Dixon is trying to misrepresent me again, and I can well understand that my enemies (who will be unmasked one day) have been actively engaged at work for some time trying to do their best to swamp me. I am acquainted with nearly all their methods so Mr. Dixon's letter is no surprise to me. I was looking for some more, even though I made it plain that I desire no controversy.

Mr. Dixon and myself belong to two opposite schools of thought and we are both differently situated. I am not a representative of Mr. Dixon's class. Mr. Dixon is of the "aristocratic class." I am of the humblest class, and I feel satisfied by election to be with the people whom neither Mr. Dixon nor his friends will call representative. But it would appear to me, sir, that some people are "swell-headed" enough to believe that they represent every body. Mr. Dixon surely does not represent me, and I have never yet felt so ambitious (aristocratically) as to represent Mr. Dixon's class. Men of the "Dixon School" stand in the way of general improvement among the common people. Their one mission is to disgust everybody who attem[pt]s to say or do anything to bring about a change in their condition. These 'lip-service' leaders must be heard and seen alone. Mr. Dixon's class does not represent ten per cent. of the negro population, hence he is like an atom in the vast immensity. Mr. Dixon's reasoning is bad and I really do not care to have him "showing his hands" any more in this fashion for the good of his own class. Isn't this charity, sir?

I never suggested any friction in the matter of our visitor, I only wrote to your paper giving an explanation, which you summarised. Surely if you had space for my letter it would have explained itself, and sober-minded men would never think that I desired anything else but harmony. I am, etc.,

MARCUS GARVEY

P.S.—What I have said orally or written I mean, hence I must stand or fall by my own expressions. Mr. Dixon cannot think for me he must just think for himself.

M. G.

To 'Churchman'—We have received your communication. It should be sent to the Editor of the "Catholic Opinion."[1] If you will send for it we will return it to you.

Printed in the *Gleaner*, Friday, 3 March 1916. Original headline has been omitted.

1. Garvey had been formerly connected with *Catholic Opinion*, the official paper of the Roman Catholic diocese of Jamaica. (*NW*, Saturday, 19 June 1920).

THE TUSKEGEE
NORMAL AND INDUSTRIAL INSTITUTE
FOR THE TRAINING OF
COLORED YOUNG MEN AND WOMEN

TUSKEGEE INSTITUTE, ALABAMA

March 2d, 1916

Mr. Marcus Garvey, Jr.,

   30 Charles St., Kingston, Jamaica.

    My dear Sir:-

    I have received your kind letter of February 4th in which you speak of the work you are carrying on in Jamaica for the Negro people, and your plan to visit the United States this spring.

    If you should come South while in this country, we shall be very glad to welcome you to Tuskegee and visit the Institute. If you come here we can then go over your plans and if I find it possible to assist you in any way, I of course shall be very glad to do so.

    I thank you for your kind references to Dr. Washington and the influence of his life and work upon the people in Jamaica.

    Yours very truly,

    Secretary.

H

Emmett J. Scott to Marcus Garvey

TUSKEGEE INSTITUTE, ALABAMA
March 2d, 1916

My dear Sir:—

    I have received your kind letter of February 4th in which you speak of the work you are carrying on in Jamaica for the Negro people, and your plan to visit the United States this spring.

If you should come South while in this country, we shall be very glad to welcome you to Tuskegee and visit the Institute. If you come here we can then go over your plans and if I find it possible to assist you in any way, I of course shall be very glad to do so.

I thank you for your kind references to Dr. Washington and the influence of his life and work upon the people in Jamaica. Yours very truly,

EMMETT J SCOTT
Secretary

H

EDSG. TLS, Recipient's copy.

Extract from the Crew List of the S.S. *Tallac*

DISTRICT, CITY OF NEW YORK,
PORT OF NEW YORK.
Mar 24 1916[1]

. . . I, *Louis Hansen*, MASTER OF THE *Am. Ste. Tallac*[2] DO SOLEMNLY AND TRULY SWEAR THAT ALL OF THE ABOVE NAMED CREW[3] HAVE RETURNED WITH ME IN SAID VESSEL TO THIS PORT EXCEPT:
H. Hoggland[4] *as per Consular Certificate Also returned Marcus Garvey, signed at Kingston, Ja., after clearing.*[5]

LOUIS HANSEN
SWORN TO BEFORE ME
THIS   DAY OF *Mar 24 1916*
B BAEHR
DEPUTY COLLECTOR

DNA, RG 36, New York, Returned Crew List. DS, Printed form with typewritten and manuscript additions. The statement pertaining to Garvey was handwritten by Louis Hansen.

　1. Date-stamped.
　2. The ship had originally left for Jacksonville, Fla., on 25 February 1916 and arrived at Kingston, Jamaica, on 1 March.
　3. A total of twenty-two crew members were listed.
　4. Discharged at Kingston, 7 March 1916.
　5. S.S. *Tallac* cleared the port of Kingston on or after 7 March 1916. The ship arrived at Belize, British Honduras, on 10 March and sailed from Belize on 15 March, arriving at the port of New York on 24 March.

Marcus Garvey to W. E. B. Du Bois

(Crisis' Office) [1]

53 W. 140th Street, New York City
April 25, 1916

Dear Dr. DuBois/

I called in order to have asked you if you could be so good as to take the "chair" at my first public lecture to be delivered at the St. Mark's Hall, 57 W 138th St. City on Tuesday evening 9th May at 8 o'clock. My subject will be "Jamaica"—a general talk ~~of~~ /on/ the phases of Negro life.

I also beg to hand you tickets[2] for same and to submit to you a circular in general circulation among prospective patrons.

I shall be pleased to hear from you immediately. Trusting you will be able to help by taking the chair. With . . .[*words illegible*] Yours . . .[*illegible*]

MARCUS GARVEY

[*Endorsement*]   Thank you
out of town [*WEBDB*]

MU, WEBDB. ALS, Recipient's copy. Written in pencil.

1. Garvey had called at the editorial offices of Du Bois's *Crisis*, the official organ of the NAACP, at 70 Fifth Avenue in New York City, but at the time Du Bois was traveling. (See Herbert Aptheker, ed., *The Correspondence of W. E. B. Du Bois*, vol. 1 [Amherst: University of Massachusetts, 1973], pp. 214–15).

2. Garvey enclosed three tickets, two in the name of Dr. W. E. B. Du Bois and one in the name of the *Crisis*.

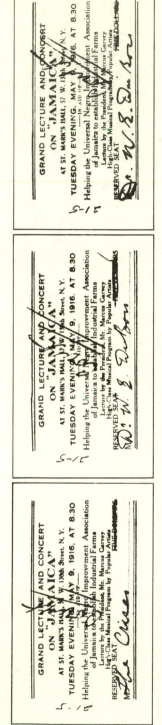

Tickets to Garvey's First Lecture in America (Source: MU, WEBDB).

Attachment

30 & 34 Charles Street
Kingston, Jamaica, W.I.
53 West 140th Street   New York,
[*April*] 191[6]

Dear Friend and Brother:

Herewith I beg to hand you tickets for a "Lecture and Concert" to be given in the St. Mark's Hall, 57 West 138th St., New York, on Tuesday night, the 9th of May, at 8 o'clock, in the interest of the Universal Negro Improvement Association of Jamaica, to help in establishing our "Industrial Farm and Institute" in that country, for helping the Negroes of that section to a higher state of educational and industrial usefulness among the people and for service to the world.

The plan of the "Farm and Institute" is to include the highest educational and industrial training, which will mean bringing the people up to cultured lines, whence they will be rendered able to understand and appreciate all the things that are necessary for the advance of the professions, trade, commerce, literature, art and world-wide industries.

We want to produce among the people a better class in the bulk—more thoughtful, more appreciative, more industrious and more international in their views as affecting established ideals—a class that can command the universal esteem and stand the contact of all classes of mankind. A certain class of graduates from this Institute will be used as missionaries to Africa with the hope of helping to bring the millions of that "wonderful" Continent into the van of civilization, which will mean so much to commerce and other industries.

I have come over to America to lecture on "Jamaica," and to raise the necessary help to enable us to put through our Institute, and this lecture and concert is for the purpose mentioned.

I send you the tickets asking your patronage and help, and if you find it impossible to use them, I beg that you send a donation to help in the work, which donation shall be treasured and remembered in the history of our effort. A donation of any amount will be highly appreciated.

It is not necessary to enumerate Jamaica's service to the United States, as in many ways the Negro people of that country have done their share in helping American capital, American enterprise and American industries, not to mention, our Negro people have helped substantially in pushing through the Panama Canal—to be the world's greatest trade route—and our people are ever willing to work under the progressive leadership of American genius.

I feel that you will not turn down the brotherly and philanthropic request for your patronage and help, but that you will send in your help as per tickets or per donation.

Should you attend you will be treated to an interesting lecture on Jamaica, as also to a good performance of Negro artists who will delight you, and I feel sure you will benefit by the lecture. With very best wishes, Your most obedient servant,

UNIVERSAL NEGRO IMPROVT. ASSO.
PER MARCUS GARVEY
PRESIDENT

On Lecture Tour, United States.
53 West 140th St., New York City.

Reference—Jamaica Club,
588 Lenox Ave., Care of W. Adams,
Treasurer.

MU, WEBDB. LS, Printed on official UNIA stationery. The organizational title, as listed in the letterhead, was the "Universal Negro Improvement Association of Jamaica." The UNIA officers included in the letterhead are printed in Appendix III.

W. E. B. Du Bois's Private Secretary to Marcus Garvey

[*New York City*] April 29, 1916

My dear Mr. Garvey:

Doctor DuBois begs me[1] to thank you for your note of April twenty-fifth and express his regret at not be able to be on hand on account of his being out of town. Very sincerely yours,

MU, WEBDB. TL, Carbon copy.

1. The name of Du Bois's private secretary has not been ascertained.

Account by W. A. Domingo[1] of Marcus Garvey's St. Mark's Church Hall Lecture

[*New York, n.d.*][2]

[*Beginning of sentence mutilated*] [many?] comical incidents, but whether this was acted or a piece of sheer, unpremeditated comedy I do not know. Considered in relation to the amo[u]nt [of] horn tooting and tom-tom beating that had preceded it and which formed a glaring contrast to what actually happened the incident which I am about to relate will live in my memory, and I feel certain in the memories of those who had witnessed it, as ~I~ one of the most amusing that I have ever seen.

He [*Garvey*] had just arrived in the United States after a "tour" of the world where, according to his own unsupported statement, he had "lectured" before large audiences in England, Scotland, Wales, Central America and the ~~United--Sta-~~ West Indies. He was short of stature and dark of complexion. His head was a perfect brach[y]cephalic type, while the /outward/ projection of his lower jaw gave him a pro[g]nathous, ape-like appearance when seen in profile. He was practically without any neck and his head sat close down upon his massive, muscular shoulders. He had a deep, broad chest and slightly protruding abdomen which were supported by spindly legs that were adorned with large widespread feet.

As I remember him now he was dressed in a much crumpled and misfitting suit of cheap light grey material. On his head was a salmon-brown soft felt hat of ancient style and appearance. The shoes he wore, although old and . . . [*several words mutilated*] straggly mustache-~~that-~~below his broad, flat nose was uneven and unkempt. Generally his appearance was repulsive, Caliban-like.[3]

Being an orator of international~~ly~~ fame he very naturally had to let /the public/ ~~us-~~ know that fact, so he had some flamboyant handbills printed which announced to all and sundry that the "Hon" ——— world-famed-orator would speak at St Mark's-Hall.

On the night in question [*9 May 1916*] I went to the hall. Although scheduled to have a regular chairman and to start at 8.30 o'clock, the meeting did not begin until after nine. The speaker of the evening, whose versatility was great, was also master of ceremonies. He was there early dressed in a tuxedo suit of antique cut, a black silk cap, hardboiled shirt and a pair of dancing pumps. The chairman not being on time, and the janitor being absent, the orator lost patience and asked a local light to preside.

According to the advertisement the lecture was to be preceeded by a concert. The artists did not acquit themselves well so the o[r]chestra was resorted to keep up ~~sp-~~ the spirit of the audience which numbered al~~l~~together about 36 persons.

The orator was visibly nervous. He kept pacing the floors all the time. The lights gave no end of trouble so that they had to depend upon the feeble rays of a few gas jets. . . . [*Several words mutilated*] bored [the] audience for about half an hour and then introduced the Hon ——— world-famous orator of the Negro race.

Shaking like an aspen leaf and with a tremor in his voice he started to deliver his oration. He hadn't gone very far when the audience began to vent its disgust by whistling and hooting. You can easily imagine the sorry figure and the pitiable spectacle the poor discomfited orator presented. He looked around in affright and pulling a manuscript from his pocket began to read. The more he read the great was the din created by the audience.

It was ~~and~~ ordeal that flesh and blood could not long endure. From all sides of the small hall came shouts of: "Sit down;" "shut up"; ["] Away with him," interspersed with catcalls and ear-splitting whistles. /While this was going on one of the musicians, a Porto Rican, calmly lit his cigarette from a flame no[t] two feet from the speaker./

To cap the climax and increase the ~~laughter of~~ mirth of the audience which was enjoying itself for every penny of the twenty five cents admission fee, a tall light-complexioned countryman of the orator mounted the stage and pointing his index finger at the audience strove in vain to quiet it. ~~Seeing that~~

Around f[rom the] back of the stage came another countryman [of the] speaker, a ~~young~~ brown-[colored youth?] of prepossing personality. Possessing [str]ong arms and a loud, penetrating voice he push the first intruder aside and shouted: "The trouble with you people is that you cannot appreciate intelligence—" He had no sooner delivered himself of this when some of the audience made a motion as if to attack him but he was saved from them as the tall man whom he had brushed aside, regained himself and retaliated in kind.

During all of this the orator made desperate efforts to speak and then even his /steel/ nerve snapped. He was near the edge of the stage which is about 3 feet from the floor and suddenly he began to sway ~~f~~ backwards and forwards. Before any ~~of those~~ one in the audience could help him he fell from off the stage and lay prostrate on the floor.

Immediately the audience's levity subsided and willing hands lifted ~~him~~ the Hon ——— orator from the floor and applied First-Aid relief. This brought the lecture or rather the concert, for the whole thing was an entertainment, /to a close./

Questioned as to what had happened the orator said that he had lost his nerve and fainted. Whether it was a genuine accident or whether it was a clever piece of stage-play to tra . . . [*mutilated*] the audience . . . [*words mutilated*] sy/m/pathy I have never [been] able to decide, but I do know that that fall was responsible for mitigating a very embarrassing and humilating ~~trag~~ incident. All through the occurrence my heart was in conflict with my responsiveness to comedy and when all is said and done I regard that incident as one of transcendent comedy tinged with a little tragedy.

WAD. AMS.

1. Wilfred Adolphus Domingo (1889–1968) became the first editor of the UNIA's *Negro World* after the paper's inception in August 1918, a position he held for eleven months before resigning in July 1919. For additional information about Domingo, see the Biographical Supplement, Appendix I.

2. Since it is not possible to date this document, its place has been assigned on the basis of the date when the event described occurred. It does not appear that Domingo wrote the document for publication.

3. A reference to the deformed and bestial native, Caliban, one of the principal characters in Shakespeare's *Tempest*.

Marcus Garvey to T. A. McCormack

53 W 140th Street,
New York, N.Y. City May 12 1916

Dear M.ᶜ.

This is to inform you that I have been in New York since the 26th of April, having stopped over at Belize British Honduras and travelling to a couple of the states of this country to have my lecture programme arranged. I delivered my first lecture here on the 9th and it will take me a few days to know the result from those who are helping me. I learned from a letter I received from Miss Ashwood that her mother left Jamaica the very day I sail[e]d of which I knew nothing   I made out that she was in Kingston and in charge of the house at Charles street. Before I sailed I paid her and handed over to a man living with one Conductor Anderson in the yard a balance of 7/- to hand over to her and I also wrote to her thinking she was in Kingston but her daughter has informed me otherwise, hence I am at a loss to know what has become of my things there. There was a table there for Reid[1] and a case for Stennett[2] as also books, papers, desk chairs, pictures, etc.

Can you find out for me from one Mr. Ricketts in Chance[r]y lane above Charles street a carpenter—Adrian knows who—if Mrs Ashwood owes any money—and how much and let me know by return mail so that I can send same and have the things redeemed. I have had some terrible experience with that woman I never knew she was going away. Please tell Mr. Ricketts that for me. If it is possible to get the home as an office even to rent the whole place find out from him and let me know so that I can send the money to pay for same or some other place. I am plan[n]ing a big programme which I feel sure will put us in a good position   You must excuse my not writing to you before . . . [*third and fourth pages of letter missing*]   Will you let me know just what is going on so that I can handle things in the proper way? I am writing to all the other officers to come together so as to redeem what has been lost.

Give my compliments to everybody. Miss Ashwood is still in Colon with her father   I do not think she can be blamed for her mother's actions. It is through her that I found out what she had done. About three members of the old board [of] management are over here and helped at the lecture.

Now let me hear from you early when I shall send you down all particulars. I leave hear for Boston in two weeks but all my letters can be address to me here at my headquarters. I noticed in the papers that the "Jamaica League" crowd who have been trying to upset the association are trying to form an association thrugh E. E. Brown to befool the Negro and make selfish capital out [of] him.[3] I will handle them when I return to Jamaica. I am writing something to the newspapers there. Yours faithfully,

MARCUS GARVEY

Write nothing to the press. The public is not entitled to know the secrets of any organization otherwise all organizations would go to nought   Let them say all they car[e.] [I] will act. They want to know so as to smash and find fault

TAM. ALS, Recipient's copy. The stationery lists "Journalist" as an additional title for Garvey. The UNIA officers printed in the letterhead have been included in Appendix III. Added to the official UNIA letterhead was the quotation, "He created of one blood all nations of man to dwell on the face of the earth," taken from Acts 17:26 of the New Testament.

   1. Before leaving for America, Garvey had left a table and fourteen chairs, on loan from the Reid brothers' restaurant, at 12 Charles Street, Kingston. Along with some magazines, this apparently comprised the furniture of the UNIA reading room. (Lionel Yard's interview with Reid, 1973).

   2. A possible reference to William Stennett, proprietor of the West India Medical and Mail Order Agency in Kingston.

   3. The Progressive Negro Association (PNA) was proposed by Rev. E. Ethelred Brown, who was also an official of the Jamaica League, in a letter on 28 April 1916 to the *Daily Chronicle*. Its first meeting took place on 20 June 1916 in the Unitarian Hall, Kingston. The association, which chose "Progress and Dignity; Justice and Fraternity" as its motto, had three aims: to foster race pride; to improve the economic, social, intellectual, and moral conditions of blacks in Jamaica; and to secure rights for all blacks. The first officers of the PNA were president, Mr. J. W. Milbourne (previously UNIA treasurer from about November 1914 to April–August 1915); vice-president, Rev. D. A. Waugh; secretary, Rev. E. Ethelred Brown; assistant secretary, Mr. C. A. Meade; and treasurer, Mr. T. C. Golding ("Association Constituted," *Daily Chronicle*, 8 August 1916). In November 1916, Rev. Brown proposed that the PNA publish a magazine, but it does not appear that this ever materialized.

Item in the *Crisis*

[May 1916]

   Mr. Marcus Garvey, founder and president of the Universal Negro Improvement Association of Jamaica, B.W.I., is now on a visit to America. He will deliver a series of lectures on Jamaica in an effort to raise funds for the establishment of an industrial and educational institution for Negroes in Jamaica.

Printed in the *Crisis* 12 (May 1916): 9, from "Along the Color Line."

Marcus Garvey to Emmett J. Scott

7. Greenwich St., Boston Mass,
June 9 1916

My dear Mr. Scott,
   I have just received your kind letter of March 2nd. in reply to my communication of 4th. February of the present year.

I left Jamaica on the 6th. of March and my Secretary has just sent on your letter for which I thank you. It is most likely that I will be in the South about August at which time I hope to meet you.[1] I am at present lecturing in Boston.

Thanking you for your kindly interest With best wishes Yours faithfully

MARCUS GARVEY

[*Endorsement*] *ackgd*

ATT, RRM. ALS, Recipient's copy. Endorsement is handwritten. Written in hand by Garvey in the body of the letterhead was the following: "On Lecture Tour U.S.A. Permanent address: 53 W. 140th St., New York."

1. Garvey later stated that, following his arrival in New York in March 1916, he "hastened to the shrine of the illustrious gentleman [Booker T. Washington] to pay his homage." (*NW*, Saturday, 10 December 1921, p. 5).

Marcus Garvey to the *Daily Chronicle*

[[1816, 12th St., N.W.
Washington, D.C. U.S.A.
18th Aug., 1916]]

TO THE EDITOR: Sir,—

It is with a great amount of alarm and regret that I learn of the destruction that has been wrought to the various crops of Jamaica by the terrible hurricane, notice of which was taken by the *Washington Times* of this city, through whose medium I learned of the sad occurrence.

I feel with the poor people of Jamaica, as it would appear that they are never free from pain and sorrow.

My deepest sympathy goes out also to the planters, whose fortitude must be commended, for they are never discouraged by disasters which occur so often. Some people say that "God is not in the wind," but if Jamaica would purge herself of some of her vices, her hypocrisy, her lack of sympathy for the struggling, I do think that disasters would be less frequent.

A country without true religion—that religion that seeks in very truth to help the poor and unfortunate, as they ought to be helped, to become better men and useful citizens—is doomed. But I do pray that my native land fall not in the category of Sodom.

I hope that all classes will unite to restore that which has been lost, and that the good men and true, and the righteous and noble of our country be not discouraged nor become weary in well-doing. With deep regret, I am, etc.,

MARCUS GARVEY

Printed in the *Daily Chronicle*, Wednesday, 30 August 1916. Original headline has been omitted.

Letter Denouncing Marcus Garvey

[[Philadelphia, U.S.A.
September 19th, 1916]]

THE EDITOR, Dear Sir,—

We the undersigned Jamaicans, residents of the United States for several years beg permission to call to your attention and the public of Jamaica a matter affecting the welfare of Jamaicans at home and abroad.

Under the caption of Journalist and President of the Universal Negro Improvement Association, Jamaica, W.I., one Marcus Garvey, Jr., is giving an extended series of lectures in this Country, pertaining to the social and economic conditions of Jamaica.

We, having attended his lectures, found them to be pernicious, misleading, and derogatory to the prestige of the Government and the people.

Among the many assertions of the speaker are the following:—

1.   Governmental misrule, causing economic depression, poverty and misery with their detrimental consequences.

2.   The falsity and hypocrisy of the existing social condition between the white and black races—to wit:

Absorption by inter-marriage of the intellectually superior and advanced blacks with whites, with the view of estranging and nullifying their usefulness to their race.

Result—Acquiescence, arrogance, and unapproachableness, on the part of these blacks who inter-marry. The white wife tires. There is an ultimate separation. Wife returns to her native land. Husband in Jamaica contributes to her support abroad.

3.   The Governmental and Commercial interests connive to keep the scale of wage so low that the labouring classes are unable to meet the necessary demands to sustain their needs and wants. The girls of Jamaica are resorting to vice and immorality through lack of industrial opportunities and poor economic conditions. Praedial larcency is rampant and the jails are filled[.] Education is restricted and limited to the children of the poorer classes causing intellectual deficiency to the masses.

4.   He drew a deplorable picture of the prejudice of the Englishman in Jamaica against the blacks, portraying hypocrisy and deceit of his attitude towards the blacks, and stated his preference for the prejudice of the American to that of the Englishman.

Mr. Editor, the above are only a few of the damaging statements being disseminated by the aforesaid Marcus Garvey, Jr., among the American public.

Further details would be a repetition of the demoralising utterances of the speaker.

The bad effects of these lectures on the minds of the American public are deplorable and are causing great indignation among Jamaicans here, who feel greatly humiliated.

Thanking you for space and hoping through this medium Jamaicans will be enlightened on the seriousness of this matter. We are,

Father Raphael,[1] O.C.G.,[2] Priest-Apostolic, the Greek Orthodox Catholic Church, Dr. Uriah Smith, Ernest P. Duncan, Ernest K. Jones, H. S. Boulin, Phillip Hemmings, Joseph Vassal, Henry H. Harper, S. C. Box, Aldred Campbell, Hubert Barclay, John Moore, Victor Monroe, Henry Booth and many others.

Printed in the *Jamaica Times*, Saturday, 7 October 1916. Original headlines have been omitted.

1. "Father Raphael" was the Greek Orthodox ecclesiastical name of Robert Josias Morgan, a Jamaican who received his education in Sierra Leone at the Church Missionary Society grammar school in Freetown, and at Fourah Bay College, Freetown, Sierra Leone. He was appointed a missionary teacher and lay reader in Liberia, but after a number of years there, he left for America where he became successively an AME minister and a deacon in the Protestant Episcopal Church in 1895. He served for a time in Wilmington, Del., and in Charleston, W. Va. For unknown reasons, he was deposed on 6 November 1908 by the Bishop of Asheville. Sometime in 1912–13 he was baptized into the Greek Orthodox Catholic Church in Constantinople after an extended visit to Russia. The Holy See of Constantinople commissioned him as priest-apostolic to America and the West Indies, with headquarters at Philadelphia. (*WWCR*; Episcopal Diocese of Delaware, *Journal* [1896], p. 26; *Lloyd's Clerical Directory*, 1898, 1910; Monroe N. Work, ed., *Negro Year Book: An Encyclopedia of the Negro, 1921–22* [Tuskegee Institute, Ala.: The Negro Year Book Publishing Co., 1922], p. 213; *ATOR*, [Feb.–Mar. 1913], p. 163; and George F. Bragg, *History of the Afro-American Group of the Episcopal Church* [Baltimore: Church Advocate Press, 1922]).

2. Order of the Cross of Golgotha, a religious fraternity founded by Father Raphael.

Article by Marcus Garvey in the *Champion Magazine*

[January 1917]

WEST INDIES IN THE MIRROR OF TRUTH
By Marcus Garvey, Jr.

I have been in America eight months.[1] My mission to this country is to lecture and raise funds to help my organization—the Universal Negro Improvement Association of Jamaica—to establish an industrial and educational institute, to assist in educating the Negro youth of that island. I am also engaged in the study of Negro life in this country.

I must say, at the outset, that the American Negro ought to compliment himself, as well as the early prejudice of the South, for the racial progress made in fifty years, and for the discriminating attitude that had led the race up to the high mark of consciousness preserving it from extinction.

I feel that the Negro who has come in touch with western civilization is characteristically the same, and but for the environment, there would have been no marked difference between those of the scattered race in the western hemisphere. The honest prejudice of the South was sufficiently evident to give the Negro of America the real start—the start with a race consciousness, which I am convinced is responsible for the state of development already reached by the race.

A Fred Douglass or a Booker Washington never would have been heard of in American national life if it were not for the consciousness of the race in having its own leaders. In contrast, the West Indies has produced no Fred Douglass, or Booker Washington, after seventy-eight years of emancipation, simply because the Negro people of that section started out without a race consciousness.

I have traveled a good deal through many countries, and from my observations and study, I unhesitatingly and unreservably say that the American Negro is the peer of all Negroes, the most progressive and the foremost unit in the expansive chain of scattered Ethiopia. Industrially, financially, educationally and socially, the Negroes of both hemispheres have to defer to the American brother, the fellow who has revolutionized history in race development inasmuch as to be able within fifty years to produce men and women out of the immediate bond of slavery, the latchets of whose shoes many a "favored son and daughter" has been unable to loose.

As I travel through the various cities I have been observing with pleasure the active part played by Negro men and women in the commercial and industrial life of the nation. In the cities I have already visited, which include New York, Boston, Philadelphia, Pittsburgh, Baltimore, Washington and Chicago, I have seen commercial enterprises owned and managed by Negro people. I have seen Negro banks in Washington and Chicago, stores, cafes, restaurants, theaters and real estate agencies that fill my heart with joy to realize, in positive truth, and not by sentiment, that at one center of Negrodom, at least, the people of the race have sufficient pride to do things for themselves.

The acme of American Negro enterprise is not yet reached. You have still a far way to go. You want more stores, more banks, and bigger enterprises. I hope that your powerful Negro press and the conscientious element among your leaders will continue to inspire you to achieve; I have detected, during my short stay, that even among you there are leaders who are false, who are mere self-seekers, but on the other hand, I am pleased to find good men and, too, those whose fight for the uplift of the race is one of life and death. I have met some personalities who are not prominently in the limelight for whom I have a strong regard as towards their sincerity in the cause of race uplift, and I think more of their people as real disciples working for the good of our race than many of the men whose names have become nationally and internationally known. In New York, I met John E. Bruce,[2] a man for whom I have the strongest regard inasmuch as I have seen in him a true Negro, a man who does not talk simply because he is in a position for which he must say or do something, but who feels honored to be a member. I can also place in this category Dr. R. R. Wright, Jr.,[3] Dr. Parks,[4] vice-president of the Baptist Union, and Dr. Triley of the M.E. church of Philadelphia, the Rev. J. C. Anderson[5] of Quinn Chapel [*AME Church*] and Mrs. Ida Wells-Barnett of Chicago.[6] With men and women of this type, who are conscientious workers, and not mere life service dignitaries, I can quite understand that the time is at hand when the stranger, such as I am, will discover the American Negro firmly and strongly set on the pinnacle of fame.

The West Indian Negro who has had seventy-eight years of emancipation has nothing to compare with your progress. Educationally, he has, in the exception, made a step forward, but generally he is stagnant. I have discovered a lot of "vain bluff" as propagated by the irresponsible type of West Indian Negro who has become resident of this country—bluff to the effect that conditions are better in the West Indies than they are in America. Now let me assure you, honestly and truthfully, that they are nothing of the kind. The West Indies in reality could have been the ideal home of the Negro, but the sleeping West Indian has ignored his chance ever since his emancipation, and today he is at the tail end of all that is worth while in the West Indies. The educated men are immigrating to the United States, Canada and Europe; the laboring element are to be found by the thousands in Central and South America. These people are leaving their homes simply because they haven't pride and courage enough to stay at home and combat the forces that make them exiles. If we had the spirit of self-consciousness and reliance, such as you have in America, we would have been ahead of you, and today the standard of Negro development in the West would have been higher. We haven't the pluck in the West Indies to agitate for or demand a square deal and the blame can be attributed to no other source than indolence and lack of pride among themselves.

Let not the American negro be misled; he occupies the best position among all Negroes up to the present time, and my advice to him is to keep up his constitutional fight for equity and justice.

The Negroes of the West Indies have been sleeping for seventy-eight years and are still under the spell of Rip Van Winkle. These people want a terrific sensation to awaken them to their racial consciousness. We are throwing away good business opportunities in the beautiful islands of the West. We have no banks of our own, no big stores and commercial undertakings, we depend on others as dealers, while we remain consumers. The file is there open and ready for anyone who has the training and ability to become a pioneer. If enterprising Negro Americans would get hold of some of the wealthy Negroes of the West Indies and teach them how to trade and to do things in the interest of their people, a great good would be accomplished for the advancement of the race.

The Negro masses in the West Indies want enterprises that will help them to dress as well as the Negroes in the North of the United States; to help them to live in good homes and to provide them with furniture on the installment plan; to insure them in sickness and death and to prevent a pauper's grave.

Printed in the *Champion Magazine* ('A Monthly Survey of Negro Achievement') 1 (January 1917): 167–68. Published in Chicago.

1. Evaluating Garvey's career in America, William H. Ferris recalled: "Then in December 1916, when I was associate editor of the Champion Magazine of Chicago, he [Garvey] came into the office with an article, which we published. He was interested in raising funds for a Tuskegee Institute to be established in Jamaica, BWI, and emphasized the economic development of the Negro." (*Philadelphia Tribune*, 27 June 1940).

2. John Edward Bruce (1856–1924), popularly known by his pen name, Bruce Grit, was a prolific writer and journalist who was called "the prince of Afro-American correspondents." He worked as the American representative and correspondent of the *African Times and Orient Review* and in 1911 was the founder and president of the Negro Society for Historical Research, the forerunner of the Association for the Study of Negro Life and History. Bruce later wrote the following account of his early meeting with Garvey:

> When Mr. Garvey first came to this country from his island home in Jamaica, B.W.I., I was one among the first American Negroes, on whom he called . . . I promised him such aid in the furtherance of his plans as I could give him, morally and substantially. We parted the best of friends. I had given him a list of the names of our leading men in New York and other cities, who, I felt, would encourage and assist him. Some of them were Clergymen; some professional men; and some of them private citizens. He called on some of these, and among them, Prof. Du Bois, who did not think well of his plan, but he kept on. (NN-Sc, JEB, B5-14).

It was not until October 1919, however, after listening to a street corner speech by Garvey on the aims of the UNIA, that Bruce was actually converted to Garvey's cause. He began writing a regular column for the *Negro World* in May 1920. He continued his work as a contributing editor for the *Negro World* until his hospitalization in the winter of 1923. For his loyalty, the UNIA knighted Bruce in 1921 as the "Duke of Uganda." In addition to his political, historical, and literary activities, Bruce worked for forty years as a messenger in the federal customs house of Westchester, N. Y. Marcus Garvey delivered the eulogy for Bruce's 1924 Liberty Hall funeral which was attended by some 5,000 mourners. (*WWCA*, vol. 1; *NYT*, 11 August 1924; DNA, RG 59, File 800-L-2, 22 April 1921).

3. Rev. Richard Robert Wright, Jr. (1878–1967), sociologist, businessman and AME clergyman, received his Ph.D. from the University of Pennsylvania in 1911 for a study of economic conditions in black Philadelphia. The son of a prominent black college president, and later a Garveyite, Wright held a research fellowship in sociology at the University of Pennsylvania and was also at various times engaged in work for the U.S. Bureau of Labor, the Carnegie Institution, and other agencies and organizations. Wright became the business manager of the AME Church Book Concern in 1909–12 and again in 1916–20; the editor of the *Christian Recorder* (1909–36); the founder, with his father, of the Citizens and Southern Building and Loan Association in 1921; and president of the Citizens and Southern Bank and Trust Co. He also served as a member of the committee to draft a new charter for the city of Philadelphia in 1917–19, and was secretary of the Colored Protective Association of Philadelphia in 1918. He was elected a bishop of the AME church in 1936 and assigned to South Africa from 1936 until 1940. Wright was also the author of many books, among them *Eighty Seven Years Behind the Black Curtain: An Autobiography* (Philadelphia: Rare Book Co., 1965); *Centennial Encyclopedia of the African Methodist Episcopal Church* (Philadelphia: AME Book Concern, 1916); and ed., *Encyclopedia of the African Methodist Episcopal Church* (Philadelphia: AME, 1944). (*WWA*, vol. 30; DNA, RG 65, files OG 3057, 308372, 329359, and 359099).

4. Rev. William G. Parks, D.D., (d. 1922) was a vice-president of the National Baptist Convention (Incorporated) and its denominational representative on the Federal Council of Churches. He was the pastor of Union Baptist Church, Philadelphia's largest black church, since 1908. (*NW*, 23 December 1922).

5. Rev. J. C. Anderson, an AME minister, studied at Hamline University in St. Paul, Minn. and the University of Chicago. He was a graduate also of Taylor University (Upland, Ind.) and later the McCormick Theological Seminary in Chicago. Anderson entered the itinerant minis-

try in Marshalltown, Iowa, in 1889, and he headed congregations in St. Paul, Chicago, and Louisville. Known as an excellent fund raiser and administrator, Anderson also served as a delegate to the AME general conferences of 1912 and 1916. (*Encyclopedia of the African Methodist Church*, pp. 24–25).

6. Ida B. Wells-Barnett (1862–1931) was a militant journalist and antilynching crusader as well as an outstanding black civic and political leader in Chicago. She founded the Negro Fellowship League in 1910 and organized the Alpha Suffrage Club, the first such group for black women. In the course of his visit to Chicago in 1916, Garvey was the dinner guest of Ida B. Wells-Barnett and her husband, Ferdinand L. Barnett, an outstanding black lawyer. (*WWCR*; DNA, RG 65, files BS 202600-14, OG 3057, 123754, 336880, 344219). In her post-humously published autobiography, *Crusade for Justice: The Autobiography of Ida B. Wells* (Chicago: University of Chicago Press, 1970), she described this meeting in the following terms:

> . . . Mr. Garvey was travelling from place to place to arouse the interest of other West Indians who were living in the United States to assist him in establishing an industrial school in Jamaica. He visited my husband's law office, and Mr. Barnett brought him home to dinner.
>
> In the course of his conversation he said that ninety thousand of the people of the island of Jamaica were colored, and only fifteen thousand of them were white; yet the fifteen thousand white people possessed all the land, ruled the island, and kept the Negroes in subjection. I asked him what those ninety thousand Negroes were thinking about to be dominated in this way, and he said it was because they had no educational facilities outside of grammar-school work. He wanted to return to his native home to see if he could not help to change the situation there. (Ibid., p. 380).

Marcus Garvey to Andrew Bonar Law

636—9th St. W.
Cincinnati, Ohio. Feb. 6, 1917

My Honorable Sir:—

I write to express the good wishes of my Association toward you, and our pleasure in learning of your elevation to the office of Chancellor of the Exchequer of England[1] and of our Empire.

My Association take[s] the deepest interest in all that tends to the success of your Government and we hold you in the highest esteem, believing you to be one of those of our statesma/e/n who ever remember the cause of our poor people and ever strive to see that they are fairly treated. Your effort, whilst Secretary for the Colonies,[2] in trying to place our men industrially,[3] will long be remembered by us, and we now beg to express our thanks for your consideration.

We pray that your Government will have success in this, your effort to suppress the military tyrants of Europe and to restore peace to the world. I remain Sir Your Obedient Servant

MARCUS GARVEY
PRESIDENT

[*Endorsement*] Thanked 26/2/17

HLRO, ABL. TLS, Recipient's copy. Correction and some punctuation marks are in Garvey's hand. Endorsement is handwritten. Typed in the body of the letterhead was the following: "Lecture Tour U.S.A. Permanent Address in America 53, 140th St. W. New York."

1. Andrew Bonar Law was appointed chancellor of the exchequer, as well as leader of the House of Commons, in Lloyd George's new government in January 1916, in return for his covert collaboration in toppling Herbert Asquith as prime minister.

2. Secretary of state for the colonies, May 1915–January 1916.

3. The reference to Bonar Law's "efforts" is unclear.

Broadside by Marcus Garvey

[*ca. 25 March 1917*]

BIG MASS MEETING
A CALL TO THE
COLORED CITIZENS
OF
ATLANTA, GEORGIA
To Hear the Great West Indian Negro Leader
HON. MARCUS GARVEY
President of the Universal Negro Improvement Association
of Jamaica, West Indies.
Big Bethel A.M.E. Church
Corner Auburn Avenue and Butler Street
SUNDAY AFTERNOON, AT 3 O'CLOCK
MARCH 25, 1917
He brings a message of inspiration to the
12,000,000 of our people in this country.
SUBJECT:
"The Negroes of the West Indies, after
78 years of Emancipation." With a
general talk on the world position of
the race.

An orator of exceptional force, Professor Garvey has spoken to packed audiences in England, New York, Boston, Washington, Philadelphia, Chicago, Milwaukee, St. Louis, Detroit, Cleveland, Cincin[n]ati, Indianapolis, Louisville, Nashville and other cities. He has travelled to the principal countries of Europe, and was the first Negro to speak to the Veterans' Club[1] of London, England.

This is the only chance to hear a great man who has taken his message before the world. COME OUT EARLY TO SECURE SEATS. It is worth travelling 11,000 miles to hear. **All Invited. Rev. R. H. Singleton, D.D., Pastor**.

Reprinted from Amy Jacques Garvey, *Black Power in America* (Kingston, Jamaica: By the Author, 1968), p. 13.

1. The Veterans' Club was founded in January 1913 and was located at Hand-court, High Holborn, in London.

HIGH·CLASS BENEFIT CONCERT
In Aid of Helping
UNIVERSAL NEGRO IMPROVEMENT ASSOCIATION
OF JAMAICA, WEST INDIES
To establish Industrial and Trades Institute

THIS ENTERTAINMENT WILL BE HELD AT
ST. MARK'S CHURCH HALL
57 W. 138th Street, New York

Tuesday Evening, June 26, 1917, 8 o'Clock
PATRONS RESERVE TICKET

R.S.V.P. ADMISSION ONE DOLLAR

Ticket for R. R. Moton (Source: ATT, RRM)

Marcus Garvey to R. R. Moton

235 West 131st. St., New York City,
June 1. 1917

Dear Doctor Moton:

I hereby beg to inform you that the Universal Negro Improvement Association of Jamaica is an organization of men of my race, formed for the purpose of helping in the uplift of our people, and that I am in America lecturing and seeking help to enable us to establish a "Trades and Industrial Institute" to help the neglected of our suffering people of our race.

A Concert is to be given at St. Mark's Hall, 57 West 138 Street, New York, on Tuesday evening, June 26, in aid of the cause, and I now take the liberty to write to you asking *your patronage and help for which I enclose tickets*, which I feel sure you will retain by way of your kind assistance.

As one of the foremost leaders of the Negro, you fully realize the difficulty of our struggle, and you can understand [*in the margin*: that] it is only by common help that those who are engaged in uplifting work can succeed.

I, therefore, send you these tickets with a conscious assurance that you will extend your patronage and help as asked. I shall be pleased to receive your reply by early mail.

203

Thanking you in anticipation of your patronage and help and with best wishes, I am Yours faithfully,

UNIVERSAL NEGRO IMPROVT. ASSO.
PER MARCUS GARVEY
PRESIDENT

ATT, RRM. TLS, Recipient's copy. Corrections are in Garvey's hand. Inserted in the center of the UNIA letterhead was the following typewritten statement: "Lecturing in United States."

Amy Ashwood to Marcus Garvey

Colon P.O. [*Panama*] 3–6–17

Dear Marcus:—

I have written you dozens of letters to your New York Address and I thought you would have replied by this as you sent me four P.C. two weeks ago, on your way to New York. I saw your friend Duhaney. I went to the Royal Mail wharf to receive a basket of fruits and he saw me and called to me. He said, he saw you in New York and you should have given him a letter for me, but, you did not turn up. If you should send a letter for me by bearer, I am situated at 120 D. Street at the corner of eight St. opposite the p[u]mping station, name of the house, Julia Margarita. Mr. Duhaney says you are looking fine.

I received a letter from my Dad last week; he is in Florida, but he advised me not to answer as he was leaving for New York. Anyway I can see from his letter that he is not in a position to help me just now. I haven't his address or I would send you same to look him up and help him for me. I can never be able to tell you of all my troubles, I have been burnt out twice since my father's absence and for one to be burnt out and to be penniless is hell. Death in such a case is the only welcome guest. Now Marcus, if you really mean to help me over to [New York], you have got to do it now. I have told you the amt. to fix my mouth. I cannot leave Colon like this. I have lost over 15 teeth, they are extracted now and only waiting on the money to put them in. I have told you the amt. it will take, not less than $200. U.S.A. to move me here. Don't worry to send articles that I sent for. I can do without them now, but send for me, a coat suit, like this suit; it must be a coat suit, and hat like this; my travelling collars are black or navy blue. If the suit is of navy blue, then the hat must be the same, but you had better make it black. One pair of boots to match, I want something nice high heels. I like the latest color in now. It is called bronze (bronze). Send the corset with it and a pair of stockings. You understand me./

One black suit, I like silk—stiff silk, a black hat like this with a white feather behind. One pair of high heel boots, bronze. One corset, straps over shoulder and a pair of stockings and corset.

I have sent you my measurement already. It will take me $200 and things I have sent for to land me in New York. If you agree let me know by return mail, as I want to know what I am about, as I must be in New York not later than August.

News.

Edna is in Jamaica again. Jim Mc.Gregor is in the states, also C. Meade[1] and Evans, nearly all the baptist boys are over there. They flew from conscription. I know you can afford to send that money for me by return mail and let me book my passage now even for July, but if you are sending it by return mail, you must write as you are my Uncle and if I produce that letter I can get my ticket that is if I have a letter to show you are my uncle and that you will meet me in the States, but you must write as if you are married. My mouth can be fixed in a week. I am only waiting on the money from you. What a nice time we are going to have when we meet eh! Marcus. We shall never cease talking of months we spent apart, I have so much news for you. You will be surprised. Arrange for me right away and send money by return mail and I shall be with you in July. I will travel on Royal Mail. I don't like the other boats. Don't fail to answer now and let me know all. We are all well. I am coming to you now Marcus. Embrace opportunity and send money and accept love and kisses from your dear

AMY

If you send parcel, let bearer borrow the Royal Mail Office telephone and get me at 247 Corporation [C]olon, or Miss Ashwood's residence so that I may know to send for parcel or letter. Amy. That's my phone Marcus.

Reprinted from *Marcus Garvey* v. *Amy Garvey*, No. 24028 (Sup. Ct. N.Y. 1920) Exhibit A. TL, Transcript.

1. C. A. Meade was elected assistant secretary of the Progressive Negro Association in Jamaica in July 1916. (*Daily Chronicle*, 8 August 1916).

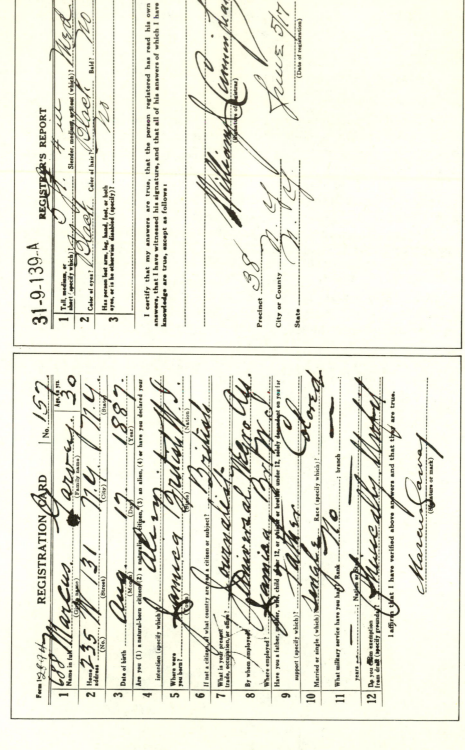

Selective Service Card of Marcus Garvey (Source: AFRC, RG 163)

R. R. Moton to Marcus Garvey

[*Tuskegee Institute, Alabama*]
June 6, 1917

Dear Mr. Garvey:—

I have your letter of recent date and the two tickets which you kindly sent me for the meeting June 26 at St. Marks Church, New York City. If I am in New York at the time, I shall make an effort to be present and to hear your lecture on conditions and needs of Jamaica. Yours very truly,

R. R. MOTON

ATT, RRM. TLS, Carbon copy.

Amy Ashwood to Marcus Garvey

Colon [*Panama*], *10,6,17*

Dearest Marcus:

Yours safely to hand and contents carefully noted. I was much surprised at your long silence. Why it is that you keep my letters so long to answer. I know there is a direct boat every week from New York.

Now let me explain my story to you. The girl Rittie left us and has gone so bad that the governor sent a police for mother to compel her to take the girl home, but since she, my mother is not in good health I must take her home. I had to get a lawyer to go to court with me, explaining all about my Dad being away and everything, and that I will be leaving here for America soon[.] I had to go to the Royal Mail office and investigate[.] I can get a passage through to New York with a stay off at Kingston[.] I can get a ship leaving here on the 23rd of August and get the other ship passing through on the [*6th?*] of September from Kingston. I shall be in Mandeville the most of the time, but send me your sister's address so that I may stay with her the few days I may have to spend in the city.

I am fretting out my heart. I cannot get passage alone, so I have arranged with a friend, Muse Marahan, to travel with me, she has f[ri]ends in U.S.A. but are not corresponding with them now, so you will have to promise to meet her with me, of course she is responsible for herself, that's just to facilitate me she will stay over to see her relatives, she is fat and just a shade lighter than I am. We are travelling as cousin's and you are our uncle. Should you meet my Dad do not mention anything to him about Rittie until I see him, as I know how much he will fret. Now promise me that. She is being kept in jail, now awaiting my departure. I have to feed her and it cost me the least 50 cents per day to feed her in there, so I had to sign a paper to the effect that according to my arrangements I will sail from here on the 23rd of August, and I don't want to lose that ship or it means trouble for me. My passage must be booked at least a month ahead of time as there are hundreds of people from here that are flocking to go away and have to be turned back weekly for the next ship. There are, I understand lots of people booked already for that month. So try and remit me Amt. to book passage, etc.

I don't think it's dear for my mo[u]th, you see Marcus, I have extracted 15 teeth and I lost five previous to that and its 20 teeth in all. It really isn't dear. It will be done just as good as over there. This Dr. is an American and English graduate. I could never pass through Jamaica like this. In fact, I can scarcely talk now without them. And you must write a nice letter as we are related to the effect that you will meet us in New York, or that you will send your wife to meet us. That letter must be showed up at the ticket office before we can get passage. I want you [to] send next month a pair of high top bronze boots for me and my travelling dress. I want a coat suit—black silk and a hat to match, but the hat must be a toque. Ask for a toque, a small hat but my head is very large. I won't worry you for anything after that. My measurement is

Bust	36	Hips	42
Waist	26	Length of skirt	33

After this I am through. I would never be able to tell you of the 1/100th part of my worries until we meet. Everything must be as I have told you. Lots of news, but I am sick at heart. Ah! Marcus, I wonder if I shall ever be happy. I wonder if after so many years of worries and sorrows I shall ever be happy[,] I shall ever find peace.

One year now since my father has not given me a cent. Poor fellow, he met it, but as soon as I get a line from him again, I shall inform you. I know he will gladly pay back after a while even a portion of this expense I am causing you. With love and kisses. Yours in love,

AMY

Reprinted from *Marcus Garvey* v. *Amy Garvey*, No. 24028 (Sup. Ct. N.Y. 1920), Exhibit B. TL, Transcript.

Josephine M. Stricker, Private Secretary to Theodore Roosevelt, to Marcus Garvey

[Oyster Bay, Long Island]
June 11th, 1917

Dear Mr. Garvey:

I am returning herewith the tickets enclosed to Colonel Roosevelt.[1] I am sorry, but so many similar requests are made of him that it is impossible to comply with them. Sincerely yours,

[JOSEPHINE M. STRICKER]

DLC, TR. TL, Carbon copy.

1. Theodore Roosevelt (1858–1919) was U.S. president from September 1901 until March 1909. Garvey's letter to Roosevelt has not survived. The tickets were probably for the concert scheduled for 26 June at St. Mark's Church Hall, the same as those that he sent to R. R. Moton.

Launching of the "Liberty League of Negro-Americans"

[Voice, 4 July 1917]

LAUNCHING THE LIBERTY LEAGUE

The Liberty League of Negro-Americans, which was recently organized by the Negroes of New York, presents the most startling program of any organization of Negroes in the country today. This is nothing less than the demand that the Negroes of the United States be given a chance to enthuse over democracy for themselves in America before they are expected to enthuse over democracy in Europe. The League is composed of "Negro-Americans, loyal to their country in every respect, and obedient to her laws."

The League has an interesting history. It grew out of the labors of Mr. Hubert H. Harrison,[1] who has been on the lecture platform for years and is well and favorably known to thousands of white New Yorkers from Wall Street to Washington Heights.

Two years ago Mr. Harrison withdrew from an international political organization,[2] and, a little more than a year ago, gave up lecturing to white people, to devote himself to lecturing exclusively among his own people. He acquired so much influence among them that when he issued the first call for a mass-meeting "to protest against lynching in the land of liberty and disfranchisement in the home of democracy," although the call was not advertised in any newspaper, the church in which the meeting was held was packed from top to bottom. At this mass-meeting, which was held at Bethel

Church on June 12, the organization was effected and funds were raised to sustain it and to extend its work all over the country.

Harrison was subsequently elected its president, with Edgar Grey[3] and James Harris as secretary and treasurer, respectively. At the close of this mass-meeting he hurriedly took the midnight train for Boston, where a call for a similar meeting had been issued by W. Monroe Trotter,[4] editor of *The Boston Guardian*.[5] While there he delivered an address in Fanueil Hall,[6] the cradle of American liberty, and told the Negroes of Boston what their brothers in New York had done and were doing.[7] The result was the linking up of the New York and the Boston organizations, and Harrison was elected chairman of a national committee of arrangements to issue a call to every Negro organization in the country to send delegates to a great race-congress which is to meet in Washington in September or October and put their grievances before the country and Congress.[8]

At the New York mass-meeting money was subscribed for the establishment of a newspaper to be known as *The Voice* and to serve as the medium of expression for the new demands and aspirations of the new Negro. It was made clear that this "New Negro Movement" represented a breaking away of the Negro masses from the grip of the old-time leaders—none of whom was represented at the meeting. The audience rose to their feet with cheers when Harrison was introduced by the chairman. The most striking passages of his speech were those in which he demanded that Congress make lynching a Federal crime and take the Negro's life under national protection, and declared that since lynching was murder and a violation of Federal and State laws, it was incumbent upon the Negroes themselves to maintain the majesty of the law and put down the law-breakers by organizing all over the South to defend their own lives whenever their right to live was invaded by mobs which the local authorities were too weak or unwilling to suppress.[9]

The meeting was also addressed by Mr. J. C. Thomas, Jr.,[10] a young Negro lawyer, who pointed out the weakness and subserviency of the old-time political leaders and insisted that Negroes stop begging for charity in the matter of their legal rights and demand justice instead.

Mr. Marcus Garvey, president of the Jamaica Improvement Association, was next introduced by Mr. Harrison. He spoke in enthusiastic approval of the new movement and pledged it his hearty support. . . .[11]

Printed in the *Voice*, Wednesday, 4 July 1917; and reprinted from Hubert H. Harrison, *When Africa Awakes: The "Inside Story" of the Stirrings and Strivings of the New Negro in the Western World* (New York: The Porro Press, 1920), pp. 9–13. The editor of the *Voice* was Hubert H. Harrison.

1. Hubert Henry Harrison (1883–1927) was a brilliant street-corner orator, lecturer, and political activist who was also considered the father of Harlem radicalism. In an account of the early history of the UNIA, Garvey declared that "he had made up his mind to return to Jamaica in the spring of 1917, when he became associated with Mr. W. A. Domingo and Mr. Hubert Harrison." (*NW*, Saturday, 10 September 1921, p. 5). Born in St. Croix, Virgin Islands, Harrison immigrated to the United States at the age of seventeen. An excellent student, Harrison attended night school while working at various menial jobs, and in 1906 he com-

pleted his studies with the highest grades. He then took a job with the post office while continuing independent study in history, sociology, literature, and other fields. In April 1907 the *New York Times* employed him as an occasional literary critic. Eventually, the post office dismissed him following the publication of an article critical of Booker T. Washington; he then joined the Socialist Party of America (SPA) having embraced the idea of socialism as the solution to the race problem.

Harrison participated with "Big Bill" Haywood, Elizabeth Gurley Flynn and Morris Hill-quit in the famous silk strike of 1913 in Paterson, N.J. He was made an assistant editor of the *Masses* under Piet Vlag and contributed articles to various journals. However, after the SPA's refusal to acknowledge racial discrimination both inside and outside the party, he severed his connections with the SPA in 1914. Thereafter Harrison concentrated his energy on promoting black independence under the slogan "Race First," and his future activities reflected his belief in the centrality of racial rather than class oppression in America.

Resuming his career as a street-corner orator, he formed the Harlem People's Forum in 1916 and shortly thereafter the Liberty League of Negro-Americans, the latter formed two days after the East St. Louis riots. In his newspaper, the *Voice*, Harrison urged violent retaliation against the white mobs. In 1918 the Department of Justice closely monitored his activities, since he was suspected of being under German influence. By 1919, many of Harrison's former supporters had already joined the UNIA, and in January 1920 Garvey appointed him associate editor of the *Negro World*. This appointment followed Harrison's editorship of the *New Negro*, which was formerly the *Clarion*, in 1919. Harrison stayed with the *Negro World* from 1920 to 1921, during which time he also held the position of commissioner of education in the UNIA. In August 1920, along with William Bridges and Edgar M. Grey, he organized the short-lived Liberty party, which nominated the Garveyite Rev. J. W. H. Eason as its presidential candidate. Although Harrison had no formal college degree, he was awarded posts as instructor in the Harlem School of Social Science (1912–14) and adjunct professor in comparative religion at the Modern School (1913–14).

In 1923, Harrison took a position with the New York City Board of Education as a roving lecturer and became a member of the Institute for Social Study and the Sunrise Club, a white intellectual society. Lecturing at New York University and other educational establishments, he became known to his colleagues as "Dr." Harrison, a tribute to his standing in the intellectual community. He continued to be politically active in Harlem, announcing in August 1924 his support for the creation of a separate black state in the U.S.A. In 1925 he organized the International Colored Unity League and edited a new journal, the *Voice of the Negro*. He also played an important role in the 1926 campaign led by several radicals to free Richard B. Moore after his arrest for organizing some black projectionists who had struck against the Lafayette Theater. In September 1926, he advocated a black police force for Harlem. A few months later, Harrison testified in the divorce case involving Marcus Garvey and Amy Ashwood Garvey. Harrison died in New York City as a result of complications arising from appendicitis. (DNA, RG 65, files BS 202600-2, 202600-667, 202600-1628, 202600-2031, 202600-2155; OG 3057, 185161, 198940, 208369, 272751, 329359; *WWCA*; *NW*, 7 January 1928; "Brief History of the Life and Work of Hubert Harrison," WPA Writer's Program, "Negroes of New York," 1939; Joel A. Rogers, *The World's Great Men of Color*, vol. 2 [New York: n.p., 1943], pp. 611–19; Wilfred D. Samuels, "Hubert H. Harrison and 'The New Negro Manhood Movement,' " *Afro-Americans in New York Life and History* 5 [January 1981]:29–41).

2. Harrison left the Socialist party after being suspended by the executive committee of the local New York party on 18 May 1914. (Philip S. Foner, *American Socialism and Black Americans: From the Age of Jackson to World War II* [Westport, Conn.: Greenwood Press, 1977], p. 217).

3. Edgar Mussington Grey (b. 1890) was born in Sierra Leone, probably the son of West Indian parents. After receiving his early education at a missionary school in Freetown, he attended Buston Grove High School in St. Johns, Antigua, BWI, and later studied at Aberdeen University in Scotland (1909–11). Earlier, in 1906, he worked as an interpreter for the United States government in Puerto Rico, and from 1907 to 1909 he served as English secretary to Don Juan Moncastro, president of the Dominican Republic. He moved to the United States in 1911 and worked first as a postal clerk and then as a bookkeeper for the Daily Lunch Corporation. Grey met Garvey for the first time on 13 May 1917, when he introduced him on the platform of a mass meeting in Harlem. In July 1918 Grey enlisted in the U.S. army, and in November of that year he was naturalized as an American citizen. Discharged from the army in April 1919, he organized the Foreign Born Citizens Political Alliance. Shortly thereafter, on 6 May 1919, Garvey employed him as general secretary of the UNIA, secretary of the New York local

division, advertising and business manager of the *Negro World*, and, after 27 June 1919, as director and assistant secretary of the Black Star Line, Inc. He severed his connections with Garvey, however, by 18 July 1919, and he was officially expelled from the UNIA on 2 August 1919. Grey was also a professional chiropractor since May 1921; he was reemployed by the post office, and in 1925 he embarked upon a career in journalism, first as associate editor of the *New York News*, and later as a contributing editor to the *New York Amsterdam News* (1926–28), and the *American and West Indian News* (1929). (*WWCA*, vol. 2; *Garvey v United States*, no. 8317, pp. 61, 80, 117–19; DNA, RG 59, file 000-612, 30 August 1921).

4. William Monroe Trotter (1842–1934), was one of the founders of the Niagara Movement in 1905 and also founder of the National Equal Rights League (NERL) in 1907, the name of which originated in 1865 when an earlier NERL had been founded. (DNA, RG 65, files BS 202600-5, 202600-667; OG 3057, 36727, 49899, 105391, 185161, 208369-A, 265716, 366523, 369936; Stephen R. Fox, *The Guardian of Boston: William Monroe Trotter* [New York: Atheneum, 1970]).

5. First published 9 November 1901.

6. Fanueil Hall, built originally in 1742, was one of the most famous sites in colonial Boston and was popularly known as the "cradle of liberty" after James Otis, the Massachusetts patriot, dedicated the remodeled building to the cause of American liberty in 1763 (Edwin M. Bacon, *Rambles Around Old Boston* [Boston: Little, Brown, 1921]).

7. The *Afro-American* of Baltimore reported in its issue of 30 June 1917 that "Herbert L. Harrison [*sic*] of N.Y. speaking under the auspices of the Liberty League in Boston suggested that the colored people rise against the government just as the Irish against England unless they get their rights."

8. The National Liberty Congress, organized and planned during the summer of 1917, was held in Washington, D.C., in June 1918. It was followed by the calling of a National Race Representative Congress for World Democracy in December 1918 in Washington, D.C. (DNA, RG 165, file 10218-153).

9. In 1917 two whites and thirty-six blacks were lynched, but the figures of blacks lynched in the years following increased to sixty in 1918, seventy-six in 1919, and it remained in the fifties for the years 1920–22.

10. James C. Thomas (b. 1889), reputed to be the wealthiest black attorney in New York, received his LL.B. from Cornell University in 1912. After eight years of private practice, he was appointed on 6 July 1921 as an assistant to the U.S. District Attorney for the Southern District of New York, and placed in charge of immigration and custom matters. Thomas resigned on 1 March 1926 to return to private practice, in the course of which he specialized in immigration law. (*WWCA*; *NYT*, 9 March 1927, 26 January 1930, and 29 November 1931).

11. What followed were the resolutions that the meeting adopted, as well as a petition that was to be presented to the U.S. House of Representatives.

Printed Address by Marcus Garvey on the East St. Louis Riots

[[8 July 1917]]

"THE CONSPIRACY OF THE EAST ST. LOUIS RIOTS."[1]
SPEECH BY MARCUS GARVEY

Founder and President of the Universal Negro Improvement Associa[*tion*] and African Communities League of Jamaica, Who has Just Completed a Tour of the United States.

This powerful speech was delivered by Mr. Marcus Garvey founder and president of the Universal Negro Improvement Association and African Communities' League of Jamaica, at the Lafayette Hall, New York, on

Sunday afternoon July 8th 1917, before a large and enthusiastic gathering of Negro Americans and West Indians, at which the Police Captain of the Borough Precinct attended by more than ten detectives, police lieutenants, and secret-service men were present. The meeting was presided over by Mr. Chandler Owen,[2] Editor of the Hotel Messenger.[3]

THE SPEECH:

"The East St. Louis Riot, or rather massacre, of Monday [*July*] 2nd, will go down in history as one of the bloodiest outrages against mankind for which any class of people could be held guilty. (Hear! hear.) This is no time for fine words, but a time to lift one's voice against the savagery of a people who claim to be the dispensers of democracy. (cheers) I do not know what special meaning the people who slaughtered the Negroes of East. St. Louis have for democracy of which they are the custodians, but I do know that it has no literal meaning for me as used and applied by these same lawless people (hear! hear!). America, that has been ringing the bells of the world, proclaiming to the nations and the peoples thereof that she has democracy to give to all and sundry, America that has denounced Germany for the deportations of the Belgians into Germany, America that has arraigned Turkey at the bar of public opinion and public justice against the massacres of the Armenians, has herself no satisfaction to give 12,000,000 of her own citizens except the satisfaction of a farcical inquiry that will end where it begun,[4] over the brutal murder of men, women and children for no other reason than that they are black people seeking an industrial chance in a country that they have laboured for three hundred years to make great. (cheers) For three hundred years the Negroes of America have given their life blood to make the Republic the first among the nations of the world, and all along this time there has never been even one year of justice but on the contrary a continuous round of oppression. At one time it was slavery, at another time lynching and burning, and up to date it is wholesome [*wholesale?*] butchering. This is a crime against the laws of humanity; it is a crime against the laws of the nation, it is a crime against Nature, and a crime against the God of all mankind. (cheers)

Somewhere in the book of life we are told that "God created of one blood all nations of men to dwell on the face of the earth," and after mankind, in scattered groups, had for thousands of years lived in their own spheres without trouble or molestation, promoting in their own way the course of peace and happiness, the white race, a party of this group, went out to enslave, conquer and rob the rights of the Peaceful. Through that system of enslavement, conquest and robbery, the black man was taken into this country where he was forced against his will to labor for the enrichment of the whiteman. Millions of our people in the early days of slavery gave their lives that America might live. From the labours of these people the country grew in power, until her wealth to-day is computed above that of any two nations. With all the service that the Negro gave he is still a despised creature in the eye of the white people, for if he were not to them despised, the 90,000,000 of whites of this country would never allow such outrages as the East St. Louis massacre to perpetuate themselves without enforcing the law which provides justice for every man be he black or white.

The blackman has always trusted the whiteman. He has always clung to him as a brotherman, ever willing to do service for him, to help him, to succor him, yet with all this the whiteman has never found it convenient to live up to the principles of brotherhood which he himself teaches to all mankind. (hear! hear!) From the time of Livingstone to the present day the blackman has always been kind to the whiteman. When there was no white-man in Africa to help the sickly and dying Livingstone, the blackman, ever true, even as Simon the Cyrenian was true, in bearing the cross of the despised Jesus, came to the rescue of the suffering Englishman, and when he was dead, faithful as they were, they bore his body for hundreds of miles across the desert and plains of Africa until they deposited his remains at a place where other whitemen could reach him to convey him to England and inter his bones in the Cathedral of Westminster Abbey. The Negro in American history from the time of Crispus Attucks[5] at Boston, the 10th Cavalry at San Juan Hill,[6] which saved the day for Roosevelt, up to the time when they stuck to Boyd at Carrizal,[7] has demonstrated to the American Nation that he is as true as steel. (cheers) Yet for all his services he receives the reward of lynching, burning and wholesale slaughter (hear, hear). It is even strange to see how the real American white people, the people who are direct de[s]cendants from the Pilgrim Fathers, allow the alien German, Pole, Italian and other Europeans who came here but yesterday to lead them in the bloody onslaught against the Negroes who have lived here for over three hundred years. When I say that the Aliens are leading the descendants of the Pilgrim Fathers against the Negroes in this country I mean to support it with as much facts as possible.

Mayor Mollman of East [S]t. Louis[8] if [no]t himself a German, is a descendant of German immigrants, he is the man to be blamed for the recent riots in East St. Louis. I say so because I am convinced that he fostered a well arranged conspiracy to prevent blackmen migrating from the South much to the loss of Southern Farmers who for months have been moving heaven itself to prevent the exodus of the labor serfs of the South into the North.

Two months ago I was in New Orleans completing a lecture tour of the United States, and on the 26th of April Mayor Fred W. Mollman arrived in the city on a trip from St. Louis. In New Orleans he was met by Mayor Behrman and the New Orleans Board of Trade. For months the Farmers of Louisiana were frightened out of their wits over the every day migration of Negroes from great farming centres of the State. They wrote to the papers, they appealed to the Governor, the Mayor and the Legislature and the Board of Trade to stop the Negroes going away, but up to the 26th of April nothing was done to stop the people excepting the Railway Companies promising to use certain restraint on the rush of people obtaining passages on the trains by Railway orders sent to them from the North. At this time Mayor Mollman arrived and the Farmers and Board of Trade met him and asked his help in discouraging the Negroes from going North and especially to East St. Louis. In an interview given out to the New Orleans press he said that the Negroes from the South were reaching St. Louis at the rate of 2,000 per week, and that they were creating a problem there. He said that some of the largest industries in the country were established in East St. Louis and there were strikes for the last few months.[9] He believed the labor conditions in East St. Louis were responsible for the number of Negro laborers going to that city. When the strikes started, he said, United States District Judge Wright issued an injunction restraining the strikers from intimidating the laborers who took their places. This order prevented uprisings and riots. "Conditions are very bad in East St. Louis" he said, "because many plants are suffering for the want of labor. However, our city is growing and we have a population of 85,000 persons. During 1916 we gained 1,600 in population.["] His interview did not make pleasant reading for the Farmers and others interested in labor in New Orleans and Louisiana so that the very next day he appeared at the Board of Trade where he met the Farmers and others and in discussing the labor exodus with them, he promised that he would do all he could to discourage Negroes from Louisiana going into East St. Louis as the city did not want them. His interview on the first day was an encouragement to the Negroes to go to East St. Louis, as there was work for them, owing to the inability of the various plants to get labor. On the second day when he was approached he said East St. Louis did not want the Negroes, and he then promised to do all in his power to prevent them going there. His remarks to the people whom he met were published under big headlines in the Newspapers, so that the Negroes could read that they were not wanted in East St. Louis, but that did not deter the blackmen of Louisiana who were looking for better opportunities in the land of their birth going about the country looking for better conditions than the South offered with lynching and jim crowism.[10] The Negroes still continued their migration North.[11] The Mayor of East St. Louis returned to the city after making his promise to the Farmers, Board of Trade and others who were interested in Negro labor. On the 5th of May the New Orleans Board of Trade elected Mr. M. J. Sanders its president, and Mr. W. P. Ross as delegates to attend a transportation conference at St. Louis to be held on May 8–9. You will remember that Ma[y]or Mollman appeared before the Board of Trade on Friday the 27th April where he made his statement of promise. The transportation conference was held at St. Louis on the 8th and 9th of May at which several prominent men interested in the labor condition of the South were present as also Messrs Sanders and Ross, from New Orleans. It isn't for me to suggest that Mayor Mollman met these gentlemen again; it is for you to imagine what further transpired while these gentlemen from the South who were so deeply interested in keeping the Negro below the Mason and Dixon line said and did among themselves while in that vicinity where Mayor Mollman held sway so much so as to be able to make a promise to keep out citizens of the United States who were not born in Germany, but in the Southland. One thing I do no[w?] know; the first riot started on May 28 after a conference of labor leaders with Mayor Mollman. On that day, May 28, crowds of white men after leaving the City Council stopped street cars and dragged Negroes off and beat them. Then the night following three Negroes and two white men were shot. An investigation of the affair resulted in the finding that labor agents had induced Negroes to come from the South. I can hardly see the relevance of such a report with the dragging of men from cars and shooting them. The City authorities did nothing to demonstrate to the unreasonable labor leaders that they would be firmly dealt with should they maltreat and kill blackmen. No threat was offered to these men because Mayor Mollman himself had promised to do all he could to drive the Negroes out of East St. Louis, and to instill fear in the hearts of the people in the South so as to prevent them coming North. On the 29th of May, a day after the first disturbance, and when three Negro men had been killed, Mayor Mollman sent a dispatch to Governor Pleasant[12] of Louisiana advising the Negroes of Louisiana to remain away from East St. Louis. This news item from the "Call" of May 31 which I will read will speak for itself.

Negroes Asked to Stay Away.

["]Baton Rouge, La., May 30. An order advising all Louisiana Negroes to remain away from East. St. Louis, Ill., was issued to-day by Governor Pleasant, following a request from Mayor Mollman of the Illinois city."

I have not seen the Louisiana papers that published that order but you can imagine for yourselves how the papers made prominent news of it so as to bring home to the Negroes of the State the very discouraging situation which the Mayor of East St. Louis helped to create. Because nothing was done to crush the originators and leaders of the first riot the Negro haters of East St. Louis took fresh courage and made their final attack on our defence-less men, women and children on Monday July 2nd which resulted in the wholesale massacre of our people. When we read in the white press a report like what I will read to you, we can conjure to our own minds the horror of the whole affair.

"East St. Louis, July 2d—Negroes are being shot down like rabbits and strung up to telegraph poles.

"The official police estimate at 9 o'clock put the number of dead at 100. They reach this total partly through reports that many victims have been pursued into creeks and shot, burned in buildings or murdered and thrown into the Mississippi. The exact number of dead will probably never be known. Six Negroes were hanged to telegraph poles in the south end of town. A reliable whiteman reports having counted nineteen Negro corpses on a side street.

"A reign of terror prevails. The police and the two companies of National guard are powerless. The companies of soldiers were powerless as they had orders not to shoot. The whites took their rifles from them telling them they might hurt some one whilst these very whites took the rifles and shot Negroes." The whole thing my friends is a bloody farce, and that the police and soldiers did nothing to stem the murder thirst of the mob is a conclusive proof of conspiracy on the part of the civil authorities to condone the acts of the white mob against Negroes. (hear! hear!) In this report we further read that as the flames of fire would drive a Negro man, wom[a]n or child from a dwelling their clothes burning the mob would set up a great shout and rifles and pistols would be fired. So far no Negro was known to escape as the whites had a merciless net about the Negroes, and the cry was, "kill 'em all." Negro faces were seen at frames of windows and when they saw what happened to those who flew from the burning structures, they dropped back into the fire rather than tempt a similar fate. (deep groan) An example of what the guardsmen encountered, and themselves enjoyed, was the beating of colored women by white girls. This sort of thing was common. It resulted in the death of several Negro women. Six girls, according to the report pursued a colored girl around the main railway station. A mob formed behind the girls who were screaming frantic epithets at the terrified black girl. "Send them back to Africa." "Kill them all." "Lynch them" shouted the young white amazons. Suddenly the crowd swept from the trail of the girl. A yell then arose. "There is one." It was a Negro walking on the railroad track. Before he realized his peril he was killed. Half a dozen pistols cracked and the man dropped without a chance to run. (groans) Two white girls, neither more than 17 years old, the report said, were cheered when they dragged a colored girl from a street car, removed her slippers and beat her senseless with the sharp wooden heels. Some reports said black women were stripped by white women for the amusement of the crowd. (Cries of shame!)

The mob and entire white populace [o]f East St. Louis had a Roman holiday. They feasted on the blood of the Negro, encouraged as they were by the German American Mayor who two months ago went to New Orleans and promised to keep the Negroes out of East St. Louis. That this man did absolutely nothing to let the people know that the law would be enforced to preserve order and ensure the peaceful lives of the black people is amply demonstrated by a report which comes from East. St. Louis, and was published in the "New York Tribune" of Saturday, July 7. Under the caption: "Citizens Blame Long Reign of Lawlessness for Riots" the paper published this bit of News. "East St. Louis, Ill., July, 6, Resignation of Chief of Police Payne of East. St. Louis and of Cornelius Hickey night Chief of police or of radical reforms will be demanded of Mayor Mollman by the citizens' committee of the Chamber of Commerce. This determination is a result of the race riots here Monday in which thirty-seven persons lost their lives. Maurice Joyce, vice-president of the Chamber of Commerce, declared to-day the rioting was the direct result of the long reign of lawlessness in East. St.

Louis. We have a police department that is incompetent and inefficient if not worse. Not only was the word sent out that law would not be rigidly enforced but the impression was allowed to spread that law violations would be winked at."[13] This gallant vice-chairman of the Chamber of Commerce who knew this even before one Negro was shot, never said a word and did nothing to bring the delinquent Mayor who ruled the city to a realization of these facts until great property damage was done to the Southern Railway Company, when their warehouse of over 100 car loads of merchandise was consumed by the flames causing a loss to the company of over $500,000, and a white theatre of over $100,000 was destroyed. It was not until property was destroyed in which the Chamber of Commerce was most interested, that the officers of that body let the Mayor know that he must do his duty. It was not through over-population or through scarc[i]ty of work why East St. Louis did not want Negroes. It was simply because they were black men. For Mayor Mollman himself said months ago that East St. Louis was badly off for laborers as many of the plants could not get hands to operate them.

I can hardly see why blackmen should be debarred from going where they choose in the land of their birth. I can not see wherefrom Mayor Mollman got the authority to discourage blackmen going into East St. Louis, when there was work for them, except he got that authority from mob sentiment and mob law. It was because he knew that he could gain a following and support on the issue of race why he was bold enough to promise the white people of Louisiana that he would keep Negroes out of East St. Louis. He has succeeded in driving fully 10,000 in one day out of the city, and the South has gone wild over the splendid performance in so much so that the very next day after the massacre the Legislature of Georgia sent out the message that their good Negroes must come home as they will treat them better than East St. Louis did. Can you wonder at the conspiracy of the whole affair? White people are taking advantage of blackmen to-day because blackmen all over the world are disunited. (Loud and prolonged cheers)

(This bit of news was published in the New York Globe, July 11th, which goes **to prove** the state of affairs in Louisiana.)

South Holds up 200 Negroes
Sheriff and Police Chief at Shreveport, La.,
Prevents Migration to Pittsburgh, Pa.

SHREVEPORT, LOUISIANA, July 11.—In their efforts to check the migration of Negro labor to the north and east, planters of this section are being assisted by Sheriff Hughes and Police Chief Gray, who last night blocked plans for the departure of about 200 Negroes to Pittsburgh.

Fred Rankin Stier, who said he was a special agent of the Pennsylvania Railroad, assisted by a local agency, recruited the Negroes.

They were boarding coaches when the officers arrived and warned the agents that if they shipped the Negroes they would be arrested under the Louisiana law prohibiting the enticing of labor.

Stier abandoned his plans and the Negroes returned home.

EDITORIAL FROM THE NEW YORK SUN

A LESSON FROM EAST ST. LOUIS.

The facts in the East St. Louis riots of July 2 are becoming clearer. They carry with them a terrible indictment of the local, county and State authorities; they offer a lesson to every community in America.

The city administration, apparently following precedents established by its pr[e]decessors, tolerated lawlessness for months, and permitted the police force to exist in a state of inefficiency and incompetence.

The county authorities allowed illegal conditions to exist, either through laziness or because of a perverted conception of the principle of home rule.

The State was serenely oblivious to the situation that was being created in an important industrial city within its bounds.

When the inevitable eruption of disorder occured, the police, enervated by a long course of lax discipline and weakened by the system under which they had been trained, were unfit to handle it. The county government apparently collapsed utterly. And [w]hen the State was compelled to intervene, it sent only 100 troops, and these it dispatched without ammunition for their rifles!

Arriving at the scene of the riots the soldiers spent hours in utter helplessness. They were too few to club the mob into submission, not armed to shoot the ringleaders; and when powder and ball were served to them, the disorder had subsided, the rioters being satiated or having run out of victims.

It is idle to say that bad Negroes or bad white[s], trades unionists or nonunionists, were responsible for these disturbances. The business of government, city, county and State, is to maintain order. If it fails to do that it fails in its principal function. For months the city of East St. Louis, the county of St. Clair and the State of Illinois by their conduct prepared the outbreak, and rendered themselves impotent in is presence.

They are doing it in England too.
RACE RIOTING IN LONDON; NEGROES' HOMES MOBBED.
Caused by White Girls' Infatuation for Black Men, Officer Testifies.

LONDON, July 2.—"In consequence of the infatuation of white girls for black men in this district some of the inhabitants are greatly incensed against colored men," said a police officer testifying to-day in West Ham Police Court adding:

"On Saturday night a gang of youths attacked a number of houses on the Victoria Dock Road where black men lived. Windows were broken and the colored people came into the streets with knives and forks, and one had a revolver. Missiles were thrown by the English lads, and great damage was done.

"Disturbances lasted until Sunday evening, when a large force of police were drafted into the neighborhood. A crowd of about 1,000 people had then assembled and stones, sticks, bottles, pokers and tongs were used on both sides." A number of arrests were made.

A colored man who appeared with his head in bandages was remanded, and several other men, some in bandages were fined or discharged.

Mr. Garvey speaks at the Lafayette Hall 131st Street and 7th Avenue, New York, every Sunday at 3 o'clock until October 1917.

The Proceeds from this Pamphlet will go towards the Fund being raised to help the Sufferers in East St. Louis. Copies can be obtained by sending to The Universal Negro Improvement Association, 235 West 131st Street, New York.

DHU. *Conspiracy of the East St. Louis Riots Speech by Marcus Garvey Delivered at Lafayette Hall, New York, Sunday, July 8th, 1917* (n.p., n.d.).

1. Thirty-nine blacks and nine whites were killed in the East St. Louis riot that erupted on 2 July 1917. The black population increased from around 6,000 in 1910 to almost 13,000 in 1917. Consequently, the local Democratic party successfully used the race issue in the 1916 election to discredit the Republicans, whom they accused of importing blacks to increase their electoral power and to use as strikebreakers. The local press also encouraged antiblack sentiment in the winter of 1916–17. Violence first occurred on 28 May 1917 following rumors that a group of blacks had killed a white man. Several blacks were injured in the ensuing attacks but there were no deaths. However, neither the mayor nor the local law enforcement authorities took precautions, and in the following weeks, both blacks and whites armed themselves for further conflict. The coroner's inquest on the 2 July riot blamed the violence on the corrupt administration of Mayor Mollman and on the inaction of the police department and the Illinois National Guard. (Ida B. Wells-Barnett, *The East St. Louis Massacre: The Greatest Outrage of the Century* [Chicago: The Negro Fellowship Herald Press, 1917]; Samuel Gompers, "East St. Louis Riots—Their Causes," *American Federationist* 24 [August 1917]: 621–26; Elliot Rudwick, *Race Riot at East St. Louis, July 2, 1917* [New York: Atheneum, 1972]).

2. Chandler Owen (1889–1967) was a leading black socialist and joint editor, with A. Philip Randolph, of the *Messenger* magazine. Born in Warrenton, N. C., Owen graduated from Virginia Union University, Richmond, Va., and in 1913 entered Columbia University in New York where he studied political science, law, and sociology, coming under the influence of the sociologist Lester F. Ward (1841–1913). In early 1916 he met Randolph and also learned of the radical ideas of Hubert H. Harrison. He frequently attended lectures given at the socialist Rand School of Social Science. In conjunction with Randolph, the two men organized the Independent Political Council in Harlem in the spring of 1916, with Owen as executive secretary. The council's purpose was to promote socialism in the black community and to support black political candidates. Later in 1916 both Randolph and Owen formally joined the Socialist party and abandoned further academic studies. They also accepted an offer to edit the *Hotel Messenger*, a magazine representing the interests of the Headwaiters and Sidewaiters Society, but in August 1917 they severed their connection with the society and began to edit their own *Messenger* magazine, endorsing and subsequently campaigning for Morris Hillquit, the Socialist party's mayoral candidate in New York. Shortly thereafter they published their first joint pamphlet, *Terms of Peace and the Darker Races* (New York: Poole Press Association, 1917), establishing their radical credentials. In September 1918 the two men were arrested for preaching sedition in wartime, and after their acquittal, Owen was drafted into the U.S. Army.

Owen was later to become one of Garvey's most avid black critics. In May 1920 he and Randolph organized the Friends of Negro Freedom, and in August 1920 Owen launched the first of several attacks on Garvey's organization which later escalated into the "Garvey Must Go" campaign led by the Friends of Negro Freedom and the *Messenger*. During this period Owen made three attempts at union organization and in November 1920 he stood as a candidate for New York assemblyman in the Twenty-first Assembly District. The reasons for his eventual withdrawal from the radicalism of the *Messenger* and the Socialist party are complex, but it is known that he was greatly disillusioned by the 1923 death of his brother Toussaint Owen, a tailor who had been impoverished by the refusal of the socialist needle-trade unions in New York to allow him membership and thus regular employment. In late 1923 Owen left New York for Chicago, where he worked as a correspondent for the *Washington Bee* and as a public relations employee for both Republican and Democratic ward politicians. By 1925 he had ceased contributing to the *Messenger* entirely. During the Second World War, he was employed by the U.S. Office of War Information in Washington, D.C. In subsequent years Owen served as a columnist for the *Chicago Daily News*, and on a number of occasions he entered the real estate business, although without much success. (DNA, RG 65, files BS 202600-33, 202600-667, 202600-1528, 202600-1617, 202600-1775; 9-12-695; 4-2-3-14; 61-570; 205613-84; OG 3057, 105400, 185161, 208369, 215915, 229849, 258421, 259364, 329359, 341761, 369443, 370980, 376475, 387072, 391060, 369936; "Chandler Owen," Federal Writers Program, New York City, "Negroes of New York," 24 May 1939; Owen, "A Program for Immediate Attack upon Bad Race Relations Between the Jewish and Negro Elements of the Population," MS [ca. 1938–39], Chicago Historical Society, Irene McCoy Gaines Papers, Box 1; Owen and A. Philip Randolph, *The Negro and The New Social Order: A Reconstruction Program* [New York: The Messenger Co., 1918]; Jervis Anderson, *A. Philip Randolph: A Biographical Portrait* [New York: Harcourt Brace Jovanovich, 1972]; Theodore Kornweibel, Jr., *No Crystal Stair: Black Life and the Messenger, 1917–1928* [Westport, Conn.: Greenwood Press, 1975]; *Daily Defender*, 7 November 1967).

3. The official organ of the Headwaiters and Sidewaiters Society of Greater New York, published January–September 1917, and edited jointly by Owen and Randolph.

4. Probably a reference to the special congressional investigating committee entitled Select Committee to Investigate Conditions in Illinois and Missouri Interfering with Interstate Commerce between these States, in October–November 1917. The committee's final report was entitled "Report of the Special Committee Authorized by Congress to Investigate the East St. Louis Riots," *House Documents*, 114, Document No. 1231, (Sixty-fifth Congress, 1918). In addition there was also a special inquiry by the Illinois State Board of Inquiry into Illinois National Guardsmen's conduct during the riot.

5. Crispus Attucks (1723?–1770) was a black American patriot and one of the leaders of the mob that triggered the Boston Massacre (7 March 1770). Attucks was one of the three men killed in the demonstration by the British soldiers. Regarded as martyrs, they were given a public funeral on 8 March 1770 at Boston's famed Faneuil Hall. (*WBD*).

6. The Tenth Cavalry was an all-black unit of the U.S. Army that was first formed after the Civil War. It was one of the four black regular regiments sent to Cuba in 1898 to fight in the Spanish-American War. Known for its bravery, it was instrumental in the successful occupation of San Juan Hill in July 1898. (Robert Ewell Greene, *Black Defenders of America, 1775–1973* [Chicago: Johnson Publishing Co., 1974], pp. 125 ff.).

7. Carrizal, Mexico, was the site of a skirmish between the Mexican militia and the U.S. Tenth Cavalry on 21 June 1916. Capt. Charles T. Boyd, who had orders to perform a reconnaissance mission, misunderstood and thought he had to pass through the town of Carrizal. The Mexican militia denied him permission, but Boyd proceeded through the town with his black troops. The Mexican forces defended the town and there were casualties on both sides (forty-two Mexicans killed, fifty-one wounded; eight Americans killed, including Capt. Boyd). The U.S. Army decided not to take any disciplinary action against the officers responsible for the incident at Carrizal. (Greene, *Black Defenders*, pp. 365–66).

8. Fred Mollman was elected mayor in 1915.

9. A reference to the strike at Aluminum Ore Corp. and the strikes in the meat-packing and transportation industries in the spring of 1917.

10. The term *Jim Crow* was first popularly used in the nineteenth century to describe Southern racial customs and regulations. Explanations of the origin of the term differ, but it appears that Jim Crow was a fictional character in a song and dance routine popular in the

1820s. The song used in the routine, "Jump Jim Crow," was popularized in 1828 in Louisville, Ky., by Thomas D. Rice (1808–1860). It gained its first racial use, however, in Massachusetts in 1841, as a colloquial term applied to the separate black railway car. (*Negro Year Book, 1918–19*, p. 196).

11. The Department of Labor reported that in eighteen months of 1916–17, black migration reached between 200,000 and 700,000. It has later been estimated that in 1920 alone close to a million blacks left the South for the North. (W. E. B. Du Bois, "Migration of Negroes," *Crisis* 16 [June 1917]:62–66; "The Shifting Black Belt," ibid., 18 [June 1919]:94–95; Ira Rosewaike, *Population History of New York City* [Syracuse: Syracuse University Press, 1972]; Daniel M. Johnson and Rex R. Campbell, *Black Migration in America: A Social Demographic History* [Durham, N.C.: Duke University Press, 1981]).

12. Gov. Ruffin Golson Pleasant (1871–1937) studied law at Harvard and Yale universities. He began practicing law in Shreveport, La., in 1899 following service in the Spanish-American War. Pleasant later served as Louisiana's attorney general (1912–16) and governor (1916–20) (*WWWA*).

13. The concluding paragraph of the article was omitted by Garvey; it continued as follows: "This condition became so pronounced recently that a certain bad element of both blacks and whites became convinced they could do just as they pleased. This led to excesses by the negroes against the whites, and was responsible for the subsequent outrages committed by whites upon the negroes."

Newspaper Report from the *Brooklyn Advocate*

[*Jamaica Times*, 22 September 1917]

AMERICA'S BITTER RACE WAR.

"The Brooklyn Advocate" contains the account of a Mass Meeting at Bethel Church, New York, described as representing "the better and thinking element of the coloured people," 2,000 in number.[1] The object was to denounce, protest against and petition against the indignities and injustices and the outrages against the coloured race in the United States, particularly in the South. The following petition was endorsed. The speakers included Mr. Marcus Garvey of this Island.

To the House of Representatives of the United States:—

"We, the Negro people of the United States, loyal to our country in every respect, and obedient to her laws, respectfully petition your honorable body for a redress of the specific grievances and flagrant violations of your own laws as set forth in this statement.

We beg to call your attention to the discrepancy which exists between the public profession of the government that we are lavishing our resources of men and money in this war in order to make the world safe for democracy, and the . . . [*remainder of sentence missing*] Just as public performances of lynching-bees, Jim-crowism and disfranchisement in which our common country abounds.

We should like to believe in our government's professions of Democracy, but find it hard to do so in the presence of the facts; and we judge that millions of other people outside of the country will find it just as hard.

Desirous, therefore, of squaring our country's profession with her performance, that she may not appear morally contemptible in the eyes of friends and foes alike, We, the Negro people of the United States, who have never been guilty of any disloyalty or treason to our government, demand that the nation shall justify to the world her assertions of democracy by setting free the millions of Negroes in the South from political and civil slavery throug[h] the enactment of laws which will either take the Negroes under the direct protection of the U.S. Congress by making lynching a Federal crime, or (by legislative mandate) compelling the several states which now deprive the Negroes of their right to self-government, to give them the suffrage as Russia has done for the Jews. We ask this in the name of the American declaration that the world shall be made safe for Democracy and fervently pray that your honorable body will not go back upon Democracy."

Printed in the *Jamaica Times*, Saturday, 22 September 1917. Original headlines have been abbreviated.

1. The exact date for the convening of the meeting has not been found.

"Among the Negroes of Harlem"[1]

[*Home News*, 3 October 1917]

A mass meeting will be held at the Palace Casino next Sunday afternoon [*7 October*] under the auspices of the Ladies' Auxiliary of the Universal Improvement League, of which Prof. Marcus is the founder. The princip[a]l speaker will be Mrs. Mary Church Terrell.[2] Prof. Marcus Garvey, late of London University, and who has been in this country for the past several months organizing branches of the league,[3] will also speak. Mrs. Irene Mormon Blackstone[4] will preside.

Printed in the *Home News* ("For the People of Harlem and the Heights"), Wednesday, 3 October 1917.

1. The title of the regular news feature published in the *Home News*, from which the printed text is an extract. The author was Cleveland G. Allen (1887–1953), the first black member of the editorial staff of the *Home News*. Born in Greenville, S.C., Allen came to New York City around 1902. He worked for several years as a publicity agent for Booker T. Washington and also contributed numerous articles to a variety of magazines and newspapers. (*WWCA*, *NYT*, 14 October 1953).

2. Mary Church Terrell (1863–1954) was a leading black educator, popular lecturer, author, and founding member of the NAACP. She was educated at Oberlin College, Oberlin, Ohio, receiving her A.B. in 1884 and her A.M. in 1888. She served as the first president of the National Association of Colored Women from 1896 until 1901, and she was the first black woman to serve on the board of education in Washington, D.C. (1895–1901 and 1906–11). She represented Afro-American women at the International League for Peace and Freedom in Zurich in 1919, and at the World Fellowship of Faiths in London in 1937. (*JNH* 39 [1954]:334–37; *WWCA*, vol. I).

3. In a later series of partly autobiographical newspaper articles, Garvey recounted the following events leading up to the launching of the UNIA: ". . . I arrived in America in the

spring of 1916, after which I started to study the sociological, economical and political status of the Negroes of America. This took me through 38 states. It was after my return from these trips to New York that I founded in New York the New York division of the Universal Negro Improvement Association." (*Pittsburgh Courier*, Saturday, 22 February 1930).

4. Irena Moorman-Blackston, president of the New York UNIA Ladies' Division and a well-known socialist, was among the small group who were present at Garvey's first public lecture in New York City. She became one of the first to buy stock in the Black Star Line steamship venture when it was launched in the spring of 1919. Moorman-Blackston was also president of the Harlem branch of the Women's National Fraternal Business Association in 1919. She sold newspapers in Harlem for a living. Later, in August 1931, she headed the Colored Women's Organization of the State of New York. (New York *Age*, 15 February 1919; *NW*, 8 September 1923, 8 August 1931).

[*Home News*, 10 October 1917]

A meeting was held at the Palace Casino last Sunday afternoon under the auspices of the New York Branch of the Universal Negro Improvement League. Fully 2,000 were in attendance. Mrs. Irene Moorman Blackstone, president of the [*ladies'*] auxiliary . . . [*illegible*] . . . and there were several musical numbers given. James O. Thomas, Jr., Professor Marcus Garvey and Mrs. Mary Church Terrell spoke.

Mrs. Terrell called attention to the opportunity that the war is giving to the Negro for a larger economic and industrial freedom. She denounced the atrocities heaped upon the Negro like the East St. Louis riot and other cases of discrimination. Over $70 was [contributed?] at the meeting toward the support of the work.

There were many . . . [*words illegible*] [distinguished?] Harlem people on the rostrum, among them John E. Bruce, Samuel Duncan,[1] . . . [*illegible*], Professor Allan Whaley[2] and . . . [*illegible*].

Among the interested visitors was Miss Ida Vera Simonton[3] who has travelled extensively in Africa. She was the first white woman to penetrate the dark regions of Africa and was keenly interested in the meeting.

Printed in the *Home News*, Wednesday, 10 October 1917.

1. Samuel Augustus Duncan (b. 1880) originally came from St. Kitts, BWI by way of Hamilton, Bermuda. Duncan arrived in America in May 1900, and he became naturalized in May 1908. He was employed in Harlem as a porter. Before joining the UNIA, he edited the *Pilot-Gazette*, a short-lived paper in Harlem. Duncan briefly seized control the UNIA from Garvey in February 1918, but after his expulsion he resumed his leadership of the West Indian Protective Society of America, which he had founded in October 1916. This rival body was also variously known as the Universal Negro Protective Association, the Universal Improvement and Cooperative Association, and the Universal Negro Protective and Co-operative Association. The society sought to aid new West Indian arrivals in New York, and it later proposed to create a separate West Indian-American regiment under joint British–U.S. supervision to fight in the First World War. After the war, Duncan wrote to the governors of Jamaica and Trinidad via the British Colonial Office in London warning them of Garvey's anti-British propaganda in the West Indies, which, he wrote, was responsible for "the recent bloody strikes in Trinidad." (PRO, FO 115/2619; NFRC, naturalization certificate).

2. Allen Weston Whaley (b. ca. 1868), formerly pastor of the People's African Methodist Episcopal Church of Chelsea, Mass., was one of the best-known black orators in America. Whaley received his A.B. in 1883 from Claflin University at Orangeburg, S.C., and his theology degree from Boston University School of Theology in 1889. Whaley also attended Harvard University's Law School in 1897–98. Author of the pamphlet, *Equal Chance and Fair Play: The*

Negro's Cause (Boston: n.p., n.d.), Whaley was appointed the national organizer of the Colored Liberty Congress which met in Washington, D.C., 21–23 June 1918, and he signed the petition submitted to the House of Representaives by the group. Whaley liked to style himself as "a professor of human rights and education." He maintained his headquarters at 36 West 135th Street in Harlem. (DNA, RG 65, files OG 3057, 295314, 344219, 366523; *Boston Herald*, 12 September 1912; letter to editor, Boston University School of Theology, 19 May 1978).

    3. Ida Vera Simonton (1870–1931), author, lecturer, and African traveler, was a native of Pittsburgh. She studied in London and Paris, and in 1906 she traveled throughout Africa. On her return to the United States, she lectured on Africa for various colleges, schools, and social clubs. Her observations on African life formed the basis of her 1912 novel, *Hell's Playground* (New York: Moffat Yard & Co.). She also spoke on behalf of women's suffrage and the Liberty Loan drives. (*WWWA*; *NYT*, 6 July 1931).

Marcus Garvey to Nicholas Murray Butler, President, Columbia University

One God!   **One Destiny!**   **One Aim!**

NEW YORK DIVISION
Universal Negro Improvement Association
AND
African Communities' League

Cable Address: "UNIANY", New York
Telephone 7976 Morningside

ISAAC B. ALLEN,[1]
President

WALTER J. CONWAY,[2]
1st Vice President

C. C. SEIFERT[3]
2nd Vice President

SAMUEL DUNCAN,
3rd Vice President

E. D. SMITH-GREEN,[4]
General Secretary

BEN. E. BURRELL,[5]
Associate Secretary

MARCUS GARVEY, JR.
International Organizer

JOHN E. BRUCE,
Chairman Advisory Board

SERENA E. DANRIDGE,
Secretary

IRENA MOORMAN BLACKSTON,
President Ladies' Division

EVA F. CURTIS,
1st Vice President

LIZZIE B. SIMS,
2nd Vice President

ETHEL OUGHTON-CLARKE,
General Secretary

CARRIE MERO,[6]
Associate Secretary

SAMUEL BRIGHT,[7]
Treasurer

2305 Seventh Avenue
NEW YORK, November 27, 1917

"He created of one blood all nations of men to dwell on the face of the earth."

My dear Dr. Butler:[8]

    At a general meeting of the Universal Negro Improvement Association of New York, I was instructed to write to you asking your help in the following matter.

The Association will be holding a State Elocution Contest among the Negro literary people of New York, in The Palace Theatre, 135th Street and Madison Avenue, on Tuesday Evening, December 18th, 1917, at 8.15 O'clock, at which sixteen young men and wom[e]n of literary training will compete among themselves for three prizes for the best rendition of various selections (prose and poetry) from standard authors, each reciter to recite only one piece for not longer than seven minutes.

My instruction is to write to you asking you to act as one of seven judges to judge the contest. I am now writing to the principals of six other Universities and Colleges asking them to judge also[.]

We write asking you to be a judge because we feel that you will help us in that capacity, but we also realize that your duties are many. We are counting on you as a judge on the occasion, but should you find it impossible to help us, we ask that you do not completely disappoint us but that you help us with the service of one of your associates in the University with whom we shall be pleased.

Feeling sure that you will help us with your presence as a judge and patron, and awaiting your early reply, With very best wishes, Yours respectfully,

MARCUS GARVEY

CM/MG

NNC, NMB. TLS, Recipient's copy. Corrections are in Garvey's hand.

1. Isaac B. Allen (1884–?), born in Barbados, BWI was president of the UNIA between 27 November 1917 and 13 January 1918. After immigrating to the United States, Allen worked as a longshoreman in New Jersey and later as a real estate agent in Harlem. He was one of several West Indian UNIA officials whom Garvey later accused of attempting to split the association in January 1918. Nevertheless, in June 1918 Allen was one of the first incorporators of the American branch of the UNIA and a delegate of the association to the National Liberty Congress of Colored Americans in Washington, D.C. He also signed the petition to the U.S. House of Representatives submitted by this congress. A year later, in June 1919, he was appointed second vice-president of the Black Star Line. The following month, however, Allen resigned from the UNIA along with several other officials; afterwards he was secretary of William Monroe Trotter's National Equal Rights League. (AFRC, RG 163, registration card 31-9-21).

2. Walter Johnson Conway (1880–1920) was an attorney who also worked as a clerk in the general post office in New York City, from 1 October 1902 until his death on 21 March 1920. He was one of the original directors of the UNIA, and he also served as the association's first vice-president from November 1917 to November 1918. (AFRC, RG 163, registration card).

3. Charles Christopher Seifert (1880–1949) was born at Christ Church, Barbados. His father was a plantation overseer who was also renowned as a mathematician in Barbados. Seifert was raised by his mother, Mary Elizabeth Green, but the books that he read in his father's library developed his lifelong interest: the study of Egyptian history. Seifert served his apprenticeship with a local architect and builder. With the encouragement of a group of British colonial civil servants, he later joined the Plymouth Brethren sect and became a missionary lecturer on behalf of the order, traveling throughout South and Central America and at the same time supporting himself as a carpenter. After spending several years at Gatun, Panama, Seifert moved to Quebec, Canada, where he continued his work with the Brethren. In September 1910 he moved from Canada to the United States, and while lecturing for the Brethren, he worked as a roominghouse operator in New York City. In all, Seifert spent nineteen years in the cause of the Brethren. He resigned in 1914 and devoted the rest of his life pursuing historical research and disseminating information about the ancient black civilizations of Egypt and Ethiopia.

In addition to his cooperation with Garvey in the early phase of the UNIA in 1917, Seifert was also closely associated with the black bibliophile Arthur A. Schomburg (1874–1938). He assembled his collection of rare books on Africa into a research library, known as the Ethiopian Historical Research Association, which later became the nucleus of his Ethiopian Research School of History. He invited as guest lecturers many noted authorities, such as the anthropologists Alexander A. Goldenweiser (1880–1940) and Franz Boas (1858–1942), and the distinguished Howard University Africanist William Leo Hansberry (1894–1965). Regular classes for adults and young people were held there. "Professor" Seifert, as he was popularly known, was elected chairman of the educational department of the Ethiopian World Federation, Local 26, in addition to being made a member of the African Students' Association of the United States and Canada. He wrote a number of booklets on ancient African history, among them, *The Negro's or Ethiopian's Contribution to Art* (New York: Ethiopian Historical Publishing Co., 1938); *The Three African Saviour Kings* (New York: n.p., 1946); and *The True Story of Aesop "the Negro"* (New York: n.p., 1946). Among Seifert's unpublished works are "Genesis of Religion and Art," "Bible Students and the Black Man's Place in World History," and "Christianity Before Christ." He was probably best known for coining the motto: "A race without the knowledge of its history is like the tree without roots." He was also the associate editor for the short-lived bimonthly *Negro Illustrated News*, edited by S. L. Logehom. (AFRC, RG 163, registration card, 31-9-140-C; interview with Mrs. Goldie Seifert; Charles C. Seifert Papers; Elmer W. Dean, *An Elephant Lives in Harlem* [New York: Ethiopian Press,. n.d.]).

4. Edward David Smith-Green (1888–1969), one of the founding members of the New York UNIA, was born at Rose Hall, New Amsterdam, British Guiana. After passing the competitive civil service examination, he was appointed to a position in the prestigious colonial customs service. However, subsequent legal charges were brought against him by the customs service and although he was eventually found innocent and acquitted by the local courts, the ensuing controversy caused him to leave Guiana shortly afterward. He migrated to the United States and was employed by the American Sugar Company in Brooklyn. Smith-Green claimed to have known Garvey since 1916 and to have had frequent, if not daily, contact with him during this time (DNA, RG 65, file BS 198940, 31 August 1921). He moved from Brooklyn to Trenton, N. J., to take a job in an ammunition factory, but Garvey invited him back to New York to accept the position of secretary of the newly incorporated Black Star Line. Garvey also appointed him executive secretary of the UNIA on 22 July 1919. At a 14 November 1919 meeting of the directors of the Black Star Line, Inc., Smith-Green recommended that the corporation increase its capital stock from $500,000 to $10,000,000, a proposal that was formally adopted on 22 December 1919.

In January 1920, Smith-Green accompanied the Black Star Line flagship S.S. *Yarmouth* on its second voyage to Cuba, but shortly after his return to America he resigned from his positions with the Black Star Line, Inc., and the UNIA.

Throughout his life Smith-Green pursued an interest in the historical study of African civilizations. At the time of his death, he left several unpublished manuscripts, among them a four-volume study, "The Black Man: A History of the Negro Race Touching upon His Origin, Achievements, and Contributions to Civilization," as well as several other manuscripts on "Christianity, White Supremacy and the Black Man," "An Analysis of Race Prejudice," and a two-volume work, "Processional: A History of the Negro Race." (AFRC, RG 163, registration card 31-9-167-A; *Gleaner*, 13 December 1919; *Garvey* v. *United States*; E. D. Smith-Green Papers; interview with Smith-Green family, June 1980).

5. Benjamin Ebenezer Burrell (1892–1959) was born at Daviton, Manchester, Jamaica. He was the fourth of six children of John S. Burrell, who was a prosperous coffee cultivator. At the age of sixteen he began writing poetry, and afterward became a country correspondent for the *Jamaica Times*, which published his annual Christmas poem. He arrived in the United States on 20 June 1917, and at first he worked in an ammunition factory somewhere in the Carolinas. He was the coauthor with Arnold J. Ford of the lyrics of the UNIA anthem, later known as the "Universal Ethiopian Anthem." Burrell did not remain with the UNIA long. In July 1920 he became, along with his brother Theophilus Burrell, one of the contributing editors of Cyril Briggs's *Crusader* magazine, the official organ of the anti-Garvey African Blood Brotherhood; he also held the position of director of historical research for this group. Burrell later became one of the organizers and founders of the Amalgamated Garment Workers Union in 1931. Along with his brother, he was also one of the founders of the Jamaica Progressive League in New York in 1936. The Burrell brothers were also active for many years in running a black history club for young people called The Gleaners at the Harlem YMCA. (Interview with

Mrs. Benjamin E. Burrell, June 1980; NFRC, naturalization file; Robert T. Kerlin, *Negro Poets and Their Poems* [Washington, D.C.: Associated Publishers Inc., n.d.]).

6. Carrie Mero (later Carrie Ledeatt) first met Garvey in October 1917 at a meeting in the Palace Casino. In November 1917 she was appointed associate secretary of the Ladies' Division of the UNIA; she was later employed as a clerk-stenographer with the UNIA and the Black Star Line, Inc. She left her various positions briefly in September 1918, but returned in April 1919.

7. Isaac Samuel Bright (b. 1888) was American born; in September 1918 he was employed as a superintendent for H. E. Zitrell in New York. (AFRC, RG 163, registration card).

8. Nicholas Murray Butler (1862–1947), president of Columbia University from 1902 until 1945, was one of the leading conservative Republicans. He was named president of the Carnegie Endowment for International Peace from 1925 until 1947. Butler was also the author of many books, including *The International Mind* (Washington, D.C.: American Peace Society, 1912), a work that gave currency to the term *internationalism*. In 1931 he was the recipient, with Jane Addams, of the Nobel Peace Prize. (*DAB*, 1946–50 supplement).

Nicholas Murray Butler to Marcus Garvey

[*New York City*] November 28, 1917

Dear Mr. Garvey:

I am very much interested in the suggestion contained in yours of the 18th. It is not certain that I myself shall be free on the evening of the 18th prox., as I may have to go to Boston on the afternoon of that day, but if I am in town I shall be very happy to act as one of the judges in the interesting contest which you describe. In case I am not in town, I am quite certain that one of my colleagues will be glad to represent me.

Thanking you for your letter and with best wishes for the success of your organization, I am, Very truly yours,

NICHOLAS MURRAY BUTLER

NNC, NMB. TLR, Carbon copy.

"Among the Negroes of Harlem"

[*Home News*, 2 December 1917]

Prof. Marcus P. Garvey, founder of the Negro Universal Improvement League, addressed a large gathering last Sunday afternoon [*25 November*], at Lafayette Hall. He spoke on "The Opportunities of the Young Negro". The meeting was held under the auspices of the New York branch of the Universal Improvement League. He will leave for Boston and other points soon and will then go to Africa, where he will organize the work among the natives there.

Printed in the *Home News*, Sunday, 2 December 1917.

[*Home News*, 5 December 1917]

A meeting of the New York Branch of the Universal Improvement League was held at Lafayette Hall last Sunday afternoon [*2 December*]. Isaac B. Allen presided. An address was made by Prof. Marcus P. Garvey.

Printed in the *Home News*, Wednesday, 5 December 1917.

Marcus Garvey to Nicholas Murray Butler

New York, December 7, 1917

My dear Doctor Butler:

I hereby beg to thank you for your very kind letter of the 28th ultimo, in which you promised to act as one of the judges for us at the Elocution Contest we are to hold in the Palace Theatre, 135th Street and Madison Avenue, on Tuesday evening, the 18th inst., at 8.15 o'clock.

When your letter was read to the Association, the spirit of jubilation was manifest throughout, as an expression of our people's gladness for your good will towards them. I will send you the program and further details and the names of the other judges within a few days. With very best wishes   Yours respectfully,

MARCUS GARVEY

MG.MEL

[*Endorsement*] RECEIVED DEC 7 1917
COLUMBIA UNIVERSITY
SECRETARY'S OFFICE

NNC, NMB. TLS, Recipient's copy. Stamped endorsement.

"Among the Negroes of Harlem"

[*Home News*, 9 December 1917]

A large mass meeting was held at the Metropolitan Baptist Church last Tuesday evening [*4 December*] under the auspices of the Negro Universal Improvement League. Addresses were made by Isaac B. Allen, Mrs. Irene Moorman Blackstone and Professor Marcus P. Garvey. Several new members joined the organization. The work that is being done has the support of the pastor, the Rev. Dr. W. W. Brown,[1] who has long felt that the Negro of

Harlem has a fine opportunity to develop into business. Branches of the league will be formed throughout the country by Professor Garvey.

Printed in the *Home News*, Sunday, 9 December 1917.

1. Rev. Willis W. Brown (1858–1930) was the pastor of the Metropolitan Baptist Church located at 143 West 131st Street in Harlem. Brown became a Baptist clergyman in 1879. In 1898 he was introduced to the young African Christian John Chilembwe and in the following decade he emerged as one of the leading clergymen in the new socially-conscious black church movement, preaching social and political activism from pulpits in Roanoke, Va., and Pittsburgh. In 1914 Brown moved to New York, where he maintained his reputation as an astute businessman and a social activist, and became a vocal sympathizer of the UNIA. (*WWCA*, vol. 2).

Marcus Garvey to Nicholas Murray Butler

New York, December 17, 1917

My dear Dr. Butler:

I write to remind you of the Contest to come off tomorrow (Tuesday) the 18th inst., at 8.15 o'clock, at the Palace Theatre, 135th Street and Madison Avenue, at which you promised to act as one of the Judges. At this function, as you have been previously informed, sixteen Negro Elocutionists will compete among themselves for three prizes of first, second and third places.

The other Judges will be Chief Justice Charles L. Guy,[1] of the Supreme Court, Chief Justice Cornelius L. Collins,[2] Associate Justice of the Court of Special Sessions, Justice Phillip J. Sinnott[3] of the Municipal Court and the Very Reverend Father John McGrath of the Church of St. Thomas the Apostle. I take pleasure in enclosing you program of the affair. With very best wishes   Yours respectfully,

MARCUS GARVEY

MG.ML

[*Endorsement*] RECEIVED DEC 18 1917
COLUMBIA UNIVERSITY
SECRETARY'S OFFICE

NNC, NMB. TLS, Recipient's copy. Stamped endorsement.

1. Charles Lewis Guy (1856–1930) won a reputation as a liberal judge on the New York Supreme Court, where he served from 1906 until his retirement in 1926. (*NCAB*, vol. 24; *New York County Lawyers Yearbook*, 1931).

2. Cornelius F. Collins (ca. 1870–1947) sereved for seventeen years as a judge in the Court of General Sessions, starting in 1912. A lifelong Tammany Hall Democrat, Collins was also active as an Irish-American, at one point touring the country to raise funds for the Irish nationalist cause. (*NYT*, 24 February 1947).

3. Philip J. Sinnott (?–1944) was a justice of the Municipal Court of New York. (*NYT*, 4 June 1944).

New York, December 20, 1917

My dear Dr. Butler;

I have it in command from the Universal Negro Improvement Association, in general meeting assembled, to convey to you the whole hearted thanks of the Association, for your very kind interest manifested in us through your attendance at our Elocution Contest held in the Palace Theatre last Tuesday night.

You can hardly imagine how highly pleased we were of your responsiveness, and you can take it that we feel exceedingly grateful for your kind consideration.

Trusting you are well, and with the very, very best wishes of the Association, I beg to remain   Yours respectfully,

MARCUS GARVEY

MG/CM

[*Endorsement*] RECEIVED DEC 21 1917
COLUMBIA UNIVERSITY
SECRETARY'S OFFICE

NNC, NMB. TLS, Recipient's copy. Stamped endorsement.

Nicholas Murray Butler to Marcus Garvey

[*New York City*] December 21, 1917

Dear Mr. Garvey:

I thank you for your cordial note of the 20th, and beg you once more to convey to the members of the Universal Negro Improvement Association my compliments upon the admirable competition which was carried out under their auspices on the evening of the 18th. I left the Hall with a new feeling of pride and satisfaction at what the members of the Association and their friends are accomplishing. Very truly yours,

NICHOLAS MURRAY BUTLER

NNC, NMB. TLR, Carbon copy.

"Among the Negroes of Harlem"

[*Home News*, 23 December 1917]

The State Elocution Contest, among negro competitors, last Tuesday evening [*18 December*], at the Palace Casino, brought out a large gathering interested in the outcome of the Contest. There were sixteen contestants, graduates and students of the various high schools and colleges in New York and vicinity, and the event took on high importance and significance by the presence of President Nicholas Butler of Columbia University, Justice Charles Guy of the Supreme Court, Justice Cornelius Collins, of the Court of Special Sessions, Justice Phillip Sinnot[t], of the Municipal Court, and Rev. John McGrath, of the St. Thomas Apostle's Church.

Before the contest opened there was an address by E. A. Johnson,[1] and musical selections from the New Amsterdam Orchestra, and the Aldama Concert Company.

After a heated contest, the following persons were awarded the prizes. First, Edward Starling Wright, who recited "The Raven", from Edgar Allan Poe; Charles S. Morris, Jr., who offered an oration entitled "The Disgrace of Democracy", from Kelly Miller,[2] and Mrs. Helen Waller McAllister, who recited "Ostler Joe". . . .

The Negro Universal Improvement League, which is located at present at 2303 Seventh Ave., plans to lease an office building where it will be better able to carry on its work. One of its objects is to open a large grocery store in Harlem and to give employment to a large number of young negro men and women. This will be the permanent organization of the association, and branches will be established throughout the country. Marcus P. Garvey is the national organizer.

Printed in the *Home News*, Sunday, 23 December 1917.

1. Edward Austin Johnson (1860–1944) became the first black member of the New York state legislature when he was elected in 1917 to represent the Nineteenth Assembly District. Born a slave near Raleigh, N. C., Johnson enrolled at Atlanta University in January 1879. He studied law at Shaw University in Raleigh, receiving his LL.B. degree in 1891 and later taught there for fourteen years. He began his Republican political career as a congressional district chairman, and also attended the Republican national conventions. In 1907, as a result of the progressive disenfranchisement of black voters, he moved to New York City where he developed a lucrative law practice and entered New York politics. During his career, Johnson also wrote a series of popular histories of black Americans. (*DAB*, supplement 3).

2. "The Disgrace of Democracy" was the title of an open letter written in 1917 by Kelly Miller (1863–1939) to President Woodrow Wilson protesting the sharp increase in wartime mob violence directed against blacks. At the time Miller was the head of the Department of Sociology at Howard University where he had also been dean of the College of Arts and Sciences from 1907 to 1918. One of the major black spokesmen in the early twentieth century, Miller was also the author of several important collections of essays. He was born in Winnsboro, S. C., and graduated from Howard University in 1886. He remained connected with that institution as a teacher for nearly forty-five years before his 1931 retirement. (*DAB*, supplement 1–2; *Negro Year Book, 1917–1918*, pp. 119–20; *Crisis* 15, no. 1 [November 1917]: 22).

[*Home News*, 9 January 1918]

On Sunday afternoon [*13 January*] Prof. Marcus P. Garvey will speak at a meeting to be held in the Lafayette Hall in the interest of the movement that he has launched in this country among negroes.

Printed in the *Home News*, Wednesday, 9 January 1918.

J. Robert Love

S. A. G. Cox

Birkbeck College

Edward Wilmot Blyden

Dusé Mohamed Ali

Booker T. Washington

Amy Ashwood

H. A. L. Simpson

E. Ethelred Brown

Emmett J. Scott

R. R. Moton

John E. Bruce

W. A. Domingo

Nicholas Murray Butler

Hubert H. Harrison

William Monroe Trotter

Ida Wells-Barnett

Eliézer Cadet

Allen Weston Whaley

William H. Ferris

Benjamin E. Burrell

Edward D. Smith-Green

Edgar M. Grey

Fred D. Powell

Jeremiah M. Certain

George Tobias

Joshua Cockburn

Maj. Walter H. Loving (left) and Roscoe Conkling Simmons on January 1918 speaking tour

Henrietta Vinton Davis

The first public meeting of the visiting Abyssinian delegation, held at the Metropolitan Church, New York City, arranged by R. D. Jonas (wearing white suit with the open jacket).

A. Philip Randolph

Chandler Owen

Cyril V. Briggs

Edwin P. Kilroe

J. Edgar Hoover

J. W. H. Eason

Chief Alfred C. Sam

Liberty Hall, Dublin

Liberty Hall, Harlem

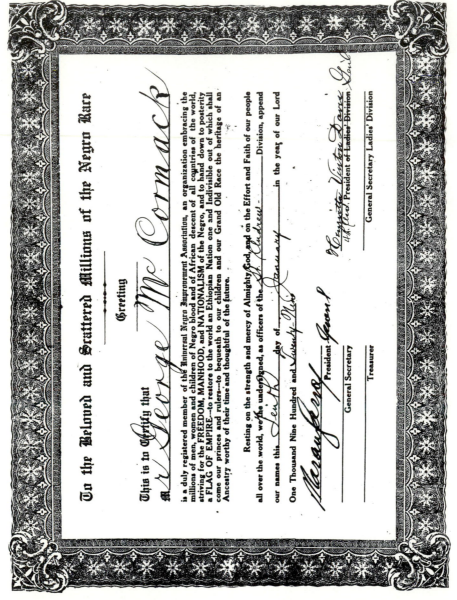

To the Beloved and Scattered Millions of the Negro Race

Greeting

This is to Certify that

Mr George Mc Cormack

is a duly registered member of the Universal Negro Improvement Association, an organization embracing the millions of men, women and children of Negro blood and of African descent of all countries of the world, striving for the FREEDOM, MANHOOD, and NATIONALISM of the Negro, and to hand down to posterity a FLAG OF EMPIRE—to restore to the world an Ethiopian Nation one and Indivisible out of which shall come our princes and rulers—to bequeath to our children and our Grand Old Race the heritage of an Ancestry worthy of their time and thoughtful of the future.

Resting on the strength and mercy of Almighty God, and on the Effort and Faith of our people all over the world, we the undersigned, as officers of the St Andrew _____ Division, append our names this _Tenth_ day of _January_ _____ in the year of our Lord One Thousand Nine Hundred and Twenty-Two

Marcus Garvey
President General

_____
General Secretary

_____
Treasurer

Henrietta Vinton Davis
4th Asst. President of Ladies' Division Gen'l

_____
General Secretary Ladies' Division

UNIA Membership Certificate

[*Home News*, 16 January 1918]

The meeting of Professor Marcus P. Garvey was held in the Odd Fellows Hall last Sunday afternoon [*13 January*] instead of at Lafayette Hall. The subject of his address was "The Burden of the Negro Woman".

Printed in the *Home News*, Wednesday, 16 January 1918.

[*Home News*, 20 January 1918]

The first program of the Negro Universal Improvement League under its new president, Samuel A. Duncan, was held in the Lafayette Hall last Sunday afternoon [*13 January*]. Marcus P. Garvey has resigned as the organizer[1] and is holding meetings Sunday afternoon at the Odd Fellows Temple.

Printed in the *Home News*, Sunday, 20 January 1918.

1. Garvey later recalled the factional split within the still nascent UNIA: "I can remember well the activities of Mr. Isaac B. Allen, Messrs. Samuel Duncan and L. Lavelle and others who had political designs and who thought that they could work them out through the newly formed organization I had created. To throw off the political influence of these men I was even forced into court, for I had to somewhat beat up Duncan in detaching him from the presidency of the newly formed division of New York." ("Garvey Tells Story of Bitter Struggles," *Pittsburgh Courier*, 22 February 1930). It should be noted, however, that Isaac B. Allen, contrary to Garvey's statement, continued to serve in an official capacity with the UNIA until sometime after the split between Garvey and Duncan, since at the time of the UNIA's June 1918 incorporation Allen was listed as one of the six UNIA directors.

[*Home News*, 23 January 1918]

The installation of the newly elected officers of the UNIA took place last Sunday afternoon [*20 January*] at their headquarters in Lafayette Hall. John E. Bruce made the address to the new officers, and those who were inducted into office were: Samuel A. Duncan, pres.; Mrs. Irene M. Blackstone, 1st vice-pres.; Pope Billups,[1] 2d vice pres.; Miss Eliza Hendrickson, 3d vice-pres; Elizabeth Jackson, fin. secy.; R. Cross, asst. secy; Samuel Bright, treas; L. A. Leavelle,[2] sergt. at-arms; chaplain, C. C. Seifert. The chairman of the Advisory Board is J. E. Bruce. A literary program was presented in which Edward Sterling Wright and Mrs. Helen McAllister took part. An address was made by Cleveland G. Allen.

Printed in the *Home News*, Wednesday, 23 January 1918.

1. Pope Barrow Billups (1889– ?), lawyer and Republican politician, was born in Athens, Ga., and educated at Florida Baptist Academy, 1904–10; Florida A & M College, Tallahassee, 1911–12; and New York University Law School, New York City, 1913–16, receiving his LL.B. in 1916. Admitted to the New York bar in 1917, he was elected a member of the assembly of the New York state legislature in November 1924 and served for one term. (*WWCA*, vol. I).

2. Louis A. Leavelle (variously spelled Lavelle) (1877–?) joined the Kentucky bar in 1901, but in 1904 he went to Harlem where he opened a law practice. He was also the president and

general manager of the Thunderer Printing-Publishing Company. He ran unsuccessfully in 1914 as a Progressive in the Twenty-first Assembly District in the Harlem assembly election. In 1922 and 1924 he was nominated for Congress by the Democratic party in the Third Congressional District in the Bronx. (*WWCA*, vol. 2; *NYT*, 24 August 1924; *Law Directory*, 1921–1944).

[*Home News*, 27 January 1918]

Marcus P. Garvey, the founder of the Negro Universal Improvement Association, and who recently resigned from the parent body, is now holding meetings at Odd Fellow's Temple.[1] Garvey came to this country from the West Indies about one year ago.

Printed in the *Home News*, Sunday, 27 January 1918.

1. Telling later how he organized the UNIA branch in New York, Garvey described it thus: "They started with thirteen members, and in the space of six months the membership had grown to 600. The politicians came, prompted by a desire to further their own ends, but they had to go, after a terrible fight which left him faced with the task of beginning all over again." (*NW*, Saturday, 10 September 1921, p. 5).

[*Home News*, 30 January 1918]

The program of the Negro Universal Improvement Association, last Sunday afternoon [*27 January*], was under the direction of Pope Billups, attorney for the Association.

Printed in the *Home News*, Wednesday, 30 January 1918.

John E. Bruce to the *New Negro*

[*ca. January 1918*]

To the Editor of The New Negro: Dear Sir:
Please grant me space to ask the editor of the Negro World the following questions:

(1)   Are you a citizen of New York or of the U.S.?

(2)   Have you any visible means of support?

(3)   Is your present organization a branch of the Jamaica Industrial School Scheme which you launched on your first arrival in America?

(4)   How much money did you collect from all sources for this work? How much did you collect in Jamaica?

(5)   What did you do with it?

(6) Have you at any time made a report in writing of all moneys received by you for the various schemes you have set on foot here, if not, why not?

(7) What became of the 1,500 pounds sterling (about $7,500) you are said to have begged in Jamaica to establish an Industrial School along the lines of Tuskegee?

(8) Have you abandoned that scheme, or is it now part of your African Communities, etc., propaganda?

(9) What Africans of light and leading in Africa are co-operating with you to establish a great Negro commercial center?

(10) How is your organization going to bring this about?

(11) What authority have you to represent the Africans?

(12) Have any of the native kings or chiefs authorized you to speak for them or their peoples?

(13) Have you any written endorsements from leading Africans in Africa supporting your present scheme?

(14) Are you aware that you are playing with fire and may get your fingers burned? And that if you were a citizen of this country instead of an unknown wandering alien with a grudge against toil, your brilliant phillipics and criticisms of native Americans of African descent m[i]ght be more effective, if you were more responsible than you now seem to be?

(15) Who are you anyhow and what is your game?

ARGUS[1]

Reprinted from the *Crusader* 5 (December 1921). The editorial headnote in the *Crusader* declared: "(What John E. Bruce thought of Marcus Garvey in 1918. When in 'The New Negro', writing under the pseudonym of 'Argus' he propounded the following questions to 'The Moses That Was to Have Been, the Judas that is.')" The caption to the reprint of Bruce's original letter read, " 'Answer, "Professor" Garvey, Answer.' " Issues of the *New Negro* have not been found.

1. Argus was the name of the newspaper established by John E. Bruce in 1884 in Washington, D.C.

Statement by John E. Bruce[1]

[New York City, ca. January 1918]

Mr Marcus Garvey   the Ciceronian orator who /has/ thrilled audiences in England   Scotland   Ireland   and Mars /by the witchery of his eloquence/   would be a much more effective critic of the public men of this country—if he had his naturalization papers signed and properly sealed.

~~Mr Garvey~~ He is a *glib* phrase maker, and a dreamer with a tolerably florid imagination ~~and.~~

/He/ has about as much influence with the 400,000,000 people of Africa who are to be consolidated under his leadership into one great, powerful and influential Negro nationality, as the Statue of Liberty, or a deaf and dumb Choctaw Indian.

Mr Garvey is fooling only the unthinking among the people of the Negro race in this city. We like to listen to the music of his mouth, because it is amusing and delightfully so. Mr Garvey will find that the Negro race is not so easily organized as he imagines it is, but that it is a pretty good meal ticket until the period of disillusionment ~~wanes~~ WANES.

It requires a ~~pretty~~ /tolerably/ big man mentally to do a tithe of the things Mr Garvey has mapped out to do to get a representative of the Negro race at the Council table after this war, when the pie is to be cut. We dont mind telling Mr Garvey now that this /is/ one dream of his that isnt going to come true except on paper or a platform, with himself ~~as the~~ and his lovely voice as the centre of attraction, and that he is wasting valuable time and energy—to say nothing of electric lights, telling our people things that will not bear the acid test, things which in the last analysis are pure buncumbe and perfervid rhetoric mixed with phrensy—and oral gymnastics. [*In the margin*: The idea is all right, but the method all wrong—all gas.]

Mr Garvey is *sui generis*. And he is a wonder, really.—A good military strategist, ~~and a~~ wise statesmen, and shrewd politicians always conceal more than they reveal when talking of their plans. But Garvey *tells all* and so we have his number. You wont do Mr Garvey too *muchee talkee*.

[*Deletion illegible*]

NN-Sc, JEB. AMS.

1. No evidence has been found that this letter was published.

Marcus Garvey to Nicholas Murray Butler

New York, February 5, 1918

My dear Dr. Butler:

Under stress of circumstances, I write, in behalf of my Association, to solicit your help in the following matter, although I fully realize the great burden that falls upon you during this time of international and national strife, when every one is called upon to do something to relieve the distress and hardships around:

In the effort to carry out the purpose of our Association in doing uplift work among our people, to bring them in line with the best in our civiliza-tion, we are now endeavoring to secure and move into a permanent building of our own, on lease, where we will be able to hold our regular meetings and lectures of instruction, but owing to the low state of our funds, we are finding it hard to carry out our plans—which plans would help us so much in the move onward, so we have decided to ask help from a few gentlemen by way of a small donation from each, to help us to meet the requirements in taking over the building on the 15th inst, so in common with the few that I am now writing to, I beg to ask if you would be so good as to give us a helping hand, and to promise us a talk of some kind later on when we are properly located in the building. Trusting to hear from you by return, With very best wishes, Yours respectfully,

UNIVERSAL NEGRO IMPROVEMENT
ASSOCIATION PER
MARCUS GARVEY

MG/CM

[*Endorsement*] RECEIVED FEB 6 1918
COLUMBIA UNIVERSITY
SECRETARY'S OFFICE

NNC, NMB. TLS, Recipient's copy. Stamped endorsement.

Nicholas Murray Butler to Marcus Garvey

[*New York City*] February 7, 1918

Dear Mr. Garvey:

I have this morning your letter of the 5th, and greatly wish it were within my power to assist your undertaking financially. I am sorry, however, to have to tell you that the demands upon me are so numerous and so constant that at the moment I am not able to add to my undertakings. Faithfully yours,

NICHOLAS MURRAY BUTLER

NNC, NMB. TLR, Carbon copy.

"Among the Negroes of Harlem"

[*Home News*, 17 February 1918]

The Equity Congress[1] held its first annual conference last Tuesday [*12 February*] at the Salem M.E. Church. At the evening session the welcome address was made by Alfred [Cosy?]. . . . Other addresses were made by D. C. Outlear, John E. Bruce, Marcus P. Garvey, James P. Simmons,

W. T. B. Richardson, and Cleveland G. Allen, and Rev. F. A. Cullen, the pastor of the church. . . .

Printed in the *Home News*, Sunday, 17 February 1918.

1. There had also been an Equity Congress formed in Harlem earlier, in 1911, to agitate for the creation of an all-black regiment within the expanded New York State Guard.

Marcus Garvey to Nicholas Murray Butler

New York, February 18, 1918

My Dear Dr. Butler:

I am sorry to trouble you so much after your good will toward us, but in this case I am acting in compliance with the overwhelming sentiment of the people I represent in regarding you as a whole hearted friend to whom they feel to look for that moral help that goes to lift the unfortunate up the ladder of progress and human development. In accordance with the sentiments of the people they have commanded me to ask you if you would be so good as to address a large meeting of the Association and its friends, in the Palace Theatre, 135th Street and Madison Avenue, on Sunday afternoon, the 3rd of March, on the subject of "Education and What It Means".

The Association has acquired the use of this hall for the purpose of creating a literary and educational center for the Negro people of this district and city, and at which place they may invite their friends of the opposite race to come and talk to them on various subjects that would tend to make us a more thoughtful and responsive people.

We are starting on Sunday the 24th inst the series of educational meetings, when the Hon. George Gordon Battle[1] will address us on the subject of "The Duty of a Citizen in the Time of War". The people therefore feel that you, as one of their best friends, will help again by addressing us on the afternoon mentioned on the topic afore mentioned;—"Education and What It Means".

In anticipation of your being present with us, we have started out already to make arrangements for the occasion, and therefore await your kind reply. With very best wishes, I beg to remain   Yours respectfully,

UNIVERSAL NEGRO IMPROVEMENT
ASSOCIATION PER MARCUS GARVEY

MG/CM

[*Endorsement*] RECEIVED FEB 19 1918
COLUMBIA UNIVERSITY
SECRETARY'S OFFICE

NNC, NMB. TLS, Recipient's copy. Stamped endorsement.

1. George Gordon Battle (1868–1949), born in North Carolina, was a prominent white lawyer in New York and a Democratic party member who maintained an active interest in the

welfare of black Americans throughout his life. Garvey later hired Battle as his legal counsel in 1924 for his appeal after his conviction on federal charges of mail fraud. (*NCAB*; DNA, RG 204, file 42-793, 30 January 1926).

Nicholas Murray Butler to Marcus Garvey

[*New York City*] February 19, 1918

Dear Mr. Garvey:

I should be most happy to accept your invitation for Sunday afternoon, March 3, were it not that I am already obligated for that afternoon in connection with a meeting which is to be held on the occasion of the visit here of the Archbishop of York.[1] Perhaps at some future time I may be able to speak to your Association and their friends. Very truly yours,

NICHOLAS MURRAY BUTLER

NNC, NMB. TLR, Carbon copy.

1. William Cosmo Gordon Lang (1864–1945), Lord Lang of Lambeth and later Archbishop of Canterbury, was appointed archbishop of York in 1908. In 1918 he visited the United States at the British government's request to explain the allied cause. (*WWW*).

"Among the Negroes of Harlem"

[*Home News*, 27 February 1918]

A large mass meeting was held at the Palace Casino last Sunday afternoon [*24 February*], under the direction of the UNIA. Rev. W. S. Holder[1] presided. Addresses were made by George Gordon Battle, J. C. Thomas, Jr., and Rev. Dr. R. C. Ransom.[2] Edward Sterling who recently won the State Elocution Contest, recited some of Paul L. Dunbar's selections, and Madam Hanley Green offered "The Black Regiment".

Printed in the *Home News*, Wednesday, 27 February 1918.

1. Rev. Wesley S. Holder was the minister of the Harlem Congregational Church at 250 West 136th Street. At one time, in October 1907, he was the vice-president of the West Indian Trading and Development Co. Later, in 1918, he was president of the New York branch of the National Equal Rights League. (New York *Age*, 3 October 1907; New York *Call*, 28 July 1919).

2. Rev. Reverdy Cassius Ransom (1861–1959) was one of the founders of the Niagara movement. Born at Flushing, Ohio, Ransom was educated at Oberlin College, Oberlin, Ohio, 1882–83, and Wilberforce University Seminary, Wilberforce, Ohio, 1883–86, where he also received his D.D. in 1898 and an honorary LL.D. in 1912. Ransom was ordained an elder of the AME Church in 1887, and subsequently served as pastor for AME churches in Pennsylvania, 1886–90; Cleveland, 1890–96; Chicago, 1896–1904; New Bedford, and Boston, 1904–07; New York, 1907–12, moving to Louisville, Ky., in 1924. During these years he played an active role in black politics as a way to combat racial discrimination, joining the revived Afro-American League, the Constitution League, and the NAACP. Transferred by Bishop Henry McNeal Turner to the prestigious AME Bethel Church in New York City, Ransom's influence grew,

despite conservative opposition, and in 1912 he was elected editor of the *AME Church Review*, a position he held until 1924. In 1924 he achieved his ambition of becoming an AME bishop. In 1920 he published "Back to Africa: A Militant Call" in the *AME Church Review* (37 [1920]: 88–89), in which he praised the passage of the Declaration of Rights at the August 1920 UNIA convention, and in subsequent editions of the magazine, he sympathized with Garvey and his movement. (*WWCA*, vol. 2; *Crisis*, 28:5 [September 1924] p. 212).

Nicholas Murray Butler to Marcus Garvey

[*New York City*] March 5, 1918

Dear Mr. Garvey

I thank you for your invitation of the 4th,[1] but I am off tomorrow for the South to be gone through the whole of March, and cannot, therefore, have the pleasure of addressing your group on the evening of Sunday, the 17th. Yours very truly,

NICHOLAS MURRAY BUTLER

NNC, NMB. TLR, Carbon copy.

1. Garvey's letter of invitation of 4 March 1918 has not been found.

Marcus Garvey to Theodore Roosevelt

New York, March 12, 1918

Honored Sir:

Please let me convey to you the happiness of my Association in the matter of your complete recovery from your recent illness.

At the last general meeting of the Association I was directed to write to you, asking your help and cooperation in the following matter:

Our Association, being representative of the educated and thoughtful of our race, desires a complete understanding between the two opposite races— the White and Black. We of the Association believe that ultimately the two races that have been so closely associated for all these centuries in the best of friendly relations will be forced to stand together in the preservation of those human rights that are every day being threatened from sources not quite friendly to the White or Black race.[1] To foster the spirit of race cooperation between the White and Black peoples of the world, we are to hold a monster meeting in the Palace Theatre, Madison Avenue & 135th Street, on Sunday afternoon, May 6 5th at 3.15 o'clock, and at our meeting we unanimously voted to ask you to deliver an address for us on the occasion on the subject of "The Whiteman's Relationship to the Blackman in the Development and Preservation of Civilization".

We feel sure that you will help us with the address on the occasion, but if the date is not convenient, we shall gladly change it to meet your convenience. With best wishes, Yours respectfully,

UNIVERSAL NEGRO IMPROVEMENT
ASSOCIATION PER MARCUS GARVEY

MG/CM

DLC, TR. TLS, Recipient's copy. Corrections in Garvey's hand.

1. An allusion to the German "Teutonic menace." Roosevelt had encouraged anti-German feeling by his jingoistic attitude towards American war preparedness in anticipation of a conflict with Germany. (Thomas G. Dyer, *Theodore Roosevelt and the Idea of Race* [Baton Rouge: Louisiana State University Press, 1980]).

"Among the Negroes of Harlem"

[*Home News*, 24 March 1918]

The Universal Negro Improvement League is staging a big debate at the Palace Casino this afternoon, the subject having to do with whether Africa should be self-governing or not. The question will be argued by the members of the league and the editors of the *Independent*.[1]

Printed in the *Home News*, Sunday, 24 March 1918.

1. No confirmation has been found in the *Independent*, or any other source, that the debate was ever held. Garvey's challenge to debate was occasioned by the *Independent's* lengthy editorial of 23 February 1918, entitled, "The Question of Africa." He objected to the following statement: "The Bolsheviki proposes to treat the African savages the same as the Alsatians and Poles and have them settle their sovereignty by a popular referendum. This is reducing democracy to an absurdity. . . . The question of sovereignty must be settled soon and settled for the present by Europe and America with little help from Africa."

Theodore Roosevelt to Marcus Garvey

[*Oyster Bay, Long Island*] April 23, 1918

My dear Mr Garvey:

The demands upon me for speeches have been so numerous, and indeed the demands upon me for every kind of service and action have become so heavy, that it is an utter impossibility for me to undertake anything additional at this time. I am very sorry but it is not possible for me to do more than I am doing.

Thanking you and expressing my regret, I am Faithfully yours,

[THEODORE ROOSEVELT]

DLC, TR. TL, Carbon copy.

Marcus Garvey to Nicholas Murray Butler

One God! **One Aim!** **One Destiny!**
New York Division
Universal Negro Improvement Association
And
African Communities' League

Cable Address: "Uniany", New York
Telephone 7976 Morningside

IRENA MOORMAN-BLACKSTON
President Ladies' Division

MARCUS GARVEY, President
and International Organizer

IRENE W. WINGFIELD,
1st Vice President

WALTER J. CONWAY,
1st Vice President

GEORGE A. CRAWLEY,[1]
Executive Secretary

JANIE JENKINS,[2]
2nd Vice President

EDWARD STERLING WRIGHT,
2nd Vice President

J. A. DAVIS
Chairman Advisory Board

R. H. ROGERS,
3rd Vice President

E. D. SMITH-GREEN,
General Secretary

JULIA E. RUMFORD
Secretary

ETHEL OUGHTON-CLARKE,
General Secretary

BEN. E. BURRELL
Associate Secretary

CARRIE MERO,
Associate Secretary

CLARENCE A. CARPENTER,[3]
Treasurer

Lafayette Building, 165 W. 131st St.
New York, April 29th 1918

"He created of one blood all nations of men to dwell on the face of the earth."

My dear Dr. Butler:

It is unfortunate that we have to appeal to you at this time, when the public and other financial demands are so many on one of your position, but as you will realize sometimes, one has to appeal to the old friend for help, when there is no one else to ask.

Thus, in keeping with an unanimous vote of our members, at our last general meeting in the Lafayette Hall, I was instructed to write to you asking your help by a small donation to assist our building fund.

We feel sure that whatsoever you can do for us, will be done. Trusting to receive your kind help, with return of list, with best wishes, I am   Yours respectfully,

Universal Negro Improvement
Association
Marcus Garvey President

NNC, NMB. TLS, Recipient's copy.

1. George A. Crawley (b. 1892) was born in Lambertville, N. J. In 1917, he was employed as a chauffeur. (AFRC, RG 163, registration card).

2. Janie Jenkins was born in Maryland; she first met Garvey in 1917 and became an officer of the UNIA during that year. In June 1919 she became assistant treasurer and a director of the Black Star Line, Inc. (*Garvey* v. *U.S.*, no. 8317, pp. 1336–40).

3. Clarence Alexander Carpenter (b. 1892) was from St. John's, Antigua, BWI. He was employed as an elevator operator. (AFRC, RG 163, registration card).

Enclosure

New York, April to June, 1918

[*Inserted*] Hon. Dr. Nicholas Murray Butler's List

Dear Friend:—

We, the undersigned officers, on behalf of the Universal Negro Improvement Association of New York, are hereby appealing to you for a little help, to enable the Association to erect its proposed $200,000 building in Harlem, for the purpose of centralizing our effort of social service uplift work among our people.

Unfortunately, we have not yet in our midst any institution worthy of the loftier and nobler purposes of a struggling race such as we are, and this building that we are to erect will be the source from which we will train and educate our people to those essentials that will make them a more cultured and better race.

Please help us to raise $200,000 for this building by writing your donation on attached subscription list. Write plainly your name, address and amount.

Thanking you in anticipation of your kind help, With best wishes, Yours faithfully,

UNIVERSAL NEGRO IMPROVEMENT ASSOCIATION

MARCUS GARVEY President	I. M. BLACKSTON President of Ladies Division
WALTER J. CONWAY 1st Vice-President	ETHEL OUGHTON CLARKE General Secretary—Ladies Division
GEORGE A. CRAWLEY General Secretary	CLARENCE A. CARPENTER Treasurer

NNC, NMB. LS, Recipient's copy. Printed on official UNIA stationery with insertion written in Garvey's hand.

Nicholas Murray Butler to Marcus Garvey

[*New York City*] April 30, 1918

Dear Mr. Garvey,

I am sorry to have to reply unfavorably to your letter of the 29th, but the pressure upon me just now is so great from every source that I am unable to make even the small contribution for which you ask. Faithfully yours,

NICHOLAS MURRAY BUTLER

[*Docket*] For Miss Wadelton's file

NNC, NMB. TLR, Carbon copy. Docketing is typed.

Report by the American Protective League to the Bureau of Investigation

NEW YORK CITY   JUNE 3, 1918

In re: GERMAN PROPAGANDA AMONG NEGROES IN HARLEM (New York) Investigation by C. E. Campbell, A.P.L.[1]

. . . I was informed by a Sargeant of the Police, badge No. 407 that there was a man by the name *Garvey* (colored) who preaches every night against the white people, generally from 134th to 137th Street and Lenox Avenue. On several occasions he has tried to overhear the conversation, but being in uniform, the man would walk away and say no more.

There are several men who speak in this district.

. . . It might be a good idea to run down these negro speakers referred to on Lenox Avenue between 134th and 137th Street, by the policeman to whom I spoke, as they may be the source of some of these rumors.[2] . . .

C. E. CAMPBELL, A.P.L.

[*Endorsements*] Negro Subv   JES

DNA, RG 165, File 10218-116/29 124X. TD. Endorsements are handwritten.

1. Formed in Chicago on 11 March 1917, the American Protective League (APL) was a veritable army of nearly 250,000 volunteer sleuths organized to assist the government in tracking down German spies. It was also designated as an auxiliary to the Bureau of Investigation. After the APL moved its headquarters from Chicago to Washington in November 1917, the War Department made Charles Daniel Frey, one of the organization's three national directors, a captain in the U.S. army and assigned him to the departmental military intelligence agency to handle cases requiring APL assistance. By April 1918, the APL liaison group had become so significant that it became a separate subsection of MI 3, responsible for counter-espionage and one of the largest sections in military intelligence operations. (See Col. Bruce W. Bidwell, "History of the Military Intelligence Division, Department of the Army General Staff," XIII-7, p. 235 [unpublished ms, 1959-61], Carlisle Barracks, Pa., United States Army Military History Institute, regraded unclassified 20 July 1979; Joan M. Jensen, *The Price of Vigilance* [Chicago: Rand McNally, 1968]).

2. The investigation was undertaken at the request of the chief of the Bureau of Investigation, Alexander Bruce Bielaski (1883–1964), in a letter of 6 April 1918. It was based on "the rumor being circulated in Harlem, New York City, concerning the treatment received by colored troops in the United States Army" (DNA, RG 165, file 10218-116/29 124X). The matter had originally been referred to the Bureau of Investigation by the Military Intelligence Section of the War Department General Staff.

Marcus Garvey to Theodore Roosevelt

New York, June 24, 1918

Dear Mr. Roosevelt:

At the last general meeting of our Association, held in the Lafayette Hall, it was unanimously voted to write to you enclosing the accompanying ticket invitations for three, you and your family, to attend our Musical and Literary Carnival to be held in the Palace Theatre, 135th Street and Madison Avenue, on Thursday evening, 27th June, at 8.45 o'clock, in aid of our Association, in helping us to do uplift work among our struggling people in New York.

If you will be unable to attend we feel that you will do your bit to help us in our struggle, as we are reserving the three seats for you. The price for each seat is one dollar; but we know you will do your best to help us.

Thanking you in anticipation of your kind help. With best wishes   Yours respectfully

UNIVERSAL NEGRO IMPROVEMENT
ASSOCIATION
MARCUS GARVEY PRESIDENT

[*In the margin*]   Please lend us a helping
hand in our struggles
M. G.

DLC, TR. TLS, Recipient's copy. Marginal note is handwritten by Garvey.

Certificate of Incorporation of the UNIA

[*New York City*] Filed and Recorded
Jul 2 1918

The Universal Negro Improvement Association, Inc.

State of New York :

: SS:.

County of New York :

WE, THE UNDERSIGNED, desiring to form a corporation, pursuant to the provisions of the Membership Corporation Law, all being of full age, at least two-thirds being citizens of the United States, and one of us a resident of the State of New York, do hereby certify and state:

First: The particular objects for which the corporation is to be formed are:

To promote and practice the principles of Benevolence, and for the protection and social intercourse of its members and for their mental and physical culture and developments and to extend a friendly and constructive hand to the Negroes of the United States.

Second: The name of the Proposed corporation is: The Universal Negro Improvement Association, Inc.

Third: The territory in which its operations are to be principally conducted is the United States, territories, and possessions.

Fourth: The place in which its principal office is to be located is the City of New York, Borough of Manhattan, in the County of New York, State of New York to wit: [*Inserted*: #165 West 131st Street]

Fifth: The number of its directors is seven-/six/:

Sixth: The names and places of residence of the persons to be directors until its first annual meeting are:—

Issac B. Allen	12 West 99th St., New York City.
Irene M. Blackstone	488 Lenox Avenue, New York City.
Walter J. Conway	130 West 142nd St., New York City.
Carrie B. Mero	143 West 140th St., New York City.
Iolanthe E. Sterrs	West 145th St., New York City.
Harriet Rogers	9 West 133rd St., New York City.
Marcus Garvey	2305 Seventh Avenue, New York City.

Seventh: The time for holding its annual meeting is on the first Monday in January in each year.

IN WITNESS WHEREOF, we have made and acknowledged this certificate this 17th day of June, 1918.

Marcus Garvey
Carrie B. Mero

Isaac B. Allen
Irena M. Blackston
Harriet Rogers
Walter J. Conway

State of New York   :
                    : SS:.
County of New York:

On this 17th day of June, 1918, before me personally came, Issac B. Allen, Irene M. Blackstone, ~~Iolanthe E. Storrs~~ Walter J. Conway, Carrie B. Mero, Harriet Rogers and Marcus Garvey to me personally known to be the individuals described in and who executed the foregoing certificate, and they severally duly acknowledged to me that they executed the same.

Chas J. H Hamilton
Notary Public
NYC. #26

~~Marcus Garvey~~
~~Carrie B. Mero~~
~~Isaac B. Allen~~
~~Irena M. Blackston~~
~~Harriet Rogers~~

State of New York   :
                    : SS:.
County of New York:

Issac B. Allen, Irene M. Blackstone, Carrie B. Mero, ~~Iolenthe E. Storrs,~~ Walter J. Conway, and Harriet Rogers, being duly sworn deposes and says that they are the persons described in and who executed the foregoing certificate of Incorporation; that no previous application has been made for the approval of said certificate; that they are all of full age; that the said Issac B. Allen, Irene M. Blackstone Carrie B. Mero, Iolanthe E. Storrs, Walter J. Conway, and Harriet Rogers, are citizens of the United States and residents of the State of New York.

Isaac B. Allen
Irena M. Blackston
Carrie B Mero
Harriet Rogers
Walter J. Conway

Sworn to before me this
17th day of June, 1918.
Chas J H Hamilton
Notary Public
NYC. #26

[*Stamped*] WALTER J CONWAY ATTORNEY
AND COUNSELLOR-AT-LAW[1]

115 WEST 135th ST., N.Y.
[*Docket*] Book 13 Page 7. [*Initialed*] JAY
MBW
[*Typewritten endorsement*] I, the under-
signed Justice of the Supreme Court of the
State of New York, do hereby approve of
the within Certificate.
[*Signed*] F. K. Pendleton/SC JSC   Dated
at New York this 27 day of June, 1918.
[*Stamped endorsement*] STATE OF NEW
YORK OFFICE OF SECRETARY OF STATE
Filed and Recorded JUL 2 1918   Francis
M. Hugo   SECRETARY OF STATE[2]

NAiDS, Book 13, Page 7 (3). TDS, with additions in the hand of Walter J. Conway.

1. Responsible for filing the incorporation papers.
2. Francis M. Hugo (1870–1931) was the secretary of state for New York from 1915 until 1920, and a member of the Republican state committee. (*NYT*, 31 December 1931).

Certificate of Incorporation of the ACL

[*New York City*] Filed and Recorded
Jul 31 1918

State Of New York)
   SS.:
County Of New York)

WE, the undersigned, all being persons of full age, and at least two-thirds being citizens of the United States, and at least one of us a resident of the State of New York, desiring to form a Stock Corporation, pursuant to the provisions of the Business Corporations Law of the State of New York, do hereby make, sign, acknowledge and file this certificate for that purpose, as follows:

FIRST: The name of the proposed corporation is AFRICAN COMMUNITIES LEAGUE, INC.

SECOND: The purposes for which it is to be formed are:
    a. To conduct grocery stores; to buy or otherwise acquire, to manufacture, market, prepare for market, sell, deal in and deal with, import and export food and food products of every class and description, fresh, canned or preserved, or otherwise, and all other food and other preparations.
    b. In connection with the foregoing, to manufacture, market and prepare for market, buy, sell, deal in and deal with, import and export tin and any products of tin, glassware and any articles of

glassware and any other article, receptacle, package or thing which may be useful in connection with the manufacture or marketing, vending or shipping of the products of the company or like products.

c. To carry on the business of restaurant keepers, caterers, tobacconists, dealers in provisions, wine and liquor dealers, and to manage and conduct restaurants and cafes in any part of the United States and in foreign countries.

d. To carry on the business of steam and general laundry and to wash, clean, purify, scour, bleach, wring, dry, iron, color, dye, disinfect, renovate and prepare for use all articles for wearing apparel, household, domestic and other linen and cotton and woolen goods and clothing and fabrics of all kinds, and to buy, sell, hire, manufacture, repair, let on hire or improve, treat and deal in all apparatus, machines, materials and articles of all kinds which are capable of being used for any of such purposes.

e. To prepare for publication, print, electrotype, bind, sell and distribute and generally deal in magazines, newspapers, pamphlets, books and publications of all kinds, and to engage generally in the business of job and book printers, book-binders, stationers, engravers and electrotypers. To apply for, purchase or otherwise acquire and to dispose of, copyrights in the United States and elsewhere. To purchase or otherwise acquire and to sell either as principal or agents and as freely as natural persons might or could do, books, magazines, music, newspapers and publications of all kinds and descriptions, stationery and stationers' supplies, and generally to carry on the business of wholesale and retail book sellers and stationers.

f. To manufacture and deal in clothing, haberdashery, boots, shoes, leather, leather goods and wearing apparel generally and any other articles which may be conveniently or advantageously handled in conjunction with the business aforesaid. To engage in the manufacture, purchase, sale, export and import of woolen, silk, cotton and other fabrics of all kinds and any and all materials used in the manufacture of clothing, wearing apparel, boots, shoes, leather goods or articles usually dealt in therewith or in connection therewith.

g. To manufacture and generally deal in stoves, furnaces, ranges, gas and electric appliances and devices of all kinds for heating purposes.

h. To make and enter into any and all manner of contracts or agreements by and with any person or persons, firm or corporation; to purchase, acquire, manufacture, sell, deal in, export or import any of the articles or merchandise aforementioned, and generally with full power to perform any and all acts connected with the foregoing purposes arising therefrom or incidental thereto, and any and all acts proper and necessary for the purposes of the business.

i. To do such other acts and to conduct such other business or businesses in connection with or resulting from the exercise of any of the powers enumerated in the preceding subdivision as may be found advantageous or desirable by the corporation so far as the same may be lawful for a corporation organized under the Business Corporations Law.

j. To take, buy, purchase, exchange, hire, lease or otherwise acquire real estate and property, either improved or unimproved, and any interest or right therein, and to own, hold, control, maintain, manage and develop the same, in connection with said business.

k. To purchase, exchange, hire or otherwise acquire such personal property, chattels, rights, easements, permits, privileges and franchises as may lawfully be purchased, exchanged, hired or acquired under the Business Corporations Law of the State of New York.

l. To erect, construct, maintain, improve, rebuild, enlarge, alter, manage and control, directly or through ownership of stock in any corporation, any and all kinds of buildings, houses, stores, offices, warehouses, mills, shops, factories and plants and any and all other structures and erections, which may at any time be necessary, useful or advantageous in the judgment of the Board of Directors for the purposes of the corporation, and which can lawfully be done under the Business Corporations Law.

m. To sell, manage, improve, develop, assign, transfer, convey, lease, sub-lease, pledge or otherwise alienate or dispose of, and to mortgage or otherwise encumber the lands, buildings, real property, chattels, real and other property of the Company, real and personal and wheresoever situate, and any and all legal and equitable rights therein.

n. To borrow money with or without pledge of or mortgage on all or any of its property, real or personal, as security, and to loan and advance money upon mortgages on real or personal property, or on either of them.

o. To purchase, acquire, hold, sell, assign, transfer, mortgage, pledge and otherwise dispose of the shares of capital stock, bonds, debentures or other evidences of indebtedness of any corporation, domestic and foreign, and while the holder thereof to exercise all the rights, privileges, ownership, including the right to vote thereon, and to issue in exchange therefor its own stocks, bonds and other obligations.

p. To apply for, obtain, register, produce, lease or otherwise acquire and to hold, own, use, operate, introduce, sell, assign, or otherwise dispose of any trade-marks, trade-names, patents, inventions, improvements, designs, licenses and processes in connection with, or secured by letters patent of the United States, or under any of the trade-marks or copyright laws of the United States or otherwise, to produce or otherwise acquire patents, inventions, improvements, licenses and processes of others for the purpose of holding, owning, using, operating or to sell, assign or otherwise dispose of the same, and to grant licenses thereto, or otherwise turn to account such patents, inventions, improvements, designs, licenses and processes, as above set forth.

q. To act as agent, commission merchant, or consignee in carrying on the businesses or purpose hereinbefore mentioned; and also as principal, agent, commission merchant, factor, or otherwise engage in every and any and all of said businesses as distributors, dealers and importers of every, any and all things which may be necessary or proper in connection with the said business, or either of any of them, and which may not be contrary to law.

r. To purchase, acquire, own and sell the plant or plants of any other corporations, associations, firm, firms, or individuals carrying on any business similar in nature to any, either or all of the businesses for which this corporation is formed, and either along, or in connection with any such other corporation or corporations or associations, firm, firms, or individuals, and all and everything necessary, suitable and proper for the accomplishment of any of the purposes, or the attainment of any of the objects, or in furtherance of any of the powers hereinbefore set forth, provided the same be not inconsistent with the laws under which this corporation is organized.

s. To conduct and transact its business in any or all of its branches in any of the States, Territories, Colonies or Dependencies of the United States, in the District of Columbia and in any and all foreign countries; to hold, purchase, mortgage and convey real and personal property without limit as to amount in any such State, Territory, Colony, Dependency, District or foreign country, but always subject to the laws thereof.

t. To do all and everything necessary, suitable and proper for the accomplishment of any of the purposes or the attainment of any of the objects, or in furtherance of any of the powers hereinbefore set forth, and to do any other act or acts, thing or things incidental or pertaining to, or connected with the aforesaid businesses, or powers, or any part or parts thereof, provided the same be not inconsistent with the laws under which this corporation is organized.

u. This corporation shall not have the power of, nor shall anything herein contained authorize or permit it to carry on the business of discounting bills, notes or other evidences of debt, of receiving deposits or buying or selling bills of exchange or issuing bills, notes or other evidences of debt for circulation as money.

THIRD: The amount of Capital Stock is Ten Thousand ($10,000) Dollars.

FOURTH: The number of shares of which the Capital Stock shall consist is Four Hundred (400) shares of the par value of Twenty-five ($25.00) Dollars each, and the amount of capital with which the said corporation shall begin business is Five Hundred ($500.00) Dollars.

FIFTH: Its principal office is to be located in the Borough of Manhattan, in the County of New York, City of New York, State of New York.

SIXTH: Its duration is to be perpetual.

SEVENTH: The number of its Directors is to be Nine (9).

EIGHTH: The names and post office addresses of the Directors for the first year are as follows:

NAMES	POST OFFICE ADDRESSES
MARCUS GARVEY	238 West 131st Street, Borough of Manhattan, New York City.
IRENA MOORMAN-BLACKSTON	488 Lenox Avenue, Borough of Manhattan, New York City.
ISAAC S. BRIGHT	278 Pulaski Street, Borough of Brooklyn, New York City.
IRENE W. WINGFIELD	237 West 40th Street, Borough of Manhattan, New York City.
JAMES PERKINS[1]	133 West 140th Street, Borough of Manhattan, New York City.
CARRIE B. MERO	143 West 140th Street, Borough of Manhattan, New York City.
CLARENCE A. CARPENTER	70 West 131st Street, Borough of Manhattan, New York City.
F. B. WEBSTER[2]	42 West 139th Street, Borough of Manhattan, New York City.

SIDNEY SMITH   110 West 133rd Street,
                               Borough of Manhattan,
                               New York City.

NINTH: The names and post office addresses of the subscribers of this certificate, and a statement of the number of shares of stock which each agrees to take in this Corporation, are as follows:

NAMES	POST OFFICE ADDRESSES	NO. OF SHARES
MARCUS GARVEY	238 West 131st Street, Borough of Manhattan, New York City.	1
ISAAC S. BRIGHT	278 Pulaski Street, Borough of Brooklyn, New York City.	1
F. B. WEBSTER	42 West 139th Street, Borough of Manhattan, New York City.	1
IRENE W. WINGFIELD	237 West 40th Street, Borough of Manhattan, New York City.	1
JANIE JENKINS	35 West 139th Street, Borough of Manhattan, New York City.	1
JAMES PERKINS	35 West 139th Street, Borough of Manhattan, New York City.	1
CARRIE B. MERO	143 West 140th Street, Borough of Manhattan, New York City.	1
JULIA E. RUMFORD	2313 Seventh Avenue, Borough of Manhattan, New York City.	1
CLARENCE A. CARPENTER	70 West 131st Street, Borough of Manhattan, New York City.	1
DAISY DUNN	598 Cortlandt Avenue, Borough of the Bronx, New York City.	1

IRENA MOORMAN-BLACKSTON	488 Lenox Avenue, Borough of Manhattan, New York City.	1
AMY HAYNES[3]	151 West 133rd Street, Borough of Manhattan, New York City.	1
JAMES HAYNES[4]	151 West 133rd Street, Borough of Manhattan, New York City.	1
HENRY DOLPHIN[5]	28 West 131st Street, Borough of Manhattan, New York City.	1
GRANZALINE MARSHALL	221 West 139th Street, Borough of Manhattan, New York City.	1

IN WITNESS WHEREOF we have made, signed, acknowledged and filed this Certificate of Incorporation in duplicate.

> Marcus Garvey (L.S.)
> Irena Moorman-Blackston (L.S.)
> Isaac S. Bright (L.S.)
> Irene W. Wingfield (L.S.)
> Janie Jenkins (L.S.)
> Carrie B. Mero (L.S.)
> Julia E. Rumford (L.S.)
> Clarence A. Carpenter (L.S.)
> James Perkins. (L.S.)
> Daisy Dunn (L.S.)
> Amy Haynes (L.S.)
> James Haynes (L.S.)
> Henry D. Dolphin (L.S.)
> F. B. Webster (L.S.)
> Granzaline Marshall (L.S.)

STATE OF NEW YORK)
) SS.:
COUNTY OF NEW YORK)

On this 26th day of July, 1918, before me personally appeared MARCUS GARVEY, IRENA MOORMAN-BLACKSTON, ISAAC S. BRIGHT, F. B. WEBSTER, IRENE W. WINGFIELD, JANIE JENKINS, JAMES PERKINS, CARRIE B. MERO, JULIA E. RUMFORD, CLARENCE A. CARPENTER, DAISY DUNN, AMY HAYNES, JAMES HAYNES, HENRY DOLPHIN and GRANZALINE MARSHALL, to me known and known to me to be the individuals mentioned and described in and who executed the foregoing Certificate of Incorporation, and they duly severally acknowledged to me that they executed the same.

JAS S. WATSON[6]
Commissioner of Deeds #235
New York City
Term expires Nov. 20/19

[Docket] Book 686 Page 43 11 [Initialed]
MBW
[Stamped endorsements] Tax for privileges of the organization of this Corporation. $[Inserted: 10–]   Under Section 180, Chapter 62, Law of 1909 AS AMENDED Paid to State Treasurer before Filing. STATE OF NEW YORK Office of SECRETARY OF STATE Filed[7] and Recorded JUL 31 1918 Francis M Hugo SECRETARY OF STATE

NAiDS, Book 686 Page 43 (11). TDS, with manuscript additions in the hand of James S. Watson.

1. James Hamble Perkins (1892–?) was born in Bridgetown, Barbados. (AFRC, RG 163, registration card).

2. Fleming Du Bignon Webster (1873–?), born in the United States, was employed as a clerk with Whitehead Brothers and Co. in September 1918. (AFRC, RG 163, registration card).

3. Wife of James Haynes.

4. James Haynes (1876–?), South Carolina-born, was from May 1915 to January 1917 intermittently employed as a laborer for the U.S. government at the Brooklyn Navy Yard. From January 1917 to October 1918 he worked as a driller. (AFRC, RG 163, registration card).

5. Henry D. Dolphin (1886–?) was born in Den Amstel, British Guiana. He was self-employed as a renovator and in February 1920 he was employed as a journalist for the *Daily Citizen*. (AFRC, RG 163, registration card).

6. James Samuel Watson (1882–1951) was chief of the corporation tax and contract divisions of the law firm of House, Grossman and Vorhaus. Born at Spanish Town, Jamaica, Watson came to the United States in 1905, becoming a U.S. citizen in 1912. He studied law at the City College of New York and New York Law School, and after receiving his LL.B. degree he was admitted to the New York bar in 1914. In 1920, he opened his own law office, and two years later he was appointed special counsel to the corporation counsel of the city of New York in the special franchise tax division. In January 1931, he became the first black justice of the municipal court of the city of New York. When he resigned after serving for almost twenty years, he was appointed president of New York City's Municipal Civil Service Commission. (*Crisis*, 34:2 [February 1931]; The Association of the Bar of New York, *Memorial Book* [New York: n.p., 1953]).

7. Filed by House, Grossman, and Vorhaus, counselors-at-law, 115 Broadway, New York City.

Constitution and Book of Laws

NEW YORK, JULY, 1918

MADE FOR THE GOVERNMENT OF THE UNIVERSAL NEGRO IMPROVEMENT ASSOCIATION, INC., AND AFRICAN COMMUNITIES' LEAGUE, INC., OF THE WORLD

IN EFFECT JULY, 1918[1]

PREAMBLE[2]

The Universal Negro Improvement Association and African Communities' League is a social, friendly, humanitarian, charitable, educational, institutional, constructive and expansive society, and is founded by persons, desiring to the utmost, to work for the general uplift of the Negro peoples of the world. And the members pledge themselves to do all in their power to conserve the rights of their *noble race* and to respect the rights of all mankind, believing always in the Brotherhood of Man and the Fatherhood of God. The motto of the organization is: "One God! One Aim! One Destiny!" Therefore, let justice be done to all mankind, realizing that if the strong oppresses the weak confusion and discontent will ever mark the path of man, but with love, faith and charity towards all the reign of peace and plenty will be heralded into the world and the generations of men shall be called blessed.[3]

CONSTITUTION
ARTICLE I.
JURISDICTION.

Section 1.   This body shall be known as the Universal Negro Improvement Association and African Communities' League. Its jurisdiction shall include all communities where the people of Negro blood and African descent are to be found. In it alone, and through the Potentate and Supreme Commissioner, hereinafter spoken of, and his successors, are vested powers to establish subordinate divisions and other organizations, whose objects shall coale[s]ce and be identical with those herein set forth, and its mandates shall be obeyed at all times and under all circumstances. To the Universal Negro Improvement Association and African Communities' League, through the authority of the Potentate, is reserved the right to fix, regulate and determine all matters of a general or international nature as affecting the objects of the organization and the membership at large.

Sec. 2.   The right is reserved to re-establish jurisdiction over any division or subordinate organization whose affairs are conducted contrary to the welfare of the Universal Negro Improvement Association and African Communities' League as required by the Constitution and General Laws.

Sec. 3.   The objects of the Universal Negro Improvement Association and African Communities' League shall be: to establish a Universal Confraternity among the race; to promote the spirit of pride and love; to reclaim the fallen; to administer to and assist the needy; to assist in civilizing the backward tribes of Africa; to assist in the development of Independent Negro Nations and Communities; to establish Commissionaries or Agencies in the principal countries and cities of the world for the representation and protection of all Negroes, irrespective of nationality; to promote a conscientious Spiritual worship among the native tribes of Africa; to establish Universities, Colleges, Academies and Schools for the racial education and culture of the people; to conduct a world-wide Commercial and Industrial Intercourse for the good of the people; to work for better conditions in all Negro communities.

Sec. 4.   A charter may be issued to seven or more citizens of any community whose intelligence is such as to bring them within respectful recognition of the educated and cultured of such a community.

ARTICLE II.
LAWS.

Section 1.   The Universal Negro Improvement Association and African Communities' League may enact and enforce laws for its government and that for subordinate divisions, organizations and societies and members throughout the jurisdiction.

Sec. 2.   The laws of the Universal Negro Improvement Association and African Communities' League shall be comprised in (a) The Constitution which shall contain the outlines, fundamental principles and policies of the organization, its jurisdiction and that of local divisions, organizations and societies, the list of officers and all matters pertaining to their duties. (b) The By-Laws, which shall contain the order of procedure in Convention, the specific duties of officers and committees, and the standing rules. (c) The General Laws, which shall contain all matters pertaining to the relations of members and local divisions and societies to each other.

Amendment to Constitution

Sec. 3.   The Constitution shall only be amended at times when such amendments tend absolutely to the further interest of the Universal Negro Improvement Association and African Communities' League and when carried by a two-thirds majority in Convention fully assembled.

Sec. 4.   By-laws and general laws may be enacted by the convention of the Universal Negro Improvement Association and African Communities' League and such laws shall be carried by a two-thirds majority.

ARTICLE III.
DEPUTIES TO CONVENTION.

Section 1.   Divisions and all kindred organizations, societies and orders subordinate to the Universal Negro Improvement Association and African Communities' League are entitled to representation in Convention; such divisions and societies sending a delegate or delegates, who shall be named deputies, as directed through the office of the President-General.

Sec. 2.   Each Deputy shall hold office for four years after election, and his office shall be honorary with his expenses paid for attending Convention by his own division, organization, society or order. He shall be entitled to one vote in Convention and no proxy shall be allowed.

ARTICLE IV.
OFFICIALS, OFFICERS, APPOINTMENTS AND ELECTIONS.

Section 1.   The Rulers of the Universal Negro Improvement Association and African Communities' League shall be a Potentate and Supreme Commissioner; a Supreme Deputy; a President General and High Commissioner; a Secretary General and High Commissioner; a High Chancellor; a Chaplain General; a Counsel General; a High Commissioner General; a Speaker in Convention and an International Organizer and High Commissioner, all of whom shall form the High Executive Council and all of whom shall be elected at the first Convention of the Universal Negro Improvement Association and African Communities' League, to be held immediately after branches or divisions of the organization shall have been established in the principal Negro Countries of the world, and all officials and officers shall hold office as herein specified.

Appointment of High Commissioners.

Sec. 2.   The Potentate and Supreme Commissioner shall appoint High Commissioners and commission them to represent the interests of the organization in all countries of the world, and they shall be controlled by the office of the High Commissioners-General.

Election of Divisional Officers.

Sec. 3.   Divisions and subordinate organizations shall elect their officers by majority vote to be approved of by the office of the Potentate and Supreme Commissioner.

Term of Office of Rulers.

Sec. 4. The term of office of the Potentate and Supreme Commissioner and that of the Supreme Deputy shall be permanent. Other officials shall hold permanent appointments, provided that their conduct conform with the interest of the Universal Negro Improvement Association and African Communities' League at all times.

ARTICLE V.
POTENTATE AND SUPREME COMMISSIONER.

Section 1. The Potentate and Supreme Commissioner shall be the invested ruler of the Universal Negro Improvement Association and African Communities' League and all its appendages. He shall be of Negro blood and race. He shall constitutionally control all affairs of the Association and League and all other societies. He shall institute social orders and societies and organizations in connection with the Universal Negro Improvement Association and African Communities' League, as determined by the said Association and League, and shall retain full power and control over their actions and jurisdiction. He shall have constitutional authority, through his high office, to suspend, reduce or relieve any officer other than the Supreme Deputy of his commission or authority of service to the Universal Negro Improvement Association and African Communities' League and subordinate orders, societies and organizations. He shall issue "articles" or "messages" from time to time to the entire body of members of the Universal Negro Improvement Association and African Communities' League on questions of moment and such "articles" and "messages" shall be respected by all those claiming allegiance to the Association and League. He shall appear in person to open the Convention and to deliver a speech which shall be called the "Potentate's Speech," and which shall be a review of the work and operations of the Association and League for the past year, as also advices for the conduct of affairs for the current or following year. He shall make his official residence at the place provided for him by the Universal Negro Improvement Association and African Communities' League. He shall marry only a lady of Negro blood and parentage, and his consort shall herself by virtue of her position be head of the female division of all organizations, societies and orders. He shall form an Executive Council to assist him in his administration out of the officials of the Universal Negro Improvement Association and African Communities' League and others elected by the Convention, and his colleagues shall be required to be loyal to him and to the Association and League. He shall be empowered to confer titles, honors, orders of merit, degrees, or marks of distinction on any person or persons who shall have rendered faithful service to the purposes of the Universal Negro Improvement Association and African Communities' League of whom he has been advised as being fit to bear such titles, honors, orders of merit, degrees or marks of distinction. He shall appoint or commission, through his office, any member or members to carry out any work in the interest of the Association and League. He shall be privileged to nominate his successor during his life time and that nomination shall be handed in a sealed envelope to the High Chancellor, who shall preserve same until the time of his death. At the time of his death his nomination shall be handed over to the Executive Council and the Executive Council shall make two other nominations before breaking the seal of the late Potentate's nomination; the nomination of the Executive Council shall be from among officials, officers, or distinguished members of the organization who have heretofore distinguished themselves in service to the Universal Negro Improvement Association and African Communities' League and whose honor, loyalty and devotion cannot be questioned. After breaking the seal of the Potentate's nomination the three nominations shall be announced to the world, and the Supreme Deputy shall call an immediate session of the Convention and then and there elect the new Potentate from the three nominees by majority vote and ballot. The election of a new Potentate shall take place two months after the demise of the former, and his investiture shall take place one month after his election. On the death of the Potentate, and on the election of another, his consort shall vacate the official residence for another to be provided by the Universal Negro Improvement Association and African Communities' League, which shall support her until her death or marriage to another party.

Sec. 2.   The Potentate's power of action in all matters shall be derived from the advice received from his Executive Council and through the officers of the Universal Negro Improvement Association and African Communities' League, which advice shall be expressive of the will and sentiment of the people, and he shall not be empowered to act in any matter of great moment without first receiving the advice of the Executive Council.

Sec. 3.   Immediately during the sitting of Convention of each year the Potentate and Supreme Commissioner shall cause to be given at his official residence or at some place of high moral and social repute an "at home" or "reception," which shall be called the "Court Reception," at which the Potentate and his Consort shall receive in presentation those distinguished ladies and gentlemen of the race and their male and female children whose character, morally and socially, stands above question in their respective communities. No lady below the age of eighteen shall be presented at the "Court Reception," and no gentleman below the age of twenty-one. No one shall be received by the Potentate and his Consort who has been convicted of crime or felony, or whose morality is not up to the standard of social ethics. No one shall pay money to be presented at Court, and no one shall be presented at Court who is not known to the President and General Secretary respectively, of the local division to which he or she belongs. All recommendations for social recognition shall be made through local divisions of the office of the High Commissioners General, who shall edit a list of "social eligibles" and present said list to the Potentate, who shall cause commands from his household to be issued to the respective parties to attend "Court Receptions." Recognition for social or other distinctions shall only be merited by previous service to the Universal Negro Improvement Association and African Communities' League by the person or persons to be honored, and no local division shall recommend anyone to be honored by the Potentate who has never done some praiseworthy or meritorious service to the organization in the carrying through of its objects, and all persons honored by the Potentate shall be so respected by all Negroes of all countries and climes.

Sec. 4. The Potentate and Supreme Commissioner and Supreme Deputy, should they at any time act contrary to the good and welfare of the Universal Negro Improvement Association and African Communities' League in refusing or neglecting to abide by or carry out the commands of the Association and League through its Constitution and through the order of its Convention shall, on proper evidence of the fact, be impeached by any member of the Executive Council through the office of the Counsel General, and they shall be tried for such irregularities, neglect, misconduct or disloyalty to the Association before the Convention, and if found guilty before the Convention by a two-thirds vote, they shall automatically forfeit the high office held by them, and the Convention shall take immediate steps to elect a new Potentate or Supreme Deputy.

Sec. 5. If the Potentate and Supreme Commissioner or the Supreme Deputy shall be charged or impeached before the Convention, the Counsel General shall prosecute them in the interest of the Universal Negro Improvement Association and African Communities' League, and the Potentate or Supreme Deputy shall have counsel to appear at the Bar of the Convention in his behalf, and such counsel shall be an active member or officer of the Universal Negro Improvement Association and African Communities' League.

Sec. 6. No Counsel excepting an Officer and active Member of the Universal Negro Improvement Association and African Communities' League shall be allowed to appear in behalf of any member charged before any "responsible body of trial" of the Association and League.

Sec. 7. Should the Potentate and Supreme Commissioner or Supreme Deputy take or receive moneys or gifts from any person or persons by way of bribes or rewards for neglecting or selling out the interests of the Universal Negro Improvement Association and African Communities' League, he shall be guilty of high crime against the Association and League, and on conviction before the Convention shall forthwith be disgraced and dismissed from the high office he holds.

Sec. 8. Any officer or official of the Universal Negro Improvement Association and African Communities' League charged and found guilty of a similar offense shall be forthwith dismissed from the office of the Association and League through the office of the Potentate or his or her Superior Officer, on the approval of the Executive Council.

Sec. 9.   No Officer or Official in the service of the Universal Negro Improvement Association and African Communities' League shall receive money or gifts on his or her account from anyone for services rendered for the Universal Negro Improvement Association and African Communities' League, but all such money and gifts shall be turned over to and shall be the property of the Universal Negro Improvement Association and African Communities League; but a purse or testimonial may be presented publicly to any Officer or Official on his or her own account as appreciation of faithful services performed for the Association and League.

Sec. 10.   All Officers, Officials and active Members of the Universal Negro Improvement Association and African Communities' League shall sign their names in approval and acceptance of the Constitution and By-Laws in a register provided for that purpose before they are installed into office.

Supreme Deputy.

Sec. 11.   The Supreme Deputy shall assist the Potentate in the discharge of his duties and shall perform the duties of the Potentate in his absence, incapacity or interregnum. He shall be the Potentate's special envoy to attend any function or ceremony that the Potentate may be unable to attend himself. He shall attend along with the Potentate the opening of convention and sit next to the Potentate. He shall be of Negro blood and his wife shall also be of Negro blood and parentage.

President General and Administrator.

Sec. 12.   The President General and Administrator shall be the working head of the Universal Negro Improvement Association and African Communities' League, and he shall be held responsible to the Potentate for the entire working and carrying out of all commands. He shall attend conventions and make a speech in reply to that of the Potentate. He shall instruct minor officers on their duties and see that such duties are properly performed.

Secretary General and High Commissioner.

Sec. 13.   The Secretary General and High Commissioner shall have in his custody all correspondence of the Universal Negro Improvement Association and African Communities' League. He shall have under control all divisional secretaries and shall conduct the general correspondence of the organization. He shall attend conventions and read reports and answer questions relative to the work of the organization. He shall be the spokesman of the Potentate and Executive Council in Convention.

High Chancellor.

Sec. 14. The High Chancellor shall be the custodian of the funds of the Universal Negro Improvement Association and African Communities' League and shall, under the direction of the President General, deposit all funds in some responsible bank. He shall give bond to the President General, which bond shall be well recognized. He shall attend convention and deliver the financial speech of the year.

Chaplain General.

Sec. 15. The Chaplain General shall be the spiritual adviser of the Potentate and Council. He shall act as the representative of the Universal Negro Improvement Association and African Communities' League in conducting the investiture of all high officials and at the conferring of titles, honors and degrees by the Potentate. He shall attend convention at its opening along with the Potentate and open the proceedings with prayers.

Counsel General.

Sec. 16. The Counsel General shall be the head legal officer of the Universal Negro Improvement Association and African Communities' League. He shall instruct all officials and officers of the Association on the law and shall conduct all cases or see to the defending of the Society before all courts of justice and appear on the Society's behalf at all times as directed by the President General.

High Commissioners General.

Sec. 17. The High Commissioners General shall be the head of the foreign High Commissioners. He shall receive their reports and report same to the Potentate and Executive Council. He shall recommend to the Potentate worthy individuals on whom commissions, titles, honors, social distinctions and degrees should be conferred.

Speaker in Convention.

Sec. 18. The Speaker in Convention shall be the chairman of the convention whose order and ruling shall be obeyed in convention according to the rules of debate. He shall prepare through his office all orders and arrangements for the convening of convention. During the rising of convention he shall receive all motions, resolutions, or matters to come before the convention which he shall have arranged in order for presentation.

International Organizer and High Commissioner.

Sec. 19.   The International Organizer and High Commissioner shall be charged with the duty of organizing all the Negro communities of the world into the Universal Negro Improvement Association and African Communities' League, and shall have under his control all local organizers who shall report to him monthly through the officers of their respective local divisions the results of their various organizing campaigns. He shall make periodic visits to all countries to ascertain and see to the proper bringing together of the world's corporate body of Negroes.

ARTICLE VI.
REQUIREMENTS OF OFFICIALS AND HIGH OFFICERS.

Section 1.   All officials and high officers of the Universal Negro Improvement Association and African Communities' League shall be Negroes and their consorts or wives shall be Negroes. No one shall be admitted to the high offices of the Association whose life companion is of an alien race.

Qualifications for Office.

Sec. 2.   The qualifications of candidates for office in the Universal Negro Improvement Association and African Communities' League shall be as follows: Registered active membership with all dues paid up; shall be a Negro; shall be proven as being conscientious to the cause of race uplift; shall not be married to anyone of alien race; shall be free from criminal conviction, and shall be of reputable moral standing and good education.

ARTICLE VII.
SALARIES AND EXPENSES.

Section 1.   The salary of the Potentate and Supreme Commissioner shall be in keeping with his high office and responsibilities, which salary shall be granted by the convention at its first sitting. The Potentate shall labor for the good and welfare of the organization, irrespective of salary or other consideration.

Sec. 2.   The Supreme Deputy shall be subjected to the same conditions on matter of salary as the Potentate.

Sec. 3.   All officials and officers of the Universal Negro Improvement Association and African Communities' League other than the Potentate and Supreme Commissioner and Supreme Deputy shall be granted salaries commensurate with the work they perform, which shall be voted by the convention.

Sec. 4.   Officers of local divisions who give their entire time to the working of their local divisions shall receive salaries for their services according to the ruling of the membership of such local division.

Transfers of Officers.

Sec. 5.   The President or any other officer of a local division in the pay of the Universal Negro Improvement Association and African Communities' League shall be subjected to annual, bi-annual or tri-annual transfers, according to the advices of the office of the Potentate and Executive Council.

ARTICLE VIII.
REVENUE, INCOMES, ETC.

Section 1.   The Revenue of the Universal Negro Improvement Association and African Communities' League shall be derived from monthly subscriptions which shall not be more than 25 cents per month, being authorized dues of each active member, donations, collections, gifts, profits derived from businesses, entertainments, functions or general amusements of an innocent nature.

Sec. 2.   The Revenue of the Universal Negro Improvement Association and African Communities' League shall be apportioned to the General Fund, which shall go to bear the general expenses of the organization for the carrying out of its objects.

Remitting of Monthly Dues by Local Divisions, Societies, Etc.

Sec. 3.   The Secretary of all divisions and subordinate organizations shall remit at the end of each month to the High Chancellor, through the Secretary-General, one-fifth of all monthly subscriptions, dues and net profits from local businesses under the control of the said division, as also from donations, grants, gifts, amusements, entertainments and other functions for the general fund of the Universal Negro Improvement Association and African Communities' League for the carrying out of its general objects.

Sec. 4.   All moneys of the Universal Negro Improvement Association and African Communities' League shall be lodged by the Chancellor in a responsible bank and drawn only on the signatures of the President General, the High Chancellor and Secretary General.

Sec. 5.   The Potentate and Supreme Commissioner shall be empowered to make donations of charity to be created from the Charitable Fund of the Universal Negro Improvement Association and African Communities' League, to worthy causes in the name of the Association and League, with the approval of the Executive Council.

Investing of Money.

Sec. 6.   The Universal Negro Improvement Association and African Communities' League and all its divisions and allied societies may invest money in any business which to the best judgment of the members of the organization are of such as to yield profit in the interest of the Association.

Sec. 7.   No investment in money or stocks shall be made by a local division or society without the consent of the membership of the said division or society.

Sec. 8.   No division shall allow any of its officers or members to use the meetings of the organization for selling stocks or shares in any personal or private concern, and any such officer or member found guilty of such offense shall be suspended for three months.

Sec. 9.   The Universal Negro Improvement Association and African Communities' League may invest its money wholly or in company with others for the good of the organization.

Sec. 10.   The Funds of the Universal Negro Improvement Association and African Communities' League as derived from all sources herein mentioned shall be used for the carrying out of the objects of the Association.

ARTICLE IX.
MEMBERSHIP.

Section 1.   All persons of Negro blood and African descent are regarded as ordinary members of the Universal Negro Improvement Association and African Communities' League, and are entitled to the consideration of the organization. Active members are those who pay the monthly dues for the upkeep of the organization, who shall have first claim on the Association for all benefits to be dispensed.

GENERAL LAWS
ARTICLE I.
CONVENTIONS.

Section 1.   The Convention of the Universal Negro Improvement Association and African Communities' League shall assemble at 1 o'clock P.M. on the first day of meeting at the headquarters building of the society set apart for that purpose, at which the Potentate and all high officers of the Association shall attend in official robes and attire. After the opening of convention the convention shall meet at 10.30 A.M. and adjourn at 10 o'clock P.M. The Potentate and Supreme Deputy shall not attend convention after its opening and after the Potentate's speech shall have been delivered. The Convention shall be held in the first week of January of each year.

Sec. 2.   No person other than officials, officers and delegates will be allowed the privilege of the floor in convention.

Sec. 3. No one shall be admitted to the Convention but a member of the Universal Negro Improvement Association and African Communities' League except on recommendation from a High Official of the Association and League. Visitors who are members of the Association may be admitted to the Visitors' Gallery by receiving a pass from the Sergeant-at-Arms, but no one shall be admitted except on a pass, to be produced at entrance.

Sec. 4. The following obligation shall be administered by the Chaplain-General to the several elected and appointed representatives and delegates before they shall enter upon their respective duties on the first day of convention: I solemnly pledge my word and honor in the presence of this convention assembled, and Almighty God, that I will, to the best of my ability, discharge the duties devolving and incumbent upon me as a member of this convention, and be loyal to the organization, the Potentate, his high office and his sacred charge—so help me God.

ARTICLE II.
ELECTING OF DEPUTIES TO CONVENTION.

Section 1. No member of a division or subordinate society shall be eligible for election as a deputy to convention unless he or she shows special qualities of interest in the uplift of the race and the progress of the Association.

Sec. 2. The election of deputies to convention shall be left entirely to divisions and subordinate societies except as hereinbefore mentioned.

Sec. 3. Divisions and subordinate societies shall send one deputy to convention representative of each one thousand members in good standing, but no division shall have more than five deputies in convention.

Sec. 4. Divisions and subordinate societies not having more than a thousand members and not less than five hundred shall send one deputy to represent their interests in convention.

Sec. 5. Divisions and subordinate societies with less than two hundred paying members shall request of the nearest division that has a deputy to have that deputy represent its interests in convention.

Sec. 6. Each division or society shall bear the expense of its own deputies.

Sec. 7. Two or more divisions with less than five hundred paying members each may join together and elect a deputy and pay his expenses jointly.

Sec. 8. Wherever local divisions or societies are sending deputies to convention they shall instruct the said deputies to bring up before the convention such motions, resolutions, general suggestions or motions of amendment as such local divisions or societies shall have decided upon and of which they shall have notified the office of the Speaker in Convention two months previous to the sitting of convention, and which notices of motions, resolutions, general suggestions and motions of amendment shall be printed on the general order of proceedings for the convention.

ARTICLE III.
EXECUTIVE COUNCIL.

Section 1. The Executive Council of the Universal Negro Improvement Association and African Communities' League shall assemble at the headquarters of the Association and shall consist of all the high officers of the Association and others elected thereto. The Potentate shall be its Chairman and the Secretary General its Secretary. It shall decide all questions arising between divisions and subordinate societies, appeals, international questions and all matters affecting the good and welfare of the organization and its members at large during the rising of convention.

ARTICLE IV.
AUDITING ACCOUNTS.

Section 1. The President General shall cause the books and accounts of the High Chancellor and subordinate officers to be audited twice a year as follows: All accounts for the six months ending July 31st within 15 days after that date, and for same period ending January 31st, within 15 days after that date. For this purpose he shall appoint an expert accountant, who shall make a thorough examination and shall submit a report to the President General, who shall cause its publication in the regular journal of the society.

Sec. 2. If said report should show any errors of importance or defalcation or misappropriation of funds of any officer, so responsible, it shall be the duty of the President General, with the consent of the Potentate, to suspend such officer or officers, and he shall instruct the Counsel General to proceed at once, legally, to secure the Universal Negro Improvement Association and African Communities' League from loss, and in accordance with the bond or bonds of said officer or officers.

Fiscal Year.

Sec. 3. The fiscal year of the Universal Negro Improvement Association and African Communities' League shall commence on the first day of June and end on the 31st day of May in each year.

ARTICLE V.
JURISDICTION AND CHARTERS.

Section 1. The jurisdiction of divisions and subordinate societies chartered by the Universal Negro Improvement Association and African Communities' League shall extend within the corporate limits of the country, state, province or township named in the charter.

Sec. 2.   Charters shall be granted to seven or more members of the Negro race in any country, state or province, providing such charter members display sufficient intelligence as to safeguard the interests of the society.

Officers of Local Divisions.

Sec. 3.   Every chartered division shall elect its own officers with the approval of the President General. The Executive Officers shall be a President, a First Vice-President, a Second Vice-President, a Third Vice-President, a President of the Ladies' Division, a First Vice-President, a Second Vice-President, a Third Vice-President, an Executive Secretary, a General Secretary, an Associate Secretary, a General Secretary of the Ladies' Division, and an Associate Secretary, a Treasurer, an Assistant Treasurer (the Assistant Treasurer shall be a lady), a Chaplain, and a Board of Trustees. There shall also be an Advisory Board, consisting of twenty-five persons elected from the general membership, the Executive Officers to be ex-officios of the Board. Only divisions with more than three hundred members shall be allowed to carry all the officers herein named. Divisions with less than three hundred members shall only carry the necessary officers for working conveniences.

Male President.

Sec. 4.   The Male President of each local division shall be responsible to the parent body of the Universal Negro Improvement Association and African Communities' League for the successful working of his division, branches, societies and orders under his jurisdiction. He shall see that all officers under his charge perform their duties, and in case of irregularities he shall exercise over his jurisdiction the right that the President General exercises over the general body. He shall preside at all general meetings of the Association.

Lady President.

Sec. 5.   The Lady President shall be given control of all those departments of the organization over which she may be able to exercise better control than the Male President, and she shall have the right to preside over any meeting called by her on the approval of the general membership, but all her reports shall be submitted to the Male President for presentation to the general membership. Each local division shall arrange the department of the organization that shall be especially controlled or supervised by the Male and Female Presidents, respectively.

Sec. 6.   The Male President shall be held responsible to the Convention and to the President General for the constitutional workings of his division.

Vice-Presidents.

Sec. 7. Vice-Presidents of the Male and Female divisions shall perform those duties assigned them by the Presidents of their respective divisions on the approval of the general membership, and the First Vice-Presidents shall perform the duties of the Presidents in their absence.

Secretaries.

Sec. 8. The Secretaries shall perform those duties assigned them by the Presidents and arranged for by the membership of their local divisions in their By-Laws, which duties shall not conflict with the laws of the Constitution. All Financial Secretaries shall be bonded.

Treasurers.

Sec. 9. The Treasurer and the Assistant Treasurer of each local division, branch, society or order of the Universal Negro Improvement Association shall receive from the Secretaries all moneys for the Association and hand over such money to the Trustees, or lodge same in the bank designated by the Association. They shall be bonded.

Trustee Board.

Sec. 10. The Trustee Board of each division shall consist of five persons with a Chairman and Secretary, the Chairman to be its Treasurer. The Trustees shall see that all moneys of the Association is lodged in some responsible bank and not drawn from the said bank except on the proper order of the membership of the division through its accepted By-Laws. The Trustees shall also have under their control the properties and real estate of the local divisions, and shall see that no one abuses the rights of such properties or estate. The chairman of the board shall be bonded.

The Honorable Advisory Board.

Sec. 11. The Advisory Board of a division shall have a Chairman and a Secretary. The board shall be a "clearing house" for all disputes, suggestions, appeals, recommendations and business matters referred thereto by the President or general membership before they are brought finally to the general body for action. The Advisory Board shall also be referred to as the Honorable Advisory Board. Any member of the Honorable Advisory Board who shall be charged and found guilty of bribery for selling the interests of the Association shall be forthwith discharged from the Honorable Advisory Board by the President. Members shall be elected to the Honorable Advisory Board from the general membership. If any member of the Honorable Advisory Board fails to attend two consecutive meetings the Chairman shall instruct the Secretary to inform the President through the Executive Secretary, and the President shall declare the member's seat vacant.

Declaring Offices Vacant.

Sec. 12.   It shall be the prerogative of the Male President only to declare an office vacant on the breach of the Constitution by any officer, or discharge a committee or its Chairman.

Term of Office of Local Divisions.

Sec. 13.   The term of office of each officer of a local division shall be three years, after which time said officer may be transferred or re-elected to his or her position.

Suspended or dismissed officers shall have no right or claim to promotion, transfer or re-election to office, and this shall not be interpreted to mean officers whose positions might have been declared vacant by non-attendance at two consecutive meetings.

By-Laws of Local Divisions.

Sec. 13a.   Divisions and subordinate societies may enact by-laws for their own government, providing the by-laws do not conflict with the Constitution and General Laws of the Universal Negro Improvement Association and African Communities' League, and such by-laws shall be submitted to the Secretary General of the Universal Negro Improvement Association and African Communities' League before its final adoption.

Committees of Management.

Sec. 14.   Chartered divisions are at liberty to appoint local committees of management to carry through the various objects of the society.

Transmitting of Reports.

Sec. 15.   Divisions and subordinate societies are obliged to transmit and make returns of all their funds to the office of the President General of the Universal Negro Improvement Association and African Communities' League, on whom it is incumbent to administer the working of local divisions irrespective of local financial considerations.

Sec. 16.   No division shall admit to active membership any person other than a Negro.

Sec. 17.   Every member of a division shall be expected to be loyal and truthful to the dictates of the Universal Negro Improvement Association and African Communities' League, and the Potentate and Supreme Commission.

Discussing the Business of the Association.

Sec. 18.   It shall be unlawful for any officer or member of the Universal Negro Improvement Association and African Communities' League to discuss the business of the Association in public or with persons who are not active members, and anyone so charged and found guilty by the Advisory Board of the division to which he or she shall belong shall forfeit his office, if an officer, and shall be suspended from the meetings of the division for three months if an active member and all charges against officers and members of a division shall be made before the Advisory Board, and the Advisory Board shall recommend to the general membership the removal of the officer or member so charged and found guilty.

Appeal to Executive Council.

Sec. 19.   If an officer shall have been removed from office by a local division for disloyalty to the organization, the secretary of the local division shall make immediate report to the President General of the entire proceedings. The officer so removed may make appeal to the Executive Council, which shall judge the appeal from the evidence given at the trial before the Advisory Board of the local division.

Plotting of Members and Officers.

Sec. 20.   Any officer or member accused of plotting against fellow officers and members of a division shall, on conviction before the Advisory Board, be removed from office and suspended for three months from active membership by the President.

Certificate of Membership.

Sec. 21.   All members of divisions shall be provided with a certificate of membership which shall set forth in brief the purpose of the organization.

Relationship of Members.

Sec. 22.   Every member of the Universal Negro Improvement Association and African Communities' League is by fraternity admitted to the brotherhood in race, and is therefore requested to treat each and every one of the race in the truest spirit of friendship and affection, and to do all that lies in his or her power to advance the cause of Afric.

Respect to Officers.

Sec. 23.   All members of the Universal Negro Improvement Association and African Communities' League are requested to show all due respect to the officers of the organization who exercise temporary power and authority in connection with the organization.

Insubordination.

Sec. 24. No officer or member is supposed to be insubordinate to those in higher authority.

Control Over Local Divisions.

Sec. 25. The Potentate and Supreme Commissioner, through his office, shall have complete constitutional control over all divisions and societies allied to the parent body of which he is the recognized head.

Presidents' Reports.

Sec. 26. The presidents of local divisions and societies shall see that their secretaries make the proper monthly reports to the office of the President General.

Sec. 27. Any division or subordinate society failing to make its monthly report to the office of the President General for two consecutive months shall forfeit its charter and the President General shall, through his office, proceed forthwith to re-establish jurisdiction over the said division or society by a re-election or appointment of new officers for its administration.

Death Tax.

Sec. 28. A death tax of 10 cents per month shall be levied on each member, which shall be separate and distinct from the regular monthly dues, and the death tax so levied by each local division or society shall be forwarded to the Secretary General of the Universal Negro Improvement Association and African Communities' League to be lodged to the credit of the Association's death fund; and on the death of a member who has paid up his or her last month's complete dues a sum of seventy-five dollars shall be granted from the death fund for his or her burial.

Arrears.

Sec. 29. No member in arrears for two months for general dues shall be entitled to receive the seventy-five dollars death grant.

Payment of Death Grants.

Sec. 30. No death grants shall be paid until a member shall have paid six months' general dues as an active member of the Association.

Sec. 31. Local divisions may advance the death grant from their treasury to facilitate immediate payment and then collect same from the office of the Secretary General of the Universal Negro Improvement Association and African Communities' League.

Death of Member.

Sec. 32.   Each local division and society shall on the death of an active member to whom death grant is due levy an extra tax of five cents on each member, to be collected immediately, which tax shall form a part of the seventy-five dollars to be paid by the Universal Negro Improvement Association and African Communities' League, and this extra tax shall be forwarded to the Secretary General to be lodged in the Death Fund.

Sec. 33.   A member's card shall be supplied each member of a division or society of the Universal Negro Improvement Association and African Communities' League and on that card shall be entered, month by month, the monthly payment of dues and death tax of the member.

Honorary Membership Cards.

Sec. 34.   All divisions and societies of the Universal Negro Improvement Association and African Communities' League shall honor the membership card of another division and give credit to the member for all payments made to the other division of which he or she was first a member.

Removal of Members.

Sec. 35.   On the removal of a member from one country, province, state, city or town to another, he shall obtain from the Secretary of his or her division a recommendation card to the Secretary of the division to which he removes, and such Secretary and his division shall do all in his or her power to assist the member as a stranger in their midst.

Sec. 36.   All officers and members of the Universal Negro Improvement Association and African Communities' League shall maintain a brotherly and friendly attitude toward one another and shall be ever willing to lend a helping hand in time of need and distress to a fellow member.

Colors.

Sec. 37.   The colors of the Universal Negro Improvement Association and African Communities' League shall be red, black and green.

Sec. 38.   Each member of the Universal Negro Improvement Association and African Communities' League shall wear on his coat or her blouse a button representative of the colors of the organization so as to be distinguished as an active member and to merit the respect and consideration of other members.

Respectability of Officers.

Sec. 39.   All officers of divisions and societies of the Universal Negro Improvement Association and African Communities' League shall be required to maintain a high order of respectability, and any officer found drunk, immoral, dishonest or disorderly in public shall be called upon by the President, and on conviction before the Advisory Board, to resign forthwith his office in the organization.

Misappropriation of Money.

Sec. 40.   No officer or member of the Universal Negro Improvement Association and African Communities' League shall retain in his possession funds or moneys intended for the Universal Negro Improvement Association and African Communities' League, and any officer or member found misappropriating the funds of the organization shall be forthwith dismissed from the service of the organization and legal proceedings taken against him to recover moneys thus misappropriated, and the President of each division shall see to the carrying out of this law.

Non-Selling of Stocks or Shares.

Sec. 41.   No officer or member of a division shall, be allowed to sell private stocks or solicit shares for any individual or private company at a meeting of the Universal Negro Improvement Association and African Communities' League.

Investing in Stocks by Local Divisions.

Sec. 42.   Each local division of the Universal Negro Improvement Association and African Communities' League through its Advisory Board may recommend to its members the taking of stocks or interest in any company or corporation whose capital, financial standing and state or national guarantee is of such as to insure the safety of such investment, but no recommendation shall be made until the Advisory Board shall have made proper investigation into the working of the company or corporation and shall then be assured of its sound standing and good possibilities.

Sec. 43.   Divisions or societies of the Universal Negro Improvement Association and African Communities' League may invest their money in self-owned business of any description or take shares in any company or corporation of good standing yielding sufficient profit as to encourage investment and whose outlook promises well.

Profits from Investments.

Section 44.   All profits derived from investments by local divisions or societies of the Universal Negro Improvement Association and African Communities' League shall go to the general fund of the local division or society to be used as hereinbefore ordered.

Auditing Accounts of Local Divisions.

Sec. 45. All local divisions and societies of the Universal Negro Improvement Association and African Communities' League shall have their accounts audited in the same way as the general body, as hereinbefore stated, and such accounts shall be presented to the office of the President General at the close of every financial year.

Charitable Fund of Local Divisions.

Sec. 46. Each local division or society shall maintain a charitable fund for the purpose of assisting distressed members or needy individuals of the race.

Loans to Members.

Sec. 47. Each local division shall maintain a fund for rendering ready assistance by way of loans of honor to active members who may be temporarily embarrassed, which loans shall be repaid with or without interest at the earliest convenience of the member, according to the ruling of the local division.

Employment Bureau.

Sec. 48. Each local division shall maintain an employment bureau for the purpose of finding employment for members of the Universal Negro Improvement Association and African Communities' League.

Building.

Sec. 49. Each local division shall maintain as far as possible a building of its own (rented, leased, or purchased), and shall maintain a general office, and shall hold a general meeting every Sunday afternoon from 3 to 6 o'clock over which the Presidents shall preside. Meetings shall also be held in the evenings of week days.

General Meetings.

Sec. 50. All divisions of more than five hundred members shall call a fortnightly general meeting, other than Sunday, for the purpose of keeping the members together.

Absent Officers.

Sec. 51. Any officer of a local division who should absent himself or herself from two consecutive meetings of the division without leave of absence shall automatically forfeit his or her office, and the division shall forthwith elect a successor.

Publishing of Reports.

Sec. 52.   All elections, changes, notices, news or reports of divisions or societies shall be published in the weekly journal of the Universal Negro Improvement Association and African Communities' League.

Journal.

Sec. 53.   The Universal Negro Improvement Association and African Communities' League shall publish a weekly journal for circulation among all Negroes, and each division and society shall be responsible for its proper distribution and circulation.

Sec. 54.   The Journal of the Universal Negro Improvement Association and African Communities' League shall be the official mouthpiece of the organization, and the editor or editors shall see and so provide that nothing contrary to the interests of the organization appears therein.

Sec. 55.   Each and every member of the Universal Negro Improvement Association and African Communities' League shall be a regular subscriber to the weekly journal of the organization, and the subscription for the journal shall be separate and distinct from monthly dues and taxes.

Right to Question.

Sec. 56.   Each member of a division or society shall, by right of membership, question the action of any officer or officers or the division as a whole doing anything contrary to the Constitution and General Laws of the Universal Negro Improvement Association and African Communities' League.

Local Organizers.

Sec. 57.   Each country that holds a general charter from the Universal Negro Improvement Association and African Communities' League shall appoint its own local organizers, whose duties it shall be to organize divisions within the said country on the authority of the office of the International Organizer.

Music.

Sec. 58.   Each division shall maintain a band of music or orchestra which shall be used at all meetings or gatherings of the organization in whole or in part, as also a well organized choir.

HYMN FOR OPENING OF MEETING.

FROM GREENLAND'S ICY MOUNTAINS

From Greenland's icy mountains,
   From India's coral strand,
Where Afric's sunny fountains
   Roll down their golden sand;
From many an ancient river,
   From many a palmy plain,
They call us to deliver
   Their land from error's chain.

II.

Shall we whose souls are lighted
   With wisdom from on high,
Shall we to men benighted
   The lamp of life deny?
Salvation, O Salvation,
   The joyful sounds proclaim,
Till earth's remotest nation
   Has learned Messiah's name.

III.

Waft, waft, ye winds His story,
   And you, ye waters, roll,
Till, like a sea of glory,
   It spreads from pole to pole.
Till o'er our ransomed nature
   The Lamb for sinners slain,
Redeemer, King, Creator,
   In bliss returns to reign.

PRAYER FOR OPENING OF MEETING.
DEDICATED TO THE UNIVERSAL NEGRO
IMPROVEMENT ASSOCIATION OF THE WORLD.
BY JOHN E. BRUCE-GRIT.

A PRAYER.

Not by might, nor by power, but by
   my spirit, saith the Lord of Hosts.—Zach. 4, v.

God of the right our battles fight,
   Be with us as of yore,
Break down the barriers of might,
   We rev'rently implore.

II.

Stand with us in our struggles for
    The triumph of the right,
And spread confusion ever o'er
    The advocates of might.

And let them know that righteousness
    [Is] mightier than sin,
That might is only selfishness
    And cannot, ought not, win.

III.

Endow us, Lord, with faith and grace,
    And courage to endure
The wrongs we suffer here apace,
    And bless us evermore.

PARTING HYMN FOR JUVENILES.

NOW THE DAY IS OVER.

Now the day is over,
    Night is drawing nigh,
Shadows of the evening
    Steal across the sky.

Jesus, give the weary
    Calm and sweet repose;
With Thy tend'rest blessing,
    May our eyelids close.

Grant to little children
    Visions bright of Thee;
Guard the sailors, tossing
    On the deep blue sea.

When the morning wakens,
    Then may I arise
Pure and fresh and sinless,
    In Thy holy eyes.

NATIONAL ANTHEM OF UNIVERSAL NEGRO IMPROVEMENT ASSOCIATION AND AFRICAN COMMUNITIES' LEAGUE—[5] TO BE SUNG ON ALL OCCASIONS.

Ethiopia, thou land of our fathers,
Thou land where the gods loved to be:

REFRAIN.

As storm cloud at night sudden gathers,
Our armies come rushing to thee.

Shall we in the fight be victorious
When swords are thrust outward to glean?
For us will the vic'try be glorious
When led by the red, black and green?

CHORUS.

Advance, advance to victory!
Let Africa be free!
Advance to meet the foe
With the might
Of the red, the black, the green.

Shall aliens continue to spoil us?
Shall despots continue their greed?

REFRAIN.

Will nations in mock'ry revile us?
Then our keen swords intercede!
And tremblings shall fall on the nations,
As eyes of mankind hath not seen,
Defeat shall meet their preparations,
And vic'try the red, black and green.
And when the great battle is ended,
The swords and the spears be laid down:

REFRAIN.

The land which their might had defended,
Shall once more become as our own.
And peace and prosperity bless us,
Our standard shall float far above us:
With warfare nor sorrow between us;
The red, and the black, and the green.

When Making Your
Will
Remember the
UNIVERSAL NEGRO IMPROVE-
MENT ASSOCIATION AND
AFRICAN COMMUNITIES'
LEAGUE
and its Objects

Bequeath Something to This
Organization to Help in
the Redemption of
the Race

DNA, RG 165, File 10218-261/52. Printed pamphlet; however, no publication data was supplied.

1. Later revised and amended, August 1920, August 1921, and August 1922.
2. Garvey later explained that the preamble "was written particularly for the purpose of winning the sympathy and support of alien races where the other objects of the association were being threatened through hostility" ("History of the UNIA," lesson 20, "School of African Philosophy," p. 2). Garvey further instructed his adherents on the preamble's use: "Whenever the purpose of the organization is challenged by foes particularly, quote the preamble of the Constitution. This should be done particularly where its enemies assail it before a Court of Law or before Governmental Authorities."
3. Cf., "For he hath regarded the low estate of the handmaiden: for, behold, from henceforth all generations shall call me blessed." (Luke 1:48).
4. The UNIA's ceremonial hymn sung at the opening of meetings. The hymn was originally written in 1701 for the Society for the Propagation of the Gospel in Foreign Parts at the time of its founding. It later became a popular hymn among black denominations.
5. Renamed in 1920 the "Universal Ethiopian Anthem." In the Declaration of Independence of the Negro Race, adopted at the UNIA convention of August 1920, article 40 resolved that the anthem "shall be considered the anthem of the Negro race." The lyrics were written by Benjamin E. Burrell and Arnold J. Ford; the music was composed by Ford.

Bureau of Investigation Report[1]

N.Y. City [*Made*] S[ep]t. 18th
[*for the period of*] Sept. 9th [*1918*]

In Re: Negro Agitators of the 3rd Precinct.

Capt. Ward[2] of the 3rd Precinct Police Station today sent me confidential employee of his, who has been attending street meetings of negro agitators in the Harlem negro district (7th Ave. above 125th St.).

Informant turned over to me a report,[3] which he had made containing an abstract of the remarks of the speakers on various evenings at these street corner meetings. He also gave me a copy of the "Negro World"[4] a newspaper whose editor has been active in speech making on the street corner. I turned all these papers over to Mr. Stephenson of this office with the request that he examine them carefully and advise me if he deemed the matter of sufficient importance to warrant further action on the part of this office.

S. B. PFEIFER

DNA, RG 65, File OG 258421. TD.

1. The Bureau of Investigation was organized in 1908 as an agency of the Department of Justice. Its original function was to investigate a wide range of criminal acts, particularly violations of land fraud and antitrust laws. During its first few years, the bureau mainly employed Treasury Department agents who had also worked for the Department of Justice. Although the 1910 White Slave Traffic Act (also known as the Mann Act) led to an increase in size, the bureau had only 141 employees as of 1914. The First World War, however, radically changed the bureau's nature and size. In July 1916 an explosion on Black Tom Island in New York harbor accelerated the bureau's growing tendency to investigate immigrants with ethnic ties to Germany and its allies. Following the U.S. entry into the war in April 1917, the bureau began a massive investigation of so-called aliens, radicals, and subversives, strictly enforcing the provisions of the broadly expanded Espionage Act. Under Attorney General A. Mitchell Palmer, the bureau also became involved in strikebreaking and other antilabor activities. The bureau's name was formally changed to the Federal Bureau of Investigation in 1935. (Max Lowenthal, *The Federal Bureau of Investigation* [New York: William Sloane Assoc., 1950]; David Williams, "The Federal Bureau of Investigation and its Critics, 1919–1921: The Origins of Federal Surveillance," *Journal of American History* 68 [December 1981]: 560–79).

2. Captain William Ward was the commander of the West 135th Street station in Harlem; he was later transferred in November 1918 to the East 25th Street station in New York for reportedly having been too lenient in the face of the many skirmishes in Harlem between black soldiers and white sailors. (*NW*, 30 November 1918).

3. A copy of this report has not been found.

4. The *Negro World* began publication on Saturday, 3 August 1918.

Newspaper Reports

[*Chicago Defender*,[1] 28 September 1918]

REPORTER SUES GARVEY

Marcus M. Garvey, editor of a little weekly paper[2] is being sued for wages due to Anselmo Jackson,[3] 23, 54 West 140th Street. Jackson, a well-known newspaper writer and reporter, was engaged by Garvey, so it is alleged, to do reporting work for his little sheet. For this service Jackson claims Garvey still owes him, hence the suit that was brought in Seventh District court.

Printed in the *Chicago Defender*, Saturday, 28 September 1918.

1. The *Chicago Defender*, founded by Robert Sengstacke Abbott (1870–1940) in 1905, grew from a few copies of handbill size into the largest black newspaper in the United States by 1920.

2. A reference to the *Negro World*.

3. Anselmo R. Jackson (b. 1896) was born in Frederickstadt, St. Croix, Danish West Indies. In November 1918 Jackson became associate editor of the *Crusader*; later in 1920 he served as contributing editor to the *Emancipator*, the short-lived weekly newspaper which W. A. Domingo edited after his break with Garvey. Jackson also edited his own publication, *Our Boys and Girls*. (AFRC, RG 163, registration card).

[*Chicago Defender*, 2 November 1918]

MARCUS GARVEY SUED AGAIN.

Marcus M. Garvey, who is still getting out a little two-page paper in Harlem, was again sued by a former employee for wages recently. Dorothy Hensen, 228 West 141st street, is the plaintiff in the suit this time, which was filed Oct. 17 in the Seventh Municipal District Court. Only recently Anselmo Jackson sued Garvey and obtained a judgment against him in the same court.

Printed in the *Chicago Defender*, Saturday, 2 November 1918.

Marcus Garvey to Nicholas Murray Butler

New York, November 5, 1918

My dear Sir:

On the instruction of my Association I am requested to make the following request of you:

Owing to recent developments arising out of the war conflict in Europe, wherein all the oppressed peoples of the world are endeavoring to formulate and present their just claims to the Peace Conference to be held after the war, we, of the Universal Negro Improvement Association, representing the spirit and aspirations of the new Negro of this Western Hemisphere, have determined to also formulate and submit to the Conference our plans for the future government of our struggling and oppressed race.

In conformity with this, we are to hold a Universal Convention of Negroes in the Palace Casino, 135th Street and Madison Avenue, New York City on Sunday night the 10th of November at 8.30 o'clock. Our Association, holding you in the highest regard as a public character in this country commands me to ask if you will be good enough to honor us with your attendance at this Convention, and to say a few words for us. If you will be unable to attend the Convention we ask that you be good enough to send us a message expressive of your feelings toward us as a struggling race. Please be good enough to let your reply reach us not later than Friday the 8th, so that we can expect you or receive your message on that date. Feeling sure that you will countenance this as coming from a race that holds you in the highest appreciation, Yours Respectfully,

MARCUS GARVEY
President
Universal Negro Improvement Association

MG/EM

[*Endorsement*] RECEIVED NOV 6 1918
COLUMBIA UNIVERSITY SECRETARY'S
OFFICE

NNC, NMB. TLS, Recipient's copy. Stamped endorsement. A similar invitation was also sent to Theodore Roosevelt.

Nicholas Murray Butler to Marcus Garvey

[*New York City*] November 6, 1918

Dear Sir:

I am most happy to make prompt reply to your letter of November 5, for although I am to be out of town on the 10th of November and cannot therefore attend your meeting in person, I am deeply interested in it and in the cause which it is to promote.

It will not do for us as a people to fix our eyes upon wrong and injustice when done to those who dwell in other lands, and to close our eyes to wrong and injustice done to those who are our own fellow Americans and fellow citizens. I cannot but think that the very principles which have animated our nation in sharing the burdens and the dangers of this war against autocracy and oppression and in helping to bring it to a successful issue, will lead our people to do full justice—economic, social and political—to the millions among us who are negroes. With best wishes for the success of your meeting, I am, Very truly yours,

NICHOLAS MURRAY BUTLER

W

NNC, NMB. TLR, Carbon copy.

Announcement in the *New York Call*[1]

[7 November 1918]

NEGROES OF THE WORLD TO HOLD CONVENTION FOR RACE'S WAR AIMS

An open convention of the Negroes of the world—of America, Africa and the West Indies—will be held in the Palace casino, 135th street and Madison avenue, next Sunday evening [*10 November*] at 8:30 o'clock, when the Universal Negro Improvement association and the African Communities league, a worldwide Negro organization, will submit to the assembled Negroes the peace conference demands and belated war aims of the Negroes of the world.

Several prominent Negroes and white friends will address the meeting, to which the public is invited.

Printed in the *New York Call*, Thursday, 7 November 1918.

1. The *New York Call* was the official organ of the Socialist party. In its issue of 16 November 1918, it reported the UNIA meeting of 10 November 1918 with the headline, "Negroes Ask Recognition, Self-Determination Principle Should Be Applied to Africa, urges Racial League" (clipping enclosed in a letter from Lt. Col. Nicholas Biddle to Brig. Gen. Marlborough Churchill, 18 November 1918, DNA, RG 165, file 10218–255/2 2-1).

Bureau of Investigation Reports

NEW YORK CITY [*Made*] Nov. 12th 1918.
[*for the period of*] Nov. 9th [*1918*]

IN RE: MARCUS GARVEY, Negro Propaganda.

Pursuant to instructions of Special Agent Blatchford based on circular furnished by Special Agent Finch[1] to the effect that there would be a mass meeting on Sunday evening November 10th at the *Palace Casino, 135th Street and Madison Avenue*, I this day endeavored to learn who was promoting the mass meeting, the object of it being held. I first visited the vicinity of the colored district which extends from about 130th Street to 145th Street taking in 5th, Lenox and 7th Avenue. I discovered, through a negro publication, "THE NEGRO WORLD," that the meeting was being held under the auspices of the *Universal Negro Improvement Assn.*, with headquarters at 36 and 38 West 135th St. I also learned that *Marcus Garvey*, who is the managing editor of the "Negro World" also bears the title of *International Organizer of the Universal Negro Improvement Assn.* I also ascertained from inquiries made in the neighborhood among colored confidential informants that this man Marcus Garvey had devoted almost every night during the summer to public speaking on the corner of 134th St. and Lenox Ave. These meetings have been the source of much complaint on the ground that they were bearing on sedition. "The Negro World" is published at the above address and is presumed to be devoted to the general uplifting of the negro race. I shall continue this investigation and attend the meet to be held tomorrow night.

D. DAVIDSON

DWM

[*Endorsement*] Noted F. D. W.

DNA, RG 65, File OG 329359. TD. Stamped endorsement. Copy of report furnished to Special Agent Finch.

1. Raymond W. Finch was the chief investigator of the New York State Legislature Joint Committee to Investigate Seditious Activities, which was known as the Lusk committee.

New York City [*Made*] Nov. 12, 1918
[*for the period of*] Nov. 9th [*1918*]

IN RE: NEGRO AGITATION Socialist activities.

. . . A convention of negroes was held, at which certain demands were formulated for presentation to the Allies at the peace conference, which resolutions we understand are to be cabled to Europe. Marcus Garvey spoke, claiming that he represented the West Indies faction. His speech bordered closely on sedition in that he prophesied a revolution of the negroes in the United States unless their demands were granted. This man's nationality and antecedents will be closely investigated, and should it be found that he is not a citizen of the U.S., an effort will be made to locate stenographic minutes of this meeting for the purpose of taking up questions of disposing of Garvey, who could easily become a menace in these times.[1]

In addition to the demands which were drawn up yesterday for submission to the peace conference, we believe this organization constitutes not so great a menace as a separate organization as it does in the position of another one of those organizations which could very easily become affiliated with other Organizations, which combined, would certainly become a menace. An effort on the part [o]f the Socialist Party of this city to create as much trouble and unrest as possible, is one exam[p]le of how this negro organization could become affiliated with a number of organizations for the purpose of concerted action.

This organization's movements will be followed from time to time, and reports sent to the Bureau. Special Agent Davidson of this Dept. has attended the convention yesterday at Harlem Casino, N.Y., and his report will be made separately.

R. W. FINCH

MJD

DNA, RG 65, File OG 258421. TD, Carbon copy.

1. A reference to the deportation provisions of the Alien Act, which was approved by Congress on 16 October 1918. The act decreed that all aliens who were anarchists, or who believed in the violent overthrow of the American government, or advocated the assassination of officials, should be barred from entering the United States. In addition, the act decreed that "any alien who, at any time after entering the United States, is found to have been at the time of entry or to have become thereafter, a member of any of the classes of aliens [above mentioned] . . . shall upon warrant of the secretary of labor, be taken into custody and deported." The act was invoked during the Red Scare of 1919–20 when Bureau of Investigation agents launched a series of nationwide raids on left-wing organizations with large alien memberships. (Robert Preston, Jr., *Aliens and Dissenters: Federal Suppression of Radicals, 1903–1933* [Cambridge: Harvard University Press, 1963]; Dominic Candeloro, "Louis F. Post and the Red Scare of 1920," *Prologue* [Spring 1979]:40–55; Leslie Fishbein, "Federal Suppression of Left-wing Dissidence in World War I," *Potomac Review* [Summer 1974]:47–68; W. Anthony Gengarelly, "Secretary of Labor William B. Wilson and the Red Scare, 1919–20," *Pennsylvania History* 47 [October 1980]:311–29).

NEW YORK CITY [*Made*] Nov. 12th 1918.
[*for the period of*] Nov. 10th [*1918*]

IN RE: MARCUS GARVEY, Negro Propaganda

Continuing my report of November 9th, I have, this day at 8 p.m., attended the mass meeting at the Palace Casino, 135th St. & Madison Ave., held under the auspices of the *Universal Negro Improvement Association and African Community League*. I visited the meeting in the guise of a newspaper reporter and the following extracts are part of a speech made by *Marcus Garvey, the International Organizer of this movement*:

"Brethren: We are assembled here tonight for the purpose of furthering our fight for that negro democracy." "We have been slaves for four hundred years and we now come not to compromise but to demand that we be recognized as a nation and a people." "We are backed by four hundred million[1] who we will mobilize if necessary and fight for what is our just rights." "Not one of the big men which include Premier Asquith, Lloyd George, Premier Clemenceau,[2] Robert Lansing[3] or President Wilson[4] and many others have mentioned the future of the negro race." "The time has come for the blackman to mobilize his forces against these whites." "We are now as civilized as our former white masters who called upon us to aid them in this present war." "Have we not attended the same schools and colleges as the whiteman not only equaling his mental strength but in many instances excelling it." "Concerning our physical strength of that they are well aware." "No nation is safe in war when part of its internal population is dissatisfied." *"I do not say there will be but there may be a revolution if we are not recognized."* "Do not follow the dictates of men like William Randolph Hearst".[5] "We are determined to get liberty even at the cost of our lives." "No nation is safe in having twelve million dissatisfied people within their borders."

Not having used shorthand I quoted the above extracts from Garvey's speech as those which I considered most important that this department have on file. Invitations for the mass meeting were sent out to *Nicholas Murray Butler, President of Columbia University, Theodore Roosevelt, Eugene V. Debs,*[6] *Morris Hillquit,*[7] *George McAneny*[8] and *Robert E. Ford of the "Irish World".*[9] Mr. Ford's letter of regret follows:—

"Dear Mr. Garvey:—

Owing to a previous engagement I will be out of the city on Sunday evening but as the son of an abolishioner who worked while a young boy in the printing office of Lloyd Garrison[10] I congratulate you and your people in an effort to formulate and present their just claims to the peace conference to be held after the war. I hope your people will reciprocate in like spirit to the aims and efforts of the people of Ireland who have been held in bondage for seven hundred years.

(Signed) ROBERT E. FORD
Irish World."

A wire of regret from George McAneny as follows:
"MARCUS GARVEY
    REGRET LEAVING FOR CHICAGO SATURDAY MORNING UNABLE THEREFORE TO ACCEPT YOUR KIND INVITATION FOR THE EVENING
GEORGE McANENY"

There was also received a letter of regret from Nicholas Murray Butler. Theodore Roosevelt, Eugene V. Debs and Morris Hillquit did not acknowledge their invitations. There were no white speakers. At the meeting there was a set of resolutions drawn which Garvey informed me would be cabled the following morning to all the European nations and to the U.S., a copy of which resolutions I quote herewith.

"BE IT RESOLVED, That we, the Universal Negro Improvement Association and African Communities League of the World, representing the interests of the New Spirited Negroes of America, Africa and the West Indies, assembled in Universal Mass Convention in the Palace Casino, New York, on Sunday November 10, 1918, hereby beg to submit the following peace aims to the Allied Democracies of Europe and America, and to the people of democratic tendencies of the world.

AND BE IT FURTHER RESOLVED, That we believe that it will only be through a proper recognition of the Negro's rights and the rights of all weaker peoples at the Peace Conference that future wars will be obviated.

AND WE FURTHER PRAY, That the Peace Conference to assemble will take cognizance of these our aims.

(1) That the principle of self-determination be applied to Africa and all European controlled colonies in which people of African descent predominate.

(2) That all economic barriers that hamper the industrial development of Africa be removed.

(3) That Negroes enjoy the right to travel and reside in any part of the world even as Europeans now enjoy these rights.

(4) That Negroes be permitted the same educational facilities now given to Europeans.

(5) That Europeans who interfere with, or violate African tribal customs be deported and denied re-entry to the continent.

(6) That the segregatory and proscriptive ordinances against negroes in any part of the world be repealed and that they (Negroes) be given complete political, industrial and social equality in countries where Negroes and people of any other race live side by side.

(7) That the reservation land acts aimed against the natives of South Africa be revoked and the land restored to its prescriptive owners.[11]

(8) That Negroes be given proportional representation in any scheme of world government.

(9) That the captured German colonies in Africa[12] be turned over to the natives with educated Western and Eastern Negroes as their leaders."

The mass meeting was attended by perhaps 2,000 negroes amongst this attendance there were perhaps three or four white men. Garvey's appearance and manner of speech is that of a West Indian.

To be continued.

D. DAVIDSON

DWM

[Handwritten endorsement] Harris 12/7/18
[Stamped endorsement] Noted F. D. W.

DNA, RG 65, File OG 329359. TD. Copy of report furnished to Special Agent Finch.

1. The figure might have originated in black American circles with Bishop Henry McNeal Turner, who stated in an 1895 speech: "They told me in the Geographical Institute in Paris, France, that according to their calculation there are not less than 400,000,000 of Africans and their descendants on the globe, so that we are not lacking in numbers to form a nationality of our own." (Henry McNeal Turner, "The American Negro and His Fatherland," address delivered at the missionary conference "Africa and the American Negro," Atlanta, 1895, reprinted in *Respect Black: The Writings and Speeches of Henry McNeal Turner*, edited by Edwin S. Redkey, [New York: Arno Press, 1971], p. 69). A more modest population figure of 261,277,000 blacks worldwide was given by the *Negro Year Book* of 1918–19, distributed as follows: "Africa 180,000,000; Southern Asia (principally the Dravidians of India) 50,000,000; Pacific Islands (Melanesians, Papuans and Negritos) 2,500,000; North America 17,777,000; South America 11,000,000" (p. 138).

2. Georges Clemenceau (1841–1929) was premier of France and minister of war from November 1917 to January 1920. As president of the peace conference in Paris, Clemenceau devoted himself to the negotiations of the peace settlement. (*WBD*).

3. Robert Lansing (1864–1928) was the U.S. secretary of state from June 1915 to February 1920, serving previously as counselor for the Department of State from April 1914. He was also appointed chief of the American delegation to negotiate peace in November 1918. His own accounts of the peace conference were later published in *The Big Four and Others of the Peace Conference* (Boston: Houghton Mifflin Co., 1921), and *The Peace Negotiations: A Personal Narrative* (Boston: Houghton Mifflin Co., 1921). (*WBD*).

4. Woodrow Wilson (1856–1924) was the twenty-eighth president of the United States, holding office from 1913–21. (*WBD*).

5. William Randolph Hearst (1863–1951) was the owner of America's most powerful newspaper chain, which was known for its sensationalistic journalism. (*WBD*).

6. Eugene Victor Debs (1855–1926) was a five-time presidential candidate for the Socialist party, and a founder of the Industrial Workers of the World in 1905. He opposed the First World War, claiming that it was imperialistic; he was arrested in June 1918 and charged under the Espionage Act following a speech in which he denounced the government for its prosecution of persons charged with sedition. Although he was sentenced to ten years in prison in 1919, the Socialist party again nominated him as its presidential candidate in 1920. (*DAB*, vol. 3).

7. Morris Hillquit (1869–1933), a Latvian-born Jewish immigrant, was one of the most important activists, theorists, and lawyers in the Socialist party. In 1900, following a split in the Socialist Labor party, he joined Debs' more moderate Socialist party of America, remaining a lifelong member. In 1917, with antisocialist and prowar feelings at a peak, Hillquit ran for mayor of New York on the Socialist ticket. Endorsed by the *Messenger* as a man "who understands the problems of an oppressed people" (1 [November 1917]:20), he drew an impressive 22 percent of the vote, larger than any previous socialist candidate. (*DAB*, vol. 2, supplement 1; Norma Fain Pratt, *Morris Hillquit* [Westport, Conn.: Greenwood Press, 1978]).

8. George McAneny (1869–1953), banker, civil service reformer, and publicist, was the executive manager of the *New York Times* in 1918 and chairman of the board of trustees of the College of the City of New York. (*WWWA*, vol. 3).

9. Robert E. Ford (1865–1919), Irish-American nationalist, inherited the management of the *Irish World* from his father, Patrick Ford. The *Irish World*, which came under heavy U.S. government pressure, made the following editorial comment after receiving the UNIA resolutions: "In a word, the five thousand negroes who made up the mass meeting that assembled in the Palace Casino last Sunday insisted that the principles of democracy, of which we hear so much these days, should be applied to men and women of their race. A democracy that makes a distinction on account of the color of a person's skin is not true democracy. It is a sham and a fraud." ("The Negro and Democracy," *Irish World*, 16 November 1918, p. 4.).

10. A reference to the editorial offices of William Lloyd Garrison's (1805–1879) journal, the *Liberator*. The *Liberator* was started in 1831 and served as the principal forum for the abolitionist movement in America. (*WBD*).

11. The Native Lands Act was passed in 1913 ostensibly to deal with the problems of farm labor shortage and the disposal of lands won in the Anglo-Boer War to black South Africans. The act restricted the purchase or use of land by natives except in the Cape area; it also diminished squatter rights, and abolished the tenancy system of farming, under which blacks farmed white-owned land in return for half of the crops. The immediate effect of the act was

the uprooting of thousands of black Africans: four million blacks were allowed eight percent of the land, while one and a quarter million whites took control of ninety-two percent. The Native Lands Act eventually provided the basis for the formal system of apartheid. (H. J. and R. E. Simons, *Class and Colour in South Africa, 1850–1950* [London: Penguin Books, 1969], pp. 130–37).

12. Togoland, Cameroon, German East Africa, and South-West Africa. Article 22 of the League of Nations covenant established three classes of mandates (A, B, and C), corresponding to various conditions. Class A mandates were territories whose independence was to be provisionally recognized until they were able to survive on their own. Class B mandates were administered directly by the mandatory power. Class C mandates were administered under the laws of the mandatory country as integral parts of its own territories. Togoland, Cameroon, and German East Africa were the Class B mandates, while South-West Africa was designated part of the Class C mandates. (Christopher M. Andrew and A. S. Kanya-Forstner, *The Climax of French Imperial Expansion, 1914–1924* [Stanford: Stanford University Press, 1981], chap. 8; George Louis Beer, *African Questions at the Paris Peace Conference* [New York: Macmillan Co., 1923]; W. Roger Louis, "The United Kingdom and the Beginning of the Mandates System, 1919–1922," *International Organization* 23 [Winter 1969]:73–96; and Louis, "The United States and the African Peace Settlement of 1919," *Journal of African History* 4 [1963]:413–33).

NEW YORK CITY [*Made*] NOV. 12th 1918.
[*for the period of*] Nov. 12th [*1918*]

IN RE: MARCUS GARVEY, Negro Propaganda.

Continuing this investigation I have this day, under the guise of a reporter from the City News, visited Marcus Garvey at the office of the "Negro World" No. 36 to 38 West 135th St. I told Mr. Garvey I would like to get a little history of himself for our files for future use in the event of a write up.

Garvey told me he was born in Jamaica, West Indies, August 17th 1888. He remained there until twenty years of age receiving a common school education and then went to England where he took a liberal course in Barbeck [*Birkbeck*] College graduating in the year 1913. He then returned to the West Indies where he took a course in journalism. He has been in the U.S. about two and a half years and contemplates returning sometime in 1919. He told me he was the International Organizer of the Universal Negro Improvement Association with headquarters at the above address and his mission in this country was to organize the black race for the benefit of future recognition. He told me black people were much wrought up over the East St. Louis riots and everyday lynchings of negroes in the south and it was their purpose to combine in order to receive adequate protection. I mentioned certain extracts from his speech of November 10th at the Palace Casino part of which he denied and part of which he confirmed. In the office of this publication, "The Negro World" there hangs the new Eth[i]opian flag which is of red, black and green. Garvey explained that the meaning of these colors were that "the black race between blood and nature to win its rights" which he characterizes as a very noble thought. I have among the negro population in this district many colored informants who will be very glad to keep me in touch with anything that may come to their notice.

D. DAVIDSON

DWM

DNA, RG 65, File OG 329359. TD. Copy of report furnished to Special Agent Finch.

    1. See also Davidson's report made for 11 November 1918 (DNA, RG 65, file OG 329359).

New York [*Made*] November 21/[*19*]18

[*for the period of*] Nov. 14/[*19*]18

RE: NEGRO AGITATION Socialist Activities.

    The following is a report made by a Police officer to his commanding officer, 38th Precinct, New York City. This precinct covers the congested colored neighborhood of New York. The report refers partly to one Garvey, editor of the Negro World, of whom I reported recently.

    "Sometime ago a Mr. Garvey, editor of the Negro World, and organizer of the Universal Negro Improvement Association addressed a meeting on the west side of Lenox Avenue between 135th and 136th Streets, from 9:10 to 10:30 p.m. His purpose is to get the four hundred million negros of the world to organize for the purpose of getting Africa which he claimed belongs to the Negros as their own nation. He said that a million and a half negros[1] were fighting on the battlefields of France, Flanders and the West.[2] He said that the colored men should go to war when called and learn how to use the gun and bayonet; he said if the white man carries a gun and bayonet and the colored man a stick, the white man would take advantage of him. He stated that the ne[g]ro should also carry a gun and bayonet and learn how to use them so that if the white man slaps his face he can use his gun and bayonet on him and put the white man under the ground. (pointing to the ground) He also stated that when the million and a half colored soldiers came back and the Universal Negro Independence Association was strong, they would ask for Africa for the negro and if it was not given the negro would go and fight and take it. He said the white man died for what he wanted years ago and he is willing to die now for the future of the Black Race.

    "On another occasion at a meeting on Lenox Avenue near 136th Street, Garvey said that now is the time to organize and get our strength together and strike the white man and get what we want; the white man now has his hands full, he can't take care of himself, that is why he has the colored man to help him; he can't interfere with us; now is the time to get together and strike at him and get what we want. I hate the white man. I am a Roman Catholic but I hate the Pope because he is a white man. If you all hated the white man as I do, we would have had our independence long ago. We once fought the white man as Zulus, with sticks, but now we will fight them with guns and bayonets, which they are teaching us how to use, and you can imagine how good we are learning when two of our men can capture 20 of the kind that are teaching us;[3] the gun, bayonet and pistol will be the right hand of the negro hereafter.

"Some people say there will be no more wars after this, but they do not know what they are talking about. England and France will go to war and then our million and a half of colored soldiers and the rest of us will drive the white English and French into the Mediterranean Sea and Indian Ocean and take Africa for ourselves. He stated that Jamaica has a population of 900,000 and 850,000 of them are colored. He said the 50,000 whites shake hands and call the negro their equal, because the whites are in the minority. What they need there is a couple of colored crackers to drive them out and make a colored republic of it. He said if the whites think the c[o]lored men are going over to fight for them they are very much mistaken, because they are coming back and there will be some Napoleons[4] among them who are going to lead the colored men to conquer the whites. The colored man ruled years ago and there was no war but since the white man rules we are always at war. Take the present war for example. If the colored man ruled now we would not have this war.["]

R. W. Finch

[*Handwritten endorsements*] IWW[5]
Negro Activities
[*Stamped endorsement*] Noted F. D. W.

DNA, RG 65, File OG 258421. TD.

1. Over two million black men served as part of the armed forces of the U.S.A., France, Britain, and Germany during the war. By November 1918, approximately 370,000 black Americans had seen service in the American Expeditionary Force in France, a figure second only to that of the French-speaking Africans. Black American troops in World War I included both combat and noncombat units. The French recruited about 620,000 colonial troops in all, with 340,000 from North Africa, 250,000 from Sudan and Senegal, and 30,000 from the West Indies. The British recruited approximately 25,000 blacks from the West Indies, most of whom served in the Dardanelles and Palestine, while another 21,000 noncombatants from South Africa enlisted with the South African Native Labor Contingent in support of the British forces in France. In the East African campaigns, the British used over 50,000 African troops, backed by an estimated one million followers. The Germans, for their part, recruited 11,000 soldiers and policemen in East Africa to protect their colonies there. Over 20,000 carriers, mainly from Nigeria, Sierra Leone, and the Gold Coast, were used in the Togoland and Cameroons by the British colonial armies. (PRO, WO 106/532; Arthur Barbeau and Florette Henri, *The Unknown Soldiers: Black American Troops in World War I* [Philadelphia: Temple University Press, 1974]).

2. The battle line on the western front did not change more than ten miles in either direction from late 1914 until early 1917; hence, most of the fighting was concentrated in the areas of France and Flanders. In the first battle of Ypres (12 October to 22 November 1914), Britain sustained over 50,000 casualties. In the second campaign (22 April to 25 May 1917), the Germans gassed thousands of French colonial troops, though the Germans failed to capitalize on the panic that they caused and did not advance the line of battle. The third battle, also known as the battle of Passchendaele (31 July to 15 November 1917), was perhaps the bloodiest, with almost 400,000 British and 300,000 German casualties sustained, but it resulted in an advance of only nine-thousand yards by the British. In December 1915, *Punch* magazine published the late John D. McCrae's poem, "In Flanders' Fields," urging his fellow soldiers to avenge the death of those lying dead in the fields at Flanders. Other poets answered McCrae's plea, and the phrase "in Flanders' fields" became a popular symbol for evoking the allied cause in World War I. (*EB*).

3. On 14 May 1918, Henry Johnson (1897–1929) and Needham Roberts, black soldiers of the Fifteenth National Guard of New York and the 369th Infantry, fought off a raiding party of twenty-four Germans without any assistance despite their serious wounds. Johnson became a hero for his refusal to allow the Germans to carry off his wounded comrade during the raid, fighting several of them with only a knife. Newspaper reports of the incident described it as the "Battle of Henry Johnson." Both men received the French croix de guerre emblem, as did the entire 369th Regiment. Following his return to New York, the injured Henry Johnson, who had been a redcap in the New York Central railroad station at Albany, was inundated with offers for a nationwide lecture tour. At his first engagement outside New York, in St. Louis, Mo., on 28 March 1919, Johnson strongly criticized white soldiers for cowardice and racism, singling out the marines for their refusal to fight in the same trenches as black soldiers. Johnson's speech was well received by his predominantly black audience but following his speech, a federal warrant was issued for his arrest on a technical charge of wearing his uniform after the prescribed date. After the incident Johnson also came under investigation by the intelligence authorities and he appears to have retracted his earlier statement. On his return to New York, he was unable to find work and was forced to rely on charity. (Greene, *Black Defenders*, pp. 174, 177; *NYT*, 29 March 1919).

4. Napoleon Bonaparte (1769–1821). (*WBD*).

5. The Industrial Workers of the World (IWW), popularly known as the Wobblies, was organized in Chicago in 1905. Its main objective was the creation of a revolutionary industrial union based on the syndicalist principle of the overthrow of capitalism by means of a general strike. The IWW organized nonskilled workers, both white and nonwhite, but after 1912 the group declined reviving briefly after America's entry into the war. By 1917 membership had reached between sixty thousand and one hundred thousand, but wartime federal repression— partially in response to several IWW organized strikes—and criminal syndicalist legislation passed by the states led to its decline, so that by 1924 the IWW was little more than a paper organization. (Melvyn Dubofsky, *We Shall Be All: History of the Industrial Workers of the World* [Chicago: Quadrangle Books, 1969]).

Capt. Edward B. Hitchcock, Postal Censorship Committee,[1] to Brig. Gen. Marlborough Churchill, Director, Military Intelligence Division, War Department

New Orleans, La. November 15th, 1918

From: Edward B. Hitchcock, Captain USA[2]
To: General Marlborough Churchill, Director[3]
   Military Intelligence Division, G.S.[4] Washington, D.C.
Subject: Original communication covered by Index No. 24651.

1.   Enclosed is an original communication from: Marcus Garvey, President & International Organizer, Universal Negro Improvement Association, Crescent Bldg., 36–38 West 135th St., New York, N.Y. to: D. B. Lewis, Corozal British Honduras covered by Index No. 24651, together with comment sheet covering it, from which you will note that same is worthy of investigation.

2.   Enclosed also formal receipt bearing the Index No. of the document, covering the withdrawal of same from the New Orleans "hold" files. Kindly sign and return as MID is charged with this document until it is replaced.

3.   The report of your findings will be awaited with interest.

EDW. B. HITCHCOCK
CAPTAIN USA
M I D REPRESENTATIVE,
NEW ORLEANS LA.

[*Signed*] by: J. C. Clark

3 Encl. L. H.

[*Handwritten endorsements*] TO MI-4B
[*Geographic Departments*]⁵ FBH
MI-10 [*Censorship*]⁶ 10-N.O.L.
Negro Subv. Prop. Ger.
REGISTERED NO. 55181
[*Stamped endorsement*] CAPT. HAYES M.I.4

DNA, RG 165, File 10218–261/3. TNS, Recipient's copy. Letter was written on official stationery of the Postal Censorship Committee, New Orleans, La.

1. The Postal Censorship Committee consisted of representatives from the Office of Naval Intelligence, the Military Intelligence Division of the War Department's General Staff, the War Trade Board, the Chief Cable Censor, and the Post Office Department. It functioned as the executive arm of the Censorship Board, which was established on 12 October 1917 in order to censor all communications between the United States and foreign countries to prevent the transmission of enemy propaganda and to gain information useful to the United States in the prosecution of the war. The Censorship Board operated stations in New York, Cristobal (Panama), San Francisco, San Antonio, Honolulu, San Juan, New Orleans, Seattle, and Manila. In addition, operational ties were maintained with American allies in Europe, the Caribbean, and Asia. The Censorship Board provided each postal censorship committee with lists of suspects prepared by the staffs of various intelligence departments and printed a consolidated version as the *Postal Censorship Book*. By the war's end, this list contained the names and addresses of more than 250,000 subjects. The Censorship Board was discontinued on 21 June 1919. (*Cable Censorship Digest*, 1933 [Washington: GPO, 1933]).

2. Capt. Edward Bering Hitchcock (1884– ?) was a journalist and author of the official biography of pre-World War II Czech leader, Edward Benes (1884–1948). Hitchcock served as a captain in the Military Intelligence Division during World War I, and during World War II he was employed in various governmental capacities with the U.S. Treasury (1942–43), the Office of Strategic Services (1943–44), and finally with the United Nations Relief and Rehabilitation Administration (1945). (*WWA*, 1946–47).

3. Brig. Gen. Marlborough Churchill (1878–1947) served as director of the Military Intelligence Division between 1918 and 1920. Prior to his appointment in August 1918, he spent five months as acting chief of staff of artillery in the American Expeditionary Forces' First Army in France; following that, in June 1918, he was appointed to the position of chief censor of the Military Intelligence Branch in Washington, D.C. He returned to Paris on special duty to the peace conference in December 1918. He resumed his position as head of military intelligence on his return to America in March 1919. (*NYT*, 10 July 1947; *Who Was Who in American History— The Military* [Chicago: Marquis, n.d.]; Harvard College, *Class of 1900, Report* [Cambridge: Crimson Printing, 1950]).

4. The Military Intelligence Division (MID) of the General Staff, which replaced the Military Intelligence Branch (MIB), was created on 26 August 1918 as part of the War Department's reorganization of the General Staff into four equal divisions, spurred by the recall from France, on 4 March 1918, of Maj. Gen. Peyton C. March to become the new military chief of staff. Potential duplication of effort between intelligence agencies of the government was adjusted at weekly liaison conferences held at the Department of Justice and attended by the director of MID and representatives of various departments. The director of MID also maintained close liaison with British and French military intelligence. Military intelligence

activities were divided into the Positive Branch and the Negative Branch. These two branches were further subdivided into sections and subsections, on the model of British military intelligence. The Positive Branch dealt with all matters pertaining to foreign countries and the military situation throughout the world, whereas the Negative Branch was concerned with uncovering or suppressing enemy activities in the United States. At the time of the Armistice, MID had in its service 282 officers, 29 noncommissioned officers and 948 civilian employees. For details of the structure and specific functions of the various organizational components of military intelligence, see Col. Bruce W. Bidwell, "History of the Military Intelligence Division Department of the Army General Staff," (unpublished MS, 1959–61), Carlisle Barracks, Pennsylvania, United States Army Military History Institute, regraded unclassified 20 July 1979; DNA, RG 165, file 10560–152, Raymond Franklin Murray, "History of the Military Intelligence Division, Central Department," 2 June 1919.

5. MI 4B was both the most important and the largest subsection within the MI 4 section (Counterespionage Among Civilian Population) of the Negative Branch. It was responsible for handling "all routine matters bearing upon civilian counterespionage within the United States and was subdivided into six main groups in order to conform generally with the six geographical departments of the Army." The Southeastern Department of MI 4B was responsible for "Negro subversion and political demagoguery." (Bidwell, part 2, pp. 386–87).

6. MI 10 was formed on 29 July 1918 in order to achieve a greater centralization and control over the proliferation of wartime censorship efforts. It became part of the Negative Branch on 6 September 1918; its chief function was to assist the director of MID in executing his increased duties as chief military censor. At its greatest strength, MI 10 functioned with fifteen different subsections, and shortly before the Armistice, it numbered over thirty officers and sixty civilian employees, plus several hundred affiliated postal and radio censorship personnel. (Bidwell, part 2, pp. 46–67).

Enclosure

Nov. 7/18

INDEX NO. *24651*

U.S. POSTAL CENSORSHIP, NEW ORLEANS, LA.

[FROM]	TO
[Marcus Gar]vey, President & Interna[tional O]rganizer; [Univers]al Negro Improvement Association, [Cresc]ent Bldg. 36–38 West 135th St., [New] York, N.Y.	D. B. L[ewis,] Coroz[al,] British Honduras.

[DATE OF] LETTER *Nov. 1st/18*	NO. OF OBJECTS ENCLOSED *13*	LANGUAGE OF LETTER *English*	DATE OF COMMENT *Nov. 7/18*

[ROUT]E	DATE	COPIES	DISPOSITION UNLESS DISPATCHED	SUBJECT	
ONI[1]	*11/8*	*4*	*Info to 3rd & 8th ND-Suspend*		NO. OF EXAMINER *1117* TABLE NO. I

[DATE OF] LETTER *Nov. 1st/18*		NO. OF OBJECTS ENCLOSED *13*		LANGUAGE OF LETTER *English*	DATE OF COMMENT *Nov. 7/18*	
C.C.C.[2]	*11/8*	0			NO. OF COMMENT WRITER *1107*	TYPED BY FS—*11/12/18*
M.I.D.[3]	*11/8*	2	*Withdraw one blank for Wash.*			
					APPROVED BY D.A.C.[9]	APPROVED BY A.C.[10]
					G. H. T.	*R. L. W.*
W.T.B.[4] P.O.[6]	*11/8*	3		*C.P.I.[5]*		
E.A.C.[7]	*11/9*	0		*Pr.6[8]*		

COMMENT

NEGRO PROPAGANDA.

Writer encloses twelve copies of an appeal to the racial instinct of the negroes, (calculated to incite hatred for the white race) by urging them to do like "The Irish, the Jews, the East Indians and all other oppressed peoples who are getting together to demand from their oppressors Liberty, Justice, Equality, and we now call [u]pon the four hundred millions of Negro people of the world to do likewise." Also informs Addressee that he sent to him 50 copies of the "NEGRO WORLD" and will send him 50 copies per week and wants addressee to do everything to help the movement at Addressee's end, so that they will have a very strong branch in BRITISH HONDURAS in a short time.

[*Handwritten endorsement*] Withdraw
[*Stamped endorsement*] CAPT. HAYES
M.I.4-41

DNA, RG 165, File 10218–261/2. D, Printed form with manuscript additions.

1. The Office of Naval Intelligence (ONI) was concerned with the movements of naval forces worldwide, the destruction or attempted destruction of shipping, and inventions of nautical interest. It monitored enemy agents' activities, a task facilitated by the Navy Mobilization Bureau which assumed responsibility for the updating and circulation of the suspects' list that also formed the basis of all postal censorship activities. (U.S. Office of Naval Intelligence, *Cable Censorship Guide* [Washington: GPO, 1933]).

2. The chief cable censor (CCC) was a naval officer appointed by the Office of Naval Intelligence to serve on the Postal Censorship Committee. Cable censors were stationed in Washington, D.C., and New York, as well as at the major coastal bases in the United States and throughout the Caribbean. Their main objective was to prevent false or demoralizing statements through the censorship of references to military and naval operations. (*Cable Censorship Guide*).

3. MID appointed its own officers at the various postal censorship stations with responsibility for censorship of all mail entering and leaving the United States.

4. The War Trade Board (WTB) was created by executive order on 12 October 1917 under the Trading with the Enemy Act, to censor all correspondence that dealt with trade, banking, insurance, and commerce, as well as communications dealing with the shipping of war-related goods.

5. The Committee on Public Information (CPI), created by executive order on 14 April 1917, was composed of the secretaries of state, navy, and war. As a member of the Censorship Board, the committee was responsible for administering the program of voluntary censorship of the press, since most incoming cables were directed to large newspapers and news associations. The chair of the committee was George Creel (1876–1953). (George Creel, *How we advertised America* . . . [New York: Harper and Brothers, 1920]; James R. Mock and Cedric Larson, *Words that Won the War: The Story of the Committee on Public Information, 1917–1919* [Princeton, N.J.: Princeton University Press, 1939]).

6. The Post Office (PO) was responsible for the administration of each censorship station. Its local representative acted as chairman of the station's censorship committee. (DNA, RG 28, file 9.21–154, 12 July 1918; and file B-588).

7. The exchange assistant censor (EAC or EX AC) dealt with the mail after it was seen by the heads of the censorship station's divisions.

8. The area of the censorship committee's press branch which handled incoming material from British Honduras.

9. The deputy assistant censor (DAC) had responsibility for supervising examiners during the first examination of the mail. The DAC also coordinated previous censorship comments on various subjects and received daily reports from examiners. (DNA, RG 28, file 9.21–154).

10. The assistant censor (AC) routed letters to the committee's appropriate division. There were six assistant censors, each in charge of separate branches—trade, social, uncommon language, registered letters, press, and special. After the mail was first checked against the censorship committee's suspects' list, and after the examiner read the letter, it was forwarded to the assistant censor for disposition to the appropriate division. (ibid.).

Theodore Roosevelt to Marcus Garvey

[*Oyster Bay, Long Island*] November 16, 1918

My dear Sir:

I am sorry, but it just is not possible for me to undertake anything additional at this time. Will you therefore be good enough to use an extract from the enclosed, which is the copy of my speech before the Negro War Council of a few days ago?[1] Faithfully yours,

[THEODORE ROOSEVELT]

DLC, TR. TL, Carbon copy.

1. Roosevelt's speech was delivered on 2 November 1918 at a fund raising benefit held at Carnegie Hall for the Circle of Negro War Relief, Inc. The meeting was presided over by W. E. B. Du Bois; speakers included Irvin Cobb, Emmett J. Scott, George E. Haynes, Adah B. Thoms, and Marcel Knecht of the French High Commission. Roosevelt's speech lauded the performance of black fighting troops in France. (DNA, RG 165, file 10218–330; *Crisis* 17 [December 1918]:87; *NYT*, 3 November 1918).

Brig. Gen. Marlborough Churchill to Lt. Col. Nicholas Biddle

[*Washington, D.C.*] November 20, 1918

From: Director of Military Intelligence.
To: Lt. Col. Nicholas Biddle,[1] 302 Broadway, New York.[2]
Subject: Marcus Garvey and Negro Propaganda.

    1.   Marcus Garvey, President and International Organizer of "The Universal Negro Improvement Association", with offices in Crescent Building, 36–38 West 135th St., New York, is circulating pamphlets which appeal to the racial instinct of the negroes and are calculated to incite hatred for the white race.

    2.   One such pamphlet urges the negroes to do like "the Irish, the Jews, the East Indians and all other oppressed peoples who are getting together to demand from their oppressors Liberty, Justice, Equality, and we now call upon the four hundred millions of Negro people of the world to do likewise."

    3.   Please have an investigation made and report to this office.

M. CHURCHILL,
BRIGADIER GENERAL, GENERAL STAFF
by: C. J. H. HAYES,[3]
CAPTAIN, U.S.A.

[*Typewritten reference*] M.I. 4–41

DNA, RG 165, File 10218–261/6 53 (50). TN, Carbon copy.

    1. Lt. Col. Nicholas Biddle (1879–1923) graduated from Harvard in 1900 and later became a prominent New York financier. During the war he served as chief of the military intelligence branch office in New York, a post that also required him to take charge of mail censorship in the city. After the war he resumed his financial career. (*NYT*, 19 February 1923).

    2. The New York branch of military intelligence, located at 302 Broadway, was established in July 1917. Similar offices were established in Philadelphia (November 1917), St. Louis (January 1918), Seattle (February 1918), Pittsburgh (April 1918), and New Orleans (July 1918).

    3. Carlton Joseph Huntley Hayes (1882–1964), a lecturer in history at Columbia University from 1907, was a captain in the Military Intelligence Division during 1918–19. (*NYT*, 4 September 1964).

NEGROES AT VERSAILLES
THE NEGRO WORLD

A Newspaper Devoted to the Interests of the Negro Race Without the Hope of Profit as a Business Investment.

VOL. I. NO. 16.   NEW YORK, NOVEMBER 30, 1918   Price 3 Cents.

CALL MADE TO—THE MEN AND WOMEN OF THE NEGRO RACE

SECOND BIG MEETING AT PALACE CASINO TO SEND DELEGATES TO EUROPE

TO ATTEND BIG MASS MEETING IN PALACE CASINO, NEW YORK, SUNDAY, DECEMBER 1.

Fellowmen of the Negro Race:

I am again requested by the Universal Negro Improvement Association and African Communities' League to issue a call to you, asking that you attend, en masse, the big mass meeting of the Negro peoples of the world, to be held in the Palace Casino, New York, on Sunday, December 1, at 8 o'clock p. m.

The time has come for us to unite. All the other races are "doing it." On Sunday night the assembled people will elect three delegates of the race to represent our interests at the Peace Conference in France.

Every oppressed group of people will be represented in some way or other at the Peace Conference.

Remember, men, the time is now. There must be liberty, justice and equality, and that can only be when the Negro takes proper steps to make his power felt.

Let there be no compromise. Let us unite to get all that is ours. At the Peace Conference great issues are to be decided, and the Negro must prepare to take his stand without faltering.

It is your duty to be at the Palace on Sunday.

Yours fraternally,
MARCUS GARVEY.
New York, Nov. 29, 1918.

NEGROES SHOULD RALLY TO SUPPORT OF REED TO OPPOSE LEAGUE OF NATIONS

There Can Be No League Until the Negro Becomes a Nation in Africa.

Speech Means Trouble—Other Democrats Will Join Republicans in Opposing Wilson's League of Nations.

WHITE MEN DO NOT BELIEVE IN THEMSELVES

Why Should Negroes Believe in Someone Else?

"Great Power Idea" Assailed—League of Nations Can't Succeed Until Striving for Supremacy Is Ended, Says Wells.

NO CERTAINTY THAT SECRET DIPLOMACY WILL BE ABOLISHED

Black Men, Believe in No One But Yourselves

France's Views on Peace Pact—Secret Diplomacy Rather Favored—Considerable Skepticism Over Society of Nations.

By PAUL SCOTT MOWRER

CABLES DISPATCHED THROUGHOUT THE WORLD HAS IMMEDIATE EFFECT ON THE JAPANESE

Good Work of Universal Negro Improvement Association and African Communities' League.

Raises Race Question—Press Wants China to Join in Demands That Discrimination Be Abolished.

Tokio, Nov. 21.—Japanese newspapers are suggesting that Japan and China raise the race question at the forthcoming peace conference so that there shall be no more racial discrimination throughout the world.

JAPAN MOBILIZING THE SENTIMENT OF YELLOW RACES

Can You Understand This, Mr. Negro?

May Advise China at Peace Conference.

WHAT HAPPENS TO PEOPLE WHEN SURROUNDED BY STRONGER RACE

Jews Shot Down in Galicia Riots.

ORGANIZED LABOR TO HOLD PEACE CONFERENCE IN PARIS

WASHINGTON, Nov. 28.

POLICE CAPTAIN WARD SHIFTED; MANY NEGRO RIOTS ARE BLAMED

An Early Issue of the *Negro World* (Source: DNA, RG 165, file 10218–261).

299

Editorial Letter by Marcus Garvey

[[New York, Nov. 29, 1918]]

Fellowmen of the Negro Race:

I am again requested by the Universal Negro Improvement Association and African Communities' League to issue a call to you, asking that you attend, en masse, the big mass meeting of the Negro peoples of the world, to be held in the Palace Casino, New York, on Sunday, December 1, at 8 o'clock p.m.

The time has come for us to unite. All the other races are "doing it." On Sunday night the assembled people will elect three delegates of the race to represent our interests at the Peace Conference in France.

Every oppressed group of people will be represented in some way or other at the Peace Conference.

Remember, men, the time is now. There must be liberty, justice and equality, and that can only be when the Negro takes proper steps to make his power felt.

Let there be no compromise. Let us unite to get all that is ours. At the Peace Conference great issues are to be decided, and the Negro must prepare to take his stand without faltering.

It is your duty to be at the Palace on Sunday. Yours fraternally,

MARCUS GARVEY

Printed in the *NW*, Saturday, 30 November 1918. Original headlines have been omitted.

Col. John M. Dunn, Acting Director, Military Intelligence Division, to Emmett J. Scott,[1] Special Assistant to the Secretary of War

[*Washington, D.C.*] November 30, 1918

Dear Sir:

Enclosed is a copy of a Postal Censorship Report, New York, Index No. 119642, concerning an agent of the Universal Negro Improvement Association, of 36–38 West 135th St., New York City. It is sent for your information. Very truly yours,

JOHN M. DUNN,[2]
COLONEL, GENERAL STAFF,
ACTING DIRECTOR MILITARY
INTELLIGENCE,
[*Initialed*] By: W. B.[3]
MAJOR, A.S.M.A., U.S.A.

1 encl.
hgb

300

NOVEMBER 1918

[Typewritten reference] M.I. 4–41
[Typewritten endorsement] MID CJHH

DNA, RG 165, File 10218–261/11 2-2. TNI, Carbon copy.

1. Scott was appointed special assistant to the secretary of war, Newton D. Baker, in October 1917, in the area of "Negro propaganda."
2. Col. John M. Dunn (1875–1931) served as acting director of the Military Intelligence Division from 22 November 1918 to 1 April 1919. (*Official Army Register, 1920; 1931* [Washington: GPO, 1920; 1931]).
3. Maj. Wrisley Brown (1883–1943) was a lawyer by profession (National University, LL.B., 1907; LL.M, 1908). In 1909 the Department of Justice made him an examiner and later in the same year he was appointed special assistant to the U.S. attorney general. In 1910, he was appointed a consulting attorney to the fledgling Bureau of Investigation, while still continuing as a special assistant to the attorney general. An expert in national banking laws, Brown represented the U.S. government at a 1914 London conference. (*WWA*, vol. 13; *NCAB*, vol. 31).

Enclosure

11/26/18

INDEX NO. *119642*

NEW YORK, N.Y.
U.S. POSTAL CENSORSHIP

FROM   TO

Amy Ashwood   *The Democratic Club*
Universal Negro Improvement Assn.,   *c/o Mr. E. Headly*
36–38 West 135th St.,   *Ancon P.O.,*
New York City.   *Canal Zone.*
DATE OF LETTER *11/20/18*   NO. OF ENCLOSURES _____
Copied by MEL

COMMENTATOR NO. *27-375*   BRANCH *Sus[pect]*. DATE *11/26/18*   LANGUAGE *English*
ORIGINAL TO *MID-ONI*   D.A.C. *MW*   A.C. *HRJ (MW)*

COMMENT
ACTIVITIES OF THE NEGROES.

Writer, who is General Secretary of the Universal Negro Improvement Association and African Communities League, says that the negro question is no longer a local one, but of the Negroes of the World, joining hands and fighting for one common cause. Writer says that the negroes know that they cannot attain Democracy unless they win it for themselves, and that some of their members are willing to give up their lives so that the others may be free.

GEG.

DIVISION	DATE	COPIES	DISPOSITION AND SIGNATURE
WTB			
MIS	11/26/18	5	*Suspend for advice of Col. Biddle—HTP*
ONI	11/26/18	3	*JJC.*
CCC			
PO			
EX. AC[1]	11/27/18		*MKS (Sig.) D.*

THIS SLIP ALWAYS TO ACCOMPANY LETTER

[*Endorsements*] LIEUT. WINTERBOTHAM
CAPT. HAYES M.I. 4-41 COPY OF THIS
ABSTRACT HAS BEEN SENT TO LIEUT. COL.
NICHOLAS BIDDLE M.I. 4

DNA, RG 165, File 10218–261/4. D, Printed form with typewritten insertions. Stamped endorsements.

1. Exchange assistant censor.

Editorials by Marcus Garvey in the *Negro World*

[30 November 1918]

ADVICE OF THE NEGRO TO PEACE CONFERENCE.

Now that the statesmen of the various nations are preparing to meet at the Peace Conference,[1] to discuss the future government of the peoples of the world, we take it as our bounden duty to warn them to be very just to all those people who may happen to come under their legislative control. If they, representing the classes, as they once did, were alive to the real feeling of their respective masses four and one-half years ago, today Germany would have been intact, Austria-Hungary would have been intact, Russia would have been intact, the spirit of revolution never would have swept Europe, and mankind at large would have been satisfied. But through graft, greed and selfishness, the classes they represented then, as some of them represent now, were determined to rob and exploit the masses, thinking that the masses would have remained careless of their own condition for everlasting.

It is a truism that you "fool half of the people for half of the time, but you cannot fool all of the people for all of the time"; and now that the masses of the whole world have risen as one man to demand true equity and justice from the "powers that be," then let the delegates at the Peace Conf[e]rence r[e]alize, just now, that the Negro, who forms an integral part of the masses of the world, is determined to get no less than what other men are to get. The oppressed races of Europe are to get their freedom, which freedom will be guaranteed them. The Asiatic races are to get their rights and a larger modicum of self-government.

We trust that the delegates to the Peace Conference will not continue to believe that Negroes have no ambition, no aspiration. There are no more timid, cringing Negroes; let us say that those Negroes have now been relegated to the limbo of the past, to the region of forgetfulness, and that the new Negro is on the stage, and he is going to play his part good and well. He, like the other heretofore oppressed peoples of the world, is determined to get restored to him his ancestral rights.

When we look at the map of Africa today we see Great Britain with fully five million square miles of our territory, we see France with fully three million five hundred thousand square miles, we see that Belgium has under her control the Congo, Portugal has her sway over Southeast Africa, Italy has under her control Tripoli, Italian Somaliland on the Gulf of Aden and Erythria on the Red Sea. Germany had clamored for a place in the sun simply because she had only one million square miles, with which she was not satisfied, in that England had five millions and France three millions five hundred thousand. It can be easily seen that the war of 1914 was the outcome of African aggrandizement, that Africa, to which the white man has absolutely no claim, has been raped, has been left bleeding for hundreds of years, but within the last thirty years the European powers have concentrated more than ever on the cleaning up of that great continent so as to make it a white man's country. Among those whom they have killed are millions of our people, but the age of killing for naught is passed and the age of killing for something has come. If black men have to die in Africa or anywhere else, then they might as well die for the best of things, and that is liberty, true freedom and true democracy. If the delegates to the Peace Conference would like to see no more wars we would advise them to satisfy the yellow man's claims, the black man's claims and the white man's claims, and let all three be satisfied so that there can be indeed a brotherhood of men. But if one section of the human race is to arrogate to itself all that God gave for the benefit of mankind at large, then let us say human nature has in no way changed, and even at the Peace Conference where from the highest principles of humanity are supposed to emanate there will come no message of peace.

There will be no peace in the world until the white man confines himself politically to Europe, the yellow man to Asia and the black man to Africa. The original division of the earth among mankind must stand, and any one who dares to interfere with this division creates only trouble for himself. This division was made by the Almighty Power that rules, and therefore there can be no interference with the plans Divine.

Cowardice has disappeared from the world. Men have died in this world war so quickly and so easily that those who desire liberty today do not stop to think of death, for it is regarded as the price which people in all ages will have to pay to be free; that is the price the weaker people of Europe have paid; that is the price the Negro must pay some day.

Let the Peace Conference, we suggest, be just in its deliberations and in its findings, so that there can be a true brotherhood in the future with no more wars.

Printed in the *NW*, Saturday, 30 November 1918.

1. The first plenary session of the peace conference opened on 18 January 1919, almost ten weeks after the signing of the Armistice on 11 November 1918. The conference was attended by seventy delegates representing twenty-seven of the victorious powers (Germany was excluded until the peace terms were ready for submission). The formal ending of the conference occurred when the League of Nations came into being on 10 January 1920.

[30 November 1918]

RACE DISCRIMINATION MUST GO.

At last the darker peoples of the world have started out to make their united demands on Occidental civilization. The world war will not have been waged in vain if the principal peace aim of Japan, representing the interests of the races who are discriminated against in the world, is upheld.

The Universal Negro Improvement Association and African Communities' League of the World, on the night of November 10, held a mass convention of American, West Indian and African Negroes in the Palace Casino, at which the Negro's peace aims were formulated and adopted, and on the Monday following cabled to Europe for circulation all over the world. But a few days after the Japanese press picked up the sentiment of the peace aims of the Negro and embodied one of the principal clauses in their declaration "That racial discrimination throughout the world shall be abolished." The report that comes from Tokio, bearing date of November 20, is as follows: "Japanese newspapers are suggesting that Japan and China raise the race question at the forthcoming Peace Conference with the object of seeking an agreement to the effect that in the future there shall be no further racial discrimination throughout the world."[1] Another report from Japan, bearing date of November 21, says that Japan is coaching China how to enter the Peace Conference.[2]

This report is very suggestive. In it can be seen immediate preparation by the yellow man of Asia for the new war that is to be wagered—the war of the races. This is no time for the Negro to be found wanting in anything. He must prepare himself, he must be well equipped in every department, so that when the great clash comes in the future he can be ready wherever he is to be found. Japan has become the acknowledged leader of the yellow races: the white races are already leading themselves; the Negro must now concentrate on his leadership, casting all his strength there, so that whenever the world again becomes disrupted he can be led into the affray under the leadership which will lead him on to real democracy. It is impossible for the world to change itself in a day through human agencies, and since human nature has not changed, it can be seen plainly that there will be many more wars before mankind will be at peace.

We hope Japan will succeed in impressing upon her white brothers at the Peace Conference the essentiality of abolishing racial discrimination. If she does not succeed, then it will be only the putting off of a thing that must come, only that it could have come about easier in peaceful settlement than by disruption among the races.

Printed in the *NW*, Saturday, 30 November 1918.

1. An Associated Press news report that appeared in the *New York Times* on Friday, 22 November 1918. The United States ambassador in Tokyo on 15 November 1918 reported to the secretary of state the following: "It is hoped by Japanese that the organization of a League of Nations will offer an opportunity to assert the equality of the yellow race, a question which underlies all discussions on the subject. With this in mind plans are being seriously discussed for an immediate alliance with China so that the two nations may work in harmony at the (Peace) Conference" (United States Department of State, *Papers Relating to the Foreign Relations of the United States 1919—The Paris Peace Conference*, vol. I. [Washington, D.C.: GPO, 1942], p. 490). On 13 February 1919, Baron Makino, plenipotentiary delegate of Japan, submitted an amendment to the Covenant of the League that read: "The equality of nations being a basic principle of the League of Nations, the High Contracting Parties agree to accord, as soon as possible, to all alien nationals of States Members of the League equal and just treatment in every respect, making no distinction, either in law or in fact, on account of their race or nationality." The last minute secret negotiations between President Wilson and Baron Makino that forced the Japanese to agree to withdraw both the amendment and their threat to decline to sign the Treaty of Peace were believed to have included, in return, the conference's acceptance of Japan's claim to the former German rights and property in China's Shantung Province (Robert Lansing, *The Peace Negotiations: A Personal Narrative* [Boston: Houghton Mifflin Co., 1921], pp. 243–56).

2. Contained in a cable report to the *New York Times* from Peking (not Japan, as stated in the editorial) dated 21 November and published in the 22 November 1918 issue.

Bureau of Investigation Reports

NEW YORK CITY [*Made*] DEC. 5th 1918
[*for the period of*] DEC. 2nd [*1918*]

IN RE: MARCUS GARVEY, Negro Agitator.

Pursuant to instructions of Special Agent Tucker based on information supplied by Special Agent Finch from a clipping in the "*New York Tribune*" of even date to the effect that at a mass meeting held by the *Universal Negro Improvement Assn.* at the Palace Casino, 135th St. & Madison Ave., and presided over by *Marcus Garvey* who is preaching agitation (in the Black Belt) in Harlem, it appears in this clipping that Garvey had preached a threat to mobilize millions of negroes, combined with Japan and take up arms for social equality. At this meeting delegates were chosen to represent the negroes at the Versailles conference. These delegates were *Asa Phillip Randolph*[1] *and Mrs. Ida B. Wells Barnett. Eliezer Ca[d]et*[2] was appointed interpreter. (All the foregoing are colored.) Garvey also preached that the next war will be between the negroes and the whites unless their demands for justice are recognized and that with the aid of Japan on the side of the negroes they will be able to win such a war. Garvey also advocated that "for every negro lynched by whites in the south the negro ought to lynch a white in the north". With this information at hand I visited the Palace Casino today and collected from the sweepings of the night before various bits of data such as ballots, programmes, etc. I also located one *Ralph A. Jefferies* of 100 West 144th St. who is employed as a porter at the Palace Casino. This man is an American born negro and very loyal. He was a spectator at the mass meeting and overheard all of the foregoing. I have invited him to visit the Bureau Office and supply Special Agent Finch with a signed statement of the things which he heard. This Jefferies also supplied me with the names of Patrolmen Murray and Maher of the 43rd Precinct Police Station with a suggestion that they may also have heard the remarks. Accordingly I visited the 43rd Precinct at 126th St. & Lexington Ave., and interviewed both these policemen neither of whom can recall with any distinction any of the details of the speech. Later on in the afternoon I located one *George Washington Mills* who is a colored informant and a it chanced that he had attended the meeting. I have known this man Mills who is colored, for the past ten years, having at one time been his immediate superior in the Pullman Company. I know him to be absolutely reliable, honest and truthful and he has also supplied me with information which I have requested he submit to the Bureau Office the following day to Special Agent Finch. From the books of the Palace Casino I have collected a list of all the meetings held there by Marcus Garvey with the amount paid for the hall on each occasion. On all of these occasions the hall was hired personally by Marcus Garvey editor of the "Negro World" the dates and amounts paid are as follows:

October 7th 1917	$20.
December 18th 1917	$20.
February 24th 1918	$20.
May 3rd 1918.	$25.
June 27th 1918.	$25.
July 12th 1918	$25
July 26th 1918.	$25
August 20th 1918.	$25.
September 3rd 1918.	$25.
November 10th 1918.	$25.
December 1st 1918.	$25.

Of the foregoing dates I personally have attended the meeting of Nov. 10th 1918, a report of which will be found on file under Marcus Garvey. From various inquiries I have made in the Black Belt, I have learned that this man although not a citizen has been and is stirring up a great deal of discontent among the loyal negro element in that district and that with the growing discontent there will sooner or later be violence. There is absolutely no danger of conflict between the whites and blacks of this neighborhood but there is a growing danger of physical conflict between the West Indian negroes and the American negroes. I understand from an informant that one *Lieut. Wm. S. Boult, U.S.A.* (a white man), made a lengthy speech which though not of a seditious nature was anything but patriotic. I will make every effort to locate this white Lieutenant. This hall is owned by the *Everhard Brewery* and has been leased for a period of 20 years to the *Fordon brothers, Morris, Irving and Joseph*. One *Aaron Lansberg* a brother in law of the Fordons, is the man who personally let out the hall to Garvey for all the meetings.

This investigation will be continued in an effort to collect as many witnesses as possible who heard the speech.

I wish to add that I have also visited *Mr. McFarlane, City Editor of the "Tribune"* who promised to have the reporter who covered the meeting visit our office to give a statement. This reporter's name is Mr. Kantor. I gave Mr. Mills one dollar to defray expenses for lunch and carfare from his home to the Bureau Office. He resides at 322 Mott Ave., Bronx.

D. DAVIDSON

DWM

[*Endorsement*] Noted F.D.W.

DNA, RG 65, File OG 329359. TD. Stamped endorsement. Copy of report furnished to Special Agent Finch.

1. Asa Philip Randolph (1889–1979), best known for his leadership of the Brotherhood of Sleeping Car Porters (BSCP), the March on Washington movement, and his prominent position for over half a century as a labor leader and a civil rights activist, was born in Jacksonville, Fla. The son of an AME minister, he was raised in a poor but well-educated family. After working in various menial jobs, Randolph left Jacksonville in 1911 bound for Harlem with the hope of becoming a Shakespearean actor. He enrolled in night school at City College in New York, and during his first year in New York, he joined the Socialist party and came under Eugene Debs's tutelage. He also met Chandler Owen, and together the two men founded the Brotherhood of Labor and the radical *Messenger* magazine, which was financed partly by the Socialist party and partly by Randolph's wife. The *Messenger* soon earned a reputation as the most militant of all black publications, sharply attacking President Woodrow Wilson's reinforcement of segregation and discrimination against black federal employees. The magazine also opposed black participation in the First World War, leading to an extensive investigation of Randolph and Owen by the Department of Justice. In August 1918 the two men were arrested and tried for violating the Espionage Act, but the judge, who considered them as young men influenced by older white socialists, released them.

In 1925, with the *Messenger* in deep financial straits, Randolph accepted a request from a group of New York-based Pullman porters to help their union. While local rank and file leaders did most of the organizing, Randolph provided important symbolic leadership and used his political contacts within the Socialist party as well as with established black leaders and white liberals to gain support for the creation of the Brotherhood of Sleeping Car Porters. The liberalized labor laws of the New Deal and the change in the era's political climate proved highly conducive to Randolph's form of charismatic leadership, with its wide appeal to morality to end discrimination in the labor movement. Finally, in 1935, the AFL granted the BSCP an international charter, and two years later, BSCP became the first black union to obtain a contract from a white employer.

By the late 1930s Randolph had become perhaps the most important black figure in the United States, through his success with the BSCP and his ability to reach a wider black and white audience as an effective orator. But he also became virulently anticommunist, resigning his nominal leadership of the Communist-influenced National Negro Congress in 1939. A year later he formed the March on Washington movement, threatening to lead 100,000 blacks on a march into the nation's capital to protest racial bias in the burgeoning war industries. Following a now-lengendary meeting with Randolph, President Franklin D. Roosevelt issued executive order no. 8802 which forbade job discrimination in industries holding government war material contracts.

After the war, Randolph led the movement to end government segregation. He secured President Truman's agreement to desegregate the armed forces when he threatened to encourage black resistance to the first-ever peacetime draft. In 1963, together with socialist colleague Bayard Rustin, Randolph helped organize the mammoth March on Washington, which took place on 28 August, and helped lead to the passage of the Civil Rights Act of 1964. Throughout the remainder of his life, Randolph remained a symbolic figure in both the labor and civil rights movements. (*NYT*, 18 May 1979; WPA Writers' Program, New York City, "Negroes of New York," Reel I; William H. Harris, "A. Philip Randolph as a Charismatic Leader, 1925–1941," *JNH* 64:4 [Fall 1979], pp. 301–15; Jervis Anderson, *A. Philip Randolph* [New York: Harcourt Brace Jovanovich, 1979]; DNA, RG 65, files BS 61-34, 202600-33, 202600-1617, 202600-1628, 202600-1754, 202600-1775; OG 3507, 185161, 208369, 234939, 258421, 265716, 329359, 338432, 341761, 369443, 369936, 370980).

2. Eliézer Cadet (1898–   ) was born at Port-de-Paix, Haiti, the son of Mesinor Pierre Cadet, a prosperous produce dealer and dyewood merchant of St. Louis du Nord. In April 1911, Cadet was enrolled at the elite school, l'Institution St.-Louis de Gonzague, in Port-au-Prince. After graduating in July 1916, he traveled to America in 1917 to pursue a course of studies in mechanics. He was employed for a time at Nitro, W. Va. It was through a chance reading of the *Negro World* on one of his frequent weekend visits to Brooklyn, then the center of the Haitian immigrant community, that Cadet learned about the UNIA. After the newspaper published a letter from him contending that blacks in the United States had been deliberately deceived about the alleged benefits deriving from America's occupation of Haiti, Cadet became a regular visitor, along with a group of other interested Haitians, at UNIA meetings in Harlem. Since neither of the other two delegates of the UNIA peace mission were able to secure passports for travel to France, Cadet became a one-man delegation. Cadet supported himself in Paris by working as an auto-mechanic with M. Jacquelin, with whom he subsequently entered into a business relationship to establish a fruit cannery in Haiti on land that Cadet proposed to secure. The Haitian concern was intended to be a subsidiary of Jacquelin Cadet & Co., and was given the name Societé des Plantations de Val Paraiso, Port-de-Paix, but the plan ended in failure. Cadet returned to Haiti in December 1919, after stopping briefly in New York in order to meet with Garvey. Cadet later became a *vodun* high priest of the cult of Damballah (the serpent god) and established himself as one of Haiti's most renowned exponents of psychic and mystical phenomena. (Interview with editor, July 1979; Legba Eliézer Cadet to editor, 11 March and 28 May 1979; l'Institution St.-Louis de Gonzague, Delmas, Haiti, annual registers; Gerson Alexis, "Billet à Eliézer Cadet," *Le Nouvelliste*, 12 July 1979).

New York City [*Made*] Dec. 14, 1918
[*for the period of*] Dec. 2 [*1918*]

IN RE: MARCUS GARVEY—Negro Agitator

Acting under orders received from Special Agent Tucker based on request from Special Agent Finch I spent the entire day in securing data on meeting held Sunday night at the Palace Casino 135th Street, where Garvey was the principal speaker. Several speeches were delivered that were evidently intended to start an uprising among the negroes.

I called at the Tribune Office for the purpose of interviewing the reporter who attended said meeting and also got in touch with owners of the property from whom we learned that the rent of the hall had been paid by Garvey in person.

For further details of this investigation see report of Agent Finch under even date.

C. P. McCARVER[1]

MO

DNA, RG 65, File OG 329359. TD.

1. In October 1919, a year and a half after becoming a special agent, Charles P. McCarver was arrested and charged with bribery and conspiracy in violation of the wartime liquor prohibition act.

NEW YORK CITY [Made] in DEC. 3, 1918
[for the period of] Dec. 3 [1918]

IN RE: NEGRO AGITATION Marcus Garvey

Mr. Louis Cantor, a reporter for the New York "Tribune" attended the Negro meeting at the Palace Casino on Nov. 10th at the same time Agent David[so]n of this office was present. Parts of Mr. Davidson's report have been read to Mr. Cantor today regarding the November 10th meeting, and Mr. Cantor states that substantially what Mr. Davidson has in his report is correct with relation to statements made by one Garvey the Negro agitator, at that meeting.

Mr. Cantor states he attended a meeting Sunday night for the "Tribune" and it was from his attendance at this meeting that the article appeared in the "Tribune" on December 2nd. At this meeting Garvey also spoke, and Mr. Cantor now states, in a little more detail what he remembers Garvey to have said at that time with relation to the Japanese question. It is Mr. Cantor's best recollection that Garvey said that the Japanese envoys or Government would be prepared to raise the race question at the Peace Conference, and foresaw a difference of opinion between the Allies and the Japanese that might result in trouble, and in that case the Negroes, if they would throw their weight on the side of the Japanese, would be able to hold the balance of power in the world. He said that the Negro had always been on the side of the white, but if conditions went on as they are going on (lynchings, etc.,) that he could not foretell what the negroes might do, and he was rather doubtful whether the negroes would continue to fight on the side of the whites.

Mr. Cantor states that the "Tribune" article reading:

> "The next war will be between the negroes and the whites unless our demands for justice are recognized . . . "

is correct in tenor, but Mr. Cantor will not say that these are the exact words used by Garvey. Mr. Cantor also states that the idea expressed in the

"Tribune" article is identical with the idea which Garvey meant to convey to the audience.

With regard to that portion of the article which states:

"With Japan to fight with us, we can win such a war. . . ."

Mr. Cantor states to the best of his belief the above is substantially correct.
With regard to that portion which states.

"The cessation of lynching is one of the principles of right our delegates will demand at the conference. For every negro lynched by whites in the South, the negroes aught to lynch a white man in the North."

is practically and substantially what Garvey said.

With regard to the statement of other witnesses that Garvey said that the man who lost arms and legs in France could have lost them in a better cause in America, Mr. Cantor in this instance is reluctant to make any statement for the reason that at the time he was engaged in conversation with some other negro at the meeting.

Mr. Cantor states that there was a negro stenographer at the meeting who recorded Garvey's remarks stenographically. Who this negro stenographer was or why this was done Mr. Cantor does not know.

We are informed also that a white man—an Army Lieutenant named *William T. Boult*—spoke from the same platform to this audience just before Garvey spoke. Lieut. Boult's topics were mostly confined to the league of nations, stating that he believed the negroes should be represented at the peace table. He told some very interesting stories, we are informed, of the heroism of soldiers in the American Army in France. His attitude in general was very patriotic and it is not to be inferred that he participated in the general attempt to stir up trouble among these people—on the contrary, his speech was entirely opposite to the tone of Garvey's.

R. W. Finch

DNA, RG 65, File OG 329359. TD, Carbon copy.

New York City [*Made*] Dec. 3. 1918
[*for the period of*] Dec. 3, 1918

In Re: Negro Agitation Marcus Garvey.

Mr. Ralph A. Jeffreys, who is employed as Porter at the Palace Casino, 135th Street between Fifth and Madison Avenue, states that on December 1st, 1918 Marcus Garvey spoke at the above mentioned hall and that his speech in substance was as follows:

"That if the American Negro did not get their rights the next war would be between the Negro and the White man and that with Japan to help the Negro they would win the war." (When he said this a lot of white people got up and left the hall, followed by the jeers of the Negroes.) "The cessation of lynching is one of the principles which our delegates at the Peace Conference will demand. For every Negro lynched by the Whites in the South the Negroes ought to lynch a white man in the North."

Jeffreys also said that before the meeting while standing alongside of Garvey (Garvey having asked him to turn on the Sign light and he having refused on the ground that he could not do it until an hour before the Meeting was scheduled to begin), Garvey told some thirty or forty people, who were around him in the hall, "That parents should learn the children to save their pennies up and to learn to use fire-arms so that when the time came they would be able to go to war against the Whites".

Garvey also told the people at the meeting "Why go over to Europe and fight for the Whites and lose an arm or a leg when you can fight for a just cause".

Jeffreys says that Garvey's following consists entirely of West India Negroes, that the American Negroes will have nothing to do with them that they think he is a "four-flusher" and "grafter" and is out to get all the money he can out of the Negroes.

Jeffreys also says that on a previous meeting, at which Agent Davidson was present and on which he has made a report, Garvey made a speech which was, in substance, as follows:

"Brothers! We are assembled here to-night for the purpose of getting together to fight for justice. We have been slaves for four hundred years and it is now time that we be recognized as a nation and a people. We are backed by 4,000,000 blacks and we will mobilize if necessary and get what is our just rights. I do not say that there will [b]e but there may be a revolution if we are not recognized. Don't follow the dictates of men like William Randolph Hearst. We are determined to get liberty even at the cost of our lives. No nation is safe when having 12,000,000 dissatisfied people in their center."

Mr. Irving Fordon, proprietor of the Palace Casino, states that Garvey used to come to him a couple of days before he wanted to hold a meeting and hire the hall. Lately Mr. Fordon insisted upon being paid before opening up the hall as in the former meetings Garvey would have to take up a collection to pay for the hall and always ran short. The latter meetings were paid for by small checks on the Negro World endorsed by Marcus Garvey, which are assumed to be checks for subscriptions, and the balance in cash.

Mr. Fordon states that formerly Garvey never got more than two or three hundred people in the Hall but at the last two meetings he had the hall jammed to its greatest capacity, which he attributes to the revolutionary character of the speeches made at the last meetings.

Garvey's following are mostly West India Negroes who make a lot of noise but never take any action.

G. Washington Mills, 322 Mott Avenue, Bronx, N.Y., who attended the meeting at the Palace Casino, 135th Street and Madison Avenue, states that at that meeting he heard one Marcus deliver a lecture, extracts of which are as follows:

> "That Japan was combining with the Negro race to overthrow the white race because the blackman was not getting justice in this country (United States). That it was time for the blackman to mob[i]lize his forces against these former white masters who were not giving the blackman a square deal. That it is a crime [to?] lynch blackmen in the south and the Negroes ought to lynch a White man in the North for every Black man they lynch in the South."

At this part of the speech a number of white men in the audience got up and left the hall and were jeered by the balance of the audience. It seemed to Mr. Mills that Garvey was trying to incite these black people to rebel against the Government, which he is not in favor of. Garvey said that there were twelve million dissatisfied black people in the United States. During the meeting a vote was taken to elect two colored delegates to attend the Peace conference at Versailles, France. A collection was taken up to defray the expense of these delegates.

R. W. FINCH

[*Endorsement*] Noted F.D.W.

DNA, RG 65, File OG 329359. TD. Stamped endorsement.

NEW YORK CITY [*Made*] DEC. 5th 1918
[*for the period of*] Dec. 3rd [*1918*]

IN RE: MARCUS GARVEY, Negro Agitator.

Continuing on my investigation of Dec. 2nd I have again visited the negro district and was supplied with a programme by colored informant, the contents of which is as follows:

PROGRAMME

1. Opening National anthem.
2. My Country 'Tis of Thee.
3. Song Miss Marshall.
4. Recitation Mr. Edw. B. Wright.
   Champion El[oc]utionist of the State of New York.
5. Song Mr. M. Davies.

6. Recitation Miss A[m]y Ashwood.

7. Address on League of Nations by Lieut. Wm. S. Boult.

8. Collection of expenses of meeting.

9. Hymn Onward Christian Soldiers.

10. Address by Marcus Garvey.

11. Distribution of ballots.

12. Appeal for expenses of delegation.

13. Collection of ballots.

14. Appeal for members and selling of newspapers.

15. Returns of election.

The balance of the day was spent in interviewing witnesses at the Bureau Office and obtaining from them statements of extracts of the speech of Dec. 1st by *Marcus Garvey*. The statements mentioned herein are on file under Marcus Garvey. Statements were obt[a]ined from *George Washington Mills, Ralph Jefferies, Irving Fordon and Tribune reporter Kantor*.

To be continued.

D. DAVIDSON

DWM

[*Endorsement*] Noted F.D.W.

DNA, RG 65, File OG 329359. TD. Stamped endorsement. Copy of report furnished to Special Agent Finch.

Lt. Col. H. A. Pakenham to Military Intelligence Division Section Four

Washington. 3/12/18

To: M.I.4.

From: Lieut. Col. H. A. Pakenham C.M.G. General Staff.[1]

Universal Negro Improvement Association and African Community League

With reference to the attached report received from London, could any information regarding the above Association and League be forwarded me for the use of the British Authorities.

BASIL S. ROWE
Lieut.
for Lieut. Col. G.S.

[*Typewritten reference*] PK. 3726

BSR.

DNA, RG 165, File 10218-261/10. TNS, Recipient's copy.

1. Lieut. Col. Hercules Arthur Pakenham (1863–1937), soldier and politician, served as liaison officer between British and American military intelligence agencies during 1918–19, and his expertise as a counterintelligence officer proved invaluable to the American General Staff. (The *Times*, 30 March 1937). Both Britain and France assigned military intelligence staff to Washington, D.C., and according to Bidwell, "the final record in regard to military intelligence cooperation among the three principal Allied nations, especially at the operational level, was notably impressive." (Bidwell, *History of the Military Intelligence Division*, pp. 258–60.) Their cooperation resulted in the preparation and maintenance of a suspect list gathered from French, British, and American sources (Ralph Van Deman, "History and Development of MI5," history file, April 1949, pp. 54–55).

Attachment

War Office Whitehall, [*London*] S.W.1.
5th November, 1918

We should like some information about the "UNIVERSAL NEGRO IMPROVEMENT ASSOCIATION AND AFRICAN COMMUNITY LEAGUE", said to be a Society to further the interests of the negro population and to act as a kind of mutual improvement Society. One of the founders, Marcus GARVEY, of 165 West 131st Street, New York, is also believed to run a newspaper called "The Negro World". Another person possibly connected with this Society is John Edward BRUCE, of 2109, Madison Avenue, New York City. This man is in regular correspondence with a mongrel Soudanese-Egyptian named DUSE MAHOMED [*Ali*], who has been living in England for many years. This man dabbles in any sort of mischievous agitation which comes to hand and out of which a little money is to be made. GARVEY corresponds with negro soldiers in the British Army, who are apparently engaged in extending the membership of this Society.

S. NEWLY
for Col. V. G. W. Kell[1]

SN/EDT

[*Address*] Lt. Col. H. A. Pakenham,
C.M.G., Military Intelligence Branch, War
Department, Washington, D.C., U.S.A.
[*Typewritten reference*] P.F.
I.510/M.I.5.D.3.

DNA, RG 165, File 10218-261/9. TDS, Recipient's copy.

1. Col. Sir Vernon George Waldegrave Kell (1873–1942) was the director of the Special Intelligence Bureau of British Military Intelligence (MI 5) from 1914 until his retirement in 1940. (*WWW*, 1941–50). First organized in 1909 with the title of Central Counter-Espionage Bureau, MI 5 worked in close liaison with American Military Intelligence. However, the term "Counter-Espionage" was replaced in 1917 by the phrase "Special Intelligence," a source of frequent confusion, since all intelligence data collected by MI 5 came from official sources and not through the employment of intelligence agents.

in MID Washington for info; rear (illegible handwritten)

CAPT.
M. I. 4

THE GREATEST MOVEMENT IN THE HISTORY OF THE NEGROES
OF THE WORLD

Enc. 2
10218-2
WAR DEPT

The Movement that means so much to every Black man and woman of the State of New York in common with the 400,000,000 of other Negroes of this Country and other Countries of the world.

The Irish, the Jews, the East Indians and all other oppressed peoples are getting together to demand from their oppressors Liberty, Justice, Equality, and we now call upon the four hundred millions of Negro People of the world to do likewise.

THE UNIVERSAL NEGRO IMPROVEMENT ASSOCIATION AND AFRICAN
COMMUNITIES LEAGUE

Wants every Black man and woman in the State of New York to became an active member of this organiza If you have pride, if you feel that by co-operation we can make conditions better in this State and other St if you believe that the Black boy or Black girl is the equal of other boys and girls of other races, then pro now by co-operating to demonstrate our Manhood and Womanhood, not by talking but by doing things.

We want 50,000 new members in this State and you must be one, for you are a Negro like all o and our battle is in common. If we have to suffer together then we must also work together for our own and welfare.

The general objects of the UNIVERSAL NEGRO IMPROVEMENT ASSOCIATION AND A CAN COMMUNITIES LEAGUE are:

To establish a Universal Confraternity among the race; To promote the sp administer and to assist the needy; To assist in civilizing the backward tribes of Af Nationalism of Independent Negro States in Africa; To establish Commissionaries or countries of the world for the protection of all Negroes irrespective of Nationality; T Colleges and Schools for the racial education and culture of our young men and wom wide Commercial and Industrial Intercourse for the benefit of the race; To work for our people in New York; To promote Industries and Commerce in the State of New of Negroes. If these objects do not appeal to you then you are dead to all sense of ra hood.

THE OFFICERS OF THE ASSOCIATION ARE

MARCUS GARVEY, President and International Organizer	BEN. S. BURRELL, Exec. Secry.	JANIE JENK
ISAAC S. BRIGHT, 1st Vice Pres.	F. B. WEBSTER, Chair. Trust. Board	AMY HAYNE
JAMES HAYNES, 2nd Vice Pres.	HENRY DOUGLAS, Chair. Adv. Board	CARRIE MER
HENRY DOLPHIN, 3rd Vice Pres.	GRANZALINE MARSHALL, Secry.	JULIA A. RUI
JAMES PERKINS, Gen. Secry.	IRENA MOORMAN-BLACKSTON,	CLARENCE A
J. THOMAS WILKINS, Ass. Secry.	Pres. Ladies Division	DAISY DUNN,
	IRENE W. WINGFIELD, 1st Vice Pres.	

Crescent Hall 36-38 W.1

Our Association meets in the ~~Lafayette Building, 165 W. 131st~~ Street, New Yo to 5.30 P. M., in hall 8. Our Office is situated in the same building ~~165 W. 131st~~. and *36-38 W. 135* call in at any time during the day.

WE WANT YOU AS A MEMBER SO PLEASE FILL IN THE FOLLOWING API
TEAR OFF.

- -

MEMBERSHIP

GENERAL SECRETARY, UNIVERSAL N
NEW YORK, ~~Lafayette Hall 165 W. 131st.~~ *Crescent Hall 36*
Please register my name as an active member
for us as a suffering people.

Name ....

Address ....

25 CENTS MUST AC(

(Source: DNA, RG 165, file 10218–261/11). Handwritten corrections by Garvey.

Handwritten corrections by Garvey.

Maj. Wrisley Brown to
Lt. Col. H. A. Pakenham

[*Washington, D. C.*] December 6th, 1918

MEMORANDUM FOR LIEUT. COL. PAKENHAM.
Subject: UNIVERSAL NEGRO IMPROVEMENT ASSOCIATION AND AFRICAN
COMMUNITY LEAGUE,—PK-3726

    1. Pursuant to your request there is appended hereto a copy of circular[1] found in M.I.D. files on the above subject.

    2. Information has been requested from Honorable Emmett J. Scott, Assistant to the Secretary of War, and a request for investigation and report on the Association and League, Marcus Garvey and John Edward Bruce, has been made from Lieut. Col. Biddle of New York. As soon as same is received it will be forwarded to you.

WRISLEY BROWN,
Major, A.S.M.A., U.S.A.

Enc.
bip

[*Typewritten reference*] M.I.4 [*Liaison
Organization*] #27
[*Handwritten endorsement*] Copy filed in
M.I.4 Organization file. 2/10/22
[*Stamped endorsement*] MID   JSB

DNA, RG 165, File 10218-261/11. TN, Carbon copy.

    1. The enclosed circular was the same as the advertisement that appeared in the *Negro World* issue of 9 November 1918, which was the same as the circular referred to in the report of Special Agent R. W. Finch, made on 12 November 1918, reprinted above.

Col. John M. Dunn to Emmett J. Scott

[*Washington, D.C.*] December 6th, 1918

Dear Sir:

    The British Intelligence have made the following inquiry. . . .[1]

    On November 30th we sent you Postal Censorship Report in reference to this Association. May we inquire if you have any additional information concerning the Association, and also Marcus Garvey of #165 West 131 Street, New York City, and John Edward Bruce of #2109 Madison Avenue, New

York City,—the two parties referred to in the inquiry received from the British office. Thanking you in advance, I am   Very truly yours,
JOHN M. DUNN,
Colonel, General Staff,
Acting Director of Military
Intelligence,
By: Wrisley Brown,
Major, A.S.M.A., U.S.A.

No enc.
bip

[*Address*] Honorable Emmett J. Scott,
Assistant to Secretary of War, State, War
& Navy Building, Washington, D.C.
[*Typewritten reference*] M.I.4 #27
[*Endorsement*] MID   JSB

DNA, RG 165, File 10218-261/13 53 (50). TL, Carbon copy. Stamped endorsement.

   1. Another reference to the letter from Col. V. G. W. Kell to Lt. Col. Pakenham of 5 November 1918, printed above.

Bureau of Investigation Reports

NEW YORK CITY [*Made*] DEC. 13th 1918.
[*for the period of*] DEC. 9th [*1918*]

IN RE: MARCUS GARVEY, Negro Agitator,

Pursuant to instructions of Special Agent Finch I have this day in company with Special Agent Taylor, made an attempt to apprehend the subject. I visited the office of "THE NEGRO WORLD" a publication of which *Garvey* is managing editor at No. 36–38 West 135th St. Upon my arrival there I was informed that Garvey was out of town but doubting this information Agent Taylor and I remained in the vicinity of his office with the possibility in view that he might arrive.

I have learned that this Garvey spoke at the Regent Theatre Baltimore, Md. on Sunday afternoon, Dec. 8th. After a lengthy stay in the vicinity of Garvey's office we returned to the Bureau Office.

To be continued.

D. DAVIDSON

DWM

DNA, RG 65, File OG 329359. TD. Copy of report furnished to Special Agent Finch.

Washington, d.c. [*Made*] 12–10–[19]18
[*for the period of*] 12–9–[19]18

IN RE: LIBERTY CONGRESS:[1]

Continuing on this case I am in receipt of a letter from *John Bowles,* colored informant which is hereby submitted:

"I am in Baltimore as you will see. I will have something to report to you in a very few days that will give you a jolt. There is more in the wind than we think. Try and make an appointment with me for not later than Monday afternoon. Important."

I then proceeded to *John Bowles home 3238 "R" St. N.W.* and was informed by his Mother that he was out looking for me. I then went to *Bladensburg, Md.* to find him but was not successful and returned to the office.

I then had a conference with *Dr. Craig*[2] who submitted the names of *Cladius M. Green* and *Herbert H. Presturidge* both of *408 Florida Ave.*, who came here from New York and were sent by *Marcus Garvey*, editor of the negro *"World" 36 & 38 W. 135th St., New York*. Their instructions were to secure a Church or hall at any cost for *Garvey* to speak in, in this city on the 16th of this month. Dr. Craig says there is something going on among the colored people and he is trying to find out who is financing this matter.

This is the first report we have had on Marcus Garvey or either of the above named and it is in its infancy. Dr. Craig has been requested to make a surface investigation and report immediately the findings in this matter.

J. G. C. CORCORAN

DNA, RG 65, File OG 369936. TD.

1. The name *Liberty Congress* derived from the conference organized in June 1918 in Washington, D.C., by Hubert H. Harrison, William Monroe Trotter, Allen Whaley, and other officials of the National Equal Rights League under the title "the National Liberty Congress of Colored Americans." The annual meeting of the National Equal Rights League that followed in Chicago, 17–19 September 1918, however, was also known in certain circles as the Liberty Congress, since it was at this meeting that the idea was presented for the convening of the National Race Representative Congress for World Democracy, which was held in Washington, D.C., 16–18 December 1918. There was yet a fourth gathering that was referred to as the Liberty Congress, namely the National Colored Liberty Conference, held in Washington, D.C., 24–29 June 1919, and organized by the NERL. (*The Guardian*, 1 June 1918, 6 July 1918; DNA, RG 65, file OG 369936).

2. Dr. Arthur Ulysses Craig (b. 1871) was employed by the Bureau of Investigation in 1919 as one of its principal undercover agents in New York City to investigate black radicals. Born in Weston, Mo., Craig received his bachelor of science degree from the University of Kansas's school of electrical engineering, Lawrence, Kans., in 1895, becoming thereby the first black electrical engineer in the United States. Craig began his teaching career at Tuskegee Institute, where he lectured in physics from 1896 until 1901. He worked as a teacher in the high schools of Washington, D.C., where he was appointed superintendent of schools for three years. He helped to originate the public playgrounds of Washington, D.C., and also was one of the founders of the Colored Social Settlement. (DNA, RG 65, files OG 3057, OG 208369; J. L. Nichols, *The New Progress of a Race* (n.p., 1929), pp. 354–56).

Postal Censorship Report

NEW YORK, N.Y.
Dec. 11 1918
INDEX NO. *123553*

U.S. POSTAL CENSORSHIP

FROM	TO
Eliezer Cadet	*Mr. Marcel Herard*[2]
Haitian Consul's Office[1]	*Inst. St. Louis de Gonzague*[3]
31–33 Broadway	*Port au Prince*
New York City	*Haiti*
DATE OF LETTER *Dec. 2 1918.*	NO. OF ENCLOSURES *6*[4]
Copied by MEH	

COMMENTATOR NO. *60–632*   BRANCH *Social*   DATE *Dec. 11 1918*
LANGUAGE *French*   ORIGINAL TO *MID ONI*   D.A.C.   A.C. *HRJ*

COMMENT
Negro Agi[ta]tion.

Writer, who is a negro, is aiding a movement to better the condition of the negro race and free them from the tyranny of the white people. He says—"I now belong to the Universal Negro Improvement Association and African Committies League—the object of this league is to work for the formation of the African Empire. The 10th of last month we held a mass meeting in the Palace Casino, there were 5 or 6 thousand people present. We voted and cabled to the capitals of the entire world the peace propositions of the blacks of the whole world. Yesterday evening Dec. 1st we held the largest meeting since Booker Washington's time. We elected two delegates and an interpreter and secretary to sen[d] to the next peace conference at Versailles to represent the interests of the black race. I was elected as interpreter & secretary. I expect that in a week or two I shall leave for France with the delegates. How, my dear [M]arcel, I am studying the administration and the history of the black race. Where I am ready I think that I shall be sent to Afric[a] to contribute to the administration of the German colonies which are to be returned to the blacks.—(English) so doing, not only will the cause of our race in Africa, but also all over the world—The next world war will be a war of races. The yellow race is mobilizing his forces, therefore we neg[ro]es of the world must organize ourselves, for we will be the balance of power in the world. Where will go our forces, where will the victory. We are not going to fight and die for the white man Liberty any more, but for the good and welfare of the negro race.".

A. W. S.

DIVISION	DATE	COPIES	DISPOSITION AND SIGNATURE
WTB			
MIB	12/12/PM	5	*Refer to British Liaison Officer & French Liaison Officer—HTP forward BMD*
ONI	12/12/18	2	*JJC*
CCC			*3 copies French Liaison Officer 12/17/18 Velay*
			4 copies British Liaison Officer JWR 12/14/18
PO			
EX.AC	12/18/18		*MKS-D*

THIS SLIP ALWAYS TO ACCOMPANY LETTER

[*Typewritten reference*] Subject Index 1-6-A
1-8-A-1
[*Handwritten endorsement*]
T de CR/FLH 47
[*Stamped endorsements*] LIEUT.
WINTERBOTHAM CAPT. HAYES M.I. 4-41
COPY OF THIS ABSTRACT HAS BEEN SENT
TO LIEUT. COL. NICHOLAS BIDDLE M.I.4.

DNA, RG 165, File 10218–261/18. D, printed form with typewritten additions. This report was originally an enclosure to a letter from Col. John Dunn to Emmett J. Scott, 2 January 1919, DNA, RG 165, File 10218–261/19 2-1.

    1. Charles Moravia was the consul general of Haiti in New York, 1916–19.

    2. Marcel Herard (1900–) was born at Petite Rivière de l'Artibonite, Haiti. After attending primary school there, he enrolled at l'Institution St.-Louis de Gonzague in Port-au-Prince, where he met and became a close friend of Eliézer Cadet. In May 1919 Herard graduated with distinction and from 1921 until 1929 he studied medicine in France at the Faculty of Medicine of Paris, specializing in otolaryngology and ophthalmology. He presented his doctoral thesis in 1929, whereupon he returned to Haiti. He practiced medicine in Haiti from 1930 until 1962, when he left to serve in Guinea at the time of that country's independence from France. In 1964 he was appointed chief of service in ophthalmology and otolaryngology at Ballay Hospital in Conakry. He returned to live in Haiti in 1967. (Interview with editor, July 1979; curriculum vitae of Dr. Marcel Herard).

    3. L'Institution St.-Louis de Gonzague was founded in Haiti in September 1890 by the Frères de l'Instruction Chrétienne, a Roman Catholic religious order from Plöermel, France.

    4. The enclosures were neither identified in the report itself nor retained.

Newspaper Report

[*Afro-American*, 13 December 1918]

A New Radical Organization

The Universal Negro Improvement Association and African Communities League, a new and radical movement held its first meeting before several hundred persons at the Regent Theatre last Sunday [*8 December*].

The object was to form a branch of the New York body in this city. Nearly a hundred persons joined during the meeting.

The organization is novel in that it aims to comprehend all colored peoples, Americans, West Indians, Africans and Indians in its membership. In addition to forming a league for political and social improvement of the Negro's condition in this country, the aim is to establish in Africa a strong Negro Nation, which could command respect for the Negro, who resides in white countries.

Mr. Marcus Garvey, the organizer, who is a fluent speaker but not always logical emphasized the part the colored race is to play in the next war between the white peoples and the yellow peoples.

"The Negroes of the world," he said, "hold the balance of power, and with whomever they cast their lot in the next war, that side wins."

The audience applauded this and there was even more applause when he said that the white people had rallied two million Negroes from United States, West Indies and Africa to help save democracy.

"If Negroes can face death to preserve the liberties of white peoples, then Negroes can face death to procure the liberties of black people."

Besides the 25 cents initiation fees that many persons paid to join the new organization, a collection was taken to send three delegates to the Peace Conference at Versailles.

Printed in the *Afro-American* (Baltimore, Maryland), Friday, 13 December 1918.

Maj. Wrisley Brown to Lt. Col. H. A. Pakenham

[*Washington, D.C.*] December 14, 1918

MEMORANDUM FOR LIEUTENANT-COLONEL PAKENHAM:
Subject: Marcus Garvey, John Edward Bruce, and the Universal Negro
          Improvement Association and African Community League.

Pursuant to your request, there is submitted herewith copy of memorandum received from the Hon. Emmett J. Scott, Special Assistant to the Secretary of War, in connection with above subjects.

WRISLEY BROWN,
MAJOR, A.S.M.A., U.S.A.

hgb

[*Typewritten reference*] M.I. 4-27

DNA, RG 165, File 10218–261/30. TN, Carbon copy.

Attachment

Washington. December 11, 1918

MEMORANDUM FOR THE MILITARY INTELLIGENCE DIVISION:

Attention of Major Wrisley Brown:

Replying to your letter of December 6th with reference to Marcus Garvey, and the UNIVERSAL NEGRO IMPROVEMENT ASSOCIATION AND AFRICAN COMMUNITY LEAGUE, and John Edward Bruce, 2109 Madison Ave., New York City, I wish to state that:

1. I wrote Marcus Garvey to come to see me for an interview. He was in my office yesterday, December 9th and I went over the whole situation with him in detail, pointing out to him that certain editorial comments and the news columns of his newspaper tend to inspire unrest among members of the Negro race, thereby disrupting the unity of purpose which should exist between the racial groups in America, etc.,

I have met this man once before.[1] He is a West Indian and represents the agitator type. He thanked me most profusely for sending for him and pointing out to him the difficulties probably ahead of him and for the frank manner in which I talked to him and for the counsel offered him. He has promised to change the general policy of his publication; I cannot say whether he will keep his promise. I shall keep an eye on it.

2[.] THE UNIVERSAL NEGRO IMPROVEMENT ASSOCIATION AND AFRICAN COMMUNITY LEAGUE [i]s a "paper organization" and has nothing back of it except the general unrest of Darker peoples who are groping their way and wondering how they are coming out of the present situation. Garvey is a "soap box orator" around New York and while he can cause a certain amount of mischief, he is not a man around whom any serious movements can be prompted. He and others are asking "What is the Negro to get out of the war"?

3. John Edward Bruce, 2109 Madison Ave., New York City, is a well-known writer for Negro magazines and newspapers. He contributes largely to West African publications and is the type of man who would correspond with one of the type of DUSE MAHOMED [Ali]. While Bruce has no widespread influence, he is favorably known to Negro readers and is one of those who is seeking at this time to "redress the wrongs of the Negro people of the world."

The activities of THE UNIVERSAL NEGRO IMPROVEMENT ASSOCIATION AND AFRICAN COMMUNITY LEAGUE, in my opinion, should not be seriously regarded.

EMMETT J. SCOTT
SPECIAL ASSISTANT TO SECRETARY OF WAR
ROOMS 144–146

EE,

[*Typewritten reference*] 2-1

DNA, RG 165, File 10218–261/27. TDS, Recipient's copy.

1. The exact date of Scott's meeting with Garvey is not known, but from Garvey's later testimony, they apparently met in 1916. According to Garvey: ". . . on his arrival [in America] he visited Tuskegee Institute on an outstanding invitation from the late Dr. Booker T. Washington. He met at the Institute the then Principal, Dr. Robert R. Moton and Professor E. J. Scott, the Secretary-Treasurer. He discussed with them the purposes of the Organization which were similar to the present aims and objects in the constitution. He received very little encouragement and left Tuskegee in continuation of a trip throughout the United States." (Marcus Garvey, "History of the UNIA," lesson 20, "School of African Philosophy," Toronto, Canada, 1937, p. 1).

Lt. Col. H. A. Pakenham to Military Intelligence Division Section Four

Washington. 16/12/18

To: M.I.4.-27
From: Lieut. Col. H. A. Pakenham C.M.G. General Staff.
re Marcus Garvey
Reference your 10218–261 of the 6th. December, I have received to-day from London a communication, copy of which I attach. It appears that the above is a fraud and that little importance can be attached to the movement named "Negro Improvement Association". It would be interesting to know who Mr. John E. Bruce of 2109 Madison Avenue is, and why he is interested in this fraud.

H. A. PAKENHAM
Lieut. Col. G.S.

HAP/BSR.
2 Enc.

[*Typewritten reference*] PK.3891

DNA, RG 165, File 10218–261/37 54X-50X. TNS, Recipient's copy.

Attachment

War Office Whitehall, [*London*] S.W.1
22nd November, 1918

In continuation of my letter No. P.F.I. 510 dated 5th November regarding the "Universal Negro Improvement Association and African Community League" DUSE MOHAMED [*Ali*] has since been questioned about various matters including Marcus GARVEY. He says that Marcus GARVEY first came to see him in 1913, saying he was from Jamaica. He was stranded in this country and DUSE MOHAMED gave him a job as a messenger in his office but as his conduct was unsatisfactory he was discharged after about three months. After that he claimed to have gone to the continent of Europe, but DUSE MOHAMED did not hear of him again until about a year ago when Mr. Bruce sent him a circular (copy attached) saying that Marcus GARVEY had claimed to be a graduate of Oxford University and asking DUSE MOHAMED what he knew about him. The latter told Mr. Bruce that GARVEY was a fraud and he afterwards heard from Bruce that he had attended the meeting advertised in the circular and had told the speaker to clear out.[1] DUSE MOHAMED'S own opinion is that GARVEY'S association is nothing but a pretext for collecting money for his own purposes and that there is no danger in the movement.

S. NEWLY
for Col. V. G. W. Kell

SN/UV
Enc. 1

[*Address*] Lt. Col. H. A. Pakenham,
C.M.G., Military Intelligence Branch,
War Department, Washington, D.C.
[*Typewritten reference*] P.F.I.
510/M.I.5.D.3.[2]

DNA, RG 165, File 10218–261/36. TDS, Recipient's copy.

1. The exchange of correspondence between John E. Bruce and Dusé Mohamed Ali has not been found among the John E. Bruce Papers.

2. British Military Intelligence was divided into two branches, one of which fell under the director of military intelligence, while the other fell under the director of special intelligence. The first branch (MI 1, MI 2, MI 3, and MI 4), collected positive intelligence from the war zone, foreign countries, and the British secret service. The second branch was responsible for the collection of negative intelligence, consisting of counterespionage (MI 5), war trade data (MI 6), press control and propaganda (MI 7), cable censorship (MI 8), and postal censorship (MI 9). MI 5 D had responsibility for coordination and direction of counterespionage throughout the British dominions and colonies, through the Special Intelligence Bureau (SIB) in London and through official correspondents, which usually consisted of the governor, colonial secretary, or the chief of police. In addition, MI 5 D dealt with the Irish situation, both in Ireland and the United States, and also with East Indian affairs. (H. John Bullock, *A History of M.I. 5: The Origin and History of British Counterespionage Service* [London: Arthur Barker, 1963]; Central Special Intelligence Bureau, Overseas Section, Report on "Special Intelligence" Organization in the Self-Governing Dominions and Colonies in conjunction with the Central Special Intelligence Bureau, October 1917 [JA, CSO 1B/5/829, Confidential and Secret Correspondence]; Winston S. Churchill, Secretary of State for War, "Reduction of Estimates for Secret Services," HLRO, 19 March 1920, Lloyd George Papers F9/2/16).

Attachment

[*ca. 13 January 1918*]

THE SALVATION OF A PEOPLE DEPENDS
ON THE LEADERS THEY PRODUCE.

Photograph.

And Every Negro

Man and Woman

Should Hear

PROFESSOR

MARCUS GARVEY

Founder of

The Universal Negro Improvement Association
Speak on the Subject of
"THE BURDEN OF THE NEGRO WOMAN"
at
ODDFELLOWS' TEMPLE[1]
2152 Fifth Avenue, Bet. 131st and 132nd Street
THIS SUNDAY AFTERNOON, JANU[AR]Y 13, 1918.
at 3 o'clock sharp.

A MAN OF DEEP THOUGHT AND NOBLE PURPOSE WHOSE PLANS
CALL FOR A RESTORATION OF THE NEGRO TO A PLACE
AMONG THE GREAT NATIONS OF THE EARTH &
PUT OFF EVERYTHING AND HEAR HIM.

Enc. 2

DNA, RG 165, File 10218–261/35. TMS, Transcript.

1. The meeting was originally scheduled for Lafayette Hall (*Home News*, 16 January 1918).

Bureau of Investigation Report

NEW YORK CITY [*Made*] DEC. 19th 1918
[*for the period of*] Dec. 16th [*1918*]

IN RE: MARCUS GARVEY, Negro Agitator.

Report received by a confidential informant is to the effect that Garvey intended holding a monster mass meeting at the Manhattan Casino, 1[3]5th St. & 8th Ave. at 8 p.m. this day. Accordingly and with instr[u]ction from Special Agent Finch I have gone to the Manhattan Casino to learn the details of the meeting. Upon my arrival there I learned from Mr. Walton, proprietor of the Casino that the hall has been hired for Monday evening December 23rd and it is specifically stated in the contract that this is for a dance and not a mass meeting. Mr. Walton is a very loyal man and showed a ready inclination to deny them the use of the hall. I thereupon requested Mr. Walton to permit them to use the hall at all times provided they pay their fees and he can best help the Government by informing us in advance of any proposed dance or meeting. The hall was hired personally by Marcus Garvey who paid a $10 deposit and is to pay the balance of $50 on the night of the affair. It is also stipulated in the contract that Walton will charge Garvey $25 an hour for every hour or part thereof that the hall is possessed after 11 p.m.

D. DAVIDSON

DWM

[*Endorsement*] Noted F. D. W.

DNA, RG 65, File OG 329359. TD. Stamped endorsement. Copy of report furnished to Special Agent Finch.

Col. John M. Dunn to Maj. W. H. Loving[1]

[*Washington, D.C.*] December 17th, 1918

Dear Sir:

It is urgently requested that you call at this office tomorrow,—Wednesday,—morning, December 18, to take up an important matter. Please ask for Captain J. S. Buhler.[2]

Thanking you in advance for your attention to this, I am Very truly yours,

JOHN M. DUNN,
Colonel, General Staff,
Acting Director of Military Intelligence,
BY: J. S. Buhler,
Captain, U.S.A.

bip

[*Address*] #915 S. Street, N.W.,
Washington, D.C.
[*Typewritten reference*] M.I.4 #27
[*Endorsement*] Delivered Dec. 17 '18

DNA, RG 165, File 10218–261/32. TL, Carbon copy. Endorsement is handwritten.

1. Maj. Walter Howard Loving (1872–1945) was a renowned military bandleader in the Philippines with the band of the 48th Infantry U.S. volunteers, which later became the Philippine Constabulary Band. He retired in 1916, but a year later, in March 1917, he returned to duty and accepted a position with the Military Intelligence Branch of the army. According to Ralph Van Deman:

> In the fall of 1917 it became evident that agents of the Central Powers were circulating among the Negro people of the United States. The method of agitation used was by word of mouth and it was evident that measures to counteract the influence of such propaganda must be taken if we were to avoid serious trouble with the Negro population. For this purpose two extremely capable and reliable Negro men [Maj. W. H. Loving and Charles Holston Williams] were selected after most careful investigation. These men were instructed to circulate among the various communities where unrest was being reported among the Negro population. They were to remain long enough in each community to determine for themselves what the real trouble was and then by conversations and formal talks in Negro churches and other meeting places to persuade the Negroes in the community that the actions being suggested to them by persons who had previously circulated among them would lead to very serious consequences if not abandoned. ("History and Development of MI 5," pp. 56–57).

In August 1919, Loving returned to the Philippines on special duty to revitalize the Philippine Band. During the Second World War, he was captured by the Japanese and executed in 1945. (Veterans Administration, Washington, D.C., file 372(214)XC 2311092; DNA, RG 165, files 10218–261, 274, 279, 280, 302, 307, 310, 322, 331, 346; RG 94, Records of the Adjutant General's Office, file 11258 PRD-93; *Crisis* 12 [June 1916]:67; *Negro Year Book*, 1921–22, p. 288; Charles H. Williams, *Sidelights on Negro Soldiers* [Boston: B. J. Brimmer Co., 1923]; Greene, *Black Defenders*, p. 143; Maidan Flores, *Philippine Constabulary Diamond Jubilee, 1901–76* [n.p., n.d.], pp. 72–77).

2. Joseph S. Buhler (ca. 1881–1961) was best known as a lawyer for several theatrical personalities and the organizer of the Wake Up America Committee, the purpose of which was to alert citizens to the perceived menace of the Axis powers. During World War I, he served as a captain in the Military Intelligence Division. (*NYT*, 19 May 1961).

HEAR
MARCUS GARVEY
AND
MRS. IDA B. WELLS-BARNETT
DELEGATE TO PEACE CONFERENCE
AT BETHEL CHURCH, BALTIMORE
Wednesday, December 18, at 8 o'clock
Auspices of Baltimore Division of Universal Negro Improvement Association, Inc., Wm. D. Rankin, President

---

Maj. W. H. Loving to the Director, Military Intelligence Division

Washington, D.C., December 20th, 1918

From: Major W. H. Loving, P.C.
To: Director of Military Intelligence.
Subject: M[a]rcus Garvey, Editor of the "The Negro World" and
          Mrs. Ida B. Wells-Barnett of Chicago.

1.   I am inclosing a synopsis of the speech[1] made by Mr. Marcus Garvey before the local branch of Universal Negro Improvement Association and African Communities League at Bethel A.M.E. Church, Baltimore, December 18th, 1918. The strongest points of Mr. Garvey's speech have been translated and I am also sending you the note book which contains Mr. Garvey's full speech and that of Mrs Ida B. Wells-Barnett together with Mrs Marie Madre Marshall's introductory remarks.[2] This book may be filed for future reference. . . .

W. H. LOVING
Major P.C., Retired.

[Endorsement] CAPT. J. E. CUTLER[3] M.M.S.

DNA, RG 165, File 10218–261/34 I 2–1. TDS, Recipient's copy. Stamped endorsement.

  1. The synopsis appears printed below.
  2. The stenographic notebook contained the original shorthand of the speeches, but attempts to decipher and transcribe it have not been successful.

3. James Elbert Cutler (1876–1959), a professor of sociology at the University of Michigan, was the author of *Lynch Law: An Investigation into the History of Lynching in the United States* (New York: Longmans Green and Co., 1905), the first scholarly attempt to explore the causes and effects of southern mob violence. In 1918–19, Cutler served as captain and later major in the Military Intelligence Division as an advisor on black troop morale. M. M. S. is the abbreviation for Military Morale Section. (DNA, RG 165, file 10218–190-1-124x; *WWWA*; letter to editor, 26 October 1978, from Yale University Alumni Records Office).

Maj. Wrisley Brown
to Lt. Col. H. A. Pakenham

[*Washington, D.C.*] December 21st, 1918

Memorandum for Lieut. Col. Pakenham.
Subject: Universal Negro Improvement Association and
African Communities League, and Marcus Garvey.

1.   Annexed hereto is the stenographic report of extracts from a speech made by Marcus Garvey at the Bethel A.M.E. Church, Baltimore, Md., December 18, 1918.

2.   Attention is called to the statement made by Mrs. Marie Madre Marshall introducing Mrs. Ida B. Wells-Barnett. It is reported to this office that Ida B. Wells-Barnett is considered a far more dangerous agitator than Marcus Garvey.[1] Both of these people are being carefully watched.

WRISLEY BROWN,
Major, A.S.M.A.

Enc.

bip

[*Typewritten reference*] M.I.4 #36
[*Stamped endorsement*] MID JSB
[*Handwritten endorsement*] Delivered
Dec. 30, '18

DNA, RG 165, File 10218–261/21. TN, Carbon copy.

1. In his report of this meeting to the director of Military Intelligence, Major Loving agreed with the assessment made of Ida Wells-Barnett. He wrote: "If passports are to be requested for the above named individuals I suggest that the record of each person be looked up before a passport is granted. I recommend this in the case of Mrs. Ida B. Wells-Barnett especially. This subject is a known race agitator." (DNA, RG 165, file 10218–302/3, 20 December 1918).

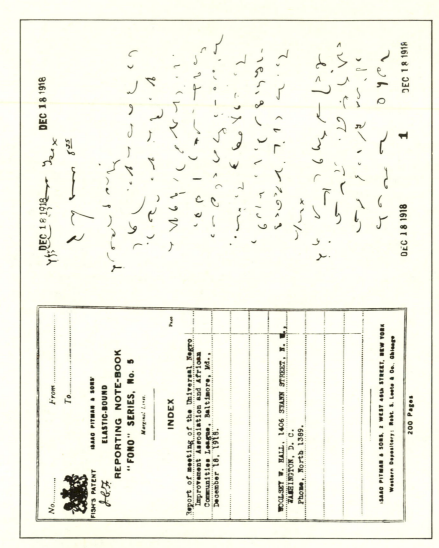

Shorthand Notes from a Speech by Marcus Garvey

Attachment

MEETING OF THE BALTIMORE BRANCH
OF THE
UNIVERSAL NEGRO IMPROVEMENT ASSOCIATION AND
AFRICAN COMMUNITIES LEAGUE.

BETHEL A. M. E. CHURCH,
BALTIMORE, MD.
DECEMBER 18, 1918.

8.35 P.M.

THE PRESIDING OFFICER. Will some[*one*] in the audience lead us in prayer?

(After prayer)

THE PRESIDING OFFICER. We are gathered here this evening under the local division of the Universal Negro Improvement Association. The association aims for the uplift of the Negro race, with which we all are identified. I want to state that the Hon. Mr. Marcus Garvey and Mrs Ida Wells-Barnett have been scheduled to speak to night. It happens that the Negro Equal Rights League, that is convening now in Washington,[1] has detained Mrs Barnett. We are expecting her though, at a later hour, but in the event of her not getting here she will be sure to be here with us on Sunday afternoon at the Regent Theatre, on Pennsylvania Avenue. But we hope she will be here, so we will at this juncture—I have the pleasure of introducing to you the Hon. Mr. Marcus Garvey, International Organizer of this organization, and General President. Mr. Marcus Garvey of New York.

MR. GARVEY: Mr. Chairman, ladies, and gentlemen: It affords me great pleasure to be here this evening to speak to you under the auspices of the Baltimore Branch of the Universal Negro Improvement Association and African Communities League. I understand that Mrs Ida B. Wells-Barnett of Chicago and myself were to be the principal speakers tonight. Mrs. Barnett was elected by the Universal Negro Improvement Association and African Communities League of America and of the West Indies on December 1st by 700 members and supporters of this organization for the purpose of representing our cause at Versailles at the Peace Conference. I was sent over by my people there to attend the National Congress of Equal Rights and affiliated societies, which has been meeting in Washington since Monday, whereat we elected nine more delegates to represent the cause of our race at this conference.

E[X]TRACTS FROM SPEECH

P.4— What the Universal Negro Improvement Association stands for—"to draw into one united whole the four hundred millions of black people of the world," etc.

P.14— But this great war has brought about a change. It has driven the men of all races to be more selfish, and Negroes, I think Negroes of the world, have been observing, have been watching carefully, and have been scrutinizing all these statesmen I have named; the statesmen of America and the statesmen of England, and in four and a half years of war, whilst observing them, whilst listening to every word that fell from their lips, we never heard one syllable from the lips of Woodrow Wilson, from the lips of Theodore Roosevelt in America, from the lips of Bonar Law or Balfour in England, as touching anything relative to the destinies of the Negroes of America or England or of the world.

P.15— Compelled to show our loyalty 100 per cent for the cause of the democracy of the oppressed peoples of Europe.

P.16— Not one has said one specific word as touching lynching, jimcrowism, and other segregation.

P.21— They have paid the price, the price of death, that their posterity might be free. Those blacks did it, those whites did it, and some of those yellow people did it, and some Hindus did it, but today all of the whites are getting their freedom. The posterity of those dead white men are today enjoying the things that they fought for—the thing, democracy, and the posterity of those brown Hindus and some of those yellow men are too, enjoying it, and by and through the same avenue the Negroes should enjoy it; but they have sent for men like DuBois and Moton to prevent us from getting it.[2] (Applause)

P.22— Whilst the Hindus are organizing for self-government; whilst they are taking this opportunity to impress upon their respective governments; whilst they sent out their representatives, elected by the people, what happened to us? Twelve millions of us were told two Saturdays ago that DuBois and Moton were in France to prevent Negroes from getting the fruits of th[ei]r sacrifices on the battlefie[l]ds.

P.30— At the moment of the landing of our great President in France, they lynched a Negro in the uniform of the United States Army.

P.33— On November 10th the Association cabled respective allies of America the Association's peace aims.

P.36—   Japan is catering to the sentiment of the darker peoples of the world.

P.37—   We, like Josephus Daniels,[3] believe that the next world war will be a war of the races, and I believe that that war will star[t] between the white and the yellow peoples. Negr[o]es should make no compromise with either the white men or the yellow men. We have become the balance of power between the white men of Europe and the yellow men of Asia.

P.39—   America cannot afford to keep within her bounds twelve millions of organized dissatisfied people.

P.41—   Can die on the battlefields of France and Flanders to give liberty to an alien race and cannot die somewhere to give liberty to himself.

P.54—   Out of this war we have produced the American, or the West Indian, or the African Napoleon who will ultimately lead the 400,000,000 black people of the world to Victory.

P.58—   Must organize to know what we are to get out of the next war and see that we get it before one sacrifice is made.

P.61—   Anglo-Saxon and American capitalists met in London and determined that "the nigger" should pay the cost of the war.

PRESIDING OFFICER: Mrs Marie Marshall will make a certain request at this juncture, before Mrs Barnett is introduced.

P.72—   MRS. MARIE MADRE MARSHALL: "My dear friends: It always happens that in—there are always traitors among the race. When it was known that Ida B. Wells-Barnett was coming to Baltimore, we—at least it was tipped off to us that there was going to be sent a spy to report her speech. You know nothing would intimidate Ida B. Wells-Barnett (cries o[f] "hear, hear" in aud[i]ence). When only a girl of nineteen years old she had the courage to write a protest against lynching, for which she had to leave her home to avoid being lynched.[4] Nothing but a girl. You know that she went across the ocean and made friends for the Negro; made friends by the millions for us, so much so that when she returned in two years after, a white methodist minister in the South had pamphlets printed and sent to Europe saying that the people who were over there talking about the treatment of the Negro in the South were liars, that they were paid, but Ida Wells-Barnett has never held her mouth.[5] You know of her visits to the White House year in and year out. You know that she has been fearless and outspoken. It can be said without successful contradiction that she is the most fearless and outspoken speaker or champion that the race has produced."

"What I want to ask you is, if there is a person near you who attempts to report this speech if you will simply make it known to us—not that she is afraid of any[th]ing, but Ida B. Wells-Barnett is scheduled to go abroad, and we know that she will tell you the true story; there will be no buying her off when she gets on the other side, or on this side for that matter. I dont want anything to be said that will have the Department of Justice or others taking measures to deprive her of her passport. You know in time of war we usually shoot spies, and it would be a good thing if by some reason the Negroes could get rid of the spies—of his writing and telling everything to the white man."

"If there is a Negro in this house who has been here for that purpose, if he attempts to report the speech you would do yourself credit to simply report the same to us" (Applause).

P.78–107—   Mrs. Ida B. Wells-Barnett's speech—Nothing of interest—Collection of $42[.]oo was taken & was started by Garvey himself giving $5. Garvey took it all, as he announced for the maintenance of the organization

DNA, RG 165, File 10218–261/33. TD. The final two sentences were handwritten by Maj. Loving.

1. A reference to the National Race Representative Congress for World Democracy, which was called by the National Equal Rights League. Delegates represented various national black organizations as well as local Equal Rights Leagues. In his report of 20 December 1918 to the Director of Military Intelligence, Maj. Loving also confused the National Race Representative Congress for the World Democracy with the National Race Congress of America (NRC), founded in Washington, D.C., on 19 September 1916, probably because the executive committee of the National Race Congress announced, on 4 December 1918, that it had named five delegates to represent it at both the Pan-African Congress and the Paris peace conference in France. The only member of the NRC delegation who succeeded in obtaining a passport from the U.S. State Department was Rev. William H. Jernagin, who arrived in Paris on 20 February 1919, a day late for the first session of the Pan-African Congress. ("The Denial of Passports," *Crisis* 17 [March 1919]:237–38; "Negro Passports Refused," *Messenger* 2 [March 1919]:4).

2. Garvey's assertion implied that both Moton and Du Bois were jointly representing the same official mission. Such an implication was erroneous, however, as Du Bois later made clear: "Neither R. R. Moton nor W. E. B. Du Bois had the slightest idea that the other was planning to sail for France, December 1, until they met in Washington on a quest for passports, November 30. They sailed together on the *Orizaba* and frankly discussed their agreements and disagreements. When they reached France, each went about his own business. Dr. Moton was sent by the President of the United States and the Secretary of War to see and talk to Negro troops. Dr. Du Bois was sent by the NAACP and the *Crisis* to gather the historical facts concerning Negro troops and to call a Pan-African Congress" (*Crisis* 18 [May 1919], p. 9). Moton's visit to France, during which he was assisted by Thomas Jesse Jones, educational director of the Phelps-Stokes Fund who had been assigned to work on black troop morale with the American Expeditionary forces, was denounced afterward by a wide cross section of the black press in America. Moton remained in France for less than a month and returned to America on 20 January 1919, while Du Bois did not leave France until 22 March 1919. (DLC,

George Foster Peabody Papers; *Crisis* 18 [May 1919]:9–10; *New York News*, 20 March 1919; R. R. Moton, "Negro Troops in France," *Southern Workman* 48 [May 1919]: 219–24; DNA, RG 120, Records of the American Expeditionary Forces, entry 241, box 6176, folder 0101–0200, no. 154; entry 244, box 6183, Moton folder; DNA, RG 165, file 10218–190; Thomas Jesse Jones, *Educational Adaptations: Report of Ten Years' Work of the Phelps-Stokes Fund, 1910–1920* [New York: Phelps-Stokes Fund, n.d.], chap. 8; Clarence G. Contee, "Du Bois, the NAACP, and the Pan-African Congress of 1919," *JNH* 57 [July 1972]:13–28; Felix James, "Robert Russa Moton and the Whispering Gallery after World War I," *JNH* 62 [July 1977]:235–42).

3. Josephus Daniels (1862–1948) was secretary of the navy from 1913 to 1921. (*WBD*).

4. Ida B. Wells-Barnett was thirty years old when she launched her famous protest against the lynching of three black men in Memphis on 9 March 1892. A coowner of the *Memphis Free Speech*, she wrote articles in her paper denouncing the crime, and she began a widespread investigation of the lynching issue. While she was in Philadelphia attending an AME general conference, a white mob destroyed her newspaper office on 17 May 1892, and it became unsafe for her to return to Memphis. (Ida B. Wells, *Crusade for Justice: The Autobiography of Ida B. Wells* [Chicago: University of Chicago Press, 1970], introduction).

5. This is a reference to Wells-Barnett's speaking tours of Great Britain in 1893 and 1894 on the problem of lynching in America during which time she helped form an antilynching committee.

Col. John M. Dunn to Emmett J. Scott

[*Washington, D.C.*] December 21st, 1918

Dear Sir:

Pursuant to understanding had with Captain Buhler of this office a representative of this Division attended the meeting of the Baltimore branch of the UNIVERSAL NEGRO IMPROVEMENT ASSOCIATION AND AFRICAN COMMUNITIES LEAGUE at Bethel A.M.E. Church at Baltimore, Md. on December 18, 1918; and there is enclosed herewith excerpts from the speech made by Marcus Garvey, and also an introductory speech made by one Mrs. Marie Madre Marshall introducing Mrs. Ida B. Wells-Barnett.

Although there are some statements made by Garvey in the annexed report which are undoubtedly intended for the purpose of agitation, the opinion expressed to this office by a reliable investigator is that Garvey should not be taken seriously but should merely be watched.

As it is the apparent intention of Mrs. Ida B. Wells-Barnett to go abroad to endeavor to act as "lobbyist", or in some other way influence action at the Peace Conference, it has been suggested that special attention be given to her record before a passport is granted her. The meeting which she is to address in Baltimore at the Regent Theatre Sunday afternoon, December 22d, will be covered by a representative from this office.

Our investigator reports also that a collection of $42.00 was taken up at the Garvey meeting, and that the first subscription, amounting to $5.00, was made by Garvey himself so as to start the collection. Garvey took all of the money, announcing that it was for the maint[e]nance of the organization. Investigator is of the opinion that Garvey cannot make much, if anything, out of these collections as they are usually small and his expenses alone in traveling would very nearly equal the amounts collected at these meetings. Very truly yours,

> JOHN M. DUNN,
> Colonel, General Staff,
> Acting Director of Military Intelligence,
> BY: Wrisley Brown,
> Major, A.S.M.A.

Enc.

bip

[*Typewritten reference*] M.I.4 #27
[*Endorsement*] MID JSB

DNA, RG 165, File 10218–261/22. TL, Carbon copy. Stamped endorsement.

Maj. W. H. Loving to the Director, Military Intelligence Division

Washington, D.C., December 23rd 1918

CONFIDENTIAL
From: Major W. H. Loving, P.C.
To: Director, Military Intelligence.
Subject: Rev. R. D. Jones (Jonas), sometimes known as "Prophet Jones".

1.   Rev. R. D. Jones,[1] a white man, who claims to have been born in Wales, addressed an audience last night, December 22nd, at the Metropolitan Church, colored, M. Street between 15th and 16th Streets, N.W. The sermon, which he was scheduled to preach, turned out to be more of an address, although he frequently referred to parts of the scripture with the idea of bearing out some of his statements. Extracts from his address are as follows:

> "I am a Welchman and was born in Wales and
> have been advocating the cause of the darker
> races for the past fifteen years".

> "During the past war I was arrested twenty-
> five times as a German spy, but was released
> each time for lack of evidence".

> "General Foch, Commander-in-chief of the
> Allied forces in France, as well as the Great
> Napoleon, were born in a small town in South-

ern France where 70% of the inhabitants of
that town are of African decent".[2]

"You do not know your strength. I am
here tonight to tell you your strength. 80%
of the population of the entire world are
composed of the darker races of the earth, and
I am going to France to take up the cause of
these darker races."

2. The reference made by Rev. Jones concerning Generals Foch and
Napoleon was no [d]oubt introduced to convince the audience that both of
these distinguished Generals are of African decent, which means in short,
that they are French negroes. Another reference to the effect that 80% of the
entire population of the world are composed of the darker races of the earth,
was made, possibly, to show the strength and power of the united dark races.
Although Rev. Jones speaks of uniting the darker races of the earth, a
propaganda carried on by the Universal Negro Improvement Association of
which Mr. Marcus Garvey of New York is president, I have never seen his
name connected with that organization. Yet the aims and aspirations of the
two men seem to be along the same line.

3. Reading between the lines it appears to me that to issue a passport to
a man of this type at this particular time would be very unwise, and I
therefore recommend against such action.

W H LOVING
Major P.C., Retired

[*Endorsement*] Isaacs 3/19/19

DNA, RG 165, File 10218–77/5 2–1. TDS, Recipient's copy. Endorsement is
handwritten.

   1. The person referred to as Rev. R. D. Jones was, in fact, R. D. Jonas (ca. 1868–?), who was
also known as "Elder R. D. Jones" and as "Prophet Jonas." For additional details on Jonas'
career, see Biographical Supplement, Appendix I.

   2. Marshal Ferdinand Foch (1851–1929), was commander of Allied forces during the final
months of World War I. He was born at Tarbes, France, in the Hautes-Pyrenees region near
the Spanish border. Napoleon was born at Ajaccio, Corsica, which belonged to the Arabs from
the ninth to eleventh centuries; it was ceded by Genoa to France in 1768. (*WBD*).

Maj. W. H. Loving to the Director, Military Intelligence Division

Washington, D.C. Jan. 5, 1919

From: Major W. H. Loving, P.C.
To: Director of Military Intelligence.
Subject: Activities Among Negroes in District of Columbia.

1. As per inclosed program marked (a), the organization known as the "Thrift Race of the World"[1] held its conference in the Colored Y.M.C.A. Building on January 1st 2nd and 3rd. Nothing of importance was transacted, and the speeches of the radicals were very tame. Mr. Hubert Harrison spoke on labor conditions the world over and made no reference to the war.

2. Circular marked (b) has been widely distributed in this city and calls attention to a Mass Meeting to be held at the Metropolitan Church January 6th. This meeting is to be addressed by Mr. Marcus Garvey of New York, President-General of the Universal Improvement Association, and editor of the "Negro World", a colored journal published weekly in New York. Considerable attention has been paid to Mr. Garvey's talks on street corners in New York lately where he urges the darker races of the earth to get together and form one great alliance. Garvey is West Indian by birth, but has spent some time in Europe. His audiences in New York are mostly composed of his own countrymen and he generally calls their attention to the treatment of the West Indians by the British. He has been recently making frequent trips out of New York, and has spoken in Chicago, Baltimore and Newport News. Strict watch is being kept over all of his meetings to see that he does not try to incite race prejudice.

3. Mr. Hubert Harrison is scheduled to address the Bethel Literary Society[2] of this city on Tuesday January 7th. He has been in this city for about ten days and is active in all of the meetings and conferences.

4. Messrs Phillip Randolph and Chandler Owen, colored, Socialists from New York, are arranging a conference in this city during the third week in this month. It appears that all of these New York "soap box orators" are beginning to invade this city, and their presence must carry some significance.

W H Loving
Major, P.C., Retired

[*Endorsement*] CAPT. J.E. CUTLER M.M.S.

DNA, RG 165, File 10218–261/26 273X(50). TDS, Recipient's copy. Stamped endorsement.

1. The Thrift Race of the World was organized in 1906 by Henry E. Bryant, president, and had headquarters in Washington, D.C., with branches in other cities. (DNA, RG 165, file 10218–261).
2. The noted Bethel Literary and Historical Association of the Metropolitan AME Church in Washington, D.C., founded in 1881.

A CALL!

To every Man and Woman in
Washington to attend the

Mass Convention

OF

NEGROES

AT

The Metropolitan A.M.E. Church

M. Street, between Fifteenth and Sixteenth Streets

Monday Night, Jan. 6

1919, at 8 o'clock sharp

HEAR

Hon. MARCUS GARVEY

President-General of the Universal Negro Improvement Association
and African Communities League, and Managing Editor of
" The Negro World " of New York

Be in time to hear the Greatest Orator of the Negro Race

Professor Garvey's reputation as an orator is world-wide, having addressed thousands in England, Scotland, France, Germany and America

BE EARLY IN ATTENDANCE TO GET SEATS

UNIVERSAL NEGRO IMPROVEMENT ASSOCIATION, Inc

Gerald Cox, Secretary-General   Jos. E. Johnson, High Chancellor

339

Maj. W. H. Loving to the Director, Military Intelligence Division

Washington, D.C., January 6th 1919

CONFIDENTIAL

From: Major W. H. Loving, P.C.
To: Director, Military Intelligence.
Subject: Marcus Garvey of New York

1.   Marcus Garvey, President-General of the Universal Negro Improvement Association, delivered a lecture last evening at the Metropolitan Church during which he stated that the Allies had forced Germany to turn over her navy including all of her Submarines and that greedy England had gobbled up the better portion of them.[1] He said that Germany was perfectly willing to give up the vessels which had failed to win the war for her and had already begun the construction of a different type of Submarine which would do the work and the world would hear from her again within the next twenty-five years. He says Germany intends to hit back. He said that the four hundred million people which composed the darker races of the earth held the balance of power and in the next war, which would be a war between races, these four hundred million people would cast their lot with the side which offers them freedom and liberty.

2.   These same remarks, if Mr. Garvey had made them less than three months ago, would have been declared seditious.[2] If by signing the armistice these remarks are not considered seditious now, it is imperative that Mr. Garvey's activities should be closely watched until the terms of peace are signed.

3.   I am keeping in touch with all of these negro demonstrations in the different cities and shall promptly report any acts which heretofore would have been considered disloyal or seditious.

W H LOVING
Major P.C., Retired

Stamped endorsement]CAPT. J. E.
[CUTLER M.M.S.]
[*Handwritten endorsement*] Negro
Subversion.

DNA, RG 165, File 10218–261/23 2-1 273X(50). TDS, Recipient's copy.

1. The destruction of the German navy was the principal postwar objective of the British Admiralty in order to ensure future British maritime supremacy. To this end, the British Admiralty established the following objectives in January 1919: surrender of the German submarine fleet, surrender or destruction of all German surface vessels interned in Allied and neutral ports, and retention by the Allies of all German colonies and their naval bases. The question of the distribution of the German fleet, however, was debated for several months at the Paris Peace Conference, with the American delegation attempting to prevent a situation of unrestrained British naval supremacy. The issue remained partially settled when the peace conference ended, but then, on 21 June 1919, the problem was largely settled by the Germans themselves, when the bulk of their fleet interned at Scapa Flow, was scuttled by crews under command of Admiral Ludwig Von Reuter (1869–1943). The question of the distribution of the remaining German fleet continued, however, and in November 1919 the British demanded that the proceeds from the destruction of German surface ships be distributed in proportion to losses incurred during the war. This plan was adopted by the Council of Four on 9 December 1919.

2. The Sedition Act of 16 May 1918, consisting of a number of amendments to section 3 of the Espionage Act of 15 June 1917, provided for a penalty of a $10,000 fine or up to twelve years imprisonment, or both, for those persons who "willfully utter, print, write, or publish any disloyal, profane, scurrilous, or abusive language about the form of government of the United States." The act also made it an offense to utter, write, or publish anything that would in any way "support or favor the cause of any country with which the United States is at war" or that might bring the United States or its constitution, armed forces or flag "into contempt, scorn, contumely or disrepute." (Amendment of 16 May 1918 to section 3 of the Espionage Act of 15 June 1917, 40 stat. 553 [1918]). A total of 2,168 persons were eventually prosecuted under the provisions of the Espionage Act, of whom 1,055 were convicted. It is possible that Garvey's statements relating to England's alleged seizure of the bulk of the German navy or his prediction of future German military retaliation may have prompted the suspicion that he was promoting the cause of an enemy of the United States. On 10 May 1920 Congress passed legislation providing for the deportation of aliens convicted under the amended Espionage Act of 1917. The 1918 amendments to the Espionage Act, however, were finally repealed by a joint resolution of Congress on 3 March 1921.

Col. John M. Dunn to Capt. John B. Trevor

[*Washington, D.C.*] January 11th, 1919

From: Acting Director of Military Intelligence
To: Capt. J. E. Trevor,[1] 302 Broadway, New York
Subject: REVOLUTIONARY AND ANTI-BRITISH VIEWS OF A NEGRO.

1. Attached hereto is a copy of a Postal Censorship Report, New York, Index #123546, which in our opinion merits special attention.[2]

2. Apparently the writer of the intercepted letter entertains most violently anti-British and revolutionary views which he is attempting to spread, and has been associated with Marcus Garvey's "UNIVERSAL NEGRO IMPROVEMENT ASSOCIATION" already the subject of considerable investigation on our part.

3. This is sent for your information and appropriate action. If you are able to obtain additional information concerning the writer and his activities, please report it promptly to this office.

JOHN M. DUNN,
Colonel, General Staff,
By: Carlton J. H. Hayes,
Captain, U.S.A.

Enc.
bip

[*Typewritten reference*] M.I.4 #41
[*Handwritten endorsement*] Negro Subversion.
[*Typewritten endorsement*] MID CJHH

DNA, RG 165, File 10218-277/4 273X(50). TD, Carbon copy.

1. John Bond Trevor (1878–1956) was appointed a special deputy attorney general of New York State to the Lusk Committee investigating subversive activity in 1919. In 1920 he was named associate counsel of the Senate Foreign Relations Committee in its investigation of Russian propaganda. (*WWWA*).

2. Similar letters, dated 11 January 1919, were also written by the acting director of Military Intelligence to W. E. Allen, acting chief, Bureau of Investigation, and to Emmett J. Scott. (DNA, RG 165, files 10218-277/2 and 10218-277/3).

Attachment

NEW YORK, N.Y. Dec. 11 1918
INDEX NO. *123546*

U.S. POSTAL CENSORSHIP

FROM	TO
Hambla,[1]	*Mr. Winifred D. Perkins,*
% *[G?]. Cox,*	% *Gov't [P]rinting Works,*
100 Wyckoff St.,	*Mt. Hope, Canal Zone,*
Brooklyn, N.Y.	*Rep. Panama*
DATE OF LETTER *Nov. 26 1918.*	NO. OF ENCLOSURES _____
Copied by GS	

COMMENTATOR NO. *58-634*   BRANCH *social*   DATE *Dec. 11 1918*
LANGUAGE *Eng.*   ORIGINAL TO *MID-ONI*   D.A.C.   A.C. *HRJ—*

COMMENT

Negro Expresses Revolutionary & Anti-British Views.

Writer states:—"—some damned pest of an official more nosey than anything else has been seizing my mail for the longest time. I was for some months General Secretary of the Universal Negro Improvement Association & African Communities League—a body of Negroes—African, American and West Indian, organized to form an African Empire on Our continent, Africa, and Great Britain & all the forces of Hell combined won't be able to snuff out the indomitable desire to do this thing—to Hell with England a hundred times, with her damned white man's burden which is hogging up the earth—We intend to kick their hind quarters out of Africa if we use up 7 million negroes in the bloody attempt—England's land stealing & other dishonest propensities has made her the Caanan of the races/ nobody loves England not even U.S.A., France hates her like hell. Germany [s]trafed her until U.S. shielded her & took her navy out of the British Museum. Imagine her ruling the waves & yet not being able to hold her own in the North Sea, her own adjacent waters. Big bluff & Braggadocio are always exposed in the long run & altho the "strafing" was completed in one instance, Japan may teach her how to commit hari-kari which i[n] this hated tongue which I am forced to speak & write means ["]suicide" The world will hear of us later & I want you to use these circulars and organize a branch among race-loving negroes—keep these plans away from those full-blooded Englishmen-Anglicized niggers—Get the young radical, revolution-inclined negro to fill out the form—Send us the detached coupon & names & address—Send them to me. ------------------

I love the U.S.A. only I hate how they treat us in the Southern States—I won't leave this country yet because my plans are not mature—I want to lead a band of insurgents some part of this world & I won't go where I want to do this thing before I am ready—But supposing Liberia could back me, were she strong enough I go this very moment & spill all the English blood procurable.—If we could buy 4 old submarines & organize 500 thousand men I would give the world a Republic of West India in about 8 months & an eternal negro holiday to boot.

If our good & christian President, Woodrow Wilson remembers his utterances England will either yield or bahg [*balk?*] & I know the next time the U.S. meets her, she get her tail cut & her wings clipped again—if England 'monkeys' at the peace table she may get kicked out of there   America & no one else won this war & what we say goes not what England covets"—

Circulars spoken of are not enclosed in letter—

NTP

DIVISION	DATE	COPIES	DISPOSITION AND SIGNATURE
WTB			
MIB	12–12–18	5	*HTP—Hold*
ONI	12–12–18	3	*JJC*
CCC			
PO			
EX.AC	12–17–18		*MKS-D*

THIS SLIP ALWAYS TO ACCOMPANY LETTER

[*Typewritten endorsement*] Copy sent to
Intelligence Officer, Canal Zone.
Jan. 4, 1919
[*Handwritten endorsements*] Copy sent to
Justice Officer, Canal Zone.
T de CR/FLH 47
[*Stamped endorsements*]
LIEUT. WINTERBOTHAM
COPY OF THIS ABSTRACT HAS BEEN SENT
TO LIEUT. COL, NICHOLAS BIDDLE M.I.4.
Delivered to D of J Jan. 8, 1918. G[*eorge*] C
V[*an*] D[*usen*]

DNA, RG 165, File 10218-277/1 304-50X. D, Printed form with typewritten additions.

1. James Hamble Perkins.

Maj. W. H. Loving to the Director, Military Intelligence Division

253 West 137th Street
New York, N.Y., Jan. 15, 1919

From: Major W. H. Loving, P.C.
To: Director of Military Intelligence.
Subject: Calling attention to The World Forum, organ of the International League of Darker Peoples.

1. I am inclosing herewith literature regarding the International League of Darker Peoples,[1] recently organized in New York City, including "The World Forum", which is the official organ of this movement.[2]
2. Among some of those identified with this movement are A. Philip Randolph, George Frazier Miller[3] and Chandler Owen, whose records are already on file in the Bureau. There is one white man prominently associated

with this movement in the person of Reverend R. D. Jonas, of Chicago, sometimes known as "Prophet" Jonas.[4]

3. This new organization seems to be organized along the same lines and for the same purpose as the Universal Negro Improvement Association of which Marcus Garvey is President-General and on which I have made several reports. The new movement is broader in conception as it includes all of the colored races of the world, while the movement headed by Mr. Garvey is a purely Negro movement.

4. It will be noted from inclosed literature that both organizations have called mass meetings for the night of January 16, 1919, and in different parts of the city. Strict vigilance is being kept on all such meetings and a full report will be made in the event that anything out of the ordinary occurs.

W H LOVING
Major, P.C., Retired

3 inclosures.

[*Handwritten endorsements*] OK SE
Negro Subversion
[*Stamped endorsement*]
CAPT. J. E. CUTLER M.M.S.

DNA, RG 165, File 10218-296/2 2-1 273X(50). TDS, Recipient's copy.

1. The International League of Darker Peoples was organized on 2 January 1919 at a conference attended by Marcus Garvey at Mme. C. J. Walker's villa, Lewaro-on-the-Hudson (*World Forum*, January 1919, p. 3). The league aimed at organizing the various black American delegates who had been elected to attend the Paris Peace Conference in order to create a united front among the delegates in France. To this end, the league adopted proposals drafted by A. Philip Randolph for submission to the peace conference on behalf of the various black groups. The officers of the league were Rev. Adam Clayton Powell, president; Isaac B. Allen, first vice-president; Lewis G. Jordan, second vice-president; Madame C. J. Walker, treasurer; A. Philip Randolph, secretary; and Gladys Flynn, assistant secretary. The league was short-lived, however, with both Powell and Walker publicly resigning their offices in early March 1919. During its existence the league's only significant activity was a conference that it arranged with the visiting Japanese publisher and editor, S. Kuroiwa (1862–1920). The meeting, held at the Waldorf Astoria in January 1919, was arranged by Randolph at Walker's request in order to seek Japanese assistance to have the race question brought up at the peace conference. (New York *Age*, 15 March 1919; DNA, RG 65, files OG 258421, OG 377483; RG 165, file 10218-296).

2. The only issue of the *World Forum* (organ of the International League of the Darker Peoples) that appeared was dated January 1919.

3. George Frazier Miller (1864–1943) was a contributing editor of the *Messenger*. Born in Aiken, S. C., Miller graduated from Howard University with a B.A. degree in 1888 and an M.A. in 1893. He also received a D.D. degree from the General Theological Seminary in 1891. From 1896 until his death, Miller was rector of St. Augustine's Episcopal Church in Brooklyn. Rev. Miller was a founder of the Niagara movement in 1905, and in 1906 he joined the Socialist party, becoming a leading proponent of the "open union." He ran as the Socialist party's candidate for Congress in November 1918 in the New York Twenty-first Congressional District, thus becoming the first black person ever nominated for Congress in New York politics. The author of numerous tracts, essays, and pamphlets, Rev. Miller served as president of the National Equal Rights League and for many years he was president of the Howard University Alumni Association. (*WWCA*, vol. 3, 1930–32; *NYT*, 11 May 1943; New York *Call*, 4 November 1918; Philip S. Foner, *American Socialism and Black Americans* [Westport, Conn.: Greenwood Press, 1977]).

4. In a report of an interview with Jonas, the Bureau's special agent in New York City disclosed:

> (Jones), with several other Methodist preachers, has formed "The League of Darker People" which he plainly states is merely a camouflaged name, the real purpose underlying the project being an attempt to band the negroes together against the inroads of Socialism and Bolshevism. In this work Mr. Jones states he comes in contact with all classes of negroes, for he is known as an active radical. Thus this new society, which is actually backed by preachers, would appear to be one sympathetic with radical propaganda, thus attracting the attention of those prominent in such agitation. In this way the Rev. Jones believes he can be of much assistance to this Department in furnishing 'inside' information. (DNA, RG 65, file OG 258421, 11 February 1919; see also file OG 377483, 12 February 1919).

Despite the league's early demise, Jonas continued to exploit its name, issuing circulars as late as October 1919, which he signed as "Secretary, League of Darker Peoples of the World." One such publication was his pamphlet, *First Call For Abyssinia* (n.p., n.d.), the cover of which bore the caption, "Magazine of the Darker Peoples of the World."

SERIOUS CALL

To every Colored Man and
Woman to attend the

Mass Convention

OF

NEGROES

OF THE WORLD

(Americans, Africans, South and Central Americans and West Indians)

At SALEM M. E. CHURCH

Corner 133rd Street and Lenox Avenue New York City

Thurs. Night, Jan. 16

1919, at 8 o'clock sharp

At this Covention **The Universal Negro Improvement Association and African Communities League,** the first Negro Organization of the World to take a stand for the Negro during the times of war and peace, will follow up the Peace Aims of the race as moved and carried by the acclamation of 7,000 of the race on the 10th of December, 1918, in the Palace Casino, which aims were filed with President Wilson and Robert Lansing of America, Right Honorable Arthur J. Balfour of England, Premier Clemenceau of France. the Italian Foreign Secretary, and other representatives of the Allied Governments This time these resolutions will be cabled right into the "Peace Conference" at Versailles, to be read into the proceedings of the day and "followed up" by the delegates of the Association, one of whom will sail immediately after this meeting.

Everybody of the Negro Race Must Attend

Hear MARCUS GARVEY

World-famed Negro Orator and Editor of "The Negro World"

And Other Prominent Men of the Race

UNIVERSAL NEGRO IMPROVEMENT ASSOCIATION, Inc.
AFRICAN COMMUNITIES LEAGUE, Inc.

Gerald Cox, Secretary-General   Jos. E. Johnson, High Chancellor

THE HUNT PRINTING COMPANY, 34 W. 130TH STREET, NEW YORK

Maj. Wrisley Brown to
Lt. Col. H. A. Pakenham

[*Washington, D.C.*] January 29, 1919

MEMORANDUM FOR LIEUT. COL. PAKENHAM:

Subject: *Universal Negro Improvement Association and African Communities League, Marcus Garvey and John E. Bruce.*

1. Further referring to your P.F. I.510/M.I. 5 D.3 in re above subject, we have received the attached letter from Major W. H. Loving and that of Mr. John E. Bruce, referred to in your note.

2. We are also sending you a copy of a booklet by John E. Bruce, entitled "A Tribute for the Negro Soldier" which was incorporated in the Congressional Records by the Hon. Walter M. Chandler, member of the House of Representatives of New York.

WRISLEY BROWN,
Major, A.S.M.A.

hgb

[*Typewritten reference*] M.I.4[*Liaison Organization*]-54 10218-261
[*Endorsement*] Delivered Jan. 31

Attachment

WASHINGTON. January 25, 1919

From: Major W. H. Loving, P.C.
To: Director of Military Intelligence.
Subject: John E. Bruce. (Bruce Grit.)

1. I am enclosing herewith a letter just received from Mr. John E. Bruce of New York City, who clearly states his relation with Marcus Garvey and Duse Mohamed, the former of New York City and editor of a Negro Journal called "Negro World", and the latter editor of the "African Times", London, England.

2. I have known Mr. Bruce for a number of years and I am inclined to have great faith in the letter herewith enclosed.

W H LOVING
Major, P.C., Retired

gr

[*Endorsement*] CAPT. J. E. CUTLER M.M.S

DNA, RG 165, File 10218-261/40 3-1. TNS, Recipient's copy. Stamped endorsement. Official stationery of War Department, Office of the Chief of Staff, MID.

Enclosure

2109 MADISON AVENUE NEW YORK CITY
January 13, 1919

My dear Major Loving:

Answering your question as to my connection with the Marcus Garvey organization, let me say with all possible emphasis that I am not a member of it, though my name was used nearly a year ago, as chairman of its Executive Committee, and this was done by Mr. Garvey, possibly out of friendship for me because I had given him $5.00—when he first came to America toward the establishment of an industrial school in Jamaica, West Indies, along the lines of Tuskegee. So I did not object to its use. I attended several meetings of the organization in this city and discovered that Garvey had departed from his original plan and had reorganized his society into a "great world movement" for the redemption and regeneration of Africa, and to relieve gullible Negroes of their surplus cash. I studied his methods and his tactics for several weeks, and when I got a line on him that would not break, I resigned my membership in the organization and wrote, and cause[d] to be written a number of articles in our race papers in criticism of his scheme which I have every reason to believe is impracticable, utopian and jackassical. I have never lost an opportunity to express myself fully and forcibly about Mr. Garvey's wild project and his seditious utterances on soap boxes, and in public meetings. I have never written a line for his newspaper since its appearance. I am very particular as to the kind of newspapers I write for. I am I trust, indeed I know, too good an American to join hands with any alien black, or white, against my country. Certainly I would not be such a simpleton as to line up with Mr. Marcus Garvey, who has no visible means of support and a most unsavory reputation in his own country from which I am informed by two reputable gentlemen friends of mine living respectively in London, England, and Lagos, West Africa, he decamped several years ago with several hundred pounds collected for the school to which I contributed $5 as I have stated.

Now as to Mr. Duse Mohamed of London, England, I have known him since 1912. I was introduced to him by letter from Mr. Caseley Hayford,[1] Barrister at Law, Gold Coast, Africa, who had endorsed me to Mr. Mohamed as his American agent and correspondent of the African Times and Oriental Review.[2] I have written many articles concerning our people for this publication and have secured many subscribers for it throughout the country. I have always found Mr. Mohamed a loyal race man and an honorable gentleman. We are both members of the Societie Internationale de Philo/lo/gie et Beaux Arts,[3] London, England, and I have been since 1905, a member of the African Society of London,[4] founded by Miss Ma/r/y Kingsley,[5] having been proposed and vouched for by its honorable Secretary, the Count de Cardi.[6]

I am, as you have known me for many years, a newspaper correspondent. I conducted a newspaper bureau in Washington in 1889, and published a newspaper there,[7] and later went West to Ohio (Cincinnati) where I was employed under Perry Heath,[8] sometime Asst. P.M.G. as a reporter of news occuring among colored people. So that I've been a professional "jiner" of all the wise and *otherwise* movements among negroes in many states, and a student of Negro-ology. When I discover a fake, I make the discovery known with a stub pen and such words in my limited vocabulary, as will properly describe the Fake and denounce the Fakir. Please do not insult me by linking my name with any movement, plan, scheme, plot or enterprise with which Marcus Garvey is identified.

I am now connected as correspondent, and contributing editor with "The African Times", London, The New York Defender, The Gold Coast Leader, Africa, The Monitor, Omaha, Nebraska—The Negro Magazine, and up to the time that the American Press Association was sold to the Western Newspaper Union,[9] I was on the staff of the Editor of the Negro page sent out by the association for use in hundreds of Negro newspapers throughout the country. I think I did you a turn in that page when you were leaving the Philippines (unbeknownst to you) and used your picture.

Please put me down as a 100% 'Merican, red hot republican, and a shouting methodist. If you can manufacture a traitor out of these "ingre-jents", send me a/the/formula, "suh". Sincerely yours

JOHN E. BRUCE "GRIT"

DNA, RG 165, File 10218-261/39 2-1. TLS, Recipient's copy. Written on the stationery of "Bruce and Franklin Publishers of Negro Literature" with manuscript additions in Bruce's hand.

1. Joseph Ephraim Casely Hayford (1866–1930) was generally regarded as the principal West African political figure of his day. Born at Cape Coast, Ghana, he was educated at the Wesleyan high school there and at Fourah Bay College in Sierra Leone, where he came under the direct influence of Edward Wilmot Blyden. Hayford began his career as a journalist and political commentator with the *Gold Coast Echo* in 1889, followed by the *Gold Coast Chronicle*, 1890–96; he was also associated with the *Wesleyan Methodist Times*. From 1902 until his death he published the *Gold Coast Leader*, the leading journal of West African nationalism during this period. He studied law in London and was called to the bar in 1906. He was nominated to the Gold Coast Legislative Council in 1916, where he remained until 1925, when he was elected to the seat for Sekondi Takoradi in 1927. He became the guiding spirit and principal organizer of the National Congress of British West Africa (NCBWA) in 1920. He was elected vice-president and also appointed leader of the NCBWA delegation to England in 1921. Hayford was also the author of several works, the most famous being *Ethiopia Unbound: Studies in Race Emancipation* (London, 1911), that played an important role in developing the ideology of West African nationalism. (*DAHB*, pp. 43–44; *Dictionary of African Biography*, pp. 253–55; J. Ayo Langley, *Pan-Africanism and Nationalism in West Africa, 1900–1945: A Study in Ideology and Social Classes* [Oxford: Clarendon Press, 1973], chaps. 3–4).

2. The American distributors of *ATOR* at the time were J. E. K. Aggrey (1875–1927), born in the Gold Coast, and John E. Bruce. Bruce was subsequently appointed the journal's general agent in the United States.

3. Founded in Paris in 1873 and formally constituted in 1875. Its official organ was the *Philomath*, published in London, 1895–1934.

4. The African Society was founded in 1901 in memory of Mary Henrietta Kingsley (1862–1900), English explorer and writer, "for enquiry into native law and custom, and for the mutual enlightenment of the black and white man"; and "to investigate the usages, institutions, customs, religions, antiquities, history and languages of the native races of Africa; to facilitate the commercial and industrial development of the continent, and to form a central institution

for the study of African subjects." Its quarterly *Journal of the African Society* began publication in October 1901 and continues to be published under the title *African Affairs*.

5. Mary Kingsley was among the first to reject the notion of African cultural inferiority. After two trips into western and central Africa, she also denounced the evils of formal British colonialism, advocating instead a return to the system prevailing in the 1880s under which contact with Africans was largely restricted to trade, and which she believed would allow Africa's social organizations to remain intact. (*DAHB*).

6. Count Charles de Cardi (? –1906) was the first honorary secretary of the African Society, after a highly successful commercial career in southern Nigeria that spanned thirty-four years. He settled in London in 1896 and shortly afterward met Kingsley. He contributed a paper to her book *West African Studies* (n.p., 1899) on the customs and religion of the Niger Coast. (*Journal of the African Society* 6 [1906–07]: 213–15).

7. Bruce was one of the editors of the *Colored American* in Washington, D.C.; prior to this, he published two other newspapers in that city, the *Sunday Item* in 1881, and the *Argus* in 1884. Bruce was also a special correspondent in Washington, D.C. for the *Progressive American* and for several other newspapers.

8. Perry Sanford Heath (1857–1927) was the editor of the *Cincinnati Commercial-Gazette*, 1894–96; he was appointed first assistant postmaster general in the McKinley administration in 1897.

9. The Western Newspaper Union acquired the American Press Association of New York in 1917.

Editorial Letter by Marcus Garvey

[[Baltimore, Maryland, 31 January 1919]]

The Negro Should be a Party to the Commercial Conquest of the World Wake Up You Lazy Men of the Race—This is The Time of preparation for All

Fellowmen of the Negro Race:

Greeting:—It is expected that the Peace Conference will adjourn about late spring,[1] at which time the representatives of the various nations of the world, now in France, will return to their respective countries. They will take back with them the new thought, the new hope—industrial and commercial expansion and conquest.

England is preparing for a great commercial warfare; so is America, Japan, France, Germany and the other nations. The next twenty-five year[s] will be a period of keen competition among people. It will be an age of survival of the fittest. The weaker elements will totter and fall. They will be destroyed for the upbuilding of the greater powers.

As a Negro, I would be untrue to myself and would be untrue to you, if I, from my observation, fail to prepare the mind of the race for this titanic industrial and commercial struggle that is in the making. This era has forced out the best races and nations. The white people have risen to the occasion. In Europe they are presenting to the world their keenest and best intellects. In Asia, the Japanese and Chinese are presenting on the stage of world affairs, men, who are as big as the age. America is also presenting extra-ordinary big men to meet the situation. The Negro can do no less than rise also to the occasion to produce of his best.

This commercial rivalry that I speak of will send the representatives of all these people into all parts of the world to conquer trade. As Germany sent out her commercial agents to conquer the trade of the world and had become so successful up to the time when war was declared in 1914, so must the Negro be prepared to play . . . [*remainder of sentence missing*]. If we are to rise as a great [people?] to become a great national force, we must start business enterprises of our own; we must build ships and start trading with ourselves between America, the West Indies and Africa. We must put up factories in all the great manufacturing centers of this country, to give employment to the thousands of men and women who will be thrown out of work as soon as the nation takes on its normal attitude. In these factories we must manufacture boots, clothing and all the necessaries of life, those things that the people need, not only our people in America, the West Indies and Africa, but the people of China, of India, of South and Central America, and even the white man. He has for hundreds of years made a market for his goods among Negroes and alien races; therefore, Negroes have the same right to make a market among white people for his manufactured goods.

The time has come when the Negro must take his stand as a man. If the white man is manly enough to put up a factory, the Negro ought to be manly enough to do the same thing. If he can, as a white man, manufacture things that other people need, then Negroes ought to be able to do the same thing. There is absolutely no monopoly in knowledge today. The equality of men has been proved and in this recent bloody conflict, and in this period of reconstruction, when all men are endeavoring to take their stand as equals, the Negro would be less than [a] man if he were to allow all the other races within another generation to present to the world the results of their efforts in rising to the ordinary human plane without his achieving a modicum of success.

The vision of some of us today is as penetrating as that of the great economists of Europe and Asia. When we can as a race settle down to business with honesty of purpose, we will be on the way to the founding of a permanent and strong position among the nations and races of the world. Commerce and industry were the forces that pushed the great German Empire to the front. As it can be remembered, during the first Napoleonic era, Germany was regarded as the pauper nation of Europe, whilst England and France had reached a high state in commerce and industry, having their merchant marines sailing to and anchoring [in] every port of the world; Germany was without steamships. The German was looked down on then, even as the Negro of the South is looked down on today; but the Germans of . . . [*mutilated*] about and applied themselves assiduously to the . . . [*muti-lated*] of these two forces. They . . . [*several words missing*] [Bisma]rck.[2] From then up to 1914 . . . [*several words missing*] that two hours before war was declared German manufactured goods, were underselling in England goods manufactured in England, America, Japan, Canada and Australia.

These are fair examples of how a people can rise to greatness when they apply themselves to any one good thing without faltering. The Negro should not falter, and, economically and industrially today, he should endeavor to lay a good foundation and continue to build and until the structure becomes impregnable.

In a word, my message to you for this week is: "Develop yourselves into a commercial and industrial people, and you will have laid the foundation for racial greatness." Your[s] fraternally,

MARCUS GARVEY

Printed in the *NW*, Saturday, 1 February 1919.

1. The conference formally ended on 10 January 1920.
2. Otto Von Bismarck (1815–1898) was the first chancellor of the German Empire and was responsible for Germany's unification under Prussian leadership. (*WBD*).

Address by Marcus Garvey

[Negro World, 1 February 1919]

MARCUS GARVEY AT THE CRESCENT HALL
BIG MEETING OF NEW YORK DIVISION OF
UNIVERSAL NEGRO IMPROVEMENT ASSOCIATION—
MANY NEW MEMBERS ADDED TO MOVEMENT

Last Sunday [*26 January*] the New York Division of the Universal Negro Improvement Association met in their hall at 36–38 West 135th street, at 3 o'clock p.m., in regular session. There was a large attendance of officers and members. Among those present were Mr. Marcus Garvey, president; Miss Janie Jenkins, president of the Ladies' Division; Mr. George Tobias,[1] second vice-president; Mr. W. Wells,[2] third vice-pres[id]ent; Miss Irene Wingfield, first vice-president of the Ladies' Division; Mrs. Hannah Nicholas, second vice-president; Mrs. G. Woodford, third vice-president; Mr. James E. Linton, treasurer; Rev. John T. Wilkins, executive secretary; Mr. Cecil Hope,[3] general secretary; Miss May Clarke, associate lady secretary; Mr. G. Cox,[4] secretary general of the parent body, and Mr. J. E. Johnson,[5] high chancellor.

The meeting was opened by the singing of the hymn, "Fr[o]m Greenland's Icy Mountains," after which the prayer of the association was read. The minutes were also read and confirmed. The next item on the agenda for the day was the address of the president. He took as his theme a passage from the speech made by President Wilson before the Peace Conference on the topic of the League of Nations.[6] The following is the passage:

"The select c[l]asses of mankind are no longer the governors of

mankind. **The fortunes of mankind are now in the hands of the plain people of the whole world. Satisfy them and you have justified their confidence not only, but established peace. Fail to satisfy them, and no arrangement that you can make will either set up or steady the peace of the world."**—President Wilson to the Congress.[7]

Mr. Garvey said President Wilson had become the spokesman of the Socialist party of the world. The passage is read by him he interpreted to be a direct compromise with Socialistic ideas. Those ideas which are now laying hold on the minds of the masses of white people all over the world. Indeed, to him, he said, the President was speaking the language of the people. He could not do better because it had been plainly demonstrated by the many upheavals in Europe and the uprisings abroad that the millions of toilers of all countries were not prepared to entrust their fortunes to any select group within their own nations. The aristocracy that once ruled the common people must be destroyed according to the will of the common people. They have started to destroy that privileged aristocracy in Russia, in Germany, in Austro-Hungary, and there is every indication that within the next ten years Great Britain will be swept by this threatening revolution.[8] The equality of man has become indisputable. There can be but one [*aristocracy?*] today and that is labor. The aristocracy of privilege . . . [*mutilated*] to defeat, and the President [*realizing?*] this, is endeavoring to save his class the world over. Hence, this significant passage that can be interpreted as rank Socialism. By the declaration of the President before the Peace Conference, it can easily be seen that labor has forced his hands. It has also forced the hands of David Lloyd George and will eventually force the hands of every statesman in Europe.

To his way of thinking, he believes Gompers[9] to be a greater force in American national life than even President Wilson, because Gompers stands out as the exponent of labor, and labor is determined to bring about a change, caring not what the cost may be, and every intelligent observer can see that that change is bound to occur except a compromise is made with labor before hand. It is this compromise that President Wilson is endeavoring to effect why he has so openly declared himself. How is it that labor has become such a force in the world? Can you not remember, ladies and gentlemen, that some years ago trades unionism was regarded as an impracticable thing? Can you not remember in the years gone by when a few men used to strike for higher wages and they were turned down by their employers and forced to accept their conditions? How is it that this change has come about then? It is because people who were imbued with the ideal of trades unionism years ago stuck to it. They were determined to fight their battles until victory came. It took them years, it took them decades, but today the victory is theirs. All has been accomplished through organization. Organization is the force that rules the world. It is that force that has changed the destiny of governments and of races. This, therefore, is a fair example to us as Negroes, that if we are to impose our wills on the powers that be, we must be as solidly organized as labor is today. If the Negro peoples of the world were organized as labor in America is organized among the whites, as it is organized in England and in France, simultaneously the President would have declared on behalf of African emancipation when he, without any reserve, made it known to his compatriots in the Peace Conference that the fortunes of mankind were now in the hands of the plain people of the whole world, who, in other words, are called workers.

I am somewhat persuaded to believe that the Negro has lost his premier chance through unpreparedness in this present war, but there is still another chance for him which, to my mind, will be in the next conflict that is sure to come. It is because I would like to see my people taking advantage of that chance when it again presents itself why I am today preparing your minds not only in America but all over the world, so that at the psychological moment as the opportunity presents itself, we may universally move as if we were one to bring home to us those things we have longed for.

What impression President Wilson is able to make on the toiling masses I am not prepared to say. But this I do know, that the masses of workers all over the world have bec[o]me so educated out of this bloody war that it takes more than a superman to infringe on their right without their detecting it. I do not mean to say by this . . . [*mutilated*] President has not spoken with the conviction of truth as touching the [workers] of the world, but from past experiences, peoples who have suffered, classes that have suffered must perforce become suspicious of anything coming from the opposite classes. For instance, D[a]vid Lloyd George[,] the Premier of England during the election of 1912, made great promises to the Irish people.[10] Home rule for Ireland was practically written on the statutes of England, and up to now those people have not gained their freedom.[11] Can the Irishman still continue to have confidence in English professions. I hardly believe that there is an Irishman in any part of the world who would lead himself to believe that the English statesman of today, when he speaks, means any good of Ireland. [As] the Irishman is suspicious of the man who has suppressed him for hundreds of years, so are the workers suspicious of the class that has kept him down for centuries. So when any one from within that class speaks in the language of the workers, it suggests that there may be enthusiasm over the declarations, but not a whole-hearted confidence.

As far as Negroes are concerned, there is absolutely no one, no nation, or no race that they can place their confidence in. We have listened to the various statesmen of the world for long enough and they have said nothing and done nothing to encourage us in the belief that they mean to be fair to our race. From the great centres of civilization news ha[s] come and are still coming which enlighten us of the fact that there can be no abiding peace until all oppression has been removed from the people. That is the fiat of the working classes of Europe. It is the fiat of the working classes of America. And all these white people mean to pay the cost of the realization of their object even by their very lives. As Negroes, we have not yet set ourselves a determination. It is because we have never been determined on any one thing for our own good why we are ignored in the world today, but as soon as we fall in line with the radical changes determined to impose our will for the sake of emancipating ourselves, then we will become a great force to be reckoned with. What other men in other ages of the race have failed to do, let us, as the Universal Negro Improvement Association and African Communities' League of the World, do today. Let us rededicate ourselves to the cause of bleeding Africa and scattered Ethiopia. Let us stretch our hands across to the brother wherever he be and say to him, even in the language of the white man of the past, "You are one of us and we must rise or fall together." Europe, when she becomes again settled, will rise and fall as she originated. Asia will rise and fall as she originated. So must Africa rise and fall as she was originated.

Let us not lose sight of the fact that as scattered children of the bleeding Fatherland, we owe a responsibility that is not light and the quicker we get to realize it, the better it will be.

At the close of Mr. Garvey's address several persons joined the association. The association meets at 3 o'clock every Sunday and at 8:15 on Wednesday and Friday nights of every week.

Printed in the *NW*, Saturday, 1 February 1919.

1. George W. Tobias (b. 1888) was a native of Grenada, BWI, who came to the United States in September 1913 from the Panama Canal Zone, where he was employed as a clerk with the Isthmian Canal Commission. When he met Garvey in May 1918, he was a clerk in the shipping department of the Pennsylvania Railroad in New York. His first position with the UNIA was as an editorial assistant with the *Negro World*; later he was elected first vice-president, second vice-president, and treasurer of the UNIA. On 17 June 1919, he was elected treasurer of the Black Star Line, Inc., a position that he retained until he was indicted, along with Garvey and two other Black Star Line officials, on charges of mail fraud in 1922. At his trial in June 1923, Tobias was acquitted. (*NYT*, 17 February 1922; AFRC, RG 163, registration card; *Garvey* v. *United States*, no. 8317 [Ct. App. 2d Cir. Feb. 2, 1925], folios 6372–3, pp. 2124–25).

2. Probably William Wells (1865– ?), who was born in Tallahassee, Fla., and was employed in 1917 as a porter by the Hulbert Motor Co. (AFRC, RG 163, registration card).

3. Cecil Hope was later, in 1933, to become the organizer of the West Indian Progressive Association in Harlem. He was also connected with the *Harlem Liberator*, the official organ of the American Negro Labor Congress organized by the Workers (Communist) party in October 1925. (DNA, RG 59, file 800. 00B, "International Trade Union Committee of Negro Workers," S/18).

4. Gerald Frederick Cox, (1885– ?) was a British subject; he was employed in September 1918 as a laborer by the Midland Linseed Co., Edgewater, N.J. (AFRC, RG 163, registration card).

5. Probably Joseph Everett Johnson, (1898– ?), American-born; he was employed in New York City as a dyer at the Holiday Kemp Co. (AFRC, RG 163, registration card).

6. Address before the second plenary session of the Paris Peace Conference on 15 January 1919.

7. The term *Congress* was frequently used in reference to the peace conference.

8. The Bolshevik revolution of October 1917 was followed in 1918 by a series of major upheavals in Eastern and Central Europe, hastened by the collapse of the Central Powers' war effort. By the summer of 1918 the Hapsburg monarchy and the Austro-Hungarian Empire had started to dissolve, and on 16 October 1918 Emperor Charles proclaimed the principle of self-determination for the nationalities of the former Austro-Hungarian Empire. Further upheavals in newly-independent Hungary and the other Balkan and Central European states

followed the final collapse of the Hapsburg monarchy. The abdication of the German emperor, Wilhelm II, took place on 9 November 1918.

9. Samuel Gompers (1850–1924) was president of the American Federation of Labor continuously from the time of its inception in 1886 (with the exception of one year, 1895) until his death in 1924. (*WBD*).

10. General elections were held in Britain in January and December 1910, and on both occasions Herbert Asquith was returned as premier. Lloyd George served under Asquith in various capacities but did not become prime minister until December 1916. Garvey was probably referring to Lloyd George's tentative agreement reached with the Irish Nationalists and the Ulster Unionists in the aftermath of the Easter Uprising of April 1916; the subsequent breakdown in the negotiations led the Nationalists to charge Lloyd George with duplicity. (Peter Rowland, *Lloyd George* [London: Barrie & Johnson, 1975], pp. 338ff.).

11. On 7 January 1919, twenty-seven representatives of Sinn Fein, the Irish republican organization, met at the Dublin Mansion to set up an Assembly of Ireland (Dail Eireann). On 21 January, the assembly issued a "Message to the Free Nations of the World" appealing for national recognition and Irish representation at the Paris Peace Conference. The assembly demanded "to be confronted publicly with England at the Congress of the Nations, that the civilised world having judged between English wrong and Irish right may guarantee to Ireland its permanent support for the maintenance of her national independence." ("Ireland's Message to the Nations" in Dorothy Macardle, *The Irish Republic* [London: Victor Gollancz, 1938], pp. 961–62). The British blocked the demand however, and it was not until 11 December 1919 that Prime Minister Lloyd George outlined the British government's plans for Irish home rule. The first reading of the Government of Ireland Bill took place on 25 February 1920 and became law on 23 December 1920. The Treaty of Partition was approved by the British Parliament on 16 December 1921, and the Irish Free State came into existence on 6 December 1922.

W. E. Allen, Acting Chief, Bureau of Investigation, to William M. Offley,[1] New York Division Superintendent

[*Washington, D.C.*] February 10, 1919

Dear Sir:—

For your information I enclose herewith photostat copy of Postal Censorship comment[2] relative to an intercepted letter from Eliezer Cadet, c/o Universal Negro Improvement Association, 36–38 West 135th Street, New York City, to H. Dorsinville,[3] Port au Prince, Haiti. Very truly yours,

[W. E. ALLEN][4]
Acting Chief

END

DNA, RG 65, File OG 244193. TL, Carbon copy.

1. Capt. William M. Offley was the chief of the New York division of the Bureau of Investigation, a position he held from May 1910 until February 1918. On the latter date he was appointed a special assistant to the attorney general, thereby becoming one of the principal officials of the bureau under its chief, A. Bruce Bielaski. Offley was reappointed superintendent of the New York division in June 1919. (*NYT*, 14 February 1918; *Register of the Department of Justice, 1926* [Washington: GPO, 1926]).

2. A copy of the Postal Censorship report was delivered to the Department of Justice on 8 February 1919.

3. Hénec Dorsinville (1881–1929), was the founder of *L'Essor* in 1917. The paper reflected his opposition to the American occupation of Haiti and strongly criticized the regime of President Sudre Dartiguenave. American authorities investigated his paper but it remained in circulation. He was later appointed an administrator with the Office of the Recorder in April 1922, and from August 1925 until November 1926 he served as minister of public education, agriculture, and employment in the cabinet of President Borno. (Letter to editor from Max Dorsinville, 23 October 1979; *Le Matin*, 20 May 1929; *L'Essor*, 20 May 1929; *Le Nouvelliste*, 17 May 1929; Hans Schmidt, *The United States Occupation of Haiti, 1915–1934* [New Brunswick, N.J.: Rutgers University Press, 1971]).

4. William Elby Allen (1882–1951) was appointed acting chief of the Bureau of Investigation on 1 January 1919, succeeding A. Bruce Bielaski. Allen had earlier served as one of the two assistant chiefs of the bureau after 1 July 1918, which was when he began his association with the bureau. He was replaced in his acting position later in 1919 by John T. Suter. (*NYT*, 3 January 1919; *State of Texas Bar Journal*, 1951).

Enclosure

NEW YORK N.Y. *Jan. 16/19*
INDEX NO. *130427*

U.S. POSTAL CENSORSHIP

FROM	TO
Eliezer Cadet	*H. Dorsinville*
c/o Universal Negro Improve-	*Director de l'Essor*
ment Association	*Angle des Rues Feron & H. Killick*
36–38 W. 135th St.	*Port au Prince, Haiti.*
New York City.	
DATE OF LETTER *Jan. 13/19*	NO. OF ENCLOSURES 6
Copied by MEL	

COMMENTATOR NO. *148-457*   BRANCH *Press*   DATE   *Jan. 16/19*
LANGUAGE *French* ORIGINAL TO *WTB-MID-ONI-CCC*   D.A.C.   A.C. *EA*

COMMENT

Writer, according to File Index 123553 (q.v.) elected interpreter and secretary to represent the *Universal Negro Improvement Assn.* and *African Committees League* at the Peace Conference, acknowledges receipt of a letter from addressee (not in file) and states that he and his president (of the Universal Negro Improvement Association) accept addressee's "generous propositions." Writer advises they [(]i.e. the Association) cannot immediately take up business with addressee for the following reasons:

1. The president is very busy establishing branches of this Assn. in all the states of the Union, and in holding meetings in various parts.

2. We have great projects to execute, we only await the results of the peace conference to know where we stand. You (addressee) shall be our

principal agent in Haiti not only to establish a branch of this Association in Haiti as in Panama, at Port de France [*Port-au-Prince?*], etc. but also you shall be our commercial and industrial agent. If our peace propositions are accepted, we shall assemble the great negro capitalists of the U.S. and establish a line of ships between the West Indies[,] America, and Africa to facilitate the exchange of raw materials for manufactured products. Our aim is to unite, to organize and to mobilize the intellectual and material forces of the 400,000,00[0] blacks of the entire world in order to impose the respect of their rights.

Writer further advises he did not receive the papers sent him by addresse[e,] one of which, writer indicates contained an article of his. He acknowledges receipt of names sent by addressee, and advises he will address communications to them after the Peace Conference.

He adds that on his return from France he may render great services to addressee's paper, and that he will "also" send addressee the names of merchants with whom he may do business.[1]

In postscript writer requests addressee to correct mistakes in the (enclosed) open letter (see below) saying: "I am certain that I have not yet the desired capacity for writing for the papers; but—I feel it a duty to denounce to the people bad cit[i]zens, and to defend my country and my race." He also announces sending addressee "more papers." The above mentioned 'Open letter' reads:

"To the Editor of *l'Essor*
Dear Sir:

The object of my discourse today is to tell you of a little incident which occurred between the *Consul Moravia*[2] and a group of Haitians at the Consulate of Haiti, general headquarters of the Haitians in New York. It was on account of a circular letter issued by the International Headquarters Universal Negro Improvement Association, African Communities League, to request gifts from friends of the African cause. The money collected was to be used for travelling expenses and in support of the delegates of the black race to the Peace Conference in France. The duty of these envoys will be to formulate before the entire world assembled the grievances of the said race against its oppressors.

"Apparently Monsieur Moravia could not be agreeable to such a movement on the part of the Young Blacks for the triumph of these will mean the complete defeat of the reactionaries and annexationists in Africa as well as in Haiti.

"Since my first article, published in the *Negro World* with the sole aim to justifying my country in the eyes of foreigners, Monsieur Moravia has had a grudge against me; he discovered in me a future antagonist to the infamous persons slandering the Haitian people and their best statesmen in order to attract the good will of the implacable enemies of our color.

"The consul used the above mentioned letter to explode the bomb of his anti-African wrath. His bombardment of threats and his balm of hy[p]o-critical advice concern us little, all his efforts will waste themselves against the solid and indestructible armour of intrepidity and of courage of the Young Blacks of the world.

"The good consul ventured to notify me moreover that I was not to count on his protection, if I set myself to defend here (in N.Y.) my country, my race, my liberty. Does this noble cavalier forget that only he and his confederates may open their mouths in Haiti? Yes, this generous man would urgently invite me to offer my life for the liberty of the French, the Italians, the Belgian assassins of my African Kindred, but naturally he protests at my lifting my voice in unison with my brothers of America, The West Indies and Africa against the wholesale massacre of pregnant women and new born infants of my own race.

"Let him know, if he does not understand, that a life without glory, without honor, without liberty is far worse than the most miserable death; may he know also that the dwelling place of the generous and brave is not here below.

"I stand for the conquest of Justice and Liberty. I am also certain that I shall not enjoy these, but my remote descendants will bring me word of them where I shall be.

["]I am going to France this week as interpreter and secretary of the delegates of the black race at the peace conference. They are mistaken if they think we shall mince the truth before the Caucasians. We, the young blacks of the Antilles, of North and South America and of Africa, have uncovered the policy of the Caucasians which consists in effecting the disunion of the 400,000,000 black[s] of the world by leading those of one country to believe that they are better than those of another and must, consequently, shun them. At heart they entertain the same amount of hatred for all.

"We have resolved to imitate the yellow race. We are in process of organizing and mobilizing our intellectual and material forces in order to be ready for the next world war which will be a race war. We shall then be the balance of power between the yellow race and the white race. Victory will incline (to the side) where our forces are thrown—We shall remain neutral only if the Caucasian gives us Justice at this peace conference.

"Down with the traitors, down with the detractors, down with the disturbers of the race.

"Long live the Union and Fraternity of the children of Ethiopia." "Your servant

> Eliezer Cadet. N.Y. 13/1/19
> c/o Universal Negro Improvement Association
> 36–38 West 135th St. N.Y.C."

Writer encloses a one dollar bill.

EBS

DIVISION	DATE	COPIES	DISPOSITION AND SIGNATURE
WTB	1/18/19	3	*Hold—LCB*
MIB	1/20/19	3	*BMD*
ONI	1/20/19	3	*CEK*
CCC	1/21/19	2	*McI.*
PO		3	*Press, Reg.* [,] *Trade ACs.*[3]
EX.AC	1/22/19		*MTP*

THIS SLIP ALWAYS TO ACCOMPANY LETTER

[*Typewritten reference*] SUBJECT INDEX
1-8-A-1 L-6-A-
[*Endorsement*] Negro Subversion

DNA, RG 38, File 20948–184, Index No. 130427. D, Printed form with typewritten additions. Endorsement is handwritten.

1. Hénec Dorsinville might have been seeking business contacts in the United States for his two younger brothers, Louis and Luc Dorsinville, both of whom were proprietors of their own import and export businesses in Haiti. Louis Dorsinville operated in the town of St. Marc, while the firm of Luc Dorsinville was located at 105 Rue du Quai in Port-au-Prince and represented the products of several American manufacturers in Haiti. Luc Dorsinville also advertised his wish in the *Negro World* "to establish good relations with all colored American Corporations and Firms" (*NW*, 5 August 1920). He was later appointed the agent of the Black Star Line in Haiti.

2. This was a reference to the United States' occupation of Haiti, which began in 1915, and would continue until August 1934, and also to those allied governments, such as Great Britain, France, Belgium, and Italy, which were demanding the annexation and partition among themselves of the former German colonial empire in Africa.

3. Assistant censors for press, registered letters, and trade.

R. Walter, Officer Administering the Government of British Honduras, to the British Ambassador, Washington, D.C.

Government House Belize
13th February 1919

Sir,

I have the honour to invite Your Excellency's attention to the enclosed copies[1] of a paper entitled the Negro World which has been finding its way to the Colony.

The object of this paper appears to be to incite racial hatred and I shou[l]d not be surprised if the paper was supported by German or Bolshiviki money.

2 I do not know whether the United States authorities are cognisant of this paper which does not seem to comply with the usual requirements regarding registration and the printing of the name of the printer and publisher.

3 While I do not think the loyalty of the people of this [*colony*] will suffer much from the inflammatory rubbish contained in this paper I do not consider its circulation here desirable and I am giving instructions with a view to putting an end to its circulation.[2]

4 You may consider it worth while to bring the paper to the notice of the U.S. Authorities. I should be glad to hear the result of such action[.] I have the honour to be, Sir, Your Excellency's most obedient humble Servant

R. WALTER[3]
Administering the Government

[*Address*] His Britannic Majesty's
Ambassador[4] Washington U.S.A.
[*Typewritten reference*] British Honduras
No. Confidential

PRO, CO 123/295, British Honduras Confidential Despatch. TL, Transcript.

1. Copies were not retained in the Colonial Office file.

2. Governor Eyre Hutson (1864–1936) subsequently cited as one of the three reported grievances leading to the Belize Riot of 22 July 1919, "the suppression by Mr. Walter, Acting Governor, in January last of an American newspaper 'The Negro World'," to which he added: ". . . the result of Mr. Walter's order was, that whereas in January last, only a few copies had been received, since the order many copies had been regularly introduced surreptitiously, and had been largely circulated and read." (PRO, CO 123/295, Governor Eyre Hutson to Viscount Milner, secretary of state for the colonies, 31 July 1919).

3. Robert Walter, CMG, (1873–1959) was the colonial secretary of British Honduras (now known as Belize); he was also the officer administering the government from March 1917 until April 1918 and again from August 1918 until May 1919. (*Dominions Office and Colonial Office List, 1929* [London: HMSO, 1929]).

4. The British ambassador in America at the time was Rufus Daniel Isaacs, the first marquess of Reading (1860–1935). His full title was "High Commissioner and Special Ambassador." "High Commissioner" signified his authority to coordinate the British war effort with the American government. (*DNB*).

R. Walter to the British Ambassador, Washington, D.C.

Government House Belize
17th February, 1919

SIR,

In continuation of my Confidential despatch of the 13th February regarding the "Negro World" newspaper, I have the honour to draw special attention to the issue of that paper dated October 26th 1918 which contained the following in large type:

"Arthur J. Balfour of England says the German(?)
"Colonies shall not be returned to Germany.[1] I agree.
"Let Balfour know that England shall not have them.

"They neither belong to England nor Germany. They are the
"Property of the Blacks, and by God we are going to have
"them now or some time later, even if all the world is to
"waste itself in blood. Half the world cant be free and
"half slave.

"Marcus Garvey"

2. Marcus Garvey is the Managing Editor of the paper in question. I have the honour to be, Sir, Your Excellency's most Obedient, humble servant.

R. WALTER
Administering the Government

[*Typewritten reference*] BRITISH
HONDURAS No. Confidential

PRO, CO 123/295, British Honduras Confidential Despatch. TL, Transcript.

1. In various speeches throughout the second half of 1918 the British foreign secretary, Arthur Balfour, opposed restoring Germany's former African colonies. (*The Times*, 9 August 1918, 17 September 1918, 24 October 1918; see also Gaddis Smith, "The British Government and the Disposition of the German Colonies in Africa, 1914–1918," in Prosser Gifford and William Roger Louis, eds., *Britain and Germany in Africa: Imperial Rivalry and Colonial Rule* [New Haven, Conn.: Yale University Press, 1967], pp. 275–99).

Maj. W. H. Loving to the Director, Military Intelligence Division

253 West 137th Street. New York, N.Y.,
Feb. 17, 1919

From: Major W. H. Loving, P.C.
To: Director of Military Intelligence, Washington, D.C.
Subject: Report of mass meetings during January, 1919.[1]

1. Inclosed herewith is a full list of important mass meetings held during the month of January, with names of speakers who delivered addresses.

2. I wish to call special attention to the increased activity in radical propaganda among the colored people since the signing of the armistice.

3. All of the speakers named on inclosed list are radicals and frequently advocate Bolshevism in their speeches. This is especially true of Mr. Hubert Harrison, who claims that "Bolshevism is the salvation of America." The conservative colored population of Washington had never been accustomed to radical addresses of this nature and when Mr. Harrison first appeared before Washington audiences the people list/e/ned at him in awed silence. Now that he has been delivering addresses there for the past six weeks, the

people have not only become accustomed to his philosophy but are applauding it. During this brief period of six weeks Mr. Harrison has developed a very large following in the city of Washington, just as he did in New York.[a]

4. With the exception of Rev. R. D. Jonas (white), all of the speakers named have, in their recent addresses, attempted to explain and defend Bolshevism to their audiences, which in most cases have been large.

5. There has been an apparent decrease in the number of such meetings during the present month, but a record is being kept and report will be rendered at the close of the month.

W H LOVING
Major, P.C., Ret.

1 incl. in dupl.

[*Handwritten endorsement*] Confidential
[*Stamped endorsements*] CAPT. J. E. CUTLER
M.M.S   CAPT. HAYES M.I.4–41

DNA, RG 165, File 10218-309/2 2-1. TDS, Recipient's copy.
   1. Col. John M. Dunn, the acting director of Military Intelligence, forwarded a copy of this report on 21 February 1919 to William E. Allen, the acting chief of the Bureau of Investigation. (DNA, RG 165, file 10218-309/3).

Enclosure

[*New York City, ca. 31 January 1919*]

RECORD OF MASS MEETINGS HELD IN DIFFERENT CITIES DURING THE MONTH OF JANUARY, 1919, AND NAMES OF SPEAKERS WHO DELIVERED ADDRESSES.

January 1, 1919.

New York City—Crescent Hall	— Marcus Garvey.

January 3, 1919.

New York City—Crescent Hall	— Marcus Garvey.
Boston, Mass.—Odd Fellows Hall	— W. Monroe Trotter.

January 4, 1919.

Washington, D.C.—John Wesley Church	— Hubert Harrison.
Newark, N.J.—Colored A.M.E. Church	— Marcus Garvey.

January 5, 1919.

New York City—Crescent Hall	— Marcus Garvey.

January 7, 1919.

Washington, D.C.—Bethel Literary   — Hubert Harrison.

January 8, 1919.

New York City—Crescent Hall   — Marcus Garvey.
Chicago, Ills.—#33, 12th St.   — Rev. R. D. Jonas.
New York City,—Palace Casino   — Rev. G. F. Miller.

January 10, 1919.

New York City—Crescent Hall   — Marcus Garvey.

January 12, 1919.

Louisville, Ky.—K. of P. Hall   — Rev. R. D. Jonas.
New York City—Forward Hall   — Chandler Owen.
New York City—Crescent Hall   — Marcus Garvey.

January 13, 1919.

New York City—Bryant Hall   — Chandler Owen.

January 14, 1919.

Washington, D.C.—Florida Ave. Church   — Hubert Harrison.

January 15, 1919.

New York City—Crescent Hall   — Marcus Garvey.
New York City—Hotel DeVan   — Rev. G. F. Miller.

January 16, 1919.

New York City—Mt. Olivet Church   — A. Philip Randolph

January 17, 1919.

New York City—Crescent Hall   — Marcus Garvey.

January 19, 1919.

New York City—Crescent Hall   — Marcus Garvey.

January 22, 1919.

New York City—Crescent Hall   — Marcus Garvey.

January 24, 1919.

New York City—Crescent Hall   — Marcus Garvey.
New York City—Met. Baptist Church   — Rev. R. D. Jonas.
Washington, D.C.—Y.M.C.A.   — Hubert Harrison

January 26, 1919.

New York City—Crescent Hall — Marcus Garvey

January 27, 1919.

New York City—Lafayette Hall — A. Philip Randolph

January 28, 1919.

Washington, D.C.—Bethel Literary — Rev. G. F. Miller

January 29, 1919.

New York City—Crescent Hall — Marcus Garvey
Washington, D.C.—Florida Ave. Church — Hubert Harrison.

January 30, 1919.

Washington, D.C.—John Wesley Church — Hubert Harrison.
Baltimore, Md.—Bethel Church — Marcus Garvey.

January 31, 1919.

New York City—Crescent Hall — Marcus Garvey.

DNA, RG 165, File 10218-309/1. TD.

Petition by Marcus Garvey

[[New York, February 21, 1919]]

. . . Gentlemen of the Congress of the United States—Greeting:

As president general of the Universal Negro Improvement Association and African Communities League, a worldwide Negro organization, fighting for the liberation of the Negro peoples of the world, I have taken the liberty to address myself to you today relative to the constitution of the proposed [L]eague of Nations.

Gentlemen. I address myself to you on behalf of the struggling people of my race, because I realize that among you are to be found men of liberal views and democratic sentiment. Some of you have impressed me as being broad in your viewpoints, even as the great fathers of the republic were when they, among themselves, protested against the tyranny forced upon them by the strong hand of an alien empire. Having before me the records of men like George Washington and Patrick Henry, men most uncompromising in their demand for liberty, for complete freedom for the oppressed, I imagine that you in this age of fuller democracy, will also live up to the teachings of these noble progenitors of human rights.

You, within a few days, will be called upon by President Woodrow Wilson to give your consent and approval to the constitution of the League of Nations, as drafted and submitted to you from the continent of Europe.[1] Sirs, in a matter of self-defense, the Negro peoples of the world look at this constitution as one of the most outrageous attempts to further enslave them. There is not one syllable, not one word, not one letter, in the drafted constitution that suggests the spirit of good will toward a struggling race such as we are. But, on the contrary, everything has been offered to all other races for development while in the nineteenth clause of this very constitution is embodied the character of pillage, robbery, wholesale exploitation, with the concurrent evil of human slaughter on the continent of Africa. I hereby beg to quote that section of the constitution, which reads as follows:

"To those colonies and territories which as a consequence of the late war have ceased to be under the sovereignty of the states which formerly governed them and which are inhabited by peoples not yet able to stand by themselves under the strenuous conditions of the modern world, there should be applied the principle that the well-being and development of such peoples form a sacred trust of civilization, and that securities for the performance of this trust should be embodied in the constitution of the league.

"The best method of giving practical effect to this principle is that the tutelage of such peoples should be intrusted to advanced nations who, by reason of their resources, their experience or their geographical position, can best undertake the responsibility, and that this tutelage should be exercised by them as mandatories on behalf of the league.

"The character of the mandate must differ according to the stage of the development of the people, the geographical situation of the territory, its economic conditions and other similar circumstances.

"Certain communities formerly belonging to the Turkish empire have reached a stage of development where their existence as independent nations can be provisionally recognized subject to the rendering of administrative advice and assistance by a mandatory power until such time as they are able to stand alone. The wishes of these communities must be a principal consideration in the selection of the mandatory power.

"Other peoples, especially those of Central Africa are at such a stage that the mandatory must be responsible for the administration of the territory, subject to conditions which will guarantee freedom of conscience or religion, subject only to the maintenance of public order and morals, the prohibition of abuses such as the slave trade, the arms traffic and the liquor traffic, and the prevention of the establishment of fortifications or military and naval bases and of military training of the natives for other than police purposes and the defense of territory, and will also secure equal opportunities for the trade and commerce of other members of the league.

"There are territories such as Southwest Africa and certain of the South Pacific isles, which, owing to the sparseness of their population, or their small size, or their remoteness from the centers of civilization, or their geographical continuity to the mandatory state, and other circumstances, can be best administered under the laws of the mandatory state as integral portions thereof, subject to the safeguards above mentioned, in the interests of the indigenous population.

"In every case of mandate the mandatory state shall render to the league an annual report in reference to the territory committed to its charge.

"The degree of authority, control, or administration to be exercised by the mandatory state shall, if not previously agreed upon by the high contracting parties, in each case be explicitly defined by the Executive Council in a special act or charter.

"The high contracting parties further agree to establish at the seat of the league a mandatory commission to receive and examine the annual reports of the mandatory powers and to assist the league in insuring the observance of the terms of all mandates."

Gentlemen, can you see anything in this section of the Constitution that breathes the spirit of good will toward my race? Can you not read between the lines and see that it is the intention of the European powers to shackle the millions of black people on the continent of Africa and to further exploit them for the development of their respective nations on the continent of Europe, which nations have been for centuries waging war one against the other, and in their jealousies and rivalries they have time over and again shocked the civilization in which we live, and not later than a few months ago they, by these very jealousies, caused 7,000,000 men to have died, fighting one against the other?[2]

My appeal to you, gentlemen, is to refuse your consent to the League of Nations as it is proposed today. The League of Nations will be the "hangman" of all future aspirants to that liberty which you fought and won for yourselves not many centuries ago. I would ask you, gentlemen, to remember the words of Patrick Henry, as uttered in the Virginia Legislature, over 140 years ago: "I care not what others may say, but as for me, give me liberty or give me death."[3] On the strength of these words American independence was declared and the greatest democracy in the world was insured.

Will you deny the native Africans of the spirit of a Patrick Henry? Should tomorrow morning the oppressed natives of Africa rise as one man and repeat the words of Patrick Henry would you, gentlemen, send out your navies and your armies in conjunction with those of England, France and Italy to crush the rising spirit of these people? I feel perfectly sure that not one man in the Congress of these United States would consent to any such a thing. But, gentlemen, could it be possible for you not to join in such a bloody war when you will have become signatories to the Constitution of the League of Nations? That is just what you are called upon to do, today, gentlemen.[4] You are called upon to sign away the liberty of fully four hundred millions of black men, women and children scattered all over the world.

In the name of the High God, in the name of all that is dear in this world, I beseech you not to become parties to this gigantic robbery of the rights of the most oppressed of God's people today.

Remember, gentlemen, that twelve millions of black Americans have aspirations just as the ninety millions of white Americans. Today all people are crying out for self-control, self-government. We, in America, realize that there can be no self-government for us here or self-control independent of that which is exercised by the constituted government as elected by all. Yet, with the control of constituted government, we fall short in getting our constitutional rights. We, therefore, desire a wider expansion. That expansion can only be realized on the continent of Africa, our ancient fatherland. Today, hundreds of us are ready to go back as missionaries[5] in the cause of freedom. Will you stop us, gentlemen, by signing the Constitution of the League of Nations, or will you give us a passport to liberty?

Remember, gentlemen, what Lafayette[6] did in helping to save the nation. Will you deny the right to another Lafayette on the continent of Africa? Gentlemen, will you deny the right of a native of Africa to express himself in the language of a Patrick Henry, and deny him the privilege of putting his language into effect? Surely not.

Therefore, I again implore you, sirs, to turn down the Constitution of the League of Nations when presented to you by President Wilson in Congress.[7]

Yours, in anticipation of your kind help. Respectfully,

MARCUS GARVEY

Reprinted from the *New York Call*, Wednesday, 26 March 1919. The original head-lines and first three introductory paragraphs have been omitted. The appeal was originally published as a front-page editorial letter by Garvey in the *NW*, 22 February 1919, under the caption: "An Appeal to the Congress of the United States to Turn Down the Constitution of the League of Nations—Every Negro Should Be Against This Damnable Thing."

1. The text of the covenant and draft of the constitution of the League of Nations was presented by President Wilson to the plenary session of the peace conference on 14 February 1919. But the covenant was not presented in final form until 18 April 1919. President Wilson had returned to the United States in February 1919 on a temporary visit, when it was announced that he would hold discussions on 26 February with members of the Senate Foreign Relations Committee and House Foreign Affairs Committee at the White House on the subject of the League covenant. (*NYT*, 16 February, 27 February 1919; Arthur S. Link, *Wilson the Diplomatist: A Look at His Major Foreign Policies* [Baltimore: Johns Hopkins University Press, 1957], pp. 129–30).

2. An estimated ten million men were killed in World War I, while another twenty million were wounded.

3. Patrick Henry (1736–1799), one of the leaders of the American Revolution, delivered the speech from which this famous quotation is taken on 23 March 1775 before the Virginia House of Delegates. (*WBD*; Charles L. Cohen, "The 'Liberty or Death' Speech: A Note on Religion and Revolutionary Rhetoric," *William and Mary Quarterly*, 3rd series, 38 [October 1981]: 702–17).

4. Garvey was quoting from a draft version of the mandate article. When first presented to the peace conference's commission on the League of Nations on 10 February 1919, it was article

17. In a later draft it became article 19, and with some slight modifications it was adopted as article 22 in the covenant's final version. The conference considered a proposal by the French delegation for an international military force capable of enforcing international law; in the final form of the league covenant, provisions were made in article 16 for the use of military sanctions but only against a member state that committed an act of war.

5. Colonial governments in Africa generally opposed Afro-American missionaries, although it appears that no specific legislative restriction directed against Afro-American missionaries as such was ever enacted. Colonial authorities disapproved of Afro-American missionaries because they felt that these missionaries would spread the subversive doctrine of "Africa for the Africans" which the Garvey movement played an important role in disseminating in Africa.

6. Marie-Joseph-Paul Yves-Roch-Gilbert du Motier, marquis de Lafayette (1757–1834), French statesman and military officer, fought in the American War of Independence from 1777 until 1782. (*WBD*).

7. Ratification of the peace treaty was defeated in the Senate by a vote of thirty-eight to fifty-three in November 1919.

Postal Censorship Report

NEW ORLEANS, LA., 2/24/19

INDEX NO. *31555*

FROM	TO
(Dr.) E. A. Sampson,	Universal Negro Improvement,
Payo Obispo,	Association of New York,
Mexico.	"The Negro World"
	36–38 West 135th St.,
	New York, N.Y.

DATE OF LETTER ??	NO. OF OBJECTS ENCLOSED 4	LANGUAGE OF LETTER English	DATE OF COMMENT 2/24/19.

ROUTE	DATE	COPIES	DISPOSITION UNLESS DISPATCHED	
O.N.I.	2/25	4	8th-3rd-N.D.	NO. OF EXAMINER 1137 TABLE NO. 1
C.C.C.	2/25	2		
M.I.D.	2/25	2	Hold	NO. OF COMMENT WRITER 1127 TYPED BY FS—2/25/19.
W.T.B.	2/25	2		
P.O.				APPROVED BY D.A.C. —— APPROVED BY A.C. G.H.T.
E.A.C.	2/24	1	N.Y.	SUBJECT Pr. 4-Mex.[1]

COMMENT

Exhorts Negroes to Strike for Freedom.

Writer sends what seems to be an advertisement, which is to be inserted, apparently in the "Negro World", and in which Writer claims to be able to cure persons addicted to the use of "poisonous drastic drugs", and promises help to those who have become financial, moral, spiritual or physical wrecks.

Writer also encourages the ladies to "have no fear for their secrets", and to send their letters to Dona VERA DE SAMPSON, in care of Writer; he also sends a list of his qualifications, which state that he is a Fellow of the British Psychological Institute, Bolton 15 Vernon St., England, a graduate of Chicago and St. Louis Colleges, etc.

Writer also encloses two pages of verses, signed by himself, dated Jan. 29/1919, Payo Obispo, and entitled: "We Will Get Our Freedom."

This attempt at poetry is an exhortation to the Negroes to fight for their freedom.

"We will endure the taunts no more,
Turn us loose on Africa's shore.
There we'll find Freedom.

Save, teach, endure, till the nerves they break,
Fight, die, and rather to dwell in Hell's Lake
Without our Freedom

Where is the Negro with Soul so dead,
Three hundred years with a Heart of lead,
Look! can't you see that embellished Light,
And know for your rights it is time to Fight?"

[Endorsement] Mr. Fulk for Justice (?)

DNA, RG 38, File 10948-184, Index No. 31555. D, Printed form with typewritten insertions. Endorsement is handwritten.

1. The press branch of postal censorship responsible for handling material from Mexico.

Colville Barclay, Chargé d'Affaires Ad Interim, British Embassy, to William Phillips, Asst. Secretary of State

[Washington, D.C.] February 24, 1919

My dear Mr. Phillips,[1]

The Acting Governor of British Honduras has invited my attention to the enclosed copy of the paper entitled "The Negro World",[2] which has been finding its way to that Colony. The object of this paper appears to be to incite racial hatred, and it is very possibly supported by German or Bolshevist money. The Acting Governor informs me that he does not consider the circulation of the paper in British Honduras desirable and he is giving instructions to prevent this.

I am forwarding you a copy of the paper, as it does not appear to comply with the usual requirements regarding registration and the printing of the name of the printer and publisher. I shall be very glad if you will inform me whether any importance is attached to this paper in the United States. Yours sincerely,

COLVILLE BARCLAY[3]

[*Typewritten reference*] No. 146
[*Endorsement*] Paper to D.J. 2-26-19 TC-LH.

DNA, RG 59, Office of the Counselor, File 800.9. TLS, Recipient's copy. Endorsement is handwritten.

    1. William Phillips (1878–1968) was assistant secretary of state from January 1917 to March 1920. (*NYT*, 24 February 1968).
    2. The copy was not retained in the file.
    3. Sir Colville Adrian de Rune Barclay (1869–1929) was appointed counselor in the British embassy at Washington, D.C. in October 1913, and promoted to chargé d'affaires in 1914. He was appointed a minister plenipotentiary on 3 May 1918. (*WWW*, 1929–40).

L. Lanier Winslow, Counselor,[1] Department of State, to W. E. Allen

Washington February 26, 1919

Dear Mr. Allen:

I take pleasure in enclosing a copy of the paper entitled "The Negro World",[2] which has found its way, among other places, into British Honduras. The object of this paper appears to be to incite racial hatred, and it is suggested that it may be supported by German or Bolshevist money. The British Government has taken steps to have it kept out of British Honduras.

The paper does not seem to comply with the usual requirements regarding registration and the printing of the name of the printer and the publisher. I should be glad to hear from you at your early convenience whether this paper has come to your attention before and if you deem it advisable to take any action towards the suppression of the same. Very truly yours,

L. LANIER WINSLOW[3]

C-H
Enc.

DNA, RG 65, File OG 185161. TLS, Recipient's copy.

    1. The office of the counselor in the Department of State was established as part of the department's reorganization in 1909. The counselor's primary role was to report to the

secretary of state on those questions requiring legal or technical skills, such as international trade agreements. Together with the three assistant secretaries, the counselor was also a member of the staff of policy advisors to the secretary of state. In 1919 the office of the counselor became the office of the undersecretary of state, and the new undersecretary was given responsibility for the department's liaison with government agencies involved in the investigation of subversive organizations and individuals both in the United States and abroad.

2. The copy was not retained in the file.

3. Lawrence Lanier Winslow (1885–1929) was assigned in February 1917 to the Department of State from his post as secretary of the American Embassy in Berlin; in November 1919 he was reassigned to the American embassy in London. (Department of State, *Register, 1930* [Washington, D.C.: GPO, 1930]; *NYT*, 27 October 1929).

Address by Marcus Garvey in Brooklyn

[*West Indian*,[1] 28 February 1919]

What is said to be the greatest movement in the history of the Negroes of the world, organized by Mr. Marcus Garvey a few months ago in New York, is spreading throughout the United States. The movement has for its standard the improvement of the coloured peoples of the entire globe despite geographical disadvantages. Mr. Garvey and his army of workers are enthusiastic over the progress of the organization and are working assiduously to further the plans of the as[s]ociation, which is called the Universal Negro Improvement Association and African Communities League. The movement is backed by thousands of Negroes in the United States and the organization has its branches in nearly every large city situated above the Mason Dixon Line.[2]

He has visited these cities and has delivered addresses to monster gatherings of coloured people and returned to New York with optimistic thoughts of the future of the darker race, or the balance of power in the world, as he termed them in his eloquent address delivered in the Harlem Casino on December 6th, and subsequently when the coloured people of New York assembled to elect three delegates to the Peace Conference.

To further the aims of the association and to properly place before the public the achievements and aspirations of the League, a weekly paper is published and is meeting with success from every direction. Mr. Garvey is a versatile writer and a forceful and convincing orator. On the 9th of January he held a large audience spell-bound for nearly two hours in Brooklyn. The speech was delivered in the John Wesley M.E. Church.

After the singing of the Negro National Anthem[3] and Mr Garvey had been introduced, he rose amid the thunderous applause of the thousands gathered to hear him speak. He told of his visits to the different cities and the success that followed, also of the spirit of co-operation that is being manifested by coloured people with whom he came in contact. He said in part:

"Whether it is in America, in the West Indies, in Central America or South America or Africa, the news is coming to us every day of the readiness of the people to cooperate with us. It is because we want you in Brooklyn to be as solid, as resolute in your determination as we are in New York city why I come to you without any scruples to let you know that if the people in Greater New York are ready, if the people in Harlem are ready, if the people in Newport News are ready, if the people in Chicago are ready, if the people in Washington are ready, and if the people in every part of the world are ready, the West Indies and Africa; you in Brooklyn must also be ready, because the four hundred millions of us scattered in all parts of the world must be so prepared that at the call for service, we must step forth to deliver ourselves into that freedom, that democracy for which we have fought in many a battle. (Hear, Hear.) The real fight of the Negro is to come. When we look on the world as it is reorganizing itself today, we cannot see any sleeping people, I mean people who are not alive to their immediate need of freedom. Whether it is the Irish people, the Polish people, the Jews, or the Hindoos, everybody is looking out to protect himself and in this case wherein men are fighting for freedom, we of the Negro race cannot afford to linger behind. Our sacrifices, as made in the cause of other people, are many. I think it is time that we should prepare to sacrifice now for ourselves, (Cheers). I cannot see why you in Brooklyn should be different from other people in that we are Negroes suffering from the same disadvan[t]ages. I would like it to go down in the history of our great world-wide movement that you in Brooklyn were not dead, were not deaf to the appeal for cooperation when made to you. And I am now making that appeal, trusting each and every one of you here will become members of the association before the meeting comes to a close.

"Organization is the force that rules the world. All peoples have gained their freedom through organized force. All nations all empires have grown into greatness through organized methods. These are the means by which we as a race, will climb to greatness. The world around us is organizing itself today. The white world of Europe is so organized as to be able to protect itself from foreign intrusion. Asia is organizing to repel the aggressor. Africa at home and Africa abroad are the only open doors that suggest exploitation and robbery to othe[r] peoples. When I say Africa at home, I mean the 280,000,000 of blacks who live on that continent that God gave us as our heritage. There we have no well organized government for protection. Because of that all the alien races of Europe have invaded that territory and they have subjugated the teeming millions to serfdom, to slavery. Africa abroad is suffering from many abuses. In America we have the lynch rope around our necks. In the West Indian islands we are relegated to the ditch of industrial stagnation. Nowhere in this br[o]ad universe are we recognized as a competent race simply because we have failed in that most essential weapon—organization. Let us be organized in Brooklyn tonight as we are organized in other parts of this country and in the West Indies (cheers.) "This war that has been won by the allied nations was fought for a great principle. It was that of giving to all peoples the right to govern themselves. Now that there is peace and the affairs of the world are to be settled, we find that every race except the

Negro will have a voice in the principle of self-determination. And why is it so? Because all of them are organized[.] In a matter of comparison, you can hardly find any race of people standing on the same political platform in the world as the Negro[.] They might suffer disadvantages, such as Poland,[4] but none of these countries suffer in the way Africa suffers. Africa of 12,000,000 square miles is the most congenial country in the world for the Negro[.] That country . . . [*several words mutilated*] gave him is to . . . [*several words mutilated*] in the East . . . [*several words mutilated*] South or Central . . . [*mutilated*] every spot that is habitable has [become?] the domain of the white man, and he has possessed himself of it, not by a matter of conquest alone, but through the easiest methods possible, simply because there has been no organized resistance. The time for the peaceful penetration of the black man's right by the white man is past, and the time for a determined resistance has come, and it is on that problem we of the Universal Negro Improvement Association stand. (Loud and prolonged cheers.) We are determined to live and die free men. (Cheers) Men who are free never admit of inroads into their rights. When such inroads are attempted, the result has always been a fight to the finish. When Germany made her inroad into the political boundaries of Northern Europe, there was an organized resistance to repel her. She has been whipped, and I am now saying to you people in Brooklyn tonight that the same methods that were used by the allied governments in whipping Germany to her knees for the intrusion she had made into the rights of other people's, is the same course we must take as a universal people to repel the aggressor on the continent of Africa. (Cheers.) Africa will be a bloody battlefield in the years to come. (Hear, hear.) We cannot tell who the foemen will be, whether he will be English, French, German, Belgian or Dutch; but there is one thing we are determined on that we are going to fight it out with him to a finish. That finish must mean victory for the Negro standard. (Wild cheers.)

Freedom has become a sacred possession to men. No race can be completely free, living as subjects of an alien race. The Negro is tired of being a subject. He is tired of being a citizen without rights, and the time is now ripe when we should guarantee freedom even at the cost of our lives. (Cheers.) One generation must die even in half to save the other generation in whole. (Cheers) As for me the spirit of Patrick Henry still moves; it is the spirit of liberty or death. There has always been one consolation for me which I have gained out of this war. I, as a young man, could have died in France, in Flanders or Mesopotamia, fighting for the brutal Belgian. Since I could have so died without achieving anything for myself after the victory, I am now resolved to try the game of dying for myself; but before I die, I feel sure that my blood shall have paid that remission for which future generations of the Negro race shall be declared free. (Cheers) Freedom of action, freedom of opportunity are the things we need, which I believe can only be gained after we shall have established an imperial power to command the respect of nations and races.

"Let us step out in Brooklyn tonight with the spirit of service. That service which the Pilgrim Fathers gave for the building up of America we must also give for the building up of our race."

Printed in the *West Indian* (Mail Edition), Friday, 28 February 1919. Original headlines have been omitted.

1. Garvey's lecture was reported by W. H. Simpson, the New York correspondent of the *West Indian*, which was published in Grenada by T. Albert Marryshow (1887–1958), the pioneer of the self-government movement in the West Indies. (*DG*, 20 October 1958).

2. The Mason-Dixon line was originally the boundary line between Pennsylvania in the North, and Maryland and present-day West Virginia in the South.

3. " 'Lift Every Voice and Sing' (National Hymn for the Colored People of America)," was originally composed in 1900 as a commemorative hymn on the anniversary of Abraham Lincoln's birth by James Weldon Johnson (1871–1938) and his brother J. Rosamond Johnson (ca. 1875–ca. 1940), and dedicated to Booker T. Washington. Both men later made an outstanding mark in the musical history of America, and their song gained such wide acceptance among black Americans that within a decade following its composition it came to be known as the "Negro National Anthem." (James Weldon Johnson, *The Autobiography of an Ex-Colored Man* [1912; reprint ed., New York: Hill & Wang, 1960]; Wayne Francis, " 'Lift Every Voice and Sing,' " *Crisis* 32 [September 1926]:234–36; Eugene Levy, *James Weldon Johnson: Black Leader, Black Voice* [Chicago: University of Chicago Press, 1973]).

4. A reference to the long-standing territorial partition of Poland between Russia, Germany, and Austria-Hungary, as well as to the problem of religious, cultural, and linguistic rights of its various minorities. By the Treaty of Saint-Germain, signed on 10 September 1919, the independence of Czechoslovakia, Yugoslavia, Poland, and Hungary was recognized, with each state obliged to give guarantees of protection for the rights and various privileges of its various minority populations.

Report by the *Afro-American*

[Baltimore, Maryland, 28 February 1919]

Garvey Urges Organization
Radical New Yorker Says Time Has Come for Colored Soldiers to Fight for Themselves

At meetings held at Bethel A.M.E. Church Monday night [*24 February*] [M]acedonia Baptist Church Tuesday night [*25 February*] and John Wesley Thursday night [*27 February*], Hon. Marcus Garvey, of the Universal Independent Improvement Association, struck telling blows in an attack upon the white man's treatment of the Negro all over the world.

Mr. Garvey, whose purpose is to organize a large branch of the association here, said:

"We Negroes have fought and died enough for white people, the time has come to fight and die for ourselves.

"From 1914 to 1918 two million Negroes fought in Europe for a thing foreign to themselves—Democracy. Now they must fight for themselves. The time for cowardice is past. The old-time Negro has gone—buried with [']Uncle Tom.'[1]

"All white people are cowards anyhow, and the greatest coward of them all is the American white man. America is the only nation outside of the Turks where the superior numbers take advantage of the inferior numbers by lynching and burning them.[2]

"Let one Negro in New York pass fifteen white men on a street corner and he will be called 'nigger.' Let one Negro pass one white man and the white man calls no names. The reason is that he is a coward and man to man is afraid of the Negro. In the same way ninety millions of whites in this country bully ten millions of Negroes.

"To get even with these cowardly whites, Negroes have got to win their freedom just as the Russians and the Japanese have done—by revolution and bloody fighting.

"Negroes in America cannot do this. They are too hopelessly outnumbered and it would be foolish to attempt it. But in Africa, where there are over four hundred millions Negroes, we can make the white man eat his salt. Africans are looking to the United States to help them organize against this emergency.

"White people give the Negro the Christian religion of brotherhood and then pay no respect to it themselves. Now they are talking about perpetual peace. But before that time there will be made of Africa one bloody battlefield.

"There will be no peace as long as all white people are up because they are white and all black people down because they are black. There will be no peace until I get where he is. If they want peace let them give every man an equal chance. Make it possible for a black man to be president of the United States or France or any other country; then we can begin to talk about perpetual peace."

Printed in the *Afro-American*, Friday, 28 February 1919.

1. Uncle Tom was the principal character in Harriet Beecher Stowe's novel, *Uncle Tom's Cabin, or Life Among the Lowly* (1852); it has since become a pejorative term denoting the behavior of any black person who sacrifices principles to curry favor from whites.

2. A possible reference to the Armenian massacres carried out by Turks during the period of the Ottoman Empire.

Editorial Letter by Marcus Garvey

[[New York, N.Y., February 28, 1919]]

Fellowmen of the Negro Race:

Greeting:—I am instructed by the Universal Negro Improvement Association, in keeping with their promise of last week,[1] to give to you the following reports as touching the Association's ac[ti]vities in the matter of having the race represented in Europe and especially in France during the time of sitting of the Peace Conference.

Mr. Eliezer Cadet was appointed High Commissioner of the Universal Negro Improvement Association and African Communities' League to represent the cause of our race in Europe. He was elected by the popular vote of the people at the great mass meeting we held in the Palace Casino, New York, on the 1st of December, 1918. He is now in France and he has delivered the following addresses to the English and French people respectively, and has also presented the resolutions to the Peace Conference, as adopted at the meeting of November 10, 1918, at the Palace Casino, New York.

Mr. Cadet will report to us from time to time of his activities in Europe, and it shall be the pleasant duty of the Association to have same made public through the medium of "The Negro World." Yours fraternally,

MARCUS GARVEY

MR. ELIEZER CADET'S ADDRESS[2] TO THE PEOPLE OF FRANCE.

Citizens of Democratic France:

We, the Negro people of the world—the world of Africa, America, of the West Indies, and of South and Central America—greet you in the spirit of liberty and true democracy.

In the terrible war of 1914–1918 we stuck by you, helping to secure for you that freedom and liberty of action that every free nation and race desire. We have fought alongside of you under the tri-color of your glorious republic, to supplant the common enemy, and now that the battle is won and France declared free, we are now asking for your consideration towards us as a section of the unfairly treated and oppressed people of the world.

You, most noble French people, have declared for universal freedom. We, of the Universal Negro Improvement Association and African Communities' League, representing the interests of our people in Africa, America, the West Indies and South and Central America, now beg to lay before you our claim for justice which, we trust will be taken cognizance of at the Peace Conference now sitting in your august and most democratic city.

We, of North America, beg to lay before you the awful institutions of lynching and burning at the stake of our men, women and children by the white people of that country, which institutions are in direct contravention of the established codes of civilization. We ask your help and interference in the stopping of these outrages, which cannot be regarded as national or domestic questions, but as international violations of civilized human rights, a perpetuation of which may again throw the world into war, as the Negroes of the world are not disposed to have their race so outraged by another through the high-handed assertion of prejudice, a thing most foolish, unnatural and inhuman.

In the West Indian Islands, millions of us are reduced to common serfdom, robbed and exploited by alien masters who pretend to love and care for us whilst depriving us of every chance that would make us a free and prosperous people. The abominable low wage system i[n] those islands can be characterized in no better language than that of wholesale industrial robbery.

In Africa, we are suffering by the millions from mal-administration, bad government, prejudice and exploitation as inflicted upon us by the many alien whites of Europe.

Our hearts and souls all over the world cry out in rebellion against these many atrocities, and we now in the name of justice call upon the democratic people of France to rise as one man to help us to throw off the burden of the oppressors. We call upon France for help, because we, to the extent of nearly two millions, left our homes in Africa, America and the West Indies, to help France in the time of her trouble. The many exploits of our soldiers on the various battlefields are proofs of our love for France.

France, oh, immortal France! We, the Negroes of the world, have helped to save thee in the time of danger. We now call upon thy children to help us in our time of need. These are some of the claims we lay before thee and before the Peace Conference. . . .[3]

MR. ELIEZER CADET'S ADDRESS TO THE PEOPLE OF ENGLAND

Most Humane and Democratic Citizens of England:

We, of the Universal Negro Improvement Association and African Communities' Le[ag]ue, representing the interests of the Negro people of the world, beg to lay before you in this time of world readjustment the claims of our oppressed race.

We, in the terrible war of 1914–1918, have followed you on every far-flung battlefield for the purpose of saving civilization and the democracies of the world. We were called out by the millions from Africa, America and the West Indies to fight, and if need be, die, to save the world. The world is now saved for the democratic people of all climes.

The Peace Conference now sitting in Paris is charged with the settling of all human wrongs. At this conference, delegates from all the democracies of the world are assembled, and especially the delegates of England. We are, therefore, asking you, the real people of England—the toilers, thinkers and electors—to so create sentiment within your country as to have your representatives in Paris to act fairly towards the Negroes of the world.

It has been a custom among the white people of Europe and America to treat the Negro's cause lightly. You can no longer, if you desire the peace of the world, afford to treat the Negro's cause lightly today, for the new Negroes of the world are determined that they, like other men, shall be completely free. We say this to you, most dear people of England, because you above all people know, through experience, the cost of liberty. When your forefathers fought and won their liberty, you in gratitu[d]e embodied their memory in prayer and in song. Your many monuments in the great city of London are proofs of your recorded gratitude for what has been done in the past by your pioneers and martyrs for the founding of your glorious empire.

Negroes, and especially the young ones, are not disposed to read your history without the hope of a like achievement for their race. We do not desire conquest, we do not desire to interfere with the rights of other people; all we desire is fair play and justice on the continents of Africa, America and on the West Indian Islands. There can be no abiding peace, we believe, so long as half of the world remains free and the other half slave. We ask you, therefore, to help us to abolish the lynching institutions and burning at the stake of men, women and children of our race in the United States of America, to abolish industrial serfdom, robbery and exploitation in the West Indies and the new slavery and outrages inflicted on our race in Africa.

We desire the abolition of all these things, because we would like to see perpetual peace on earth. Remember, men and women of England, that Negroes are people like Europeans and Asiatics. Whatever is good for either the whites of Europe or the yellows and browns of Asia, should be good also for the blacks, in that "God created of one blood all nations of men to dwell on the face of the earth."

We, therefore, further beg that the democracy of your common country instruct the delegates of the empire in Paris[4] to remember the peace aims cabled to your capital on the 11th of November, 1918, and which we placed in the hands of your Foreign Secretary, the Right Honorable Arthur J. Balfour.

Introducing Mr. Eliezer Cadet to the Press of France
Warmly Received by French Journalists.

The following credentials were handed Mr. Cadet as introducing him to the French Newspaper Fraternity:

To the Gentlemen of the Newspaper Press of France:

Greeting—This is to introduce to you Mr. Eliezer Cadet, of New York City, New York, United States of America, native of the Free Republic of Haiti, the duly accredited representative in France of the Universal Negro Improvement Association and African Communities' League of the world. He is commissioned to represent the cause of our world-wide movement before the Peace Conference now sitting in Paris and wheresoever it may sit hereafter until peace is fully established.

Mr. Cadet is authorized to take part in any deliberation pertaining to the good and welfare of the Negro race, as the representative of the Universal Negro Improvement Association and African Communities' League.

He is recommended to all governments, their delegates and representatives at the Peace Conference for kind and considerate treatment. The Universal Negro Improvement Association and African Communities' League shall hold itself responsible for the findings of Mr. Cadet on any matter pertaining to the cause which he is herein accredited to represent, and shall honor his name as attached to any document in common with others issued jointly or otherwise in the interests of the Negro peoples of the world.

Mr. Cadet is especially recommended to the press fraternity for assistance in laying the grievances of our race before the democratic peoples of Europe and the world through the med[i]um of the various liberal newspapers of France.

The Universal Negro Improvement Association and African Communities' League, owners and controllers of the newspaper known as THE NEGRO WORLD, with universal circulation, feels that the members of the press fraternity of France will accommodate Mr. Cadet and help him in every way to lay the Negro's cause before the great French people.

Any treatment accorded Mr. Cadet shall be regarded as a similar treatment towards the Universal Negro Improvement Association and African Communities' League of the World, representing the interests of the millions of black men, women and children of Africa, America, the West Indies, South and Central America.

In testimony whereof we, as officials and duly elected officers of this association and league, append our names and the seals of the organization, this fifteenth day of [*February*], one thousand nine hundred and nineteen.

> (Signed) MARCUS GARVEY,
> President-General
> JOSEPH JOHNSON,
> High Chancellor
> JULIA E. RUMFORD,
> Acting Secretary-General

Printed in the *NW*, Saturday, 1 March 1919. Original headlines have been omitted.

1. The issue of the *Negro World* for Saturday, 22 February 1919, has not been located.

2. The addresses which Cadet took to Europe were probably written by Garvey.

3. There followed a listing of the peace aims approved at the Universal Mass Convention held at the Palace Casino in New York on Sunday, 10 November 1918; the list was cabled the next day to the heads of the Allied governments and also to the peace conference in Paris.

4. The British Empire's delegates to the peace conference consisted of the five plenipotentiary delegates of Great Britain and the delegates representing the British dominions (Canada, Australia, South Africa, New Zealand, Newfoundland) and India.

NOTICE ᵀᴼ ᵀₕₑ COLORED POPULATION OF HARLEM

THE UNIVERSAL NEGRO IMPROVEMENT ASSOCIATION AND AFRICAN COMMUNITIES' LEAGUE, INC.

HAS OPENED A FIRST-CLASS

LUNCH ROOM. RESTAURANT. TEA ROOM AND ICE CREAM PARLOR

AT

56 West 135th Street

Three Floors Adjoining the Lincoln Theatre, New York

AND THE PATRONAGE OF THE PUBLIC IS SOLICITED

Special Dinner Every Sunday Night
BEST DISHES SERVED NIGHT AND DAY

Negro World, 1 March 1919

Fund Raising Appeal

[*Negro World*, 1 March 1919]

To the Readers and Friends of the Negro World of America, the West Indies, Central and South America, and Africa:

Greetings:—I am requested by the Universal Negro Improvement Association to make a direct appeal to you for some financial help to enable

"The Negro World" to fulfill its mission of conveying to all the scattered people of our race the aims and purposes of the Association.

For six months the Association has been publishing this paper at a great financial loss. We started out with a circulation of three thousand copies a week, and today we are in the neighborhood of fifty thousand. This paper stands for an ideal and not for commercial greed or profit. Because of that we have refused to carry certain advertisements that would in any way libel the reputation of the race.

In comparing "The Negro World" with the other colored newspapers of America and other countries of the world, you will find that from an advertising standpoint we stand singularly clean. We have refused to carry advertisements that tell our people to "bleach their black skins," or to "straighten their kinky hair." Other newspapers of the race draw incomes of from $500 to $5,000 a year for carrying these advertisements. If a million dollars were involved instead of five hundred or one thousand, we would not carry any such advertisements. Through such a policy that Association has to pay the full cost of production and in some instance we have given away the newspaper and have not even received returns from certain sections of the world to which it has been sent. Yet, we gladly continue, so that all the people of the race might know of the movement that we hope will one day permeate the entire Negro world—the world of Africa, of America, of the West Indies and of Central and South America.

Three thousand dollars must be raised immediately to place the paper on a sound financial basis. This three thousand dollars must be raised in two weeks, and I am, therefore, requested to ask that every reader of the paper and every friend send direct to the office, a dollar donation to help the paper. It will be a dollar well spent, because it will contribute to the building-up of a great newspaper institution—an institution that will one day bestow unlimited benefits on those who have helped to build it.

If there is to be a united sentiment among all the people, if there is to be unity of action in everything, then there must be a medium through which this sentiment must be created, and the greatest medium for creating sentiment in the world today is that of the newspaper.

"The Negro World" is now spreading itself all over the world; but to keep the press going and to speed up the production, we must have the necessary money as capital, so that the Universal Negro Improvement Association is not asking for too much when it asks for one dollar from each reader to make up three thousand dollars in two weeks.

Wherever you are when this reaches you, whether it is in the South of America, West, the Middle West or the Eastern States, send in your dollar; if you are in the West Indian Islands, send in your dollar; if you are in Central and South America, send in your dollar; if you are in Africa, send in your dollar; and let us report to you that we have received at the end of two weeks the three thousand dollars to put the newspaper on a sound basis.

Send your dollar addressed to the General Secretary of the Universal Negro Improvement Association, 36–38 West 135th street, New York, N.Y., U.S.A.

Feeling sure that you will respond to this appeal, as requested. Yours fraternally,

(Signed) MARCUS GARVEY,
Managing Editor of
"The Negro World["]

P.S.—Send all donations addressed to General Secretary, Universal Negro Improvement Association, 36–[3]8 West 135th street, New York City.

Printed in the *NW*, Saturday, 1 March 1919, and passim.

ALL NEGRO COMMUNITIES of the WORLD

(of America, Africa, the West Indies, Central and South America)

ARE REQUESTED TO FORM THEMSELVES INTO BRANCHES OF THE

UNIVERSAL NEGRO IMPROVEMENT ASSOCIATION and AFRICAN COMMUNITIES' LEAGUE OF THE WORLD

FOR THE CONSOLIDATION OF THE SENTIMENT AND ASPIRATIONS OF THE 400,000,000 OF THE NEGRO RACE.

ORGANIZE FOR RACIAL PROGRESS, INDUSTRIALLY, COMMERCIALLY, EDUCA-TIONALLY, POLITICALLY AND SOCIALLY
ORGANIZE FOR THE PURPOSE OF FOUNDING A GREAT NATION

Any Seven Persons of Liberal Education of the Negro Race Can Organize Among Themselves and Apply to the International Headquarters for Necessary Instructions and Charter.

INTERNATIONAL CONVENTION OF DEPUTIES

From the Branches of the Association in Every Country in the world Will Assemble on 1st of August, 1920, to Elect

HIS SUPREME HIGHNESS, THE POTENTATE, HIS HIGHNESS, THE SUPREME DEPUTY,

AND OTHER HIGH OFFICIALS

Who Will Preside Over the Destiny of the Negro Peoples of the World Until an African Empire Is Founded.

Address All Communications to

UNIVERSAL NEGRO IMPROVEMENT ASSOCIATION AND AFRICAN COMMUNITIES' LEAGUE, INC., 36-38 WEST 135th STREET   NEW YORK, UNITED STATES OF AMERICA

MARCUS GARVEY, D. S. O. E.
PRESIDENT-GENERAL

SECRETARY-GENERAL

JOSEPH E. JOHNSON,
HIGH CHANCELLOR

Negro World, 1 March 1919

SERIES OF

Important Meetings!

A Call to All

NEGROES

If you want to hear things about your race
If you want to be among those who are doing things to make the Negro race
a power in the World
If you want to learn about the Founding of a great Negro Nation
Then attend the Series of Meetings to be addressed by

MARCUS GARVEY

World-Renowned Negro Orator and Managing Editor of the "Negro World"

AT THE

UNIVERSAL RESTAURANT

56 West 135th Street, next to the Lincoln Theatre

EVERY NIGHT

FROM **9** TO
SUNDAY   SUNDAY   **MARCH 16**
NIGHT   NIGHT

Big Programme for Everybody

SUBJECTS

Sunday Night, 9th at 8 o'clock, "Report of the Negro High Commissioner at
the Peace Conference"
Monday Night 10th, "The Future of the American and West Indian Negro
in Africa
Tuesday Night 11th, "The possibilities of a Negro Nation."
Wednesday Night 12th, "America and The Negro."
Thursday Night 13th, "The West Indies and the Negro"
Friday Night 14th, "My stay among the Whites in Europe"
Saturday Night 15th, "The Negro in the next War"
Sunday Night 16th, "The Negro's Sway on the World."

Americans, Africans and West Indians and Negroes of all countries are requested
to attend these meetings.
Admission Free.

THE HUNT PRINTING COMPANY   56 W. 135TH STREET NEW YORK

(Source: DNA, RG 65)

385

E. J. Kerwin to the Chief, Bureau of Investigation

Pine Bluff, Ark. [*Made*] March 12, 1919
[*for the period of March*] 12 [*1919*]

IN RE: COMPLAINTS BY CITIZENS OF WABBASECKA, ARK. RELATIVE TO FEELING BEING CREATED BETWEEN NEGROES AND WHITE ACCOUNT OF CHICAGO DEFENDER[1] AND NEGRO WORLD PUBLISHED IN NEW YORK.

CHIEF DEPARTMENT JUSTICE,
Bureau of Investigation:

Am enclosing you a copy of newspaper published in New York of date February 22, 1919 called the Negro World at its top in big black letters the following: NO LEAGUE OF NATIONS. Strong article on f[ro]nt page being an appeal to Congress of the United States to turn down the Constitution of the League of Nations being a signed article. From a perusal of the paper you can see what it is as it is not necessary to here mention editorial and article after article.

The complaint I received enclosing me copy of this paper is from one of our best citizens who lives in the country and one of our oldest. He says there is no danger immediate or otherwise from our old time darkey but from the present younger crowd. And desires to know if there is any means whereby the circulation of this sheet and the Chicago Defender can be stopped or something done I believe his daughter is Postmistress at Wabbasecka and his name is R. J. WATKINS.

E. J. KERWIN[2]

Enclosure Paper.

DNA, RG 65, File OG 185161. TD. Copy of the report was furnished to "McElveen, [*in*] Memphis."

1. More than any other black newspaper, the *Chicago Defender*, edited by Robert S. Abbott, played a major role in attracting southern blacks to the North during the period of the "Great Migration." The paper's national edition was aimed primarily at southern blacks, and it carried prominent reports of southern lynchings and violence, as well as advertisements for well-paying jobs in the Chicago area. Between 1916 and 1918 the *Defender's* circulation increased from 10,000 to 93,000, despite several attempts to ban it from the southern mails. As the paper came under increasing attack, it was distributed by black Pullman railway porters, black stage shows, clandestine labor-recruiting agents, and returning World War I veterans. By 1920 the *Defender* reached an estimated circulation of 283,571. (Frederick G. Detweiler, *The Negro Press in the United States* [Chicago: University of Chicago Press, 1922]; *DAB*; *WWCA*; *NYT*, 1 March 1940; Metz T. P. Lochard, "Robert S. Abbott, 'Race Leader,' " *Phylon* [1947]:124–28).

2. Edwin J. Kerwin (? –1931) was admitted to the Arkansas bar in 1904. He was elected to the General Assembly of Arkansas in 1911, and later became a county judge. During World War I, he served in the Department of Justice. (*Bar Association of Arkansas, Proceedings* [n.p., 1932]).

Eliézer Cadet to the UNIA

[[Paris 13 March 1919]]

To the Universal Negro Improvement Association and the African League Committee.

Since my arrival in Paris, this is the first opportunity that I have had to talk with you, Dear Comrades.

The only error that I see that we have committed was not to give a proper emphasis to the influence of President Wilson on the Peace Conference and on Europe. The liberal French press is afraid to wound the susceptibility of England and America in publishing the request of the Blacks. Do not worry, my dear fellow citizens, I want that the nine articles be published; nevertheless, I await an answer from the Peace Conference. I do not follow the policy of Pessoa, from Brazil.[1] I try at first the path of persuasion; depending upon the result I will know what to think. Our nine points have been delivered directly to the President and to the Secretary of the Peace Conference[2] on Monday the 9th. On the 10th, I went to demand an answer[;] they promised to get it for me as soon as possible. We ought to realize that our movement is already known in all parts of the World. Thus our adversaries try to group themselves together in order to prevent a united organization.

The advice which has been suggested to us by our eminent friends from England and France would be to try to make a union with all the American associations which loudly demand the same rights and are in the process of organizing.

I was surprised in speaking to our men from all parts of Africa, the Antilles, Central, North, and South America, at Liverpool, Havre and Paris, to see that they all were animated with the same spirit, even greater enthusiasts than the members of the Universal Negro Improvement Association.

The Caucasians have recognized this feeling and they tremble. John Bull says: let us begin to starve them. The day after the signing of the armistice, its Parliament declared that negroes should be rejected as workers and as Businessmen in England, although the voracious animal everyday gobbles up more and more of the wealth of the negroes of the world.[3] Let us wait for the day of indigestion and its stomach will burst.

I have noticed during my four days in London that color prejudice is much more intense in this city than in the North of the United States. There are black soldiers there who are awaiting ships. Everyone can see the truth and justice of the observations of our president made from time to time concerning the situation of races in England.

In France, it is the natural goodness and the joyous qualities of the people which mitigates the foolish resentments, as few as they are, toward blacks.

The French use ridicule against blacks, while the Anglo-Saxons offer them hatred.

Yesterday evening, while returning from Mr. P[e]ssoa's home, I met some women in the streets. They said aloud: Look at that negro. That one apears intelligent. At times they laughed and called me names. At times they irritated me; at other times, I paid no attention. I can say that I was well received in offices, as a representative and that I was always listened to with respect and excitement.

My dear friends, let us always work for the expansion of our Association whether it be in Africa, in the Antilles, in Central, North or South America.

In the spirit of unity, I pay my respects to you all.

ELIÉZER CADET

Printed in *L'Essor* (Port-au-Prince, Haiti), Thursday, 8 May 1919. Translated from the French original. Original headlines have been omitted.

1. Epitácio da Silva Pessoa (1865–1942), the noted Brazilian statesman and jurist, was the head of the Brazilian delegation to the Paris Peace Conference. He assumed the presidency of Brazil in July 1919, a post he held until 1922. (*NYT*, 24 February 1942; *Nôvo Dicionário de Historia do Brasil*, 2d ed. [1971]).

2. As the host country, France furnished both the president and the secretary general of the peace conference. The president was Georges Clemenceau, French premier, and the secretary general was Paul Eugene Dutasta (1873–1925).

3. No record of a declaration to restrict the presence of black persons in Great Britain has been found in the proceedings of the British Houses of Parliament. It may have been inspired by the British postwar demobilization policy of returning unemployed colonials to their homelands.

W. E. Allen to Alfred Bettman, Department of Justice

Washington. March 14, 1919

Memorandum for Mr. Bettman[1]

The attached letter from Mr. Lanier Winslow, State Department, with newspaper entitled "The Negro World", is submitted for such comment as you care to make. It appears, after an examination of the Department as well as the Bureau files, that no information has heretofore been received with respect to this paper. Respectfully,

W. E. ALLEN
Acting Chief

[*Printed*] ADDRESS REPLY TO CHIEF,
BUREAU OF INVESTIGATION, AND REFER

TO INITIALS. [*Handwritten insertion*] HBL.
[*Typewritten reference*] HBL-LOB

DNA, RG 65, File OG 185161. TNS, Recipient's copy.

1. Alfred Bettman (1873–1945) served as special assistant to the U.S. attorney general in charge of sedition prosecutions from 25 October 1917 to 13 May 1919. He helped to draft wartime legislative restraints on aliens, though he later became an outspoken critic of the Red Scare raids against aliens. (*DAB*, Supplement 3).

Alfred Bettman to W. E. Allen

[*Washington, D.C.*] *March 17, 1919*

MEMORANDUM TO MR. ALLEN:

In regard to the attached relating to a newspaper entitled THE NEGRO WORLD, I do not see anything therein upon which this Department can base any action whatever. There is, [*erasure*], in a democratic form of government like ours the right to agitate to influence governmental policy, and so far as appears on the face of this newspaper, the publishers have not gone beyond that. Respectfully,

[ALFRED BETTMAN]

[*Typewritten reference*] AB-MM

DNA, RG 65, File OG 185161. TN, Carbon copy.

W. E. Allen to L. Lanier Winslow

Washington. March 18, 1919

Dear Sir:

Your letter of the 26th ultimo, enclosing copy of the paper entitled "The Negro World", has received careful attention. An examination of our files discloses that no previous complaints have been received concerning this publication and it is the opinion of the Department that no action need to be taken at the present time toward its suppression. Yours very truly,

W. E. ALLEN
Acting Chief

[*Printed*] ADDRESS REPLY TO CHIEF,
BUREAU OF INVESTIGATION, AND REFER
TO INITIALS. [*Handwritten insertion*] HBL
[*Typewritten reference*] HBL-LOB
[*Endorsement*] Took British Em. 3–21–19
[TC?]LH

DNA, RG 59, Office of the Counselor, File 800.9-71. TLS, Recipient's copy. Handwritten endorsements.

Bureau of Investigation Report

NEW YORK CITY [*Made*] MARCH 20, 1919
[*for the period of*] [*illegible*]

In re: NEGRO ACTIVITIES.

A. Philip Randolph, et al. Bolshevist Activities."The Messenger" publication.

Pursuant to urgent telephone call this morning from our informant in Negro matters, the Rev. R. D. Jonas, I met him in the Woolworth Building where he informed me that while he was in Randolph's office to-day a telegram was received from *Roger N. Baldwin*,[1] former director of the National Civil Liberties Bureau now confined in the Essex County Jail, Newark. The telegram stated in effect that Randolph should be on his guard against a spy in his organization—the name of a negro, Thomas Swan,[2] was given as the suspect. Randolph immediately made provisions to keep everyone out of his office expecting our informant.

Just how Baldwin got information in this respect we are unable to state. However, from day to day he keeps closely in touch with various radical organizations, included among which are *The Negro Improvement Association* and allied Negro radical groups, and it is believed therefore that one of the negros who make regular trips to him at the jail may have communicated the information outlined a[bove.]

R. W. FINCH

DNA, RG 65, File OG 258421. TD.

1. Roger Nash Baldwin (1884–1981), author and social reformer, was the director of the National Civil Liberties Bureau, the forerunner of the American Civil Liberties Union. He was also the founder of the Bureau of Conscientious Objectors and the American Union Against Militarism. Baldwin was incarcerated in the Essex County jail in Newark, New Jersey, on 11 November 1918 as a result of his refusal to be drafted. After nine months of imprisonment, he was released on 19 July 1919. (*WBD*; Peggy Lamson, *Roger Baldwin, Founder of the American Civil Liberties Union: A Portrait* [Boston: Hougton Mifflin, 1976]).

2. Thomas Wallace Swann was connected with several black newspapers and magazines in various parts of the United States. He was the leader of the Chicago chapter of the Negro National Anti-Taft League in 1908. Later he served as organizing secretary of the Illinois Commission for the National Half-Century Anniversary of Negro Freedom in 1915. Swann was also an officer of the International League of Darker Peoples in January 1919. (*WWCA*).

L. Lanier Winslow to Colville Barclay

[*Washington, D.C.*] March 21, 1919

Dear Barclay:[1]

Mr. Phillips turned over to me your letter of February 24th, No. 146, which relates to the paper "The Negro World" which has been finding its way to the Colony of British Honduras.

I took the matter up with the Department of Justice and they are of the opinion that no action is feasible at the present time towards its suppression. Very sincerely yours,

[L. LANIER WINSLOW]

C-H
[TRC?]. HLH

DNA, RG 59, Office of the Counselor, File 800.9-71. TL, Carbon copy.

1. Colville Barclay relayed the reply to Robert Walter, the colonial secretary of British Honduras, stating that the U. S. Department of Justice had "taken up the matter of the *Negro World*" and that "no action is feasible at the present time toward its suppression." (PRO, CO 123/295, Barclay to Walter, 22 March 1919).

Editorial Letter by Marcus Garvey

[[New York, March 27, 1919]]

Fellowmen of the Negro Race:

Greeting:—To you I write this week trusting you are still of good cheer. Since my last message to you, the revolutionary world has taken on new activities. The Russian people have issued a proclamation of sympathy and good will towards the laboring peoples of the world.[1]

Hungary has declared for a new form of government in alliance with Russia.[2] All this means revolution among the whites. They have not yet stopped killing out themselves because the masses are not yet free.

We are not very much concerned as partakers in these revolutions, but we are concerned in the destruction that will come out of the bloody conflict between capital and labor, which will give us a breathing space to then declare for our freedom from the tyrannical rule of oppressive over-lords.

Egypt has sounded the note of liberty. All Negroes are allied with Egypt; not for the delivering of Egypt to an alien rule, but to make Egyptians free so that Africa might be redeemed for the Africans.

The "Pieces Conference" because of its unholy intent in depriving men of their liberty has made no headway for the restoration of peace; on the contrary, it is fomenting more wars, and in another twenty-five years the dream of the framers of it, whose intent is to shackle the now unliberated peoples of the world, will be regarded as the nightmare of Bolshevism. Bolshevism, it would appear, is a thing of the white man's making, and whatever it means is apparent, it is going to spread until it finds a haven in the breasts of all oppressed peoples, and then there shall be a universal rule of the masses.

Wherever you be today, in America, Africa, Canada, the West Indies, South or Central America, let your cry be "liberty or death." Prepare your minds, your hearts and your swords for the next world war. It will come whether it is to be between Asia and Europe, or Europe and Africa, be assured that it will come, and at that time we hope every black man will be ready to take care of himself.

Fight the good fight therefore, and be always in readiness for the bugle call of Mother Africa. Yours fraternally,

MARCUS GARVEY

Printed in the *NW*, Saturday, 29 March 1919. Original headlines have been omitted.

1. A reference to the founding congress of the Third (Communist) International held in Moscow, 2–6 March 1919, which promulgated the *Manifesto of the Communist International to the Proletariat of the Entire World.*

2. A reference to the formation on 21 March 1919 of the short-lived Hungarian Soviet Republic under Alexander Garbai, president, and Béla Kun, minister of foreign affairs. On 24 April 1919 *The Times* published the text of an alliance between the Soviet republics of Hungary, the Ukraine, and Russia. After the creation of the Hungarian Soviet Republic, the western powers organized a blockade of Hungary and gave further aid to the advancing Rumanian forces. On 1 August 1919, the Béla Kun regime fled the country, and on 4 August the invading Rumanian forces took Budapest.

Synopsis of UNIA Meeting

[*Negro World*, 29 March 1919]

A cable message was received in this city on Monday morning [*24 March*] by the Universal Negro Improvement Association and African Communities' League of the World from the Hon. Eliezer Cadet, the High Commissioner of this world-wide movement, who was elected by 7,000 American, African, West Indian and South and Central American Negroes in the Palace Casino on December 1, 1918, to represent the race as a delegate to the Peace Conference. He sailed from America with the knowledge of the Negro people as made known through publicity. On his arrival in Paris at the Peace Conference he presented the aims of the race, which were well received. He further made known to the French people the conditions of lynching and burning of men, women and children in America because they are black, and W. E. B. Du Bois has repudiated his statements by defeating his articles in the French newspapers.[1] For supporting Mr. Eliezer Cadet, the President-General of the Universal Negro Improvement Association called a mass convention of American, African, West Indian, Canadian and South and Central American Negroes within 24 hours' notice, and on Wednesday night 3,000 of the representatives of the 400,000,000 of the race assembled at the Mother Zion A.M.E. Church, New York, while hundreds were unable to gain entrance, and there, in the most spirited and patriotic manner, denounced the reactionary leader, W. E. B. Du Bois, and upheld Eliezer Cadet.

The meeting was the most orderly, intellectual and racial ever held in New York City.

The meeting was presided over by Mr. Chandler Owen, associate editor of "The Messenger."[2] The principal speaker of the evening was Mr. Marcus Garvey, President-General of the Universal Negro Improvement Association and managing editor of The Negro World. The other speakers were Miss A[m]y Ashwood, who recited "The Colored Soldiers," from Paul Lawrence Dunbar; Mr. W. A. Domingo, literary editor of The Negro World; Mr. Asa Philip Randolph, editor of "The Messenger," and Professor Allan Whaley, of Boston, national organizer of The Equal Rights League.

The following resolution was moved and carried and cabled to the French press:

"Resolved, That 3,000 American, African, West Indian, Canadian and South and Central American Negroes, in mass convention assembled, express the complete support of Mr. Eliezer Cadet, their elected representative at the Peace Conference, and register their complete repudiation of Dr. W. E. B. Du Bois for placing obstacles in the way of the elected representative efficiently discharging his already difficult duties on behalf of the Negro race. This resolution was carried unanimously with acclamation."

Two hundred and four dollars was given in a voluntary collection to help the delegate combat Dr. Du Bois. Full report of the speeches delivered will be published in the next issue of The Negro World. All those who have not yet contributed to the Delegates' Fund are asked to send in their help to Mr. Joseph E. Johnson, 38 West 135th Street, New York, High Chancellor of the Universal Negro Improvement Association.

Printed in the *NW*, Saturday, 29 March 1919. Original headlines have been omitted.

1. The reference in the "cable message," which was not published, remains unclear, though it might have been due to either Eliézer Cadet's faulty English expression or inaccurate translation from Cadet's original French. Cadet's cable, which would have been dispatched from Paris on either 22 or 23 March 1919, coincided with Du Bois' own departure for the United States on 22 March. In December 1920, Du Bois referred to the charge made against him as follows: "Of Garvey's curious credulity and suspicions one example will suffice: In March 1919, he held a large mass meeting at Palace Casino which was presided over by Chandler Owen and addressed by himself and Phillip Randolph. Here he collected $204 in contributions on the plea that while in France, W. E. B. Du Bois had interfered with the work of his 'High Commissioner' by 'defeating' his articles in the French press and 'repudiating' his statements as to lynching and injustice in America! The truth was that Mr. Du Bois never saw or heard of his 'High Commissioner', never denied his nor anyone's statements of the wretched American conditions, did everything possible to arouse rather than quiet the French press and would have been delighted to welcome and cooperate with any colored fellow-worker" (*Crisis* 20 [December 1920]: 58–60).

2. The *Messenger* first began publication in November 1917. During the next fifteen months, however, only two more issues, January 1918 and July 1918, appeared, due to financial difficulties, paper shortages, a printers' strike, and harassment and investigation of the paper by New York authorities. Regular publication resumed in March 1919, although on a few subsequent occasions it failed to appear. The last issue of the *Messenger* was May–June 1928.

SOLDIERS and CIVILIANS, LOOK!

GREAT CHAMPION OF THE NEGRO SOLDIER
C O M I N G

On Wed., May 14, '19
At 8:15 P. M.

The Great NEGRO Historian, Author, Scholar and Journalist, will deliver his Master Address

"The Negro Soldier in France"
—AT THE—
ACADEMY OF MUSIC
UNDER THE AUSPICES OF THE
PHILADELPHIA BRANCH OF THE NATIONAL ASSOCIATION FOR THE ADVANCEMENT OF COLORED PEOPLE

Come and hear the man who outwitted the American prejudice in Paris and held the great Pan-African Congress—the man who was followed all over France by detectives—the man who gathered material for history of the Negro in the World War despite the greatest hindrances. If you miss this, you miss the greatest treat of the year.

MISS CLEOTA COLLINS, Lyric Soprano.
MISS MARIAN E. ANDERSON, Contralto,
and the ST. CECELIA TRIO
Will render Musical Numbers.

**POPULAR PRICES
WITHIN REACH OF ALL** -:- **TICKETS 25c to $1.00**

DR. W. E. B. DUBOIS

On Sale at Davis' Drug Store, 1537 South Street; Tribune Office, 526 South 16th Street; Isadore Martin, 6 N. 12nd Street; Dr. J. Max Barber, 3223 Woodland Avenue, etc.

(Source: *Philadelphia Tribune*).

Addresses Denouncing W. E. B. Du Bois

[*Negro World*, 5 April 1919]

ENTHUSIASTIC CONVENTION OF 3,000 AMERICAN, CANADIAN, WEST INDIAN, AFRICAN, SO. & CENTRAL AMERICAN NEGROES DENOUNCED DR. W. E. B. DU BOIS CHARACTERIZED AS REACTIONARY UNDER PAY OF WHITE MEN— RESOLUTION CARRIED UNANIMOUSLY

In our last issue we gave a synopsis of the meeting of the Universal Negro Improvement Association and African Communities League, held at Mother Zion A.M.E. Church on March 25, for the purpose of denouncing the recent reactionary attitude of Dr. W. E. B. Du Bois with regard to his opposition to the resolutions which appeared in the Negro world of March 1, 1919, and which were presented by Mr. Eliezer Cadet to the Peace Conference and also to determine the most effectual means of protecting the Association's elected delegate. In this issue we are prepared to give, as promised, a full report of the speeches delivered. The meeting was attended by fully 3000 Negroes and several white men representing the Department of Justice. The meeting was opened with the singing of the hymn "From Greenland's Icy Mountains," after which a very inspiring prayer was offered by the Rev. John S. Wilkins, executive secretary of the association. . . .

The chairman[1] before introducing the next speaker took advantage of the opportunity of explaining his psychological view of the efficient members of the Department of Justice, and hoped that the heads of the Department of Justice were doing their duty in crushing autocracy and establishing universal democracy, so that a little may be able to reach the Southern lands. He then introduced the next speaker, Mr. Marcus Garvey, President-General of the Universal Negro Improvement Association and African Communities League.

Mr. Marcus Garvey said: "Mr. Chairman, Ladies and Gentlemen: on behalf of the Universal Negro Improvement Association and [U].N.I.A. and African Communit[i]es' League, this meeting was called. Owing to a cable report sent us on Monday morning [24 March] by our representative, Mr. Eliezer Cadet, now in France, representing the interest of 12,000,000 American, 10,000,000 West Indian Negroes, and 280,000,000 Africans, for which representation he was elected by 7,000 American, African, West Indian, and South and Central American Negroes, at a mass meeting in the Palace Casino on December 1, 1918. The cable tells us that he has published certain articles in the French papers[2] expressing the sufferings of our people and the outrages committed in America, and Dr. W. E. B. Du Bois has repudiated his statements by defeating his article in the French paper. (For Mr. Eliezer Cadet's Speech in France, and resolutions presented to Peace Conference, read The Negro World of March 1, 1919).

Because Mr. Cadet presented these aims to the French people and to the Peace Conference and got the hearing and sympathy of the French people and the Peace Conference, Dr. Du Bois, who left this country, and who was never elected by any one except by the capitalistic class, because of the favorable impression of our aims upon the minds of the French people, has come out to attack them in the French papers.

Men and women, I am indeed glad to see how we are assembled here tonight and to hear the acclamations given to the type of new Negroes, who spoke previous to me. These are men ranging in age from eighteen to thirty-two; men who would have died in this bloody war if it had continued another two years. If the war had continued for two weeks longer I would have had to go to France and Flanders to die for the Belgian. According to the law I would have been compelled to go. I know there are going to be more wars within the next twenty-five years, and Negroes will be called upon. But the Negro is prepared to emancipate himself on the continent of Africa. The time has come for the emancipation of all peoples, whether Russians, Germans, Poles or Jews. Already the Egyptians are fighting for their freedom, and it will not be surprising to hear India also striking the blow for complete emancipation. Egypt is now striking, and I pray Almighty God to be on the side of Egypt. What is good for the white man by way of freedom is also good [*for*] the black man by way of freedom. Why should Europe emancipate herself and keep Africa under the heel of oppression. Africa must be for the Africans, and them exclusively. Dr. Du Bois desires internationalization of Africa[3] for the white man, the capitalistic class of white men. Cannot these hand-picked leaders see that under the League of Nations certain places will be oppressed by mandatories, and unless the entire constitution of the League of Nations be repealed internationalization will be the control of Africa? France, Belgium and Italy have already realized their positions in Africa, because two millions of blacks have gone back to Africa as soldiers. Italy has already lost her individual nationalistic control[4] which she had prior to the outbreak of war. This Government got Dr. Du Bois to go to France so that when he returns and everything is settled they can say, "It i[s] you who asked for these things." Men and women of America, West Indies and Africa. Are you prepared to live in slavery everlasting? "No!" shouted the audience.

A UNIVERSAL MESSAGE.

The time has come for us to proclaim our freedom, and we must say to the white peoples of the world that the millions of Negroes who fought in the war are now getting ready to emancipate themselves on the continent of Africa. There will be a revolution not in America, but in Africa. I want the members of the Department of Justice to understand that we mean nothing that will keep the Negro from being regarded as a loyal American citizen, but we acknowledge no constitutional law at present existing in Africa. You, of the Department of Justice, know that three hundred years ago you left your country, went down into Africa and brought 40,000,000 of us here. You told Queen Elizabeth that your object was to civilize and christianize us and on this pretence she signed the charter to empower you to do so.[5] For two hundred years you enslaved us, and now we are going to use the same civilization and christianity that you brought us out here to get, to make Africa free. In America you acknowledged our civilization when you held us up in the subway for our registration cards[6] (laughter). You acknowledged us in the great war. You recognized our civilization when 2,000,000 of us were sent to fight and die in France and Flanders, while you were here in America. When you called us you told us that we were going to fight for world wide democracy and since all the other peoples have liberated themselves, we are going to get in line and liberate ourselves also.

We speak tonight, not in the spirit of cowardice, but as men who died in France in 1914–1918, and since we could have died in France we can now die right here. We remember the words of Patrick Henry one hundred and forty-three years ago in the Virginia Legislature, when he was endeavoring to lay the foundation of independence. "I care not what others may say, but as for me, give me liberty or give me death," and now as a new people representing a new sentiment we will say: "We care not what others may say, but for us give us liberty or give us death." If there are to be white kings, white emperors and white czars, there must also be Negro men representing the same dignitaries. The spirit of the age is freedom; the spirit of the age is liberty; the spirit to sanctify by the blood of the martyr, and I feel quite sure that there are no cowards among you men and women in this church tonight.

Liberty Exploited and Robbed

The object of America, for which George Washington and Patrick Henry fought 140 years ago, are today cast aside and disregarded. Young men and young women, awake! Be ready for the day when Africa shall declare for her independence. And why do I say Africa when you are living in the West Indies and America? Because in these places you will never be safe until you launch your protection internally and externally. The Japanese and Chinese are not lynched in this country because of the fear of retaliation. Behind these men are standing armies and navies to protect them. Such is the case with Frenchmen and Englishmen, but Negroes, representing an undignified and unorganized nation, are lynched, because they know the best that can be done is to hold a mass meeting. It is truly said that we have no original right in America. If the Poles and Hungarians require a national home with national government—and Australia and Canada are white men countries— then it is requisite for 400,000,000 Negroes to have a national home and a national government, and, as I was asked in England and Scotland and Germany what I was doing there, we will also be able to ask somebody, "What are you doing here?"

Objects of the U.N.I.A.

Ladies and gentlemen, I want you to realize that the Universal Negro Improvement Association and African Communities League, the organization which I have the honor to represent, is a worldwide movement that is endeavoring to unite the sentiment of our people. Our objective is to declare Africa a vast Negro empire. We can see no right in Belgium's retention of the Congo. We are going to wait until peace is completely restored, and then will we work Belgium out. And when we ask Belgium, "What are you doing there?" America will have nothing to do with it. Under the League of Nations when Africa revolts America will have to call upon Negroes to fight Negroes, therefore the League of Nations must be defeated by every Negro in America, or it will mean that Africa will have to fight the combined nations of the world.

Unanimity of Spirit.

I thank you, ladies and gentlemen, for the spirit of your responsiveness, which is proof that you disfavor the reactionary activities of Dr. Du Bois in

France. A few minutes after we received the cable we sent our representative what assistance we had, and told him that in forty-eight hours we would call a meeting to stand by him. And we have done so. This is the spirit of the association. In forty-eight hours, twenty-four hours or twelve hours we will be able, I trust, in some future time to call a meeting of 400,000,000 Negroes all over the world and let them know what we mean by it.

AN ALL-IMPORTANT MESSAGE.

We are waiting for the next world war—that racial war which Josephus Daniels, Secretary of the Navy, spoke of thirteen months ago. And we are telling the white people of the world to give Negroes liberty and democracy before it comes. If you do not do it, let me say to you that when the 900,000,000 of yellow and brown peoples of Asia line up against the white ones of Europe and America not a Negro will be found fighting on either side.

We wish to enlighten the sentiment of the 400,000,000 of our people for the next world war. Sixty million Huns outraged civilization for four and a half years, and the other whites were unable to beat them until they called out the American Negroes to assist. And we helped so splendidly that Roberts and Johnson alone were able to bring back twenty captives. This shows exactly the spirit of the Negro. We have made 2,000,000 Napoleons in this war—nay, 2,000,000 Wellingtons—therefore there must be a Waterloo; and I say to you young men; middle-aged and old men, that I can see in you a Napoleon surveying the bridge of Lodi; a Brutus reading in his tent at Phillippi; a Richard Coeur de Lion bearing down upon the armies of Saladin; a Crown Prince storming the forts of Verdun, and a Marshal Joffre marshaling the French artillery in counterattack, winning the day, to the everlasting glory of France. I can see in you women a Florence Nightingale, going among the soldiers of the Crimean battlefield. Nay, a Negro Florence Nightingale going among the black soldiers on the battle plains of Africa; a Joan of Arc leading black men on to victory. This is the spirit of the American Negro; this, I think, is the spirit of all Negroes.

Negroes of the West Indies, let me tell you that the Universal Negro Improvement Association will expect you to go back to those islands and teach the doctrine of the association. Let them know that they are lynching and burning black men in the South simply because they are black. We want you to do that because we are starting to organize the Negroes of the world. The people in British Honduras are already starting to organize themselves. There our papers are held up in the post office. But I am going down there for two weeks, and I know they will not be able to stop me from speaking.[7] In Jamaica there are 900,000 black people and 15,000 white ones, who are telling the blacks that there is no difference between black people and white people, and at the same time exploiting and robbing them. They are trying to keep our papers away, and saying they must not be circulated. The British government has paid us a compliment by sending to Africa to know if the Negro World is circulated and what effect it has on the sentiment of the people.[8] I am going to spend six months more here, and the next six months will be to clean up the entire West Indian islands.

This is an age in which we must stand up for our constitutional rights[.] Let your brothers and sisters in the West Indies know that the white man has no privilege, pre-eminence or monopoly over them. I want you to understand clearly that I am not telling you to do anything unconstitutionally.

There are several reasons why we are holding this meeting in the church. We are here because God has always been with the Negro and the Negro with God. We are here because we want the blessing of God. At the crucifixion, white men got hold of Christ, beat him and mocked him but, unlike these, Simon, the Cyrenean, a Negro, took his cross and carried it. Jesus, whom we helped, is now in heaven. If man can be grateful, we know the Divine is much more grateful. When the Divine was in trouble we helped Him, and now that we are in trouble we know that he will help us.

Ladies and gentlemen, I am now going to appeal to you to give as liberally as possible to this worthy cause. Your help is required to fight this reactionary leader. At the Palace Casino you gave $220 to fight your noble cause. It will take $780 to fight it and bring your representative back.

M. Cadet's article is already disputed by Dr. DuBois in the French papers, so therefore give as liberally as you can.["]

IMPORTANT RESOLUTION

The chairman upon calling upon W. H. Domingo to move the resolution decided upon to be cabled to the French press, he said: "In rising to move this resolution I desire to preface it. I have favored, honored and respected for many years the person against whom this resolution is directed, but in view of the fact that he changed his face and wrote a certain editorial called "Clothed Faces,"[9] I am compelled to dishonor and disfavor him." . . . [10]

A. P. Randolph: "I must felicitate both you and myself of seconding this resolution, which is calculated to demonstrate to the world that we are a people here." The resolution was again read, this time by the chairman and was unanimously carried with acclamations. . . .

The meeting came to a close at 11.30 p.m., followed by the singing of "Onward, Christian Soldiers."

Printed in the *NW*, Saturday, 5 April 1919.

1. Chandler Owen presided over the meeting. In his speech, he decried official policy: " . . . With regard to the refusal of passports for delegates to the Pan-African Conference, there has been something wrong, and singularly wrong, about that. Only 'good niggers' could get them, all Negroes were denied; Moton, Du Bois and Walton, men who were qualified to the satisfaction of Colonel House, men who positively would not discuss lynching, peonage, disfranchisement and discrimination, were able to get passports." (*NW*, 5 April 1919). W. A.

399

Domingo also denounced Du Bois as "the mouthpiece of the government," and he urged his audience to "repudiate any kind of selected leadership," and to "continue in the great movement with impartiality and self-interest." (ibid.).

2. A search of French newspapers failed to reveal the publication of any articles by Eliézer Cadet.

3. Du Bois actively campaigned for an international system of administration of the former German colonies in Africa. His plan was outlined in "Memoranda on the Future of Africa," which he presented on 11 November 1918 to the NAACP Board of Directors. The plan called for a greatly enlarged Central African state consisting of the former German colonies, Portuguese Africa and Belgian Congo. (DLC, NAACP, Pan-African Congress file, container 385; also published as "The Future of Africa," *Crisis* 17 [June 1919]: 119–20). James Weldon Johnson, NAACP field secretary, discussed this plan at the special NAACP meeting, "Africa in the World Democracy," held at Carnegie Hall on Monday, 6 January 1919. ("Africa at the Peace Table and the Descendants of Africans in our American Democracy," *Africa in the World Democracy* [New York: NAACP, 1919], pp. 14–15). However, the final resolutions of the Pan-African Congress called for international protection or oversight instead of international administration. (See the *Washington Bee*, 29 March 1919; *Chicago Defender*, 24 May 1919).

4. There is no evidence that Italy lost control of any territory held at the outbreak of World War I either in Europe or Africa, although in the final territorial settlement reached at the peace conference, Italy was forced to accept reduced territorial gains both in Africa and Europe. (Robert L. Hess, "Italy and Africa: Colonial Ambitions in the First World War," *Journal of African History* 4 [1963]:105–26).

5. Queen Elizabeth I (1533–1603) initially expressed shock at the reports of John Hawkins' first slaving expedition in 1562; after Hawkins showed her the profit sheet of his venture, not only did the queen grant him forgiveness but, more importantly, she became a substantial investor in all his subsequent slaving voyages. Thereafter, the English queen promoted her country's participation in the early transatlantic slave trade by granting the "Senegal Adventurers" a royal charter in 1588; moreover, her encouragement of the slave trade was connected to England's growing challenge to Spain's economic and military dominance of the period. (For Garvey's later elaboration on the same subject, cf., *Minutes of Proceedings . . . Speech Presenting the Case of the Negro for International Racial Adjustment by the Hon. Marcus Garvey, D. C. L.*, [London, June 1928], pp. 10–11; James Walvin, *The Black Presence: A Documentary History of the Negro in England* [New York: Schocken Books, 1972], chaps. 2–3; Eric Williams, *From Columbus to Castro: The History of the Caribbean, 1492–1969* [London: n.p., 1970]).

6. On 3 September 1918, the Department of Justice began a three-day search of New York City in an attempt to round up "slackers" who were turned over to local draft boards for registration. Although "slacker raids" were frequently conducted throughout the United States during 1917–18, the New York raids of 3–5 September 1918 were by far the most controversial. According to figures released by the attorney general, 21,402 persons from Manhattan, Brooklyn, and the Bronx were apprehended and detained. (*NYT*, 6 September 1918).

7. Garvey left the United States circa 25 February 1921 on a visit to Cuba, Jamaica, and Central America. He returned on 12 July 1921.

8. The importation of the *Negro World* into the Gold Coast was not prohibited until 1921, under order by the governor, No. 1 of 1921, (National Archives of Ghana, Confidential Minute Paper 6805/23). However, Ordinance No. 18 of 1920 in Sierra Leone prohibited the importation of seditious books, newspapers, or other printed material (PRO, CO 96/614, 15 October 1920), possibly a response to the circulation of the *Negro World* in that colony.

9. The correct title of the editorial was "Close Ranks," in which Du Bois urged blacks to be patriotic: "Let us, while this war lasts, forget our special grievances and close our ranks shoulder to shoulder with our own white fellow citizens and the allied nations that are fighting for democracy. We make no ordinary sacrifice, but we make it gladly and willingly with our eyes lifted to the hills." (*Crisis* 16 [July 1918]: 3).

10. At this point Domingo read to the meeting the resolution that appears in the preceding document.

Capt. John B. Trevor to Brig. Gen. Marlborough Churchill

NEW YORK CITY April 5th, 1919

From: Office of M.I.D., 302 Broadway, New York
To: Director of Military Intelligence
Subject: Negro Agitation.

1. From a confidential source[1] I have received some information which is summarized hereinunder in regard to the subject. According to my informant this agitation goes far beyond the redress of the alleged grievances of our negro population. It aims at Pan-Negroism and a combination of the other colored races of the world. As a colored movement it looks to Japan for leadership; as a radical movement it follows Bolshevism and has intimate relations with various socialistic groups throughout the United States. With this latter connection it naturally sympathizes with and has relations with the Irish, the Jews and Hindus. In fact all of the alleged oppressed nationalities. The program is Liberty, Justice and Equality.

2. This movement is noteworthy from the fact that it marks a transfer of leadership from the more conservative leaders to others of a radical type. The matter is put very clearly in an article headed, "Radicalism and the Negro" which appeared in the "Negro World" of March 1st. Heretofore the negro has been conservative. This is mainly because he has been under the leadership of his preachers who "find it convenient to hide their ignorance under a cloak of sanctity while soothing their followers with the Shibboleths of a /dead/ politically past". From these "/Ambassadors/ of a hereafter" negro leadership is being transferred to the heads of various negro educational institutions. These new leaders, although better educated than their predecessors, are nevertheless more incapable of giving voice to any real radical opinions because of the economic necessities of their existence. Most of them, Booker Washington, Moton, DuBois, Pickins,[2] Kelly Miller, etc. are connected with make their living from institutions which largely exist as a result of the philanthropy of industrial magnates who endow the majority with more important negro schoolsx x x x Thus, in the church and in the school negroes are taught all the servile virtues which develop an unhealthy respect for conservatism". The new leaders attempt to remedy this by teaching through newspapers, periodicals, organizations, lectures, and more intimate and private propaganda for the adoption of a truly radical program. It is difficult to say how far they have been successful, but there is no doubt they have been able to seduce a good many negroes.

3. Example of the methods employed by the radicals in their endeavor to secure the leadership is afforded by the conference of delegates from nine states which met at the New Zion A.M.E. Church on West 136th Street, New York on the 20th and 21st of March, for the purpose of forming a "Federation of Colored Organizations in the United States"....[3]

4. The new "Federation of Colored Organizations in the United States" is only one among a number of radical negro organizations most of which are of recent origin and founded for similar purposes. The following are some of these:

The Universal Negro Improvement Association and African Communities League.

This is Marcus Garvey's association and its organ is his newspaper, the "Negro World". Its headquarters is in New York and it has branches in Chicago, Baltimore, Washington, Newport News, Jamaica, British Honduras, Trinidad and Panama and some of the small West Indian Islands. . . . [4]

5. Among the negro newspapers and magazines "The Negro World", "The Messenger" and "The Crisis" have been already mentioned. "The Negro World" published by Marcus Garvey's organization, the "Universal Negro Improvement Association" is in financial straits and Garvey has been issuing pleas for its better support. This does not look as though Garvey is having all the success he would like. . . . [5]

6. In dealing with the position of negroes in the United States the principal theme of journals and speakers is abuse of the white man. The topics which most frequently come up are lynching, the Jim Crow laws, the political status of the n[e]gro, their economic position, and their treatment by labour unions.

The position of the n[e]gro in the West Indian Islands and other British colonies is considered to be no better than it is in the United States, and frequent complaints on this subject are made in the n[e]gro newspapers and magazines. Persons attending the recent conference in the New Zion Church wanted to bring up the question of the n[e]groes in British possessions, but they were ruled out of order, as the meeting was only a preliminary one for organization. The "Negro World" in its issue of the first of March states that "in the West Indian Islands millions of us are reduced to common serfdom, robbed and exploited by land masters who pretend to love and care for us whilst depriving us of every chance that would make us a free and prosperous people.["] On the 13th of March Garvey delivered a lecture on "The West Indies and the Negro".

The new Pan-African agitator regards the African continent as the motherland and centre from which to form the great nation of the four hundred million negroes of the world. In the first instance, they look towards the independent or semi-independent negro states. The "Crusader" has an article on Liberia as a possible centre for militant negroes in Africa. It thinks that "with the Liberian literal [*littoral*] effectively guarded against foreign invasion, the position of Liberia would be fairly impregnable and that through pre-war propaganda an alliance with the Mohammedan forces of North and Central Africa could easily be achieved. Is the Western negro ready to venture? Is he willing to make the necessary sacrifices for freedom and a redeemed Africa?"[6] The same journal has an article headed "Basuto-land, the Hope of the Black Race".

The negro agitators are of course very indignant at the idea that the late German colonies should be placed under white tutelage, and the "Challenge"[7] in an article headed "Must there be another war to settle the African question?" complains that "the British mean to preserve inviolate their Imperial policy of annexation after each war in which the eagle of St. George spreads his wings". The troubles in Egypt have given a fresh impetus to the Pan-African ideas.

7. The following extract from the "Negro World" illustrates the encouragement which the negro agitators derived from the Bolshevist and Socialist movements:—

> "As you will all realize this is a time of active aggression on the part of the oppressed. In the various theatres of discontent you will see the teeming millions of unsettled workers agitating for the overthrow of the privileged classes among them. Whether it is in Russia, Germany, Austria, France, or in England, it can be seen as plain as daylight that the time of the privileged reactionary is passed and the time for the free man has come. What the toilers are doing in Germany, what they have already done in Russia, are indications of the fact that the world in this period of reconstruction will never be the same as it was prior to 1914. The spirit of liberty, of freedom, is now permeating the world from one end of the given creation to the other. You will find men assembled for the purpose of agitating the cause of liberty. Are black men going to be indifferent to this spirit that is so much abroad. Surely not".

In the same paper it is stated that "on the subject of Africa the only government that believes in freedom for the natives of that continent is that of Bolshevist Russia, which incorporates its belief into its Declaration of Rights. The others, like the United States, Italy, Japan, England, and France, are all in favour of the infamous League of Nations (Plague of Abominations) which proposes to subject Africa to perpetual, unresisting exploitation". The "Negro World" also laments the false stories circulated about Bolshevist misdeeds. In an article headed "Get out of Russia" the "Messenger" rails against the intervention of the Allies. The "Messenger" also notices in a satirical article the statement made by Dr. Simons before the State Senate Committee that there is a negro member of the Russian Bolshevist cabinet.

8. The negro agitators have made common cause with the Socialists and have established intimate connections with them. They have a strong socialist organization in Harlem and put up a colored man named [George] Fraser Miller at the recent election for Congress. One of his keen supporters was a negro named Domingo,[8] who speaks at both radical and Irish meetings. At a meeting to celebrate the first anniversary of the Bolshevik Government, Domingo was introduced as one of the most active workers in the election campaign. . . . [9]

The negro journals also contain many references indicating the close alliance between the negro agitators and the Socialists. Thus, to take one instance, the "Negro World" says that the only white press in the country that demands negro rights uncompromisingly is composed of radical Socialist newspapers and magazines like the "Call", "The Liberator", "The Nation", "The Public", "Solidarity", "The Rebel Worker", and "Freedom".[10]

10. The degree to which negro agitators rely upon Japan as the leading coloured nation deserves special notice. The following is from the "Negro World":

"When the American Secretary of the Navy, Josephus Daniels, said that the next war will be a war of races, he was thinking wisely. It will indeed be so. With the rising militarism of Asia and the standing militarism of Europe one can foresee nothing else but an armed clash between the white and yellow races. When this clash of millions comes, an opportunity will have presented itself to the negro people of the world to free themselves. At that time, whether you are born an American negro, West Indian negro, or African negro, there will be no time to think of anything else but negro liberty on the Continent of Africa. It will be through the winning of the day for African arms that the negroes both of America and the West Indies will be rendered safe for all times."

Again, from the same journal:—

"The next war will be between the negroes and the whites, unless our demands for justice are recognized. With Japan to fight with us we can win such a war." . . . [11]

12. The negro agitators strove hard to get representatives to the Peace Conference but apparently the State Department has not met their views in regard to passports as they have not left. The case of Mr. Jernigan,[12] however, appears to be an exception as in some way he has managed to get across.

Garvey's organization, the Universal Negro Improvement Association, held a mass meeting in the Palace Casino, New York, and elected Philip Randolph and Mrs. Ida E. Wells Barnett to represent the negroes at the Conference, and Eliezer Cadet, a native of Haiti, to be their interpreter. Neither Randolph nor Mrs. Barnett were able to get permission to go, but the organization succeeded in sending over Cadet, "despite the attitude of the State Department". They now style him their "High Commissioner". There is a copy of a letter published in the "Negro World" of the 1st March, introducing Mr. Cadet to the French newspaper fraternity. Other issues of the "Negro World" state that Cadet is doing very well and has succeeded in placing before the Conference the peace aims of his organization, representing all the negroes of the world. I should imagine, however, that the part played by Mr. Cadet is less prominent than Garvey would wish his readers to believe. . . . [13]

JOHN B. TREVOR
Captain, U.S.A.

T/S

[*Typewritten reference*] #27961
[*Handwritten endorsement*] Negro
Subversion
[*Stampled endorsements*] CAPT. DALRYMPLE[14]
M.I.4 [*Liaison Organization*]-46 CAPT. J. E.
CUTLER M.M.S.

DNA, RG 165, File 10218-324/1 273X(50). TDS, Recipient's copy.

1. The report originally came from British Military Intelligence in New York City, which agreed to supply the Military Intelligence Division of the army with copies of its reports on black radical activities in America. Rev. R. D. Jonas, working as a British undercover agent, prepared the reports.

2. William Pickens (1881–1954) was best known for his work as field secretary of the NAACP. After graduating from Talladega College, Alabama, (B.A., 1902), he attended Yale University (B.A., 1904) and Fisk University, Nashville, (M.A., 1908). Pickens taught at Talladega College between 1909 and 1914 and at Wiley University, Texas, 1914–15. In the latter year, he was appointed dean at Morgan College, Baltimore, becoming vice president in 1918. In 1920, he began a lengthy association with the NAACP; he resigned in 1942 to become director and chief of the Interracial Section of the Savings Bond Division, U.S. Treasury Department. (*WWWA*, 1951–60; DNA, RG 65, files BS 61-23, 158260-1, 202600-39, 202600-667, 202600-1628, 202600-1778; OG 132476, 292778).

3. A one-page description of the Federation of Colored Organizations followed.

4. Several paragraphs discussing the following organizations have been omitted: the National Race Congress, the National Equal Rights League, the International League of the Darker Races, and the NAACP.

5. The final paragraphs of the fifth section contained a description of the following publications: *Messenger, Challenge, Crusader, New York News, Amsterdam News,* and *Chicago Defender.*

6. The *Crusader* was first published in September 1918 and continued monthly until January–February 1922. Unfortunately, none of the surviving issues contains the article referred to in the above report. For additional information on the role played by the *Crusader*, see the note on Cyril V. Briggs in the Biographical Supplement, Appendix I.

7. The *Challenge* was a monthly magazine edited and published in Harlem by William Bridges. None of the three surviving issues of the magazine contains the article referred to in the report. Elsewhere in the report the *Challenge* was called "another very extreme magazine" whose "tone is highly anti-British." The magazine's motto was: "It fears only God."

8. At the time, W. A. Domingo was still editor of the *Negro World*.

9. Two sentences at the end of the eighth section concerning other participants in the election have been omitted; also omitted is the beginning of the next section, which discussed the National Association for the Promotion of Labor Unionism among the Negroes.

10. Of these papers, the *Rebel Worker* and *Solidarity* were officially aligned with the IWW, and the *Call* with the Socialist party. Max Eastman's *Liberator* was an independent pro-Soviet paper that later became the *Communist;* however, the *Nation* and the *Public* were independent, liberal-oriented publications. *Freedom*, which was published in New York, described itself as "a journal of constructive anarchism."

11. Two pages concerning the attempts of black leaders to align with the Japanese have been omitted; the section pertaining to Negro Women's Clubs has also been omitted.

12. Rev. William Henry Jernagin (b. 1869), a Mississippi-born clergyman, was president of the National Race Congress. Educated at Meridian College and Alcorn Agricultural and

Mechanical College, Jackson, Miss., he was ordained in 1890, and he achieved local recognition as a pastor for several Mississippi Baptist churches. In 1906 he moved to Oklahoma City to take a position there; he also served as president of the local Baptist educational board. After he was elected president of the State Constitutional League of Oklahoma, he became involved in a campaign for equal rights while he was the managing editor of the *Oklahoma Tribune*. In 1912 he left Oklahoma to become pastor of Mt. Carmel Church, Washington, D.C., where he remained active in the ministry and in the National Race Congress. (*WWCR*, vol. 1).

13. The final two paragraphs of the twelfth section, one on William Monroe Trotter and the other on William Harrison of Chicago, have been omitted.

14. William Earl Dalrymple (b. 1891) was a lieutenant in the aviation section of the Signal Reserve Corps. (*Official List of Officers' Reserve Corps of the Army of the United States, August 31, 1919* [Washington: GPO, 1919]).

W. E. Allen to William M. Offley

[*Washington, D.C.*] April 7, 1919

Dear Sir:—

It has been reported to this office that the March 22, 1919, issue of "The Negro World" (Vol. 2, No. 6), published at 36–38 West 135th Street, New York, contains matter believed to be violation of the Federal law.

It is therefore suggested that the issue of the paper in question be secured and examined. Very truly yours,

[W. E. ALLEN]
Acting Chief

[*Typewritten reference*] MDA:END
[*Endorsement*] Hoover[1]

DNA, RG 65, File OG 185161. TL, Carbon copy. Endorsement is handwritten.

1. John Edgar Hoover (1895–1972) entered the Department of Justice in July 1917 and in November 1918 he was promoted to the position of special attorney in the naturalization division; on 1 July 1919, he was made special assistant to the attorney general and assigned to the newly created General Intelligence Division, primarily to provide justification for those deportation cases on which he had gathered information. Hoover became assistant director of the Bureau of Investigation in 1921, and in May 1924 he was promoted to the position of director, which he held until his death in May 1972. (*WWWA; NCAB;* Max Lowenthal, *The Federal Bureau of Investigation;* Sanford Ungar, *FBI* [Boston: Little, Brown & Co., 1975]; *Annual Report of the Attorney General of the United States for the Year 1920* [Washington, D.C.: GPO, 1920], pp. 172–80; Michael R. Belknap, "The Mechanics of Repression: J. Edgar Hoover, the Bureau of Investigation and the Radicals, 1917–1925," *Crime and Social Justice* 7 [Spring–Summer 1977]: 49–58).

Bureau of Investigation Reports

New York City [*Made*] April 15, 1919
[*for the period of*] April 10 [*1919*]

IN RE: "THE NEGRO WORLD." PROBABLE BOLSHEVIK PROPAGANDA.

This investigation is based on a letter from the Chief, initialed M.D.A., file #185161, dated April 7, 1919, which states in substance that report had come to the attention of the office that the March 22, 1919 issue of this publication was reported to contain matters in violation of the Federal Law.

Pursuant to instructions received from Special Agent Tucker I this day called at the publication office of this paper, 36[–]38 West 135th Street, where I secured a copy of the issue on the day of March 22, 1919 and brought same to the office of this Bureau.

W. H. POLING[1]

DNA, RG 65, File OG 185161. TD.

1. William H. Poling was admitted to the New York Bar in 1909, and was a member of the New York County Lawyers' Association, 1914–18. A year and a half after becoming a special agent, he was arrested and charged in October 1919 with conspiracy to violate the provisions of the wartime liquor prohibition act. (*NYT*, 23 October 1919).

New York City [*Made*] April 15, 1919
[*for the period of*] April 11 [*1919*]

IN RE: "THE NEGRO WORLD." PROBABLE BOLSHEVIK PROPAGANDA.

I this morning took up this matter with Assistant Superintendent Baker[1] for further instructions and he advised me to turn the matter over to Special Agent Finch.

I accordingly turned over the matter to Agent Finch and also the copy of this publication and such information as I had in the matter.

Investigation closed.

W. H. POLING

DNA, RG 65, File OG 185161. TD.

1. Joseph A. Baker served for ten years in the New York office of the Department of Justice, and for five years as New York assistant superintendent of the Bureau of Investigation, retiring in 1919. (*NYT*, 30 December 1919).

Eliézer Cadet to the UNIA

[[19 April 1919]]

Wilson Dominates In France

. . . I did not think that it was necessary to expedite a report to this honorable body prior to the accomplishment of my preliminary duties; things do not go as quickly as we like to think.

I was obliged to spend four days in London, having been fooled by the newspapers *The Telegraph*, [T]*he Times*, and [T]*he Daily News* which had promised me that they would publish my articles before my departure, if they were allowed to do so,—to return them to me in the opposite event. Nothing has been published, nothing has been returned to me. After two days and upon the complaint that I made to them, they all responded to me that they had already examined the issue. I had not wished to remain in London any longer. Before my departure, I asked Mr. Duse Mohamed [A]li to kindly take care of my articles.

You know why they have taken all these precautions: there are in London thousands of black soldiers, from Africa and America and as many colored men from the Orient. I have spoken to several of them at the colored soldiers' Club where I spent several hours in the company of an officer, who later became my good friend.

All these heroes are animated with the same spirit of liberty and democracy for their brethren and their race, and many of them have been punished for having openly expressed this opinion to their officers.

On 1 March, I landed in Paris in the company of one of my friends, Mr. Frederic Guilbaud. We had to walk all day long and for a good part of the night in search of a hotel where we could stay and receive our friends and visitors. The following day was spent looking for a typesetter to print 1st *the articles and letters* that I had translated into French for inclusion in the newspapers, and 2nd *the 9 points*[,] before being communicated to the plenipotentiaries of the Peace Conference. I spent several days before succeeding in speaking to the editors of the newspapers.

On the 3rd, I had an interview with Mr. Tertulien Guilbaud[1] to whom I explained the purpose of the association[,] "The New Negro." Upon his request I explained to him the purpose of Dubois who made the mistake of publishing the name of the Haitian representative as president of the commission without explaining the true situation to this honorable man.[2]

On 6 May [*March*], after the printing of my 9 points, I called upon the Cuban delegate, at that time suffering from influenza.[3] He received my letter and informed me that he would be ready to receive me as soon as his health would permit him to do so.

That same day, the honorable Baron Makino[,] the representative from Japan[,][4] agreed to an interview for the following day the 7th. Upon arriving there, the Baron, with great interest[,] listened to my statement. He replied that our movement was to be taken seriously and that it was important that we be united. Dealing with our 9 points, the Baron made me see that representing Japan, it would not be proper for himself to present the text to the Peace Conference.

After this interview, I went to the editorial offices of the liberal French newspapers. First[,] at the "Matin"[5] I chatted for an hour with the Director and the editor on questions which interested us. They were deeply touched to hear of my statement concerning the atrocities committed against our brethren in the Southern States of the U.S.A[.]; but they openly replied to me that they could publish nothing on this subject before I would be called by the Conference to submit our 9 points.

You can see by this, my dear comrades, that *the "liberal" French newspapers work under the whip of the Peace Conference which is itself under the whip of Wilson.*

Take what I tell you as fact: President Wilson is the sole omnipotent of the Peace conference. The great European powers do not have confidence in themselves. They can say or do nothing without the approval of this powerful "Metternick" of the present hour.[6]

The nations outside of the 5 great Powers[7] are in such a minority at the Peace Conference, that they are as powerless as the portraits which are hung on the wall in the conference room. Within the five Commissions designated to study and settle the different affairs concerning the interests of the World, only five Representatives were accorded to each of the Small Nations, while the five Great Powers each had twenty and England even more because of its Colonial Empire.[8] Therefore, you can see, my dear comrades, that the Small Nations will always be overrun.

Mister Epétacio Pessoa, from Brazil, vigorously attacked this dishonest policy, in the name of the small Nations, last week.[9] I guess that it would be better policy to change the intentions of these Masters by persuasion because now the five great Powers are on the verge of driving the small ones outside of the Peace Conference.

Yesterday I received an invitation from the Brazilian Delegate for an interview today; but this afternoon, I received another letter of apology from the delegate announcing to me that he is ill and that as soon as he recovers, he will come to see me. I delivered our nine points directly to the President and to the Secretary of the Peace Conference after 7 March. On Monday the 10th I returned for an answer and they replied to me that he would write me as soon as possible. Do not worry about the publication of the articles. If the "Petit Parisien", the "Presse"[10] and the "Intransigeant"[11] which have promised to publish them for me as soon as possible do not keep their word and after the answer of the Peace Conference will be received[,] I will know what I must do.

I count on seeing the other plenipotentiaries and eminent men. I do not have a minute to lose Yours fraternally

ELIÉZER CADET

Printed in *NW*, 19 April 1919; reprinted in *L'Essor* (Port-au-Prince, Haiti), Thursday, 8 May 1919. Translated from the French original.

1. Tertulien Guilbaud, a former minister of justice in the Haitian government, was offered the presidency of Haiti in 1915 by its congress, following the assassination of President Vilbrun Guillaume Sam and the subsequent American occupation of the country, but he declined. In 1919 he was appointed Haiti's minister plenipotentiary to the Paris Peace Conference.

2. On 27 January 1919 Du Bois wrote to the chairman of the NAACP board of directors from Paris, stating that the "Haytian and Liberian delegates to the Peace Conference are with us" (DLC, NAACP). Four days later, on 31 January, the NAACP was further informed by a cablegram from Du Bois: "Two of our Delegates Haiti, Liberia Sit in Peace Conference" (ibid.). On 16 February the *New York Times* reported that among the delegates attending the Pan-African Congress was "Tertullian Guilbaud of Havana," while on 21 February, an Associated Press dispatch announced that the Pan-African Congress was "headed by Dr. W. E. B. Du Bois, the Foreign Minister of Liberia and T. Guilbaud, the Minister of Hayti in Paris" (DLC, NAACP).

3. Antonio Sánchez de Bustamante y Sirvén (1865–1951), prominent international lawyer and member of the International Court of Justice at the Hague, was the head of the Cuban delegation to the Paris Peace Conference. When Cuba became a republic in 1902, Bustamante was elected senator in the new national legislature, a position he held until 1918. He was appointed in 1921 to the Permanent Court of International Justice at the Hague, serving there until his retirement in 1939. (*NYT*, 26 August 1951).

4. Count Nobuaki Makino (1861–1949), Japanese statesman and diplomat, represented Japan at the peace conference where he was one of the so-called Big Five. He also exerted considerable influence on the future Emperor Hirohito. During the revolt of the Japanese military in 1936, an attempt on his life was narrowly thwarted. (*NYT*, 26 January 1949; *WBD*).

5. *Le Matin*, a daily morning newspaper in Paris, was founded in 1884.

6. Prince Klemens Wenzel Nepomuk Luthar von Metternich (1773–1859), Austrian statesman and diplomat, was the architect of the concert of Europe by which means European monarchs sought to halt the spread of democratic ideas and nationalistic movements unleashed by the French Revolution. (*WBD*).

7. The five were the United States, France, Great Britain, Japan, and Italy.

8. Diplomatic negotiations at the peace conference were conducted by numerous commissions and subcommissions. In January 1919 the Supreme Allied Council had decided to allow representatives of the smaller nations with "special interests" to participate in two of the five principal areas of decision making: war guilt and international labor legislation. Subsequently, several additional commissions were created and the seventeen small nations were allocated a limited number of representatives, in most cases five. (*EA*).

9. On 3 March 1919, at a meeting of the Representatives of the Powers with Special Interests, Epitácio Pessoa, the head of the Brazilian delegation, read a resolution protesting the Supreme Allied Council's allocation of only five representatives to members of the group on the financial and economic commissions. (*NYT*, 14 February 1942). His resolution called for the total to be increased to ten. The French president of the group, Jules Cambon (appointed as part of France's host obligations) subsequently proposed that the Supreme Allied Council decide on the question of representation, and his proposal was unanimously adopted. Subsequently, the council ruled that representation for the group on the two commissions should remain at five.

10. *La Presse*, a Parisian daily newspaper.

11. *L'Intransigeant*, founded in 1880, was the largest evening newspaper in Paris throughout the post–World War I era.

Newspaper Report

[*New York Call*, 27 April 1919]

Negroes Plan to Found Ship Line
Project Will Be Discussed at Palace Casino
Rally Tomorrow Night

The Universal Negro Improvement Association and African Communities League, recognizing, according to its president-general, Marcus Garvey, that this is a "selfish age," will hold a mass meeting at the Palace Casino, 135th Street and Madison Avenue, tomorrow night to prove the Negro has caught the spirit.

According to Garvey, the Negroes are anxious to go back to Africa and the West Indies and create empires of their own as strong as that of the yellow and the white man. To go back, they need ships.

Therefore, at this mass meeting the founding of the "Black Star Line" will be attempted.[1] The proposed steamship line will operate between American ports and those of Africa, the West Indies, Central and South America.

Printed in the *New York Call*, Sunday, 27 April 1919.

1. The *Negro World* of 3 May 1919 reported that the UNIA "has opened a special account with the Corn Exchange Bank, 125th Street and Lenox Avenue, to receive lodgment of the Black Star Line" (*Garvey* v. *United States*, no. 8317 [Ct. App., 2d Cir. Feb. 2, 1925], p. 1308). The same announcement reported that the secretary of the line was "W. T. Mitchell" and that the treasurer was George W. Tobias. The former was actually Uriah T. Mitchell, a Jamaican who at the time also held the position of UNIA secretary. However, a few weeks later Mitchell resigned from the UNIA, after temporarily serving as a member of a three-man committee auditing the UNIA's accounts. The committee also charged Garvey before New York Assistant District Attorney Edwin P. Kilroe, alleging financial mismanagement and collection of money from UNIA members under false pretenses.

Bureau of Investigation Report

New York City [*Made*] May 28, 1919
[*for the Period of*] May 28 [*1919*]

IN RE: Negro Activities The Black Star Line.

Our attention has been called to a notice which appeared in the "Negro World" of April 26th, reading:

"Every Negro Man and Woman in the States of New
York and New Jersey Is Hereby Notified

That a monster convention of the race is called for Sunday night, April 27, 1919, at 8.30 o'clock at the Palace Casino, New York, Cor. Madison

Avenue and 135th Street. *The Universal Negro Improvement Association and African Communities League, Inc. of the World.*

Marcus Garvey
World-Famed Orator Will Speak at This Convention.

The move to inaugurate the First Line of Negro Steamships to run between America, Africa and the West Indies, South and Central America, to compete in the new world trade, will be launched at this convention.

Everybody Must be There at 8:30 Sharp to Get Seats."

The meeting was held as advertised. There was besides Garvey, one other speaker, named *A. H. Whale[y]*. After the meeting Garvey said privately that their purpose was to inaugurate the *Black Star Line* of vessels to sail between New York and the West Indies, and then to Liberia. This was the first meeting for the purpose and something between $7,000 and $8,000 was collected in the form of cash and pledges. When they have a certain amount of money they propose to get a charter under the American flag, and later on transfer the ship or ships to the Liberian flag.[1] After the charter has been procured they propose to take the matter up with the Japanese bankers and get financial backing from them.

There have been other references of late to negro steamship lines. *John W. Howard*, a negro radical who edits the Philadelphia "Ledger," is contemplating propaganda for a line to Africa under the Liberian flag.[2] *R. W. Hunter & Co.*, the colored bankers of Chicago,[3] who appear to be mixed up with radical activities, are also said to be interested in prom[o]ting a shipping line between New York and Liberia.

M. J. Davis[4]

DNA, RG 65, File OG 258421. TD.

1. It was and still is a common practice for merchant ships to register under the Liberian flag, since Liberian law exempts shipping companies from taxes on profits and imposes few maritime regulations.

2. The only black newspapers published in Philadelphia at this time were the *Philadelphia Tribune*, the *Philadelphia Courant*, and the *Public Journal*; there was no newspaper with the title, "Philadelphia Ledger," though there was a *Public Ledger*, but it was both owned and edited by whites. "The African Steamship and Saw Mill Company" was incorporated in Philadelphia on 24 March 1919 by A. White, W. D. Winston, and Lewis Williams. The original incorporators ceased their involvement by 1921, when the records listed as president and secretary AME Bishop W. H. Heard and Dr. W. L. Jordan respectively.

3. The R. W. Hunter Banking and Industrial Company was one of the first private black banks organized in Chicago, located near 48th and State Streets. However, the bank's president, R. W. Hunter, formerly of Alabama, went bankrupt sometime in 1919. No corroboration of R. W. Hunter's involvement in the promotion of a shipping line has been found. (Abram L. Harris, *The Negro as Capitalist: A Study of Banking and Business among American Negroes* [Philadelphia: American Academy of Political and Social Science, 1936]).

4. Mortimer J. Davis (ca. 1896–1973) joined the Department of Justice in January 1917 and was a member of the Bureau of Investigation until 1925, when he left to become the assistant director of the fraud prevention department of the National Association of Credit Management. Davis also served as an aide to J. Edgar Hoover and Attorney General Harlan F. Stone (*NYT*, 19 July 1973).

Editorial Letter by Marcus Garvey

[[Biltmore Hotel, Detroit, Mich.,
June 4, 1919]]

Fellowmen of the Negro Race.

Greeting:—Through pressure of work I was rendered unable for several weeks to send to you the accustomed message of cheer and good will. Today I write to you from the City of Detroit, bidding you be steadfast in your hope of the glorious future that awaits us.

The Universal Negro Improvement Association is now starting in earnest to cover the entire world in its campaign to inaugurate "The Black Star Line."

Two Million Dollars ($2,000000) must be raised in four months, starting from Sunday the 8th inst., and I trust that every man, woman and child in these United States, Canada, South and Central America, the West Indies and Africa, will respond in the true spirit of this universal appeal.

"The Black Star Line" must be floated on the 31st of October of the present year. It is a great task, but it can and must be achieved. The Two Million Dollars will be raised in the following manner:

One Million Two Hundred and Fifty Thousand Dollars among the colored people of the United States, by each person donating to the Universal Negro Improvement Association One Dollar or more; Two Hundred and Fifty Thousand Dollars in the West Indies, by each person donating Twenty-five Cents or more; Three Hundred Thousand Dollars in South and Central America, by each person donating Fifty Cents or more; Two Hundred Thousand Dollars on the Continent of Africa by each . . . [*mutilated*] twenty-five cents or more.

[*Beginning of sentence mutilated*] . . . to be owned by the people and . . . [*mutilated*] of the people, and not owned and controlled by any private corporation or individual. Every Negro can be a member of the Universal Negro Improvement Association, hence, every Negro can by majority vote determine how "The Black Star Line" shall be operated. A line of steamships owned by and operated in the interest of the people is necessary for the fuller economic and industrial development of the race.

The Universal Negro Improvement Association takes the place of a guardian for the people and is bound to administer all its holdings solely in the interest of the people.

There will be no speculation in "The Black Star Line," except that which will be to the people as a whole. Like the property of a nation or of a state, the properties of the Universal Negro Improvement Association are the people's, hence no private dividends.

The Universal Negro Improvement Association is determined to lift the American Negro, the African Negro, the West Indian, South and Central American and Canadian Negroes to a higher plane of economic independence, and to this effort every man and woman of color should lend support.

Let us all unite and make "The Black Star Line" a huge success, thereby demonstrating the ability of the Negro in this age of reconstruction to in some way take care of himself.

To those of you who are in the city of New York, I extend an invitation to meet me at the Palace Casino, 135th street and Madison avenue, on Sunday night, June 8, at 8.30, and those of you who are located in other parts of these United States, the West Indies, Canada and South and Central America, you may expect to see me in person shortly to explain completely the aims and objects of the world-wide movement of the Universal Negro Improvement Association, which is endeavoring to do so much for each and . . . [*mutilated*]. With very best wishes, Yours fraternally.

MARCUS GARVEY

Printed in the *NW*, Saturday, 7 June 1919. Original headlines have been omitted.

Rear-Admiral A. P. Niblack, Director of Naval Intelligence, to W. E. Allen

[*Washington, D.C.*] June 8th, 1919

CONFIDENTIAL
My dear Mr. Allen:

For your information and file there is attached hereto, a copy of the newspaper known as "the Negro World", which copy was issued under date of May 31st, 1919.[1] Very truly yours,

A. P. NIBLACK,[2]
Rear-Admiral, U.S.N.
Director of Naval Intelligence
[*Signed by*] G M Baum[3]
By direction

Enclosure No. 20845-1-
Copy of newspaper

[*Typewritten reference*] A-I APN:MB
[*Endorsement*] PAF.

DNA, RG 38, File 20948-184. TLS, Carbon copy.

1. Before its transmission to the bureau, the copy of the *Negro World* was circulated within ONI by Lt. H. L. Thompson with an accompanying memorandum (DNA, RG 38, file 20948-184). On 4 June, Lt. Comdr. Randolph H. Miner, called "attention . . . to the tone of the publication and to its extreme views" (ibid.).

2. Rear-Adm. Albert Parker Niblack (1859–1929) was commander of the Atlantic fleet during the First World War and in October 1920 he was appointed naval attaché to the American Embassy in London. (*WWWA*, vol. 1).

3. George Martin Baum (1883–1968) served with ONI from December 1918 until December 1920. He later served as a naval attaché in Berlin, Oslo, Copenhagen, and Stockholm. (Office of Naval Intelligence, Personnel Records).

Editoral Letter by Marcus Garvey

[[Montreal, Canada, June 10, 1919]]

Fellowmen of the Negro Race!

Greeting:—I write to inform you that just at this time the Universal Negro Improvement Association is preparing itself for a great battle to offset the enemies of our cause. For some time a number of political grafters and conscienceless crooks have been trying to gain control over the sentiment of our people, for the purpose of exploiting and robbing them of their hard earned mites. Some have formed companies and corporations, have sought to ingratiate themselves into the good graces of the members of our organization and our supporters by pretending to be so much interested in the cause and our people. These crooks have been blocked at every turn, in many instances have been prevented from robbing the people. These men are of the kind who have robbed the race in the past by starting corporations that existed only for a year or eighteen months. We can remember the history of so many fake Negro enterprises and it was because of that we refused to allow certain individuals to use the patronage of the Universal Negro Improvement Association to rob the people. Because these designers did not succeed in getting the executives of our association to help them to exploit the people for personal ends they have organized a campaign of lies and villification against the association. These robbers and "white men's niggers" have gone to white men to lie about us so as to have our cause interfered with. They went to and wrote to the police headquarters of New York, saying that the bombs that were manufactured and sent through the United States mails to certain individuals as reported in the newspapers a few days ago,[1] were manufactured by me and posted from the office of THE NEGRO WORLD. The police department investigated and in two minutes found the whole thing to be a manufactured lie.

These crooks and Negro traitors did not stop there. They went to the State Attorney of New York and told him a great many lies. He has summoned me to appear before him on the 12th for what reason I do not know, only that I have sufficient information to know the ones who are, unfortunately, of our race, being paid to do all kinds of dirty work to hamper the Universal Negro Improvement Association. The names of these traitors will be published in THE NEGRO WORLD in bold black type in the next week or two. Some of them joined the association for the purpose of carrying out the designs as explained. They have been expelled from the association and their names will be published so that the world might know them. I feel sure that the Negro people of the world have settled in their minds already how they will deal with their traitors. I have mentioned the facts.

I may say this to you fellowmen, that the Universal Negro Improvement Association has accomplished so much within the last six months that it is now impossible for any traitors, foreign or domestic, to prevent it from achieving its useful purposes.

The Universal Negro Improvement Association is the people's movement and I as one of its leaders fear no man or government in putting
through the just claims of the 400,000,000 of our people, who are suffering
all over the world.

The new Negro is no coward. He is a man, and if he can die in France or
Flanders for white men, he can die anywhere else, even behind prison bars,
fighting for the cause of the race that needs assistance.

I say to you men, be of good cheer. The Negro now or at some time will
have to give his martyrs or offer his sacrifice before the race can be redeemed.

I shall write to you later to keep you informed of the actions of these
traitors. With best wishes, Yours fraternally,

MARCUS GARVEY

Printed in the *NW*, Saturday, 14 June 1919. Original headlines have been omitted.

1. On 30 April 1919, a New York City postal clerk read a newspaper description of the
incident involving a bomb received through the mail by former Senator Thomas W. Hardwick
of Georgia (previously the chairman of the U.S. Senate Immigration Committee). Recalling
that he had withdrawn similarly wrapped packages from the mail because they lacked postage,
the clerk alerted the New York police to remove them. After this incident, federal and local
authorities increased their surveillance of radicals in the New York City area. The intercepted
bombs were mailed to a total of thirty-six persons, including A. Mitchell Palmer, Oliver W.
Holmes, Jr., John D. Rockefeller, and J. P. Morgan. (*NYT*, 1 May 1919; Stanley Coben, *A.
Mitchell Palmer: Politician* [New York: Columbia University Press, 1963]).

Eliézer Cadet to *L'Essor*

[10 June 1919]

LETTER FROM FRANCE
THIS MAN IS JUPITER

Our correspondent Eliezer Cadet sends us the following remarks:

The cables must have informed you that the pact of the League of
Nations has been adopted and that Mr. Wilson's plan has prevailed on every
line, as the headlines of the 29 April 1919 issue of *Le Matin* have conveyed.[1]

France, Belgium and Japan had amendments to propose during the
formulation of this pact; they even drew these amendments up, but since
Wilson dominates things here, these amendments have been rejected[2] and
you are about to see how.

I was the only black to attend this solemn meeting. The honorable Mr.
Tertulien Gui[l]baud was ill with influenza for a few days and the plenipotentiary from Liberia was no longer there.[3]

Because of what I saw and heard at this plenary meeting, I concurred
with the diplomats of the small powers, that the other nations of the world,
with the exception of the four great allied powers, were invited to the
conference only as pure camouflage.

How well I understand those indignant words of Gabriele d'Annunzio,[4] pronounced from a balcony in Saint Mark's Square in Venice and reported in the 29 April 1919 Intransigeant: "Each combattant must retake his position today. . . . I have spent two hours in readying my machine-gun and placing the bombs on my airplane of Vienna.[5] . . . We will no longer hope, we want. Repeat this word (the crowd repeated: we want). . . . Our leaders have closed their book on the table of tricksters, on the page of deceit and lies. . . . We will reopen it at the page where we wrote with the blood of Montello. . . . We must pose a second[6] question to Italy: Are you ready to fight again? We must pose a single question to the people of Venice: Are you ready to suffer again?"

What shocked me the most during the course of the meeting was the attitude of the strong toward the little peoples of the Americas. While the delegates from Uruguay, Honduras, and Panama put forth their view on certain clauses of the league and especially on art. 21 concerning the Monroe doctrine,[7] there was, let us say, a general uproar which arose in the hall. Mr. D. Lloyd George left his seat to go and congratulate Baron Makino who had just said that: "the Japanese government and Japanese people do not ask to speak out at the Peace Conference today, but they proclaim that they will never cease in insisting so that in the future it may accede to their request[,]" the request to recognize the principle of the *Evolution of the Races*, because "a race which today is very backwards may tomorrow come to be a power of the first class and as a consequence it will not accept the injustice of the inequality of its race with all the others."

Indeed[,] several other plenipotentiaries left the room under the pretext of going outside to take some air. The motions of the so-called small states were not even translated for those who did not understand French, such as Mr. Wilson[.] Mr. Clemenceau no longer even put the motions to a vote.

Honduras maintained that the Monroe Doctrine was not sufficiently explicit; Uruguay proposed the establishment of a Pan-American alliance for the defense of the weak countries of the New World; it sanctioned the signing of commercial treaties etc. among the American republics . . .

After Baron Makino had given up immediate acceptance of his amendment, it was France's turn to beat a retreat in front of Mr. Wilson's will who nevertheless forced the acceptance of the recognition of the Monroe Doctrine without discussion.

This league, which was voted upon unanimously, is nevertheless a sham. Mr. Wilson was able to obtain a unanimous vote by making concessions elsewhere to the great powers. In this setting, this man is Jupiter.

Printed in *L'Essor* (Port-au-Prince, Haiti), Tuesday, 10 June 1919. Translated from the French original.

1. The original headline in *Le Matin*, 29 April 1919, read: "Le pacte de la Ligue des Nations est adopté/ Le projet de M. Wilson l'emporte sur toute la ligne/La France, la Belgique et le Japon n'insistent pas pour le vote immédiat de leurs amendements." ("The League of Nations

Pact is adopted/The plan of Mr. Wilson prevails on every line/France, Belgium and Japan do not insist on voting immediately on their amendments.").

2. The French amendment to the League's covenant, presented on 27 April 1919, was eventually withdrawn. It was designed to further French security by calling for the creation of a permanent organization that could provide military enforcement of the covenant's provisions. The Belgian amendment, which was defeated, concerned the choice of Geneva instead of Brussels as the seat of the League.

3. The Liberian delegation was headed by C. D. B. King, secretary of state and president-elect of Liberia. The other delegates were C. B. Dunbar, Secretary of State H. A. Miller, and Henry F. Worley, the American-appointed financial adviser to the Republic of Liberia. In a report to the U.S. Department of State, Worley mentioned the activities of Cadet:

> His card reads Eliezer Cadet, Grand Commissaire en France, representing the Universal Negro Improvement Association . . . He also is said to represent 'The Negro World' of New York of which Marcus Garvey is the managing editor. He left several copies of the publication with the Liberian Delegates and each containing large headlines and inflammatory wording, emphasizing the wrongs of the Negro Race, calling on them for retaliation, and prophesying a day of judgment and retribution for the American people. Cadet called on Secretary King and endeavored to arouse in him some sort of movement but I think did not receive much encouragement. Secretary King asked him, if the American Negroes were so thoroughly dissatisfied with the social and political conditions in America, why they did not go to Liberia, which is a Negro Republic founded by the United States, and become citizens there where they would have social and political equality. (DNA, RG 59, file 763.72119/5119, H. F. Worley to William A. Phillips, Paris, 2 May 1919).

4. Gabriele d'Annunzio (1863–1938) was a respected Italian poet, novelist, and soldier. When the allied leaders, particularly President Wilson, opposed Italy's claim to the city of Fiume during the peace conference, d'Annunzio, accompanied by a few hundred soldiers in September 1919, seized control of Fiume and occupied it for fifteen months against the wishes of the Italian government and other allied powers. After his occupation of Fiume ended, d'Annunzio became a strong supporter of Benito Mussolini (1883–1945). (WBD).

5. The French original read "mon avion de Vienne."

6. L'Intransigeant's version of d'Annunzio's speech read "seule" ("single") rather than "seconde" as reported by L'Essor.

7. The American peace delegation hoped to include in the peace treaty an article or declaration safeguarding the general principles of the Monroe Doctrine. This led to an attempt by Dr. Policarpo Bonilla, the Honduran delegate, to include in the final treaty an official definition of the doctrine, which had never previously been defined. In Bonilla's opinion, the Latin American countries' acceptance of the League of Nations meant that henceforth the United States should, like the great European powers, be excluded from interference in Latin America. (NYT, 31 January, 23 March, and 14 June 1919).

Meetings of the UNIA

[*Negro World*, 14 June 1919]

NEWS ITEM

The Universal Negro Improvement Association scored a tremendous hit at the Palace Casino on Sunday evening, June 1, to a vast audience. Mrs. Peters[1] brought a message directly from West Africa to Africans abroad.

The meeting was started with its usual excellent musical program, followed by an address of welcome by the general secretary of the organization, Mr. Edgar M. Gray.

Mr. Gray held his audience for about thirty-two minutes under a storm of applause, when he repeatedly scored the present oppressive system of government that applied to Negroes, and called upon all Negroes to prepare themselves for the conflict of some day to come.

Miss Henrietta Vinton Davis, the National and International Organizer,[2] was then introduced, and with her usual earnestness and intelligence proceeded to discuss the present status of the Negroes of the world, and held out and discussed a bright future at not a very distant date.

Mrs. Peters was then introduced. She proceeded to discuss all phases of African life, and especially the economic, social, judicial and tribal phases of it. She declared that from observation and investigation the people of interior Africa always have been governed under the most refined judicial system of law, and that the social system of African life might be called a socialistic one. The speaker dwelled largely upon the natural obedience of the African to law, order and authority, and further stated that the honesty of the people was so remarkable that one might always leave one's property unguarded or unprotected and be assured of its safety upon one's return.

She stated by implication that the time-honored tradition in America that the Negro was a natural and rabid rapine did not seem to hold true in the land of the Negro's origin, since she had traveled many thousands of miles in the interior of Africa, and her only guards were half-dressed, half-naked Negroes, as they are found in their clime.

After a very brilliant discussion of the entire field of missionary life the speaker brought her discourse to a climax when she stated that the African was not lacking in the preparation and organization for the great conflict to come, for which the Universal Negro Improvement Association was so arduously and persistently endeavoring. Her remarks were brought to a close under a storm of constant applause exemplifying that the Negro was anxious at all times to receive a message from his fatherland.

Printed in the *NW*, Saturday, 14 June 1919.

1. Henrietta E. Peters and her husband, Rev. R. E. Peters, were black missionaries of the AMEZ church in the Gold Coast from 1915 until 1925. (David H. Bradley, *History of AME Zion Church* [Nashville: Parthenon Press, 1956]).

2. Henrietta Vinton Davis (1860–1941), elocutionist and dramatist, was born in Baltimore, Md., the daughter of musician Mansfield Vinton Davis. She attended public schools in Washington, D.C., where she soon displayed her dramatic prowess. At the age of fifteen she was employed as a teacher with the Maryland public schools; later, she was employed with the Louisiana Board of Education, but she returned to Washington, D.C., to attend her ailing mother. In 1878 she entered the Office of the Recorder of Deeds as a copyist, first under George A. Sheridan, and afterward under Frederick Douglass, who held the position from 1881 to 1886. She continued to pursue her interest in the dramatic arts, however, studying privately with various teachers in Washington, D.C., New York City, and at the Boston School of Oratory.

On 25 April 1883, she made her first dramatic appearance in Washington, D.C., introduced by Frederick Douglass. A few weeks later, under the management of James M. Trotter and William H. Dupree, she embarked on a successful tour of several eastern cities. Her repertoire included dramatic readings from Paul Laurence Dunbar, Mark Twain, and Shakespeare. In 1884, she resigned her position with the Office of the Recorder of Deeds to pursue her dramatic career. She married Thomas T. Symmons, who became her manager. In 1893, she established her own dramatic company in Chicago and produced the play "Dessalines" by William Edgar

Easton, a young black playwright. In a letter to Ignatius Donnelly (1831–1901), the outstanding Populist leader, Davis expressed her support of the Populist party platform as presented in the 1892 conventions in St. Louis and Omaha and volunteered to lecture on the party's behalf.

In April 1912, accompanied by contralto Nonie Bailey Hardy, Henrietta Vinton Davis toured Jamaica, giving performances throughout the island. Later that year she also took over the management of Kingston's Convent Garden Theatre. While in Jamaica, she organized the Loyal Knights and Ladies of Malachite, a black American benevolent society. Around March 1913, both women left Jamaica for Central America, where they performed in Panama and Costa Rica before returning to the United States. It was while she was in Costa Rica, however, that Davis met a Jamaican woman who donated a piece of land in Jamaica to her in order to build a school for girls. Davis conducted several fund raising efforts for this project over the next several years, until she became associated with the UNIA in 1919. On 27 June 1919, she was listed as one of the original directors of the Black Star Line as well as the second vice-president of the corporation. Throughout the peak years of the UNIA, she remained among the movement's top leadership, and in 1924 Garvey sent her as part of the final UNIA delegation to Liberia in order to try to negotiate an agreement for land with the Liberian government. She died on 23 November 1941 at St. Elizabeth's Hospital in Washington, D.C. (Minnesota Historical Society, St. Paul, *Ignatius Donnelly Papers*, Roll 104, 158, vol. 116, p. 158; Washington, D.C., Vital Records Office, death certificate; *Cleveland Gazette*, 9 February 1884; A. F. Richings, *Evidence of Progress among Colored People* [Philadelphia: A. S. Ferguson, 1896], p. 422; Monroe Alphus Majors, *Noted Negro Women: Their Triumphs and Activities* [Jackson, Tenn.: M. V. Lynk Publishing House, 1893], pp. 102–08; *Jamaica Times*, 13 April 1912, 17 August 1912, 23 March 1913; *Daily Chronicle*, 8 November 1915, p. 9; *New York Age*, 29 March 1919; William Seraile, "Henrietta Vinton Davis and the Garvey Movement," unpublished manuscript, 1981; Errol Hill, "Henrietta Vinton Davis," in Helen Chinoy and Linda Jenkins, eds., *Women in the American Theatre* [New York: Crown Publishers, 1981]).

[*Negro World*, 14 June 1919]

AFRICAN SPEAKER THRILLS NEW YORK AUDIENCE— TELLS OF NATIVE POWER

Sunday evening, June the 8th, despite the inclemency of the weather, an audience of over two thousand persons assembled at the Palace Casino to attend the weekly mass convention staged by the Universal Negro Improvement Association in the interest of the Black Star Line. Mr. Edgar M. Grey, general secretary of the organization, presided. After the singing of the opening ode the chairman made a short, eloquent and inspiring address, which was liberally interspersed with applause from the audience.

The next speaker was the well-known elocutionist, Miss Henrietta Vinton Davis, of Washington, D.C., who made the rafters of the huge Casino resound with her thrilling eloquence. At the close of her address the chairman introduced as the next speaker Mr. Cooper, a native of Liberia, West Africa.

Mr. Cooper literally took the house by storm by his unsuspected eloquence. With picturesque phraseology he graphically told his audience of some of the latent powers of the Negro race in its native habitat. The audience showed its appreciation for the many good things it had listened to during the evening by its hearty response to the appeal made for funds for the Black Star Line.

A much enjoyed portion of the program was the musical items, which were given by persons who had volunteered their services. This consisted of two vocal solos and one flute and piano solo.

The envelope method of collecting for the Black Star Line was largely omitted because of a direct appeal made by the chair, which resulted in a mass collection to the table.

Newport News, Sunday, June 7, 1919.—This city was roused from its usual calm by the appearance of Mr. Marcus Garvey, the world-famed orator of the race, organizer and president-general of the Universal Negro Improvement Association, and managing editor of THE NEGRO WORLD, who addressed a huge audience which filled our largest local theatre to capacity today.

Expectation had been at fever heat to both see and hear this famous orator, and although the meeting had been called and advertised within twelve hours, it was impossible to find a vacant seat in the auditorium of the building in which he spoke. Mr. Garvey lived up to his reputation as in purest English that flowed from his lips without interruption, he told his audience of the objects and founding of the organization and newspaper which he represented. He said that in this travels throughout most of the countries of Western Europe, the islands of the West Indies, republics of Central and South America, and over thirty States of the American Union from what he saw of the plight of his people he was convinced that oppression was not the peculiar monopoly of any individual country, but the common misfortune of all Negroes. His experiences, he said, had made him determined to fight without fear of consequences for the rights of his race in all parts of the world, and to that end he had founded the Universal Negro Improvement Association and African Communities League, out of which grew THE NEGRO WORLD, which was today regarded as the foremost journalistic champion of the race in any country. At the close of his address, which was rapturously received by his hearers, he made a powerful and eloquent appeal for funds for the purpose of establishing the Black Star Line. The audience heartily responded, and the following persons subscribed:

A Friend	$ .10	Caesar Barron	.50
W. S. Creeper	1.00	Mrs. Will James	.25
James A. Morris	1.00	J. W. Purdy	.50
Mattie Daries	.50	Ned McKeiver	.50
Howard Goodwin	1.00	Geo. Thomas	
G. W. Rogers	1.00	Alonzo Boone	1.00
W. H. Schoefield	1.00	W. G. Dickens	1.00
W. A. Walters	1.00	Miss Mary Jackson	1.00
Thos. Lewis	.63	A Friend	.25
Joseph Johnson	1.00	Robert Warren	.05
Joe Lewis	1.00	W. McGovin	.25
H. E. Howell	1.00	Charlie Thort	1.00
F. H. Howell	1.00	Batorn Evans	.50

W. Sanders	.25	L. L. Jackson	1.00
Lizzie Jones	.25	George Sayles	.25
Mrs. A. L. Ridgell	.25	Joseph Pittman	1.00
George Lipscomb	.25	Peter Clement	.50
J. H. Ridgell	.25	William Bowles	.25
J. R. Rasberry	.50	Alonzo Taylor	1.00
Lena Roole	1.00	James Hopkins	.25
Samuel Anderson	.25	Elkines Clement	1.00
James Croom	.25	W. Jones	
George Duglins	.25	Lillie George	.03
Jim Wynn	.50	George McDonald	2.00
Ozel Potts	.50	Harrington Williams	2.00
Joseph Gilliam	[torn]	W. M. McClark	1.00
Roscoe Sanders	[torn]	Charlie Grevious	1.00
Richard Gray	.25	Eadie Dane	.75
W. Walke	1.00	George Wilkins	1.00
William Price	.25	R. A. Battle	1.00
Ollie Charity	.50	George Effort	
Lillie Brown	.25	M. Herbert Spence	1.00
C. J. and Lillie Clayton	1.00	Morris Dodson	1.00
L. C. Hamlin	.25	A. G. Dodson	1.00
J. H. Robinson	1.00	Roy Gwathey	1.00
J. Wilkerson	.50	Theodore T. Taylor	5.00
C. G. Bucum	1.00	M. J. Norman	1.00
J. B. Seldon	1.00	Miller H. Hynes	1.00
Y. C. Mattay	.25	Miles Key	.25
Bettie Morgan	.15	Beverly Anderson	1.25
Henry W. Gibson	.50	Mrs. W. T. Powell	.25
N. W. Mulderbee	.50	Charles H. Spratleis	1.00
R. Hundley	1.00	Norman Baker	.25
C. C. Jones	1.00	L. W. Sleeper	1.00
B. McRimmes	.50	Priscilla Thomas	.50
F. Grece	.23	Geo. Edwards	.55
Joseph Wright	.50	Robert Tucker	1.00
Albert Tumbling	.50	John McRimmon	.50
Roas Love		C. W. Penny	.50
Mrs. Agnes Bluden	.50	Mrs. Maggie H. Brown	.25
M. M. Green		Arthur Mantley	1.00
Walter Edward Cherry	.50	L. A. Porter	1.00
L. M. Johnson	.25	Julia Orr	0.25
Thomas Jones	1.00	L. Bryant	.10
Ben Scales	1.00	James Day	1.00
W. H. Jackson	1.00	George Strawss	1.00
Tom Matherson	.05	Flemming Prime	.73
Annie Alexander	1.00	Joe Harrial	.25

John Hill	1.00	Henry Corbin	1.00
A friend	.20	Edwin Flowers	1.00
Hugh McKethan	1.00	James Jelks	1.00
F. L. Anderson	.05	Mrs. Nannie Clark	1.00
Henry Gibbs	1.20	Van Jordan	1.10
F. Strickland	1.00	J. R. Warren	.25
R. T. Kaersenhaut	1.00	Tom Carlon	
George Hill	1.00	T. C. Scott	.25
Isaac Watson	1.00	T. C. Chandler	.50
R. Jennett	.25	Willie Jordan	1.00
Jane Byrd	.25	J. Bethea	
Littleton Cartie	1.00	J. Briggs	1.00
William Parson	.50	Hettie Sanders	.25
Andrew Bailey	.25	Frank Simpson	1.00
Charlie Cartwright	1.00	A. S. Brown	1.00
J. C. Chanix	1.00	Arthur Williams	1.00
J. Hall	.50	J. C. Hill	.25
Leander Clarke	1.00	John Simpson	1.00
Alex Quilles	1.00	A friend	.20
John Hinsor	.50	W. C. Taylor	
B. Harris	1.00	Moses Brunson	
Eddie Johnson	2.00	J. J. Alston	.50
W. Alexander	1.00	Benney Bethea	1.00
O. Dudley	1.00	Wilson Lockhart	.25
Charles Porter	1.00	Henry Lockhart	5.00
William Rhodes	.50	William Rodd	.05
W. S. Lockhart	.75	James Smith	.50
J. H. Brown	1.00	Alex McRimon	1.00
Cleveland Robinson	1.00		

Printed in the *NW*, Saturday, 14 June 1919.

Editorial in the *Negro World*

[14 June 1919]

"DIVIDE AND RULE."

With the arrival of warm weather Lenox avenue, New York as during the past three summers, is nightly being infested with several soap-box and step-ladder orators. This, if not used for subversive purposes, is a healthy sign of intellectual curiosity on the part of the audiences who listen to the various speakers. However, every good thing is susceptible of being used in such a manner as to destroy its intrinsic excellence. The fact that public speaking is to be encouraged both for the benefit of the orators and their hearers is no reason why it should be abused by ignorant, irresponsible and mercenary individuals. A public speaker should conceive his functions as that of disseminating information or of formulating opinions. To do either of these properly it is necessary that the speaker himself should be informed and his opinions worthy of public assimilation. Mere ability to coin pleasant sounding phrases, give illustrations of doubtful appropriateness and make sweeping assertions does not by any stretch of imagination justify a speaker engaging the attention of passers-by. In New York, within the last few weeks, one or two new faces have appeared on the avenue as public speakers, and so far as we have been able to see, they have not contributed very much to the intellectual probity of the Negro race. Instead, some of them in their zeal to hold public attention by any and every unscrupulous means have thrown every canon of good taste overboard and abandoned the ordinary dictates of common sense that should govern one in discussing any question calling for delicacy of treatment. Obviously the new tactics of discussing the West Indian and American question along purely nationalistic lines must be taken as eloquent testimony of the intellectual impoverishment of those speakers, who in order to attract a crowd resort to the most disgusting and vulgar form of billingsgate and abuse imaginable. Perhaps the Negro speakers who indulge in this race-disrupting pastime are merely rendering service for wages already received, or perhaps (and this is a charitable view) they are merely imitating a certain white man who started out along that line on Lenox avenue this season.[1]

We extremely regret that Negroes who essay to leadership should permit themselves to be consciously or unconsciously tools for white men whose aspirations for leadership among Negroes can only be achieved by first breaking up the race into sectional or color groups. Feeling that the sound common sense of the rank and file of our people cannot be tampered with, we will remind them of the old Roman maxim which was used by the Caesars and is today being so efficiently used by Great Britain in order to solidify imperialism upon various and diverse national groups: "Divide and rule."

Printed in the *NW*, Saturday, 14 June 1919.

1. This referred to Rev. R. D. Jonas.

Arden A. Bryan to the *Negro World*

[14 June 1919]

To the Editor of The Negro World:

I notice a certain college professor has given us food for thought concerning Egypt, part of our fatherland, Africa. This white man, says the Globe, tells a story that a handful of white men and loyal Hindu troopers for three days fought off thousands of rebel natives until relief came from Cairo.

He says this shows how little progress civilization has made against the dark frontiers since the dawn of recorded history.

Cairo and Alexandria represent modern civilization and the north shore of Africa, but in the days of Rome, Carthage represented civilization there before them. So much of modern Africa was civilized then, as today. In the East, European civilization is maintained only by force of arms or trade, as in the case of India and China, and could be overswept, swallowed and obliterated in a day by that older civilization of the East.

With all its vaunted inventions, all its improvements in alleviating life and then making i[t] miserable in prolonging life and taking it, Europe is unable to break its bounds. The white writer concludes with, "Perhaps the trouble is with European civilization."

Just so, I can assure him. If Europe will let Africa alone, and if his cousin, the English, will stop meddling with Asiatic and African affairs, then there will be no more cause for uprisings in the East. Keep out of Africa! Keep out of Asia! Stop trying to tell the other fellow how to run household affairs. He will not tolerate your interference, especially when he is much riper than you, and he sees and knows you are advising him terrible destruction.

Africa has given her Ethiopic alphabet to the now modern world as a guide which shows Africa was in the lead or is the leader of civilization. We like the Irish claim: Withdraw your forces, which rule us only by tyrant subjugation, not only England but all Europe, and we will prove to the world that Africa, at home and abroad, is capable of self-determination.

ARDEN A. B[RY]AN[1]

Printed in the *NW*, Saturday, 14 June 1919. Original headline has been omitted.

1. Arden A. Bryan (1893–1971) was the first field secretary and sales manager of the Black Star Line, a position that he held from the summer of 1919 until early 1921, except for a brief interlude in 1919–20 when Harry R. Watkis held this position. Born in Bridgetown, Barbados, Bryan worked for three years in Panama before migrating to the United States in 1914. When he joined the UNIA, he was employed as an elevator operator in New York City. Known also as "Socrates," a nickname that Garvey is said to have given him, Bryan was made UNIA commissioner for Connecticut in 1921–22; for a period he was also foreign affairs editor of the *Negro World*. Bryan was the organizer in 1933 of the Nationalist-Negro Movement and African Colonization Association, with himself as president, Charles B. Cumberbatch as secretary, and Adina Grant as treasurer. Its aim was to try to obtain the former German colony of Cameroon as a concession from the League of Nations for the purpose of black American colonization. (*Garvey* v. *United States*, pp. 1379–1401; AFRC, RG 163, registration card; interview with the editor, 1971).

Robert Lansing, Secretary of State, to A. S. Burleson, Postmaster General

WASHINGTON June 14, 1919

The Secretary of State presents his compliments to the Honorable the Postmaster General[1] and has the honor to transmit the enclosed communication for consideration and such action as may be required.

[ROBERT LANSING]

[*Typewritten reference*] 5A
[*Endorsements*] Solicitor   HCH

DNA, RG 28, File B-398. TN, Recipient's copy. Endorsements are handwritten.

1. Albert Sidney Burleson (1863–1937) was appointed postmaster general by President Wilson in March 1913. Burleson later acknowledged receipt of this letter from Lansing, and replied that the complaint of the British Guiana government "will receive careful attention." (A. S. Burleson to Robert Lansing, 28 July 1919, DNA, RG 28, file B-398; *NYT*, 25 November 1937).

Enclosure

AMERICAN CONSULATE.
Georgetown, Guiana, May 9, 1919

CONFIDENTIAL.
SUBJECT: Requesting inf[or]mation for the British Guiana Government concerning certain publications issued in the United States.

Sir:

I have the honor to advise that recently certain publications have been received in this colony from the United States, evidently issued by Negro publishers, which appear to adopt a policy of antagonism to the white race, and which are causing the British Guiana Government some anxiety. The Government would like to prevent their receipt and distribution, but owing to the fact that the black population is several times that of the white and includes some prominent persons such as officials, lawyers, doctors and ministers, they are uncertain as to the advisability of taking the necessary steps here to prevent their circulation.[1]

The Inspector General of Police called at the consulate in connection with the matter and enquired as to whether any action had been taken in the United States to investigate the nature of these publications, stating that they were becoming alarmed as to what might result from an unrestricted circulation in the colony of these papers on account of the nature of some of their articles. Being unable to advise him as to the situation in connection with these papers in the United States, I informed him that I would be glad to present the matter confidentially to the Department of State and request such information as it might be able to supply, provided his Government considered it advisable.

I am enclosing herewith a copy of a communication received from the Colonial Secretary[2] in which he states that His Excellency would be much obliged if confidential enquiries could be made in the United States concerning these papers, and enclosing four copies of publications for my information. Unfortunately these papers cannot be transmitted as it was requested that they be returned after perusal.

The papers enclosed were as follows:

"The Crusader" of April, 1919, Vol. 1, No. 8, published monthly by Cyril V. Briggs,[3] at 2299 Seventh Avenue, New York, N.Y.

"The Negro World" of February 8, 1919, Vol. 1, No. 26, Marcus G[ar]vey, Managing Editor, published at 36–38 West 135th Street, New York, N.Y.

"The Monitor"[4] of March 15, 1919, Vol. IV, No. 37, published by the Rev. John Albert Williams[5] at Omaha, Nebraska. A weekly publication.

"The Christian Recorder"[6] the Official Organ of the African Methodist Church of March 20, 1919, Vol. LXVI, No. [3]3, published weekly at 631 Pine Street, Philadelphia, Pennsylvania.

I have read these papers carefully and am unable to find anything objectionable in "The Monitor" and "The Christian Recorder", but the "Crusader" and "The Negro World" both have articles that would appear antagonistic to the white race, and it is these two papers that the Inspector General of Police considered dangerous if circulated freely among the Negro population of the colony. It appears that the publishers forward these publications in packages addressed to local persons who act as agents or distributors.

I shall be glad if the Department can supply the confidential information requested by His Excellency, the Officer Administering the Government. I have the honor to be, Sir, Your obedient servant,

G. E. CHAMBERLIN[7]
Consul

Enclosure: Letter from the Colonial
Secretary, May 3, 1919.
[*Address*] THE HONORABLE THE
SECRETARY OF STATE, WASHINGTON,
D.C.
[*Typewritten reference*] No. 282.

DNA, RG 28, File B-398. TLS, Carbon copy.

1. The secretary of state for the colonies, Lord Milner, advised the governors of the West Indian colonies that "in view of the existence of some unrest among the coloured population of

the West Indies, [they] should be prepared . . . to approve of the exercise of stricter control over the press by means of legislation giving power to suppress any publications of a character either seditious or calculated to incite to crime" (PRO, CO 318/349, Secretary of State, 10 September 1919, file 46872). On 13 September 1919, the acting governor in British Guiana introduced a special seditious publications ordinance, modeled on the Straits Settlements Ordinance No. 11 of 1915. It was met with a wave of protest, however, causing it to be amended on 26 September 1919, and finally withdrawn after its second reading. In February 1920, a new seditious publications bill was again introduced, but it was never formally enacted. Special seditious ordinances, however, were passed in the Bahamas (Act 28/1919), Grenada (Ordinance 6/1920), the Leeward Islands (Act 9/1920), St. Vincent (Ordinance 19/1920), and Trinidad and Tobago (Ordinance 10/1920). (See W. F. Elkins, "Marcus Garvey, the *Negro World*, and the British West Indies, 1919–1920," *Science and Society* 36:1 [Spring 1972]:63–77).

2. A reference to George Ball Green (b. 1872), assistant colonial secretary of British Guiana, (*Colonial Office List*, 1924 [London: HMSO, 1924]).

3. Cyril Valentine Briggs (1887–1966) was a leading black communist and a vocal critic of Marcus Garvey. (See Biographical Supplement, Appendix I).

4. The *Monitor*, a black newspaper published in Omaha, Neb., began publication on 3 July 1915 and ceased publication on 11 January 1929.

5. Rev. John Albert Williams (1866–1933) was the rector of the Episcopal Church of St. Philip the Deacon in Omaha, Neb., a position he held for thirty years. Born in Canada, he grew up in Detroit. He received his bachelor of divinity degree from Seabury Western Theological Seminary in 1891 and was ordained an Episcopal priest in the same year. He was appointed the historian of the diocese of Nebraska in 1906, and the associate editor of the *Crozier*, the official journal of the Nebraska Episcopal diocese in 1909, and editor-in-chief in 1912. Williams became the missionary bishop of Haiti in 1921. (*New Era*, 29 September 1922; *Crisis*, 7:2 [December 1913]: 66).

6. The *Christian Recorder* is the oldest surviving black newspaper in the United States. As the organ of the African Methodist Episcopal church, it evolved from a monthly magazine started by the New York Conference of the AME in 1841. By 1848 sufficient support was received for weekly publication and its official name became the *Christian Herald*. The present name was adopted in 1852, under the editorship of Jabez Campbell. In 1919 the journal was edited by Rev. R. R. Wright, Jr.

7. George Ellsworth Chamberlin (b. 1872) was appointed American consul at Georgetown, British Guiana, 24 April 1914, serving there until September 1919. (*U.S. Department of State Register, 1924* [Washington: GPO, 1924]).

Enclosure

COLONIAL SECRETARY'S OFFICE,
Georgetown, Demerara, 3rd May, 1919

CONFIDENTIAL

COPY.

Sir:

With reference to the interview which the Inspector General of Police had with you upon the subject, I am directed by the Officer Administering the Government[1] to transmit herewith copies of the following publications issued in the United States:

"The Crusader"
"The Monitor"
"The Recorder"
"The Negro World"

It would seem desirable that some enquir[i]es should be instigated with a view of determining whether or not any action should be taken to restrict the circulation of any of these publications which appear to adopt a policy of antagonism to the white race, and His Excellency would be much obliged if you will cause confidential inquiries to be made in the United States concerning these papers.

I will be glad if you will return the papers after perusal. I have the honor to be, Sir, Your obedient servant,

GEO BALL-GREENE,
Acting Colonial Secretary

[*Address*] G. E. Chamberlin, Esquire,
Consul of the United States of America,
Georgetown.
[*Typewritten reference*] No. 2183.

DNA, RG 28, File B-398, TL, Transcript.

1. Sir Cecil Clementi, CMG (1875–1947) was colonial secretary of British Guiana from 1913 until 1922. (*WWW*, 1941–50).

Editorial Letter by Marcus Garvey

[[New York, June 18, 1919]]

Fellowmen of the Negro Race, Greeting:

Last week I wrote to inform you that the Universal Negro Improvement Association was preparing itself for a battle to offset the designs of its enemies in their attempt to interfere with the success of our world-wide movement.

Today I am able to inform you that whilst I was away from New York on a lecture of the States of Michigan, Virginia and of Canada several traitors of the race plotted to use the office of the District Attorney of New York to intimidate and scare the officers of the association left behind. Fortunately, on my way to Canada from Virginia, I stopped off in New York for a couple of hours and then I found that there was half a dozen summons issued for the secretaries of the association to appear before the Grand Jury.

I hastened down to the District Attorney, accompanied by one of the secretaries of the association, and got him to issue a summons for me also. The hearing was dated for Monday, the 16th, as I had to speak in Canada and was unable to reach New York for the original date of the 12th. On Monday several officers and myself went to the District Attorney in answer to the summons. We were there confronted by four Negro traitors (stool pigeons) who had gone to the District Attorney and told him all that the Universal Negro Improvement Association ever did and all that it never did. He had on his desk copies of The Negro World. He was presented with the Constitution of the organization and everything else that the traitors thought would have done harm to the organization. The District Attorney was so well informed about the association that for that matter he could have been one of the highest officers. He was able to tell in his own way the history of the association from the information he got from the stool-pigeons. His purpose was to return an indictment against Marcus Garvey on the charges of the four traitors. All the books and documents of the association were presented to the District Attorney and he, when he found that the men had "fallen down" on the first charge they made, asked them what next. They said that if they were to see the records and the books of the association they could prefer their charges. The officers of the association consented and at 11 o'clock the books, papers and documents of the association were laid before the four traitors wherefrom to find their charge against Marcus Garvey. They had the use of the books and documents of the association until 4 o'clock, at which time the District Attorney returned to place his indictment upon the charges of the traitors. They failed to find any charge and the District Attorney dismissed the matter. The attorney was very much against the idea of a Black Star Line and then I was forced to tell him that even as there is a White Star Line[1] owned by white men, there is going to be a Black Star Line owned by black men.

The Universal Negro Improvement Association has thus scored a victory over the four traitors, William Bridges[2] and their accomplices, whose names will be published in bold black type in the next issue of The Negro World.

On Sunday night [*22 June*] their names will be on exhibition at the Palace Casino, 135th street and Madison avenue, New York, so that every member of the race may know the Benedict Arnolds of our cause.

The association has pledged itself to give the people a "Black Star Line" and they are going to have it in spite of all. The Negro means to combat the white man's right to stop him from doing what he wants to do. This is a free for all age and black, white and yellow men shall have their rights irrespective of the opposition of either.

The Universal Negro Improvement Association has become too strong all over the world to be defeated in the State of New York. What doesn't satisfy us with the district authorities then we shall take to the State authorities. What doesn't satisfy us with the State authorities, then we shall take to the National authorities, and when questions involving the destiny of the Negroes of the world can't be settled by the national authorities of the countries of the world, then there is the African battlefield for which the Negroes of the world are preparing.

Some people take ten years to get even with their enemies. The Universal Negro Improvement Association is prepared to wait one hundred years, but the next world war is not so far distant—Negroes of the world, prepare; Yours fraternally,

MARCUS GARVEY

Printed in the *NW*, Saturday, 21 June 1919. Original headlines have been omitted.

1. "The White Star Line" began sailing to the United States from Liverpool in June 1849. It later sailed the British-Australian route as "The Liverpool White Star Line" of Australia.

2. William Bridges (1891– ?) and Hubert H. Harrison founded the Liberty party of America in August 1920. Born in Jackson, Fla., Bridges worked in a Harlem hotel as a waiter during the war. In 1917 he became a member of the Socialist party's People's Educational Forum which met informally in Harlem. In 1918 he founded the *Challenge*, which he published until late 1919, when he helped to found the National Negro Realty and Holding Co., Inc. He eventually drifted away from his relationship with the Liberty party and became associated with Tammany Hall; in the meantime, after a visit to the Socialist party headquarters in Wisconsin in September 1920, where he received a warm welcome, Bridges returned to Harlem and made several speeches urging black voters to support the Socialists. (DNA, RG 65, files Misc. 22274; BS 202606-1531; OG 208369, 211979, 256421, 258121, 272751, 329359, 369342, 374214, 390776; *NW*, 19 June 1920).

Newspaper Report

[*World*, 19 June 1919]

DISTRICT ATTORNEY SINKS "THE BLACK STAR LINE." HEAD OF NEGRO STEAMSHIP PROJECT PROMISES NOT TO COLLECT ANY MORE FUNDS

"The Black Star Line," advertised as "a fleet of steamships to trade in the interests of the colored race," by the Universal Negro Improvement Association and the African Communities League, with headquarters at No. 38 West 135th Street, was torpedoed and sunk yesterday by Assistant District Attorney Kilroe.[1] He instructed Marcus Garvey, colored, President of both organizations to refrain from collecting any more funds. Garvey promised to refrain.

According to Mr. Kilroe, who has examined Garvey and his "General Ladies' Secretary," Amy Ashwood, also colored, of No. 552 Lenox Avenue, Garvey has collected about $3,000 in this city and throughout the United States and Canada. The investigation was made at the request of a committee of the association, who complained that Garvey's organizations were about bankrupt.

The committee, headed by U. T. Mitchell of No. 79 West 141st Street, told Mr. Kilroe that Garvey had been selling bonds with little security back of them and had taken in about $2,000. Garvey said about $320 had been raised for the "Black Star Line" and all but $150 had gone to cover expenses "which came up." Garvey also is managing editor of the Negro World.

Printed in the *World*, Thursday, 19 June 1919.

1. Edwin Patrick Kilroe (1883–1953) graduated from Columbia University with an LL.B. degree in 1906 and a Ph.D. in 1913. He was appointed a deputy attorney general of New York in 1916, a position that he held until 1923. In March 1921, Kilroe was convicted in a bigamy case of conspiracy to obstruct justice, but the following December the conviction was overturned and Kilroe resumed his office until his resignation in 1923. A lifelong Irish-Catholic Democrat,

Kilroe served for many years as the unofficial historian of Tammany Hall. In 1941 he was elected a director of Twentieth Century-Fox, having previously served as its legal counsel. (*NYT*, 31 March 1921, 30 December 1922; 28 December 1923, 10 July 1953).

Marcus Garvey to the News Editor of the *World*

NEW YORK June 19, 1919

Dear Sir:

On the 32nd page of your paper of today's date there appeared a news article under the caption of "District Attorney Sinks the Black Star Line".

I hereby beg to inform you that your newspaper has misrepresented the truth to the reading public, and for that matter a mass meeting of Negroes is called for Sunday night the 22nd inst at 8.30 P.M. o'clock in the Palace Casino, 135th Street and Madison Avenue to give the lie to the public/ation/ and in all fairness to you, I ask that you send a reporter to the meeting to glean the facts for yourself as the veracity of the paper will be attacked by the principleal speaker of the evening. Yours truly,

Universal Negro Improvement Association
MARCUS GARVEY
President

NNC, *W*. TLS, Recipient's copy. Corrections and additions in Garvey's hand.

Rear-Admiral A. P. Niblack to W. E. Allen

WASHINGTON 20th June, 1919

My dear Mr. Allen:

Enclosed for your information is a report relating to radical agitation aimed at negro labor submitted to this Office by the Bureau of Ordnance[1] under date of June 17th. Very truly yours,

A. P. NIBLACK
Rear-Admiral, U.S.N.
Director of Naval Intelligence.
[*Signed by*] G M Baum
By direction.

[*Typewritten reference*] GFS*MAM
[*Handwritten endorsements*] Noted by
J[ohn] T. S[uter][2] EmR DG
[*Stamped endorsements*] NOTED J. E. H.
NOTED F.D.W.

DNA, RG 65, File OG 3057. TLS, Recipient's copy.

1. The Bureau of Naval Ordnance, Washington, D.C., was responsible for the design, production, issue, and maintenance of supplies for the U.S. Navy. However, since the production and inspection of war material created labor problems, the bureau also coordinated labor relations for the Navy Department, maintaining liaison with the War Labor Policy Board, the War Labor Board, and the War Department.

2. John T. Suter succeeded William Elby Allen as assistant chief of the Bureau of Investigation in April 1919. (Dept. of Justice Personnel Records).

Enclosure

OFFICE OF NAVAL INSPECTOR OF ORDNANCE

New Jersey District, Old Post Office Building
New York City. June 14, 1919

From: Lieut. Edward L. Tinker, U.S.N.R.F.[1]
To: Bureau of Ordnance.
Subject, Radical Agitation Aimed at Negro Labor.

1.   Copies of the "Crisis" and the "Messenger",[2] negro radical magazines, were recently forwarded, and the attention of the Bureau was called to an organized agitation of the negro among negroes. Since that time many new facts have been ascertained.

2.   Many new negro organizations have been formed, and those already existing have taken on a new lease of life; while all are unanimous in demanding political equality and social recognition for the negro, a goodly number advocate revolution and the Soviet form of government as the only solution of the negro problem.

3.   A partial list of those organizations, together with their chief movers and official organs are given below.

> A. THE UNIVERSAL NEGRO IMPROVEMENT ASSOCIATION AND AFRICAN COMMUNITY LEAGUE, of which Marcus Garvey (negro) is the promoter. Its headquarters are in New York and their League publishes an ultra radical sheet known as the Negro World. . . .[3]

4. Many signs point to the facts that all these negro associations are joining hands with Irish Sinn Feiners, Hindu, Egyptians, Japanese and Mexicans. . . .[4]

5. A glance at the names of the white backers of these black associations show that they are all under the tutelage of radicals and socialists who, through their agents and the emissaries and literature of the Civil Liberties Bureau[5] and Worker's Defence Union[6] are doing their best to inflame the negro mind and cause serious unrest.

6. In conclusion the attention of the Bureau is invited to the fact that the Negro is a very emotional race with marked lack of self control. If he be continuously inflamed by recitals of his wrongs and incited to action by all the various influences mentioned, there is grave danger that serious negro disorders may result. This, however, is what some of ~~the~~ /his/ white advisors probably wish for.

EDWARD L. TINKER

DNA, RG 74, File 34034-951-1000. TDS, Recipient's copy.

1. Lt. Edward L. Tinker (b. 1880) served as the assistant inspector of ordnance as of 1 February 1919. (*Register of Commissioned Officers of U.S. Navy, 1919* [Washington: GPO, 1919]).

2. Copies of the *Negro World* (21 and 28 June 1919) and the *Messenger* (July 1919) were sent by Tinker to the Bureau of Ordnance. (Lt. Edward L. Tinker to Bureau of Ordnance, Navy Department, 1 July 1919, DNA, RG 74, file 34034-951-1000).

3. Other black organizations and "radical organs" listed by Tinker were the League of Democracy, New York City; National Colored Liberty Conference, Boston; the People's Movement and Unity Club, Chicago; the National Association for the Promotion of Labor Unionism among Negroes led by Chandler Owen and A. Philip Randolph; the NAACP, the *Messenger*, and *Chicago Defender*.

4. The "signs" consisted of an address in March 1919 in Chicago by "Rev. Pat. H. O'Donnell, an Irish Sinn Feiner" before a meeting of the People's Movement and Unity Club "at which were present 500 negro soldiers and a goodly number of Hindus"; the membership of W. E. B. Du Bois in the League of Small and Subject Nationalities, in which Lajpat Rai "the Hindu revolutionary leader . . . who was arrested here and charged with plotting a rebellion in India, is a prominent member"; and the conference in New York City between Kuroiwa, the Japanese publisher on his way to attending the Peace Conference, and "Phillip Randolph, the negro editor of the Messenger and several other ultra radical negroes."

5. The National Civil Liberties Bureau (NCLB) was formed on 2 July 1917 out of the Bureau of Conscientious Objectors organized by Roger Nash Baldwin, who was at the time also executive director of the American Union Against Militarism (AUAM). Baldwin directed the new organization, with L. Hollingsworth Wood as chairman and Norman Thomas as vice-chairman. In January 1920, the NCLB changed its name to the American Civil Liberties Union. (Lamson, *Roger Baldwin, Founder of the American Civil Liberties Union*).

6. The Workers' Defense Union had a very brief existence; it published only two bulletins, on 15 April and 26 May 1919. (DNA, RG 165, file 10110).

Debate between Marcus Garvey and William Bridges

[*Negro World*, 21 June 1919]

WILLIAM BRIDGES, STEPLADDER AGITATOR ON LENOX AVE., CHASED OFF AVENUE AS TRAITOR TO RACE

On Saturday night last [*14 June*], Lenox avenue, New York city, was crowded with thousands of people at the corner of 138th street, where Mr. Marcus Garvey, President of the Universal Negro Improvement Association, met Mr. William Bridges, editor of a little magazine that he sells on the avenue every night after haranguing the passers-by for hours.

Bridges has made it a custom to attack prominent public men and institutions on the avenue, to impugn things against them, thereby catering to those who may take delight in scandalizing the reputation of others. All last summer this man Bridges succeeded in abusing some of the noblest members of the race and was able to "get away with it," but last Saturday night he met his Waterloo at the hands of Mr. Marcus Garvey whom he had attacked in his absence from the city on a tour of the country. On Mr. Garvey's arrival from Canada he consulted with the members of the New York Division of the Universal Negro Improvement Association and it was decided that he would appear on the avenue at a public mass meeting to challenge Mr. Bridges. Mr. Garvey served notice on Bridges at 12 o'clock Saturday that he was to gather all his facts against the association and the president and to tell them to the people on the avenue at 9 o'clock that night. At 9 o'clock a huge crowd gathered and Mr. Garvey was introduced to the people by Mr. Wa[l]ter Farrell, the Associate Male Secretary of the New York local.[1] Mr. Garvey was greeted with cheers. On taking the platform he explained to the assembled multitude that the meeting was called for the purpose of answering one William Bridges, a stepladder orator of the avenue, who for over two years has been attacking the reputation of prominent public men and organizations for the purpose of finding a way to sell a lot of literary rubbish he publishes under the name of "The Challenge."

Mr. Garvey said that before he addressed the people he would offer the platform to the man Bridges for half an hour to tell what he knew about the Universal Negro Improvement Association and its president. Bridges was afraid to appear, but public opinion forced him to take the stand.

During the half-hour that was given Bridges to speak, the people awaited anxiously to hear what was wrong with Mr. Garvey or the organization, but Bridges was unable to reveal anything new except the old-time white man's propaganda of Negroes being unable to do anything except led by him—the white man. Bridges said that the association could not achieve the things it had set out for itself; that Mr. Garvey had robbed the people and that he would be indicted by the District Attorney. Bridges, in the course of his remarks, revealed the fact (because he was not sensible enough to handle the situation) that he and others had been plotting to injure Mr. Garvey and the association. Bridges, who pretended to be a Democratic vote-getter, has been trying for some time to popularize himself among the people on the avenue in Harlem, but failed for two years to gain the confidence of anyone. Mr. Garvey, who is not a politician but a pro-Negro, in the space of a few months was able to rally around him over 10,000 people in Harlem as members and supporters of the Universal Negro Improvement Association. This was too much for Bridges and the little politicians of the district, so they plotted to have the District Attorney indict Mr. Garvey, as revealed through the senseless prating of Bridges on the avenue.

Bridges was visibly nervous all through his rambling talk to the people. Some hooted him and Mr. Garvey had to ask the people to give the man a fair chance to speak.

When his half-hour was up he was hissed from the stand and Mr. Garvey was again introduced. He was cheered to the echo as he resumed the stand. In a most brilliant speech he explained the strength of the association and challenged any man, or even government, to break the association. He cited the fact that he had been before the public in Harlem for just twelve months with the association. In that space of time he had built up a worldwide movement and that others whom he met a year ago in Harlem were still at the same place and that the man Bridges for several years had done nothing else but sell trashy magazines to the people.

Mr. Garvey was acclaimed when he referred to Bridges as a "beast in the image of God," citing the following "that immediately after slavery a white man wrote a book in which he asserted that the "Negro" was a beast in the image of God,"[2] claiming the following arguments: "That the nation was about to admit into full fledged citizenship 4,000,000 of black people to enjoy equal rights with 30,000,000 of whites and that these blacks had never done anything on their own initiative; that they had never built any government of their own, never constructed any steamships, railroads, or built any buildings or institutions, while the whites had contributed everything to civilization. That the Negro was capable of doing anything only when forced or put to work like the horse, mule, cow or donkey; that the horse when harnessed will perform work of its master, so does the Negro when put to labor; that the lower animals could do nothing on their own initiative and neither does the Negro, hence the Negro was but a beast in the image of God.["] Mr. Garvey said that the audacity of that white man who wrote that was above question; but here is a Negro, William Bridges, coming before enlightened American, West Indian and African Negroes at this time to tell them that they cannot do anything except when led by the white men. Mr. Garvey shouted that if there was a beast in the image of God, then that beast was William Bridges. The thousands on the avenue cheered Mr. Garvey in the declaration for over five minutes.

Mr. J. Certain,[3] one of the Vice-presidents of the New York Division of the association, a native of Florida, said that he was ashamed of Bridges who had disgraced the glorious State of Florida by being born there.

Miss Amy Ashwood asked the thousands who assembled for three cheers for the Universal Negro Improvement Association and the people cheered wildly for several minutes. At this stage a man by the name of Gibson attempted to make a remark in support of Bridges and he was saved from injury by the members of the association when they saw that the crowd was bent on mobbing him. The man ran away and left his hat. After this the meeting came to a close and the crowd quietly dispersed.

Printed in the *NW*, Saturday, 21 June 1919.

1. Walter Napier Farrell (b. 1884) was born in the British West Indies; in 1918 he was employed as a porter by Proser Brothers of New York City. (AFRC, RG 163, registration card).

2. Garvey was referring to the title of the book by Charles Carroll, *The Negro a Beast; or, In the Image of God* (St. Louis: American Book and Bible House, 1900), a work which attempted to revive the theory that blacks possessed an apelike nature, which it interpreted as a sign of a preadamic creation. Carroll's book is regarded as the ultimate extension of religious racism in America, and was the subject of refutation by several authors, such as Henry Parker Eastman, *The Negro, His Origin, History and Destiny* . . . (Boston: Eastern Publishing, 1905). For additional information, see George M. Frederickson, *The Black Image in the White Mind: The Debate on Afro-American Character and Destiny, 1817–1914* (New York: Harper & Row, 1971).

3. Jeremiah M. Certain was a vice-president of both the UNIA and the Black Star Line. He was born in Florida, and when he met Garvey in early 1919, he was self-employed as a cigar manufacturer in Passaic, N. J. Certain later formed the Gold Dollar Cigar Manufacturing Co. in 1921. (*NW*, 1 January 1921). (*Garvey* v. *United States*, pp. 1290–1311).

Address by Marcus Garvey at the Palace Casino

[*Negro World*, 21 June 1919]

Over three thousand persons, members and friends of the Universal Negro Improvement Association, assembled at the Palace Casino, 135th street and Madison avenue, New York City, Sunday evening, June 15, to greet Mr. Marcus Garvey, president-general and International Organizer of the association, who has just returned to the city after an extended lecture tour in Michigan, Virginia and Canada.

Mr. Edgar M. Grey, general secretary of the association, called the meeting to order a few minutes after nine o'clock, by the singing of the opening hymn, "From Greenland's Icy Mountains." After a few brief remarks by the chairman, a musical program consisting of one violin solo by Master William Wilkinson, accompanied by his sister, Miss Edith Wilkinson, and a piano solo by Miss Irene Callender was rendered. Mr. George Tobias, treasurer of the association, was next presented to the audience and surprised his hearers and friends by revealing unsuspected talent as a reader, when he gave an impressive rendition of Wendell Phillips' great oration on Toussaint L'Overture. [1]

The next speaker introduced was Miss Henrietta Vinton Davis, the popular and talented elocutionist of Washington, D.C., who, as a tribute to the children who had so splendidly entertained for the evening, recited a poem entitled "Little Brown Baby with Sparkling Eyes," written by Paul Lawrence Dunbar, poet laureate of the Negro race.

In order to make the recitation as realistic as possible, Miss Davis used for the occasion a large colored doll manufactured by Berry & Ross, [2] who had very kindly loaned it for the occasion. At the end of the recitation Miss Davis made a stirring appeal for support for the factory that was doing so much to inculcate a spirit of race pride in the Negro race.

Following this the chairman asked for a silver collection, which was heartily and liberally responded to. Taking as his theme, the subject of race pride, the chairman then made a few short and cryptic remarks in which he pointed out that the principal concern of the race was not so much in finding out how to die but in learning how to live.

At the close of his address the chairman then introduced as the next speaker the person whose commanding personality was responsible for the vast assemblage that evening, Mr. Marcus Garvey. Mr. Garvey began his address by thanking all those who had supported the officers of the association, while he was absent touring the West, Canada and the South. He then told how efforts were being made by enemies of the association to discredit both himself and the organization. He specifically named Mr. William Bridges, editor of the "Challenge Magazine," and a well known stepladder orator on Lenox avenue, as having assailed him in many ways while he was away. On his return to the city he had taken up the gauntlet and challenged the editor of the "Challenge" to meet him in open debate, which Mr. Bridges at first declined, but under pressure of public opinion was compelled to accept. Mr. Garvey then outlined the debate which had taken place the night before at the corner of 138th street and Lenox avenue, and which he assured his audience resulted in the complete and inglorious defeat of his opponent. The speaker also told of the plots engineered against himself and the organization by a cabal of envious and malicious individuals, who being incapable of thinking internationally, were doing everything of an underhand nature to wreck the organization; but inasmuch as the organization had firmly established itself in a majority of the States of the Union, the islands of West Indies, several republics of South and Central America and on the west coast of Africa, it was next to impossible for any group of men or any government to entirely destroy it. He was there that evening, he said, for the purpose of defending himself and the organization, and to give a detailed explanation of the feasibility of the Black Star Line project.

He then roused his audience to the highest pitch of enthusiasm when he recited to them the prowess of the black race and how it was possible for the scattered millions of Negroes all over the world to accomplish the liberation of Africa by supporting the plans of the Universal Negro Improvement Association and African Communities League. Dramatically striking his chest, Mr. Garvey convincingly assured his hearers that all cowardice had departed from his anatomy, "for," he said, "if I could have died on the field of Flanders of France in the white man's cause, I can die in America fighting for myself and my race." At this a storm of applause rent the building. Men and women rose to their feet and handkerchiefs were waved over head as every individual vied with his neighbor to show that the orator had transmitted the spirit of courage from himself to the entire audience.

After scathingly condemning those who were opposing the organization as "white men's niggers" and cowards, the speaker told of the great work that was being done by the Newport News branch, which had pledged itself to subscribe $100,000 for the purpose of making the Black Star Line a reality. At the close of his address, which lasted for over an hour and generously applauded throughout, Mr. Garvey made an eloquent and impressive appeal for funds to help the Universal Negro Improvement Association and African Communities' League in the prosecution of its many plans for the liberation of the Negroes of the world and the founding of a Negro nation on the continent of Africa. The audience showed their sincere appreciation of the evening's exercises by subscribing most liberally.

Printed in the *NW*, Saturday, 21 June 1919. Original headlines have been omitted.

1. Wendell Phillips (1811–1884), noted orator and abolitionist, delivered his oration on Toussaint L'Ouverture before audiences in New York and Boston in 1861. The text of his speech was first published as a pamphlet in 1863 and later in his *Speeches, Lectures and Letters* (Boston: Walker, Wise & Co., 1864). (*NCAB*).

2. The Berry & Ross Toy and Doll Manufacturing Co. was a black enterprise located in Harlem.

Draft of a *World* News Report

[*New York, 22 June 1919*]

BLACK STAR LINE

Marcus Garvey, President of the Universal Negro Improvement Association, who promised Assistant District Attorney Kilroe to collect no more funds to inaugurate "The Black Star Line" of steamships "to trade in the interest of the negro race", yesterday cleared decks for action, ordered full speed ahead and sent a warning shot over the bow of the legal craft in the form of a challenge to Mr. Kilroe, the World and others to/"come out" and/sink his prospective fleet if they dare.

A summons sent by Mr. Kilroe to Garvey at his headquarters, No. 38 West 135th Street, to appear before him yesterday, was treated by the "Admiral" of the "Black Star" fleet as a "scrap of paper" and tossed to the trade winds—he did not appear. On the contrary he announced by printed circular, that he would appear on the bridge at the Palace Casino, /135th Street and Madison Avenue,/ tonight at 8:30 [*inserted* McNevin[1] cover] and fire a broadside at the enemy.

"A challenge to District Attorney Kilroe, the lying New York World and the negro traitors, Mitchell, Cox, Johnson, Robinson[2] and Bridges", says the circular in letters mast high. "A dare to stop the inaugurating of the Black Star Line. Marcus Garvey issues the challenge. The New Negro shall meet this foe on any battle ground. There shall be freedom and true Democracy for all. Be early and get seats."

Learning of this circular Mr. Kilroe, from the deck of the legal craft, wigwagged to Garvey to come aboard yesterday, but got no signal in reply. He then ordered a flotilla of "plain clothes" destroyers to weigh [in at the?] dock at the Palace Casino pier tonight with [the] instructions to sink the

"Black Star" fleet if Garvey fires any fund-collecting shells in the direction of the audience. He also semaphored the detective commanders of the flotilla to depth-bomb the meeting if they discover evidences of any submarining /by Garvey/.

The negroes named in Garvey's "challenge" are members of a committee of the Negro Improvement Association who complained to the District Attorney that they had found the organization, under Garvey's leadership, to be bankrupt, though it has collected about $3,000. Garvey was examined by Mr. Kilroe and said he had taken in $320 for the "Black Star Line" and had only $150 of it, the rest having gone for "expenses."

When Garvey ignored his subpoena Mr. Kilroe said he might seaplane up to the meeting in person tonight as he believed the circular is a criminal libel, though he considers the "Black Star" only a phantom fleet.

JOHNSON

[*Endorsement*] Please save copy if not used,
for day desk

NNC, *W*. TMS. Insertions and endorsement are handwritten.
 1. A staff reporter of the *World*.
 2. Norman Albert Robinson (b. 1882) was born in the United States. He was employed by the Post Office Department until 1945. (AFRC, RG 163, registration card).

World News Memorandum

[*New York, 22 June 1919*]

Memo for Mr. Smith
 McNevin says Marcus Garvey spoke /tonight (Sunday)/ at a meeting of 1500 negroes at the Palace Casino, 135th Street and Madison Avenue, claiming he has been libelled by the World and threate[ni]ng to sue for $100,000. The meeting was under the auspices of the Universal Negro Improvement Association and the African Consumers' League. A collection to defray expenses was taken up—25 cents from each person.

 Garvey said the Black Star Line is not on the verge of bankruptcy but would have /its/ flag flying over at least one ship of its fleet on Oct. 31.

 He attacked President Wilson, saying the President "proved false to democracy when he permitted lynchings in America."

PORTER

[*Endorsement*] Mr. [Gavin?]

NNC, *W*. TN, Carbon copy.

Certificate of Incorporation of the Black Star Line, Inc.

[New York, 23rd day of June A.D. 1919]

We, the undersigned, in order to form a corporation for the purposes hereinafter stated, under and pursuant to the provisions of an Act of the Legislature of the State of Delaware, entitled "An Act Providing a General Corporation Law"[1] (approved March 10th, 1899) and the Acts amendatory thereof and supplemental thereto, do hereby certify as follows:

FIRST: The name of this Corporation is Black Star Line, Inc.

SECOND: Its principal office and place of business in the State of Delaware is to be located in Wilmington, County of New Castle. The agent in charge thereof is the Charter Service Corporation, 206 West Ninth Street, Wilmington, Delaware.

THIRD: The specific objects for which it is formed are as follows, namely:

> For the purpose of building for its own use, equipping, furnishing, fitting, purchasing, chartering, navigating or owning steam, sail or other boats, ships, vessels or other property, to be used in any lawful business, trade, commerce or navigation upon the ocean, or any seas, sounds, lakes, rivers, canals or other waterways and for the carriage, transportation or storing of lading, freight, mails, property or passengers thereon.

In general to do any and all things and to exercise any and all powers necessary or advisable to accomplish one or more of the purposes of the corporation or which shall at any time appear to be conducive to, or for the benefit of, said corporation in connection therewith which may now or hereafter be lawful for the corporation to do or exercise under and in pursuance of the laws of the State of Delaware, or of any other law that may be now or hereafter applicable to the corporation.

To conduct its business in any or all of its branches, so far as permitted by law, in the State of Delaware and in any other state of the United States of America, and in any territory, dependency, colony or possession thereof and in the District of Columbia, and in any foreign country, and in connection therewith, to hold, possess, purchase, mortgage, and convey real estate and personal property, and to maintain offices and agencies either within or anywhere without the State of Delaware.

FOURTH: The waters to be navigated are:

The Atlantic Ocean along the entire eastern seaboard of the United States, and the Dominion of Canada, Newfoundland and about Cuba, Porto

Rico and West Indian Islands, Central and South America, including the gulfs, bays, sounds, harbors and roadsteads along said coasts and adjacent thereto, and such navigable rivers as flow therein; the Pacific Ocean along the entire western seaboard of the United States, British Columbia, and Alaska, Lower California, Mexico, Central America and South America, including the gulfs, bays, sounds, harbors, and roadsteads along said coasts and adjacent thereto, and such navigable rivers as flow therein; the Gulf of Mexico and Panama Canal, the Gulf of California, Puget Sound, the Great Lakes, and all navigable waters and canals that flow therein, or may hereafter be constructed connecting any of the aforesaid waters, and all navigable inland waters of the United States, and of the Dominion of Canada; and also along the entire seaboard of the Continent of Africa, including the gulfs, bays, sounds, harbors, and roadsteads along said coasts and adjacent thereto, and such navigable rivers as flow therein; and those of such other continents as may hereafter be determined; it being the purpose of this provision to permit the Corporation to conduct its business in any part of the world, as far as may be permitted by law.

FIFTH: The amount of the total authorized capital stock of this corporation is Five Hundred Thousand ($500,000) dollars, divided into one hundred thousand (100,000) shares of five ($5.00) dollars each. The amount of capital stock with which it will commence business is One Thousand ($1,000.00) dollars, being two hundred (200) shares of the par value of Five ($5.00) dollars each.

SIXTH: The names and places of residence of each of the subscribers to the capital stock are as follows:

Names	Residences	No. of Shares
Marcus Garvey,	238 W. 131 St., N.Y.C.	40
Edgar M. Grey,	158 W. 141 St., N.Y.C.	40
Richard E. Warner,[2]	2412 7th Ave., N.Y.C.	40
George Tobias,	174 W. 136 St., N.Y.C.	40
Janie Jenkins,	35 W. 139 St., N.Y.C.	40

SEVENTH: The existence of this corporation is to be perpetual.

EIGHTH: The private property of the stockholders shall not be subject to the payment of corporate debts to any extent whatever.

NINTH: The directors[3] shall have power to make and to alter or amend the by-laws, to fix the amount to be reserved as working capital, and to authorize and cause to be executed mortgages and liens upon the real and personal property of this corporation.

With the consent in writing and pursuant to a vote of the holders of a majority of the capital stock issued and outstanding, the directors shall have authority to dispose in any manner of the whole property of this corporation.

The by-laws shall determine whether and to what extent the accounts and books of this corporation (other than the stock ledger) or any of them shall be open to the inspection of the stockholders, and no stockholder shall have any right of inspecting any account or book or document of this corporation, except as conferred by law, or the by-laws, or by resolution of the stockholders.

If the by-laws so provide and by vote of a majority of the whole Board the said directors shall have power to designate two or more of their number to constitute an executive committee, which committee shall for the time being, as provided in said resolution, or in the by-laws of this corporation, have and execute any or all of the powers of the Board of Directors in the management of the business and affairs of this corporation, and have power to authorize the seal of this corporation to be affixed to all papers which may require it.[4]

The signers of the Certificate of Incorporation being all the Incorporators, shall have the direction of the affairs and of the organization of the corporation, and may hold meeting or meetings in person or by proxy and at such meeting or meetings elect directors and take such steps as are proper to obtain the necessary subscriptions to the stock, and to perfect an organization of the corporation.

The stockholders and directors shall have power to hold their meetings and keep the books, documents and papers of the corporation (subject to the provisions of the statute) outside of the State of Delaware at such places as may be from time to time designated by them.

This corporation may in its by-laws, confer additional powers upon the directors supplemental to the powers and authorities expressly conferred upon them by the statute.

This corporation reserves the right to amend, alter, change or repeal any provision contained in the certificate of incorporation, in the manner now or hereafter prescribed by statute, and all rights conferred on stockholders herein are granted subject to this reservation.

It is the intention that the objects, purposes and powers specified in the third paragraph hereof shall, except where otherwise specified in said paragraph, be nowise limited or restricted by reference to or inference from the terms of any other clause or paragraph in this Certificate of Incorporation, but that the objects, purposes and powers specified in the third paragraph and in each of the clauses or paragraphs of this Charter shall be regarded as independent objects, purposes and powers.

We, the undersigned, do make, file and record this Certificate and do certify that the facts herein stated are true, and we do respectfully agree to take the number of shares of stock hereinbefore set forth, and have accordingly hereunto set our hands and seals this 23rd day of June A.D. 1919.

MARCUS GARVEY	(Seal)
EDGAR M. GREY,	(Seal)
RICHARD E. WARNER,	(Seal)
GEORGE W. TOBIAS,	(Seal)
JANIE JENKINS,	(Seal)

In the presence of:

Jas. S. Watson.

State of New York,

County of New York, ss:

Be It Remembered, that on this 26 day of June, A.D. 1919, personally came before me, the subscriber, a Notary Public for the State of New York, County of New York, Marcus Garvey, Edgar M. Grey, Richard E. Warner, George Tobias and Janie Jenkins, parties to the foregoing certificate of incorporation, known to me personally to be such, and severally acknowledged that they signed, sealed and delivered the said certificate as their act and deed, and that the facts therein stated are truly set forth.

Given under my hand and seal of office the day and year aforesaid.

JUNIUS MCD. GREEN,
Notary Public,
New York Co.
Reg. 256
10189

Reprinted from *Garvey* v. *United States*, No. 8317 (Ct. App., 2d Cir. Feb. 2, 1925), Government's Exhibit 1.

1. After the passage in 1899 of the Act Providing a General Corporation Law, the state of Delaware became particularly attractive for businesses due to its simple procedure for incorporation, its low corporate income tax, and the special privileges that it offered corporations for enlarged capitalization and the authority to adjust their internal management and financial organization.

2. Richard E. Warner, (b. 1883) a free-lance journalist, had been the managing editor of the *New York News* before his introduction to Garvey by Edgar M. Grey in mid-June 1919. He served for four weeks as executive secretary of the UNIA and secretary of the Black Star Line, after which he resigned; he was subsequently employed as a prohibition agent by the Internal Revenue Service on 25 August 1921, but he lost his job in 1927 after he was indicted for fraud on a charge of collecting money from prohibition law violators. (*Garvey* v. *United States*, pp. 144, 150, 182–83; AFRC, RG 163, registration card).

3. The first meeting of the incorporators of the Black Star Line was held on 27 June 1919, when the following directors were elected: Marcus Garvey, Edgar M. Grey, Richard B. Warner, George Tobias, Jeremiah M. Certain, Henrietta Vinton Davis, and Janie Jenkins.

4. The officers elected at the initial board of directors' meeting were: Garvey, president; Certain, first vice-president; Davis, second vice-president; Tobias, treasurer; Warner, secretary; Grey, assistant secretary; and Jenkins, assistant treasurer.

Editorial Letter by Marcus Garvey

[[New York, June 24, 1919]]

Message to Negro People of the World
President-General of Universal Negro
Improvement Association Writes

Fellowmen of the Negro Race:

Greeting:—It is with a heart full of gladness that I write to you this week. The news has come across the wires that there is to be peace. The Huns have signed.[1] This ushers in a new era, the era of preparedness for all peoples.

The proudest people in Europe five years ago are today humbled. It is not suggestive that they shall remain always humbled, for they are known to be great intriguers and fighters. They shall intrigue another world war, and if they of themselves do not do it, some one else will do it.

I am now asking the Negro peoples of the world to prepare for such a war to free Africa from the thraldom of the white man, who neither wants black men in England, Germany, France nor America.

We should all glory in the defeat of the Huns in 1918. It shall be a stepping stone to fuller independence for Negroes in the future. I am also pleased to report to you that the Universal Negro Improvement Association has succeeded in having incorporated the great enterprise known as "The Black Star Line, Inc." Within a few days the corporation shall place on the market $500,000 of common stock at the par value of $5.00 a share.

The association, through its many branches all over the world, will assist this corporation to float "The Black Star Line" on the 31st of October, and I am asking every Negro in every part of the world to make the Black Star Line a success.

The letters that are pouring in to us from all quarters of the Negro world relate the fact that our race is in no mood to be tampered with.

The entire race is now in dead earnest, and all of us mean either to live together or die all together—and there are 400,000,000 of us to die—too many to be defeated.

To those of you fellowmen in New York, Brooklyn and Philadelphia, I hereby beg to return my grateful thanks for the splendid manner in which you rallied to my support when the traitors of our race and cause tried to drag my name and that of the association into disrepute.

Last Sunday night [22 June] the thousands who assembled at the Palace Casino, New York, proved to one and all that the new Negro is really on the stage of action and means to stay there and play his part.

The men, URIAH T. MITCHELL, of Jamaica, British West Indies; NORMAN ROBINSON, of America; GERALD COX, of St. Lucia, British West Indies, and JOSEPH JOHNSON, of America, assisted by WILLIAM BRIDGES, who plotted to have the district attorney of New York stop the onward march of the Universal Negro Improvement Association, were ignominiously defeated and their names have passed on as the Benedict Arnolds of the race. Future generations of Negroes shall read of them in disgust and contempt.

The district attorney of New York was lied to by these men, two of whom were previously expelled from the association. It is the old time game of the Negro trying to "do up" the Negro; but this time it was not the individual, it was the principle of lynching an entire race, and the lynchers were to be Negroes.

Now let us all take new courage to fight the battle through, realizing that even within our ranks we have some of the most deadly foes.

Again I bid you be of good cheer and ask that you do your best to float "The Black Star Line" in October. With best wishes, Yours fraternally,

MARCUS GARVEY

Printed in the *NW*, Saturday, 28 June 1919.

1. The formal signing of the peace treaty was not held until 28 June, but this coincided with the actual publication date of the *Negro World* issue.

Bishop C. S. Smith to A. Mitchell Palmer, Attorney General

Detroit, Mich., June 25, 1919

Dear Sir:—

Your attention is directed to the enclosed copy of the "Negro World"[1] for the reason that, in my judgment, it is the organ of an Association whose methods are calculated to breed racial and international strife.

The editor of the "Negro World" was in Detroit June 1, 1919, and I had a lengthy interview with him at my home. As the result of the interview, I am firmly convinced that he is an adventurer and a grafter, bent on exploiting his people to the utmost limit.

"The Black Star Line" project is a fake pure and simple.

Marcus Garvey, the editor of "The Negro World" and the promoter of the "Black Star Line" scheme, is a Negro and a native of Jamaica, British West Indies.

He is in every respect a "Red", according to the sense in which that term is used in the common parlance of the day. He should either be required to discontinue his present vicious propaganda and fake practices or be deported as an undesirable. Sincerely yours,

C. S. SMITH[2]

[*Address*] To the Honorable Attorney
General,[3] Department of Justice,
Washington, D.C.
[*Handwritten endorsements*] EmR   DG.
JEH
[*Stamped endorsements*] Noted F. D. W.
NOTED J. E. H.

DNA, RG 65, File OG 185161. TLS, Recipient's copy. Written on the stationery of the Commission on After-War Problems.

1. Attached to the letter was the editorial, "The Negro At Bay," from the *Negro World* issue of 21 June 1919 which was written in response to an editorial of the same title published in the *Nation*, 14 June 1919.

2. Bishop Charles Spencer Smith (1852–1923) was the chairman of the Commission on After-War Problems created by the African Methodist Episcopal church. He was the presiding AME bishop of Michigan, Canada, and the West Indies. Born in Canada, Smith migrated to Kentucky where he became a teacher under the auspices of the Freedmen's Bureau. He was licensed to preach in 1871 at Jackson, Miss., and ordained an AME minister in 1872. He was elected a member of the Alabama House of Representatives 1874–76, and he was often a delegate to Republican national conventions. He founded the AME Sunday School Union in 1882, and in May 1900 he was elected to the position of bishop. He visited West Africa and South-West Africa in 1894, and during the next twenty-six years he was a frequent visitor to Africa and the West Indies. (*Crisis*, 20:2 [June 1920], pp. 90–92; *WWWA*).

3. Alexander Mitchell Palmer (1872–1936) was appointed U.S. attorney general on 5 March 1919, a position he held until the close of President Woodrow Wilson's administration in March 1921. Prior to his appointment he served as alien property custodian in the Department of Justice. It was during his tenure as attorney general that the suppression and prosecution of radicals, known as the Red Scare, was carried out. (*DAB*, Supplement 2; Stanley Coben, *A. Mitchell Palmer*).

Meeting of the UNIA

[*Negro World*, 28 June 1919]

Palace Casino, 135th Street and Madison Avenue, New York City, was packed to the doors on Sunday night, June 22, when Mr. Marcus Garvey, President General of the Universal Negro Improvement Association, appeared for the purpose of vindicating himself and the organization which he represented against an alleged libelous report of his interview with District Attorney Kil[roe] which appeared in the New York World Thursday, the 19th inst.

The stage of the huge Casino was liberally decorated with the Stars and Stripes, while at the northern corner was a huge sign about six feet in height on which was printed in large black and red letters the following:

"TRAITORS TO THE RACE
"URIAH T. MITCHELL
"NORMAN ROBINSON
"GERALD COX
"JOSEPH JOHNSON
"assisted by
"WILLIAM BRIDGES.

"These are the men who have tried to have the District Attorney of New York stop the BLACK STAR LINE."

The meeting was called to order promptly at 9 o'clock, with Mr. Edgar M. Grey, General Secretary of the organization, in the chair. After the singing of the opening ode, "From Greenland's Icy Mountains," and the offering up of prayer, a musical program was rendered.

Miss Irene Callender entertained the vast audience with an excellent piano solo, followed by a vocal solo by Miss Dorothy Trottman, which received such tremendous applause that Miss Dorothy encored in a splendid duet in conjunction with her sister, Miss Lillian Trottman.

At the close of the program the chairman made a very instructive and eloquent ten minute address in which he pointed out very convincingly the difference between the leadership of the Universal Negro Improvement Association and that of other organizations. "That difference," said he, "resides in the fact that this is the first organization entirely composed of Negroes for which leadership had not been chosen by white people; but instead its leadership is not alone chosen by the led, but was controlled and dictated to by its entire membership." The speaker ended his address with a dignified and eloquent peroration which was profusely endorsed by the audience with loud exclamations of "Hear, Hear!"

Follo[wi]ng this the audience was appealed to for a silver collection for the purpose of carrying out the aims of the Universal Negro Improvement Association. At this point a policeman and several other white men, apparently representatives of the District Attorney's office, attempted to prevent the collection from being taken up, but were promptly dissuaded by Mr. Grey, who explained the legal aspects of the situation.

The next speaker introduced was the famous and widely traveled e[loc]utionist, Miss Henrietta Vinton Davis, of Washington, D.C., who was greeted with applause.

Miss Davis paid a touching tribute to the courage, intelligence and self-sacrificing leadership of Mr. Marcus Garvey, which she followed up by reciting the valor of first the native Jamaican Negro troops,[1] who volunteered for the war, and who through their charges over the hot Palestinian deserts and up the Mesopotamian [Mo]untains made it possible for the Jewish dream of a restored Jerusalem to become a reality.

She then turned to the question of the brave black boys who fought for America and with their blood watered the tree of freedom in the vine-clad valleys and the snow-capped mountains of France. She pointed with telling effectiveness to the fact that the Negro under whatever flag you find him, is noted for his loyalty to that flag. In conclusion, she assured her hearers that the "Black Star Line," regardless of the opposition directed against it, regardless of traitors within and enemies without, would be a reality on the 31st of October, in the year of our Lord, One Thousand Nine Hundred and Nineteen.

The chairman resumed the platform and briefly introduced as the principal speaker of the evening, the world-famed orator, scholar and leader, Mr. Marcus Garvey, who on rising became the cynosure of all eyes, and was given a tremendous ovation. In opening, Mr. Garvey pointed out that he appeared that evening for the purpose of vindicating his personal honor and the honor of the association he was representing. If any one, said he, expected to see a trembling, cowardly Negro that evening, that one was mistaken, for as he had told his hearers on many previous occasions, all fear had departed from his heart and he was determined that no power on earth, whether it was a district attorney or a group of envious little Negro traitors and conspirators, could prevent the Universal Negro Improvement Association from carrying its objects to a successful conclusion. He had been subpo[e]naed to the district attorney's office along with the secretary of the ladies' division, Miss Amy Ashwood, and after the books had been examined and the affairs of the organization investigated he had been completely exonerated.

The enemies of the organization thought that they could score a victory by having the organization disrupted and himself slandered, and by giving it questionable publicity in the daily press. This they had not succeeded in doing, nor will they succeed in their villainous scheme of frustrating us in our attempt to float the Black Star Line. No power on earth whether it be the district attorney or those miserable traitors of the Negro race, whose names are displayed on the sign, would ever succeed in their vile intention, for with God's help the Black Star Line would be floated if necessary in a sea of blood. He had told the district attorney that his organization was legally incorporated in the State of New York, and that it was supported by over four thousand members in this State, not to speak of millions of Negroes in other parts of the world. He had told the district attorney just as white men were conducting a fleet of vessels called the White Star Line, the four hundred million Negroes of the world were determined to start and operate a line of vessels to ply between Africa, the West Indies, Central and South America, and the United States, under the name of "The Black Star Line."

Waving a typewritten letter in his hand he told the audience that one firm of African merchants by the name of Agamazong, Taylor & Co. had offered to ship not less than 50,000 tons of African produce as soon as the Black Star Line became a reality. Mr. Garvey, with emotional eloquence, evoked considerable enthusiasm among his hearers when he pointed out that the Black man was an essential Democrat, for from the time of Jesus Christ on Calvary it was the Black man who came to the assistance of the Redeemer. The Jews had spat upon Him, the Roman soldiers had pierced His side with a spear, but it was the Black man in the person of Simon the Cyrenean, who bore the Cross up Calvary's rugged height. That record had been carefully preserved by the Black men of today who, coming from Africa, the West Indies and the United States, had vicariously given up their lives on the battlefields of Palestine, Flanders and France in order that the world should be free from Prussian Tyranny. Turning his eyes upward and raising his arms in supplication, the speaker said: "Jesus Christ, even as we were with you in your painful and bloody journey through the garden of Gethsemane, be with us in this our hour of trial!" Immediately the house was in uproar. Young and old seemed to have caught the spirit of the prayer and showed it by their vocal responses. Mr. Garvey spoke for over an hour, during which time the house was frequently rent by loud exclamations of "Hear, hear," and at one time, when appealed to for a test of its allegiance to the cause, stood up to a man. Great satisfaction was exhibited when the speaker announced that the Black Star Line would be made a reality on October 31, 1919, even if they had to use part of the money they hoped to get from the $100,000 libel suit that had been instituted against the New York World. Pointing out the need of finance to combat the insidious and pernicious attacks being made upon himself and the association, Mr. Garvey made a touching appeal for a defense fund, which was liberally subscribed to in the form of $5, $2 and $1 bills, not to mention the smaller monetary denominations.

The meeting was then brought to a close after announcement had been made of a similar mass convention to be held on the following Sunday [29 June].

Printed in the *NW*, Saturday, 28 June 1919. Original headlines have been omitted.

1. The Jamaican contingent represented two-thirds of the total British West Indies Regiment. They were distributed among eleven battalions, two of which (the First and Second Battalions), received their training in Egypt and saw action in Palestine in August and September 1918 as part of the Egyptian Expeditionary Force. They were also the first allied troops to advance from the east bank of the Jordan River to Amman. After the war, the entire regiment, including those who fought in France, east Africa, and Mesopotamia, was commended by Lord Haig (1861–1928) for its bravery. (*HJ*, 1919).

UNIA Libel Action

[*Negro World*, 28 June 1919]

The Universal Negro Improvement Association of the World, through its New York office, has instituted libel action against the New York World for $100,000 and against the Harlem Home News for $25,000 for maliciously publishing articles[1] they knew to be manufactured and untrue against the association and its president.

Printed in the *NW*, Saturday, 28 June 1919. Original headline has been omitted.

1. The issues of the Harlem edition of the *Home News* for 1919 have not been preserved.

Maj. W. H. Loving to Capt. J. E. Cutler

[*New York City*, 28 June 1919]

Memo for Captain Cutler:

I am sending you a copy of the Negro World of last week[1] and one for this week.[2] The one for last week is evidently the one you wanted to see. The District Attorney had Marcus Garvey on the carpet last week for selling stock of a company that [h]as not been incorporated. "The Black Star Line" has since been incorporated as can be seen by the head lines in the issue of the Negro World for June 28th.

W. H. LOVING

[*Endorsement*] Negro Subversi[on]

DNA, RG 165, File 10218-317/7 273X(50). TNS, Recipient's copy.

1. Issue of 21 June 1919.
2. Issue of 28 June 1919.

Memorandum by Edward O'Toole of the *World*

[New York City] June 30, 1919

Marcus Garvey, president of the Universal Negro Improvement Association, and president of the African Communities League, both organizations of which were founded by him about eleven months ago and incorporated under the laws of the state of New York, is, according to three members of the organizations recently appointed by him as an auditing committee, mismanaging the funds of the two organizations and collecting money from the mem/b/ers under false pretenses. The three making the charges against him are J. E. Johnson, 35 West 139th Street, Norman Robinson, 55 West 137th Street, and U. P. Mitchell, for two weeks secretary of the Black Star Steamship Line, which Garvey alleges he is trying to float.

The three just named were appointed to audit the accounts of the societies and upon their finding . . . [*deletion illegible*] irregularities in the way of concealed expenditures, they asked Gravey for certain papers and books which he held, and the latter refused, bringing charges of disloyalty against them and calling them vile names.

Papers which were available show that Garvey had up to May 1st a balance of $264.50, $200 of which was deposited in the Corn Exchange Bank. According to the three, Garvey has sold to members, promissory notes, which he terms bonds, to the amount of about $4,000 for the avowed purpose of starting a Black Star line of steamships, but in reality, according to the committee of three, to pay the expense of a restaurant at 56 West 135th Stre[e]t which Garvey opened some time ago in the name of the organization of which he is president and which is now practically bankrupt, according to the three; largely, they say, because of his mismanagement.

These three took the matter up with the District Attorney's office and the action brought by Assistant District Attorney Kilroe in which Garvey was warned to cease collecting money for the steamship line led to the publication /of the story/ in the World and the Harlem Home News, for which Garvey is threatening to sue. According to these three men, Garvey asserted in a recent issue of the Negro World of which /he/ is the editor and proprietor that he expected to get a judgment for $100,000 from the World and one of $25,000 from the Harlem Home News, and that the money thus obtained would be sufficient to float the Black Star Steamship Line.

According to the three, Garvey is the sole officer of the two organizations? He is cha[ir]man of the Board of Directors of both societies, but a directors' meeting has never been held, /they/ say, ~~these three~~ because ~~of the fact that~~ there are no directors. The society had on May 1st 334 financial members who paid dues of $.35 per month and 153 non-paying members. Most of the membership in the two organizations, they say, is made up of foreign born negroes over whom Garvey holds an unusual sway. Despite the warning of Assistant District Attorney Kilroe, they declare that Garvey has been collecting money every Sunday for the Black Star Line and has recently applied to have the line incorporated in the state of Delaware. The three say they are in favor of such a steamship line but /that/ they object to the "unlawful and autocratic methods of Garvey".

EDWARD O'TOOLE

NNC, *W*. TMS, Carbon copy.

Editorial Letter by Marcus Garvey

[[Portsmouth, Va., July 9, 1919]]

Fellowmen of the Negro Race:

Greeting: I take great pleasure in writing to you this week from the city of Portsmouth, Va. I have been lecturing through the State of Virginia for fourteen days, and I must say that the people all through have been most responsive to the new doctrine being taught that of preparedness and action in this, the age of unceasing activity.

The city of Newport News has responded most splendidly to the call of the Universal Negro Improvement Association. At that end I found an enthusiastic people anxiously waiting to receive us and to show their fullest appreciation of the work we have started in the interest of our down-trodden people.

The great enterprise of the Black Star Line is receiving great support in Virginia, and I feel sure that by the splendid start made by the people in their sections that our steamship line will become one of the most prosperous ones afloat after October 31.

Let all of us rally to the colors of the Universal Negro Improvement Association and help make the Black Star Line a possibility in October. Five hundred thousand dollars of common stock have been placed on the market at $5. per share, and I now ask every Negro all over the world to send in at once to The Black Star Line, Inc. 38 West 135th Street, New York, and secure as man[y] shares of stock as possible. A five dollar investment in the Black Star Line today may be worth one hundred dollars six months from now. Write right away and purchase your shares in this great Negro enterprise.

Feeling sure that every man, woman and child of the race will invest in this line of Negro steamships. I beg to remain, yours fraternally,

MARCUS GARVEY

Printed in the *Despatch* (Panama), Wednesday, 20 August 1919. Original headlines have been omitted.

Robert Adger Bowen, Bureau of Translation,[1] Post Office, to William H. Lamar, Post Office Solicitor

[*New York City*] July 10, 1919

Attention of James A. Horton, Esq.[2]

My dear Judge Lamar:[3]

Thinking that it may interest the Department of Justice,[4] I call attention to the systematized campaign conducted by The Negro World and Marcus Garvey in behalf of The Black Star Line. Nominally this is a steamship line in the interests of negroes, and negroes through out the country are being urged to buy shares at $5.00 a share "which may be worth one hundred dollars six-months from now." It seems that even among the negroes themselves Marcus Garvey and his scheme has come under suspicion, and it is possible that this may be deservedly so. The Negro World and Marcus Garvey are working the racket for all it may be worth—to them. Very truly yours,

[ROBERT A. BOWEN][5]

[*Typewritten reference*] RAB:MR

DNA, RG 28, File B-240. TL, Carbon copy.

1. The Bureau of Translation was established as part of the post office in New York City, under Section 19 of the Trading with the Enemy Act of 6 October 1917, empowering the postmaster general to restrict the mailing of foreign language publications (Section 19, Public Law No. 91, 65th Congress). The Bureau of Translation also inherited the functions established earlier by the New York Post Office to implement the postal surveillance required by the Espionage Act of June 1917. Since the provisions of the act were restricted to the period when the United States was at war, postal surveillance was conducted after the war's end through the use of a section of the Espionage Act, which declared "any matter advocating or urging treason, insurrection, or forcible resistance to any law of the United States" to be "nonmailable." (Section 2, title 12). Several black periodicals, in addition to the *Negro World*, were examined for possible denial of mailing privileges: the *AME Zion Quarterly Review, Afro-American, Amsterdam News, Boston Guardian, Challenge, Chicago Defender, Crisis, Messenger,*

New York Age, New York News, Pittsburgh Courier, and *Veteran*. (DNA, RG 28, file B-588, "War Activities of the Post Office Department").

2. James Albert Horton (1886–1964) was appointed principal assistant attorney in the Office of the Post Office Solicitor in March 1917. He resigned from the Post Office Department on 30 June 1919 to become a special investigator with the Bureau of Investigation. (*WWA*, 1946–47).

3. William Harmong Lamar (1859–1928) was appointed solicitor for the Post Office Department in May 1913. The war activities of the solicitor consisted mainly of enforcement of the postal provisions of the Espionage and the Trading with the Enemy Acts. Lamar resigned from the Post Office in March 1920 to enter private practice in Washington, D.C. (*WWWA*).

4. The Post Office solicitor was required, in addition to his other duties under the Espionage Act, to bring to the attention of coordinate federal departments violations which the Post Office found. Under the Trading with the Enemy Act, the Post Office solicitor also acted as the coordinator of the collective efforts of the Post Office Department with the work of the Military Intelligence division, the Office of Naval Intelligence, the Bureau of Investigation, and the Committee on Public Information.

5. Robert Adger Bowen (1868– ?) was a literary editor in the years between 1894 and 1910. Bowen was one of the original staff of three charged with the supervision of the Bureau of Translation; he became its director in 1918. (*WWA*.)

Bureau of Investigation Report

New York City [*Made*] July 10, 1919
[*for the period of*] July 10, [1919]

IN RE: NEGRO ACTIVITIES MARCUS GARVEY, ET AL. "BLACK STAR LINE"

Referring to a previous report on the formation of a "Black Star Line" among the negroes, I call attention to a copy of the "Negro World", a New York weekly publication, for July 12th. This contains a full-page "ad" offering for sale the stock of this steamship line. It states that the "Line" was incorporated under the State laws of Delaware with a capitalization of $500,000.: that it is the result of effort on the part of the *Hon. Marcus Garvey*, and that it will be "a direct line of steamships—to be owned, controlled and manned by negroes, to reach the negro peoples of the world." The stock is selling at $5 par on a basis which they call "The Liberty Loan Selling Plan",[1] i.e., on a partial-payment basis.

Garvey, who has also been the subject of many former reports, is probably the most prominent Negro radical agitator in New York. As before set out, we have been told that he is a native of the West Indies, the founder of the *Universal Negro Improvement Association and African Communities League*, 36 West 135 St. New York, from which address is also directed the *"Black Star Line,*["] as well as the publishing of the "Negro World," of which Garvey is Managing Editor. He is an exceptionally fine orator, and some of his speeches during the war period were of a character to cause the local police to close up some of his meetings. His associates are *A. Philip Randolph, Chandler Owen* and *George Frazier Miller*, publishers of "The Messenger" and teachers at the Rand School,[2] New York.

It is surprising to note the excitement which Garvey is causing among the negro element in New York thru this steamship proposition. With the promise of "participation in the world's trade" he has induced these negroes to part with their money up to the present to the extent of $25,000 we are informed. A list of contributors published in his newspaper indicates that his campaign is nation-wide, the out of town negroes being handled thru the mails. This last feature has undoubtedly been looked into by the Post Office Department.

The general trend of Garvey's newspaper has been gone into in previous reports. This issue above mentioned contains attacks upon the Peace situation, characterizing the League of Nations as a "vile thing"; much favorable comment regarding Soviet rule, and several advertisements of radical meetings, one particularly, scheduled for July 13th, at the Palace Casino, called "RED HOT PROTEST MASS MEETING" to protest suppression of the outspoken Negro publications by Burleson of Texas."[3] The speakers will be *Elizabeth Gurley Flynn*,[4] *George Frazier Miller, A. Philip Randolph, Chandler Owen* and *W. A. Domingo*, all negroes excepting Flynn.

Another very important situation which the writer desires to call to the Department's attention is a notice, in large, black type contained in the Negro World, reading:

PRINCE RENDIVA GEBRAU
OF THE ABYSSINIAN COMMISSION[5] WILL SPEAK AT THE
Palace Casino, 135th St. & Madison Ave. Sunday Night [*13 July*] at 8:30

An informant known to this office, in negro circles, came into this office today to protest against the holding of this meeting. He stated, in effect, that this is nothing more than a political trick on the part of Garvey, who desires not only to convey the effect that the Prince represents an element of his type, but also Garvey "has his eye" on Abyssinia in connection with his steamship proposition should it ever materialize, having in view no doubt securing the official aid of the diplomatic and commercial interests of Abyssinia to further it. Our informant advises that Garvey has often stated that Abyssinia would be a likely place for the negro steamships to run to.

I advised our informant that this department was powerless to interfere in such matters as the holding of the meeting. He stated, however, that he would make an attempt to interview Capt. Morrison[6] (white), said to be the manager of Prince Gebrau while in this country, explain the radical element which Garvey represents and have Garvey's meeting either called of[f] or offset by a previous mass meeting, on Sunday afternoon, at one of the large negro churches in this city. The informant stated that he would like to refer Capt. Morrison to the writer for a reference as to sincerity of purpose, etc. I advised our informant that I would be glad to talk with the Captain over the telephone, in an unofficial capacity, however, and only as regards the personal character of the informant. Up to this writing I have not heard from Captain Morrison.

This is a matter which I believe might interest our State Department, for I doubt whether the Prince knows the real motives and activities of Garvey and his ilk. The fact that the Prince has consented to lecture here under Garvey's auspices, besides being taken as an insult by the patriotic, American negroes, would indicate that Garvey has undoubtedly misrepresented his status to the Prince.

M. J. DAVIS

[*Stamped endorsement*] Noted F. D. W.
[*Handwritten endorsement*] DG.

DNA, RG 65, File OG 329359. TD.

1. Garvey's "Liberty Loan Selling Plan" was modeled on the U.S. government's World War I Liberty Loan Drive to which black Americans had contributed generously. The *Negro Year Book of 1918–1919* (pp. 45–50) estimated that their support of the various Liberty Loan, Liberty Bond, and Thrift Stamp drives amounted to more than $225 million. (Charles Gilbert, *American Financing of World War I* [Westport, Conn.: Greenwood Press, 1970]).

2. Randolph and Owen began teaching at the Rand School of Social Science on 14 April 1919. Their course was entitled "Economics and Sociology of the Negro Problem," which consisted of six weekly lectures. (New York *Call*, 25 March 1919). The Rand School was founded in 1906 by George D. Herron, a Christian socialist minister, and his wife, the daughter of the abolitionist Carrie Rand. Located on East 15th Street near Fifth Avenue, the school provided a socialist education for workers and labor leaders, but after the Herrons moved to Italy in 1906, they left the school to the American Socialist Society to operate. The school subsequently acquired a wider liberal arts curriculum and attracted, at various times, the talents of Charles A. Beard, Clarence Darrow, John Dewey, Alexander Kerensky, Bertrand Russell, Norman Thomas, Scott Nearing and W. A. Domingo. In 1917, its publication of Scott Nearing's *The Great Madness* led to an indictment of the American Socialist Society under the Espionage Act, which resulted in a $3,000 fine. On 21 June 1919 the Lusk Committee raided the school and seized its records and publications (*NYT*, 22, 23, 24 June 1919). Following the raid, the school was charged by the Lusk Committee with providing subsidies to black radicals and with cooperating with Ludwig C.A.K. Martens, head of the Russian Bureau and "unrecognized" ambassador of the Soviet Union. The Lusk Committee filed a suit to revoke the school's charter but the State Supreme Court dismissed it for lack of evidence. In later years, the Rand School became the established center for the Socialist party's "old guard." Membership in the school progressively declined, and in 1956 it was closed. (Norma Fain Pratt, *Morris Hillquit* [Westport, Conn.: Greenwood Press, 1978], pp. 79–81; Daniel Bell, *The Tamiment Library* [New York: New York University Libraries, 1969]; Murray B. Seidler, *Norman Thomas: Respectable Rebel* [Syracuse: Syracuse University Press, 1961]; and Julian J. Jaffe, *Crusade Against Radicalism* [Port Washington, N.Y.: Kennikat Press, 1972], chap. 5).

3. The issue of the *Messenger* for May–June 1919 was the first issue to come to the attention of the Post Office Bureau of Translation. On 15 May 1919, Bowen wrote to the Post Office solicitor indicating "certain items of objectionable import" in the magazine. The succeeding July issue of the *Messenger* was detained by the postmaster at New York City under the amended Espionage Act of 16 May 1918. The issue was finally accepted for mailing on 8 July 1919 after the Post Office solicitor's ruling. Throughout 1919 the *Messenger* was denied permanent second-class mailing privileges, being granted only a temporary permit by the post office in New York City. A permanent second-class permit was not granted until mid-1921. (Theodore Kornweibel, *No Crystal Stair: Black Life and the Messenger, 1917–1918* [Westport, Conn.: Greenwood Press, 1975], p. 87). The circular advertising the *Messenger* meeting did not use the word "suppression," nor were the words cited in the second half of the quotation accurate. The following were the actual words used: "10,000 Harlem Citizens will protest against the unjust interference with Negro Publications in Mails by Burleson of Texas" (N-Ar, LC, Box 7, File 18). The meeting, called to protest the delay of the *Messenger's* July issue by the post office, was moved to the Rush Episcopal Church at 58 West 138th Street, where over a thousand people reportedly attended, after the Palace Casino's owners refused to permit its use, resulting in the closing of the hall by the police. (*Harlem Home News*, 6 July 1919.) The

Messenger continued to be refused second-class mailing privileges, but no other issues were detained in the mails, nor was any other black newspaper or magazine ever detained.

4. Elizabeth Gurley Flynn (1890–1964), labor activist, joined the IWW in 1906 and was a participant in all the major IWW strikes. She helped to found the Workers' Liberty Defense Union in 1918 and during the immediate postwar years she was involved in the defense efforts for the political and trade-union radicals during the Red Scare of 1919–20. (Gary Fink, ed., *Biographical Dictionary of American Labor Leaders* [Westport, Conn.: Greenwood Press, 1974], pp. 108–09).

5. After visiting England, France, and Italy, an official Abyssinian delegation arrived in the United States on 5 July 1919 "to congratulate the American people for winning the great war." President Woodrow Wilson formally received the delegates on 14 July at the White House. The delegation was headed by Dajazmach Nadao, and included Kantiba Gabrou (mayor of Gondar, the former capital of the Ethiopian Empire), Ato Herouy (secretary of the municipality of Addis Ababa), and Ato Sinkae (aide to the chief of the delegation). On the eve of their departure, the delegates were refused admittance to a farewell dinner at the National Democratic Club and at the Republic Club in New York City, where H. H. Topakyan, former consul general of Persia, was to have officially entertained them. The refusal came after club officials learned that the guests were black. It was suggested at the time that the principal purpose of the Abyssinian visit was to gain U.S. support for Ethiopia's desire to join the League of Nations. ("Impressions of the Abyssinian Commission on Colored Americans," *Baptist World* 1 [23 November 1919]: 2; *Crisis* 18 [September 1919]: 158–59; New York *World* 7, 23, 26 July 1919, 1, 4 August 1919; *NYT*, 6, 8, 15, 16 July, 17 August 1919; DNA, RG 65, file OG 388462).

6. Capt. Paul Rex Morrissey was assigned by the American government to escort the Abyssinian mission during its visit.

A. M. Dockery, Third Asst. Postmaster General, to William H. Lamar

Washington July 11, 1919

The Solicitor.

Inclosed please find copies of the June 7, 14, 21 and 28, 1919, issues[1] of the "Negro World" a publication admitted to the second class of mail matter at New York, N.Y.

I will thank you to advise this office whether these copies contain any matter that is unmailable under the law.

A M DOCKERY[2] HL
Third Assistant

Inc. D

ABB-m
[*Printed*] IN YOUR REPLY REFER TO C.D.
NO. [*Typewritten insertion*] 187166

DNA, RG 28, File B-500. TNS, Recipient's copy.

1. The issues were not retained.
2. Alexander Monroe Dockery (1845–1926) was the third assistant postmaster general from 17 March 1913 until 31 March 1921. He was formerly a member of Congress from Missouri (1882–98), and its governor (1901–05). (*WWWA*).

John T. Suter, Acting Chief, Bureau of Investigation, to P. J. Barry, Chicago

[*Washington, D.C.*] July 12, 1919

Dear Sir:

I am in receipt of your communication of July 3, 1919, in which you inclose a copy of the publication "THE MESSENGER" for the current month.

While this publication has frequently been called to my notice, I nevertheless desire that you keep in touch with its circulation in your territory and that particular attention be given to the activities of the negro radicals, particularly "*Marcus Garvey*". Very truly yours,

[JOHN T. SUTER]
Acting Chief

[*Typewritten reference*] [. . .]-GPO
[*Endorsement*] Noted F.D.W.

DNA, RG 65, File OG 329359. TL, Carbon copy. Stamped endorsement.

William M. Offley to the Chief, Bureau of Investigation

14th Floor. Park Row Bldg.
New York City July 14, 1919
Attention Mr. Hoover.

Dear Sir:

Referring to your request for reports concerning certain designated radicals[1] in this city, I beg to advise you that Marcus Garvey, a neg/r/o, who in November, 1918, could be found care "The Negro World", 36–38 West 135th Street, was born in Jamaica, West Indies, August 17, 1888, [*1887*] where he resided until twenty years of age, at which time he went to England and graduated from Bardeck [*Birkbeck*] College in 1913. He then returned to the West Indies, and subsequently came to the United States, where he has been between two and a half and three years, and has made the statement that he contemplates returning to Jamaica during the present year.

As to his activities I beg to refer you to the following reports:

Special Agent Davidson for November 9th, 10th and 12th, and December 2nd, 3rd, 9th and 16, 1918.

Special Agent Finch for November 13th and 14th, and December 3rd (two reports), 1918.

I also enclose two "dodgers" advertising meetings to be held in this city at which Garvey would speak. Very truly yours,

WM M. OFFLEY
Division Superintendent

Encs.
[*Typewritten reference*] WMO JFD
[*Handwritten endorsement*] HWG
[*Stamped endorsement*] Noted F.D.W.

DNA, RG 65, File OG 329359. TLS, Recipient's copy.

1. A reference to the list of eight "radicals" about whom John T. Suter, acting chief of the Bureau of Investigation, requested information. Marcus Garvey was one of the eight. (John T. Suter to William M. Offley, 12 July 1919, DNA, RG 65, File OG 5523).

Maj. W. H. Loving to Brig. Gen. Marlborough Churchill

253 West 137th Street.
New York, N.Y., July 16, 1919

From: Major W. H. Loving, P.C.
To: Director of Military Intelligence, Washington, D.C.
Subject: Conditions among Negroes in New York City.

The following recent incidents in New York City are reported for your information. . . .

Meeting Announced by Universal Negro Improvement Association to Introduce Abyssinian Nobleman.

On the night of the 13th of July a large crowd assembled at Palace Casino to hear Duke Dedjazzmatch Nadao, of Abyssinia, who had been advertised to speak by the above organization. He is now stopping at the Waldorf-Astoria in New York and Marcus Garvey, the chief spirit of the Universal Negro Improvement Association had obtained the promise of this nobleman to speak to the colored people of Harlem. But again the authorities intervened and ordered the owner of the hall not to open the doors. This was the second time on the same day (Sunday, July 13th) that meetings had been prevented at Palace Casino, the same thing having occurred to the Socialists during the early afternoon. Following so soon after the first occurrence, the resentment of the people ran very high. However, there was no outburst of disorder, although many of the crowd lingered around the hall for more than an hour expressing their opinion of the government. No other effort has as yet been made to have Duke Dedjazzmatch address a Negro audience.

W H Loving
Major, P.C., Retired

[*Endorsement*] MAJOR J.E. CUTLER

DNA, RG 165, File 10218-345/1 50X. TDS, Recipient's copy. Stamped endorsement.

Robert Adger Bowen to William H. Lamar

[*New York City*] July 18, 1919
Attention of James A. Horton, Esq.

My dear Judge Lamar:

THE NEGRO WORLD of July 19th bore in large black type on its first page two editorials in which coming war between the Blacks and Whites was prophesied so that the negroes might establish themselves as a nation in Africa.

THE CRUSADER for August has a leading editorial along the same lines—Government of the Negro—by whom and for Whom?

I refer to this matter as another evidence of Negro race consciousness.

The Crusader also, on page 31, has an article which draws comfort from certain editorials on the Negro appearing in recent issues of The Nation, The Call, The Liberator, and The New Republic. Very truly yours,

[ROBERT ADGER BOWEN]

[*Typewritten reference*] RAB:MR

DNA, RG 28, File B-500. TL, Carbon copy.

Editorial Letter by Marcus Garvey

[[New York, July 18, 1919]]

ALL NEGROES SHOULD GET READY TO PROTECT THEMSELVES IN THE FUTURE
UNIVERSAL MOVEMENT GETTING STRONG ALL OVER THE WORLD.

Fellowmen of the Negro Race:

I have to return thanks to you for the splendid spirit you are manifesting in all quarters as touching the aims and purposes of the Universal Negro Improvement Association.

Our organization is making millions of converts every month. Africa, the West Indies and South and Central America have fallen into line with us in America, and we can foresee the day twenty or thirty years hence when four hundred millions of us will march down the line hand-in-hand to establish liberty and true democracy.

My appeal is to every member of the race in every part of the world. The Universal Negro Improvement Association realizes that the war of 1914–1918 is over, but all Negroes must prepare for the next world war. There is bound to be more wars because human nature has not changed. Stronger nations and races are still robbing and exploiting the weaker ones. So long as the Negro is oppressed all over the world there can be no abiding peace. Four hundred million Negroes are now suffering from the injustices of the white man, and for that reason we cannot entertain any idea of peace that does not mean equality for all peoples. Negroes must now combine with China, India, Egypt, Ireland and Russia, to free themselves in the future.

Our Fatherland, Africa, is bleeding, and she is now stretching forth her hands to her children in America, the West Indies and Central America and Canada to help her.[1] We must help her, therefore I hereby ask every Negro in the world to get ready for the next war, twenty, thirty or forty years hence. The next world war shall find Negroes fighting together to free our common fatherland. Now is no time for the Negro to be divided between two opinions. We must be pro-Negro now and always. The white man has been pro-white for thousands of years; the yellow man is now pro-yellow; this is the time, therefore, for us to be pro-Negro, and without offense to any one.

I am asking all Negroes to invest in the Black Star Line. This line of steamships will be operated to the exclusive interests of Negroes. In the near future if you want to leave America, the West Indies, South and Central America for more prosperous fields, the Black Star Line will be at your service. You can buy shares now at $5.00 each, so please buy as many as you can.

With very best wishes for your success, Yours fraternally,

MARCUS GARVEY

Printed in the *NW*, Saturday, 19 July 1919.

1. The reference was taken from Ps. 68:31, "Princes shall come out of Egypt; Ethiopia shall soon stretch out her hands unto God."

Statement of Edgar M. Grey

[*New York City*] July 18, 1919

(Copy)

Statement in Relation to Black Star Line Inc. and Marcus Garvey[1]

Statement of: Edgar M. Grey.
Made to: Mr. Thomas Mahoney.
On: July 18, 1919.
Steno: Hooper.

Edgar M. Grey, 249 West 138th Street, New York City, N.Y., General Mail Secretary, Universal Negro Improvement Association African Communities League, and Assistant Secretary of the Black Star Line Incorporated.

The Black Star Line was incorporated under the laws of the State of Delaware, $500,000 at $5. a share. Mr. Marcus Garvey made a trip to Virginia in the interest of the Black Star Line, for the purpose of selling the stocks. He took one stock book with him, and had two more mailed to him. The stubs from the stock certificates, which he issued down there, but claims he has lost, thereby preventing us, as officers, from being able to make the proper entries in the ledger of the Black Star Line Corporation as to the amount of stocks issued in the south.

About $500. from the sale of stocks was collected here by the officers of the Corporation, the New York end, which moneys this man has spent in the liquidation of debts not incurred by the Black Star Line, but by the Universal Negro Improvement Association, which is a distinct Corporation.

Day before yesterday, against the wishes of the Secretaries of the Corporation, he paid to N. Radus and Sons, whose offices are located at 78 Bowery, $266.44, out of the receipts of the Black Star Line for the liquidation of a debt outstanding against the restaurant, owned and operated by the Universal Negro Improvement Association and African Communities League.

At the outset of the Incorporation of this Black Star Line, we directed that under the law it was only legal to issue stock certificates when a Federal Revenue Stamp, to the extent of 1% on a dollar, appeared on the face of the stock certificate. This gentleman proceeded to Virginia and issued about $1200 worth of stock without such revenue stamp appearing on the face of the certificates. Up to this time he has not been able to, he says, produce the stubs from the stock certificates which were issued in Virginia, consequently the proper entries of the sale of such stocks have not been entered by either Secretary of the Corporation in any accountable ledger of the Corporation.

Against the wish of the Secretary, and only with the coerced consent of a majority of the Board of Directors, this gentleman took the stock certificates south, and issued them without any proper entries being made. It was legislated, at the time of his leaving for the south, by the Board of Directors, a majority present, that an account of his expenditures and receipts for the Black Star Line should be kept by the Treasurer of the Corporation—who accompanied him to the south—which was to be supervised by the said President, Marcus Garvey. Up to this time no such report has been kept or made to the Directors of the Black Star Line Inc. and more than two thirds of the moneys received from sales of shares of the Black Star Line has been spent in the liquidation of debts not incurred by the Black Star Line, before its actual Incorporation, or since, over the protest of both of the Secretaries of the Black Star Line. At this time, contrary to the Articles of Incorporation, no account has been opened with any bankers for the Black Star Line.

[EDGAR M. GREY]

DNA, RG 165, File 10218-373/3. TD, Transcript.

1. This statement, and the one following, were collected from assistant district attorney Kilroe by Inspector Melvin J. McKenna of MID's New York office; McKenna sent the statements on 8 October 1919 to Capt. W. L. Moffat, Jr., who forwarded them to the director of Military Intelligence in Washington, D.C. on 9 October. Kilroe planned to present the statements to the New York County grand jury for its investigation of the Black Star Line. (DNA, RG 165, file 10218-373).

Statement of Richard E. Warner

[*New York City*] July 18, 1919

COPY

STATEMENT IN RELATION TO BLACK STAR LINE INC.
AND MARCUS GARVEY

Statement of: Richard E. Warner
Made to: Mr. Thomas Mahoney
On: July 18, 1919
Steno: Hooper.

Richard E. Warner, 2412 Seventh Avenue, New York City, Executive Secretary of the Universal Negro Improvement Association, and Secretary of the Black Star Line Inc.

All of the statement made by Mr. Grey, I concur with and I have more to tell.

As a member of the Universal Negro Improvement Association, I was elected to the office of Executive Secretary of said Association on the same principles which any organization would elect its officers. The Black Star Line having been incorporated under the laws of the State of Delaware on June 27, 1919, it became necessary that the officers of the Universal Association be made offi[c]ers of the Black Star Line. Mr. Garvey decided to make a tour to Virginia, and wanted me, as Secretary of the Black Star Line, to sign up a book of certificates and give him to carry—accompanied by the General Ladies Secretary—which I refused to do. I told him in an open meeting of the Board of Directors that if that stock book was taken south, either the Secretary or Treasurer of the Corporation must go with it, and that under no consideration will I sign my name to a book of certificates to be sent away under the supervision of someone else. This protest was not adhered to and one Mr. Tobias, the Treasurer at the 11th hour accompanied Mr. Garvey, Miss Henrietta V. Davis, 2nd Vice President and Miss Amy Ashwood, General Ladies Secretary on this trip.

He arrived in Virginia on Sunday morning June 29th, and spoke at Newport News in the interest of the Black Star Line. He sent[,] Monday morning, by telegraph via Western Union, to the Corn Exchange Bank, $440. and asked that that go towards the liquidation of outstanding indebtedness, which was not all incurred by the Black Star Line Inc.

Finding that he was bent on misappropriating the funds collected by the Black Star Line, I not only continued to protest, but forwarded him by Special Delivery, my resignation as Secretary of the Black Star Line, a copy of which resignation is herewith attached.[1]

Further, having in hand certain moneys which were collected from the membership in New York, and seeing the slip-shod-methods that were being used, I called upon 1st Vice President, Mr. Jeremiah M. Certain to place such moneys, for safe keeping, in the Empire City Savings Bank, jointly between said Mr. Certain and myself, until Mr. Garvey's return and a meeting of the Board of Directors be held, for the reason that his being in the south, no account could be opened in the name of the Black Star Line without the signature of the proper officers.

This was done with full knowledge of not only Mr. Certain, but the other Directors in New York, and as a safeguard for myself, in preventing the expenditures of any moneys, whatever, for purposes other than for which it was collected.

Since his return, I have pressed my claim to be relieved of the duties of Secretary. At the meeting of the Board of Directors held Wednesday night, July 16th, said resignation was not accepted. The day prior to the meeting he ordered[,] contrary to the By-laws of the Corporation and without the knowledge and consent of the majority of the Directors, the payment of $266.44 to N. Radus & Sons, for fixtures for the restaurant of the Universal organization, which is a distinct proposition from that of the Black Star Line Inc.

He has also had outstanding receipt, held by members of the Universal, for moneys loaned by them, running into the hundreds of dollars, and in order to liquidate said indebtedness, he has requested that certificate for shares in the Black Star Line be issued these members as payment for their loans, borrowed before the inception of the Black Star Line and dating as far back as March, April, May and June. This I absolutely refused to consider, and over my protest, said certificates are being issued by the Treasurer, Mr. George Tobias.

[RICHARD E. WARNER]

DNA, RG 165, File 10218-373/4. TD, Transcript.

1. Not found.

Marcus Garvey to Dusé Mohamed Ali

Crescent Bldgs.
36/38 West 135th Street, N.Y.
July 18, 1919

My dear Mr. Mohamed,

I expect to be in England for three weeks in the month of November of this year from the 10th to the 29th to speak in London, Manchester and Liverpool in the interest of the Universal Negro Improvement Association and African Communities League[1]

I would like to secure the Royal Albert Hall in West Kensington, South West London for a mass meeting for about the 13th or 14th of November and to secure Caxton Hall for the 18th.

Will you be good enough to find out the charges on the Royal Albert Hall, as also the Caxton Hall and let me know by return mail.[2]

Let me know also if you can undertake the arranging for these meetings for us. If you cannot handle them please put me in touch with Mr. Hutchinson,[3] so that I may ask him to take up this matter.

Trusting to hear from you by return, I am, Yours respectfully

(sgd) MARCUS GARVEY,
President

NN-Sc, JEB. TL, Transcript; an enclosure in Dusé Mohamed Ali to John E. Bruce, 12 September 1919.

1. Garvey did not visit England in 1919 as planned.
2. Dusé Mohamed Ali informed Bruce in a second postscript to his letter: "I got a letter from your friend Marcus Garvin [*sic*] copy enclosed. Of course I did not answer, as it did not require an answer."
3. Probably W. F. Hutchinson, coeditor of the *African and Orient Review*. Hutchinson, one of Ali's close associates, was originally from the Gold Coast. (Ian Duffield, "Some American Influences on Dusé Mohamed Ali," paper presented at UCLA, Colloquium on Pan-African Biography, 12 April 1982).

Notice in the *Negro World*

[19 July 1919]

Wanted
10,000 Intelligent Young Negro Men

and women of ambition to take advantage of the following: The Universal Negro Improvement Association wants 10,000 leaders to send into new fields. A six-month course of instructions will be necessary for each applicant.

Apply now in writing to

GENERAL SECRETARY, UNIVERAL NEGRO
IMPROVEMENT ASSOCIATION,

38 W. 135TH ST. NEW YORK CITY.

Printed in the *NW*, Saturday, 19 July 1919.

Statement by Marcus Garvey

[*Negro World*, 19 July 1919]

EXTRAORDINARY ANNOUNCEMENT FOR EVERYBODY
ALL POLITICIANS SHOULD TAKE NOTICE.

Owing to growing misunderstanding as touching the political affiliation and sympathy of the Universal Negro Improvement Association of the world,[1] I hereby beg to state for the information of all concerned that this organization has absolutely no association with any political party. We do not accept money from politicians, nor political parties. We have never accepted any and we do not want any from that source. Republicans, Democrats and Socialists are the same to us—they are all white men, and to our knowledge, all of them join together and lynch and burn Negroes.

We are Negroes, and we want it clearly understood that persons who endeavor to use the name of the Universal Negro Improvement Association or the name of the "Negro World" for enhancing their individual political fortunes do so without the approval of the association or the management of the "Negro World."

The Universal Negro Improvement Association and the "Negro World," its official organ, are supported by the hard earned dimes and dollars of the Negro people of the world, and to them alone do we owe an obligation. We ask that all politicians and political organizations take notice of this announcement. The only pol[i]tics that we indulge in and are supporting is that of the New Negro Party of all the world. We are four hundred million strong in such a party.

(Signed) Universal Negro Improvement Assn.
MARCUS GARVEY, President General

Printed in the *NW*, Saturday, 19 July 1919.

1. Garvey possibly felt that the clarification was necessary as a result of his break with W. A. Domingo, the former editor of the *Negro World*, who was also closely identified with the Socialist party. (Philip S. Foner, *American Socialism and Black Americans*, pp. 307–09; Harold Cruse, *The Crisis of The Negro Intellectual: From Its Origins to the Present* [New York: William Morrow, 1967] pp. 128–32).

Letter to the Editor, *Negro World*

[*ca. 19 July 1919*] Portsmouth, Va.

To the Editor of the Negro World,
Dear Sir:

Through Mr. P. H. Thornton of this city I have been a reader of your paper for some time, and because of its attitude on public questions and the work of the Universal Negro Improvement Association, I decided to become a member. I notice that you give prominence to the address of a friend of mine, Mr. Lacy, before the National Convention of the A. F. of L.

I admire the spirit of Mr. Lacy very much, also that of the convention; but I fail to see how the black man can ever get justice so long denied him in that organization. I have been with the A. F. of L. for five years, and have visited their National Convention, also the Virginia State Conventions, and have made request after request through resolutions for justice to my race.

At the Buffalo Convention of November 12 to 24, 1917, I introduced resolution No. 57, which sought to have colored organizers in the field; but this resolution was never heard from after it was referred to the finance committee for action. However, not to be daunted, Southern Negroes have begun to see that they can utilize the same methods used by white men for achieving the things they desire. To this end the National Brotherhood Workers of America was chartered in Washington, D.C., on March 21, 1919. We have added to the Brotherhood, 4,578 members, Newport News turning in 105 riveters, and 50 chippers, corkers, blacksmith helpers and laborers. We have locals in Florida and Atlanta, Ga., and all of the railway shops through the Northeastern districts of Virginia are almost solidly organized. It is because of this that the A. F. of L. was willing to make concessions to the Negroes. The Brotherhood is composed of black men and women, and we are working to develop a consolidated union with a general view towards upbuilding our people industrially. Before we started, the colored mechanic was not desired in the international unions; but now those same unions are making overtures to get them in.

However, we are determined not to sell our hard earned birthright for the proverbial mess of pottage. Trusting you will give this letter publicity I am, Yours fraternally,

WALTER GREEN

Printed in *NW*, Saturday, 19 July 1919.

Robert Adger Bowen to William H. Lamar

New York, N.Y. July 24, 1919
Attention of James A. Horton, Esq.

My dear Judge Lamar:

I send you the July 26th issue of THE NEGRO WORLD, and call attention to that editorial *Race First* which closes with these words:—

"It is true that all races look forward to the time when spears shall be beaten into agricultural implements, but until that time arrives it devolves upon all oppressed peoples to avail themselves of every weapon that may be effective in defeating the fell motives of their oppressors.

"In a world of wolves one should go armed, and one of the most powerful defensive weapons within the reach of Negroes is the practice of Race First in all parts of the world." Very truly yours,

ROBERT A. BOWEN

[*Typewritten reference*] RAB:MR
[*Endorsement*] Jacket & index Nicholson
assign space

DNA, RG 28, B-500, *NW*. TLS, Recipient's copy. Endorsement is handwritten.

Enclosure

[[*Negro World*, 26 July 1919]]

RACE FIRST!

PERHAPS no phrase has done more to consolidate the sentiment of the Negroes of the world than that summed up in the two words: "Negro First." If we remember correctly, the slogan was coined by the well-known lecturer and scholar, Hubert Harrison.[1] It is a succin[c]t paraphrase, for purposes of Negro propaganda and advancement, of the practices of all other races, particularly the white race.

Reasonably interpreted it means that in the situation of racial strife existing Negroes should give their own racial concern precedence over all other matters when such preference does not make for perpetuating racial inefficiency or causing individual loss while enriching exploiters who operate under the camouflage of race loyalty. In other words, all things being equal, Negroes should give preference to members of their own race so as to conserve their resources to enable them more effectively to combat those forces that oppose them on racial grounds only.

The present condition of Negroes forces them to assume an essentially defensive role; hence, practicing the principles of "Negro first" does not mean an abandonment of common sense or a disregard of individual interest; instead, the best defensive is sometimes achieved through employing tactics of offense, and individuals can better gain what they want by pooling their interests. The essence of "race first" is, therefore, co-operation among Negroes to protect themselves against the attacks of truculent and race-prejudiced white men. *This may be a new doctrine for Negroes, but it has been consciously practiced by Caucasians and others from time immemorial.*

It is the principle of race first aggressively misapplied that white men the world over practice when they discriminate against Negroes. But it is the same principle defensively and intelligently applied that makes the Chinese a self-sufficient people, although forming but a very small percentage of the population of New York, the West Indies and other territories outside of China where they reside. The same principle partially accounts for the power and influence of the Jewish race, which power and principle seem to be in inverse proportion to the number of Jews in the world.

It may be argued that race first is racial selfishness, and as such will not remove the reasons that called it into being; but this argument loses its validity when recognition is taken of the fact that certain problems seem to suggest their own remedies. Fire is regarded or reputed to be an effective agent in fighting, while steel is principally relied upon to cut steel. *To say that because Negroes are the victims of organized race first sentiment on the part of white people they should not organize along lines of race first to defend themselves is to inferentially condone their present oppression and counsel meek submission to its perpetuation.* Failure on the part of the oppressed to organize in terms of self as opposed to similar kinds of organizations on the part of their oppressors must naturally make their oppression more thorough. "Race First," "Negro First," or whatever the shibboleth adopted by Negroes may be, finds its highest justification in the practices and methods of their oppressors.

It is true that all races look forward to the time when spears shall be beaten into agricultural implements,[2] *but until that time arrives it devolves upon all oppressed peoples to avail themselves of every weapon that may be effective in defeating the fell motives of their oppressors.*

In a world of wolves one should go armed, and one of the most powerful defensive weapons within the reach of Negroes is the practice of Race First *in all parts of the world.*

Printed in *NW*, Saturday, 10 April 1920. The editorial appeared originally in *NW*, 26 July 1919; it was reprinted in *NW*, 10 April 1920 with this explanation: "This week we are reproducing an editorial written on July 26th last year by Mr. W. A. Domingo, at present editor of The Emancipator, under the caption, "Race First!" It makes quite interesting reading. Comment of our own is unnecessary. Each reader may furnish his own. H.[*ubert*] H. [*arrison*]." This editorial, marked "Exhibit #8," formed part of the file of exhibits attached to a 11 May 1921 letter from J. Edgar Hoover to William L. Hurley, Dept. of State. (DNA, RG 59, 000-612).

    1. Harrison would make use of the slogan in *When Africa Awakens* (New York: Porro Press, 1920), in support of his criticisms of the Socialist party's attitude to black Americans: "we say Race First, because you have all along insisted on Race First and class after when you didn't need our help" (p. 79 ff). The phrase contained an echo of Woodrow Wilson's "America First" speech delivered in April 1915 on the subject of America's neutrality vis-à-vis the conflict in Europe.

    2. A paraphase of Mic. 4:3.

Richard E. Warner to Marcus Garvey

2412 Seventh Ave.
New York City, Aug. 1st, 1919

Sir:

    Below is an itemized account as to how the $275.00 credited to House Grossman and Vorhaus, Lawyers for the Black Star Line, Inc., which money was borrowed from the Universal Negro Improvement Assn; was finally disbursed for the Universal.

    June 30th: Salaries to the Office Employes by Checks as follows:

W. A. Domingo, $20.00; Edgar M. Grey, $18.00;
A. G. Coombs $15.00; Mrs. Leadett,[1] $11.00;
Mrs. Whittingham, $9.00; R. E. Warner, $20.00
      Total $93.00

"30th: Salaries to Restaurant Employes by Checks as follows:

Two Waiters @ $12.00 each   24.00
One Cook @ $12.00   12.00

    "30th: Check to Printer for Paper issued to
    Mr. Grey   150.00
      Total $279.00

    It is believed your Check Book will verify said amounts, all of which you are very well acquainted. Courteously yours;

R. E. WARNER

Reprinted from *Garvey* v. *United States*, No. 8317 (Ct. App., 2d Cir. Feb. 2, 1925), Defendant's Exhibit RRR.

1. Carrie Ledeatt, formerly Carrie Mero.

William H. Lamar to Frank Burke, Assistant Director and Chief,[1] Bureau of Investigation

Washington Aug. 1, 1919

Dear Sir:

There is inclosed for your information copies of communications received from Consular G. E. Chamberlin and Acting Colonial Secretary Geo. Ball-Greene of Georgetown, Demerara, which were received from the Department of State. Very truly yours,

W H LAMAR
Solicitor

Inc.

[*Typewritten reference*] RW-FZ
[*Endorsement*] Negro Publications

DNA, RG 65, File OG 359561. TLS, Recipient's copy. Endorsement is handwritten.

1. Frank Burke (1869–1942) served as a U.S. government secret service agent for a total of forty-three years. In July 1919 he was appointed chief of the Bureau of Investigation; he resigned in July 1920. Afterward he served briefly as a special assistant to the attorney general and also as a special agent for the bureau, and later he accepted the position of manager of the investigative department, U.S. Shipping Board. (Dept. of Justice Personnel Records).

Dedication of UNIA Liberty Hall

[*Negro World*, 2 August 1919]

LIBERTY HALL DEDICATED AT GREAT MASS MEETING MARCUS GARVEY DEFIES HIS ENEMIES—BLACK STAR LINE GOING OVER THE TOP.

Sunday, July 27 was a memorable day in the history of the Universal Negro Improvement Association, for it was on that day that the organization moved into its new home, the old Metropolitan Baptist Church, 138th street, between Lenox and Seventh avenues, which has since been renamed "Liberty Hall."[1] A great crowd assembled in the hall on Sunday evening in response to a call that had been issued by Marcus Garvey, the president general of the association. The meeting was called to order at nine o'clock with the opening ode and prayer, and was presided over by Miss Henrietta Vinton Davis. The following program was rendered: A vocal solo by Mrs. Allen; a flute solo by Mr. Portius; a vocal solo by Miss Ash,[2] and a piano solo by Miss Callendar; all of which received the unstinted applause of the audience. Miss Davis then spoke for a few minutes on the meaning of liberty and why it had been selected as the name of the new hall. She took occasion to refer to the recent Washington riots[3] and lauded the colored people, particularly the women, for their fearlessness in the face of brutal and unprovoked attacks made upon them by white sailors, soldiers and civilians.[4] At the close of her address a silver collection was asked for and liberally subscribed by the audience.

The next speaker introduced was William H. Ferris, author of "The African Abroad," who lauded the organization and its founder. He related the military history of the Negro race from the time of Herod[o]tus down to the present day, and exhorted his hearers to have faith in themselves and the possibilities of the race. Another flute solo was rendered and Mr. Garvey was introduced. As he rose to his feet he was greeted with thunderous applause. Mr. Garvey said that perhaps that speech would be the last one in many years, as he was apprehensive that certain si[ni]ster forces in the community that were trying to have him removed from the s[ce]ne might have their aims achieved. He said that at 10.30 the next morning [28 July] he would have to appear before District Attorney Kilroe. He enjoined upon the members of the association and its supporters to see that the splendid ideals for which it stood survived even if he became a victim of the malice of his enemies. When he was away in the South he left two scoundrels in charge of the office and it appears as if these two men, both occupying official positions, had used the knowledge they gained of the aims and objects of the Universal Negro Improvement Association to assist the white men of the country, especially District Attorney Kilroe, to hound and persecute him. However, the time had come for the Negro race of offer up its martyrs upon the altar of liberty even as the Irish had given a long list from Robert Emmet[5] to Roger Casement.[6] The principles of the Universal Negro Improvement Association were spread all over the world, and the removal of one leader would result in his place being taken by a hundred more. It was clearly the intention of white men, who fear the awakening of the Negro, to scatter the sheep by striking the shepherd. At one time Mr. Garvey asked those in the audience who were willing to sacrifice their lives for their race to stand and the vast gathering rose to its feet. He mentioned also that Mr. Edgar M. Grey, an ex-officer of the association, whom he had intended to prosecute, had apparently been instrumental in bringing about his present plight. After speaking for considerably over an hour an appeal was made for funds, while stock in the Black Star Line was offered for sale. This brought the meeting to a very successful close.

Printed in the *NW*, Saturday 2 August 1919.

1. Liberty Hall was also the name of the Dublin headquarters of the Irish Transport and General Workers' Union (ITGWU). The union established an office in 1909, following its formation in December 1908. In 1912, the union moved its headquarters to Dublin's North-

umberland Hotel, 18 Beresford Place, and renamed it Liberty Hall. The radical Irish socialist, James Connolly (1868–1916), described it as "the fortress of the militant working class of Ireland" (*Workers' Republic*, 8 April 1916; reprinted in James Connolly, *Labour and Easterweek* [Dublin: Sign of Three Candles, 1949], edited by Desmond Ryan, p. 175). The decision to proceed with the Easter Rising of 1916 was made at the meeting in Liberty Hall of the military council of the secret Irish Republic Brotherhood. (Cathal O'Shannon, ed., *Fifty Years of Liberty Hall: The Golden Jubilee of the Irish Transport and General Workers' Union, 1909–1959* [Dublin: ITGWU, 1959]). The UNIA Liberty Hall was located at 120 West 138th Street on the southeastern corner of Lenox Avenue and 138th Street. The adjoining property of 140 West 138th Street was acquired by the UNIA in April 1920, doubling the size of the original space. The original property was acquired from the Metropolitan Baptist Church for a purchase price of $27,000; the second property was purchased for $23,000. (New York County Clerk, Deeds and Mortgages, serial no. C 13319, liber 3101, p. 219; serial no. C. 7826, liber 3248, p. 113). In a magazine article ("Back to Africa," *Century* 105 [February 1923]: 539–48), W. E. B. Du Bois described the renovated Liberty Hall as "a long, low unfurnished church basement, roofed over," and also "a low, rambling basement of brick and rough stone . . . designed as the beginning of a church long ago, but abandoned." However crude it appeared, Liberty Hall became the spiritual tabernacle for the entire UNIA, inspiring UNIA divisions everywhere to establish Liberty Halls as meeting places in their communities.

2. Ida Estina Ash was third vice-president of the UNIA Ladies' Division. (*NW*, 11 October 1919).

3. The Washington riot erupted on 19 July 1919 and continued until 22 July. On 21 July, four persons were killed and eleven others were wounded seriously, some of them possibly fatally; ten of the dead and injured were white, while five were black. (Arthur Waskow, *From Race Riot to Sit-In, 1919 and the 1960s* [Gloucester, Mass.: P. Smith, 1966]).

4. Black resistance during the Washington riot, as well as during the Chicago riot, the other major racial disturbance of the summer of 1919, provided the focus for numerous expressions of racial pride in the black press. (Robert Kerlin, *Voice of the Negro* [1920, rpt. New York: Arno Press, 1968]).

5. Robert Emmet (1778–1803) was the leader of the abortive Irish rising of 1803. The rising began prematurely when the British discovered a concealed store of arms and ended in total confusion. Emmet was captured on 25 August 1803, found guilty of treason, and hanged on 20 September 1803. For many generations, he was considered one of Ireland's most romantic heroes. (*WBD*; Henry Boylan, *A Dictionary of Irish Biography* [Dublin: Gill and Macmillan, 1978], pp. 100–1).

6. Sir Roger David Casement (1864–1916), a former consular official with the British Foreign Office, returned to Ireland in 1912 and became associated with the Irish National Volunteers in 1913. He opposed the conscription of Irishmen to fight in World War I on England's behalf. He visited Germany in November 1914 to try and gain assistance in the fight for Irish independence, and while in Germany, he published a series of anti-British pamphlets and tried unsuccessfully to recruit Irish prisoners-of-war to fight on the side of Irish independence. A participant in the planning of the Irish Easter Rising, Casement sailed for Ireland aboard a German submarine on 12 April 1916. He landed in County Kerry, but the ship accompanying him was captured along with its cargo of German weapons intended for the Irish rebels. Casement was captured on 24 April, was subsequently tried for treason, and sentenced to death on 29 June. His appeal was denied and he was hanged at Pentonville prison in England on 3 August 1916. (*WBD*; Brian Inglis, *Roger Casement* [London: Hodden and Stoughton, 1973]; Benjamin Lawrence Reid, *The Lives of Roger Casement* [New Haven, Conn.: Yale University Press, 1976]).

Article in the *Negro World*

[2 August 1919]

Two Negro Crooks Use Office Of Deputy District Attorney Kilroe To Save Themselves From Jail

Last Monday [*28 July*] Mr. Marcus Garvey was ha[u]led before District Attorney Kilroe of New York to be indicted by the Grand Jury in preparation for eliminating him from the sphere of activity in the interest of his race. This made the sixth time Kilroe called Garvey, and every time Kilroe has failed to indict him, for Kilroe has all along been depending on the perjured statements of Negro vagabonds and scoundrels to indict an honest and honorable man. Kilroe wants to get Mr. Garvey out of the way because he is a thorn in the side of the white vagabonds who have robbed, exploited and murdered the Negro. Kilroe has kept the company of Negroes who have robbed the Universal Negro Improvement Association so as to get them to frame up against Mr. Garvey. In the examination last Monday Kilroe said, "If I don't get you it will not be my fault," and for the sixth time the District Attorney had the wrong information. Mr. Garvey went to Kilroe on Monday backed by thousands of Negroes in New York City. He made a speech at Liberty Hall on Sunday night before thousands of the members of the Universal Negro Improvement Association, whilst thousands gathered outside of the hall unable to get entrance and thousands turned away. For the first time in the history of the Negro they stood behind their leader and pledged their lives and their money. Kilroe is endeavoring to get Mr. Garvey out of the way because he realizes that to strike the shepherd he will scatter the sheep, but he is mistaken, for on Sunday night fully one thousand young men promised to avenge the life or the imprisonment of Marcus Garvey on a frame-up by white men. Negroes from all over the world made it their lifetime promise in America, Africa and the West Indies to get even with the white man for at any time tampering with that leadership upon which they depend for victory. Kilroe tried to make out that Mr. Garvey should not be president of the association, and Mr. Garvey asked him, "Do you think you are going to tell Negroes whom they should elect or not?" Kilroe fails to realize that Mr. Garvey does not represent the fawning, cringing, begging Negro whom he is accustomed to deal with, but that he represents the new type who means to get even with any white man who plays the fool. Kilroe fails also to realize that the Universal Negro Improvement Association and the Black Star Line is not a New York proposition, but a world-wide movement that may one day sweep a "few" Irishmen off their feet in the West Indies and Africa, if Kilroe plays the fool in New York by misusing his office as Deputy District Attorney to persecute honest Negro leaders. Mr. Garvey told him that he was waiting for the opportunity to expose the di[r]t that surrounds the District Attorney's office when he, Kilroe, could associate himself with and offer protection to men who had robbed the Universal Negro Improvement Association and the institutions it controls.

During the absence of Mr. Garvey in the South for two weeks he left behind in New York two men to represent him, one as General Secretary of the New York Local of the association and the other as Executive Secretary, the two vagabonds robbed the association and its allied corporations, and when Mr. Garvey returned to New York he started an investigation to have the men arrested and then they sought the aid of Kilroe, who offered them immunity if they would frame up Mr. Garvey. Kilroe admitted that he prevented Mr. Garvey getting a warrant for the arrest of Edgar M. Grey. Kilroe is shielding this man, who is a disgrace to the Negro race, in that he and Richard E. Warner during the absence of Mr. Garvey from New York did things that even the devil ought to be ashamed of.

If it costs the Universal Negro Improvement Association a million dollars through the strength of its membership all over the world, it will force Kilroe's hands to play a fair game. Mr. Garvey is longing for the opportunity of going before a jury of white Americans so as to be persecuted, as Kilroe feels sure he will succeed in having done, at which time the Negro peoples of the world will get the evidence they are waiting for to finally indict the white man's sense of justice.

Printed in the *NW*, Saturday, 2 August 1919.

Complaint of Edwin P. Kilroe against Marcus Garvey

CITY OF NEW YORK,
COUNTY OF NEW YORK
4th day of August–1919[1]

CITY MAGISTRATES' COURT OF THE
CITY OF NEW YORK,
IST DISTRICT, BOROUGH OF MANHATTAN

CITY OF NEW YORK,
COUNTY OF NEW YORK   SS.:

Edwin P. Kilroe OF NO. 408 Manhattan Avenue STREET, AGED [*blank*] YEARS, OCCUPATION Assistant District Attorney BEING DULY SWORN, DEPOSES AND SAYS THAT ON THE 2nd DAY OF August–1919, AT THE CITY AND COUNTY aforesaid

Marcus Garvey, did wilfully and malicious violate the provisions of Section 1340 of the Penal Law of the State of New York, in that he did cause to be printed and publ[is]hed in a weekly newspaper a statement in which statement the defendant exposed deponent to hatred, contempt, ridicule or obloquy, the same injuring deponent in his business or occupation under circumstances as follows.

Deponent further says that on the said date he was an Assistant District Attorney of the County and City of New York and in such capacity he was legally investigating the affairs of an organization known as the "Black Star Line" of which concern the defendant is President, for the reason that complaint had been made that the affairs of the said comp[an]y had been conducted in an illegal manner.

That under date of August 2nd 1919 in a newspaper known as the "Negro World" and of which newspaper the defendant is Managing Editor, there was printed and published on Page 2 of the said newspaper a statement headed "Two Negro Crooks use Office Of Deputy District Attorney To Save Themselves From Jail"

That the said newspaper and said printed statement therein is hereto attached and made part of this complaint.

Deponent further says that the said printed statement is false and libelous and caused to be published by the defendant in order to expose deponent as aforesaid.

Wherefore deponent asks that a warrant issue and the defendant be apprehended and dealt with according to law.

EDWIN P. KILROE

GEORGE W. SIMPSON[2]

City Magistrate

SWORN TO BEFORE ME, THIS 4th DAY OF
August 1919

People v. *Garvey*, No. 126535 (Ct. Spec. Sess., N.Y. County Ct. Aug. 9, 1920). TDS.

1. Garvey was indicted a second time on 28 August 1919 on an identical charge of criminal libel in the Court of General Sessions, New York County (Indictment No. 126535), but both indictments were subsequently amalgamated. When the case finally reached trial on 9 August 1920, Garvey filed a retraction statement and published a public apology on the front page of the *Negro World*.

2. George W. Simpson (1870–1951) served one term as state senator before being appointed as a temporary magistrate in 1918. The following year, and again in 1929, he was appointed to a full term. During his judicial term, Simpson handled cases involving commercial fraud. (*NYT*, 18 August 1951).

Newspaper Report

[*New York Call*, 8 August 1919]

NEGRO EDITOR IN COURT TO MEET CHARGE OF LIBEL

Marcus Garvey, editor of the Negro World and president of the Universal Negro Improvement Association, appeared yesterday before Judge Simpson in the First District Court to answer to the charge of libelling Assistant District Attorney Edwin Kilroe in the August 2 issue of the Negro World. Two attorneys appeared for Garvey and at their request, the case was postponed till August 28.

Garvey was arrested last Monday [*4 August*] in his office, 36 West 135th street, on a warrant sworn out by Kilroe, in which the latter declared Garvey had libelled him. . . .[1]

Printed in the *New York Call*, Friday, 8 August 1919. Original headlines have been abbreviated.

1. The remainder of the report consisted of both a direct quote and a paraphrase of the *Negro World* article, "Two Negro Crooks Use Office of Deputy District Attorney Kilroe to Save Themselves from Jail," printed above.

Capt. Henry G. Sebastian to Col. Alexander B. Coxe

Washington. August 9, 1919

MEMORANDUM FOR COLONEL A. B. COXE.[1]

Subject: Activities of Department of Justice on Negro Question.

1. In compliance with your instructions to me this morning, I had a conference with Mr. Burke, Assistant Director -in- Chief of the Bureau of Investigation, Department of Justice, to ascertain what efforts they are making to cover the Negro Question in any comprehensive manner.

2. Mr. Burke informed me that at first they paid little attention to propaganda among the negroes for the reason that they did not consider it a very serious matter. Later developments, however, have caused the Department to take more active steps and yesterday they employed a negro man as a special agent to cover activities within the District of Columbia. They have also instructed their Special Agents in the field throughout the United States to take such steps as they deem practical to obtain reliable information on this subject and, wherever possible, to employ reliable negroes who are in touch with the various negro lodges and associations to make full and

confidential reports on any propaganda that may be circulated or promoted among the negro race.

3. In connection with the investigation, Mr. Burke suggested that it might be well for the Military Intelligence Division to cover this field where it is practicable for them to do so as oftentimes Intelligence Officers may be in position to obtain information which could not be obtained by the Department of Justice Agents. Mr. Burke indicated that he would appreciate any information or assistance that the Military Intelligence Division might be able to give him in handling this question.

HENRY G SEBASTIAN[2]
Captain, Inf., U.S. Army

Mgw

[*Endorsement*] NOTED: A. G. CAMPBELL[3]

DNA, RG 165, File 10218-361/3. TDS, Recipient's copy. Stamped endorsement.

1. Lt. Col. Alexander B. Coxe (1872–1965). (*U.S. Army Register*, 1919).
2. Capt. Henry G. Sebastian (1890– ?). (*U.S. Army Register*, 1918).
3. Lt. Col. Arthur G. Campbell (1884– ?). (*U.S. Army Register*, 1919).

Frank Burke to Joseph A. Baker, Acting New York Division Superintendent

[*Washington, D.C.*] August 11, 1919

Dear Sir:

I have succeeded in obtaining the services of a Negro informant by the name of Dr. A. U. Craig who has in the past furnished valuable information to this office concerning the various movements among the Negro population in the city of Washington.

I am instructing Dr. Craig to proceed to New York and to report to you for the purpose of making inquiry into the activities eminating from New York of a radical nature among the Negro element in the country at large. Dr. Craig will work under cover and will endeavor to obtain information concerning the various leading Negro agitators in New York and the publications with which they are connected. I desire that any assistance that you may be able to offer him be furnished and have instructed him to confer with you upon all matters of importance. Very truly yours,

[FRANK BURKE]
Assistant Director and Chief

[*Address*] J. A. Baker, Esq., Acting Division
Superintendent, P.O. Box 241, City Hall
Station, New York, N.Y.

DNA, RG 65, File OG 258421. TL, Carbon copy.

C. B. Treadway, Special Agent-in-Charge, Jacksonville, Florida, to Frank Burke

Room 317 Federal Building
Jacksonville, Florida
August 11, 1919

Dear Sir:

I am enclosing a negro newspaper published at 38 W 135 St, New York City, called "The Negro World".

This copy was found in the hands of a negro by the name of S. P. Norris at Cocoa, Fla., and other copies were being distributed by him.

Such literature as this is causing a great deal of unrest among the negroes in this section and particularly those negroes who are trying to find some gr[ie]vance against the white people. The man who signs himself Marcus Garvey, seems to do most of the writing for this paper and the whole trend seems to be an advertisement to sell stock in the Black Star Line, Incorporated, which purports to be a Steamship Line to be owned and controlled and manned by negroes, which may be only a scheme to defraud by getting ignorant negroes to subscribe for this stock.

Mr. John A. Fiske, who maintains a hardware store at Cocoa, Florida, will keep this office informed concerning further distribution of this paper. Yours very truly,

C B Treadway
Special Agent-in-Charge

CBT/B

[*Handwritten endorsement*] EmR
[*Stamped endorsements*] File j.e.h. Noted
F.D.W.

DNA, RG 65, File OG 185161. TLS, Recipient's copy.

J. Edgar Hoover, Special Assistant to the Attorney General, to Frank Burke

WASHINGTON, D.C. August 12, 1919

MEMORANDUM FOR MR. BURKE

I am attaching hereto a memorandum which I have prepared relative to the investigation which Dr. Craig, the Negro informant, is to make while in New York City. I would appreciate it if you would look the same over and make any additions which I may have overlooked in the preparation of the memorandum. Respectfully,

J. E. HOOVER

[*Typewritten reference*] JEH/FWC
[*Handwritten endorsements*] Negro
Activities in New York City   OK FB will
see Craig when in NY
[*Stamped endorsements*] FILE J. E. H.
Noted F. D. W.

DNA, RG 65, File OG 258421. TNS, Recipient's copy.

Attachment

[*Washington, D.C.*] August 12, 1919

MEMORANDUM

The following are the principal phases of the Negro movement into which inquiry should be made:

1.   "The Messenger", published at 2305 7th Avenue, New York City. Editors, A. P. Randolph and Chandler Owen. Business Manager, Victor Daly.[1] Contributing Editors W. A. Domingo, William N. Colson[2] and Mr. G. F. Miller. The last mentioned is stated to be a prominent Negro preacher in New York. Domingo is the author of a pamphlet outlining a radical campaign among the Negroes.[3] "The Messenger" is stated to be the Russian organ of the Bolsheviki in the United States and to be the headquarters of revolutionary thought.

Inquiry should be made as to the citizenship of all persons connected with the editorial staff of this publication, together with their associates and business connections. Particular attention should be given to ascert[a]ining whether any of these persons are in any way connected with Max Eastman,[4] agents of the Bolsheviki in the United States, or the I.W.W. The income of this publication from its advertising and subscriptions should be definitely ascertained and any private source of re[v]enue should be fully inquired into.

2.   The Universal Negro Improvement Association, located at 36–38 West 135th Street, New York City. The prime mover i[n] this organization seems to be Marcus Garvey. "The Negro World" is the official organ of this Association. There appears to be an intense feeling existing between Garvey and the group supporting "The Messenger". The same information to be obtained as outlined above for "The Messenger" should likewi[se] be determined in connection with "The Negro World" and the Universal Negro Improvement Association. . . .

[J. E. HOOVER]

[*Typewritten reference*] JEH/FWC

DNA, RG 65, File OG 258421. TD.

1. Victor Daly, a lieutenant in the black 367th Infantry, was awarded the French croix de guerre. He was employed as the business manager of the *Messenger* after his demobilization. His book, *Not Only War: A Story of Two Great Conflicts* (Boston: Christopher Publishing House, 1932), "dedicated to the Army of the Disillusioned," was the first novel written by a black author about the war. During the 1930s, Daly worked for the U.S. Employment Service in Washington, D.C. (*NYT*, 15 May 1921; Hugh M. Gloster, *Negro Voices in American Fiction* [New York: Russell and Russell, 1948], pp. 217–18).

2. William N. Colson (1890–1923) enlisted in the U.S. Army on 15 June 1917, and was commissioned a second lieutenant in the U.S. Infantry four months later. After his duty in France, he returned to the United States on 15 March 1919, enrolled as a law student at Columbia University, and also became a contributing editor of the *Messenger*. His article in the July 1919 issue, "Propaganda and the American Negro Soldier," exposed the treatment of black soldiers in France and discussed the altered racial attitudes of black veterans. Congressman James F. Byrnes (1879–1972) of South Carolina, in a speech in the House of Representatives, cited his article as an example of "the activities of the IWW among the negroes in America." (AFRC, RG 163, registration card; DNA, RG 15, Veterans Administration pension file, XC-627-541; State of New York, Department of Health for the City of New York, Bureau of Records, death certificate, filed on 23 March 1925, No. 3505; *Congressional Record—House*, 25 August 1919 [Vol. 58, Part 5, 66th Congress, 1st sess.], pp. 4302–06).

3. "Socialism Imperilled, or The Negro—A Potential Menace to American Radicalism." The manuscript was among the documents seized in the Lusk Committee's raid of the Rand School of Social Science. The manuscript was received in evidence at the committee's hearing on 27 June 1919, and it was reprinted in its entirety in the final report of the Lusk Committee, *Revolutionary Radicalism*, pp. 1489–1510. It does not appear that Domingo ever published the manuscript as he originally intended. Domingo's argument expanded upon the thesis advanced earlier by A. Philip Randolph and Chandler Owen in their article, "The Negro—A Menace to Radicalism." (*Messenger* [May–June 1919]:20). (*NYT*, 30 June, 4 August 1919; W. A. Domingo, "Socialism, The Negroes' Hope," *Messenger* 2 [July 1919]:22).

4. Max Eastman (1883–1969) American socialist, writer, and editor of *The Masses* (1913–17) and *The Liberator* (1918–22). (*WBD*).

John W. Creighton, Special Assistant to the Attorney General, to A. Caminetti, Commissioner General of Immigration[1]

[*Washington, D.C.*] August 13, 1919

My dear Mr. Caminetti:[2]

Will you kindly advise me whether or not the case of Marcus Garvey of New York City has ever been called to your attention relative to the institution of deportation proceedings against this subject. Respectfully,

[JOHN W. CREIGHTON][3]
Special Assistant to the Attorney General

[*Typewritten reference*] JEH/FWC

DNA, RG 65, File OG 185161. TL, Carbon copy.

1. On 4 March 1913 the bureau was transferred to the Department of Labor from the Department of Commerce. In 1933, executive order no. 6166 united its various functions into the Immigration and Naturalization Service, and it became part of the Department of Justice in 1940.

2. Anthony J. Caminetti, (b. 1854) rose to prominence on the basis of his vigorous opposition to Asian immigration to California, which he claimed undercut the wages of white workers. The Wilson administration appointed him commissioner-general of immigration in 1913, and during the Red Scare of 1919–20, Caminetti played a prominent role in the deportation of alien radicals. Under the provisions of the Alien Law of 1918, deportation hearings were handled administratively without the necessity for a trial hearing. (Robert K. Murray, *Red Scare*, paperback ed. [New York: McGraw-Hill, 1964], p. 14).

3. John T. Creighton (b. 1884) served as an attorney in the office of the attorney general (September 1919–July 1920), and special assistant to the attorney general (May–August 1919). (Dept. of Justice, Personnel Records).

Frank Burke to Joseph A. Baker

[*Washington, D.C.*] August 15, 1919

Dear Sir:

My attention has recently been called to the particularly aggressive activities of Marcus Garvey, editor of THE NEGRO WORLD. I have been informed that Garvey is not an American citizen and for that reason would be amendable to the immigration laws relating to deportation.

I therefore desire that you immediately forward to me a complete summary upon all of the information in your files upon the activities of this subject and prepare for me at the earliest moment a case for deportation in line with the instructions set forth in the confidential letter forwarded to you on the 12th instant. Very truly yours,

[FRANK BURKE]
Assistant Director and Chief

[*Address*] J. A. Baker, Esq., Acting Division Superintendent, P.O. Box 241, City Hall Station, New York, N.Y.
[*Typewritten reference*] JEH/FWC

DNA, RG 65, File OG 185161. TL, Carbon copy.

Robert P. Stewart, Assistant Attorney General, to William Bauchop Wilson, Secretary of Labor[1]

[*Washington, D.C.*] Augu[st 15, 1919]

Sir:

I have the honor to transmit [for your?] action under the immigration laws [an anonymous] letter relative to alleged unlawful [activities on the]

part of Marcus Garvey, claimed to be [a citizen of] Great Britain. Respectfully,

For the Attorn[ey General]
(Sig[ned by) ROBERT P. STEWART][2]
Assistant Atto[rney General]

Inc. 8057.
[*Typewritten reference*] RPS–198940-2

DNA, RG 60, File 198940-2. TL, Carbon copy.

1. William Bauchop Wilson (1862–1934) was formerly a representative from Pennsylvania in the U.S. Congress; he was appointed secretary of labor in 1913. He also served on the Council of National Defense throughout the period of the war. (*WWWA*; Gengarelly, "Secretary of Labor William B. Wilson," pp. 311–29).

2. Robert P. Stewart (1876–1936) served as assistant attorney general from 1919 to 1921. (Dept. of Justice, Personnel Records).

Enclosure

New York City   August 11th 1919

Gentlemen,

As an American citizen I beg to direct your attention to the activities of Marcus Garvey, a negro subject of Great Britain, who is carrying on a very serious and intensive agitation among Southern Negroes as well as those of Africa and the West Indies. Garvey is president of the Universal Negro Improvement association with an alleged membership of nearly 6,000 members in New York besides branches in Africa, Canada, the West Indies and Central and South America /and other parts of the U.S.A./. The organization publishes a newspaper, "The Negro World", with Garvey as editor which has an alleged circulation of over 25,000 copies in various parts of the world, including the United States. So inflamatory and intemperate is its tone that it has been barred from Trinidad, Br Guiana, Antigua and Br Honduras.

It is the avowed object of the Association to stir up armed revolt among the natives of Africa and, if possible, among those of the West Indies.

The recent riots in Chicago & Washington have aided this propaganda immensely and Garvey has capitalized it to the extent of openly advising Negroes of Africa and the West Indies to kill whites in retaliation. This was written above his signature. He has also founded a Black Star Line to further dislocate the labor market by a inducing Negroes to return to Africa. He also entertains visions and hopes of smuggling [or?] shipping arms to Liberia & other African points for the purpose of "freeing Africa[."] This is written for the purpose of finding out if th[er]e is no law to stop this open incitation to rebellion which if realized will do irreparable harm to Negroes themselves.

At present your department is hounding Hindu nationalists[1] and while another group openly uses the United States as a base for revolutionary propaganda.

483

Garvey has no following other than deluded foreign Negroes and the most ignorant of American Negroes, but if not checked now his movement will gain momentum as the man knows his people's ignorance, psychology & weakness and plays upon them.

He is vulnerable along the following lines:

(1) He has manipulated the funds of the Black Star Line to liquidate debts of two other corporations of which he is also president.

(2) His accounts have never been audited and will disclose gross mismanagement and dishonesty.

(3) He uses the mails to circulate the newspaper which has /an/ advertisement of the Black Star Line which is obviously a fraud

(4) Co-operation with the British colonial office & secret service and will easily break his propaganda oin British territory.

(5) He is liable to the Mann white Slave Act[2] since he has traveled out of New York with his secretary and on his return has slept at her house regularly.

(6) He is wanted in Jamaica his native country [on a?] criminal charge besides having been arrested and in an in Costa Rica (Pt Limon) from which country he is an alleged fugitive of Justice.

In order to remove him with out creating the impression /of persecution/ among his deluded followers the writer would suggest

(1) that the circulation of the paper be impeded in the United States while the British government bars it in its colonies.

(2) Establish the fact of dishonesty on his part by employing a *Negro accountant* to go over his figures-/books./

(3) Issue releases his to the Negro press warning Negroes against bogus schemes of African repatriation and Negro Steamship Corp. Point the exam[ple of] the Chief Sam fiasco.[3]

So as to disabuse your mind as to personal animus against the man I will say that at present the district attorney of New York is investigating him but are apparently inclined to "go easy" but he uses it to make a martyr of himself and extract money from his dupes. A hint from your department or active co-operation showing that he toured the United States in 1916 collecting money for a bogus school in the West Indies will do much to removing a growing menace.

Believing that a hint to the wise is sufficient, I am, yours for speedy action

Enclosed copy (marked both sides) is from The Negro World, Aug 2nd, 1919

[*Address*] Department of Justice Washington D.C.
[*Endorsement*] STEWART [*illegible*]

DNA, RG 60, File 198940-2. AL, Recipient's copy. Stamped endorsement.

1. Between 1914 and 1917 East Indian nationalist and revolutionary organizations used the United States, especially California, as a base for activities directed against British rule in India. Chief among these groups was the Ghadar party, a revolutionary group which, with German assistance, had shipped both men and arms from the United States to India. Recognizing the Ghadar threat, Britain pressured the U.S. government to suppress the group's activities since it had violated U.S. neutrality law through its dealings with German officials in America. The American government, however, resisted the British pressure until its entry into the war. Consequently, in Chicago in October 1917 and in San Francisco in April 1918, thirty-three German and Indian defendants, including members of the Ghadar party's central committee, were convicted of conspiring to violate U.S. neutrality law. In addition to Ghadar activists, however, the American government also suppressed the activities of the less radical Indian nationalist, Lajpat Rai, whose publications the U.S. Censorship Board banned from the mails and whom various American intelligence services questioned in 1917 and 1918. At the end of World War I, the government also helped delay his return to India at Britain's request. (DNA, RG 165, file 10560-152, "The Hindu Conspiracy, the Ghadar Society, and Indian Revolutionary Propaganda"; N. G. Rathore, "Indian Nationalist Agitation in the United States: A Study of Lala Lajpat Rai and the India Home Rule League of America, 1914–1920," Ph.D. diss., Columbia University, 1965; Joan M. Jensen, "The 'Hindu Conspiracy': A Reassessment," *Pacific Historical Review* 46 [1979]: 65–83).

2. The Mann or White Slave Traffic Act, passed in 1910, prohibited the transportation through interstate or foreign commerce of any female for the purpose of prostitution or any other immoral purpose.

3. "The first Negro Steamship of the Twentieth Century" was how the purchase of the steamship *Curityba* (later rechristened S.S. *Liberia*) in New York in February 1914 by Chief Alfred Charles Sam, a Gold Coast African, was described by the distinguished West African educator, writer, and clergyman, Orishatukeh Faduma (1857?–1946). Faduma was also one of Sam's close collaborators (*Sierra Leone Weekly News*, 3 October 1914). Sam's career in America foreshadowed, in many significant respects, the subsequent appearance of Marcus Garvey, who arrived in the United States less than two years after Sam's departure for West Africa. For additional information on Chief Alfred Sam's career, see the Biographical Supplement, Appendix I.

Louis F. Post, Assistant Secretary of Labor, to A. Mitchell Palmer

Washington August 16, 1919

Sir:

I have the honor to acknowledge the receipt of your letter of the 15th instant (RPS—198940-2), transmitting copy of an anonymous letter relative to the alleged unlawful activities of Marcus Garvey, claiming to be a negro subject of Great Britain, and to state that the matter will be given proper consideration with a view to determining whether or not this man is subject to the immigration laws. Respectfully,

LOUIS F. POST[1]
Assistant Secretary

HMC/FE

[*Typewritten reference*] 54735/136[2]
[*Endorsement*] File HSR

DNA, RG 60, File 198940-3. TLS, Recipient's copy. Endorsement is handwritten.

1. Louis Freeland Post (1849–1928), writer, journalist, and reformer, served as assistant secretary of labor from 1913 to 1921, and was largely responsible for preventing the deportation of 3,000 alleged subversives arrested during the Palmer Raids in January 1920. (Dominic Candeloro, "Louis F. Post and the Red Scare of 1920," *Prologue* [Spring 1979]:40–55).
2. After conducting exhaustive searches, Immigration and Naturalization Service (INS) disclosed that it was unable to locate file 54735/136, "relating to Marcus Moziah Garvey born August 17, 1887, at St. Ann's Bay, Jamaica, British West Indies." It concluded that "this file is no longer in existence." (Letter from Stanley E. McKinley, INS, to the editor, 3 August 1978, file no. CO-2 12-C).

A. Caminetti to John W. Creighton

Washington August 16, 1919
(Attention of Mr. Hoover)

My dear Mr. Creighton:

I desire to acknowledge your letter of the 13th instant, concerning one Marcus Garvey of New York City and to advise that this case has never been called to the attention of the Bureau with a view to the institution of warrant proceedings. It is desired to add that a letter has been received this morning from R. P. Stewart, Assistant Attorney General, with which is transmitted copy of an anonymous letter concerning the alleged unlawful activities of this man. Very truly yours,

A. CAMINETTI
~~Assistant~~-Commissioner-General

[*Printed*] ADDRESS REPLY TO COMMIS-
SIONER GENERAL OF IMMIGRATION AND
REFER TO NO. [*Typewritten insertion*]
54735/136
[*Handwritten endorsement*] Hoover
[*Stamped endorsement*] NOTED J. E. H.

DNA, RG 65, File OG 329359. TLS, Recipient's copy.

Robert Adger Bowen to William H. Lamar

NEW YORK, N.Y. August Sixteenth 1919

My dear Judge Lamar:

I am in receipt of your letter[1] (WHL-FMK) of the 15th this morning.

It will be a pleasure to me to keep you personally informed of all that I may find in the Negro press. I am sending you at once copies of material I have already furnished the Department of Justice, and a little summary of the situation which I was asked to write by Mr. Keohan for his and Mr. Garvan's[2] information

Curiously enough, since the rioting, the negro press has not been particularly indiscreet. . . . I am watching all these publications carefully, and shall keep you personally informed of any transgressions or mischief-breeding influences. I am, Yours very truly,

ROBERT A. BOWEN

[*Typewritten reference*] RAB:PVF

DNA, RG 28, File B-240. TLS, Recipient's copy.

1. This letter has not been located.
2. Francis Patrick Garvan (1875–1937) served as assistant attorney general under A. Mitchell Palmer during the period of the Red Scare. Garvan was in charge of the newly created General Intelligence Division of the Department of Justice to investigate radical subversion. (*WWWA*).

Attachment

New York, N.Y. July 2, 1919

RADICALISM AND SEDITION AMONG THE NEGROES AS REFLECTED IN THEIR PUBLICATIONS

A general survey of the field of negro publications will give a very fair idea of the dangerous influences at work upon the negro, and the concerted effort, abetted by certain prominent white publicists, to arouse in the negro a well-defined class-consciousness, sympathetic only with the most malign radical movements. It will be the purpose of this brief summary to show that the negro editors and writers—and some of them are not without a marked ability—are fully alive to the influence they possess over their readers as well as to the fact that in their hands the negro masses may be made to assume a very dangerous power. Some of the ablest of these writers have gone beyond the point where advocacy of moderation and temperate counsel any longer contents them. They preach violence and "direct action." They urge affiliation with the I.W.W. as an organization peculiarly fitted to the negroes needs and his nature. The ablest of them all advocate Bolshevism among the negroes and the establishment in this country of Bolshevik rule. Even upon the subject of lynching, where the negro might reasonably count upon the sympathy of the more discerning, the attitude of these writers has become one of threatening and retaliation. It is not putting it too strongly to state that the cumulative effect of the various negro publications is to foster a sense of resentment and race antagonism, in which effort, ever since the entry of this country into the recent war, there has been increasingly employed the tone of menace and the threat of violent resistance.

To ignore all this as the ante-bellum characteristics of the plantation negro preacher is, I am convinced, to go very far astray of the mark. There is bombast and nonsense to be found in the negro publications of today, but when their editors and star contributors write of lynchings and race discrimination in the fray—when they write of their wrongs as they see them, it is in a mood very different from bombast and nonsense. And the negro himself knows it! He means business, and it would be well to take him at his word. . . .

The radical movement in the negro press has become remarkably accelerated during the past six months. To combat what was considered the too conservative character of such papers as The New York News, The Amsterdam News, and such magazines as The Crisis, sponsored in part by Oswald Garrison Villard,[1] of The Nation, /and/ The Crusader, there came into being The Negro World, an avowedly radical sheet, /which/ in its issue of *May 24, 1919* bore an editorial condemning the conservative character of most of the negro press with the notable exception of the infamous monthly, The Messenger. When it is remembered that the least offensive of the negro publications still is offensive in its attitude of racial antagonism an idea may be had of the character of The Negro World to whom the names of Booker Washington and Moton are synonymous with a craven subservience to the white man. . . .

In this necessarily brief, though I hope not altogether inadequate survey of the field of negro publications and of those tendencies of which they are the significant exponents, the salient facts are that, permeating even the negro masses, there has been aroused a dangerous sense of racial antagonism which is being thoroughly exploited by their leaders of the press, at least. The attitude is not one of wholesome endeavor to alleviate and correct the wrongs under which the negro labors. Rather is it one of increasing defiance and organized alignment with the most destructive forces of our political life today. The publications referred to in this paper, as well as such others as The Crusader, The Crucible, and others not mentioned, are not the out-put of "childish" minds, however ill-reasoned and absurd they may often be. The purpose of this summary has entirely failed of its mark if it has not made clear the fact that the negro is rapidly being made strongly race conscious and class conscious, and that to him his way of salvation is felt to lie not in conformity to the law but in defiance and antagonism of it, while of popular opinion he is encouraged to become increasingly more insolently scornful. It is not, in my opinion, an attitude that the government can safely ignore. . . .

ROBERT ADGER BOWEN

[*Typewritten reference*] RAB:MR
[*Handwritten endorsements*] EmR X Negro
Activities Negro Publications

DNA, RG 65, File OG 359561. TDS. Recipient's copy. A carbon copy located in DNA, RG 28, File B-240, has the following endorsement written in Bowen's hand: "Prepared for W[*illiam*]. F. Keohan at his request. B[*owen*]."

1. Oswald Garrison Villard (1872–1949) was the grandson of abolitionist William Lloyd Garrison and a lifelong activist in many liberal causes. He was associated with the Niagara movement and became one of the founders of the NAACP. Chairman of the executive board at its inception, Villard became treasurer in 1914. Although sometimes in conflict with the more radical members of the NAACP, Villard continued for many years to give crucial financial support to the association. (*NCAB*; *JNH* 35 [January 1950]: 105–06; Charles Flint Kellogg, *NAACP: A History of the National Association for the Advancement of Colored People*, vol. 1, 1909–1920 [Baltimore: Johns Hopkins University Press, 1967]).

Frank Burke to Joseph A. Baker

[*Washington, D.C.*] August 18, 1919

Dear Sir:

I am enclosing herewith a photostatic copy of a communication received in this Department concerning certain radical Negro Publications which have a circulation abroad.

Will you kindly make necessary inquiry into the publications referred to, two of which I know are published in your city, namely "The Crusader" and "The Negro World". Very truly yours,

[FRANK BURKE]
Assistant Director and Chief

Inclosure 7570[8?]

[*Typewritten reference*] JEH/FWC

DNA, RG 65, File OG 359561. TL, Carbon copy.

Brig. Gen. Marlborough Churchill to
Gen. Peyton Conway March, Chief of Staff

Washington August 20, 1919

MEMORANDUM FOR THE CHIEF OF STAFF:[1]

Subject: The Negro Situation.

1. There is submitted herewith memorandum on "The Negro Situation", prepared by Major J. E. Cutler just prior to his demobilization, with which is submitted final memorandum prepared by Major W. H. Loving, Philippine Constabulary at the time, just prior to his relief from duty with the Military Intelligence Division.[2]

2. These memoranda are considered important because they represent the views of two specialists who have devoted all their time for the past year to the study of this subject. Major Cutler is considered an absolutely impartial expert in sociology. Major Loving has always been regarded as one of the best types of "white man's negro" and the fact that he has, himself, recently shown an indication to criticise the handling of the negro situation by the War Department is considered as having an important bearing on the seriousness of the situation.

M. CHURCHILL
Brigadier General, General Staff,
Director of Military Intelligence

Encls.
ch

[*Endorsement*] Noted by C of S and Sec
War Returned by C of S Aug. 21. 19

DNA, RG 165, File 10218-361/12 2-1. TDS, Recipient's copy. Endorsement is handwritten. Copies of the memoranda were also submitted to the acting chief of the Bureau of Investigation, "in view of the seriousness of the negro situation," on 19 August 1919. In the letter of transmission, however, the director of Military Intelligence "requested that no reference to Major W. H. Loving be made public," and that "Major Loving has rendered most excellent service and it would be unfortunate if he should be made to suffer because of his willingness to assist us in the study of the negro problem" (DNA, RG 165, File 10218-361/8).

1. Gen. Peyton Conway March (1864–1955) served in France before being recalled to become chief of staff and President Wilson's chief military advisor on 20 May 1918. (*NCAB*).

2. Major Loving asked to be relieved of his duties on 31 August 1919 to return to his position as conductor of the Philippine Constabulary Band.

Attachment

[*Washington, D.C.*] August 15, 1919

CONFIDENTIAL.   (COPY)

MEMORANDUM FOR THE DIRECTOR OF MILITARY INTELLIGENCE.

Subject: The Negro Situation.

1. Radical propaganda has made noteworthy headway among the colored people in this country during the past three months. Since the demobilization of the colored organizations, the grievances of colored officers and enlisted men against white officers for alleged discriminatory treatment, and the absence of color prejudice among the French, as noted by the colored soldiers in A.E.F., have become matters of common knowledge among the colored people of this country. As a consequence, there is now a more fertile soil in which to plant seeds of extreme radicalism. The avidity with which the newspaper-reading negroes are buying and reading a periodical like THE MESSENGER demonstrates this fact.

2. The attached copy of a final report made by Major W. H. Loving, P.C., Retired, who has served as an agent of M.I.D. during the emergency, is believed to be a conservative and judicious statement by a colored man of the change that has taken place in the attitude of the colored people. It is the result of thoughtful consideration of the problems involved and an intimate knowledge of the growing influence of radical publications and of a new type of radical race leader.

3. The doctrines preached by I.W.W. agitators and radical socialists are daily winning new converts among the negroes, particularly among the younger and more irresponsible element. The long continued propaganda, as, for example, that carried on by the National Association for the Advancement of Colored People, urging the colored people to insist upon equality with white people and to resort to force, if necessary, in order to establish their rights, is now bearing abundant fruit. Beyond a doubt, there is a new negro to be reckoned with in our political and social life.

4. The emphasis which has been laid upon the principles of democracy and the self-determination of racially defined peoples, during the progress of the war, has not been without its effect upon the colored people of this country. They have become more sensitive than ever with regard to the practice of lynching, even though the victims of lynchings are not negroes exclusively, and with regard to "Jim Crow" regulations. It is true, also, that while hostilities were on, in the effort to make the Liberty Loan drives effective and to secure the patriotic cooperation of the entire citizenship, the colored people were led to expect a modification, or possibly removal, of some of the discrimination of which they complain. The fact that their expectations are not being realized is a source of disappointment and embitterment.

5. The recent race riots in Washington and in Chicago exemplify the new spirit animating an increasing proportion of the colored people. "Fight for your rights" is the new s[lo]gan. This office is informed that very generally throughout the country the negroes are purchasing firearms and ammunition. It is reported that negroes in the South are writing to friends in the North, asking that purchases be made for them. In Washington and elsewhere "defense funds" have been started, contributions to which are more or less openly solicited, on the plea that it is necessary for negroes to *defend* themselves against the aggressions of the whites.

6. One of the most unfortunate results of the riots in Washington and in Chicago is the fact that so many of the negroes are convinced that they won out against the whites in the riots, that they showed their superiority over white rioters and over the police, that even the troops were unable to do much against them. This attitude on their part, it is believed, may be productive of some very serious race clashes in the near future.

7. The fallacy in the statement that negroes, by insisting upon their rights and by *fighting* for them, will break down race prejudice, seems to be entirely over-looked at this time, even by most of the more thoughtful and better informed negroes.

8. In this final report by Major Loving, referred to in paragraph 2, there is evidence that he has himself, through familiarity with the activities of radical leaders and with their teachings, changed his viewpoint somewhat, at least temporarily. While he firmly believes that the colored people would be far better off without these self-styled race leaders who are springing up and teaching a socialistic radicalism, nevertheless, he seems inclined to feel that action to safeguard the interests of the colored people which could and should have been taken by the Government during the emergency has not in all cases been taken, hence agitation and the strongest pressure that the colored people can muster, short of actual hostilities, is now their only recourse. In this respect, he probably typifies the attitude of a considerable proportion of the more thoughtful and substantial negro citizens.

9. The present situation seems, beyond a doubt, to constitute a critical juncture in the history of the colored race in this country. It is conceivable that this may mark the beginning of what usually happens when a people native to the temperate zone comes in contact with a people native to the tropical zone, to which the record of the colored race in this country has hitherto been a notable exception. It is certain that the capacity of the citizens of this country to govern themselves will be severely tested during the next few years, with regard to this as well as other matters. . . .

16. It is possible that so brief a sketch of the present situation as is here given draws a picture which is somewhat out of proportion. Perhaps it gives an unwarranted impression as to the extent and predominance of radicalism among the colored people. It is difficult for any one who knows the negro at his best to believe that any considerable proportion of the colored population, outside of the younger, more or less irresponsible element, will be

misled by unsound doctrines and self-appointed radical race leaders. Yet, unquestionably there is a potential and impending danger in the present situation which may not wisely be disregarded, particularly in view of the existing general social and industrial unrest. There is a race consciousness among the colored people today which is of recent origin and which is susceptible to direction and manipulation by those who have sinister motives. . . .

(Sgd.) J. E. CUTLER
Major, U.S. Army

mgw

Attachment

New York, August 6th 1919

From: Major W. H. Loving, P.C.
To: Director of Military Intelligence, Washington, D.C.
Subject: Final Report On Negro Subversion.[1] . . .

Universal Negro Improvement Association

The avowed object of this organization is to awaken race consciousness among Negroes of the United States and Africa, with the aim of gradually bringing about a unity of purpose between the Negro peoples of both continents. The scheme is very broad in scope and includes the establishment of closer relations between all the colored races of the world with a view to their mutual cooperation. This work is being carried on by clever propaganda directed principally by Marcus Garvey, a West Indian Negro whose office is at #36 West 135th Street, New York City. Mr. Garvey has been the subject of many previous reports to your office. This movement, like most others of its character, originated in New York City and has a weekly newspaper, The NEGRO WORLD, as its official organ. This organization holds periodical mass meetings which are usually well attended but the scope of its plan is too broad to determine at this time the extent of any influence it may exercise in accomplishing its desired results. I have ascertained that there has been considerable correspondence between the officers of this organization in New York and prominent colored men in foreign countries. Its leaders are all radical but most of them are lacking in the intellectual equipment possessed by the young Negroes in the Socialist Party and those at the head of the League for Democracy. This, however, is not true of Marcus Garvey and W. A. Domingo, who are very able young men. This organization is too young as yet to give it any special significance other than the fact that it has aligned itself with the radical forces now active throughout the country. It should be borne in mind, however, that correspondence and exchange of views between American Negroes and prominent colored men in other countries such as Africa, India, China, Japan and the West Indies, will no doubt have its effect in due time in establishing a closer relationship between the colored races of the world. I am informed that after the peace has been ratified it is the intention of this organization to raise funds and send agents to the countries named above to spread the propaganda. This is to be accomplished not by public lectures, but by establishing personal relations of friendship with the more radical natives in each country and leaving to them the work of getting the message to the masses. . . .

W H LOVING
Major, P.C., Retired

[*Handwritten endorsement*] Confidential
[*Stamped endorsements*] NOTED:
A. G. CAMPBELL
NOTED: M. CHURCHILL   MAJOR J. E.
CUTLER

DNA, RG 165, File 10218-361/1 190X. TDS. Recipient's copy.

1. A copy of Major Loving's final report was submitted to the British Cabinet on 7 October 1919 by the Directorate of Intelligence of the British Home Office as Special Report No. 10 (Secret), entitled "Unrest Among the Negroes." (PRO, CAB. 24/89, GT 8289).

Bureau of Investigation Report

NEW YORK CITY AUG. 22, 1919

IN RE: "NEGRO WORLD" Negro Activities.

Based upon the Chief's letter of August 18th, initialed JEH, attached to which was photostat copy of communications from the Acting Colonial Secy. at Georgetown, Demerara, British Guiana, sent to the U.S. State Department, regarding the circulation in that country of negro publications originating in the United States, namely "The Crusader," ["]The Monitor," "The Recorder" and "The Negro World," and following instructions of Special Agent Scully,[1] I this day have gathered the following information on the "Negro World." It might be mentioned here that "The Monitor" and "The Recorder" are not New York publications and therefore will not be reported upon by the writer. A separate report is being made on the "Crusader."[2]

The editorial page of the "Negro World" states that it is issued from 36 W. 135th [S]tr., N.Y. daily, published by the *Universal Negro Improvement and African Communities League*, Marcus Garvey, Managing Editor and W. A. Domingo, Literary Editor (the latter, I believe is no longer affiliated with the paper.) It is impossible to give any data upon this paper without going into the activities of Marcus Garvey, its manager and leading spirit.

This paper first came to our attention during the elections of 1918, when Garvey, his association, and the paper came out squarely in support of all candidates on the Socialist ticket, particularly three negroes running for U.S. Congress and State assembly. Those, by name, are George Frazer Miller, A. Philip Randolph and Chandler Owen. All were defeated.[3] Retaliating for its support of the Socialist Party, the New York "Call", Socialist Daily, in an editorial thanked the "Negro World" and since that time has been on very friendly terms. The "Call's" comment reads

> "The new negro is here and there will be many more of them to enrich the Socialist movement in the United States. . . .[4]

An informant who is considered probably the best in negro circles in the United States, known to the writer, but not in the employ of this Bureau, states that he considers Garvey and the "Negro World" the largest and most dangerous figure in Negro circles to-day. In commenting upon Garvey's cleverness, trickery and quick rise in the political field among the negroes, he cited the fact that the subscription list of the "World" rose from 1,000 to its present 50,000 mailing list within one year. He stated also that Garvey's office on 135th Str. is sort of a clearing house for all international radical agitators, including Mexicans, South Americans, Spaniards, in fact blacks and yellows from all parts of the world who radiate around Garvey, leave for their destinations, agitate for a time, and eventually return to Garvey's headquarters.

Altho the "Negro World" in the past has, thru writings, shown its sympathy with Socialism and particularly with Bolshevism, Garvey has been clever enough to see the error of his tactics in entering the field upon a partisan political standpoint. He has made a recent tour of the South, particularly Virginia, and it may or may not be significant that the Washington riot broke out shortly after his return here. Since returning he has, thru the "Negro Worl[d,"] come out upon a platform of straight pro-Negroism, disclaiming affiliation with any political party, stating that his only work is to aid in supporting the New Negro Party of the world, which, he states, is 400,000,000 strong. In the "Negro World" for July 18th [*19th*], Garvey in a printed letter, states that his organization is gaining millions of converts every month, and adds to this statement the daring prophesy:

> "The U.N.I.A. realizes that the war of 1914–8 is over, but all negroes must prepare for the next world war . . . So long as the Negro [*is oppressed*] all over the world there can be no abiding peace. . . . .

> Negroes must now combine with China, India, Egypt, Ireland and Russia to free themselves in the future. Our Fatherland, Africa, is bleeding, and she is now stretching forth her hands to her children in America [*, the West Indies and Central America and Canada to help her*]."

Our informant has promised to try and obtain the name of the man who handles the international exchange of correspondence and magazines for Garvey.

I called upon Col. Thwaites of the British Provost Guard[5] to-day in connection with this case, and he furnished me with a 26 page report upon the general negro situation, which I have turned over to Agent Scully, who states he will have it copied and forwarded to Washington.

Subsequently, I went to the General Post Office and interviewed Mr. Bowen of the foreign language translating section and Mr. Weller. The former advises that the Negro World has only lately come in for second-class mailing privileges, previously having been sent as regular mail.[6] Altho persons granted the second-class privilege are required to file a certificate of ownership, Mr. Weller informed me that this will not be done by the "World" until next October, having applied too late for the last statutory ti[m]e, in April.

M. J. DAVIS

WED

[*Endorsement*] A. C. DUNNE. M.I.4 9/20/19

DNA, RG 165, File 10218-261/59. TD. Stamped endorsement.

1. Charles J. Scully (? – 1952), chief of the Radical Department of the Bureau of Investigation, played a prominent role in the deportation of Emma Goldman, Alexander Berkman, and self-styled Soviet Ambassador Ludwig C.A.K. Martens. (*NYT*, 15 February 1926, 6 August 1952).

2. The report was filed on 29 August 1919 (DNA, RG 65, file OG 387162).

3. The black Socialist candidates collected from 5 to 12 percent of the total vote cast. (Michael L. Goldstein, "Black Politics in New York City, 1890–1920." [Ph.D. diss., Columbia University, 1973], pp. 336–41).

4. The material omitted pertained to an article in *NW*, 9 November 1918, which detailed the aims and objects of the UNIA and ACL. This section of the report also contained quotations from Garvey's speech of 1 December 1918 and a notice about a meeting for the Black Star Line for 27 April 1919.

5. Lt. Col. Norman Graham Thwaites (1872–1956), British intelligence officer, was sent to New York to serve as assistant provost-marshal with British military intelligence, and was promoted to a full provost-marshal in November 1919. He was in close correspondence with U.S. authorities involved in the investigation of alleged subversive activities in New York. In 1920 British military intelligence closed the New York office and Thwaites returned to England. (*The Times*, 27 January 1956; *WWW*; Norman Graham Thwaites, *Velvet and Vinegar: Autobiographical Reminiscences* [London: Grayson & Grayson, 1932]; and Lusk Committee Papers, box 2, file 4).

6. The *Negro World* was entered as second-class matter 16 April 1919 at the New York Post Office.

Memorandum by the Bureau of Translation, Post Office

[*New York City*] August 22, 1919

NEGRO WORLD

Published at New York, N.Y., by the Universal Negro Improvement Association and African Communities League, Marcus Garvey, Managing Editor.
Issue of June 7, 14, 21, 28, 1919.
Referred by the Third Assistant Postmaster General, July 11, 1919. Letter enclosed.

MEMORANDUM

. . . The columns of these issues appear to be taken up first with matters[1] that tend to instil into the minds of negroes of this and other countries that they have been greatly wronged and oppressed by the white races and that they can only hope for relief and redress through concerted and aggressive action on their part; and, second, the promotion of an organization styled "The Universal Negro Improvement Association And African Communities League;" of which the editor, "Hon Marcus Garvey, D.[S].O.E." announces himself to be "President and International Organizer." See advertisement on last page of each issue.

Among other projects of this Association is the establishment of "The Black Star Line," presumably to transport negroes to Africa, or other countries, and for this purpose "$2,000,000. must be raised in four months starting from Sunday the 8th instant ["] (June, 1919).

It may also be noted that the bona fide character of these enterprises and of "Hon. Marcus Garvey's" good faith, have been questioned by several members of his race: also, that investigations have been made in regard to them by the "District Attorney of New York." See references made thereto on pages 1–2, columns 1–2, issue of June 21, 1919.

ws-h

DNA, RG 28, File B-500. TD.

1. The material excerpted mentions the following *Negro World* articles: "Negroes! Read, Mark, Learn and Inwardly Digest. Bolsheveki Say Freedom of Negroes at Hand. Can This Be Possible?" (*NW*, 7 June 1919); "White Lynchers and Liars Spreading Alarm," (ibid., reprinted from the New York *World* and the *Messenger*, n.d.); "New War Planned by Irish, Germans, and Bolshevikis," (*NW*, 7 June 1919); "What Say Negroes? Shall They Have Died in Vain?" (ibid.; reprinted from *New York Call*, n.d.); "Message to Negro People of the World," (*NW*, 28 June 1919); "Revolt Threat by Negroes," (ibid.); "Gun, Ballot and Strike Are Weapons of Negroes, Says Army Officer [Maj. Joel E. Spingarn], Advising Latter," (ibid.); and "Negroes Be Ready For Next War," (ibid.).

UNIA Meeting at Carnegie Hall

New York City, August 25th, 1919

MEETING OF UNIVERSAL NEGRO IMPROVEMENT ASSOCIATION AND THE AFRICAN COMMUNITIES LEAGUE OF THE WORLD.[1]

Verbatim report of Speeches.
by
William [F.] Smart,

Certified Shorthand Reporter.

MASS MEETING
-of-
THE UNIVERSAL NEGRO IMPROVEMENT ASSOCIATION AND THE AFRICAN COMMUNITIES' LEAGUE OF THE WORLD.

Carnegie Hall, 57th St. & 7th Avenue,
New York City, Monday, Aug. 25, 1919, 8:30 p.m.

CHAIRLADY:

MISS HENRIETTA VINTON DAVIS, International Organizer, of Washington, D.C.

SPEAKERS:

Hon. Marcus Garvey, D.S.O.E., President-General of League and President of Black Star Line, Inc.
Dr. M. N. Shaw, of Boston, Mass.
Rev. J. W. H. Eason,[2] of Philadelphia.

THE CHAIRLADY: We will now open by singing "From Greenland's Icy Mountains". (Prayer).

The Chairlady called the meeting to order at 8:40 p.m.

THE CHAIRLADY: The very pleasant duty of welcoming you to this splendid edifice is incumbent upon me in the name of the Universal Negro Improvement Association and the African Communities League.

We are gathered here for a very serious purpose, and that is to carry forth the great project that has been undertaken by the Universal Negro Improvement Association and the African Communities' League—the launching of the first ship of the Black Star Line, on October 31st. (Applause).

We have prepared a program for you, and I now take very great pleasure in introducing to you, with a musical selection, Mr. Steel. (Song).

We will now be favored with a solo by Miss Ash. (Solo).

We will now be favored with a recit[at]ion by Miss Ashwood, our General Secretary. (Recit[at]ion—"The Colored Soldiers".)

(Great applause as Capt. Cockburn,[3] the First Commander of the Black Star Line, appeared on the stage).

CHAIRLADY DAVIS: This is Captain Cockburn of the Black Star Line. (Applause).

We will now be favored with a solo by Mr. Bradley. (Song).

ADDRESS OF CHAIRLADY.

CHAIRLADY DAVIS: We are very glad to have so many people who are interested in the Universal Negro Improvement Association and African Communities League to be present with us tonight in Carnegie Hall, New York City, but you are but a modic[um] of the many negroes who are interested in this great organization.

Tonight the negroes in Africa, our fatherland, the negroes in Central America, and South America, and the West Indian Islands, are offering up their prayers for our success here tonight. (Applause).

This great organization was founded in the City of New York about twenty-one months ago, by the Hon. Marcus Garvey. (Applause). From the small number of thirteen earnest, serious-minded negroes, we have grown to in numbers to about 5,500 members in that short time in the City of New York. (Applause).

We have branches of this Association in many of the other States of the Union, in all the Islands of the West Indies, in all the countries of that vast continent, South America, and all the countries of our fatherland, Africa; (applause); and we are here to emphasize the work of the twenty-one months that we have worked so assiduously here and elsewhere for the growth of this organization, for the carrying out of the ideas and ideals of the Twentieth Century negro who is now occupying the center of the stage. (Applause).

After this great World War, in this period of reconstruction, the negro has come into the ideal of his own solidity, the ideal of his own unity, no matter what country he may have been born in, no matter what flag may have floated over him, the negro, although patriotic and loyal and faithful to all the flags under which he has served, yet he feels the time has come when he must stand forth among the other races of the world, among the other darker skinned people of the world; he must stand forth and ask, in fact he must demand his rights in this reconstructive period. (Great applause).

We are here tonight, having representatives from every country, every island, every State where the negro lives, representatives are here tonight speaking for their own countries, for their own islands; but they are standing firm, solidly, as negroes. (Applause).

We are here tonight to renew our pledges, to stand more firmly on the platform of this great organization that takes in all the negroes, whether he be a French negro, a Spanish negro, an Italian negro, a German negro, (laughter), or an Irish negro (great laughter)—whether he speak the Spanish language or sing the Italian language, as Mr. Bradley has so beautifully done for us tonight—we are here standing on the platform of the brotherhood of the Universal Improvement Association and African Communities League. (Applause).

We have many other speakers on the program, and it is not my purpose to stand here tonight to take up the time. You have me with you always. You hear from me always; and we will ask that the ushers wait upon the friends in the two upper galleries and receive from them their contribution for this splendid cause. Those who have paid an admission fee to come into this hall, we are not asking you to contribute, but we think it no more than right that the friends who have come here to join in with us, should contribute something towards the expenses of this meeting.

We are glad to have you here. This is but an initial meeting of many meetings that shall be held for the Universal Negro Improvement Association and African Communities League. It is well that we meet together. It is well that we stand together shoulder to shoulder and arm to arm, ready to stretch forth that arm in defense of our own race now. The negro has fought every battle but his own. (Applause).

The time has come, the time is at hand, the hour is near, and the negro must fight for the negro. (Applause).

Do they think that when our brother is lynched in Florida, that we do not feel it in New York? Do they think that when our brother is taxed beyond endurance in the British Islands, that we do not feel it in New York? Do they think that when our brother in the interior of Africa is mal-treated, misused and robbed, that we do not feel it in New York?—No, a thousand times no. Our brothers' woes are our woes, and we are here tonight. (Great applause).

I now take very great pleasure in introducing to you that man among men, that fearless man who dares to look a white man in the eye and tell him what he thinks of him. (Applause). The old-time cringing negro has played his part and passed off the stage of action. (Applause).

The new negro is here, a man, a full-fledged man, asking, demanding his rights of the powers that be—the Hon. Marcus Garvey.

MARCUS GARVEY (President-General of League and President of the Black Star Line, Inc.) (The whole audience here rose). Lady Chairman, Ladies and Gentlemen: I am here tonight to represent the interests of the Universal Negro Improvement Association and African Communities League of the World.

I am here, not representing 100,000 people in New York of the race, but 15,000,000 negroes in the United States of America; 15,000,000 negroes in the West Indian Islands, and the negroes of South and Central America, and the 280,000,000 on the continent of Africa. (Applause).

We speak tonight from Carnegie Hall to the 400,000,000 of our people scattered all over the world.

We are here because the times demand that we be here. We are now living in a world that is reorganizing itself. It is reorganizing itself out of a bloody war as fought for four and one-half years, a war in which men were called out from all parts of the world, from the four corners of the world, to die for the sacred cause of democracy; to give liberty to all mankind; to make all men free; and in the war as fought for 4 1/2 years, they took out 2,000,000 black men from America, from the West Indies and Africa, to fight for this farcical democracy they told us about; and now we are, after winning the fight, winning the battle, we realize that we are without democracy; and we come before the world, therefore, as the Universal Improvement Association, to demand our portion of democracy (applause); and we say woe betide the man or the nation who stands in the way of the negro fighting for democracy!

We stand here tonight as the Universal Negro Improvement Association, on the same uncompromising platform as the Irish stand, as the Hindu stands, as the Egypti[a]n stands, and we say "We shall not yield one inch of our rights until we get all belonging to us". (Applause). For three hundred years, the white tyrant of the world encompassed us as slaves and made us peons. Between 1914 and 1918, a new doctrine was taught to the world, the doctrine of right.

To maintain that doctrine, thousands of negroes out of 2,000,000 called, died on the battle-fields of France and Flanders. We died there gladly, thinking that we were shedding our blood for a real cause. After that blood is shed we now realize that it was a farcical cause; that we have found out our mistake before it is too late; we say we shall continue the war until we get democracy. (Applause).

We stand here determined and absolute in our rights. President Woodrow Wilson entered this war on the principle of democracy. He mobilized the strength of this country for that sacred cause. England, that great Anglo-Saxon Empire or Nation, heralded to the world that she was fighting the cause of humanity, and caused President Wilson to deliver to her the strength of the American Nation; and through the declaration of England, the negroes scattered in the West Indies, in Central America, and Africa, rallied to the colors of the Allied Nations.

We fought, and after the battle what was done to us? They mobbed us in Liverpool, in London and Manchester. The English in Wales stopped the funeral procession of the West Indian negro, smashed the coffin, cut off the head of the dead man and made a football of it (cries of "Shame"). The British did that in Great Britain.

In America, below the Mason and Dixon Line, what did they do to Mary Turner?[4] Oh, I will not repeat because it is common knowledge to the world.

Now, in the face of the continuity of such outrages, how can the new negro of today, that same negro who fought in France and Flanders be satisfied with this farcical democracy in the world? (Applause and Cries of "No").

We shall not be satisfied. Therefore we declare this: We, who have survived the war, that the same blood our brothers gave in France and Flanders to free the whites, the Belgians and the Serbians, the same blood we are prepared at any time to shed in the ema[nc]ipation of the negro race. (Great applause).

The white man of the world has been accustomed to deal with the Uncle Tom cringing negro. Up to 1918, he knew no other negro than the negro represented through Booker Washington. Today he will find that a new negro is on the stage representing the spirit of the [*omission*].

We are fifteen millions in America; we are fifteen or twenty millions in the West Indies; and two hundred and eighty millions on the continent of Africa, and we have declared for a free and independent race.

In this re-construction period, when the Irishman is striking homewards towards Ireland to make Ireland a free and independent country, when the Hindu is striking homeward toward India to make India a free and independent nation and empire, the negro says—the negroes of the world say "We are striking homewards towards Africa to make her the big black republic" (applause), and in the making of Africa a big, black republic, what is the barrier? The barrier is the white man; and we say to the white man who now dominates Africa, that it is to his interests to clear out of Africa now (applause), because we are coming, not as in the time of Father Abraham, 200,000 strong, but we are coming 400,000,000 strong (applause); and we mean to re-take every square inch of the 12,000,000 square miles of African territory belonging to us by right divine. (Applause).

They say to us in East St. Louis, "We do not want you here". They say to us in Chicago, "We don't want you here". They say to us in Washington "We don't want you here", in America—They say to us in Liverpool, "We don't want you here", and so in Manchester and Cardiff, and in other parts of Great Britain—the audacity of the white man after keeping the negro in America in slavery for 250 years! That negro, through his sacrifice, through his blood, has made America what it is today. (Great applause).

That same audacious white man kept the negro in the West Indies in slavery for 230 years, and through the blood and sacrifice of the West Indian negro, the British Empire became a possibility; and the Englishman says "We don't want you—I don't want you in Liverpool, in Manchester or in London—black man". Aint it time now for the black man to think of turning to the white man and saying "I don't want you here"? (Applause). And if we have come to that stage in America, where the white man is in America ninety million whilst we are only fifteen, and if he says it in England where he dominates the country, must we not say /it/ therefore in the world where we dominate by numbers? That is the question; and as the Englishman asked the negro in Liverpool and Manchester what he is doing there, so the new negro means, within the next 20 years, to ask the white man in the continent of Africa, "What are you doing here?" (Applause).

This African question is one that every negro must understand now or never. Every American negro and every West Indian negro must understand now that there is but one fatherland for the negro, and that is Africa. (Applause). And as the Germans fought and struggled for the fatherland of Germany; as the Irishman is struggling and fighting for the fatherland of Ireland, so must the new negro of the world fight for the fatherland of Africa (applause), because if we allow the white man to continue in his old-time ways, it will mean that in the next fifty years there will be very few negroes left in the world. (Laughter.)

You remember what the white man did to the North American Indian. What he did—he exterminated him. When the white man wanted to find a place and the Indians stood in his path, he cleared the Indians from his path; and today the Indian is underground. When he did that, he was building up civilization for himself. He was building a new world for himself. He succeeded in building the new world, but what happened? Between 1914 and 1918, the white man of the world destroyed what it took him 2,000 years to build. (Applause). And today he is where he was two thousand years ago (applause).

Therefore, he is going to restart something. What is that something? He is going to restart that thing he started hundreds of years ago—exterminating and robbing all those who stand in his way; and not long ago you remember what he did to us. Three hundred years ago only, he made slaves of us; and at the time when he made slaves of us, he was better off than he is now (laughter), because he was not nearly bankrupt. Today he is a bankrupt (laughter). The Englishmen is a bankrupt. The Frenchman is a bankrupt. The German, the Austrian, the Russian—all are bankrupts (laughter); AND YOU KNOW a hungry man makes no fuss. If a man is hungry and he sees bread in his way he is going to take it and grab it, caring not to whom it belongs. A bankrupt man is like a hungry man.

It means, therefore, that the one country in the world that has wealth, mineral, agricultural and otherwise, is the great continent of Africa, and this arch-lover of the world—his eyes are now centered on the Continent of Africa. The Englishman's eyes are centered on the Continent of Africa. The Frenchman's eyes are centered on Africa; so with the Italians and the Germans; but the poor Germans have not a look-in. (Laughter).

It is their fault, anyhow. The Kaiser had no right to start any war; but anyhow, the wars that the Kaiser started suited our purpose (great applause); and therefore we are not indebted to the Kaiser at all. We have no fault to find with this man at all because in four and a half years he had negroes in New York who, in 1913 used to work for $20 a week—he helped them to get $80 a week. (Laughter and Applause). And if he had kept up this thing a little longer, some of us would have been better off tonight. But anyhow, he was defeated, and who defeated him—the black man. (Applause). It took the black man to whip the Kaiser's soldiers, and up to now there is not a more glorious record in the history of the war than the record of those two boys from the New York 15th (applause)—Needham Roberts and Johnson have proved to the Kaiser that the negro is more than a match for the German soldier; but Needham Roberts and Johnson were fighting somebody else's battle, and even though they knew they were fighting for someone else, they did half of their best, now. (Applause).

Now, when those boys and the four hundred millions of us start to fight for ourselves, what will happen? (Great applause). That is the question—that is the question for the white man to solve; and if he takes my advice, he will solve it quick (applause), because the new negro means business.

If any Englishman, if any German, if any Frenchman, if any white American man thinks that the new negro is going down on his knees to beg anything to-day, he makes a big mistake (Applause).

We are out to get what has belonged to us, politically, socially, economically and in every way (applause); and what fifteen millions of us can not get, we will call in the four hundred millions to help us get. (Applause).

Hence the Universal Negro Improvement Association comes before you tonight, not representative of any one section of negroes in the world, but of all the sections.

We are as much American as we are British; we are as much British as we are French; we are as much French as we are German (laughter)—because there is a terrible mix-up (laughter). We did not mix ourselves up; they mixed us up (laughter).

In the fight of the Universal Negro Improvement Association, as the Chairlady said to you a while ago, this Association was first founded on the Island of Jamaica, and 21 months ago was founded in the United States of America. We started in New York with thirteen members, and in the space of 21 months, what has happened? We have made 5,500 members in the district of Harlem alone. We are scattered with twelve branches, and some of the branches out of New York are stronger than the New York branch.

We are at places like Virginia, /In/ Newport News, Virginia, there are 5,000 members there (applause). We have branches of our Association in 25 States of the Union. We have branches of our Association in every West Indian Island (laughter) and Central America, and more than all men, we stand doubly strong on the West coast of Africa. (Applause).

All that we have to do in New York is to press the button, and later on—(great applause)—and later on we really mean to press the button.

Those crackers of the South who have been lynching our brothers and sisters, our mothers and our fathers and our children for over 15 years, they have been doing that thing, because they realize that in America there are ninety millions of white people, whilst there are only 15,000,000 of black. They realize by strength of numbers they will be able to take advantage of us;

and they have been getting away with their cowardice, because we were not an organized people; but in the next few months we will be so organized so that when they ~~launch-a-ne~~ lynch a negro below the Mason and Dixon Line, if we can not lynch a white man there, and since it is not safe to lynch a white man in any part of America, we shall press the button and lynch him in the great continent of Africa. (Great applause and much excitement).

From time immemorial, we have been told that the white man represents God (laughter); that the angels are white (laughter); that the very Heavens are draped in white; and all that is pure, all that is good and sublime, is white. They were able to tell us that for 300 years. Now, I wonder [if] they have the nerve to continue to think that they can tell us that now. (Laughter). We have caught the new doctrine. The white man says that everything that is pure is white. The yellow man of Asia is saying that everything that is pure is yellow. The black man is saying that everything that is pure is black (applause); and according to the white man's doctrine, if the Beings who preside over the two worlds other than this one, and I mean the eternal worlds, the one called God, and the one called the devil, if those two Beings have the semblance of mankind, then, as the white man has been saying all the time that the devil is black, and God is white, we are going to say that God is black and the devil is white (laughter), because if you are to compare men by their ways, if you are to compare the Dieties therefore, that have connection with man both ways, we can easily see who is the devil today. Why? Tell me how many people the blacks have killed within recent years on their own initiative? I can not think of any. How many have the whites killed, of their own initiative—over ten millions, just a few days ago, and they were not satisfied in doing the killing themselves. They had to call out two million black men to help them kill (applause); and because we were unable to help ourselves, because we had no organization, we had to go out and kill, even though we had no cause against those who were killing. (Cries of "No" and applause). But why were we not organized—because we had negroes of America like Booker Washington, to be succeeded by Russey [Russa] Moton. We had negroes in the West Indies like those frothy negroes there who have been always bowing down to white men, because we had not the right kind of negroes in Africa, and therefore, the white man found us napping in 1914, and he was able to say, "Come on here, negro of America, go fight and die"; "Come out here, West Indian negro, go fight and die"; "Come out here African negro and fight and die. You are fighting for democracy", and we had to go.

But there is one thing we are going to do now. We are going to so organize ourselves all over the world that when the white men say—any white man wants a black man to die in the future, they have to tell us what we are going to die for. (Applause).

The first dying that is to be done by the black man in the future will be done to make himself free. (Applause). And then when we are finished, if we have any charity to bestow, we may die for the white man; but, as for me, I think I have stopped dying for him. I do not know what you have to say about that (uproar and cries of "Yes"). Thank you. Therefore, all of us who are here representing the spirit of the new negro (cries of "We do" and applause), and that therefore will give the lie to the New York Times of a few days ago, that published yesterday, that published some news from Washington wherein it said that in New York City there is a movement led by the Bolshevists and the I.W.W. and the movement is striking out to make the negro independent.[5] I want to answer the Times from Carnegie Hall tonight. The Times seems to believe (applause)—the Times still seems to believe that they are dealing still with Booker Washington.

Now, I hope the Times will correct that wrong impression and go out tomorrow morning and tell the world as was told on Sunday, that the new negro need no other leadership but his own (applause). We are in this Universal movement that is encircling the world. We are neither Democrats nor Republicans nor Socialists nor Bolshevists nor I.W.W.'s (applause), because whether we are Democrats, Republicans, Socialists or I.W.W.'s, all of them are white men, and when they were robbing us from Africa, they robbed us with all parties—Republicans, Socialists, Democrats, ~~Soci~~ I.W.W.'s, and everybody settled us and brought us here (laughter); therefore, we are not going to waste time over the white man's politics. All the time we have to waste is with pro-negro politics (applause).

We belong to a new party—the party that means we will never stop fighting constitutionally—in countries like America and Africa, where we respect no constitution we will continue to fight, and fight until we make ourselves a great people—the new race that is to be (applause).

My allegiance to America has been questioned. Now, let me answer that accusation from Carnegie Hall. If there is one country in the world I love, that country is America. (Applause). Why do I love America? Because America was founded upon the principles of liberty, and America has always offered the opportunity and inducements to all peoples who were in search of liberty to come here and agitate the question of liberty. (Applause).

America helped the Irish. America helped the Jew. America helped the people of the Eastern states of Russia to air their grievance to the world, and for those principles I love America—and for those principles only. (Applause).

And, as the Irish came and spoke from this Carnegie Hall; as the Russians came and spoke from this Carnegie Hall; and some will get what they agitated for—and the Irish are going to get theirs—so do we come tonight to agitate so as to get ours.

The Irish have been fighting for over 700 years to free Ireland. From the time when Robert Emmett, when he lost his head, to the time of Roger Casement, Ireland has been fighting, agitating and offering up her sons as martyrs.

As Emmett bled and died for Ireland, so we who are leading the Universal Negro Improvement Association, are prepared at any time to free Africa and free the negroes of the world. (Applause).

So I trust that everybody understands the platform on which the Universal Negro Improvement Association stands. It is on a platform of manhood rights. We say if it is right for the white man to rule, to dominate, if it is right for the yellow man of Asia to rule and dominate, it is time for the negro to rule and to dominate (applause), because God created of one blood all nations of men to dwell upon the earth. He never said to the white man,— "You are to be the perpetual master and lord, and negroes must be your slaves". Although the white man had been so bad and wicked as to write a thing called the Bible and put in there and say that black men shall be hewers of wood and drawers of water" (applause and laughter)—The white man put that there and expects that 20th Century negroes to believe that (laughter). Now, we believe in everything in the Bible except that. (Cries of "No").

Now, if there is any one man in the world, whether he is an American white man or an English white man, or a French white man who thinks he can get me to chop his wood, let him come—or draw his water—let him come.

So, I want you all to understand, therefore, that the Universal Negro Improvement Association stands on a platform of manly rights. We want to see our men occupying positions in the world as white men are occupying; (Applause); as Asiatic men are occupying. We want to see our women occupying positions and stations in life as white women and yellow women are occupying (applause).

We say that the time for the negro woman to leave the kitchen is now (applause); and we of the Universal Negro Improvement Association swear by everything that is in this creation, swear by the Almighty God, that we are going to make a new race out of this negro race (applause); and that brings me to our great proposition known as the Black Star Line. (Applause).

There is [a] corporation organized and chartered by the State of Delaware, known as the Black Star Line; and fortunately, or unfortunately, I am also President of that corporation, and also President of the Universal Negro Improvement Association. (Applause).

I am lending my influence, the influence I have in America, and the influence I have in the West Indies, Central America and South America, places where I have lived and travelled for years before I came to America—I am using my influence to make the Black Star Line a possibility on the 31st of October of this year. (Applause).

That corporation is capitalized at $500,000. Within a few months its capital will increase to $10,000,000 (applause); and we are now putting on the market the $500,000 of common stock of par value of $5.00 a share, and we are asking every negro in New York City to own as many shares as possible in the Black Star Line. If you cannot own 100 shares, own 50; if not

50, own 20, 10, 5 or one; but we want every negro in Carnegie Hall tonight to be a stockholder in the Black Star Line, so as to be one of its owners. (Applause).

The West Indian negroes in the West Indies, and the South American negroes and Central American negroes are doing their part. We are selling as many shares through our branches in the West Indies and in Central Africa [*America?*], as we are selling in America; and tonight I am asking when the ushers present to you the application slips for stocks, to write your names down, and put down as many shares as you can afford to buy. Pin your money on to the application blank. The usher will give you a receipt for the money, and tonight or tomorrow or any day of this week you can get your stock certificates. Those of you who can remain behind long enough, you can get your certificates from the Treasurer here tonight. Those of you who can not wait to get your stock certificates, you can call at our office, 56 West 135th Street tomorrow, or any day next week, and get your stock certificate; but tonight we want every one of you to subscribe for shares in the Black Star Line, as the ushers hand you subscription blanks, and I want you to do it quietly while Dr. Shaw will speak.

I am called an orator, but Dr. Shaw is a greater orator, and you are going to hear him tonight. (Applause)

The things I can not touch on, the things I can not touch on because I am not an American citizen, Dr. Shaw will touch on because he is an American citizen. (Applause). I am not an American citizen not because I do not want to be an American citizen. I would have been too glad to become an American citizen tomorrow morning, but time will not permit me, because in the very near future I will have to travel into other parts of the world; and with the Universal Negro Improvement movement, the country that has the most negroes under her flag today is Great Britain, and I was born under the flag of Britain. (Applause). Britain kept me a slave for 230 years, and Britain will have to tell me the reason why; and when I go to Britain I do not want them to say to me "You are an American citizen", because those Britons are the greatest camoufleurs in the world. When they wanted the help of America, there is nobody as dear as the American. When the American wants justice, there is nobody so hideous as the American; but I say Brittonain will have to tell me why she kept me a slave for 230 years.

If David Lloyd George, if Herbert Asquith, if Bonar Law, and Arthur J. Balfour think that I, standing here tonight, [am] afraid of them, then wait until I get in London when I meet them in the Royal Albert Hall. (Applause). They might have succeeded in driving those Africans and West Indian negroes out of London, but they will have do some driving to get me out (applause), because they say—"You are a British subject; you are a British citizen"; and I shall claim my right of citizenship, and I shall go to Trafalgar Square, as Mrs. Pankhurst[6] went there; as Ramsay MacDonald[7] went there; as all the other fighters for the cause of liberty went there. I shall go to Clapham Common, Hyde Park, Trafalgar Square, and I will go also to the Royal Albert Hall and tell the white man in England what I think of him; and I feel sure that the Bonar Law and A. J. Balfour class, when they are ready to fight the negroes of Africa, they will have to fight themselves, when I am through with the English workman.

My duty is to let the English workman know that his cause is the negro's cause; (applause); and that he has absolutely no right to fight the negro, to make Balfour, Bonar Law, and those idle bluffing class, continue to fool the world.

So I am going to take my seat now.

I want every one of you here to subscribe for as many shares in the Black Star Line as possible. Buy them up tonight, writing your names down, or addresses, and the number of stocks you want and pass the money and the application blanks to the ushers. I thank you. (Applause).

CHAIRLADY DAVIS: While you are all subscribing for your 100 shares of stock in the Black Star Line, we will be favored with a selection by the Acme Quartette, who have so kindly volunteered to help us out on the program tonight. The Acme Quartette can be engaged other evenings—that is their business, to entertain people, and by applying at 56 West 135th Street, the headquarters of the Universal Negro Improvement Association and African Communities League, you can engage their services. We will now be favored by the Acme Quartette. (Applause).

(Songs by the Quartette—"Going to play all over God's Heaven").

CHAIRLADY DAVIS: We know that you all have enjoyed that. The only original music that the American people have ever produced is the music of the negro (applause); wrung from the hearts of a sorrowing people have come these songs of jubilee. After the Rev. Dr. Shaw shall have addressed you, we will have another selection by the Quartette.

I now take very great pleasure in introducing to you the Rev. Dr. Shaw, the great pulpit orator.

REV. DR. SHAW:[8] Lady President, President-General and Friends: The hour is far spent. The time in this hall is limited, and it is absolutely impossible to do justice to the subject before me in the time that is left to us here.

The great purpose, the outcome and end of this effort tonight particularly is to secure purchasers for stock in the Black Star Line, for the past thirty nights stocks have been on sale, and have been bought up every night, by blocks of it; and this is the great night for the cleaning up of the balance of the stock in the hands of the managers of this Company for New York.

I have that in mind and must reserve the detail of the discussion that I proposed to have here tonight, for Thursday night at Liberty Hall[.] Thursday night I shall enter fully into the subject and be able to do justice, I hope, to myself, if not to the subject.

At last the worm has turned, and we are here in Carnegie's Hall for business, for definite, colossal business. We are here to lay a foundation deep enough, wide enough, to take the idea of our expansion, and of the colossal superstructure outlined by the President; and therefore it is necessary that we should, first of all, stand together and independent, distinctly from other peoples.

It was Mr. Taft who said not long since, that the negro of America must be treated in this country as a distinct people. He has since that time swallowed that up a dozen times over. In his remarks on the Chicago riot lately, the ten[o]r was an entirely different one.[9] The key-note was also different, and consequently the song was an absolute new thing; and not only Mr. Taft too, but the white people of this country among whom there are a number of very decent men—I can not speak of the white race of America and forget that Sumner and Garrison and Phillips and Melville Storey[10] and Pilsbury,[11] and those men, belonged to it, but I am very cautious about universal statements because they are difficult of proof; and therefore I am contended, and it is enough to say that the vast majority of the white people of this country, and of England, and of that European tribe who have had their hands on the throat of the negroes for centuries, are coming now into their own, and it is just as easy to suspend the Falls of Niagara by the palms of two hands, as to stop the doom that God Almighty has passed upon Anglo-Saxonism today. (Applause).

There is no way out for Anglo-Saxonism—doomed eternally, and doomed by a righteous God, whether they believe in his existence or not. (Applause).

The new negro has nothing in the world to fear. He is standing upon the platform of fair play, a square deal and justice to all mankind (applause); and we want to inform Anglo-Saxonism from Carnegie Hall tonight, that the Universe is built, established and suspended upon the principles of eternal justice and righteousness, and he has got to face that fact or else—

The American negro of today wants the white people of this country to know that we have taken their words long enough, and do not intend to go upon their say-so, a minute longer. (Applause).

Whether or not the claim to almost divinity that they arrogate to themselves, the power of initiative and of management, all of which they declare, are centered in their race, that the negro is absolutely devoid of the power of initiative; that the Holy Spirit is incapable of inspiring them to leadership and to the management of their own affairs, as it has inspired the Anglo-Saxon—whether that thing is true or not, the state of affairs in the world today testifies.

Not since God said "Let there be light and there was light" was there so much confusion and mix-up as we have under the regime and authority of Anglo-Saxonism today. (Applause)

An East Indian poet, speaking from the rostrum of Tremont Temple in Boston not long ago said that Occidental civilization had converted men into money-making machines, and had burned out all of their souls; and that is as true as any word written between the covers of the Good Book.

The facts of the case and the condition of affairs prove that. The white man has lost his soul. As a race, he has lost his humanity. He ~~has~~ is a hard, unrelenting taskmaster, determined to grind out of the darker races the ounce of flesh, the pound and the blood with it. Just so his position is fortified, it matters little or nothing to him who suffers. Just so, Mr. Anglo-Saxon is well provided for. (Applause).

This is probably one of the most peculiar Falls in America, this coming Fall. It finds the American Government upside down. One thing, however, that Woodrow Wilson settled for us is in locating the Democratic Party as a National power, 100 years behind (laughter). What he has done in this Administration has fixed that party for the next 100 years to come (laughter). . . .

I was elected President of the delegation of negroes appointed in Washington to visit France in the Peace Conference. Mr. Wilson's administration refused us passports, and did not want us to go to France for fear we would tell the truth in Europe, of the negro situation here, and explain to Europe that Mr. Wilson does not represent a democracy (applause); but that he actually and in truth, and in fact, represents the most rabid plutocracy that curses God's earth today. (Applause).

I say, he denied us the right to go, but I declare before my God, that if I had been in Versailles, I would have tried to get a little more for America than he got. (Applause).

The Republican Party is the party of our race, up to perhaps tonight, but it will not be so tomorrow. We have no party—no party. We have none.

We are acting as the Association for the improvement of colored people, and the Leagues of Africa, and the Independent Political Equal Rights Leagues of this country are going to do our best sparing neither means nor pain, to organize our people, to be absolutely independent, and to cast no ballot for any party that will not guarantee—I do not mean promise, for we have been promised it from the days of reconstruction until tonight, but that was all.

We want the 13th, 14th and 15th Amendments of the Constitution of this United States of America enforced, and taken down from the shelf (applause); and until the Republican Senate now in Washington, until the members of the Republican Party now in Congress in Washington, and before November of this year, get a law through that will enforce those amendments, so that negroes in New Hampshire, as well as negroes in Texas, shall have the right of the ballot, and the right to vote for according to the dictates of their conscience, we want—I have only five minutes yet left—I want those five minutes to announce further that the negro has not only decided not to be attached to any political party as such, but to stand off for that party that will guarantee him his manhood rights. We want no favors. (Applause). We want a man's part, a citizen's share. We have no regard for the color of citizens. All Americans must be measured by their soul—"For the mind is the standard of the man"; and until that is done, and you have got it to do now, or else we will stand in the way of any man's election, and any party going into power on the mere say-so, which is not the breath with which it is uttered.

The last suggestion that we have to make is to give the American people notice that negroes have refused to die alone—now. (Applause) Not only will we seek an opportunity to revenge our wrongs, where we are in the majority in Africa, but every man that lifts a hand against a negro must die with that negro. (Great applause).

Another of my advice to my people is that after we shall have forced Congress, and we must do that if it costs us the last drop of blood we have to make those amendments of the war, those war amendments, active and vital laws, we know that after the Supreme Court has passed upon it, and Congress and the Senate have ratified laws, that men who go to Alabama will be met with Southern crackers, but we will take the law and everything in their hands, and shoot them down at the polls. We know that.

Therefore, we advise our people not to be offensive, not to assault, not to insult, and not to be aggressive, but to be absolutely prepared to be on the defensive. (Applause).

In marching down to a Southern pooll hall /place/ to cast his ballot, it beho/o/ves every negro to go with two Smith & Wessons, one in each hip pocket. (Applause). He must also have two razors, one in each coat pocket (laughter); for the Southern cracker's conscience is in his hide, and you have to go there to get it. Those are facts, and they are sad but true, and the negro today has made up his mind to defend his home, to defend his life, to defend those who are dependent upon him—"For no man can die better than facing fearful odds, for the ashes of his fathers and the Temple of his Gods." (Applause).

I urge you—in conclusion, I urge you to come Thursday night where I shall have an opportunity to talk for at least sixty minutes upon this vexed question, this question, at boiling point. We are to decide now. We are to take no steps backward, but to go constitutionally, to go seriously, to go stubbornly, to go forward earnestly.

Here is a fact I want you to know. Mr. Wilson thought he could dodge the issue of getting European representatives to listen to the negro story about facts here. It has been mooted that the next and very first meeting of this League of N[a]tions, is /to/ take place in Washington some time before this winter. We are going to spare no pains to get one solid million negroes present at that meeting in Washington—yes, one million (applause) negro men shall be in Washington whenever it meets there—this year, next year or five years to come. The only way that he will succeed, or anybody else, in keeping those European representatives from hearing us,—the thing must never come here (applause), and it must never meet in times of peace, for we have got the money, and more than that, we are going to have our own Black Star Line to carry us by the hundreds wherever under the great sun that League of Notions shall meet (laughter). They will have to hear us and we will see to it, and when they refuse, we will turn as of yore, to God, and He will not deny us the hearing we want (Applause).

MARCUS GARVEY: Now, friends, we have here tonight on the platform, one of the officers of the Philadelphia Division of the Association, the Philadelphia branch of the Universal League, which stands as strong as the New York Division, and I want you to hear a word or two from its representative; but before he speaks, and before the Quartette sings again, I want you to realize that the expenses for this hall are very heavy, and you have not yet supplied the quota necessary to liquidate it, and I am asking the ushers to wait on you, and whatsoever you can give to defray the expenses, so as not to involve us in debt, you will do it tonight. The ushers will wait on you, and those of you who have not yet bought your stocks, if it is not convenient for you to buy while the ushers wait on you, at the close of the meeting you can meet the Secretary and Treasurer of the Black Star Line outside the door in the vestibule, and they will sell you all the stocks you want; but whilst the other speakers speak, you can still buy from the ushers, so the collection will be taken up and then the Quartette will sing.

(Song by the Quartette "They tell you once, they tell you twice, there are sinners in hell for shooting dice".)

CHAIRLADY DAVIS: We will now have a selection from that famous 15th Regiment Band. (Selection by band).

We will now have a short address by Dr. J. W. H. Eason, President of the Philadelphia Branch of the Universal Negro Association and African Communities League.

REV. J. W. H. EASON: Mr. Honored Sir, Honored Sirs, Ladies and Gentlemen: A new scene is before us tonight.

An old negro put his foot out one day and it was extremely large. A man came along and intentionally stepped upon it. The old negro said "Excuse me, boss, for having my foot in the way". The young negro, the new negro, had his foot out. A man came along and intentionally stepped on it, and mashed it. The new negro looked in his face and said "What the hell do you mean?" (Applause).

My friends, we represent tonight that class of our people who believe in doing right to everybody, and then demanding the same from everybody we come in contact with. (Applause). I, for one, have spent thirty years in preparing to preach the Gospel, and I find that I can best preach the Gospel of the Son of God by telling all of my people everywhere to live right, do right, and fight like hell. (Great applause).

It is a delight for me to be here tonight. I am extremely busy. We have just put on a drive in Philadelphia for ten thousand new members of the Philadelphia Division (applause); and Honored Sir, when the new year dawns upon us, we will be able to send you a telegram, wherever you may be, that the 10,000 mark in Philadelphia has been reached; and not only that, my friends, but we are striving there, and I have the distinguished honor to be the Executive Secretary of the People's Campaign Committee—we already have something that has never been heard of in the history of Philadelphia before, and I am glad to state that a large number of other people have already granted our request, and we are starting to elect a negro magistrate, and two negro councilmen. (Applause).

I do not know anything about politics. I speak straight from the shoulder, and they tell me in order to be a good politician, you have to be a trickster; but I do know something about "negrotics", and I am in the thing to advance our people, and I believe that the Negro Improvement Association and the African Communities League will meet our requirements better than any organization anywhere in the world (applause).

I have had an opportunity of being a student of the affairs of my people, and of the other people, for that matter, and I have found out that it was a part of the defined plan that under the leadership of this, our President, that the negroes throughout the world should be called together, not for the purpose of doing any harm to anybody, but in order to keep anybody from doing any more harm to us. (Applause).

I am delighted to be here tonight. I have heard enough to send me back to Pennsylvania inspired, and from time to time I shall be glad to come back to New York and speak to you here, or at Liberty Hall, or at any other place where I can get an audience of people.

God bless you; may Heaven smile upon you; but remember that you have got to work out your own /soul's/ salvation, by working together. (Applause).

MARCUS GARVEY: We are going to dismiss, but I want you to remember what I said. Those of you who have not bought your stocks inside, you can buy your stocks from the Secretary o[r] the Treasurer in going out. Now, the band will play for us whilst we all stand. We will sing America. "America— My Country 'Tis of Thee"—(Song).

Then Dr. Shaw will dismiss us in prayer.

DR. M. N. SHAW (Boston, Mass): Dismiss us, we beseech Thee, our Father, with Thy benediction, and Thy grace. Cause Thy great face to shine upon us, and be gracious unto us. Lift Thou up the light of Thy countenance upon us and grant us peace and good success. We ask it in Jesus' name. Amen.

MARCUS GARVEY: Now, all of you who have not bought your stocks, be sure to buy them there and you can come out to Liberty Hall next Sunday night [*31 August*]. (Cheers).

(The meeting adjourned at 11:00 o'clock p.m.)

Sm-ga

N, New York (State) Legislature, Joint Legislature Committee to Investigate Seditious Activities (Lusk Committee) Papers, Part One, Box 4, Investigations File 1.

1. Bureau of Investigation Special Agent C-C attended the meeting and, in a report dated 26 August 1919, stated the following: ". . . Attendance about 2500 composed with but few exceptions of forei[gn] Negroes, men and women and no children, from the West Indies,

Central America and South America, etc. . . . Shares for the Black Star Steamship were sold. *The Negro World* was sold as well as circulars were given out concerning the Black Star Steamship Co." (DNA, RG 65, file OG 329359).

2. James Walker Hood Eason (1886–1923) was perhaps the most prominent black American clergyman ever to become involved in the leadership of the UNIA. Named for one of the most distinguished AME Zion bishops, Eason was born in North Carolina where he attended the denomination's undergraduate institution, Livingstone College. After graduating in 1912, he attended Hood Theological Seminary where he had James E. K. Aggrey (1875–1927) of the Gold Coast as one of his teachers. Eason completed his theological training in 1915 and served briefly as the pastor of a church in Charlotte, N.C., before moving to Philadelphia. He joined Varick Memorial Church in Philadelphia but withdrew in 1918. Eason took several of the church's members with him to form the People's Metropolitan AME Zion Church. At the time of the Philadelphia riot in July 1918, Eason participated with other black ministers in organizing the Colored Protective Association to protect black residents of Philadelphia from further violence. In August 1919, Eason joined forces with Garvey and the UNIA after becoming disillusioned with the NAACP which he had joined previously. However, Eason's use of the People's Church facilities in Philadelphia for UNIA organizational meetings led to a physical conflict with some church members and later an embittered legal battle. Shortly after joining the UNIA, Eason was elected the first UNIA chaplain-general, a post he held until he was elected to the position of "Leader of American Negroes" at the UNIA's first International Convention of the Negro Peoples of the World in August 1920.

Renowned as the "silver-tongued Eason" for his remarkable oratorical gifts, the flamboyant cleric-politician was nominated in November 1920 as the black presidential candidate of the Harlem-based Liberty Party which had been organized by Hubert H. Harrison, William Bridges and Edgar M. Grey. Eason was shot and killed by UNIA supporters in New Orleans in 1923. (*Philadelphia Tribune*, 27 September 1919; *NW*, 28 August 1920; DNA, RG 60, file 203677; DNA, RG 65, files BS 198940-107, 198940-171; OG 208369, 208369-A, 317834, 329359; Randall K. Burkett, *Black Redemption: Churchmen Speak for the Garvey Movement* [Philadelphia: Temple University Press, 1978], pp. 51–63).

3. Joshua Cockburn (b. 1876) became a highly successful Harlem real estate broker after his career as a seaman. Born in Nassau, the Bahamas, BWI, Cockburn began his nautical career on the Royal Navy's vessel, *Richmond*, serving there for three and one-half years. After studying navigation, he became a second mate in Liverpool in 1900, and a first mate in 1910 while serving on the West African coast on the S.S. *Egerton* with a largely African crew. In 1915 he received his master's certificate, and during the war, he again served with the Royal Navy. In 1918, however, he immigrated with his family on the S.S. *Eboe* to the United States arriving in New York on 18 October 1918. (*Lloyd's Register of Shipping, 1918–19*). In July 1919, after reading a newspaper article about Garvey's difficulties with Assistant District Attorney Kilroe over the acquisition of a ship for the Black Star Line, he sought out the UNIA leader and introduced himself as an experienced ship captain. Cockburn immediately became involved in the negotiations and eventual purchase of the S.S. *Yarmouth* and received $1,600 commission for his role as a broker. On 19 September the Black Star Line formally hired him as captain at a monthly salary of $400 to begin on 1 November. In the interim he was paid a partial salary, and during this period Cockburn accompanied Garvey on a promotional tour for the sale of stock in the Black Star Line, Inc. In 1922 Cockburn reentered the real estate business in Harlem while continuing to work as a shipping agent, and in 1924 he filed a declaration of intention to become a U.S. citizen (Letter to editor, 12 November 1981, from General Register and Record Office of Shipping and Seamen, Cardiff; *WWCA*; *NW*, 25 October 1919; *NYT*, 10 February 1924, 23 March 1937, 8 June 1937; *BM* 2 [August 1937]:19, *Garvey v. U.S.*, pp. 292–423; DNA, RG 65, file BS 198940; AFRC, Naturalization certificate, no. 149266).

4. Mary Turner, a black woman from Valdosta, Ga., was lynched along with her husband. The couple was accused of planning the murder of a white man, Hampton Smith, on whose farm they were tenants. Two other black men, Will Head and Will Thompson, were lynched a few days earlier in connection with the same incident. (*NYT*, 20 May 1918).

5. The article appeared in the *New York Times* on 24 August 1919, and was headlined "Negroes of World Prey of Agitators." The article referred to "a negro newspaper, published in New York" which "praises Lenin and Trotzky" and called for similar leaders "to emancipate the black people of the earth."

6. Estelle Sylvia Pankhurst (1882-1960), revolutionary feminist, suffragist, author, and socialist. (David S. Mitchell, *The Fighting Pankhursts: A Study in Tenacity* [London: Cape,

1967]; and Estelle Sylvia Pankhurst, *The Suffragette Movement: An Intimate Account of Persons and Ideals* [1931, rpt. ed., London: Virago Press, 1977]).

7. James Ramsay MacDonald (1866–1937) was prime minister of the first British Labor government of 1924 and leader of his party from 1922 until 1931 when he became head of the coalition National government. (*DNB*).

8. Rev. Dr. Matthew A. N. Shaw (1870–1923) was born in Jamaica; he received his early training at Calabar College and later migrated to the United States, where he practiced medicine. For twenty-four years he was the pastor of the Twelfth Street Baptist Church in Boston. He was elected president of the National Equal Rights League of America and was one of the signers of the petition that the National Liberty Congress of Colored Americans submitted to the U.S. House of Representatives in June 1918 (DNA, RG 65, file OG 336880, RG 165, file 10218–130; *NYT*, 25 November 1920; *Crisis* 28, no. 1 [May 1924]: 27).

9. William Howard Taft (1857–1930) was the twenty-seventh president of the United States (1909–1913). On 28 May 1919, he argued against the assertions of Sen. James A. Reed (1861–1944) that the "black and yellow races" would have enough representation in the League of Nations to endanger whites. Taft further declared that Reed's view was intended to dissuade Southern senators from voting in favor of U.S. participation in the League of Nations. However, no speech by Taft concerning the Chicago race riots has been found. (*WBD*; Henry H. Pringle, *The Life and Times of William Howard Taft: A Biography* [1939; reprint ed., Hamden, Conn.: Archon Books, 1964]).

10. Moorfield Storey (1845–1929), author and civil rights lawyer, served as the first president of the NAACP. Storey was a life member of the Association for the Study of Negro Life and History and a member of its executive council. (*DAB*; *JNH* 15 [January 1930]:123–24).

11. Parker Pillsbury (1809–1898) was a prominent reformer and an abolitionist. (*DAB*).

APPENDIXES

APPENDIX I

Biographical Supplement

Dusé Mohamed Ali

Born in Alexandria, Egypt, Duse Mohamed Ali (1866–1945) was the son of a Sudanese mother and an Egyptian father, Abdul Salem Ali, an officer in the Egyptian army who was later killed during an abortive nationalist uprising in 1881–82. He claimed that he was brought to England at the age of nine by an officer with whom his father had studied at the French military academy. Duse Mohamed eventually lost contact with his family. He also lost all knowledge of Arabic, becoming unable to speak or write it. According to his later testimony, the non-Arabic name *Duse* was derived from the surname of the French officer who brought him to England ("Leaves from an Active Life," *The Comet*, 12 June 1937, p. 7). In another account, Duse Mohamed claimed that this officer was the only surviving member of the French branch of the Duse family, which also included Eleonora Duse (1859–1924), the famous Italian-born actress. He adopted the Duse name during his early theatrical career in England, probably because it carried the stage appeal of the popular actress who owed her reputation as a major artist to her roles in plays adapted from the novels of Alexander Dumas, a writer whom Duse Mohamed highly praised. (Duse Mohamed, "The Coloured Man in Art and Letters," *T. P. Magazine* [June 1911]: 400). Duse Mohamed made his debut on the English stage in 1885, at the age of nineteen, in the theatrical company of Wilson Barrett, with whom he also toured the United States and Canada. While in the United States, he left the company and worked for several years as a clerk. In 1898 he returned to England to resume his dramatic career, touring the British Isles in the theatrical company of Sir H. Beerbohm Tree in his production of *Antony and Cleopatra*. In 1902 in the city of Hull he staged his own productions of *Othello* and *The Merchant of Venice*, playing the parts of Othello and the Prince of Morocco. He also founded the Hull Shakespeare Society.

Duse Mohamed's theatrical career ended in 1909 when he launched his career in journalism in London. His articles on Egyptian nationalism and racial oppression were then published by the *New Age*, an influential Fabianist weekly and leading socialist literary journal, edited by Alfred Richard Orage (1873–1934). In 1911, Duse Mohamed achieved considerable prominence with the publication of his book, *In the Land of the Pharaohs*, a short nationalist history of Egypt financed by Orage, but cribbed largely from the writings of Wilfred Scawen Blunt, Theodore Rothstein, and the Earl of Cromer. Although the critics initially praised *In the Land of the Pharaohs*, the book's success was soon undermined by the discovery of extensive plagiarism. The ensuing furor ended Duse Mohamed's connection with the *New Age*, but did not lessen the book's considerable impact among black intellectuals of the period. During the dispute Duse Mohamed was elected a corresponding member of the Negro Society for Historical Research, which was founded in 1911 at Yonkers, N. Y., under the guiding influence of John E. Bruce and Arthur A. Schomburg.

During 1911, John Eldred Taylor, a Sierra Leonian merchant trader whom Duse Mohamed had met at the Universal Races Congress in London, approached him with a proposal for publishing a trade paper to be called *African Times*. Duse Mohamed refused the offer, but soon launched his own publication: the *African Times and Orient Review*.

ATOR quickly became a publicity outlet for Duse Mohamed's own business schemes, and his primary tool for interesting British credit and banking concerns in trade with West African farmers and merchants. Very little came of such schemes, however, and Duse Mohamed's numerous business appeals to the Colonial Office were also rejected. At the same time, Duse Mohamed was active in a number of social and political causes. He was one of the founders of the Anglo-Ottoman Society and vice-president of the Central Islamic Society, both of which formed part of his important involvement with the Ottoman issue, Pan-Islamism, and Egyptian nationalism. He was also said to have been associated with "Barikat Islam" and to have been awarded the honor of the Imperial Ottoman Mejidie (OIM) by the Turkish Sultan.

The First World War led to the temporary suspension of *ATOR*, and it did not resume publication until January 1917. That same year Duse Mohamed tried to interest the British Colonial Office in a scheme to raise a £12–16 million war loan among the people of British West Africa as part of a proposed National Relief Fund. British officials turned down his proposal, although they secretly investigated its feasibility. Duse Mohamed was, in their opinion, "a pushing journalist who makes a great parade of loyalty but whose past is somewhat shady." While refusing him permission to travel to West Africa, British officials kept a close watch on his activities in England since, in their view, he was "rather inclined to pose as the champion of any dark skinned man with a grievance" (PRO, CO 554/35/55259).

Following the war, Dusé Mohamed Ali, now using the accented "Dusé" he adopted in March 1917 (*ATOR*, 4:3 [Mid–March 1917]), proposed to establish a native bank to help African traders overcome the barriers erected by the European trading monopoly, but once again his scheme was rejected by the Colonial Office. He took his plan to Lagos, Nigeria, in July 1920, but he found that the target amount of £5 million could not be raised. Undaunted, Dusé Mohamed attempted to advance his banking scheme by writing to his longtime American friend, John E. Bruce. Bruce was involved himself in an import-export company dealing in colonial produce and goods. Early in 1921 Dusé Mohamed left England for the United States where he became a director of the Intercolonial Corporation, but within a few months both his banking scheme and the newly formed corporation collapsed. He supported himself in the United States by lecturing and writing for the black press, including Garvey's *Negro World*. A decade later, Samuel A. Haynes wrote that the *Negro World* "gained distinction also under the editorship of the great Egyptian author and historian Dusé Mohamed" ("Through Black Spectacles," *NW*, 15 April 1933, p. 4). In addition Dusé Mohamed also accepted a position with the UNIA as head of African Affairs. He also tried to persuade black businessmen to provide an emergency loan to the Liberian government.

Dusé Mohamed Ali resumed his attempts at pan-African business ventures in 1923, but they proved unsuccessful. Finally, in 1931, while traveling in west Africa, he settled in Nigeria and became manager and editor of *The Comet*. In 1933 the paper's circulation reached 4,000, making it the largest Nigerian weekly; finally, in 1944, it became a daily. Although its circulation declined as a result of competition from Nnamdi Azikiwe's *West African Pilot*, it remained a viable concern. Dusé Mohamed Ali continued as managing director until his retirement in 1943 at the age of seventy-seven. He died in Lagos on 26 February 1945.

Sources: DNA, RG 59, Dusé Mohamed Ali to President C. D. B. King, 28 February 1921, file 882.512/5; RG 165, file 10218-261/47 and 10218-364/19; Federal Writers Program, New York City, "Negroes of New York," Claude McKay, "The Negro Historical Society of New York"; "The 'African Times and Orient Review'," *Gold Coast Leader*, 31 August 1912, p. 5; William H. Ferris, "A Colored American's Estimate of the A. T. O. R.," *African Times and Orient Review*, 14 April 1914, pp. 77–78; Imanuel Geiss, *The Pan-African Movement*, trans. by Ann Keep (New York: Africana Publishing Co., 1974), pp. 221–28; Michael D. Biddiss, "The Universal Races Congress of 1911," *Race* 13 (1971): 37–46; Ian Duffield, "Dusé Mohamed Ali: His Purpose and His Public," in Alistair Niven, ed., *The Commonwealth Writer Overseas* (Brussels: Libraire Marcel Didier, 1976); Duffield, "John Eldred Taylor and West African Opposition to Indirect Rule in Nigeria," *African Affairs* 70 (July 1971): 252–68; and Duffield, "The Business Activities of Dusé Mohamed Ali: An Example of the Economic Dimension of Pan-Africanism, 1912–1945," *Journal of the Historical Society of Nigeria* 4 (June 1969): 571–600; Nnamdi Azikiwe, *My Odyssey: An Autobiography* (London: C. Hurst, 1970).

Cyril V. Briggs

Cyril Valentine Briggs (1887–1966) was born at Brown Pasture, Nevis, in the British Leeward Islands, on 28 May 1887, the son of Louis and Marion Briggs. He was educated at Basseterre, St. Kitts, in Wesleyan and Baptist parochial schools, which were restricted to the native children of color. Briggs left school at the age of sixteen and worked for nearly a year as a subreporter with the *Basseterre Weekly Advertiser* and the *Basseterre Daily Express*. Before leaving St. Kitts, he was influenced by reading the works of Robert Green Ingersoll (1833–1899), the man many considered to be the greatest English language orator of his day. Ingersoll's questioning of the tenets of Christian belief, as well as his eloquence and irreverent wit, impressed Briggs, as did the discovery of various books on imperialism in the library of his early mentor, Rev. Price, a Baptist clergyman in St. Kitts.

Briggs immigrated to New York on 4 July 1905. Shortly after the New York *Amsterdam News* began publication in 1911, he joined the staff, working for several months in 1912 as the society reporter. During 1912–13 he was promoted successively to sports and theater editor; and, in 1914, he became associate editor and the writer of the paper's editorials. He also held the position of city editor, and, in actuality, was the paper's managing editor. He married Bertha Florence of Talcott, W. Va., in January 1914. The next year he resigned from the *Amsterdam News* to found a magazine for the Harlem business community, called the *Colored American Review: A Magazine of Inspiration*. The venture proved short-lived, and Briggs rejoined the staff of the *Amsterdam News* in June 1916. Briggs was again editor in all but name, that title officially belonging to James H. Anderson (1868–1931) the paper's founder and publisher. After America's entry into the European war, Briggs used his editorials to denounce the policy of black American support for the war effort. He also demanded that the principle of self-determination enunciated in President Wilson's Fourteen Points be applied by granting territorial independence to black Americans and Africans. (" 'Security for Life' for Poles and Serbs, Why Not for Colored Americans," *Amsterdam News*, 19 September 1917). Briggs's editorial was reprinted without comment in several black newspapers, and it received a large number of favorable letters. However, his opposition to the war effort as a battle for the imperialist redivision of territorial spoils brought pressure from U.S. Military Intelligence against the *Amsterdam News*'s publisher. In March 1918 Briggs resigned after refusing to accept censorship of his news columns.

Soon after his resignation, several black supporters offered financial assistance for Briggs to publish his own journal. Chief among them was J. Anthony Crawford, the president of the Inter-Colonial Steamship Co., Inc. With Crawford's backing, Briggs founded the monthly *Crusader* magazine in September 1918.

Following the appearance of the *Crusader*, Briggs received a letter from George Wells Parker (1882–1931), a medical student in Omaha and scion of one of that city's oldest black families. Parker, Rev. John Albert Williams, and John E. Bruce, had founded The Hamitic League of the World. Briggs, Parker, and Williams soon agreed to support each other, with Parker and Williams pledging to promote the *Crusader* in Omaha, while Briggs agreed to publicize the league and to promote Parker's book, *Children of the Sun*, through notices in the *Crusader*. Moreover, the *Crusader* announced in April 1919 that it was the "Publicity Organ of the Hamitic League of the World."

The New York branch of the league was organized in July 1919 and it numbered among its members John E. Bruce, Arthur Schomburg, and Briggs. The editorial office of the *Crusader* on Seventh Avenue in Harlem was also designated the eastern office of the league in August 1919, and the following month the *Crusader* reported that "a large number of the prominent citizens of British Guiana organized a branch of the Hamitic League of the World recently, and word comes that branches are soon to be formed in Nigeria and Panama" (*Crusader* 2 [September 1919]: 12).

The *Crusader* discontinued its designation as "Publicity Organ of the Hamitic League of the World" after August 1920, and in the late spring or early summer of 1921 it became the "Organ of the African Blood Brotherhood" (ABB). The formation of the ABB had been announced in October 1919 in the *Crusader*, and it later declared that its chief aims were organized self-defense against wanton white attacks, advancement of black rights and "immediate protection and ultimate liberation of Negroes everywhere" (*Crusader* 5 [October 1921]). Briggs was the organizer, executive head, and "Paramount Chief" of the Supreme Executive Council of the ABB. Charter members consisted of West Indian radicals such as Theophilus Burrell (international secretary), Benjamin E. Burrell (director of historical research), Richard B. Moore (educational director), W. A. Domingo (director of publicity and propaganda), Claude McKay, Arthur Reid, Grace P. Campbell, and Joseph P. Fanning.

Briggs's principal objective in organizing the ABB, however, was to combat the spread of Garvey's influence (see "Race Catechism" in *Crusader* 1[November 1918], reprinted in Monroe N. Work, ed., *Negro Year Book 1918–1919*, p. 100). Even though Briggs had sympathized with some aspects of the Garvey movement, the ABB became the first, and for some time the only, black radical group to challenge Garvey. Briggs actually invited Garvey to join the ABB, but as in all subsequent offers of cooperation, Garvey responded with a rebuff. However, in 1921 a number of leading Garveyites defected from the UNIA and joined the ABB's ranks, among them Rev. James D. Brooks (UNIA secretary-general), Bishop George Alexander McGuire (UNIA chaplain-general), and Cyril Crichlow (UNIA stenographer and commissioner to Liberia).

At its peak, the ABB numbered about seven thousand dues-paying members, organized through a system of "posts" (such as the New York "Menelik Post") located throughout the United States and the West Indies. The post with the largest membership, however, was located in West Virginia. The ABB's program called for "(1) a Liberated Race in the United States, Africa, and elsewhere; (2) Absolute Race Equality; (3) the Fostering of Racial Self-Respect; (4) Organized and Uncompromising Opposition to the Ku Klux Klan and anti-Negro Organizations; (5) a United Negro Front; (6) Industrial Development along Co-operative Lines; (7) Higher Wages for Negro Labor, Shorter Hours and better living conditions; (8) Education; and (9) Co-operation with those other Darker Races and with those white workers who are fully class-conscious and are honestly working for a United Front of all Labor" (*Summary of the Program and Aims of the African Blood Brotherhood, Formulated by 1920 Convention* and African Blood Brotherhood letterhead).

Possessing fraternal and benevolent features, and referring to itself as a "revolutionary secret Order," the ABB not only practiced an initiation ritual for new members, but also divided its membership on the basis of "seven degrees, the first being given upon entry, the next five for educational progress, the last and Seventh for Superlative Service" (Arthur Preuss, *A Dictionary of Secret and Other Societies* [St. Louis, Mo.: B. Herder Book Co., 1924], p. 4). Moreover, the ABB inaugurated a sick and death benefit insurance fund for members in November 1923. Previously, Briggs had attempted to start a chain of cooperative stores for ABB members on the Rochdale plan, hoping to operate twenty-five stores in different cities and possibly use them as a means of increasing ABB membership. The initial idea was proposed in July 1923, with the suggestion of starting a bank, but due to a lack of funds, the scheme was never put into operation, though it received extensive publicity among ABB members.

In November 1921, Briggs launched a ten-thousand-dollar fund drive to finance a weekly newspaper to be named the "Liberator." Although Briggs claimed to have the support of "153 Negro organizations and churches, newly federated to present a solid front to the foe" (*Crusader* 5 [November 1921]: 12), he failed to raise the necessary funds. But once again the primary purpose behind the attempt centered on Briggs's conflict with Garvey. Three successive issues of the *Negro World* (8, 15 and 22 October 1921) featured an advertisement which declared that Briggs, who was undeniably light-skinned, was actually a "white man . . . claiming to be a Negro for Convenience." Briggs's response was swift: Garvey was immediately charged and arrested for criminal libel. At a court hearing on 11 November 1921, Garvey was forced to retract his statement and to publish an apology.

The membership of the ABB reached its peak in the late summer of 1923 as a result of the campaign Briggs conducted to organize the United Negro Front Conference in New York City on 23–24 March 1923. The conference, which elected Dr. M.A.N. Shaw as president and Briggs as secretary, brought together the ABB, the Friends of Negro Freedom, the NAACP, the National Equal Rights League, the National Race Congress, and the International Uplift League. At the end of the conference, representatives of the six participating organizations signed a concordat and called for an All-Race Assembly. Instead of the All-Race Assembly convening at Louisville, Ky., on 5–12 November 1923 as originally announced, the gathering became subsumed under Kelly Miller's All-Race Conference (commonly known as the Negro Sanhedrin), which was held at Chicago during the week of 11 February 1924, with Cyril Briggs as secretary. The Negro Sanhedrin, however, suffered an early demise.

The ABB was also represented at the farmer-labor conference in July 1923. When support for the ABB slipped in the fall of 1923, however, members of the Supreme Executive Council turned increasingly toward the Workers party of America so that the ABB became, in effect, the Harlem "Negro Branch" of the new Communist party. But from early on, the two rival factions that made up the Workers party vied eagerly for the ABB's political support. Rose Pastor Stokes (1879–1933) and Robert Minor (1884–1952), each representing what they claimed was the official wing of the Workers party, paid numerous visits to the ABB, which affiliated with the faction led by Rose Pastor Stokes. With the exceptions of W. A. Domingo and Claude McKay, the ABB's entire Supreme Executive Council joined the ranks of the party by September–October 1923. Their recruitment marked the first Communist breakthrough among blacks in America. Until that time, there had been only two black American Communist party members, Otto E. Huiswood and one Hendricks, who were simultaneously members of the ABB. Huiswood held the position of ABB National Organizer.

Briggs probably joined the Workers party as early as May 1921, since he was present at the party's second session on 23–26 December 1921, as a New York delegate and one of two delegates representing the ABB. The following year, in March 1922, Briggs was employed in the national office of the Friends of Soviet Russia, a Communist front group which served as the financial branch of the Workers party. He was elected a subdistrict organizer of the Yorkville branch of the Workers party in November 1922, with his salary once again paid by the Friends of Soviet Russia.

In the fall of 1923, the ABB was integrated into the Workers party, which donated the funds for the ABB to open a forum in Harlem. The ABB was dissolved some time in 1924, though the exact date is not known. It was replaced by the American Negro Labor Congress (ANLC) in October 1925, with Briggs as its national secretary and editor of its official organ, *Negro Champion*. But, in 1927, Briggs returned to the West Indies, where he carried out organizational work in Trinidad. He made several visits to the United States, and in 1928–29 he was listed as a member of the national advisory committee of the Workers School in New York.

At the Sixth International Convention of the Communist Party of the United States (CPUSA) held in March 1929 in New York, Briggs was elected to the central executive committee. He was also appointed a member of the national committee of the International Labor Defense in 1929 and in 1932 joined them as part of the national Scottsboro Boys' defense campaign. In November 1930, at its St. Louis convention, the ANLC became the League of Struggle for Negro Rights (LSNR) and Briggs was again a member of the national committee, as well as editor of the *Liberator*, the successor to the *Negro Champion*. Briggs was elected to the national council of the LSNR in October 1933. However, the ANLC and the LSNR were judged failures, and the Communist party decided to build a new organization, the National

Negro Congress (NNC), which was founded in Chicago on 14 February 1936. Two years later, Briggs became a member of the national council of the NNC, but that same year he also became embroiled in a dispute with James W. Ford, the principal black CP figure, for whom he had acted as a ghost-writer for a number of years. In the meantime, Briggs continued as a member of the party's Negro Commission along with Ford, Theodore Bassett, A. W. Berry, and Harry Haywood.

Between 1932 and 1938, Briggs published his *Crusader News Agency* (CNA), which was a press service "giving national and international news of the liberation struggles of the Negro people," and which succeeded Briggs's mimeographed weekly *Crusader Service* that appeared briefly after August 1923. In 1936, Briggs was appointed a contributing editor of the *Negro Worker*, the official organ of the International Trade Union Committee of Negro Workers organized at Hamburg, Germany, by the Red International of Labor Unions in 1930.

The CPUSA expelled Briggs in 1939, along with Richard B. Moore and other black communists, including Hank Johnson, Manning Johnson, Otto Hall, and James Campbell, allegedly for their "Negro nationalist way of thinking" (*Pittsburgh Courier*, 7 November 1942). Following their expulsion, Briggs and Moore opened the Frederick Douglass Bookstore in Harlem. He later moved to Los Angeles in 1944 to become managing editor of *Now*, the magazine formerly known as the *War Worker*. Prior to the magazine's demise in 1946, Briggs was hired in November 1945 by the *California Eagle*, the venerable black newspaper published in Los Angeles by Charlotta Bass (1874–1969), who in the early 1920s had been co-president of the Los Angeles UNIA and who was later also to become the Progressive party's vice-presidential candidate in 1952. Briggs was soon made managing editor of the *California Eagle*, a position he held until 1948. Between 1948 and 1950 Briggs was also vice-president of S. Alexander Company, Inc., a black plastering and investment company.

In 1948 Briggs formally rejoined the Communist party and became an active member of the Ella Mae Wiggins Club of the Los Angeles County Communist party. In December 1950, however, Briggs began operating underground as a result of the anticommunist crusade that was then sweeping the country. A leader of the CP underground in Los Angeles in the spring and summer of 1951, Briggs moved briefly to Portland, Ore., where he remained for several months. After returning to Los Angeles, he functioned as a member of the Southern California District Communist party's Negro Commission and as a member of the party's West Adams Club, Moranda Smith Section. Briggs was employed as an editor with the Los Angeles *Herald-Dispatch* in the late 1950s. Cyril Briggs died of a heart attack on 18 October 1966 at the age of seventy-eight and was buried in Los Angeles.

Among Briggs's more important published writings during his years of Communist agitation are "The Negro Question in the Southern Textile Strikes," *The Communist* (June 1929): 324–28; "Further Notes on Negro

Question in Southern Textile Strikes," ibid., (July 1929): 391–94; "Our Negro Work," ibid., (September 1929): 494–501; "The Negro Press as a Class Weapon," ibid., (August 1929): 453–60; "Negro Revolutionary Hero Toussaint L'Ouverture," ibid., (May 1929): 250–54; "The Decline of the Garvey Movement," ibid., (June 1931): 547–52; "The Black Belt Republic Plan," *Harlem Liberator*, 1 August 1932; "How Garvey Betrayed the Negroes," *Negro Worker* 2 (August 1932): 14–27; with Eugene Gordon, *The Position of Negro Women* (New York: Workers' Library Publishers, 1935); and, with Harry Haywood, *Is Japan the Champion of the Colored Races?* (New York: Workers' Library Publishers, 1938).

Sources: Emory University Library, Theodore Draper Papers, Cyril V. Briggs to Theodore Draper, 7, 17, 24 March, 8 April, 1 May, 4 June 1958; California State University, Long Beach, Library, Dorothy Healey Papers, Cyril V. Briggs, MS, "On the Negro Question," (Southern California District of the Communist Party, U.S.A., November 1959); AFRC, RG 163, registration card no. 3699, 5 June 1917; DLC, NAACP Papers, "Conference, Sanhedrin, 1922–24," administrative file, subject file 1910–40, container C-232; DJ, FBI file 61-1015, "African Blood Brotherhood—Negro Radical Activities," New York, 1922–23; DJ, FBI Los Angeles, files 100-33476 and SAC 100-53953; New York, file 100-107599, bureau file 100-375204, and 100-421978; DJ, INS file 23-42987, and file 2307-76178; DNA, RG 65, file OG 387162; DNA, RG 165, files 10218-349 and 10218-364; NN-Sc, Vivian Morris, "Position of African Blood Brotherhood, *Amsterdam News* and *New York Age* on War of 1917," Federal Writers Program,"Negroes of New York"; Carl Offord, "An Account of the African Blood Brotherhood," ibid.; Theodore Draper, *American Communism and Soviet Russia* (New York: Viking Press, 1960), pp. 315–56; Joel A. Rogers, *World's Great Men of Color* (New York: published by the author, 1946; rpt., New York: Collier Books, 1972), vol. 1, p. 9; U.S. Congress, House, Special Committee on Un-American Activities, *Investigation of Un-American Propaganda Activities in the United States*, 78th Congress, 2d Sess., on H. Res. 282, 1944; and *Guide to Subversive Organizations and Publications*, 82nd Congress, 1st Sess., House Document no. 137; Theodore G. Vincent, *Black Power and the Garvey Movement* (Berkeley, Calif.: The Ramparts Press, n.d.), pp. 74–85; R. M. Whitney, ed., *Reds in America* (New York: Beckwith Press, 1924), pp. 35, 189–205; WWCR, vol. 1; "Along the Color Line—Social Uplift," *Crisis* 11 (December 1915): 61; "Angry Blond Negro," *New York News* (clipping, n.d.); Cyril V. Briggs, "Africa for the Africans," *Crusader* (September 1918), reprinted in the *Lagos Weekly Record*, 5 and 12 October 1918; Roger E. Kanet, "The Comintern and The 'Negro Question': Communist Policy in the United States and Africa, 1921–1941," *Survey* (Autumn 1973): 86–122; "Programme of the African Blood Brotherhood," *The Communist Review* (London, England), April 1922, pp. 449–54; Philip S. Foner, "Cyril V. Briggs: From the African Blood Brotherhood to the Communist Party," paper presented at the Annual Conference of the Association for the Study of Negro Life and History, Los Angeles, California, 12–15 October 1978; and Cyril V. Briggs, MS, "Autobiography (Notes)."

W. A. Domingo

Wilfred Adolphus Domingo (1889–1968) was the editor of the *Negro World* from the paper's inception in August 1918 until he resigned in July 1919. Born in Kingston, Jamaica, Domingo was the youngest child of Francisco and Alice Domingo. His father, who was Spanish, owned and operated a large fleet of hansom cabs in Kingston. His mother was from St. Thomas parish in eastern Jamaica.

Domingo and his elder brother and sister were orphaned at an early age and were brought up by their mother's brother, Adolphus Grant, a master butcher in St. Ann's Bay. Domingo received his education at Calabar School and the Kingston Board School, which was run by one of the island's most renowned teachers, J. G. Peet. After leaving school, Domingo worked for his uncle, but a short time later he took a job as an appentice tailor in Kingston, where he met Marcus Garvey, who was still a relative newcomer to the city.

An avid reader, Domingo also frequently contributed articles to the local press under various pseudonyms on the controversies of the day. Along with Garvey, he was an ardent supporter of S. A. G. Cox's National Club, and both Garvey and Domingo were for a brief time the club's first and second assistant secretaries, respectively. They also collaborated in writing the pamphlet, *The Struggling Mass*, that dealt with S. A. G. Cox's political struggle against the governor of Jamaica in 1910. Domingo introduced Garvey to the writings of Edward Wilmot Blyden, especially *Christianity, Islam, and the Negro Race*, a work which from that time was to affect Garvey's entire racial outlook.

With his uncle's financial support, Domingo left Jamaica in August 1910 for Boston, where he lived with his sister who ran a boarding house for Jamaicans. Planning to study medicine, Domingo began attending a special night school in Boston. He soon abandoned the idea of a medical career, and he moved to New York in 1912. The following year he began a speaking and writing campaign on behalf of a democratic constitution for Jamaica, one that would allow universal adult suffrage, civil service reform, free labor unions, and political self-government.

In 1915 Garvey wrote to Domingo from Jamaica to tell him that he had been invited to visit the United States by Booker T. Washington. After Garvey arrived in New York early the following year, he immediately contacted Domingo. In addition to advising him, Domingo also introduced Garvey to several prominent black figures in New York City. In July 1917, Domingo helped organize the British Jamaicans Benevolent Association in New York, a group similar to the Jamaica Club he had established earlier in Boston.

After America's entry into World War I, Domingo claimed religious exemption from the selective service draft, though by this time he had already been strongly influenced by radical socialist ideas then circulating in Harlem. When, in September 1918, he received an enlistment notice, he claimed to be conscientious objector. Meanwhile, Domingo had developed strong political ties with A. Philip Randolph, Chandler Owen, Richard B. Moore, and other blacks associated with the Socialist party organization of the Twenty-first Assembly District in Harlem, and also with the Rand School of Social Science.

During this same period, although he never became a member, Domingo participated in meetings of the fledgling New York UNIA in 1917–18. In particular, he assisted Garvey through his knowledge of parliamentary procedure. In the summer of 1918, when Garvey was about to start the *Negro World*, Domingo introduced him to the printer who produced the Socialist party's *New York Call*, Henry Rogowski. This made the publication of the *Negro World* possible, since Rogowski agreed to extend Garvey the necessary credit. Garvey also asked Domingo to write two lead editorials each week for the paper. Shortly after the *Negro World* began publication, Garvey asked Domingo, who was then employed by the post office, to take over as the editor. Domingo later claimed credit for coining the slogan, "Africa's Redemption," which appeared early in the *Negro World's* editorial columns.

Since Garvey had initially given him a free hand, Domingo used the *Negro World* to propagate socialist views. Domingo himself had already become a member of the Socialist party's Speakers' Bureau in New York, and the manuscript of his projected pamphlet, *Socialism Imperilled*, had been seized in the Lusk Committee raid on the Rand School on 21 June 1919. Garvey responded to this by having Domingo "tried" before the executive committee of the UNIA on charges of writing and publishing editorials that were not in keeping with the UNIA program. As a result Domingo resigned as editor in July 1919. In his resignation statement, Domingo later claimed that he described Garvey's methods as "medieval, obscure and dishonest," while he also referred to the Black Star Line venture as "bordering on a huge swindle." (W. A. Domingo to the Editor, "Mr. W. A. Domingo's connection with the UNIA," *Gleaner*, 15 June 1925). After his split from Garvey, Domingo resumed his connection with Randolph and Owen, who made him a contributing editor of the *Messenger* magazine. In the spring of 1920 Domingo and Richard B. Moore teamed up to publish the short-lived *Emancipator*, a weekly socialist newspaper. Its ten issues, however, mainly criticized Garvey and the finances of the Black Star Line. After the *Emancipator* failed in late May 1920, Domingo joined forces with Cyril Briggs's *Crusader*, while at the same time he became an active member of the African Blood Brotherhood. But unlike the majority of the key ABB leaders, Domingo never joined the Workers (Communist) party in 1923.

A frequent platform speaker for the People's Education Forum (the main public outlet of the socialist radicals in Harlem), Domingo was forced nonetheless to end his affiliation with the *Messenger* group after Chandler Owen's vitriolic attack on West Indians in 1923, issued in the course of advocating Garvey's deportation from America.

Little is known about Domingo's political acivities between 1923 and 1936. During this period Domingo prospered in business as an importer of West Indian foods. He had learned the wholesale food trade while working with an English importer after leaving his job with the post office. In 1936, he helped to found the Jamaica Progressive League (JPL), an organization modeled on the Irish Progressive League and made up of patriotic Jamaicans in New York City who were demanding political self-government for Jamaica. The first president of the JPL was the writer Walter Adolphe Roberts (1886–1962). Other founding members included Dr. Lucien Brown, A. Wendell Malliett, Mrs. Ivy Essien, James O'Meally, Rev. Ethelred Brown, Thomas R. Bowen, Mrs. T. D'Aguilar, and Ben and Theophilus Burrell.

As vice-president of the JPL, Domingo spent approximately six months in Jamaica in 1937–38, along with Roberts. Their visit preceded the widespread labor rebellion that erupted in May 1938 in the island, a fact that assisted the JPL in raising funds in New York for the legal defense of workers arrested during the disturbances. In addition to addressing the Jamaican branch of the JPL, both men also acted as advisers to the group that formed the nucleus of the future People's National party (PNP), headed by Norman Washington Manley. The PNP was officially formed in 1939.

Shortly after returning to New York, Domingo received an invitation from the PNP in Jamaica to become its organizing secretary, an offer that Domingo accepted on the condition that it was only for six months. Upon his arrival in Jamaica, however, on 6 June 1941, Gov. Sir Arthur Richards ordered him arrested aboard ship and placed in an internment camp, where he joined a number of Jamaican labor leaders. Domingo was declared a potential threat to the colonial government, despite the fact that he had earlier publicly expressed his support for the British war effort. The governor produced as evidence a number of censored letters that Domingo had written from New York in which he predicted that there would be a revolution in Jamaica after his arrival.

A lengthy campaign to secure Domingo's release from detention was launched by his associates in Jamaica and New York, with legal help from the American Civil Liberties Union. Domingo was finally released after serving twenty months in detention, but he was forced to remain in Jamaica for an additional four years when the U.S. government denied him a visa. During this period, Domingo worked actively for the PNP and wrote regular articles for the local press, most importantly for *Public Opinion*, the main voice of the Jamaican self-government movement.

Domingo returned to New York in 1947, where he continued to campaign for Jamaica's independence. He later became an outspoken critic of the abortive West Indian Federation in the 1950s, a stance that went against that of the PNP leadership in Jamaica. Permanently incapacitated by a stroke in December 1964, Domingo died on 14 February 1968. He is buried in Woodlawn Cemetery in the Bronx, New York.

Sources: AFRC, RG 163, W. A. Domingo, Selective Service registration card, no. 409; NFRC, naturalization declaration, no. 154792; DNA, RG 65, file OG 258421; DJ-FBI, file 65-35099; DS, Diplomatic Post Records, London Embassy, file 800 B., "Jamaica Progressive League," 1936–39, file 811.11, Domingo, Wilfred Adolphus; DS, file 800.20211 Domingo, W. A./3; DS, file 844 D.00/42, "Political Developments in Jamaica," 16 July 1941; DS, Records of the Anglo-American Caribbean Commission, United States Section, file E11-9, box 15, "W. A. Domingo"; TNF, Amy Jacques Garvey Papers, W. A. Domingo to A. J. Garvey, 15 January 1961; *WWCA*, vol. 2; Walter G. McFarlane, *The Birth of Self-Government in Jamaica, 1937 to 1944* (Kingston, Jamaica: published by the author, 1957); K. W. J. Post, *Arise Ye Starvelings: The Jamaica Labour Rebellion of 1938 and Its Aftermath* (The Hague: Nijhoff, 1978); "Bolshevism Taught to Negroes," *NYT*, 30 June 1919; W. A. Domingo, "Jamaica Fights for Freedom," *The African* 2 (October 1943): 5, 16; "Mr. W. A. Domingo's Connection with the U.N.I.A.," *Gleaner*, 15 June 1925; A. M. Wendell Malliet, "My Contemporaries: W. A. Domingo," *American Recorder*, 16 February 1929; N. W. Manley, "A Tribute to W. A. Domingo," *Daily Gleaner*, 22 February 1968; "Walter Adolphe Roberts, 1866–1962—Memorial Number," *Jamaica Historical Society Bulletin* 3 (December 1962), n.p.; Richart Hart, MS, "Notes of the

Recollections of W. A. Domingo of Dr. Robert Love and S. A. G. Cox, Made in the Internment Camp, 1942–43"; W. A. Domingo to Edmund D. Cronon, Madison, Wis., 17 April 1957;
Interviews with the editor: Karl Domingo, Freeport, Long Island, N. Y., 1972; Eulalie Man-
hertz Domingo and Doris Domingo, New York, N. Y., 1978; and Mrs. Mabel Domingo, New
Rochelle, N. Y., 1978.

R. D. Jonas

R. D. Jonas, variously known as "Elder R. D. Jonas" and as "Prophet
Jonas," was born Rupert Deveraux Griffith in Tredegar, Wales, around 1868.
He came to America with his father when he was six years old; after working
briefly as a food caterer in Chicago, he turned to religious evangelism. In
October 1903 Jonas joined the Christian Catholic Church in Zion, the theo-
cratic sect founded by John Alexander Dowie (1847–1907) in Zion City, Ill.
Through Dowie's influence, Jonas claimed to have developed an interest in
the advancement of the black race. He traveled widely throughout the
American South and Mexico, and later he established short-lived community
stores in Indianapolis and Chicago. In April 1917, he was suspected of being
an agent for German propagandists; he was arrested in St. Louis and fined
for interfering with federal military recruiting. This incident led him to
publish a pamphlet critical of Germany, *Kaiser: The Anti-Christ and his Fall*
(n.p., n.d.), written after his earlier series of pro-German pamphlets, *New
Freedom and Food for Yellow Peril* (n.p., n.d.), and *The Rothschilds and Their
Allies, the Dominating Influence of Great Britain* (n.p., n.d.). Jonas' volte-face
also resulted in his employment in late 1917 by U.S. military intelligence in
Chicago as an informer on suspected "Negro subversion," an area it saw as
one of the objectives of German propaganda in the United States. The
district military intelligence office in Springfield, Ill., also assigned Jonas to
inform against IWW activities and pro-German agitation. After nearly five
months of intelligence work, the Chicago military intelligence office discontinued his employment.

Jonas traveled extensively thereafter, giving lantern slide shows of
southern black migration to the North and advocating a scheme for the
colonization of black Americans in Mexico. In August 1918 Jonas opened a
black employment office in Philadelphia for a short time. He transferred his
activities to New York City in late 1918, where, under the guise of a minister,
he organized a group of carefully selected black Baptist and Methodist
ministers into the International League of Darker Peoples in January 1919.
Simultaneously, he offered his sevices to the Bureau of Investigation in New
York as an informer against black radicals. This offer followed an earlier one
he had made to U.S. military intelligence in New York, who recommended
him to liaison officials of British military intelligence stationed in New York
City. The British office employed Jonas as an informer and assigned him to
investigate black radicals, especially A. Philip Randolph and Chandler
Owen, as well as suspected Japanese agents. While British military intelligence paid Jonas, U.S. military intelligence shared the information he supplied to the British. Jonas' frequent reports, containing extensive data about

the most significant black radical organizations in America and their inter-connections, rank as the single most important source on the subject. Jonas remained on the payroll of British military intelligence until April 1920, when the British Military Mission's office in New York, military intelligence's operational cover, closed. Thereafter he continued to send regular reports on the black movement to the British Embassy in Washington, D.C., hoping his compensation would continue.

In July 1919, Jonas assumed the roles of escort and publicist for the visiting Abyssinian delegation. He continued to exploit this association when he organized the Ethiopian Society of U.S.A. in January 1920, which he announced in his pamphlet, *First Call for Abyssinia* (n.p., n.d.). Later in 1920, Chicago police held him as a material witness against Grover Cleveland Redding, the self-styled leader of the "Star Order of Ethiopia" and "the Ethiopian Mission to Abyssinia." Redding's burning of the American flag set off the so-called "Abyssinian Riot" on 20 June 1920 in Chicago when the "Abyssinians" shot and killed two persons, one of whom was a white Amer-ican sailor who had tried to prevent Redding's burning of the flag. Jonas had known Redding since July 1917 in Chicago; they became reacquainted during the visit of the Abyssinian delegation to America in the summer of 1919. Redding was tried and convicted of murder and hanged on 24 June 1921.

As a result of the Abyssinian riot, Jonas' role as an undercover agent was exposed, forcing him to cease his association with black radicals. Under the name "Rev. Rupert D. J. Griffith," he began to lecture on behalf of the Pro-League Independents and the newly formed Woodrow Wilson Foundation on the subject of America's participation in the League of Nations. Jonas undertook an extensive speaking tour of the South during 1921 for the League, however, he was suspected of being engaged in *Sinn Fein* propa-ganda work during this time. After 1921 Jonas disappeared without any further trace.

Sources: DNA, RG 60, file 158260; RG 65, files BS 202600-9-41, BS 215985, OG 44062, OG 258421, OG 377483; RG 165, files 10218-77, 10218-296, 10218-302, 10218-388, 10218-407; Christian Catholic Church in Zion Archives, Zion City, Illinois, application for membership, Chicago, 28 September 1903; Chicago Commission on Race Relations, *The Negro in Chicago: A Study of Race Relations and a Race Riot in 1919* (Chicago: The University of Chicago Press, 1922), pp. 59–64, 480–93; "Abyssinia and America," *Survey* (3 July 1920); and "A Spy Exposed," *Crusader* 2(July 1920): 8.

Joseph Robert Love

Joseph Robert Love was born at Nassau, Bahamas, on 2 October 1839, and educated at the St. Agnes Parish School and the Christ Church Grammar School in Nassau. After graduating, he taught for a period on Providence Island, where he was also a lay preacher in the Anglican church. Love left the Bahamas in 1866 for the United States, and in 1871 he was ordained an Episcopal deacon. In September 1872 he was placed in charge of St. Augus-tine's Mission in Savannah, Ga., by the Board of Missions of the Episcopal church; the following year he was appointed deacon of the Episcopal diocese of Georgia. Love wanted to establish, with the assistance of northern white abolitionists, a church training school to serve Savannah's fourteen thousand black freedmen. (J. Robert Love, "Mission Work among the Freedmen," *Spirit of Missions* [July 1873]: 409). While in Savannah, Love met Bishop Henry McNeal Turner (1834–1915), the foremost exponent of black nationalism in America. When he left Savannah, Love had become one of the South's most popular black preachers. In 1876 he was ordained an Episcopal priest in Buffalo, N. Y., where he served as rector of St. Philip's Church. Following his ordination, Love attended medical school at the University of Buffalo and graduated in 1879. Love was appointed to the Episcopal diocese of Western New York in 1881, but he soon left to join the Haitian Episcopal mission under the direction of Bishop James Theodore Holly (1829–1911), the first Afro-American bishop consecrated by the Episcopal Church. Holly assigned Love to the Bel Air Mission, a congregation of English-speaking West Indian immigrants in Port-au-Prince. By July 1881, Love's success with the mission prompted Bishop Holly to initiate plans for a permanent medical station in the capital. However, by September, a serious breach developed between these men, and after a great deal of ecclesiastical litigation, Love was formally deposed in September 1882. Love tried for a time to organize his own church in Port-au-Prince; however, he later accepted an appointment from Haitian president Lysius Solomon as the Army physician. Two years later, Florville Hyppolite, a new Haitian president, accused Love of "fomenting domestic strife." In spite of the intervention on his behalf by Frederick Douglass, who had recently been appointed U.S. consul-general to the Republic of Haiti, Love was deported.

Dr. Love traveled to Jamaica where he built a significant career as a radical journalist and social reformer. He became a champion of Jamaica's school teachers with his aggressively nationalist newspaper, the *Jamaica Advocate* (1895–1905), which became the official publication of the Jamaica Union of Teachers. Dr. Love described the *Jamaica Advocate* as "the literature of political and social freedom." He wrote the bulk of the material since the paper had no regular contributors. Marcus Garvey later declared that "one cannot read his [Dr. Love's] 'Jamaica Advocate' without getting race consciousness" (*Gleaner*, 17 February 1930). Significantly, while Garvey still resided there, the *Jamaica Advocate* carried a weekly report from St. Ann, as part of its weekly feature, "News from the Parishes."

Love, who frequently referred to himself as "decidedly black," became famous as a controversial exponent of the race issue in Jamaica. In a letter to John E. Bruce, Dr. Love asserted: "I am wedded the older I grow to the idea of the independent self-sustaining efforts of the race to lift itself up. However far short we may fall of the achievements of the whites (and I am by no means certain that we will fall short at all) the exertions will develop our powers and bring out of us the good that is in us" (NN-Sc, JEB, Love to Bruce, 30 July 1897).

Unrivaled as a public speaker, Dr. Love lectured frequently in Jamaica on Phillis Wheatley and Toussaint L'Ouverture. A lengthy *Gleaner* editorial praised Love: "It was the first appearance of Dr. Love on a public platform in Jamaica and he scored a success that assured him a crowded house whenever he chooses again to appear. He is a natural orator of great ability; one capable, without apparent effort, of swaying the emotions, and riveting the attention of the intellectual faculties of his auditors. . . . [Love] proved himself [a] powerful and eloquent exponent of the rights and wrongs of his down-trodden race" ("Toussaint L'Ouverture," *Gleaner*, 12 October 1898).

Dr. Love was active as an organizer of various benevolent societies in Jamaica. He also played an important role in support of the Trinidadian barrister, Henry Sylvester Williams (1869–1911), secretary of the London-based Pan-African Association, who visited Jamaica in March 1901. Williams held several meetings to discuss the work begun by the Pan-African Conference held in London in July 1900. At one of the association's local branch meetings, he reportedly "pointed out as grievances in Jamaica, no black or coloured man sat on various Boards which he named, nor rose to the sub-inspectorship in the police force" ("The Pan-African Association," *Jamaica Times*, 13 April 1901). Dr. Love was also a member of the Anglo-African Association.

Dr. Love became a champion of popular rights and representative government in Jamaica. In August 1898 he organized the People's Convention for the purpose of "celebrating in a sympathic and useful manner the sixtieth anniversary of the abolition of slavery" (*Jamaica Advocate*, 30 July 1898). Held annually in the old capital of Spanish Town on 1 August, the People's Convention soon became a forum of representative opinion for the Jamaican community to discuss subjects such as popular education, taxation, land distribution, voter registration, and citizenship. After the establishment of the People's Convention, Love also organized the Jamaica Association in early 1899. Both organizations had "for their object the protection of the rights and interests of the people of Jamaica." He justified his political interventions, since "the people's rights have been invaded by the Government whose duty it is to protect them" (*Jamaica Advocate*, 6 April 1899).

Love took an active role in the January 1899 by-election campaign of Alexander Dixon for the St. Elizabeth seat in the Legislative Council, making Dixon the first black Jamaican to be elected to the colonial legislature. Love also played an important part in the island-wide political agitation that erupted in 1899–1900 following the governor's introduction of official members to fill the four seats in the Legislative Council that had been dormant since 1884. By this means the governor used a permanent majority of government-appointed members to neutralize the votes of the elected members. Dr. Love helped organize the political delegation that was sent to England to protest the change in the constitution back to the old system of crown colony rule that the British colonial secretary Joseph Chamberlain

(1836–1914) had proposed. This system had been introduced after 1865 and continued until 1884.

In 1900 Love was elected to the Kingston City Council, and he served as chairman of some of its most important committees. In 1906 he won a seat in the St. Andrew Legislative Council by a large majority. Shortly after his election, however, he became seriously ill. For a brief time in 1907, he was well enough to edit the *Jamaican*, a semiweekly which first appeared in May 1907. He visited England for medical treatment, but his health continued to decline steadily, forcing him to retire from his Legislative Council seat and active political life in 1910.

Dr. Love died on 21 November 1914. In an editorial entitled, "The Passing of Dr. Love," the *Jamaica Times* gave the following assessment of Dr. Love's career in Jamaica:

On the constructive side Dr. Love failed, so far as organizations and institutions remain to attest his deed, but he did this for Jamaica as a whole, he breathed life into the political existence of the people; the masses as apart from the classes remained in their political sensibilities after 1865 as apathetic as sodden leather. He changed that. He roused them to feel they were British also, and had a claim on political life. This he did more than any other man (*Jamaica Times*, 28 November 1914).

Sources: The Church Historical Society Library and Archives, Austin, Texas, the Domestic and Foreign Missionary Society Papers, the Haiti Papers, 1855–1939; George Arents Research Library, Syracuse University, Gerritt Smith Collection, J. Robert Love to All Friends of the Church, 13 August 1873; J. Robert Love to Hon. Gerritt Smith, Rochester, N. Y., 30 August 1873; PRO, CO 137/604/30238, 2 November 1899; *WWJ*, 1919–20; David M. Dean, *Defender of the Race: James Theodore Holly, Black Nationalist Bishop* (Boston: Lambeth Press, 1979); Rev. Dr. J. Robert Love, *Is Bishop Holly Innocent?* (Port-au-Prince, Haiti: n.p., 1883); Love, *Proofs of Bishop Holly's Guilt* (Port-au-Prince, Haiti: n.p., 1883); W. Adolphe Roberts, "Robert Love," in *Six Great Jamaicans: Biographical Sketches* (Kingston: The Pioneer Press, 1951), pp. 70–85; John W. Blassingame, "Before the Ghetto: The Making of the Black Community in Savannah, Georgia, 1865–1880," *Journal of Social History* 6 (Fall 1972): 463–88; J. Robert Love, "Mission Work Among the Freedmen," *Spirit of Missions* (July 1873): 409–12; "Letter from J. Robert Love," *Christian Recorder*, 30 March 1876; Love, "The Debt of the Negro Race," *Gleaner*, 15 August 1894; "The Phillippo, Knibb, and Burchell Memorial Fund Association," *Gleaner*, 15 August 1894; Love, "Obituary of the Hon. Fredrick Douglass," *Jamaica Advocate*, 2 March 1895 [hereafter cited as *JA*]; "Plain Words to the Negro Population," *JA*, 28 December 1895; "The Colour for Colour Question," *Gleaner*, 14 January 1896; "The Phillippo, Knibb & Burchell Memorial Fund Association," *Gleaner*, 2 August 1897; "A Proposed Convention—Circular," *JA*, 30 July 1898; "The People's Convention, 1st August 1898," *JA*, 13 August 1898; "Toussaint L'Ouverture," *Gleaner*, 12 October 1898; "St. Elizabeth Election," *JA*, 7 January 1899; "[Alexander] Dixon vs. [J. V.] Calder," *JA*, 14 January 1899; "Mr. Chamberlain and the British West Indian Negro," *JA*, 25 March 1899; "The Duty of Our Representatives and of Ourselves," *JA*, 1 April 1899; "Emancipation Day—The People's Convention," *JA*, 5 August 1899; "People's Convention . . . ," *JA*, 30 September 1899; "The Negro's Chief Enemy," *JA*, 7 October 1899; "The Political Situation," *Gleaner*, 13 October 1899; "The People's Convention," *Jamaica Times*, 10 August 1901; "The Platform of the People's Convention," *Jamaica Times*, 8 October 1901; "The Pan-African Association," *Gleaner*, 30 March 1901; "The Pan-

African Association," *Gleaner*, 11 April 1901; "The Pan-African Association," *Jamaica Times*, 13 April 1901; "Some Character Sketches—Dr. Love," *Gleaner*, 20 June 1908; "Passing Away of Dr. J. Robert Love, Journalist, Orator and Politician," *Daily Chronicle*, 13 November 1914; "Passing Away of Dr. J. R. Love," *Gleaner*, 23 November 1914; "The Death of Dr. Love . . . ," *Jamaica Times*, 28 November 1914; "Things Which the 'Jamaica Advocate' Would Like to See," *JA*, passim.

Chief Alfred Sam

Chief Alfred Sam's career in America foreshadowed the Garvey movement in many significant respects. Contemporaries called him a "modern Moses" (*African Mail*, editorial, 5 June 1914, p. 359), "the self-styled Moses of the colored race" (*Gold Coast Leader*, 2 May 1914), and the "Moses of the movement" (*Literary Digest*, 21 March 1914). Nevertheless, the details of his life story remain a mystery, and today we know little more than his contemporaries who speculated on his claims to land ownership and alleged status as a chief. In August 1919, an anonymous writer to the United States attorney general suggested that the government could check the spread of Garveyism by issuing "releases to the Negro press warning Negroes against bogus schemes of African repatriation and Negro Steamship Corp.," and he urged officials to "point to the example of the Chief Sam fiasco" (DNA, RG 65, file 198940-2). Moreover, the *Chicago Defender*, on 20 September 1919, complained that "Garvey's proposition (for the Black Star Line) is similar to the one tried on the American public a few years ago by Chief Sam, a notorious confidence man." Finally, in a report on the spread of Garveyism in his area prepared at the request of the British Foreign Office, the British consul in Galveston, Texas, recalled the Chief Sam movement, noting that "many negroes from Oklahoma and Texas, with quite a few of the West Indian negroes, at the solicitation of 'Chief Sam' took stock in the steamer 'Liberia,' which sailed from Galveston some seven years ago for Africa" (PRO, FO 115/2619). Later, Garvey's critics would use the fateful misadventure of Sam's African movement to disparage Garvey's program of African redemption. At another level, Sam represents an important figure in the succession of West African trader-nationalists who traversed the American commercial scene during the interwar years in search of financial support, which they frequently found among black Americans, to escape the near-monopoly which British trading firms exerted over the West African import and export markets.

Alfred Charles Sam (ca. 1879/80–1930s?) was the son of Akosua Buaa and Nana Kwayke (alias James Kwakye Sam), a chief of Akyem Takyiman near Akropong in the Akyem Abuakwa district. Because of the Asante-Akyem War, the family was forced to move to the Akyem Swedru area at a place called Apaso near the town of Ewisa situated in the western Akyem region of Ghana. Sam's father wanted him to become a teacher, and he sent him to the Basel Evangelical Mission's (BEM) day-school at Kyebi. Sam received further education at the Begoro Basel Middle School, and the BEM catechist

institute at Akropong, Akwapim, where his father expected him to become a
BEM missionary worker. But, in 1900–01, at the age of twenty-one, Sam
temporarily left his missionary career to become a produce trader in cocoa
beans and crude rubber. This change coincided with the economic boom
created by the cocoa revolution in the Gold Coast. Sam used his newly-
acquired money to secure passage to America.

During his early years in the produce business, Sam had met Rev. John
Drybault Taylor (b. 1873), a Cape Coast Fanti missionary who had recently
returned from studying at the Boydton Institute, a religious school in Virginia, and the Shiloh Bible School in Maine. At Boydton, Taylor had read
Tongues of Fire, the organ of the Holy Ghost and Us Bible School, a
fundamentalist utopian sect founded by Frank Weston Sandford (1862–
1948). Sandford's sect, which later became The Kingdom Inc., flourished
between 1895 and 1911 at Shiloh, a hilltop along the Androscoggin River, near
Durham, Me. After reading *Tongues of Fire*, Taylor transferred to Shiloh
Bible School, where he learned of the sect's long-cherished dream of missionary evangelism in Africa. Taylor returned to the Gold Coast in the spring
of 1901, with the assistance and blessing of Frank Sandford and the Shilohites. Later, Rev. Taylor helped Chief Sam to plan his United States visit in
1910.

In the months preceding his departure, Sam began to correspond with
Rev. Charles E. Holland, general secretary and superintendent of the sect at
Shiloh. Upon his arrival in America on 3 September 1911, Sam was met in
Brooklyn by two members of the Shiloh sect, and later in the same month, he
attended the annual harvest convention at Shiloh, where he was baptized.

Sam realized the main goal of his American visit when he established the
Akim Trading Co. on 15 July 1911 under the laws of New York State. The
company's prospectus described Sam as "President having over 11 years
experience in West African Trade," and made it clear that the Akim Trading
Co. was purely a commercial concern with interest in trading produce and
provisions between Africa, Europe, and the United States. The prospectus
also claimed that the company owned "20 Square miles of territory in Gold
Coast to be developed in the near future," and that the directors of the
company had "decided seriously that this is the first Negro Corporation ever
conceived amongst the race, and they desire to buy their own ship which will
carry our freights and passengers from and to West Africa, and by this the
Directors had put Mr. Alex. Morgan a shareholder in this Company in the
Navigation School in New York so as when he is through they can buy him
their own ship at once to carry on with this movement." The prospectus
concluded that "the civilised Negro is responsible to develop Africa [as] his
right." It appealed for "assistance from both ends," but it announced that a
special offer of stock at a reduced price had been extended as an inducement
"for our Brethren in Africa to get into this movement" (PRO, FO 115/1803,
Negroes in West Africa, enclosure).

As promised in his prospectus, Sam departed from New York on 10 February 1912 to return to West Africa, where he planned to establish "African Factories." He was also returning to West Africa, however, as a missionary convert of the Shiloh Kingdom. The leader of the Shiloh sect wrote to Rev. Alan F. Sherrill, dean of the Atlanta Theological Seminary, as follows: "You will be glad to learn that the African King has since written full of faith and courage. Reports souls, and a remarkable miracle a blind man's eyes opened thru faith in the Son of God." (AFRC, U.S. Department of Justice, Federal Prison System, Southeast Regional Office, Correspondence of Frank W. Sandford, general file, [hereafter cited as AFRC, FWS]).

Sam also established the Akim Trading Co. in several towns in the Gold Coast and soon succeeded in persuading a number of Africans to take shares in the company. More importantly, Sam purchased sixty-four square miles of land, which he described as rich in mahogany, rubber, gold, and soil, from Ohene Kwame Dokyi of Akyem-Abuakwa for £600, his savings from over a decade of produce trading. Sam's land was located in the Akan interior lowlands at Apoli, approximately sixty miles from Cape Coast. He called his new property *Asuboi*, meaning the union of two rivers, since the land was situated near the confluence of the rivers Pra (Bosumpra) and Birim at a distance of about five and a half miles (see map). According to Sam's own estimate, this acquisition brought the amount of land he had either leased or purchased to a total of 180 square miles, a figure which included rubber and gold concessions.

Sam advertised in the *African League* newspaper published at Buchanan, Grand Bassa, Liberia, with the caption "Agricultural Lands in Africa and How to Obtain Them." From its headquarters in Jackson, Miss., the *African League* Publishing Co. promoted Liberian colonization. Sam's advertisement came to the attention of two influential black leaders in Oklahoma, Dr. P. J. Dorman, a prominent black physician in Mantee, and "Professor" J. P. Liddell of Weleetka, who wrote for details about land for Afro-American settlement. Dorman had been the president of a 150-member emigration society in Oklahoma since 1909. He had also frequently consulted the editor of the *African League*, J. H. Green, about black immigration to Liberia. Moreover, when Dorman wrote to Sam, he had been trying to charter a boat from the Bacon Steamship Co. of New York for such a purpose.

Sam brought Dorman and Liddell's inquiry before several of the Akyem chiefs (Kwamin Affanu, Kwamin Anoky, and Yao Broby) and, according to Sam's testimony, they agreed to receive the prospective black American colonists and to offer land for settlement. News of the favorable response reached Dorman and Liddell and quickly spread to the several all-black towns of Oklahoma. Consequently, the Akim Trading Company's commercial aims now encompassed the new goal of Afro-American immigration to the Gold Coast.

Before Sam left once more for the United States on 15 December 1912, he was obliged to relinquish temporarily his position as chief of Brofoyedru, and to appoint his cousin, Osai Kwamin, as regent until he returned. Sam had inherited the chieftainship from his uncle, in keeping with the customary law of the Akan people governing maternal-nephew inheritance and succession (see family tree of Alfred Charles Sam). His uncle had inherited his position from Sam's grandfather, who was "Chief of Obosse [Ofuasi] and Appasu [Apaso], West Akim." When, in March 1916, Sam was appointed chief of Apaso, his birthplace, by *Omanhene* Kofi Ahinkora, paramount chief of Akyem-Bosome state (1874–1917 and 1921–23), the British governor of the Gold Coast objected on the ground that "Sam is not a person who can very wisely be made chief" (National Archives of Ghana, ADM 11/1776, Palaver Books, Cape Coast Castle, 20 March 1916).

Sam arrived in Boston on 8 February 1913 aboard the S.S. *Arabic* from Liverpool. He severed his connection with his former business associates and the original Akim Trading Co. and launched the Akim Trading Company Ltd., on 27 March 1913, under the laws of the state of South Dakota, capitalized at one million dollars. In addition to Sam, the directors of the new company were: Joseph D. Taylor, Cape Coast; Michael V. Ofori, Larteh, Gold Coast; Moses T. Early, Monrovia, Liberia; John P. Samoah, Larteh, Gold Coast; and J. K. Asare, Aburi, Gold Coast.

Returning on 19 April 1913 to Shiloh, Sam told his missionary mentors of his work in West Africa on behalf of the faith. From Maine he traveled to Oklahoma at the invitation of Liddell, Dorman, and others interested in African emigration. He arrived at Wetumpka on 12 May 1913, and sixty-four persons enrolled as members of Sam's new enterprise at his first meeting at Mantee. Indeed, so enthusiastic was the response among blacks that an African movement rapidly began to take shape. Within six months 184 emigration clubs mushroomed throughout Oklahoma and the Southwest, and they eventually raised $72,000 through stock purchases. Each share was sold for $25 and entitled its holder to free transportation to the Gold Coast. In addition, various stockholders advanced personal loans totaling nearly $12,000. These stockholders included not only a large number of prosperous black farmers but also respected business and professional men.

While the prospectus of the Akim Trading Co. Ltd. urged "the emigration of the best Negro farmers and mechanics from the United States to different sections in West Africa," its major concern was African "economic independence." Therefore it proposed to develop trade by creating its own "Ethiopian Steamship Line" (*Sierra Leone Weekly News*, 23 January 1915).

Opposition to Sam's African movement in Oklahoma was immediate. On 2 September 1913 Sam was arrested at Boley under a warrant for disturbing the peace. Later that month, he was arrested a second time in Boley and charged with fraudulently receiving money. However, Sam was vindicated

FAMILY TREE OF ALFRED CHARLES SAM

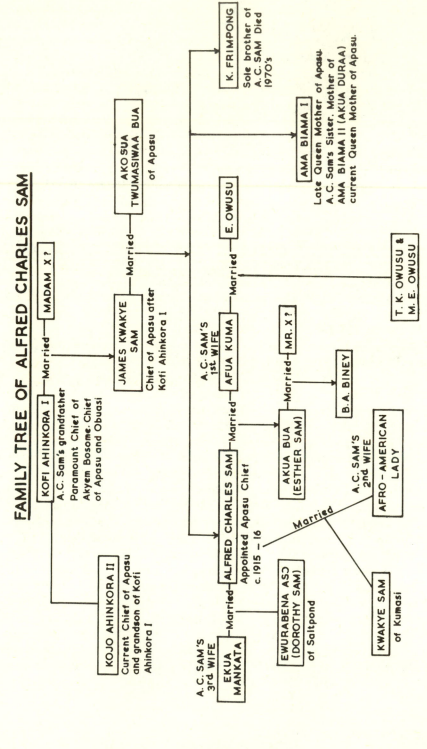

KOFI AHINKORA I — Married — **MADAM X ?**

A.C. Sam's grandfather Paramount Chief of Akyem Bosome. Chief of Apasu and Obuasi

KOJO AHINKORA II

Current Chief of Apasu and grandson of Kofi Ahinkora I

JAMES KWAKYE SAM — Married — **AKOSUA TWUMASIWAA BUA** of Apasu

Chief of Apasu after Kofi Ahinkora I

K. FRIMPONG

Sole brother of A.C. SAM Died 1970's

AMA BIAMA I

Late Queen Mother of Apasu. A.C. Sam's Sister. Mother of AMA BIAMA II (AKUA DURAA) current Queen Mother of Apasu.

E. OWUSU — Married — **AFUA KUMA**

A.C. SAM'S 1st WIFE

T. K. OWUSU & M. E. OWUSU

ALFRED CHARLES SAM — Married — **AKUA BUA (ESTHER SAM)** — Married — **MR. X ?**

Appointed Apasu Chief c. 1915 – 16

B. A. BINEY

Married — **AFRO–AMERICAN LADY**

A.C. SAM'S 2nd WIFE

A.C. SAM'S 3rd WIFE

EKUA MANKATA — Married — **EWURABENA ASO (DOROTHY SAM)** of Saltpond

KWAKYE SAM of Kumasi

S40

on 26 September when he was acquitted of all charges. During this time, the governor of Oklahoma, the state's attorney general, and the Seminole County attorney investigated Sam, but no evidence of fraud could be found. At the same time, the matter was referred to the U.S. postmaster general for investigation of mail fraud.

Meanwhile, on 30 September 1913, Sam brought a delegation from Oklahoma to New York to arrange for the purchase of a ship. The company's white business agent, A. E. Smith, met the delegation in New York on 2 October and collected the proceeds of stock sales from the presidents of the emigration clubs in Oklahoma. Sam made a first payment of $5,000 on the German-built steamer *Curityba*, which was owned by the Cuban Maritime Co. The money was paid to the representative of the Cuban company, the Munson Steamship Line, which stipulated that the final payment on the purchase price of $69,000 was due in February 1914. As it turned out, however, Sam paid the outstanding balance in cash on 15 January 1914.

Sam and an advance party of delegates returned to New York from Oklahoma at the end of January to take possession of the *Curityba*. Upon his arrival, however, Sam faced an intensive and protracted investigation by Post Office officials looking for evidence of mail fraud. They eventually found that all the stock had been sold by personal solicitation, and that Sam's use of the mails had been comparatively small. Since there was no "definite information to disprove the claims of Sam, as to his being a Chief and as to his representations concerning land to be allotted by the native Chiefs and his ownership of the sixty-four square miles of land," the investigators concluded that the case did not involve any fraudulent use of the mails.

Nonetheless, the Post Office inspector who conducted the investigation recommended that the case be transferred to the Kansas City Division of the Post Office for additional investigation. (DNA, RG 59, file 811.7111/63). The case was further investigated in Oklahoma, but the United States attorney at McAlester, Okla., finally concluded that "the facts did not warrant criminal prosecution in that district." The case was therefore returned to the New York Division of the Post Office, and, on 23 August 1914, the acting United States district attorney decided that "it would not be possible to secure a conviction in this case." (DNA, RG 59, file 811.7111/78).

The consistently negative outcome of these investigations proved a severe setback to British officials who wanted the United States government to halt the African movement by prosecuting its leader. The first Akim Trading Co. came to official notice in the Gold Coast in November 1912, but a subsequent police investigation of the allegation that Sam had obtained money under false pretenses failed to disclose any substantiating evidence. The British ambassador in Washington, D.C., Sir Cecil Arthur Spring-Rice (1859–1918), asked that the U.S. government "do all in its power to prevent the departure for the Gold Coast Colony of 'Chief Sam' and his followers," since, in the British view, "the entire scheme is fraudulent and . . . the intending emigrants are foredoomed to disappointment" (DNA, RG 59, file

811.7111/49). British officials also used the press to discredit Sam's land claims in the Gold Coast, hoping to give the public the impression that Sam's scheme was a gigantic swindle. Furthermore, they sought to discourage prospective immigrants with warnings about the adverse climate and unhealthy conditions in the Gold Coast. Finally, they urged Akim Trading Co. officials to resign their positions and to institute legal proceedings against Sam and the ship in order to recover their investment.

Sam contended, however, that the British wanted to end the African movement for other reasons: first, British firms in the Gold Coast dreaded the prospect of African commercial competition; second, British officials feared that black Americans would introduce skills among native laborers that would make them less economically dependent; third, the British desired to keep their African trade from being diverted from London and Liverpool to America; and, fourth, British colonial administrators feared that black Americans would disturb the racial peace of the West African colony.

Sam's many legal, diplomatic, and political entanglements created considerable delay and expense. The *Curityba* spent the month of February tied up in the Erie Basin in Brooklyn with forty black delegates and shareholders from Oklahoma aboard. The work of refitting the vessel for its African service began in March, but the extortionate charges demanded by the contractors soon forced Sam to approach his friends in Maine for assistance. The Shilohites sent Captain L. S. McKenzie and members of the Kingdom crew to New York to bring the *Curityba* to Portland, Me., and they promised that they would make the necessary repairs without cost. The offer was especially generous since the sect had been experiencing financial hardship, a situation exacerbated by Frank W. Sandford's conviction for manslaughter in December 1911 and his ten-year sentence in the Atlanta Federal Penitentiary. The charges grew out of the tragic 15,000-mile voyage that Sandford and his followers embarked on to Africa and the North Atlantic in 1910–11, during which six persons aboard ship perished from malnutrition and disease. In February and April 1914, Sandford wrote letters to Chief Sam in Maine regarding "Missionary operations" and "directions concerning our teachers and caplain [*sic*] doing missionary work on passage." Sam replied on 26 April 1914, and from his prison cell Sandford instructed his stenographer "to make up a good letter" to be sent to Sam. His instruction also contained the salutation: "Precious precious brother from 'Guiana' [Gambia?] My love to your people for whom we gladly *suffer. God loves Africa*." (AFRC, FWS).

While workers refitted the *Curityba* in Portland, Sam awaited the outcome of his application to register the ship with the British Board of Trade. The British government, however, seized the opportunity to force Sam to change his existing plans by threatening to deny the *Curityba* British registry. The British vice consul in Portland, J. B. Keating, thus persuaded Sam to reduce the number of delegates for the impending voyage to no more than sixty and to consider them purely as an investigating party rather than colonists. The amount of time they would be permitted to remain in the Gold Coast would be determined by the colonial authorities. Sam also consented to restrict the use of the ship to trading and to carrying freight. In return, Keating finally signed the provisional registration papers for the *Curityba* on 20 May 1914. Despite Sam's drastic modifications, the British government enacted an unprecedented ordinance in the Gold Coast compelling each Afro-American immigrant to deposit five pounds as a security bond (Ordinance No. 4 of 1914, "An Ordinance to make provision to regulate the immigration of persons not born in any part of West Africa" *Legislative Council Minutes*, 18 March 1914).

After receiving a set of British colors, Sam and his party rechristened the vessel the S.S. *Liberia*, making it "the first Negro Steamship of the Twentieth Century" (Orishatukeh Faduma, *Sierra Leone Weekly News*, Saturday, 3 October 1914). The party finally sailed from Portland on 3 June 1914, headed for Galveston, Tex., where over two hundred of Sam's followers had been waiting patiently for the preceding six weeks for the ship's arrival. The *Liberia* arrived at Galveston on 17 June, under the command of Captain L. S. McKenzie and a crew of Kingdom volunteers, and it remained at Galveston for the next two months while Sam tried to raise additional funds in Texas and Oklahoma to meet the trip's expenses.

Sam still communicated with the incarcerated Rev. Frank Sandford, writing him various letters on 20, 24, and 26 June, 17 July, and 5 September 1914 (AFRC, FWS). Sandford wrote to Captain McKenzie on 24 June "concerning our agreement with African Chief, etc." (ibid.). On 31 July, Sandford also wrote to Sam in Galveston regarding "Missionary interests" and referred to the possibility that he "may have to recall our party on board about to sail" (ibid.). The *Liberia* sailed from Galveston on 20 August, with its exploration party of forty-six delegates, including Sam's Afro-American wife and their son, Kwakye Sam. When the vessel reached Pensacola, Fla., the Kingdom crew decided to return to Maine, though Ira Benford, the chief engineer, stayed with the *Liberia* for the remainder of its voyage to Africa. The rest had left due to the outbreak of war in Europe, the cleavages that had developed aboard ship between blacks and whites, and their alarm over an outbreak of dysentery which claimed one crew member's life. Sam hired a new crew mainly of Cape Verdeans at Pensacola for the transatlantic crossing. The *Liberia* arrived at Havana on 13 September, and left again on 29 September. On 8 October, the *Liberia* arrived at Bridgetown, Barbados, where she finally received a permanent certificate of British registration. Sam and his colleagues also addressed an enthusiastic public meeting on 16 October, at the Bridgetown YMCA Hall. Before leaving Barbados, Sam wrote to Sandford, who received his letter on 28 October in Atlanta.

The delegates set out across the Atlantic on 22 October and reached the West African coast on 4 November. When the *Liberia* stopped at Cape Verde's Mayo Island, a neutral port, to pick up a cargo of salt, the British auxiliary HMS *Victorian* seized the ship as a prize on 19 November, despite the fact that the *Liberia* was flying the British flag as a duly registered British ship. It was later alleged that the ship's German-made Marconi wireless radio made her suspect. The *Liberia* was forced to abandon part of her cargo and escorted to Freetown, Sierra Leone, where British authorities detained her for four weeks awaiting the outcome of the Sierra Leone Supreme Court's decision. On 21 December, the court ruled that the *Liberia* was not a prize ship, but by then the group's resources had been severely depleted. The ship's wireless apparatus was seized as a "war precaution" on 24 December by order of the British Admiralty without compensation, although at first it was agreed in principle that compensation would be paid.

Despite these setbacks, the presence of Sam and the Afro-American delegates had come to be regarded by several important West African contemporaries as the first step in the long-awaited regeneration of Africa. The wave of nationalism that swept over the intellectual elite in West Africa could be accounted for by the movement's aims of economic and racial independence for Africans, which one newspaper later described as "the great scheme for the upbuilding of the blackman's country by the blackman" (*Gold Coast Leader*, 3 June 1916). However, the upsurge of nationalist consciousness was also stimulated by the British colonial authorities' heavy-handed opposition to the venture, particularly as demonstrated in the hasty passage of the Gold Coast immigration ordinance aimed at the Afro-Americans.

From Freetown, the *Liberia* finally reached the Gold Coast at Axim on 7 January. The following day Rev. John Drybault Taylor met the party at Cape Coast. After spending six days there, the *Liberia* left for Saltpond, its final destination, where Sam and his party were treated to a rousing durbar by the entire royal court, presided over by Ohene Nana Kurantsi III, chief of Saltpond. Kurantsi III ordered that every man and woman should make a donation towards a hospitality fund for the Afro-Americans. Later, the sum of one hundred and sixty pounds was presented to the visitors.

For six weeks Sam led an expedition inland to survey the proposed site at Apoli in the Birim Valley. His party left Saltpond on 25–26 January, and they arrived, on 1 February, at Apaso, Sam's birthplace. The party then trekked to Akyem-Swedru, where the *omanhene* received them on 6 February while they waited for the opening of the road to Apoli, eighteen miles away. The delegates next visited Nsuaem [Oda], on 11 February, where they were received by Ohene Attafuah; on 15–16 February, they left Akyem-Swedru and stopped at Aduasa where they were received by Chief Achampong. The following day the delegates finally reached Apoli and were received by Ohene Kwame Dokyi, the person from whom Sam had purchased the sixty-four square miles of land. The delegates inspected the land to determine suitable sites for future settlements and made preliminary attempts at clearing it in order to start a plantation.

Although rich in natural resources and fertile soil, the unhealthy climate and environment of the Akyem district resulted in a high incidence of malaria among foreigners. After a number of the exploratory party fell ill, Sam and

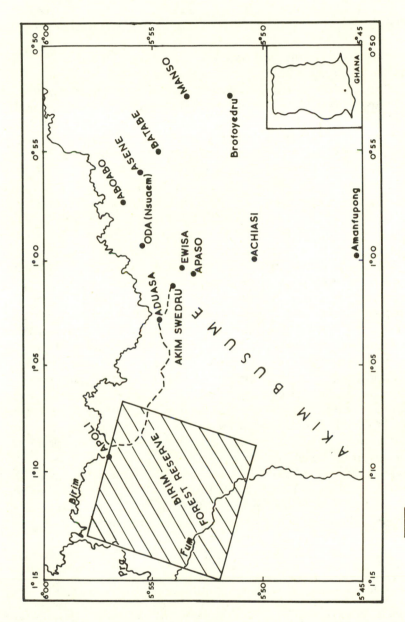

64 sq mile ASEQUOI Land proposed for Afro American settlement (1914 – 15)

---- Swedru – Apoli path constructed for Afro Americans 1914 – 15

the surviving members were forced to make their way back to the coast from Apoli, only to find a discontented group aboard the *Liberia* at Anamboe, suffering from a shortage of food and other supplies. The captain and crew of the ship also openly rebelled for the same reason. In addition, the crew had obtained judgments in the court at Cape Coast against Sam for nonpayment of wages.

Sometime in May–June 1915 Sam left the group at Anamboe for Cape Coast, on one of his many futile attempts to secure coal for the ship, but after this the delegates claimed that they received no further communication from him. Sam was accused, moreover, of absconding with the group's immigration deposit money. Stranded and without food, coal, or cash, though cared for as best they could by Ohene Amonu V and his people, the majority of the emigrants left the Gold Coast aboard S.S. *Abosso*, a merchant vessel bound for Liverpool. They arrived in the United States during the first week of September 1915. In 1916 it was reported that the Akim Trading Co. Ltd. was reorganized under a new name, The African Emigration and Trading Co. (*Gold Coast Leader*, 3 June 1916). The liabilities of the S.S. *Liberia* were eventually paid off by the Universal Transportation Co., Ltd., of Toronto, Canada, and the vessel was towed back to North America in 1916.

However, some of the Afro-Americans settled in Cape Coast, Winneba, Accra, and some even traveled to Nigeria, introducing among the local Africans a variety of impressive technical skills. In time, one of the visitors who remained in the Gold Coast constructed an engine-driven boat that plied the coastal waters between Saltpond, Cape Coast, and Amisano. Another Afro-American set up a tobacco plantation at the town of Afransi, about seventy kilometers from Saltpond. The Afro-Americans also introduced the local people to the techniques of manufacturing gunpowder as well as gin (Akpeteshie), using palm wine. Some of the Afro-Americans also attempted to start a rubber plantation at Amanfopon, but attacks of malaria soon ended their effort. Local people continued the plantation, however, and vestiges of some of the old rubber farms started by the Afro-Americans can still be found in the forest of Amanfopon.

It is generally believed that Chief Sam went into self-exile in Liberia, via the Ivory Coast. News of his death in Monrovia sometime in the 1930s was communicated by letter to his nephew in the Gold Coast. It is also believed that Sam left fairly substantial property in Liberia. In the view of Ghanaians, Chief Sam was a genuine political and economic nationalist.

Sources: DLC, Booker T. Washington Papers, container 944, Alfred C. Sam, Ayivebi, Western Akyem, to Booker T. Washington, ca. February 1915; National Archives of Ghana, Cape Coast Regional Archives, Cape Coast, Ghana: Acc. No. 179/65—"American Negro Immigrants"; DNA, RG 59, file 811.7111, "Fraudulent Use of Mail. U.S."; RG 65, file Misc. 8027, "In Re: Alfred C. Sam, Alleged Scheme to Defraud," February 1914; RG 85, Records of the Immigration and Naturalization Service, T843, Passenger and crew lists of vessels arriving at Boston, 1891–1919, 2 February 1913; PRO, CO 96/540, "Land Acquisition by Negroes from U.S.A.," "Akim Trading Co.," CO 96/552, "Negro Emigration from U.S.A."; CO 96/554, "Negro Emigration from U.S.A.," FO 115/1804, "Negroes in West Africa"; State of South Dakota, Bureau of Administration, Office of Records Management, Articles of Incorporation of the Akim Trading Co. Ltd., 27 March 1913, file no. 45167, box no. 445; Bureau of Corporations, State of New York, Certificate of Incorporation of the Akim Trading Co., 21 July 1911, book 362, p. 697; William E. Bittle and Gilbert Geis, *The Longest Way Home: Chief Alfred C. Sam's Back-to-Africa Movement* (Detroit: Wayne State University Press, 1964); E. A. Boateng, *A Geography of Ghana* (Cambridge: Cambridge University Press, 1959); Norman L. Crockett, *The Black Towns* (Lawrence, Kans.: The Regents Press of Kansas, 1979); Hans W. Debrunner, *A History of Christianity in Ghana* (Accra, Ghana: Waterville Publishing House, 1967); Edward Reynolds, *Trade and Economic Change on the Gold Coast, 1807–1874* (New York: Longmans, 1974); Arnold L. White, *The Almighty and Us: The Inside Story of Shiloh, Maine* (Fort Lauderdale, Fla.: published by the author, 1979); Gustav K. Deveneaux, "O. Faduma," *Dictionary of African Biography*, vol. 2, pp. 65–66; Orishatukeh Faduma, "American Negroes and the Gold Coast," *African Mail*, 29 May 1914; "What the African Movement Stands For," *African Mail*, 25 September, 2 October 1914; "The African Movement," *African Mail*, 20, 27 November, 4 December 1914, 12, 19 March 1915, 7, 14 May 1915, 13, 20, 27 August 1915, 10 September 1915; W. N. Gleason, "Africa," *The Golden Trumpet* 1 (October 1912):4–5, (November 1912):19, (Christmas 1912):30, (New Year's 1913):46, (February 1913):58, (October 1914):271; N. H. Harrison, "John Drybault Taylor," *The Everlasting Gospel* 1 (8 January 1901):19–20; H. C. Jenkins, "The Dark Continent," *The Golden Trumpet* 1 (Easter 1913), "An Appeal from Africa," *The Golden Trumpet* 1 (May 1913):96–98; J. Ayo Langley, "Chief Sam's African Movement and Race Consciousness in West Africa," *Phylon* 32 (Summer 1971):164–78; "Maine and Africa," *The Everlasting Gospel* 1 (25 January 1901); "Mr. Sandford's Account, Written from the Federal Prison at Atlanta, Georgia, of His Arrest and Journey South," *Portland Evening Express and Advertiser* 7 (February 1912); "Rev. Orishatukeh Faduma," *American Missionary* 58 (January 1904):13–16; Frank Sandford, " 'They Have Never Heard the Story of the Babe of Bethelehem,' " *The Everlasting Gospel* 1 (15–23 January 1901):32–35; Mrs. F. W. Sandford, "Why I Love Africa," *The Golden Trumpet* 1 (June 1913):106–107; J. D. Taylor, "More About Africa," *The Everlasting Gospel* 1 (23–29 January 1901):49–50, " 'Tell the Story Regardless of the Cost,' " *The Everlasting Gospel* 1 (29 January–2 February 1901):49; "J. D. Taylor, an African," *The Everlasting Gospel* 1 (3–16 February 1901):76; *The Golden Trumpet* 1 (Special Issue on Africa, June 1913):105–16; K. Affrifah, "Akyem, 1700–1874: A Study in Inter-State Relations in Pre-Colonial Gold Coast," Ph.D. diss., University of London, 1976; John Bannon, "Social Order: What Four Maine Utopias Can Teach Us," honors paper, Department of Government, Bowdoin College, 1977; Scott Cowger, "The Religious Community of Shiloh," unpublished paper, Swathmore College, December 1978; Sydney H. French, "Chief Sam and His 'Back to Africa Movement,' " NN-Sc, Federal Writers' Program, New York, "Negroes in New York," 19 September 1939; Rev. Frank S. Murray, "History of Shiloh, Maine," unpublished MS, chap. 34; interviews by Mr. James Anquandah, University of Ghana, Legon, for the editor, 1980, with: Fred Agyemang, Accra; Joseph Kwamena Baffoe, Saltpond; Justice Acquah Felbah (formerly Nana Kurantsi III, Chief of Saltpond), Saltpond; Efua Kuma (alias Mary Appiah, first wife of Chief Alfred Sam), Akyem Swedru; Akua Twumansiwaa Buaa (alias Esther Sam, daughter of Chief Alfred Sam by his first wife), Akyem Swedru; Akua Duraa (alias Amma Polua Biama II, currently Queen mother of Apasu, and niece of Chief Alfred Sam and daughter of Chief Sam's sister, Amma Biama I, late Queen mother of Apasu), Apasu; Kojo Anokye (eyewitness of Afro-Americans' visit of Apasu in 1915), Apasu; Opanyin Ofosuhene, Amanfopon; Timothy Kwame Owusu (son of Efua Kuma, formerly Ambassador of Ghana to the Republic of Sudan and high commissioner to Malawi), Akyem Swedru; and M. E. Owusu (son of Efua Kuma), Akyem Swedru; letter from Nana Oware Agyekum II, Omanhene Akyem Busume, Akyem Swedru, Ghana, to the editor, 2 December 1980; and Rev. Frank S. Murray, pastor, Fair Haven Chapel, Essex, Mass., to the editor, 25 May 1980.

APPENDIX II

Because it has not been possible to establish conclusively Garvey's authorship of the letter signed "Umbilla," it has been placed in the appendix. However, its date of publication, contents, and general style strongly suggest that Garvey was the author. This letter and the response to it are important for what they may reveal about Garvey's outlook and activity immediately following his arrival in England in 1912.

"Umbilla"[1] to the *Jamaica Times*

[[*London?*, 20, 6, '12]]

THE BLACKMAN'S PAST AND FUTURE

Sir,—

"Recognised and compensated," will both these condition[s] be occupied by the blackman in the world forty years hence? Particularly in countries under British dominion. Recognition of a race must come through their voluntary effort under the three essential equipments of man, viz-improved moral, physical and mental condition. The savage rudiment of morality is simplicity itself and therefore more respected than the ethics of our progressive civilisation. Life near nature, nature so rugged and imposing; so majestic and grand. The pyramids of Egypt, Thebes the great city with her fallen statues, obelisks and porticos, the present impartial account of modern travellers, convey to the mind the great physical and mental achievements of men in those days. The black runner before an Egyptian chariot, Hannibal's legions across the Alps; a fe[u]dal castle, the battle axe, mace, spear and armour, seen in the British Museum are a silent display of the physical force of those who have passed on. Today is not that vigorous force called strength but the quick force of penetration, mental ability, that irresistable current that takes the place that physical development once commanded.

The brain in the blackman has arrived at a state of development, that has undoubtedly placed the conclusions of many writers in the shade. He is now desirous of making his contribution to the benefit of history. In every branch of progressive development his efforts are portrayed. Will he be recognised and allowed his place in this our present temple of light, to stand and say, may I be allowed to speak; will you all hear and for the harmonious human standards that emblem, Peace; will you all justify my cause.

This problem is of great moment, therefore it is right and necessary for the intelligent negro in every country in the world, to be a possessor of the records of the year[s] 1861 to 1865. Such a book should be in every negro home along with his Bible, that he may read of those apostles of human right, Henry Clay, Daniel Webster, Sumner, Wendell Philips, Lloyd Garrison, and others. Ancient history does not record such epics as those of the British cruiser chasing the slave-traders on the African coast, exposed as they were to the malignant fever by which thousands have passed away? Nor that mother, sister, father, son, and brother, had contended on the bloody field of battle for the Emancipation of the blackman. Sacrifice of such magnitude should never be overlooked or forgotten by him, but should be used as a means to allay any misunderstanding that will surely occur as the black man's intellectual progress advances.

The young blackman in Africa and elsewhere, is so assiduous after knowledge and training that in two score years, instead of the nude African, in the mines and cotton fields of South Africa and Uganda, or the semi-nude negro in the cane fields of Demerara, we will see a [sober clad] black man. The present condition of the intelligent black youth in the West Indies is such, that he is actually unable to live under his present financial condition. He will have to solve the problem. "But where will he solve it." In Africa? Not in an official capacity or as an employer or labourer, but as an independent pioneer, an adventurer who is determined to wrest from nature comfort, wealth, happiness. That determined few will gradually increase in number and as Australia, Canada and New-Zealand so will West Africa reverberate to the incessant stroke of the axe, hammer and saw; her rivers will be controlled and her forests will yield, to the young impulse of the regenerated blackman. The African native has gradually yielded to the effect and method of the christian doctrine expounded to him by his black brother from the West Indies. Jamaica I think is destined to carry the bond of fellowship light and unity to the Motherland. The first black Missionary[2] was sent from her shores, and many follow. Her soldiers have gone to Africa and conquered.[3] Now has arrived the moment for her physical and industrial energy to be displayed! Jamaica of all the West Indies would be justly proud of her sons, and laurelled would she be if through her effort she could place a black adopted daughter into the group that forms the sister nations of the British Empire.—But how? Yours, etc.,

UMBILLA

Printed in the *Jamaica Times*, Saturday, 31 August 1912. Original headlines have been abbreviated.

1. Garvey arrived in England sometime in the spring of 1912 (the exact date is uncertain), but it was consistent with the letter's date. The reference in the letter to the British Museum also suggests that it was written in England.

2. In 1844 the first missionary group of Jamaicans and their Baptist supervisors arrived in Fernando Po; it marked the first African missionary undertaking utilizing West Indian agents. (Bela Vassady, Jr., "The Role of the West Indian Black Missionary in West Africa, 1840–1890," Ph.D. diss., Temple University, 1972).

3. A reference to the West India Regiments, first formed in 1795 and used in the nascent colony of Sierra Leone at the end of the eighteenth century. The West India Regiments served in British West Africa throughout the nineteenth century, most importantly in the Ashanti Wars of 1863–64 and 1873–74. (Abba Karama, "The Origin of the West Indies Regiments," *Science and Society* 35 [Spring 1971]: 58–62; Christopher Fyfe, *A History of Sierra Leone* [London: Oxford University Press, 1962]).

R. M. Stimpson to the *Jamaica Times*

[[10 North Parade, Kingston. 2.9.12]]

Sir,—

I have read with much interest the letter which appeared in your issue Aug. 31st., entitled "The Black Man's Past and Future." The story of the blackman is one which lies deep down in my heart and a subject to which I have given much time and thought. That the blackman has had a past history no student of to-day will dare deny. His history has been in most instances dimly written, but with a keen vision it may be read. In others, it is written in letters of Blood. Your correspondent asks if the subject of his letter will be "Recognised and Compensated" ["]in forty years hence." The answer lies with the blackman himself. In the fierce struggle for existence and Supremacy as we find it today, no one has time to "Recognise and Compensate" any but those who are able to demand it. Has the blackman the "Grit" to place his claims conspicuously before the world and demand "Recognition and Compensation?" Time will tell. In short, if he has the "Goods" it is his business to "produce" them. Japanese, Chinese and other backward races have done that, will the blackman follow? It is ridiculous to expect the Germans, Britons and Franks to leave their Guards and attend to the business of others. See how they treat their colonists who are not of their blood; Germany is to-day in a death-struggle in its Eastern and Western African spheres of influence in trying to subjugate the natives. Surely not to "Recognise and Compensate" them. The same story may be told of other European nations who hold spheres of influence in the blackman's country, and they too are not there to "Recognise and Compensate" those natives living in such "spheres." Is the story different in these West Indian Islands? Study the situation, and you will find it only too plain; study it in the United States of America and you find the process the same, only a little more exaggerated. As it unfolds itself to me, the United States of America are conquered territories—conquered by the white man, and he lives up to the knowledge that the blood of his fathers was spilled for them and he must make good. Those who are not of his blood but are in residence in these conquered territories subjects—serfs and Vassals! For these he has no time to "Recognise or Compensate" in any measure except as it shall suit his particular purpose; Read the recent correspondence between the Secretary of State and our Governor. See what is implied. I believe that the problem of the blackman will be solved, as other back-ward races have solved theirs. But the solution lies in his own hand, and "recognition and compensation" avail him until such time as he claims it by his own endeavour—not before. He must realise it now, and ever, and that only on African soil can he come into his own. Britons, Teutons, Gauls and others have had their like stages of development as the blackman, not less irksome, but they have proved themselves crafts-men. Before I go let me remind the blackman that in order to prove himself as others before him have done, he must be armed with *Education*, *Character* and *Wealth*. Yours, etc.,

R. M. STIMPSON[1]

Printed in the *Jamaica Times*, Saturday, 14 September 1912. Original headlines have been omitted.

1. Dr. Robert M. Stimpson (b. 1886) held the position of medical officer of health for the parish of St. Elizabeth; he was also medical officer in charge of the Mannings House for Destitute Children. (*HJ*, 1918).

APPENDIX III

This list of UNIA office holders was compiled from documents covering the period of the present volume which indicated some change of UNIA offices and/or the appearance of newly appointed officials. The list does not attempt to establish any hierarchy of UNIA offices, nor the precise period when each office was held. Names have been standardized and biographical information regarding the various individuals may be found in the annotations that appear in the volume.

OFFICERS OF THE UNIVERSAL NEGRO IMPROVEMENT ASSOCIATION AND AFRICAN COMMUNITIES' LEAGUE

27 August 1914

President and Traveling Commissioner	Marcus Garvey
Secretary-General	T. A. McCormack
Associate Secretary	Adrian A. Daily

[*Source:* Marcus Garvey to Travers Buxton, 27 August 1914, Brit. Emp. s.19, D/2/6, ASAPS, RHL.]

23 October 1914

President and Traveling Commissioner	Marcus Garvey
Secretary-General	T. A. McCormack
Associate Secretary	Adrian A. Daily
President, Ladies' Division	Eva Aldred
Vice-President, Ladies' Division	Mrs. G. Livingstone
Associate Secretary, Ladies' Division	Amy Ashwood

[*Source: Gleaner*, Friday, 23 October 1914.]

28 January 1915

President and Traveling Commissioner	Marcus Garvey
Vice-President	Thomas Smikle

Secretary-General	T. A. McCormack
Treasurer	J. W. Milburn
Associate Secretary	Amy Ashwood
Board of Management	E. E. Reid
Board of Management	J. M. Reid
Board of Management	T. T. Brown
Board of Management	Alfred Uriah Peart
Board of Management	Indiana Garvey Peart

[*Source: Gleaner*, Thursday, 28 January 1915.]

11 *February 1915*

President and Traveling Commissioner	Marcus Garvey
Secretary-General	T. A. McCormack
Associate Secretary	Adrian A. Daily
Associate Secretary	Amy Ashwood
Board of Management	Alfred Uriah Peart
Board of Management	Indiana Garvey Peart
Board of Management	Amy Aldred
Board of Management	Gwen Campbell
Board of Management	J. R. Murdock
Board of Management	T. T. Brown
Board of Management	E. E. Reid
Board of Management	J. M. Reid

[*Source: Gleaner*, Thursday, 11 February 1915.]

12 *April 1915*

President and Traveling Commissioner	Marcus Garvey
Vice-President	Thomas Smikle
Secretary-General	T. A. McCormack
Associate Secretary	Adrian A. Daily
Treasurer	J. W. Milburn
President, Ladies' Division	Eva Aldred
Associate Secretary	Amy Ashwood
Board of Management	Marcus Garvey
Board of Management	Thomas Smikle
Board of Management	T. A. McCormack
Board of Management	Adrian A. Daily

Board of Management	E. E. Reid
Board of Management	T. T. Brown
Board of Management	J. R. Murdock
Board of Management	Alfred Uriah Peart
Board of Management	Arthur McKenzie
Board of Management	J. M. Reid
Board of Management	A. Knight
Board of Management	Robert Cross
Board of Management	Eva Aldred
Board of Management	Amy Ashwood
Board of Management	Gwen Campbell
Board of Management	Connie Phillips
Board of Management	Indiana Garvey Peart
Board of Management	Amy Aldred

[*Source:* Marcus Garvey to Booker T. Washington, 12 April 1915, BTW, DLC; and enclosure, "The Universal Negro Improvement and Conservation Association and African Communities' League," n.p., n.d., BTW, DLC.]

3 August 1915

Treasurer	J. R. Murdock

[*Source: Daily Chronicle*, Tuesday, 3 August 1915.]

April 1916

President and Traveling Commissioner	Marcus Garvey
Secretary-General	T. A. McCormack
Associate Secretary	Adrian A. Daily
President, Ladies' Division	Eva Aldred
General Secretary, Ladies' Division	Amy Ashwood

[*Source:* Marcus Garvey to "Dear Friend and Brother," April 1916, WEBDB, MU.]

12 May 1916

President and Traveling Commissioner	Marcus Garvey
Vice-President	Thomas Smikle
Secretary-General	T. A. McCormack
Associate Secretary	Adrian A. Daily
Treasurer	J. R. Murdock
President, Ladies' Division	Eva Aldred
Associate Secretary	Amy Ashwood

[*Source:* Marcus Garvey to T. A. McCormack, 12 May 1916, TAM.]

27 November 1917

President	Isaac B. Allen
International Organizer	Marcus Garvey
First Vice-President	Walter J. Conway
Second Vice-President	C. C. Seifert
Third Vice-President	Samuel A. Duncan
General Secretary	Edward D. Smith-Green
Associate Secretary	Ben E. Burrell
Secretary	Serena E. Danridge
Treasurer	Isaac Samuel Bright
President, Ladies' Division	Irena Moorman-Blackston
First Vice-President, Ladies' Division	Eva F. Curtis
Second Vice-President, Ladies' Division	Lizzie B. Sims
General Secretary, Ladies' Division	Ethel Oughton-Clarke
Associate Secretary, Ladies' Division	Carrie B. Mero
Chairman, Advisory Board	John E. Bruce

[*Source:* Marcus Garvey to Nicholas Murray Butler, 27 November 1917, NMB, NNC.]

29 April 1918

President and International Organizer	Marcus Garvey
First Vice-President	Walter J. Conway
Second Vice-President	Edward Sterling Wright
General Secretary	Edward D. Smith-Green
Executive Secretary	George A. Crawley
Associate Secretary	Ben E. Burrell
Secretary	Julia E. Rumford
Treasurer	Clarence A. Carpenter
President, Ladies' Division	Irena Moorman-Blackston
First Vice-President, Ladies' Division	Irene W. Wingfield
Second Vice-President, Ladies' Division	Janie Jenkins
Third Vice-President, Ladies' Division	R. Harriet Rogers
General Secretary, Ladies' Division	Ethel Oughton-Clarke
Associate Secretary, Ladies' Division	Carrie B. Mero
Chairman, Advisory Board	J. A. Davis·

[*Source:* Marcus Garvey to Nicholas Murray Butler, 29 April 1918, NMB, NNC.]

2 July 1918

Director	Isaac B. Allen
Director	Irena Moorman-Blackston
Director	Walter J. Conway
Director	Carrie B. Mero
Director	R. Harriet Rogers
Director	Marcus Garvey

[Source: Certificate of Incorporation of the UNIA, 2 July 1918, Book 13, Page 7 (3) NAiDS.]

31 July 1918

Director	Marcus Garvey
Director	Irena Moorman-Blackston
Director	Isaac Samuel Bright
Director	Irene W. Wingfield
Director	James Perkins
Director	Carrie B. Mero
Director	Clarence A. Carpenter
Director	F. B. Webster
Director	Sidney Smith

[Source: Certificate of Incorporation of the African Communities League, Inc., 31 July 1918, Book 686, Page 43 (11), NAiDS.]

Pre–5 November 1918

Third Vice-President	Henry Dolphin

[Source: "The Greatest Movement in the History of the Negroes of the World," n.p., n.d. Enclosed in memorandum from Wrisley Brown to Lt. Col. Pakenham, 6 December 1918, File 10218-261/11, RG 165, DNA.]

5 November 1918

President and International Organizer	Marcus Garvey
First Vice-President	Isaac Samuel Bright
Second Vice-President	James Haynes
General Secretary	James Perkins
Executive Secretary	Ben E. Burrell
Associate Secretary	John Thomas Wilkins
Secretary	Granzaline Marshall
Treasurer	James E. Linton
Assistant Treasurer	Daisy Dunn

First Vice-President, Ladies' Division	Irene W. Wingfield
Second Vice-President, Ladies' Division	Janie Jenkins
Third Vice-President, Ladies' Division	Amy Haynes
General Secretary, Ladies' Division	Carrie B. Mero
Associate Secretary, Ladies' Division	Julia E. Rumford
Chairman, Advisory Board	Henry Douglas
Chairman, Trustee Board	F. B. Webster

[*Source:* Marcus Garvey to Nicholas Murray Butler, 5 November 1918, NMB, DLC.]

30 *November 1918*

President and International Organizer	Marcus Garvey
First Vice-President	Jeremiah Certain
Second Vice-President	George Tobias
Third Vice-President	William Wells
General Secretary	Cecil Hope
Executive Secretary	John Thomas Wilkins
Associate Secretary	Walter Farrell
Secretary	Granzaline Marshall
Treasurer	James E. Linton
President, Ladies' Division	Janie Jenkins
First Vice-President, Ladies' Division	Irene W. Wingfield
Second Vice-President, Ladies' Division	Hannah Nicholas
Third Vice-President, Ladies' Division	G. Woodford
General Secretary	Amy Ashwood
Associate Secretary, Ladies' Division	May Clarke
Chairman, Advisory Board	Henry Douglas
Chairman, Trustee Board	F. B. Webster

[*Source: NW*, Saturday, 30 November 1918.]

1 *February 1919*

President	Marcus Garvey
Second Vice-President	George Tobias
Third Vice-President	William Wells
High Chancellor	Joseph E. Johnson
General Secretary	Cecil Hope
Secretary General, Parent Body	Gerald Cox
Executive Secretary	John Thomas Wilkins

Treasurer	James E. Linton
President, Ladies' Division	Janie Jenkins
First Vice-President, Ladies' Division	Irene W. Wingfield
Second Vice-President, Ladies' Division	Hannah Nicholas
Third Vice-President, Ladies' Division	G. Woodford
Associate Secretary, Ladies' Division	May Clarke

[*Source: NW*, Saturday, 1 February 1919.]

1 March 1919

Acting Secretary-General	Julia E. Rumford

[*Source: NW*, Saturday, 1 March 1919.]

ca. 1 June 1919

International and National Organizer	Henrietta Vinton Davis
General Secretary	Edgar M. Grey

[*Source: NW*, Saturday, 14 June 1919.]

15 June 1919

Treasurer	George Tobias

[*Source: NW*, Saturday, 21 June 1919.]

ca. 27 June–9 July 1919

General Secretary	Edgar M. Grey
Executive Secretary	Richard E. Warner

[*Source: NW*, Saturday, 2 August 1919.]

19 July 1919

President and International Organizer	Marcus Garvey
First Vice-President	Jeremiah Certain
Third Vice-President	William Wells
Associate Secretary	Walter Farrell
Secretary	Granzaline Marshall
Treasurer	George Tobias
President, Ladies' Division	Janie Jenkins
First Vice-President, Ladies' Division	Irene W. Wingfield
Second Vice-President, Ladies' Division	Hannah Nicholas
Third Vice-President, Ladies' Division	G. Woodford
General Secretary	Amy Ashwood

Associate Secretary, Ladies' Division May Clarke

Chairman, Advisory Board Henry Douglas

Chairman, Trustee Board F. B. Webster

[*Source: NW*, Saturday, 19 July 1919.]

Officers of the Rival Universal Negro Improvement Association

20 January 1918

President Samuel A. Duncan

First Vice-President Irena Moorman-Blackston

Second Vice-President Pope Billups

Third Vice-President Eliza Henrickson

Assistant Secretary R. Cross

Financial Secretary Elizabeth Jackson

Treasurer Isaac Samuel Bright

Sergeant at Arms Louis A. Leavelle

Chairman, Advisory Board John E. Bruce

Chaplain C. C. Seifert

[*Source: Home News*, Wednesday, 23 January 1918.]

APPENDIX IV

BUREAU OF INVESTIGATION SUMMARY OF THE MINUTES OF BLACK STAR LINE BOARD OF DIRECTORS' MEETINGS, 27 JUNE–8 AUGUST 1919 (Excerpt)

Stock selling plans (from Minute Book):

It has already been shown that MARCUS GARVEY and the other 4 incorporators [*Edgar M. Grey, Richard E. Warner, George Tobias, Janie Jenkins*] assigned their subscription of 40 shares each—200 in all—to the Universal Negro Improvement Association on June 27, 1919, the date of incorporation. This stock never was issued or paid for, notwithstanding it was the declared capital with which they were to commence business.

At a second meeting of the Board of Directors held June 27, 1919, the President (MARCUS GARVEY) stated it was his intention to visit the State of Virginia and that during his stay there stocks should be sold starting on Sunday, June 29th, and further that stocks should be sold at the Palace Casino in New York at the same time. Edgar M. Grey (Director and Assistant Secretary) was empowered to do so.

At a meeting of the Board of Directors August 1, 1919, the President (MARCUS GARVEY) stated the time was at hand for a proper organized campaign for the selling of the stock of the corporation.

At a meeting of the Board of Directors August 8, 1919, it was resolved that a Rally be given by the BLACK STAR LINE for the swelling of its funds by the sales of stock. . . .

[*Source:* Thomas P. Merriless, Expert Bank Accountant, Bureau of Investigation, Department of Justice, "Summary Report of Investigation of Books and Records of The Black Star Line, Inc., and the Universal Negro Improvement Association, involving Marcus Garvey, Elie Garcia, George Tobias, and Orlando M. Thompson, in Violations of Sections #215 and 37 U.S.C.C., under the title 'US vs Marcus Garvey, et al,' " New York City, N. Y., October 26th, 1922, pp. 8–10, Records of the Federal Bureau of Investigation, United States Department of Justice, Washington, D.C.]

INDEX

A Note on the Index

An asterisk(*) precedes annotated biographical entries found in the text. A page number followed by an *n* with a digit indicates that the entry appears in the numbered footnote cited. An entry that appears both in the text and in a footnote on the same page is indicated by the page number only. Bibliographical information can be found in the annotations that accompany the text.

When there are variant spellings of a name, the accepted spelling of the name is used; in other instances, where there is no generally accepted usage, the spelling which seems most correct is indexed. Variants have not been indexed. Women are indexed under their name that first appears in the text; married names are indicated by parentheses in the index, as, Ashwood, Amy (Garvey). Cross-references to both maiden and married names are supplied in the index. Titled persons are indexed by their title, with the family name following in parentheses.

Government agencies are listed in the index by name. However, cross-references to their appropriate cabinet-level department are also provided, as, United States Department of Justice, *See also* Bureau of Investigation.

Abbott, Robert S., 282n.1, 386n.1

Abyssinia, 455–456, 457n.5, 459, 460, 532. *See also* Ethiopia

Abyssinian Riot, 532

Africa: for Africans, lxx, lxxxvi–lxxxvii, lxxxviii, 370n.5, 374–375, 396, 402, 503; Biblical references to, 57, 58, 59, 60–61; as black empire or republic, lxxv, lxxxvi–lxxxvii, 11, 303, 397, 439, 502, 503, 551; as cause of World War I, 303; as center of civilization, li–liii, lxxxvii, 60–61, 425; colonized, 288, 290n.12, 303, 351n.5, 425n.1; control of, 303, 396, 400n.3; described, 58–60; Du Bois on, 396, 400n.3; emancipation of, lxx, xc, 438; German colonies of, 288, 290n.12, 303, 319, 362–363, 400n.3, 403, 425n.1; Great Britain in, 303, 343, 541–542, 543–544; immigration to, xlvi–xlvii, 303, 538, 539, 541–546; Italy in, 303, 396, 400n.4; League of Nations mandates in, 290n.12, 362–363, 367–369, 369–370n.4, 396, 400n.3; missionaries in, xlvii, 170n.1, 189, 369, 370n.5, 419, 536–537, 538, 549, 550n.2; nationalism in, 544; *Negro World* in, 399, 400n.8; redemption of, xliv, lii, lxviii, lxix, lxxix, lxxxiii, lxxxvii, 291, 303, 319, 356, 391, 402–403, 529, 536; return to, xlvii (*see also* Black Star Line; Sam, Chief Alfred Charles); self-determination of, lxxviii, lxxxix, lxxxvi, 288, 425; UNIA in, xcvi. *See also* Abyssinia; Egypt; Ethiopia; Liberia

African Blood Brotherhood, lxx–lxxi, 227–228n.5, 523–525, 529; aims of, 523–524; and the Communist Party, 525; insurance in, 524; membership of, 523, 524. *See also* Briggs, Cyril V.; *Crusader*

African Communities (Imperial) League: capital stock of, 252; directors of, 252–253; imperialistic functions of, lix–lxi; incorporated, cxiv, 248–255; purposes of, lix–lxi, 248–252; shareholders of, 253–254. *See also* Universal Negro Improvement Association and African Communities League

African Emigration and Trading Company, 546